The Harlem Renaissance 1920–1940

Series Editor

Cary D. Wintz
Texas Southern University

A Garland Series

Contents of the Series

#35593914

The Emergence of the Harlem Renaissance

Edited with introductions by

Cary D. Wintz
Texas Southern University

GARLAND PUBLISHING, INC.
New York & London
1996

Library of Congress Cataloging-in-Publication Data

The emergence of the Harlem renaissance / edited with introductions
  by Cary D. Wintz.
      p. cm. — (The Harlem Renaissance, 1920–1940 ; 1)
    Includes bibliographical references.
    ISBN 0-8153-2212-7 (alk. paper)
     1. American literature—Afro-American authors—History and criti-
cism. 2. American literature—20th century—History and criticism.
3. Harlem (New York, N.Y.)—Intellectual life—20th century. 4. Afro-
Americans—Intellectual life. 5. Harlem Renaissance.   I. Wintz,
Cary D., 1943–   . II. Series.
PS153.N5E47   1996
810.9′896073—dc20   96-19348
                                   CIP

Printed on acid-free, 250-year-life paper
Manufactured in the United States of America

Contents

1926 *Opportunity* Literary Contest

1927 *Opportunity* Literary Contest

1932 *Opportunity* Literary Contest

CRISIS LITERARY CONTESTS

The 1923 *Crisis* Prize

Series Introduction

The Harlem Renaissance was the most significant event in African American literature and culture in the twentieth century. While its most obvious manifestation was as a self-conscious literary movement, it touched almost every aspect of African American culture and intellectual life in the period from World War I to the Great Depression. Its impact redefined black music, theater, and the visual arts; it reflected a new more militant political/racial consciousness and racial pride that was associated with the term "New Negro"; it embodied the struggle for civil rights that had been reinvigorated by the founding of the N.A.A.C.P. and the ideology of W.E.B. Du Bois; and it was an aspect of the urbanization of African Americans that first attracted public attention in the early twentieth century with the black migration.

Within this context it is difficult to pinpoint the chronological limits of the Harlem Renaissance. Generally the consensus among scholars is that the Harlem Renaissance was an event of the 1920s, bounded on one side by World War I and the race riots of 1919 and on the other side by the 1929 stock market crash. Some, however, have either greatly expanded or sharply restricted the time span of the movement. In 1967 Abraham Chapman wrote that he saw elements of the Renaissance in Claude McKay's poetry of 1917 and even in W.E.B. Du Bois's poem, "The Song of the Smoke," which was published in 1899.[1] Nathan Huggins argued that the Renaissance began during the years between the beginning of World War I and 1920, when the center of power in the African American community shifted from Tuskegee to Harlem, and he saw the Harlem Riots of 1935 as the end of the movement.[2] John Hope Franklin, on the other hand, wrote as late as 1980 that the Harlem Renaissance extended into the 1960s; more recently he has modified that concept, and now speaks of a first and second phase of the Harlem Renaissance, with the latter phase extending into the 1940s and beyond; he also observes that African American literary creativity was not confined to Harlem, but spread across the entire country[3] Benjamin Brawley, the preeminent African American literary historian contemporary to the Harlem Renaissance, downplayed the concept of the "so-called Negro literary renaissance," which he felt was centered around the publication of Carl Van Vechten's *Nigger Heaven* in 1926 and which he argued had no significant positive influence on African American literature.[4] Finally, Sterling Brown, one of the Harlem Renaissance poets and later a literary scholar, denied that Harlem was ever the center of a black literary movement.[5]

For the purposes of this collection the Harlem Renaissance is viewed primarily as a literary and intellectual movement. While theater, music, and the visual arts are looked at briefly, the focus is on African American literature, the assessment and criticism of this literature, and the relation of this literature to the political and social issues confronting African Americans in the early twentieth century.

The Harlem Renaissance was a self-conscious movement. That is, the writers and poets who participated in the movement were aware that they were involved in a literary movement and assumed at least partial responsibility for defining the parameters and aesthetics of the movement; black scholars and intellectuals were also aware of the Harlem Renaissance (even if they railed against it) and attempted to define the movement in terms both of literature and the political and social implications of that literature. While it was self-conscious, the Harlem Renaissance lacked a well-defined ideological or aesthetic center. It was more a community of writers, poets, critics, patrons, sponsors, and publishers than a structured and focused intellectual movement. It may be best conceptualized as an attitude or a state of mind—a feeling shared by a number of black writers and intellectuals who centered their activities in Harlem in the 1920s and early 1930s. The men and women who participated in the movement shared little but a consciousness that they were part of a common endeavor—a new awakening of African American culture and creativity; other than that what bound them together was a pride in their racial heritage, an essentially middle-class background, and the fact that all, to a greater or lesser degree, were connected to Harlem at the time that Harlem was emerging as the cultural, intellectual, and political center of black America.

Within this context, the Harlem Renaissance may best be conceptualized as a group of black writers and poets, orbiting erratically around a group of black intellectuals positioned in the N.A.A.C.P., the Urban League, and other African American political and educational institutions. These older intellectuals supported the movement, criticized it, attempted with varying success to define it, and served as liaison between the writers and the white publishers, patrons, and critics who dominated the business of literature in the United States in the 1920s. Complicating and enriching this mix was the fact that the lines between the various types of participants were not clearly drawn. James Weldon Johnson, for example, was a major promoter of the movement and a poet and novelist in his own right; Jessie Fauset, the most prolific novelist of the period, also served as literary editor of *The Crisis* and actively promoted the careers of young black writers; Countee Cullen, Sterling Brown, and Gwendolyn Bennett wrote regular literary columns, while Wallace Thurman, Langston Hughes, and several other writers attempted to publish literary magazines; and Carl Van Vechten, a white promoter of African American literature, worked closely with the Knopfs to publish black literature, authored the best-known novel of Harlem life, and almost singlehandedly created the white fascination with Harlem and African American life that characterized the 1920s.

With this definition it becomes a little easier to define the parameters of the movement. The Harlem Renaissance began in the early 1920s, when Jean Toomer published *Cane* and African American writers and intellectuals began to realize that something new was happening in black literature. The movement extended well into the 1930s and included the works of Zora Neale Hurston, Claude McKay, and Langston Hughes that were published in that decade. As long as they and other writers consciously identified with the Renaissance, the movement continued. It did not, however, encompass the younger writers like Richard Wright, Frank Yerby, or Ralph Ellison, who emerged in the 1930s and 1940s. Like so much else, these boundaries are not exact. Antecedents to the Harlem Renaissance are clear in the first two decades of the twentieth century; likewise it is easy to place some of Langston Hughes's work from the 1940s and 1950s in the Renaissance.

The goal of this series is to reprint articles and other materials that will delineate a clear picture and foster an understanding of the Harlem Renaissance. Three types of materials are included in this series. First, and most important, are the critical and interpretive materials on the Harlem Renaissance written by participants in and contemporaries of the movement. These firsthand accounts will assist readers in understanding the efforts of Harlem Renaissance writers, poets, and critics to define the movement and enable readers to glimpse the dynamics of the movement. Second, this series includes a retrospective look at the Harlem Renaissance through the eyes of participants and contemporaries, as well as by writers and critics who were involved in post-Renaissance black literature. Finally, the series presents a sample of the scholarly analysis and criticism of the movement from the 1950s through the early 1990s. The selections come from articles, essays, columns, and reviews in periodical literature; selections from memoirs, novels, histories, and books of criticism; and essays from scholarly journals. These materials are supplemented by a selection of previously unpublished materials, including letters, speeches, and essays. Not included are the literary works of the Harlem Renaissance. There are a number of anthologies of African American literature that already serve that purpose well.

This series also reflects one of the major problems confronting the study of the Harlem Renaissance in particular and African American history in general—the difficulty of accessing needed source materials. For years the study of African American history was handicapped by the fact that many of its primary sources had not been preserved or were not made available to scholars. If they had been preserved, they were housed in scattered collections and often incompletely processed and catalogued. The sharp increase in interest in African American history during the last thirty years has improved this situation enormously, but problems still persist. This series is in part an effort to make material related to one aspect of African American history more available to students and scholars. Unfortunately, it also suffers from the problem that some resources, even when located, are not readily available. For this reason a number of items by James Weldon Johnson had to be excluded; likewise, a very valuable retrospective on the Harlem Renaissance that was published initially in *Black World* is missing here. In the future, perhaps these and other barriers that impede research in African American history will be lifted.

As in any project of this nature there are scores of persons who have provided valuable support and assistance; it is impossible to name them all here. I want to especially thank Leo Balk and Carole Puccino of Garland Publishing. Leo with patience and firmness guided this series to completion; Carole worked diligently to arrange permissions for the publication of the material that appears here. In addition, I want to thank Paul Finkelman, who played a key role in helping me conceptualize the scope and nature of this project. Wolde Michael Akalou, Howard Beeth, Merline Pitre, and my other colleagues and students at Texas Southern University provided valuable feedback as the project developed. I also had wonderful assistance from the staff at the libraries

I visited while collecting the material for this series. I want to especially acknowledge the staff at the Harry Ransom Humanities Research Center at the University of Texas at Austin, the Beinecke Library at Yale University, and the Heartman Collection at the Robert J. Terry Library at Texas Southern University; in addition, librarians at the Fondren Library at Rice University, the M.D. Anderson Library at the University of Houston, the Perry Casteñeda Library at the University of Texas at Austin, and the library at the University of Houston, Clear Lake helped me track down the copies of the more elusive journals and periodicals used for this collection. I also want to thank Kathy Henderson and and Barbara Smith-Labard, who helped arrange for permission to publish previously unpublished materials from the collections at the Harry Ransom Humanities Research Center. Finally, research for this project was supported in part by a Travel to Collections grant from the National Endowment for the Humanities.

Cary D. Wintz

Notes

1. Abraham Chapman, "The Harlem Renaissance in Literary History," *CLA Journal* 11 (September 1967): 44–45.
2. Nathan Irvin Huggins, ed., *Voices from the Harlem Renaissance* (New York: Oxford University Press, 1976), 6–10.
3. John Hope Franklin, *From Slavery to Freedom: A History of Negro Americans*, 5th ed. (New York: Alfred Knopf, 1980), 383; John Hope Franklin and Alfred A. Moss, Jr., *From Slavery to Freedom: A History of African Americans*, 7th ed. (New York: McGraw-Hill, Inc., 1994), 379–80.
4. Benjamin Brawley, *The Negro Genius: A New Appraisal of the American Negro in Literature and the Fine Arts* (New York: Dodd, Mead, 1937), 231–68.
5. Sterling Brown, "The New Negro in Literature (1925–1955)." In *The New Negro Thirty Years Afterward*, ed. by Rayford W. Logan, Eugene C. Holmes, and C. Franklin Edwards (Washington, D.C.: Howard University Press, 1955).

Further Reading

Cooper, Wayne F. *Claude McKay: Rebel Sojourner in the Harlem Renaissance*. Baton Rouge: Louisiana State University Press, 1987.
Douglas, Ann. *Terrible Honesty: Mongrel Manhattan in the 1920s*. New York: Farrar, Straus, and Giroux, 1995.
Ferguson, Blanche E. *Countee Cullen and the Negro Renaissance*. New York: Dodd, Mead, 1966.
Hemenway, Robert E. *Zora Neale Hurston: A Literary Biography*. Urbana: University of Illinois Press, 1977.
Huggins, Nathan Irvin. *Harlem Renaissance*. New York: Oxford University Press, 1971.
———, ed. *Voices from the Harlem Renaissance*. New York: Oxford University Press, 1976.
Hull, Gloria T. *Color, Sex, and Poetry: Three Women Writers of the Harlem Renaissance*. Bloomington: Indiana University Press, 1987.
Kerman, Cynthia Earl, and Richard Eldridge. *The Lives of Jean Toomer: A Hunger for Wholeness*. Baton Rouge: Louisiana State University Press, 1987.
Levy, Eugene. *James Weldon Johnson: Black Leader, Black Voice*. Chicago: University of Chicago Press, 1973.
Lewis, Dadid Levering. *W.E.B. Du Bois: Biography of a Race, 1868–1919*. New York: Henry Holt, 1993.
———. *When Harlem Was in Vogue*. New York: Vintage Books, 1981.
Marable, Manning. *W.E.B. Du Bois: Black Radical Democrat*. Boston: Twayne Publishers, 1986.
Rampersad, Arnold. *The Life of Langston Hughes*. Vol 1. *I, Too, Sing America: 1902–1941*. New York: Oxford University Press, 1986.
———. *The Life of Langston Hughes*. Vol 2. *I Dream a World: 1942–1967*. New York: Oxford University Press, 1988.
Singh, Amritjit. *The Novels of the Harlem Renaissance: Twelve Black Writers, 1923–1933*. University Park: The Pennsylvania State University Press, 1976.
Sundquist, Eric J. *To Wake the Nations: Race in the Making of American Literature*. Cambridge: Harvard University Press, 1993.
Tillery, Tyrone. *Claude McKay: A Black Poet's Struggle for Identity*. Amherst: The University of Massachusetts Press, 1992.
Wintz, Cary D. *Black Culture and the Harlem Renaissance*. Houston: Rice University Press, 1988.

Volume Introduction

A series of events occurred in the mid 1920s that signaled the birth of the Harlem Renaissance. First was the appearance of a handful of books written by African American authors and published by white-owned mainstream commercial presses. The significance was not the appearance of the books but the fact that for the first time since Houghton Mifflin, Doubleday, and Dodd and Mead published the works of Charles W. Chesnutt and Paul Laurence Dunbar at the turn of the century, mainstream commercial publishers were willing to print the novels and poetry of Black authors. First, in 1922, Harcourt, Brace and World published James Weldon Johnson's anthology, *The Book of American Negro Poetry*; then later that same year it published Claude McKay's collection of poetry, *Harlem Shadows*. In 1923 Jean Toomer published his experimental novel, *Cane*, and in 1924 Jessie Fauset published her first novel, *There Is Confusion*; Boni and Liveright published both. Also in 1924, Alfred Knopf published Walter White's novel, *The Fire in the Flint*. The appearance of these books signaled a dramatic increase of black literary activity.

The appearance of new books and new writers generated excitement in the African American intellectual community. This led to two other developments. First, both *The Crisis* (the monthly magazine of the N.A.A.C.P.) and *Opportunity* (the Urban League's journal) began publishing African American poetry and literature and offered prizes for outstanding new works of Black literature. Both W.E.B. Du Bois, editor of *The Crisis*, and Charles S. Johnson, editor of *Opportunity*, were committed to the development of African American literature; Du Bois hired novelist Jessie Fauset as literary editor of *The Crisis*, while Johnson, in March, 1924, organized a literary banquet at the Civic Club that served to introduce Harlem's new corps of young writers to the New York literary world. At this event, Paul U. Kellogg, publisher of *Survey Graphic*, was so impressed with the talent of the Harlem writers that he asked Howard University professor Alain Locke to edit an issue of *Survey Graphic* dedicated to the art and literature of the "New Negro." This issue, which came out in March, 1925, was the second development that helped define the emerging Harlem Renaissance.

Finally, the event that further stimulated the Harlem Renaissance was the publication in 1926 of Carl Van Vechten's sensational and controversial novel of Harlem life, *Nigger Heaven*. *Nigger Heaven* was an instant best-seller, and it helped stimulate the fascination with Black life that was so much a part of the United States in the 1920s.

The popularity of jazz and the blues, of black nightclubs and speakeasies, of Black musical theater, of "slumming" in Harlem at the Cotton Club, and of ersatz images of African America like the *Amos and Andy* radio show all seemed to grow out of the craze that *Nigger Heaven* created. The publication of *Nigger Heaven* and subsequent novels and short stories by black writers that captured the exotic underlife of Harlem were controversial and divisive. Du Bois condemned *Nigger Heaven* and similar works for depicting blacks in the unflattering contexts of poverty, crime, and vice; others praised these works for their honest look at the life of the lower classes, and for capturing the local color of the Harlem slums. In spite of the criticism, Van Vechten helped to popularize black literature, and he fed the "Negro vogue" that was an essential part of the Harlem Renaissance.

This volume contains material related to the emergence of the Harlem Renaissance. First it contains a series of essays written between 1910 and 1925 that stressed the importance of developing African American literature and culture and responded to the literature that emerged in the early 1920s. This material includes book reviews, biographical sketches of the new young writers, and essays and speeches that assess the significance of the emerging literary movement. Second, this volume reprints the entire March, 1925 issue of *Survey Graphic*. This issue, subtitled "Harlem: Mecca of the New Negro," more than any other single publication lay the foundation for the Harlem Renaissance by placing the work of a variety of young writers in the context of the New Negro consciousness. Locke would publish an expanded version of this issue a year later as *The New Negro*, the first of many anthologies of Harlem Renaissance literature. Also included is a selection from the prologue of *Nigger Heaven*. This selection illustrates the aspects of this book that most offended Du Bois, and that so appealed to others. Finally, this volume reprints material related to *The Crisis* and *Opportunity* literary contests from their inception in the early 1920s to their end. The contests represented one of the efforts of African American intellectuals and institutions to promote and support (and later to influence) the development of African American literature.

The Emergence of the
Harlem Renaissance

The Negro in Literature and Art

THE NEGRO is primarily an artist. The usual way of putting this is to speak disdainfully of his sensuous nature. This means that the only race which has held at bay the life destroying forces of the tropics, has gained therefrom in some slight compensation a sense of beauty, particularly for sound and color, which characterizes the race. The Negro blood which flowed in the veins of many of the mightiest of the Pharaohs accounts for much of Egyptian art, and indeed, Egyptian civilization owes much in its origins to the development of the large strain of Negro blood which manifested itself in every grade of Egyptian society.

Semitic civilization also had its Negroid influences, and these continually turn toward art as in the case of Nosseyeb, one of the five great poets of Damascus under the Ommiades. It was therefore not to be wondered at that in modern days one of the greatest of modern literatures, the Russian, should have been founded by Pushkin, the grandson of a full blooded Negro, and that among the painters of Spain was the mulatto slave, Gomez. Back of all this development by way of contact, comes the artistic sense of the indigenous Negro as shown in the stone figures of Sherbro, the bronzes of Benin, the marvelous handwork in iron and other metals which has characterized the Negro race so long that archeologists today, with less and less hesitation, are ascribing the discovery of the welding of iron to the Negro race.

To America, the Negro could bring only his music, but that was quite enough. The only real American music is that of the Negro American, except the meagre contribution of the Indian. Negro music divides itself into many parts: the older African wails and chants, the distinctively Afro-American folk song set to religious words and Calvinistic symbolism, and the newer music which the slaves adapted from surrounding themes. To this may be added the American music built on Negro themes such as "Suwanee River," "John Brown's Body," "Old Black Joe," etc. In our day Negro artists like Johnson and Will Marion Cook have taken up this music and begun a newer and most important development, using the syncopated measure popularly known as "rag time," but destined in the minds of musical students to a great career in the future.

The expression in words of the tragic experiences of the Negro race is to be found in various places. First, of course, there are those, like Harriet Beecher Stowe, who wrote from without the race. Then there are black men like Es-Sadi who wrote the Epic of the Sudan, in Arabic, that great history of the fall of the greatest of Negro empires, the Songhay. In America the literary expression of Negroes has had a regular development. As early as the eighteenth century, and even before the Revolutionary War the first voices of Negro authors were heard in the United States.

Phyllis Wheatley, the black poetess, was easily the pioneer, her first poems appearing in 1773, and other editions in 1774 and 1793. Her earliest poem was in memory of George Whitefield. She was followed by the Negro, Olaudah Equiano—known by his English name of Gustavus Vassa—whose autobiography of 350 pages, published in 1787, was the beginning of that long series of personal appeals of which Booker T. Washington's *Up from Slavery* is the latest. Benjamin Banneker's almanacs represented the first scientific work of American Negroes, and began to be issued in 1792.

Coming now to the first decades of the nineteenth century we find some essays on freedom by the African Society of Boston, and an apology for the new Negro church formed in Philadelphia. Paul Cuffe, disgusted with America, wrote an early account of Sierra Leone, while the celebrated Lemuel Haynes, ignoring the race question, dipped deeply into the New England theological controversy about 1815. In 1829 came the first full-voiced, almost hysterical, protest against slavery and the color line in David Walker's *Appeal* which aroused Southern legislatures to action. This was followed by the earliest Negro conventions which issued interesting minutes, and a strong appeal against disfranchisement in Pennsylvania.

In 1840 some strong writers began to appear. Henry Highland Garnet and J. W. C. Pennington preached powerful sermons and gave some attention to Negro history in their pamphlets; R. B. Lewis made a more elaborate attempt at

3

Negro history. Whitfield's poems appeared in 1846, and William Wells Brown began a career of writing which lasted from 1847 until after the war. In 1845 Douglass' autobiography made its first appearance, destined to run through endless editions up until the last in 1893. Moreover it was in 1841 that the first Negro magazine appeared in America, edited by George Hogarth and published by the A. M. E. Church.

In the fifties William Wells Brown published his *Three Years in Europe*; James Whitfield published further poems, and a new poet arose in the person of Frances E. W. Harper, a woman of no little ability who died lately; Martin R. Delaney and William Nell wrote further of Negro history, Nell especially making valuable contributions to the history of the Negro soldiers. Three interesting biographies were added to this decade to the growing number: Josiah Henson, Samuel G. Ward and Samuel Northrop; while Catto, leaving general history, came down to the better known history of the Negro church.

In the sixties slave narratives multiplied, like that of Linda Brent, while two studies of Africa based on actual visits were made by Robert Campbell and Dr. Alexander Crummell; William Douglass and Bishop Daniel Payne continued the history of the Negro church, while William Wells Brown carried forward his work in general Negro history. In this decade, too, Bishop Tanner began his work in Negro theology.

Most of the Negro talent in the seventies was taken up in politics; the older men like Bishop Wayman wrote of their experiences; William Wells Brown wrote the *Rising Son*, and Sojourner Truth added her story to the slave narratives. A new poet arose in the person of A. A. Whitman, while James M. Trotter was the first to take literary note of the musical ability of his race. Indeed this section might have been begun by some reference to the music and folklore of the Negro race; the music contained much primitive poetry and the folklore was one of the great contributions to American civilization.

In the eighties there are signs of unrest and different conflicting streams of thought. On the one hand the rapid growth of the Negro church is shown by the writers on church subjects like Moore and Wayman. The historical spirit

4

was especially strong. Still wrote of the *Underground Railroad*; Simmons issued his interesting biographical dictionary, and the greatest historian of the race appeared when George W. Williams issued his two-volume history of the *Negro Race in America*. The political turmoil was reflected in Langston's *Freedom and Citizenship*, Fortune's *Black and White*, and Straker's *New South*, and found its bitterest arraignment in Turner's pamphlets; but with all this went other new thought; a black man published his *First Greek Lessons*, Bishop Payne issued his *Treatise on Domestic Education*, and Stewart studied Liberia.

In the nineties came histories, essays, novels and poems, together with biographies and social studies. The history was represented by Payne's *History of the A. M. E. Church*, Hood's *History of the A. M. E. Zion Church*, Anderson's sketch of *Negro Presbyterianism* and Hagood's *Colored Man in the M. E. Church*; general history of the older type by R. L. Perry's *Cushite* and the newer type in Johnson's history, while one of the secret societies found their historian in Brooks; Crogman's essays appeared and Archibald Grimke's biographies. The race question was discussed in Frank Grimke's published sermons, while social studies were made by Penn, Wright, Mossell, Crummell, Majors and others. Most notable, however, was the rise of the Negro novelist and poet with national recognition; Frances Harper was still writing and Griggs began his racial novels, but both of these spoke primarily to the Negro race; on the other hand, Chesnutt's six novels and Dunbar's inimitable works spoke to the whole nation.

Since 1900 the stream of Negro writing has continued. Dunbar has found a worthy successor in the less-known but more carefully cultured Braithwaite; Booker T. Washington has given us his biography and *Story of the Negro*; Kelly Miller's trenchant essays have appeared in book form; Sinclair's *Aftermath of Slavery* has attracted attention, as have the studies made by Atlanta University. The forward movement in Negro music is represented by J. W. and F. J. Work in one direction and Rosamond Johnson, Harry Burleigh and Will Marion Cook in another.

On the whole, the literary output of the American Negro

5

has been both large and creditable, although, of course, comparatively little known; few great names have appeared and only here and there work that could be called first class, but this is not a peculiarity of Negro literature.

The time has not yet come for the great development of American Negro literature. The economic stress is too great and the racial persecution too bitter to allow the leisure and the poise for which literature calls. On the other hand, never in the world has a richer mass of material been accumulated by a people than that which the Negroes possess today and are becoming conscious of. Slowly but surely they are developing artists of technic who will be able to use this material. The nation does not notice this for everything touching the Negro is banned by magazines and publishers unless it takes the form of caricature or bitter attack, or is so thoroughly innocuous as to have no literary flavor.

Outside of literature the American Negro has distinguished himself in other lines of art. One need only mention Henry O. Tanner whose pictures hang in the great galleries of the world, including the Luxembourg. There are a score of other less known colored painters of ability including Bannister, Harper, Scott and Brown. To these may be added the actors headed by Ira Aldridge, who played in Covent Garden, was decorated by the King of Prussia and the Emperor of Russia, and made a member of learned societies.

There have been many colored composers of music. Popular songs like Grandfather's Clock, Listen to the Mocking Bird, Carry Me Back to Old Virginia, etc., were composed by colored men. There were a half dozen composers of ability among New Orleans freedmen and Harry Burleigh, Cook and Johnson are well known today. There have been sculptors like Edmonia Lewis, and singers like Flora Batson, whose color alone kept her from the grand opera stage.

To appraise rightly this body of art one must remember that it represents the work of those artists only whom accident set free; if the artist had a white face his Negro blood did not militate against him in the fight for recognition; if his Negro blood was visible white relatives may have helped him; in a few cases ability was united to indomitable will. But the shrinking, modest, black artist without special encouragement had little or no chance in a world determined to make him a menial. So this sum of accomplishment is but an imperfect indication of what the Negro race is capable of in America and in the world.

Annals of the American Academy of
Political and Social Science,
September 1913

THE NEGRO "RENAISSANCE"

BY LLOYD MORRIS

RECENTLY there appeared in the newspapers an item reporting the endowment of a chair to the memory of Ira Aldridge in the new Shakespeare Memorial Theater at Stratford-on-Avon. The funds for this memorial were contributed entirely by colored citizens of the United States in appreciation of the place held by one of their race as a great tragedian in theatrical history. Aldridge died nearly seventy years ago, and the honor which his memory is now receiving serves to remind us that the contemporary contribution of the colored race to the arts is not lacking in a long and honorable tradition. Indeed, it is no exaggeration to say that the "Negro renaissance" of the last few years is rather a renaissance of interest on the part of a white audience than a renaissance of production on the part of Negro artists.

The names of Roland Hayes, Paul Robeson, and Charles Gilpin are thoroughly familiar to lovers of music and the theater. Yet few of their white admirers are apt to think of them as being other than exceptional; as being, in fact, the first members of their race to distinguish themselves in the more serious realms of music and drama. It does not derogate from the honor due them that this impression is false.

Their predecessor, Ira Aldridge, was a picturesque and romantic figure who, seventy or eighty years ago, achieved European celebrity as the "African Roscius." The accounts of his early life are conflicting. One reports him as a mulatto born in Maryland and apprenticed to a German ship carpenter. Another states that he was the son of a native of

Senegal who was brought to America as a slave, became a Christian, and was later pastor of a church in New York City.

Whatever Aldridge's early life may have been, it is known that he became the servant of Edmund Kean, the famous Shakespearean actor, and that he accompanied Kean to England in the early years of the nineteenth century. Later he returned to America and appeared on the stage in Baltimore without success. He again went to England and made his debut at the Royalty Theatre in London in the role of Othello. He was an instantaneous success and achieved wide popularity. In 1852 he essayed the role of Aaron in "Titus Andronius," and at Belfast he played Othello to the Iago of Edmund Kean. Before his death in 1867 Aldridge had toured Europe, had been decorated by the Emperors of Austria and Russia and the King of Prussia, and had been elected a member of several of the great European academies.

When we speak of the contemporary Negro renaissance, it is of literature that we usually think first, for the contribution of colored writers to recent American fiction and poetry has been substantial and significant. Nearly all readers of poetry have become acquainted with the verse of James Weldon Johnson, Countee Cullen, Langston Hughes; nearly everyone who has been concerned with the general revival of poetry in America appreciates the valiant service to art of William Stanley Braithwaite, the critic and anthologist.

Similarly, many readers of fiction are familiar with the names of W. E. B. Du Bois, Claude McKay, Wallace Thurman, Walter White, Nella Larsen Imes, Jessie Fauset. Moreover, long before the younger Negro novelists had begun writing, discerning readers had already discovered the works of Charles W. Chesnutt, the most distinguished of modern American colored novelists, and those of Paul Laurence Dunbar, to whom recognition came chiefly as a poet.

A contemporary of Phillis Wheatley, Benjamin Ban- of colored writers to our literature as an isolated phenomenon. The literary tradition of the colored race is, as we are apt to forget, not only creditable but passably long. The first Negro writer of distinction of whom we have any record was Juan Latino, professor of Latin at the University of Granada, who published a volume of Latin poems in 1573, and a work dealing with the Escorial in 1576. Latino's first work was thus published twenty years before the earliest published work of Shakespeare. In northern Europe the first Negro to receive a degree from a university was Jacobus Elisa Joannes Capitein, who was made a Doctor of Philosophy by the University of Leyden, and whose thesis for his degree, which ironically enough was a defense of slavery, was published in 1742.

From the time of Latino to the present day the contribution of the colored race to literature has been abundant and unbroken. Negroes have written in Arabić, French, Portuguese, Russian, German, and Spanish. Two writers with colored blood, Pushkin and Dumas, were among the most eminent of nineteenth century European men of letters. Frederic Marcelin, some of whose novels merit translation into English, wrote with distinction of the life of his people in Hayti. And the most celebrated of contemporary Brazilian writers of fiction, Machado de Assis, was a Negro.

The literary tradition of the Negro in the United States begins with Jupiter Hammond, who lived on Long Island, and who, about 1760, began publishing broadsides in verse. A much more picturesque figure, however, was Phillis Wheatley, a Negro slave who was sold in Boston, whose "Poems on Various Subjects Religious and Moral" was first published in London in 1773 and has since been republished in fifteen editions, the last of which appeared in 1915. The title page of the first edition of her work announces its author as "Negro servant to Mr. John Wheatley, of Boston, in New England." Her verse was sufficiently meritorious to bring her a letter of congratulation from George Washington, and it is pleasant to know that her increasing poetical reputation won her her freedom.

A contemporary of Phillis Wheatley, Benjamin Banneker, similarly attracted the attention of a President. Banneker published, during the years from 1791 to 1796, a series of almanacs which revealed a considerable knowledge of astronomy. President Thomas Jefferson, the foremost of intellectual liberals in America, sent a copy of one of Banneker's almanacs to his friend, the French philosopher Condorcet, to illustrate his contention that the Negro had the same potentialities as the white man.

A little after Phillis Wheatley there emerged another slave poet named George Horton, whose volume of verse, "The Hope of Freedom," was published in 1827. Following Horton, the next Negro poet to achieve any considerable distinction was Mrs. Frances Harper, whose verse had so widespread a vogue as to sell in the tens of thousands of copies. Mrs. Harper's work was especially popular with the Abolitionists, and she forms a link between the earlier and later colored writers in this country, for she published a novel as late as 1893, when Chesnutt and Dunbar were first beginning to publish.

Mention of the Abolitionists suggests the part which they played in the development of at least one phase of the literary production of the colored race. Under their inspiration more than one hundred slave narratives, some only narrated and some actually written by escaped slaves, were published in England and this country before the Civil War. The most celebrated of slave narratives were the three volumes written by Frederick Douglass: "Narrative of the Life of Frederick Douglass," published in 1846; "My Bondage and My Freedom," published in 1855, and "Life and Times of Frederick Douglass," published in 1882.

The first volume of fiery protest against slavery was "Walker's Appeal Addressed to Colored Citizens of the World," which was first published in 1829 and ran through three editions. It urged the slaves to rise against their white masters; as may be supposed, copies were promptly destroyed in the South whenever located, and the book has become exceedingly rare.

The first novel of Negro life in America was written by a fugitive slave named William Wells Brown. It was published in England in 1852 under the title of "Clotelle: or the President's Daughter." When it was published in the United States the title, for obvious reasons, was changed to "Clotelle: or the Colored Heroine." Eleven years later Brown published another volume, "The Black Man: His Antecedents, His Genius and His Achievements." Meanwhile, in 1857, another novel of Negro life appeared: "The Garies and Their Friends," by Frank J. Webb, which carried an appreciative introduction by Harriet Beecher Stowe. These two novels have claims to be considered the predecessors of the many contemporary novels by colored authors which study the relation between the colored and white races in our civilization.

The period after the Civil War saw the publication of a large number of propaganda race novels by colored writers, most of which were privately printed. It witnessed likewise the publication of a large controversial literature attempting to establish that principle of equality of potentiality which Jefferson affirmed to Condorcet. The first important volume of this kind was Major Martin R. Delaney's "Principles of Ethnology," published in 1879, and perhaps the most recent is Dr. Du Bois's "The Gift of Black Folk," published five years ago.

The attention which has been focused upon the novels and poetry of contemporary colored writers has obscured the contribution made by Negroes to other departments of literature and scholarship. For colored writers have written admirable books upon almost every variety of subjects: folklore, sociology, criticism of the arts, history, embryology, African and Polar exploration, law, classical languages and literatures, and philosophy, among them.

The contribution to historical literature begins as early as 1855 with William C. Nell's "The Colored Patriots of the American Revloution." The contribution to scientific literature begins in 1847 when Richard Hill, Jamaica Negro, collaborated with P. H. Gosse, the father of Edmund Gosse, on "Birds of Jamaica." This volume was followed four years later by Gosse's "A Naturalist's Sojourn in Jamaica," which made liberal acknowledgment of his indebtedness to Hill.

The first book on exploration by a Negro was Major Martin R. Delaney's report of an expedition sent to explore the Niger Valley, which was published in 1861; the most famous is Matthew Henson's "A Negro Explorer at the North Pole," for which an introduction was written by Peary.

Professor W. S. Scarborough, of Wilberforce University, published a Greek reader in 1881 which for many years was a standard college textbook. He had been fired to distinguish himself as a classical scholar by having, in his childhood, run across Henry Clay's sarcastic statement that when he had heard a Negro conjugate a Greek verb or decline a Greek noun, he would believe in the potential equality of the Negro mind to the white.

The only Creole grammar in English was written by a Negro scholar, J. J. Thomas, and although it was published in 1869 it has not been superseded. Two standard works on law, Scott's book on interstate extradition and Cosey's book on land titles, are the work of Negro authors. In the field of physics there is Robert T. Browne's "The Mystery of Space, A Study of the Hyperspace Movement." In pedagogy, there is Gilbert H. Jones's "Education in Theory and Practice." And a Negro graduate of West Point, Colonel Charles Young, has written a standard work on military tactics, "Military Morale of Nations and Races."

The contemporary Negro renaissance in the arts is making a significant and interesting contribution to our culture; there is no longer any doubt of that. But that it is a renaissance of anything more than our interest in the work of colored writers and artists is doubtful. The tradition of creative expression and of scholarship among the colored race is too old to be still considered new.

12

SOME THINGS NEGROES NEED TO DO *

BY CARTER G. WOODSON

Editor of the *Journal of Negro History*

THERE are certain things the Negroes in this country must do if they hope to enjoy the blessings of real democracy, if it ever comes.

In the first place, we need to attain economic independence. You may talk about rights and all that sort of thing. The people who own this country will rule this country. They always have done so and they always will. The people who control the coal and iron, the banks, the stock markets, and all that sort of thing, those are the people who will dictate exactly what shall be done for every group in this land. More than that, liberty is to come to the Negro, not as a bequest, but as a conquest. When I speak of it as a conquest, I mean that the Negro must contribute something to the good of his race, something to the good of his country, and something to the honor and glory of God. Economic independence is the first step in that direction.

I was in Washington the other day and a man told me that the colored people were about to have a new bank there

---

* Excerpts from an address at Hampton Institute, November 5, 1921

—"and they have two already," he said. I answered, "They should have had ten banks forty years ago." Two banks among a hundred thousand Negroes! We must learn to take these things more seriously.

I was speaking to a gentleman the other day about the organization of an insurance company, and he was telling of the wonderful things we have done in the way of insurance. After he had summarized the receipts of the various companies now organized among Negroes it was just a little modicum, so to speak, compared with the great achievements in insurance on the part of members of the white race. Here we are, rejoicing over these little things, and we have hardly begun to make a beginning.

Then we must have educational independence. If the Negro is not going to become an educational factor among his own people, then education is not the leverage to lift him, in the sense it has lifted other people; for a man is educated when he can do without a teacher, when he can and will develop and grow without the stimulus of instruction. So must it be with a race. If we are not going to reach that point some day in our lives when we shall be able to go out and establish schools and become persons well rounded in philosophy and science and history and what-not, and be able to help one another; if we are not going to prepare ourselves here, three generations from slavery, to do that work for ourselves, then we cannot say that education has done for our group what it has done for others.

Then the Negro needs to develop a press. Some of us never read a Negro newspaper—and some are not worth reading. A few, however, tell the story of the Negro in a cool, calm way. They tell of the strivings of the Negro in such a way as to be an inspiration to youth. Every Negro ought to read the publications of his own race.

I was impressed in California to find that, although there are only ten thousand Japanese in San Francisco, they have two daily papers—only ten thousand, but they have two daily papers of eight pages each. We have over ten million in the United States and we have not yet developed a real daily newspaper. We should not complain if the white papers do not tell our own story. We complain because they publish our crimes and tell of the evils that we do but do not say anything of our achievements in those lines that tend to stamp us as people of the world. We must learn to tell the story ourselves. It is our duty to develop a press.

We should also develop a literature. Negroes should read some things written by their own people that they may be inspired thereby. You will never be a George Washington or a Thomas Jefferson—you will never be a white man—but you will be a Negro, and we must realize that there are. certain things in the Negro race worth developing. Those things may be worth as much to the world as the things of the white race when they are properly developed. We must cease trying to straighten our hair and bleach our faces, and be Negroes—and be good ones.

In this literature you will get the inspiration you need to be like Frederick Douglass, Booker Washington, S. Coleridge-Taylor, or Paul Laurence Dunbar. If you can contribute to the world what those men have you will have no reason to regret that you cannot be a George Washington or a Thomas Jefferson, because you will still be identified with some of the greatest men who have ever appeared in the history of the world.

The Negro must learn to preserve his own records. He must learn the value of tradition. I was speaking to a teacher the other day. I wanted to get some information as to his people. I asked him who his grandfather was. "I am not sure," he said, "what my grandfather's name was." It may be that some of you do not know your grandfathers. You have not thought they were worth while. Although they perhaps could not read and write, they contributed much to the making of the race. They made it possible for you to be where you are to-day. They bore the burden and heat of the day. Some of them achieved a great deal more than some of us could have achieved.

If you should go to Cincinnati and speak with some of the old citizens—those who lived there before the Civil War—they would tell you that the Negroes of Cincinnati achieved more prior to the Civil War than they have since. There was a man who had patented a cord-bed which became popular throughout the United States, just as the spring-bed is popular to-day. In the exploitation of that patent he built up a large business and employed scores of white men and Negroes. He was worth thousands of dollars.

There was a Negro who went from this State—a Negro from Richmond, Va., who had worked in a blacksmith shop. His master permitted him to sell the slack of the coal. He accumulated a large sum of money, about $15,000, and he went to his master and purchased himself. He then went North and settled finally in Cincinnati. He knew the coal business and entered that business there. The people thought they would run him out of business and they said, "We coal dealers will get together and lower the price of coal to such an extent that he will be ruined." This Negro was wise. He sent mulattoes around to fill all his orders at the white coal yard, so that his supply would be kept on hand. The white coal dealers exhausted their supply and there came a great freezing. No coal could get through up the river and the railroads had not been constructed. This Negro had all his coal on hand. Nobody else could get any, and he sold out at a handsome profit. He then had so much money to enlarge his business that they never thought of combining against him again. That was in 1869. That Negro was worth something like $60,000. There isn't a Negro in Cincinnati to-day worth $60,000.

We have a wonderful history behind us. We of the *Journal of Negro History* shall have going the rounds soon a lecture on the ante-bellum period, setting forth the stories of Negroes who did so much to inspire us. It reads like the history of people in an heroic age. We expect to send out from time to time books written for the express purpose of showing you that you have a history, a record, behind you. If you are unable to demonstrate to the world that you have this record, the world will say to you, "You are not worthy to enjoy the blessings of democracy or anything else." They will say to you, "Who are you, anyway? Your ancestors have never controlled empires or kingdoms and most of your race have contributed little or nothing to science and philosophy and mathematics." So far as you know, they have not; but if you will read the history of Africa, the history of your ancestors—people of whom you should feel proud—you will realize that they have a history that is worth while. They have traditions that have value of which you can boast and upon which you can base a claim for a right to a share in the blessings of democracy.

Let us, then, study this history, and study it with the understanding that we are not, after all, an inferior people, but simply a people who have been set back, a people whose progress has been impeded. We are going back to that beautiful history and it is going to inspire us to greater achievements. It is not going to be long before we can so sing the story to the outside world as to convince it of the value of our history and our traditions, and then we are going to be recognized as men.

16

NEGRO LITERATURE FOR NEGRO PUPILS

BY ALICE DUNBAR-NELSON

THE ancient Greeks, wishing to impress upon their children the greatness of Hellas, made the schoolboys memorize Homer, particularly those passages dealing with wars and conquests. The Romans saturated their youth with Roman literature, history, and law. The Hebrew children of all ages are versed, grounded, and crammed with the Mosaic and Rabbinical law. The Chinese child learns volumes of Confucius. The French child recites La Fontaine, even before he can read. Spain drives home the epic of the Cid to the youth of her land—and so on, through all history, ancient and modern; each land, each nation, impresses most painstakingly upon the rising generation the fact that it possesses a history and a literature, and that it must live up to the traditions of its history, and make that literature a part of its life.

The reason for this is obvious. If a people are to be proud and self-respecting they must believe in themselves. Destroy a man's belief in his own powers, and you destroy his usefulness—render him a worthless object, helpless and hopeless. Tell a people over and over again that they have done nothing, can do nothing, set a limitation for their achievement; impress upon them that all they have or can hope to have is the product of the minds of other peoples; force them to believe that they are pensioners on the mental bounty of another race,—and they will lose what little faith they may have had in themselves, and become stultified non-producers. Any parent or teacher knows how disastrous is the result of telling a child how splendidly some other child has done, and asking why he does not go and do likewise. The one so adjured usually does the exact opposite, in a bitterness of resentment and gloom, it being one of the vagaries of human nature to act contrariwise.

All this is by way of reminding ourselves that for two generations we have given brown and black children a blonde ideal of beauty to worship, a milk-white literature to assimilate, and a pearly Paradise to anticipate, in which their dark faces would be hopelessly out of place. That there has not been a complete and absolute stultification of the efforts of the race toward self-expression is due only to the fact that we are a people of peculiar resiliency and combativeness. The effect of this kind of teaching is shown in the facts that the beautiful brown dolls, which resemble their tiny play-mothers, still have some difficulty in making their way into the homes of our people; that some older religionists still fondly hope that at death, and before St. Peter admits them into Paradise, they will be washed physically white; that Negro business enterprises are still regarded with a doubtful eye; and that Negro literature is frequently mentioned in whispers as a dubious quantity.

There is a manifest remedy for this condition, a remedy which the teachers of the race are applying gradually, wherever the need has been brought to their attention. We must begin everywhere to instill race pride into our pupils; not by dull statistics, nor yet by tedious iterations that we are a great people, and "if you do not believe it, look at this table of figures, or at the life of so-and-so." Idle boasting of past achievements always leaves a suspicion in the mind of the listener that the braggart is not sure of his ground and is bolstering up his opinion of himself. But we will give the children the poems and stories and folk lore and songs of their own people. We do not teach literature; we are taught by literature. The subtlest, most delicate, and lasting impressions of childhood are those gained by the chance poem, the eagerly absorbed fable, the lesson in the reader, the story told in the Sunday-school lesson. The fairy prince and the delectable princess have their charm, as opening up a vista into an enchanted land, but the poem that touches closely the heart of a child, and belongs to it because of its very nearness to his own life, is the bit of literature that lifts him above the dull brown earth and makes him akin to all that is truly great in the universe.

Three pictures project themselves upon the screen of memory, deeply suggestive of the futility of some of our efforts to reach child-life. One is that of a plaintive child, to whom the world of books was the real world, hugging to her thin little breast a big book of poetry, and passionately praying ,"Oh, please, dear Lord, let me grow up and write things, because none of us have ever written anything, and we ought to, dear Lord, because its *awful* that we don't write stories or things." Now this was a Southern child in a Southern city in a school taught by colored teachers, and her eager little soul was convulsed with shame that her own people had never accomplished anything in the realm of the books she loved.

The second picture shows a young girl teaching in a Southern city before it was supplied with modern sewerage, when to dig even eighteen inches in the ground brought one to water. The

Second-Reader lesson cheerfully told of the joys of storing red apples in the cellar to eat when the snow was on the ground. To explain snow to these children in a semi-tropical clime was a feat requiring Herculean efforts, and the modicum of impression made was tempered by open skepticism on the faces of the boys. But when the cellar problem was attacked all faith in the teacher's omniscience was blown to the four winds. What, a room underground? Why, everyone knew that you couldn't even dig a grave without its filling with water, much less have a whole room under ground! Prudence and decorum went to the winds, and the little teacher mopped her agitated forehead and prayed for Second Readers with Southern stories in them.

Third: a splendidly equipped school in a sea-side town. The windows of all the rooms on one side of the building overlooked the Atlantic Ocean, and every pane of glass framed a perfect vignette of cloud and wave and white-winged fishing smack, driving before the wind, or lying at anchor with graceful spars silhouetted against a myriad-hued sky. Yet every child in the art classes was busily painting apple orchards in full bloom, it being spring, and time for the apple orchards of New England and inland places to flower into whiteness and pinkness. There are no apple trees anywhere near this sandy strip of white coast that is pounded by the great waves, and spring for that section means the shy wild flowers that bloom in heaped sand dunes, or brilliant marsh-mallows flushing amidst swaying reeds. It means little saucy-frocked fishing smacks running through white-capped ultramarine waves. Yet in all that school not a child had been told to look out of the window and see the beauties of his own environment. They were copying the reputed beauties of a land miles inland.

These three pictures stand out in my mind because it seems to me that they symbolize the kind of teaching that we do so much of in some of our schools—the colored child, hungry for information, and yet ignorant of the history and achievements of its own race; pupils forced to insult their budding intelligence with an unnecessary situation; youthful artists turning their backs on the beauties about them and copying the counterfeit landscapes which they have never seen. It is high time that we throw off the shackles which convention binds around our educational methods and "let down our buckets where we are."

Every teacher in a colored school is a missionary. More than the mere instilling of so much knowledge in the heads of the pupils must he or she teach many other things, character through pride of race being one of the greatest. For the youth who is proud of his race and will endeavor to live up to its traditions, and will hesitate to do mean things lest they sully the escutcheon. As we have said before, the sentiment of pride and honor fostered in the Negro youth will fire his ambition, his desire to accomplish, even as others of his race have done before him. It is only the exceptional case, the overmastering genius who is thrilled with the desire to conquer because no other has done so. The ordinary one—and there are so many more of him than there are of any other kind—needs encouragement from the deeds of others.

But statistics mean nothing to children; they are colorless things, savoring too much of tables in arithmetic to be deeply intriguing. The child mind must have concrete examples, for it is essentially poetic and deals in images. It is not enough to say that black men fought in the Revolutionary War to the extent of so many in so many regiments. But there are a number of well-told, crisply narrated stories of Crispus Attucks, and even some narrative poems celebrate the first blood shed in the Revolutionary War. It is not enough to say that black slaves, from Massachusetts to Maryland, stood by the Nation when red-coated Tories overran the land. Dunbar's spirited ballad of "Black Samson of Brandywine" will fix the idea in the youthful mind, even as "Paul Revere's Ride" has fixed the date of the battle of Concord and Lexington in the minds of generations of young Americans, white and black, from Maine to California.

It is well for Negro children to know that the delightful fables of Æsop are the satires of a black slave, and that the author of the incomparable "Three Muskateers," which rejoices the swashbuckling instincts of the adolescent, was of Negro descent. There are exquisite little nature lyrics particularly snow scenes, by Pushkin (obtainable in translation) as perfect in their picturization, in a way, as those of Bryant, or that of Lowell's "First Snowfall"; and it would make the young chests swell with pride to know that these are the work of one of the greatest of Russian poets—an acknowledged Negro.

Apart from these exotic instances, the children might well be taught the folk tales of the race, as rich in content and moral lesson as can be found in any folk tales, from Æsop and Reynard the Fox to Uncle Remus. There is a mine of suggestion in Alphonso Stafford's "African Folk Stories." That classic, "The Seedling," by Dunbar, has delighted the little folks of a generation, with its botanical lesson encouched in delicate verse, and the inevitable moral admonition, which all children secretly love, at the end.

By the side of Maggie Tulliver we may place Zora, of

"The Quest of the Silver Fleece (DuBois)"; against Sparta-
cus and his address to the gladiators, is Dessalines and his defiant reminiscences; thrilling rescue stories might be matched
by the rescue of the lad in Durham's "Diane"; or by the round-
up scene from "The Love of Landry" (Dunbar), to give the
proper Western flavor to the boy or girl in love with the Bill
Hart type. In company with "The Charge of the Light Bri-
gade" is the "Second Louisiana," and the "Finish of Patsy
Barnes," (Dunbar), for those who love the small boy who overcomes obstacles for the sake of the mother ill at home. Thanksgiving is commemorated by Braithwaite as delightfully as ever Stevenson "gave thanks for many things" not to mention "Christmas," by Dunbar or similar poems by those others who have followed in his tread.

And the winged words of Booker Washington and
Frederick Douglass! The biographies of those who have accomplished great things in the face of heavy odds! Romances
of lives as thrilling as the romances which have grown up
around Lincoln and Daniel Boone! The girl, Phyllis, and the
lad, Paul! How much finer for the Negro boy and girl to know
of these lives, and of the work they did; to read the burning,
living words that are the work of their own blood and kin; to
feel that the lowly ones of the cabins in the country, or the
tenements and alleys in the city, may yet give to the world some
gift, albeit small, that will inspire and ennoble countless dark-
faced children struggling up towards the light.

Assuredly we will teach our boys and girls, not only their
own history and literature, but works by their own authors. We
will, ourselves, first achieve a sense of pride in our own productions, with a fine sense of literary values which will not allow
us to confuse trivialities and trash with literature. We will
learn to judge a thing as good, because of its intrinsic value and
not because it is a Negro's! We will be as quick to throw away
valueless stuff written by a black man or woman, as if it were
written by a white man or woman. In other words we will recognize but one absolute standard, and we will preserve for our children all that approximates that standard, and teach them to
reverence the good that is in their own because it is good.

And by so doing, we shall impress most deeply upon the
young people of our race, by our own literature, that most valuable of all lessons:—

> "Be proud, my race, in mind and soul:
> Thy name is writ on glory's scroll
>   In characters of fire;
> High, midst the clouds of Fame's bright sky,
> Thy banner's blazoned folds now fly,
>   And Truth shall lift them higher."

bingers of the new period into which Negroes appear to be emerging. Significantly, these are for the most part young writers, with a technique that is modern, and with the burning enthusiasm of a new race. They have the spirit. And it is not surprising that Claude Mackay whose "If We Must Die" has appeared in practically every Negro paper, and Countee Cullen, Jean Toomer, Gwendolyn Bennett and Langston Hughes, whose names already are becoming familiar, are well under twenty-five years. "A people that is producing poetry," says Robert T. Kerlin, "is not perishing, but is astir with life, with vital impulses, with life giving visions." It was this strange force that captured Zona Gale when she read Georgia Douglas Johnson's "Bronze." But both Mr. Kerlin and Miss Gale are speaking from a background of literary experience. In the September-October number of the *American Review* Dr. Robert E. Park, one of the leading sociologists of the country, clothes these same observations with a new interest and importance. "Freedom," he says, "has not given him (the Negro) the opportunity for participation in the common life of America and of the world that he hoped for. Negroes are restless and seeking. We are all restless, as a matter of fact. In some respects . . . the Negro, like all the other disin-

herited peoples, is more fortunate than the dominant races. He is restless, but he knows what he wants. The issues in his case, at least, are clearly defined. More than that, in this racial struggle he is daily gaining not merely new faith in himself, but new faith in the world. Since he wants nothing except what he is willing to give to every other man on the same terms, he feels that the great forces that shape the destinies of peoples are on his side."

The "dark ages" of Negro poetry are being left behind and along with this period has gone the muddled psychology of a distracted and overwhelmed race. These voices now speaking have caught not only the inspiration of newer ideals but the new spirit of Negro life.

Negro Life and Its Poets

There are new voices speaking from the depths and fullness of the Negro's life and they are har-

OUR BOOK SHELF

"Cane"
By Jean Toomer
(*Boni and Liveright, New York City*) .. ....
Price $2.00

Jean Toomer

The recent publication of "Cane" marks a distinct departure in southern literature and at the same time introduces a writer of extraordinary power in the person of Jean Toomer. Few books of recent years have greater significance for American letters than this "first" work of a young Negro, the nephew of an acting reconstruction governor of Louisiana. Fate has played another of its freakish pranks in decreeing that southern life should be given its most notable artistic expression by the pen of a native son of Negro descent.

It is a notorious fact that the United States south of the Mason and Dixon line has been, in the words of Mr. Mencken, a "Cultural Sahara." First torn and rent by the ravages of one of the most destructive civil strifes in all history, the states of the former confederacy have either used up their creative powers in mending the wreckage or have consumed them in the blighting fires of race hatred. The white South, with few exceptions, has sacrificed art for propaganda. Great art, like great deeds, cannot flourish in a land of bigotry and oppression. The great exception to this general indictment of the white South, Joel Chandler Harris, drew his material and his inspiration for his "Uncle Remus" stories from the unembittered and kindly lips of a former slave.

The Negro, altho immersed in the miasma of southern prejudice, because of his natural gentleness of soul and kindness of heart, suffers less from its pestilential influence than his white brother. Behold Paul Laurence Dunbar singing the plaintive songs of his people in immortal verse before the smoke of battle had cleared from the fields of Gettysburg and the Wilderness. Yet the Negro has been too conscious of his wrongs, too sensitive to oppression to be able to express the beauty of his racial life or to glorify his native soil. He has likewise resented the use of his folk-life for artistic purposes. It has been conceded that the varied life of the Negro in America, especially his folk-life, offers almost unparalleled opportunities for the brush of the artist and the pen of the poet. Max Rheinhardt, the world's premier dramatic director, during his recent visit to this country, stated that the chief contribution of America to the drama of tomorrow would be its development of Negro folk-drama. But what has been the attitude of the Negro himself? Unqualified opposition to the utilization of his mass life in fiction, in music, or in drama.

What has this attitude meant? It has robbed the race of its birthright for a mess of pottage. It has damned the possibilities of true artistic expression at its very source. It has enabled the white artist to exploit the Negro race for personal recognition or commercial gain. Instead of a faithful and sympathetic portrayal of our race-life by our own artists, we have been the victims of this alien exploitation, with the

result that caricatures of the race have been accepted as bona fide portraits.

Art is *self-expression*. The artist can only truly express his own soul or the race-soul. Not until Rene Maran, a Negro, had pictured the native life of Africa in "Batouala," did the dark continent find a true exponent of its wrongs and of its resentment against a cruel bondage. The white missionary or itinerant visitor had always described the natives in the light of his own preconceived prejudices.

America has waited for its own counterpart of Maran —for that native son who would avoid the pitfalls of propaganda and moralizing on the one hand and the snares of a false and hollow race pride on the other hand. One whose soul mirrored the soul of his people, yet whose vision was universal.

Jean Toomer, the author of "Cane," is in a remarkable manner the answer to this call. Sprung from the tangy soil of the South, he combines the inheritance of the old Negro and the spirit of the new Negro. His grandfather, P. B. S. Pinchback, was acting governor of Louisiana and later settled in Washington where his grandson, Jean Toomer, was born in 1894. Thus his childhood was spent in a home where dramatic incidents of slavery, of the Civil War and of Reconstruction, were household traditions. The "Song of the Sun," one of the several exquisite lyrics that appear in "Cane," shows the deep affection which young Toomer has for the old South:

"An everlasting song, a singing tree,
Caroling softly souls of slavery,
What they were, and what they are to me,
Caroling softly souls of slavery."

A youth rich in wide human experience and marked by a natural love for solitude followed. Later came an opportunity to teach at a small school in Georgia, where he secured the contacts with life in the South which were to give him his final inspirations for the book which is the subject of this criticism. "I felt strange, as I always do in Georgia, particularly at dusk. I felt that things unseen to men were tangibly immediate. It would not have surprised me had I had a vision. . . . When one is on the soil of one's ancestors, most anything can come to one."

"Cane" is not to be classified in terms of the ordinary literary types, for the genius of creation is evident in its form. Verse, fiction, and drama are fused into a spiritual unity, an "aesthetic equivalent" of the Southland. It is not a book to be intellectually understood; it must be emotionally, aesthetically felt. One must approach it with all of his five senses keenly alive if appreciation and enjoyment are to result. No previous writer has been able in any such degree to catch the sensuous beauty of the land or of its people or to fathom the deeper spiritual stirrings of the mass-life of the Negro. "Cane" is not OF the South, it is not OF the Negro; it IS the South, it IS the Negro—as Jean Toomer has experienced them. It may be added that the pictures do not pretend to be the only possible ones in such a vast panorama of life. "The Emperor Jones" was a study of one Negro as Eugene O'Neill saw him. That only. So with "Cane." It cannot be justly criticized because it does not harmonize with your personal conceptions, Mr. Reader!

"Cane" has three main divisions. The first division is laid in the land of cane, cotton and sawdust piles—Georgia. The second part deals with the more sophisticated life of the Negro "world within a world" in Washington. The third section is an intense drama of all the complicated elements of southern life, with its setting also in Georgia.

The writer will be pardoned for expressing his decided preference for the sketches, stories, and poems which comprise part one. Here the matchless beauty of the folk-life of the southern Negro is presented with intriguing charm. It is realism—not of the reportorial type found in "Main Street" writing—but the higher realism of the emotions. Here we have that mysterious, subtle and incomprehensible appeal of the South made all the more interesting because of the discordant and chaotic human elements submerged there. Of course, one is conscious of the protest of those who confuse superficial and transitory political and economic conditions with the underlying eternal elements. Those with an eye for beauty, an ear for music, and a heart for emotion, while abhorring the temporary victimizing of the South by unscrupulous demagogues, must still appreciate the fundamental Beauty which is revealed in "Cane."

The power of portraiture is unmistakable. No effort is made to create ideal characters or to make them conform to any particular standard. Here we have the method of Maran and all great artists. The characters appear in all of their lovable human qualities. We love them and yet pity them for human weaknesses for which not they but their ignorance and environment are largely responsible. It is not a question of morality but of life.

Toomer appreciates as an artist the surpassing beauty, both physical and spiritual, of the Negro woman and he has unusual facility of language in describing it. There is "Karintha at twenty, carrying beauty, perfect as the dusk as the sun goes down." A wayward child of nature whose tragedy was that "the soul of her was a growing thing ripened too soon." Of "Carma" it is said, "She does not sing; her body is a song." I prefer "Fern" to all the other portraits because the author has succeeded in conveying exquisite physical charm coupled with an almost divine quality of inarticulate spirituality. Sufficient tribute has never before been paid to the beauty of the Negro woman's eyes. Visitors from foreign lands have frequently pointed out this unique glory of our women. Is it any wonder? For do not their eyes express from mysterious depths the majesty of lost empires, the pathos of a woman's lot in slavery, and the spirit of a resurgent race? Fern's eyes. "Face flowed into eyes. Flowed in soft cream foam and plaintive ripples, in such a way that wherever your glance may momentarily have rested, it immediately thereafter wavered in the direction of her eyes. . . . If you have ever heard a Jewish cantor sing, if he has touched you and made your own sorrow seem trivial when compared with his, you know my feeling when I followed the curves of her profile, the mobile rivers, to their common delta." But her eyes were not of ordinary beauty. "They were strange eyes. In this, that they sought nothing—that is nothing that was obvious or tangible or that one could see. . . . Her eyes, unusually weird and open, held me. Held God. He flowed in as I have seen the countryside."

Mention must also be made of "Blood Burning Moon," a short story which closes this first section. Its splendid technique and striking theme are attested by the fact that O'Brien has included it in his collection of the best short stories of 1923.

A series of impressionistic views of Negro life in Washington, D. C., follows in the middle section of "Cane." Again one must be cautioned that the beauty of the work must be captured thru the senses. Seventh Street is a "crude boned, soft-skinned wedge of nigger life breathing its loafer air, jazz songs and love, thrusting unconscious rhythms, black reddish blood into the white and white-washed wood of Washington." Thickly scattered thru these pages are unforgettable "purple patches" which reveal the animate and inanimate life of You Street thru the sensitive emotional reactions of a poet. It must also be said that the style is more labored and sometimes puzzling. One feels at times as if the writer's emotions had out-run his expression. Is it that Mr. Toomer's highest inspiration is to be found in the folk-life of his beloved Southland and that his unmistakable distaste for the cramped and strictly conventionalized life of the city Negro restricts his power

of clear and forceful language? There is not the same easy rhythmic cadence of expression here as in the first division. There are also a few apparent irrelevancies (for the reader) in the text which add nothing to the total effect and detract from the artistic value of the whole. "Box Seat" which reaches high points of excellence in the portraiture of "Muriel," "Dan," and "Mrs. Pribby," and in its dramatic narrative style, limps at times with obscure writing. The thoughts attributed to "Dan," on page 124, are a case in point and strain the demand of art to the breaking point. The remaining narratives in this division are of great merit but on the whole are not of the same excellence as his chapters of Georgia life.

The drama of "Ralph Kabnis" closes the book and marks a return to Georgia. This is no ordinary drama. It can only be likened to the grimly powerful work of the Russian dramatists. Only Eugene O'Neill in America has written anything to measure up to its colossal conception. One competent critic has stated that only the Moscow Art Theatre could do justice to such a drama. It is to be hoped that a Negro Theatre will immediately arise capable of producing "Kabnis" and other plays sure to follow from Toomer.

"Kabnis" is the fitting climax to a remarkable book. Here are placed upon the stage the outstanding factors in the inner circle of Negro life. The traditional Negro is there—the Negro of the past—mute, blind, motionless, yet a figure of sphinx-like mystery and fascination. There is a type of young Negro, attractive, frivolous, and thoughtless. Then there is Kabnis himself, the talented, highly emotional, educated Negro who goes south to elevate his people but who lacks the strength of mind and character to withstand the pressure of the white South or the temptations within his own group. Finally, there is Lewis. "He is what a stronger Kabnis might have been. . . . His mouth and eyes suggest purpose guided by an adequate intelligence." Yet he does not understand these black people of the South and they do not understand him. In the end he flees from the situation without in any way helping his people who needed his help.

Evidently the author's implication is that there must be a welding into one personality of Kabnis and Lewis: the great emotionalism of the race guided and directed by a great purpose and a super-intelligence.

"Cane" leaves this final message with me. In the South we have a "powerful underground" race with a marvelous emotional power which like Niagara before it was harnessed is wasting itself. Release it into proper channels, direct its course intelligently, and you have possibilities for future achievement that challenge the imagination. The hope of the race is in the great blind forces of the masses properly utilized by capable leaders. "Dan goes to the wall and places his ear against it. That rumble comes from the earth's core. It is the mutter of powerful and underground races. . . . The next world savior is coming up that way."

MONTGOMERY GREGORY,
Washington, D. C.

*   *   *

THE YOUNGER LITERARY MOVEMENT

W. E. B. DuBois and Alain Locke

I

THERE have been times when we writers of the older set have been afraid that the procession of those who seek to express the life of the American Negro was thinning and that none were coming forward to fill the footsteps of the fathers. Dunbar is dead; Chesnutt is silent; and Kelly Miller is mooning after false gods while Brawley and Woodson are writing history rather than literature. But even as we ask "Where are the young Negro artists to mold and weld this mighty material about us?"—even as we ask, they come.

There are two books before me, which, if I mistake not, will mark an epoch: a novel by Jessie Fauset and a book of stories and poems by Jean Toomer. There are besides these, five poets writing: Langston Hughes, Countée Cullen, Georgia Johnson, Gwendolyn Bennett and Claude McKay. Finally, Negro men are appearing as essayists and reviewers, like Walter White and Eric Walrond. (And even as I write comes the news that a novel by Mr. White has just found a publisher.) Here then is promise sufficient to attract us.

We recognize the exquisite abandon of a new day in Langston Hughes' "Song For a Banjo". He sings:

Shake your brown feet, Liza,
Shake 'em Liza, chile,
Shake your brown feet, Liza,
    (The music's soft and wile).
Shake your brown feet, Liza,
    (The Banjo's sobbin' low),
The sun's goin' down this very night—

LANGSTON HUGHES

Might never rise no mo'.

Countée Cullen in his "Ballad of the Brown Girl" achieves eight lyric lines that are as true as life itself. There is in Claude McKay's "If We Must Die" a strain martial and mutinous. There are other echoes—two from dead poets Jamison and Cotter who achieved in their young years long life if not immortality. But this essay is of two books.

The world of black folk will some day arise and point to Jean Toomer as a writer who first dared to emancipate the colored world from the conventions of sex. It is quite impossible for most Americans to realize how straight-laced and conventional thought is within the Negro World, despite the very unconventional acts of the group. Yet this contradiction is true. And Jean Toomer is the first of our writers to hurl his pen across the very face of our sex conventionality. In "Cane",* one has only to take his women characters seriatim to realize this: Here is Karintha, an innocent prostitute; Becky, a fallen white woman; Carma, a tender Amazon of unbridled desire; Fern, an unconscious wanton; Esther, a woman who looks age and bastardy in the face and flees in despair; Louise, with a white and a black lover; Avey, unfeeling and unmoral; and Doris, the cheap chorus girl. These are his women, painted with a frankness that is going to make his black readers shrink and criticize; and yet they are done with a certain splendid, careless truth.

* Boni & Liveright, New York.

Toomer does not impress me as one who knows his Georgia but he does know human beings; and, from the background which he has seen slightly and heard of all his life through the lips of others, he paints things that are true, not with Dutch exactness, but rather with an impressionist's sweep of color. He is an artist with words but a conscious artist who offends often by his apparently undue striving for effect. On the other hand his powerful book is filled with felicitous phrases — Karintha, "carrying beauty perfect as the dusk when the sun goes down",—

"Hair—
Silver-grey
Like streams of
stars"

Or again, "face flowed into her eyes —flowed in soft creamy foam and plaintive ripples". His emotion is for the most part entirely objective. One does not feel that he feels much and yet the fervor of his descriptions shows that he has felt or knows what feeling is. His art carries much that is difficult or even impossible to understand. The artist, of course, has a right deliberately to make his art a puzzle to the interpreter (the whole world is a puzzle) but on the other hand I am myself unduly irritated by this sort of thing. I cannot, for the life of me, for instance see why Toomer could not have made the tragedy of Carma something that I could understand instead of vaguely guess at; "Box Seat" muddles me to the last degree and I am not sure that I know what "Kabnis" is about. All of these essays and stories, even when I do not understand them, have their strange flashes of power, their numerous messages and numberless reasons for being. But still for me they are partially spoiled.

JEAN TOOMER

Toomer strikes me as a man who has written a powerful book but who is still watching for the fullness of his strength and for that calm certainty of his art which will undoubtedly come with years.

It had been my intention when I began this essay to discuss also Miss Fauset's novel. But Mr. Locke has sent us such an admirable and discriminating disquisition on this book that I gladly yield to him.

—W. E. B. D.

II

THE novel that the Negro intelligentzia have been clamoring for has arrived with Jessie Fauset's first novel, "There is Confusion".* What they have been wanting, if I interpret rightly, is not merely a race story told from the inside, but a cross section of the race life higher up the social pyramid and further from the base-line of the peasant and the soil than is usually taken. We scarcely realize how by reaction to social prejudice we have closed our better circles physically and psychologically: it is not always the fault of the novelist that he can depict only the peasant type and his urban analogue, the Negro of the slums. But here in refreshing contrast with the bulk of fiction about the Negro, we have a novel of the educated and aspiring classes. Miss Fauset has, however, not made the error of growing rootless flowers or exploring detached levels. Indeed she has sketched a Negro group against a wide social background of four generations—almost as much perspective as can be gotten on any social group in America, and moreover has not glossed over the slave régime,

* Boni & Liveright, New York.

its ugly facts and its uglier consequences, though she has treated it incidentally as part of the genealogy and heredity of her characters. It is essentially a novel of blood and ancestry such as might be expected to come from the Philadelphia tradition which the author shares, and the Philadelphia scene which is part of her story. Yet it is too contemporary, not merely in incident, but in the phase of the race problem which it reflects, to be a period novel, a resurrection of the past. On the contrary it throbs with some of the latest reactions of the race situation in this country upon the psychology and relations of colored and w h i t e Americans of the more intelligent classes. It is this delineation of the problem as seen from the heights of r e s p e c tability and from at least a plateau of culture that sharply differentiates Miss Fauset's novel from others.

Joanna Marshall— more a heroine than most heroines, since she actually focusses and dominates in turn the life of her family, t h e estrangements and marriages of her brother and of her lover — is a strange c h a r a c t e r at war against herself. One part stoic, one part artistic, one part human with an emotional intensity and sincerity that is not Caucasian, she achieves success in her art at the very instant of her greatest disillusionment; but not before she has played unconscious havoc with several lives by her ambition and unswerving devotion to the ideals of success.

Complicated as these lives are at almost every turn by the peculiar handicaps and confusions of color, it is well for the artistry and the worth of the book that the *primary confusions are those more universal ones of human nature and its type-psychologies.* The atmosphere of the book is that of

JESSIE FAUSET

Quaker faith and sober optimism, and its constructive suggestion is that of an eventual mutual understanding and coöperation through the discipline of experience. It is as though two antithetic sides of life, male and female, white and black, had each to work out its own chastening and enlargement through sorrow and disillusionment to find itself, late but not always too tragically late, able to rise from the level of confusion to the level of coöperation and understanding.

The book has what I maintain is the prime essential for novels with such subject matter—social perspective, social sanity. A problem novel without this is either a raw and brutal cross-sectioning or medicated and unpalatable propaganda. F r o m these two evils, the book happily and skillfully escapes. Of the style, one may say, that it fits the subject —and in this day of the confusion and compounding of styles, what can be better said? Certainly it sustains with interest a story that is more heavily ballasted with truth than two or three of the usual run of social novels that sail on a breezy style to the heavens of "six best sellers". So that it can be confidently commended to that increasing band who, thank God, want truth with their fiction, and who will welcome especially upon the race question and its reactions on the best types and classes of colored folk, a social document of sterling and intimate character.   —A. L.

III

THESE, then, are the two books of the younger Negro Movement; read them and enjoy them as I have done and spread the glad tidings.   —W. E. B. D.

The subject "Negro" like the subject "sex" has been tabooed in polite circles, and the stripping off of the veil within the last two years follows with stern consistency our modernistic trend in literature as well as in life. There are three shows on Broadway with or about Negro characters and another planning appearance. Periodicals for the general reading public are carrying with increasing frequency stories and discussions of this long pocketed element of the population.

For a large measure of this new and generally distributed curiosity the numerous formal interracial bodies, with their discussions and study groups, are responsible. It is perhaps fortunate that interest in the Negro is a stamp of liberal-mindedness. But sharing with these formal agencies is the undoubted influence of the new group of young Negro writers who have dragged themselves out of the deadening slough of the race's historical inferiority complex, and with an unconquerable audacity are beginning to make this group interesting. They are leaving to the old school its labored lamentations and protests, read only by those who agree with them, and are writing about life. And it may be said to the credit of literary America, that where these bold strokes emancipate their message from the miasma of race they are being accepted as literature. A good instance of this may be noted in the quite unqualified appraisal of the work of Eric D. Walrond, one of this new group, by the editor of *Success* in introducing him to its nationwide circulation. There was no racial coddling or philanthropic condescension in the statement:

> "*Success* takes pleasure in presenting this new, young master of vivid narrative, believing that in him eventually is the making of one of the greatest novelists and short story writers of our day. . . . *The Godless City* is a portrait of a modern Pompeii that even Pliny could not have equaled—bald, brilliant descriptions of men and manners—or lack of manners, which ever you chose."

Jean Toomer, author of the exotic "Cane," is at work on a second volume and two other novels by Negro writers are about to appear. This is a healthy state for race relations. This freedom of discussion and new curiosity may well be regarded a first effectual blow in the destruction of those barriers of mutual ignorance and prejudice, hatred and fear, which long have throttled understanding.

The New Generation

There has been manifest recently a most amazing change in the public mind on the question of the Negro. There is a healthy hunger for more information—a demand for a new interpretation of characters long and admittedly misunderstood. The moderate success of books like "Black and White," "Birthright," "Nigger," followed by the even more daring departure, both in style and content, in books like "Holiday" and "Cane" is enormously significant. They point to a gentle awakening among a large mass of the reading public which until recently would take its pictures from virulent Negro baiters only, or remain indifferent.

A PAIR OF YOUTHFUL NEGRO POETS

BY ROBERT T. KERLIN

THE success of a Negro youth of twenty years in winning the second place in the American Poetry Society's contest, open to all undergraduates in American colleges, will draw fresh attention to Negro talent in the poetic art. His production, "The Ballad of the Brown Girl," will, I predict, more than fulfill whatever expectations any reader may have in taking it up, and will evoke surprise not unmixed with admiration. The whole effect will linger, pleasurably, teasingly.

The ballad is in line with the brilliant tradition created by the modern masters who sought, distantly, to imitate the antique manner—Coleridge, Scott, Morris, Rossetti. Not less original, nor less successful than these masters, is young Countee P. Cullen, the author of this ballad. To bestow such praise may be a disservice both to author and to reader but if one is to say anything one can say no less. I still leave room, I think, for surprise and delight of a keenly esthetic quality.

But having said thus much of his prize poem (which it is to be hoped has been made generally accessible to the public ere this) I wish to devote a little space to Mr. Cullen's previous work in verse as it has come to my notice from time to time in *The Crisis;* and with his name I wish to join that of another young Negro poet, likewise a contributor to *The Crisis*—Mr. Langston Hughes. They are friends and kindred spirits, yet with individual and distinctive merits. I will present two or three lyrics from each, with a reserve of comment. For who can miss the singing quality and lyrical artistry in such verses as these?

ROAD SONG

This will I say today,
　Lest no tomorrow come;
Thy words are singing birds
　That strike my faint lyre dumb.
This will I vow thee now,
　Lest vows should go unsaid:
Thou art unto my heart
　A song to wake the dead.
This oath I take to break
　When fails the lover's code:
To fare as thou, and share
　With thee each winding road.
Thus do I deal my seal,
　No alien one may break;
Thy mouth to mine, as south
　The long lone trail we take.

32

To a different tune runs the next. It suggests—and several other pieces I have from Mr. Cullen confirm the impression —that his lyre is rich in notes, and that as yet we have heard but easy preludes.

DAD

His ways are circumspect and bound
　　With trite simplicities;
His is the grace of comforts found
　　In homely hearthside ease.
His words are sage and fall with care,
　　Because he loves me so;
And being his, he knows, I fear,
　　The dizzy path I go.
For he was once as young as I,
　　As prone to take the trail,
To find delight in the sea's low cry,
　　And a lone wind's lonely wail.
It is his eyes that tell me most
　　How full his life has been;
There lingers there the faintest ghost
　　Of some still sacred sin.

So I must quaff Life's crazy wine,
　　And taste the gall and dregs;
And I must spend this wealth of mine,
　　Of vagrant wistful legs;
And I must follow, follow, follow
　　The lure of a silver horn,
That echoes from a leafy hollow,
　　Where the dreams of youth are born.
Then, when the star has shed its gleam,
　　The rose its crimson coat;
When Beauty flees the hidden dream,
　　And Pan's pipes blow no note;
When both my shoes are worn too thin
　　My weight of fire to bear,
I'll turn like Dad, and like him win
　　The peace of a snug arm-chair.

In the pieces I shall present from Mr. Hughes, two years the senior of his friend, I wish to exhibit or at least suggest, not so much the diversity of his talent as its particular bent. Hence I will give a free-verse specimen and two melodies of the Negro folk variety.

BEGGAR BOY

What is there within this beggar lad
　　That I can neither hear nor feel nor see,
That I can neither know nor understand,
　　And still it calls to me?
Is not he but a shadow in the sun—
　　A bit of clay, brown, ugly, given life?
And yet he plays upon his flute a wild free
　　tune,
As if Fate had not bled him with her knife!

DANSE AFRICAINE

The low beating of the tom-toms,
The low beating of the tom-toms,
    Slow . . . . slow
    Low . . . . slow—
    Stirs your blood.
        Dance!
A night-veiled girl whirls softly
    Into a circle of light,
    Whirls softly . . . . slowly,
Like a wisp of smoke around the fire—
    And the tom-toms beat,
    And the tom-toms beat,
And the low beating of the tom-toms
    Stirs your blood.

SONG FOR A BANJO DANCE

Shake your brown feet, honey,
Shake your brown feet, chil',
Shake your brown feet, honey,
Shake 'em swift and wil'—
        Get way back, honey,
        Do that low-down step.
    Get on over, darling,
        Now! Step out
        With your left.
Shake your brown feet, honey,
Shake 'em, honey chil'.

Sun's going down this evening—
Might never rise no mo'.
The sun's going down this very night—
Might never rise no mo'—
So dance with swift feet, honey,
    (The banjo's sobbing low),
Dance with swift feet, honey—
Might never dance no mo'.

Shake your brown feet, Liza,
Shake 'em, Liza, chil',
Shake your brown feet, Liza,
    (The music's soft and wil').
Shake your brown feet, Liza,
    (The banjo's sobbing low),
The sun's going down this very night—
    Might never rise no mo'.

Those of us who are demanding of the Negro poet something as distinctly African, and as pre-eminent, as the spirituals of the Southern plantation may at any time find it offered us. There are preluding notes to be heard even now, and the aspiration to achieve the great lyrical tragic drama of which not only slavery but subsequent history furnishes the rich material, is not wanting. The soul of the Negro that is expressing itself by the voice of Roland Hayes, and through the acting of Charles Gilpin, is groping its way to the mastery of a more articulate expression—the art of Æschylus and of the author of Job and the author of the Passion Play of Oberammergau.

The Debut of the Younger School of Negro Writers

INTEREST among the literati of New York in the emerging group of younger Negro writers found an expression in a recent meeting of the Writers' Guild, an informal group whose membership includes Countee Cullen, Eric Walrond, Langston Hughes, Jessie Fauset, Gwendolyn Bennett, Harold Jackman, Regina Anderson, and a few others. The occasion was a "coming out party," at the Civic Club, on March 21—a date selected around the appearance of the novel "There Is Confusion" by Jessie Fauset. The responses to the invitations sent out were immediate and enthusiastic and the few regrets that came in were genuine.

Although there was no formal, prearranged program, the occasion provoked a surprising spontaneity of expression both from the members of the writers' group and from the distinguished visitors present.

A brief interpretation of the object of the Guild was given by Charles S. Johnson, Editor of *Opportunity,* who introduced Alain Locke, virtual dean of the movement, who had been selected to act as Master of Ceremonies and to interpret the new currents manifest in the literature of this younger school. Alain Locke has been one of the most resolute stimulators of this group, and although he has been writing longer than most of them, he is distinctly a part of the movement. One excerpt reflects the tenor of his remarks. He said: "They sense within their group—meaning the Negro group—a spiritual wealth which if they can properly expound will be ample for a new judgment and re-appraisal of the race."

Horace Liveright, publisher, told about the difficulties, even yet, of marketing books of admitted merit. The value of a book cannot be gauged by the sales. He regarded Jean Toomer's "Cane" as one of the most interesting that he had handled, and yet, less than 500 copies had been sold. In his exhortations to the younger group he warned against the danger of reflecting in one's writings the "inferiority complex" which is so insistently and frequently apparent in an overbalanced emphasis on "impossibly good" fiction types. He felt that to do the best writing it was necessary to give a rounded picture which included bad types as well as good ones since both of these go to make up life.

Dr. W. E. B. Du Bois made his first public appearance and address since his return to this country from Africa. He was introduced by the chairman with soft seriousness as a representative of the "older school." Dr. Du Bois explained that the Negro writers of a few years back were of necessity pioneers, and much of their style was forced upon them by the barriers against publication of literature about Negroes of any sort.

James Weldon Johnson was introduced as an anthologist of Negro verse and one who had given invaluable encouragement to the work of this younger group.

Carl Van Doren, Editor of the *Century,* spoke on the future of imaginative writing among Negroes. His remarks are given in full elsewhere in this issue.

Another young Negro writer, Walter F. White, whose novel "Fire in Flint" has been accepted for publication, also spoke and made reference to the passing of the stereotypes of the Negroes of fiction.

Professor Montgomery Gregory of Howard University, who came from Washington for the meeting, talked about the possibilities of Negroes in drama and told of the work of several talented Negro writers in this field, some of whose plays were just coming into recognition.

Another visitor from Philadelphia, Dr. Albert C. Barnes, art connoisseur and foremost authority in America on primitive Negro art, sketched the growing interest in this art which had had such tremendous influence on the entire modern art movement.

Miss Jessie Fauset was given a place of distinction on the program. She paid her respects to those friends who had contributed to her accomplishments, acknowledging a particular debt to her "best friend and severest critic," Dr. Du Bois.

The original poems read by Countee Cullen were received with a tremendous ovation. Miss Gwendolyn Bennett's poem, dedicated to the occasion, is reproduced. It is called

"To Usward"

Let us be still
As ginger jars are still
Upon a Chinese shelf,
And let us be contained
By entities of Self. . . .

Not still with lethargy and sloth,
But quiet with the pushing of our growth;
Not self-contained with smug identity,
But conscious of the strength in entity.

If any have a song to sing that's different from
　　the rest,
Oh, let him sing before the urgency of Youth's
　　behest!

And some of us have songs to sing
Of jungle heat and fires;
And some of us are solemn grown
With pitiful desires;
And there are those who feel the pull
Of seas beneath the skies;

And some there be who want to croon
Of Negro lullabies.
We claim no part with racial dearth,
We want to sing the songs of birth!

And so we stand like ginger jars,
Like ginger jars bound round
With dust and age;
Like jars of ginger we are sealed
By nature's heritage.
But let us break the seal of years
With pungent thrusts of song,
For there is joy in long dried tears,
For whetted passions of a throng!

Among the guests present were Paul Kellogg,
Editor of the *Survey*; Devere Allen, Editor of
The World Tomorrow; Freda Kirchwey and
Evans Clark of the *Nation*; Mr. and Mrs. Frederick
L. Allen of Harper Brothers; Mr. and
Mrs. Arthur B. Spingarn; Mr. and Mrs. Horace
Liveright; L. Hollingsworth Wood; Mr.
and Mrs. Eugene Kinckle Jones; Georgette
Carneal; Georgia Douglas Johnson of Washington,
D. C.; Louis Weitzenkorn of the
New York *World*; A. Granville Dill; Mr. and
Mrs. George E. Haynes; Mr. and Mrs. Graham
R. Taylor; Mr. and Mrs. John Daniels; A. A.
Schomburg; Eva D. Bowles of the Y.W.C.A.;
Mr. and Mrs. Jesse Moorland; Mr. and Mrs.
Walter Bartlett; Talcott Williams; Mr. and Mrs.
Arthur C. Holden; Mr. and Mrs. James H.
Hubert; Ottie Graham; Eunice Hunton; Anna
L. Holbrook; Crystal Bird; Dr. and Mrs. E. P.
Roberts; J. A. Rogers; Cleveland Allen, Mrs.
Gertrude McDougal; William Andrews; Mabel
Bird; Dr. and Mrs. Matthew Boutte; William

Holly; Roger Baldwin; Mary White Ovington;
and others, numbering about one hundred and ten.
Of those who could not come Oswald Garrison
Villard, Editor of the *Nation,* wrote:

"Nothing would give me greater pleasure
than attending the dinner to be given to the
young Negro writers on the 21st, but unhappily
it is necessary for me to be out of
town on that date."

From Herbert Bayard Swope, Editor of the
New York *World*:

"I am heartily in sympathy with the purpose
of your dinner on the 21st and I should
be glad to go were it any other date but that.
You have my best wishes for the complete
success of your 'coming out' party."

Dorothy Scarborough, author of "In the Land
of Cotton," said:

"I think your plan an admirable one, and
I send you my heartiest good wishes for the
success of all your writers. I have always
taken a great interest in the talents which
your race possesses, and I rejoice in your
every achievement."

George W. Ochs Oakes, Editor of *Current
History,* wrote:

"I wish to commend you for the steps
that have been taken in this direction and
believe that it will do a great deal to stimulate
serious intellectual and literary work
among the Negroes. I have found evidences
of striking literary capacity and fine intellectual
expression among the young Negro
writers who have contributed to our magazine."

The Younger Generation of Negro Writers

By CARL VAN DOREN

I HAVE a genuine faith in the future of imaginative
writing among Negroes in the United
States. This is not due to any mere personal interest
in the writers of the race whom I happen
to know. It is due to a feeling that the Negroes
of the country are in a remarkable strategic position
with reference to the new literary age which
seems to be impending.

Long oppressed and handicapped, they have gathered
stores of emotion and are ready to burst
forth with a new eloquence once they discover adequate
mediums. Being, however, as a race not
given to self-destroying bitterness, they will, I
think, strike a happy balance between rage and
complacency—that balance in which passion and
humor are somehow united in the best of all possible
amalgams for the creative artist.

*Remarks at the Dinner of the Writers' Guild, held at
the Civic Club.*

The Negroes, it must be remembered, are our
oldest American minority. First slavery and then
neglect have forced them into a limited channel
of existence. Once they find a voice, they will
bring a fresh and fierce sense of reality to their
vision of human life on this continent, a vision
seen from a novel angle by a part of the population
which cannot be duped by the bland optimism
of the majority.

Nor will their vision, I think, be that solely
of drastic censure and dissent, such as might be
expected of them in view of all they have endured
from majority rule. Richly gifted by nature with
distinctive traits, they will be artists while they
are being critics. They will look at the same
world that the white poets and novelists and dramatists
look at, yet, arraigning or enjoying it, will
keep in their modes of utterance the sympathies,
the memories, the rhythms of their ancient stock.

That Negro writers must long continue to be
propagandists, I do not deny. The wrongs of

their people are too close to them to be overlooked. But it happens that in this case the vulgar forms of propaganda are all unnecessary. The facts about Negroes in the United States are themselves propaganda—devastating and unanswerable. A Negro novelist who tells the simple story of any aspiring colored man or woman will call as with a bugle the minds of all just persons, white or black, to listen to him.

But if the reality of Negro life is itself dramatic, there are of course still other elements, particularly the emotional power with which Negroes live—or at least to me seem to live. What American literature decidedly needs at the moment is color, music, gusto, the free expression of gay or desperate moods. If the Negroes are not in a position to contribute these items, I do not know what Americans are.

The Spirit of Phyllis Wheatley

A Review of "There Is Confusion"
By Jessie Redmon Fauset
(*Boni and Liveright, New York. Price* $2.00)
By MONTGOMERY GREGORY

I HAVE here on my desk the first editions of two noteworthy books, both written by Negro women, and both having a significance far beyond their intrinsic merit. The publication of this modest brown volume of verse in 1773 marked the first accomplishment in literature by an American Negro and it may, therefore, be said to mark the beginning of Negro culture in the United States. The fact that it won not only personal recognition for a slave girl, Phyllis Wheatley, but also recognition of the intellectual capabilities of her race, made it necessary for a "committee of the most respectable citizens of Boston," headed by Governor Thomas Hutchinson and John Hancock, to attest publicly "that she had been examined by some of the best judges and thought qualified to write them"! No other fact in those early days had such a devastating effect upon the doctrine of Negro inferiority as the publication of this slender book of verse more than a century and a half ago.

This other book in its attractive orange jacket is Jessie Redmon Fauset's novel, "There Is Confusion," just off the press of Boni and Liveright. It is also a "first" book, being the first recognized novel written by a Negro woman and, in fact, the first treatment in fiction of the educated strata of Negro urban life. Is it strange that several well known critics express surprise that a standard novel should be written by a woman of the black race or that the cultured group of that race described in the novel actually exists? As yet no "committee of respectable citizens" has been formed to examine her, although she was the object of curious, if polite, attention at a recent dinner attended by the literary "big-wigs" of New York. However, these gentlemen are unanimous in saying that this novel presents to white America a milieu of its civilization of which it has been totally ignorant and they gladly welcome this opportunity of "looking in" on the actual life of the more cultured class of Negroes. Here lies the great value of this novel, in interpreting the better elements of our life to those who know us only as domestic servants, "uncles," or criminals. The tremendous potentiality of such an influence was indicated in the recent statement of Horace Liveright, that a large proportion of the orders coming from Great Britain during a recent month for publications of his firm were for "There Is Confusion." This modern Phyllis Wheatley is winning a new understanding for the Negro and a wider respect and recognition for him throughout the world of culture.

Miss Fauset's novel has perhaps an even greater value to the Negro himself. It is a sincere effort to view the life of the race artistically—objectively. Heretofore we have either imbibed the depreciatory estimates of our enemies or gulped down the uncritical praise of our friends. We have not dared to see ourselves as we really are nor have our artists treated our life as material to be objectively moulded into creations of beauty. Our writers of the younger school have been the first to catch this sound point of view and upon their strict adherence to it in the future depends the successful development of Negro art and literature. Even Miss Fauset occasionally errs in this respect

41

and diverts the reader's interest from her story into bypaths of special pleading against race prejudice.

Then, again, the success of such writers as Jessie Fauset and Jean Tooner is ample proof that true merit can surmount the barriers of race prejudice and that the doors of the literary world are at least ajar for the talented and ambitious youth of the race. Both of these writers also offer the lesson that the more ambitious works cannot be attained by sudden flight, but only by long and patient apprenticeship in the writing of short stories.

Technically "There Is Confusion" more than reaches the level of the better class of contemporary American fiction. The romance of Peter Bye and Joanna Marshall, etched on the interesting background of the family life of the cultured Negroes of Philadelphia and New York, is well conceived and skilfully executed. The plot holds the interest of the reader unflaggingly to the end. There are fewer faults of construction than might be expected in a "first" novel. It may be said, however, that the latter part of the story is the least convincing. For example, although there is practically no mention of the World War throughout the main part of the novel, it suddenly appears, apparently to enable several of the characters to straighten out their careers and to offer the opportunity for a dramatic conclusion. The characters are cleverly drawn, especially that of Maggie Ellersley who, like Brutus, although not intended to be the leading figure in the story, certainly appeals to the reviewer as the finest achievement of the author. On the other hand, the white Byes, young Meriweather Bye and his grandfather seem to make their entrance on the stage as supernumeraries and to add little of value to the novel.

This is not the place to retell this splendid story of Negro life. It is sufficient to say that Jessie Fauset has created a novel of unusual power and exceptional artistry and in doing so she has not only reflected credit upon herself but has likewise rendered her race an inestimable service. It may be safely predicted that this is only the beginning of a successful career as an outstanding American novelist.

I cannot refrain from wondering why there was so much "confusion" in the typesetting room of the publishers of this novel. Perhaps the "printer's devil" got loose among the type and was responsible for the errata, some of which are indicated on the fly-leaf of the book!

Finally, permit me to make an earnest plea for a practical appreciation of Miss Fauset's achievement. "There Is Confusion" should be read by every intelligent Negro in America and it should be brought to the attention of every high school and college student in the race. We cannot expect the leading publishers of this country to continue to accept the works of our writers unless the demand for them is sufficient to justify the enormous expense involved. If our poets, novelists, and dramatists are to succeed we must form a large reading public for the products of their pens. Let the slogan be: *Read the works of our own writers first!*

THE NEGRO IN LITERATURE

WILLIAM STANLEY BRAITHWAITE

TRUE of his origin on this continent, the Negro was projected into literature by his neighbor. He was *in* American literature long before he was a part of it as a creator. I ought to qualify this last, perhaps, by saying, that as a racial unit during more than two centuries of an enslaved peasantry, the Negro's creative qualities were affirmed in the *Spirituals*. In these, as was true of the European folk-stock, the race gave evidence of an artistic psychology; without this artistic psychology no race can develop vision which becomes articulate in the sophisticated forms and symbols of cultivated expression. Expressing itself with poignancy and a symbolic imagery unsurpassed, indeed, often unmatched, by any folk-group, the race in servitude was at the same time both the finished shaping of emotion and imagination, and also the most precious mass of raw material for literature America was producing. Quoting the first, third and fifth stanzas of James Weldon Johnson's *"O Black and Unknown Bards,"* I want you to take it as the point in the assertion of the Negro's way into literature:

O black and unknown bards of long ago,
  How came your lips to touch the sacred fire?
How, in your darkness, did you come to know
  The power and beauty of the minstrel's lyre?
Who first from midst his bonds lifted his eyes?
  Who first from out the still watch, lone and long,
Feeling the ancient faith of prophets rise
  Within his dark-kept soul, burst into song?

What merely living clod, what captive thing,
  Could up toward God through all its darkness grope,
And find within its deadened heart to sing
  These songs of sorrow, love, and faith and hope?
How did it catch that subtle undertone,
  That note in music heard not with the ears?
How sound the elusive reed so seldom blown,
  Which stirs the soul or melts the heart to tears?

There is a wide, wide wonder in it all,
  That from degraded rest and servile toil
The fiery spirit of the seer should call
  These simple children of the sun and soil.
O black slave singers, gone, forgot, unfamed,
  You—you, alone, of all the long, long line
Of those who've sung untaught, unknown, unnamed,
  Have stretched out upward, seeking the divine.

Because it was possible to sing thus of a race: of a race oppressed, illiterate, and toil-ridden, it became also by some divine paradox irresistibly urgent to make literary material out of the imagination and emotion it possessed in such abundance.

I can do no more than outline the Negro in literature as he has been treated by American writers of mixed nationalities. I present this word *nationalities* because, though American by a declaration of a unity, one must not overlook the deep and subtle atavistic impulses and energies which have directed, or misdirected, the imagination, in creating character and experience, atmosphere and traits, in the use of the Negro as literary material.

The first conspicuous example, and one which has more profoundly influenced the world than any other, of the Negro in literature was "Uncle Tom's Cabin." Here was a sentimentalized sympathy for a downtrodden Race, but one in which was projected a character, in Uncle Tom himself, which has been unequalled to this day. The Negro in literature had its starting point with this book. Published in 1852, it foreran for many years the body of literature which began during Reconstruction and lasted until the publication of Thomas Dixon's "The Leopard's Spots," which began, and was the exponent, of an era of riot and lawlessness in literary expression. Between the Civil War and the end of the century the subject of the Negro in literature is one that will some day inspire the literary historian with a magnificent theme. It will be magnificent not because there is any sharp emergence of character or incidents, but because of the immense paradox of racial life which came up thunderingly against the principles and doctrines of Democracy and put them to the severest test that they had known. It was a period when, in literature, Negro life was a shuttlecock between the two extremes of humor and pathos. The Negro was free, and was not free. The writers who dealt with him for the most part, refused to see the tragedy of his situation and capitalized his traits of humor. These writers did not see that his humor was a mask for the tragedies which were constantly a turbulent factor in his consciousness. If any of the authors who dealt with the Negro during this period had possessed gifts anywhere near approaching to genius, they would have penetrated this deceiving exterior of Negro life, sounded the depths of tragedy in it, and have produced a masterpiece. Irwin Russell was the first to versify the superficial humor of this Race, and, though all but forgotten today by the reading world, is given the characteristic credit by literary historians for discovering and recording the phantasies of Negro humor. Thomas Nelson Page, a kindly gentleman with a purely local imagination, painted an ante-bellum Negro in his fiction which was infinitely more truthful to the type contemporaneous with his own manhood during the restitution of the over-lordship of the defeated slave owners in the Eighties. Another writer, who of all Americans made the most permanent contribution in dealing with the Negro, was Joel Chandler Harris. Much as we admire this lovable personality, the arts of his achievements were not in himself, but in the Race who supplied his servile pen with a store of fertile folk material. Indeed, the Race was its own artist, and only in its illiteracy lacked the power to record its speech. Joel Chandler Harris was the divinely appointed amanuensis to preserve the oral tales and legends of a Race in the "B'rer Rabbit" cycle.

The three writers I have mentioned do not by any means exhaust the list of writers who put the Negro into literature during the last half of the Nineteenth century. Mr. Howells added a shadowy note to his social record of American life with "An Imperative Duty" and prophesied the Fiction of the "Color Line". But his moral scruples—the persistent, artistic vice in all his novels—prevented him from consummating a just union between his heroine with a touch of Negro blood and his hero. It is useless to consider any others because there were none who succeeded in creating either a great story or a great character out of Negro life. Two writers of greater importance than the three I have named dealing with Negro life, are themselves Negroes, and I am reserving discussion of them for the group of Race writers I shall name presently. One ought to say, in justice to the writers I have mentioned, that as white Americans it was incompatible with their conception of the inequalities between the races to glorify the Negro into the serious and leading position of hero or heroine in fiction. Only one man, that I recall, had both the moral and artistic courage to do this and that was Stephen Crane in a short story called "The Monster". But Stephen Crane was a man of genius and, therefore, could not besmirch the integrity of an artist.

With Thomas Dixon, "The Leopard's Spots", we reach a distinct stage in the treatment of the Negro in fiction. In this book the Color Line type of fiction is, frankly, and viciously used for purposes of propaganda. This Southern author foresaw an inevitable consequence of the intimate contact and intercourse between the two races, in this country. He had good evidence upon which to base his fears. He was, however, too late with his cry for race purity—which meant, of course, Anglo-Saxon purity. The cry itself ought to have shamed all those critics who approved it; whose consciences must have taken a twinge in recollecting how the Saxon passion had found so sweetly desirable the black body of Africa. Had Dixon been a thinker, had his mind been stored with the complex social history of mankind, he would have saved himself a futile and ridiculous literary gesture. Thomas Dixon, of a quarter of a century ago, and Lothrop Stoddard of to-day, are a pair of literary twins whom nature has made sport of, and who will ultimately submerge in a typhoon of Truth. For Truth is devastating to all who would pervert the ways of nature.

Following "The Leopard's Spots", it was only occasionally during the next twenty years that the Negro was sincerely treated in fiction by white authors. There were two or three tentative efforts to dramatize him. Sheldon's "The Nigger," was the one notable early effort. And in fiction Paul Kester's "His Own Country" is from a purely literary point of view, its outstanding performance. This type of novel failed, however, to awaken any general interest. This failure was due, I believe, to the illogical ideas and experiences presented, for there is, however indifferent and negative it may seem, a desire on the part of self-respecting readers, to have honesty of purpose, and a full vision in the artist.

The first hint that the American artist was looking at this subject with full vision was in Torrence's "Granny Maumee". It was drama, conceived and executed for performance on the stage, and therefore had a restricted appeal. But even here the artist was concerned with the primitive instincts of the Race, and, though, faithful and honest, in his portrayal, the note was still low in the scale of racial life. It was only a short time, however, before a distinctly new development took place in the treatment of Negro life by white authors. This new class of work honestly strove to endow the Negro with many virtues that were still with one or two exceptions, treating the lower or primitive strata of his existence. With one or two exceptions referred to, the author could only see the Negro as an inferior, superstitious, half-ignorant and servile class of people. They did recognize, however, in a few isolated characters an ambitious impulse,—an impulse, nevertheless, always defeated in the force of the story. Again in only one or two instances did these authors categorically admit a cultured, independent layer of society that was leavening the Race with individuals who had won absolute equality of place and privilege with the best among the civilized group of to-day.

George Madden Martin, with her pretentious foreword to a group of short stories, called "The Children of the Mist,"—and this is an extraordinary volume in many ways—quite believed herself, as a Southern woman, to have elevated the Negro to a higher plane of fictional treatment and interest. In succession, followed Mary White Ovington's "The Shadow," in which Miss Ovington daringly created the kinship of brother and sister between a black boy and white girl, had it brought to disaster by prejudice, out of which the white girl rose to a sacrifice no white girl in a novel had hitherto accepted and endured; Shands'

"White and Black", as honest a piece of fiction with the Negro as a subject as was ever produced by a Southern pen—and in this story, also, the hero, Robinson, making an equally glorious sacrifice for truth and justice, as Miss Ovington's heroine; Clement Wood's "Nigger", with defects of treatment, but admirable in purpose, wasted though, I think, in the effort to prove its thesis on wholly illogical material; and lastly, T. S. Stribling's "Birthright", more significant than any of these other books, in fact, the most significant novel on the Negro written by a white American, and this in spite of its totally false conception of the character of Peter Siner. Mr. Stribling's book broke new ground for a white author in giving us a Negro hero and heroine. He found in the Race a material for artistic treatment which was worthy of an artist's respect. His failure was in limiting, unconscious as it was on the part of the author, the capacity of the hero to assimilate culture, and in forcing his rapid reversion to the level of his origin after a perfect Harvard training. On the other hand, no author has presented so severe an indictment as Mr. Stribling in his painting of the Southern conditions which brought about the disintegration of his hero's dreams and ideals.

Three recent plays should here be mentioned, of the Negro put into literature by white authors: I refer to O'Neill's "Emperor Jones," and "All God's Chillun Got Wings," and "Goat Alley". In all these plays, disregarding the artistic quality of achievement, they are the sordid aspects of life and undesirable types of character which are dramatized. The best and highest class of racial life has not yet been discovered for literary treatment by white American authors; that's a task left for Negro writers to perform, and the start has been made.

In closing this phase of my paper let me quote in extenuation of much that I have said in the foregoing a passage from an article in a recent number of "The Independent," which reads:

"During the past few years stories about Negroes have been extremely popular. A Magazine without a Negro story is hardly living up to its opportunities. But almost every one of these stories is written in a tone of condescension. The artists have caught the contagion from the writers and the illustrations are ninety-nine times out of a hundred purely slapstick stuff. Stories and pictures make a Roman holiday for the millions who are convinced that the most important fact about the Negro is that his skin is black. Many of these writers live in the South or are from the South. Presumably they are well acquainted with the Negro, but it is a remarkable fact that they almost never tell us anything vital about him, about the real human being in the black man's skin. Their most frequent method is to laugh at the colored man and woman, to catalogue their idiosyncrasies, their departure from the norm, that is, from the ways of the whites. There seems to be no suspicion in the minds of the writers that there may be a fascinating thought life in the minds of the Negroes, whether of the cultivated or of the most ignorant type. Always the Negro is interpreted in the terms of the white man. White-man psychology is applied and it is no wonder that the result often shows the Negro in a 'ludicrous light.'

I shall have to run back over the years to where I began to survey the achievement of Negro authorship. The Negro as a creator in American literature is of comparatively recent importance. All that was accomplished between Phyllis Wheatley and Paul Lawrence Dunbar, considered by critical standards, is negligible, and of historical interest only. Historically it is a great tribute to the Race to have produced in Phyllis Wheatly not only the slave poetess in 18th century Colonial America, but to know she was as good, if not a better poetess, than Ann Bradstreet whom literary historians give the honor of being the first person of her sex to win fame as a poet in America.

Negro authorship may, for clearer statement, be classified into three main activities: Poetry, Fiction, and the Essay, with an occasional excursion into other branches. In the drama, practically nothing has been achieved, with the exception of Angelina Grimké's "Rachel," which is notable for its sombre craftsmanship. Biography has given us a notable life story, told by himself, of Booker T. Washington. Frederick Douglass's story of his life is eloquent as a human document, but not in the graces of narration and psychologic portraiture which has definitely put this form of literature in the domain of the fine arts. In philosophic speculation the Negro has made a valuable contribution to American thought; indeed, with Einstein endeavored to solve the complicated secrets of infinity, in Robert Brown's "The Mystery of Space,"

a work, which, but for the discernment of a few perceptive critics, has failed to win the recognition it deserves. In aesthetic theory and criticism the Negro has not yet made any worth-while contribution though a Negro scholar, Professor W. S. Scarborough, has published a Greek grammar which was adopted as a standard text book. In history and the historical monograph there has been in recent years a growing distinction of performance. It is now almost a half century since Williams's history of the Negro Race was published, and Trotter's volume on the Negro in music. The historical studies of to-day by Dr. Carter Woodson are of inestimable service in the documenting of the obscure past character and activity of Negro life; and Benjamin Brawley, who, beside his social history of the Negro, has written a study of the Negro in art and literature and a valuable "History of the English Drama." The literary contributions of the Negro have only begun, but the beginning is significant. His accomplishment has been chiefly in imaginative literature, with poetry, by far, the prominent practice. Next to poetry, comes fiction; and though his preoccupation runs back nearly a century, he gives promise in the future of a greater accomplishment in prose fiction. In the third field of the Negro's literary endeavor, the essay, and discursive article, dealing chiefly with racial problems, there has been produced a group of able writers assaulting and clearing the impeded pathway of racial progress.

Let us survey briefly the advance of the Negro in poetry. Behind Dunbar, there is nothing that can stand the critical test. We shall always have a sentimental and historical interest in those forlorn and pathetic figures who cried in the wilderness of their ignorance and oppression. With Dunbar we have our first authentic lyric utterance, an utterance more authentic, I should say, for its faithful rendition of Negro life and character than for any rare or subtle artistry of expression. When Mr. Howells, in his famous introduction to the "Lyrics of Lowly Life," remarked that Dunbar was the first black man to express the life of his people lyrically, he summed up Dunbar's achievement and transported him to a place beside the peasant poet of Scotland, not for his art, but precisely because he made a people articulate in verse.

The two chief qualities in Dunbar's work are humour and pathos, and in these with an inimitable portrayal, he expressed that era of conscious indecision disturbing the Race between the Civil War and the nineteenth century. No agitated visions of prophecy burn and surge in his poems. His dreams were anchored to the minor whimsies, to the ineffectual tears of his people deluded by the Torch of a Liberty that was leading them back into abstract bondage. He expressed what he felt and knew to be the temper and condition of his people. Into his dialect work he poured a spirit, which, for the first time, was the soul of a people. By his dialect work he will survive, not so much because out of this broken English speech he shaped the symbols of beauty or the haunting strains of melody, but because into it he poured the plaintive, poignant tears and laughter of the soul of a Race.

After Dunbar many versifiers appeared all largely dominated by his successful dialect work; I cannot parade them here for tag or comment. Not until James W. Johnson published his Fiftieth Anniversary Ode on the emancipation in 1913, did a poet of the Race disengage himself from the background of mediocrity. Mr. Johnson's work is based upon a broader contemplation of life, life that was not wholly confined within any racial experience, but through the racial he made articulate that universality of the emotions felt by all mankind. His verse possesses a vigor which definitely breaks away from the brooding minor undercurrents of feeling which has previously characterized the verse of Race poets. Mr. Johnson brought, indeed, the first intellectual substance to the content of poetry and a craftsmanship which, less spontaneous than that of Dunbar's, was more balanced and precise.

Two other poets have distinguished themselves, though not to the same degree as Mr. Johnson. Fenton Johnson is one of those who began with a very uncertain measure of gifts, but made a brief and sudden development, only to retire as suddenly into the silence; the other poet, Leslie Pinckney Hill, has published one creditable book which has won for him a place among Negro poets, but which is the result of an intellectual determination to verse-making rather than the outpouring of a spontaneous poetic spirit.

Let me here pay tribute to a woman who has proven herself the foremost of all women poets the Race has so far produced: Georgia Douglas Johnson is a lyricist who has achieved much and who ought to achieve a great deal more. She has the equipment which nature gives in endowing the poetic spirit; her art is adequate but to say this is not to be satisfied with the best use of her gifts. A capture by her of some of the illusive secrets of form would often transmute her substance into the golden miracle of art.

I come now to Claude McKay, who unquestionably is a poet whose potentialities would place him supreme above all poets of the Negro Race. But I am afraid he will never justify that high distinction. His work may be easily divided into two classes: first, when he is the pure dreamer, contemplating life and nature, with a wistful and sympathetic passion, giving expression with subtle and figurative music to his dreams; secondly, when he is the violent and angry propagandist, using his natural poetic gifts to clothe arrogant and defiant thoughts. When the mood of "Spring in New Hampshire" or the sonnet "The Harlem Dancer" possesses him, he is full of that desire, of those flames of beauty which flower above any or all men's harming; in these are the white dreams which shine over the Promised Land of the Race's conquest over its enemies; it is the literature of those magnificent Psalms against which all the assaults of time dissolve, and whose music and whose vision wash clean with the radiance of beauty. How different, in spite of the admirable spirit of courage and defiance, are his poems of which the sonnet "If We Must Die" is a typical example. Passion is not a thing of words,—it is an essence of the spirit! He who slaves and burns with beauty is a more triumphant conqueror than he who slaves with a sword that the victim might break.

*   *   *

Too green the springing April grass,
Too blue the silver speckled sky,
For me to linger here, alas,
While happy winds go laughing by,
Wasting the golden hours indoors.
Washing windows and scrubbing floors.

Too wonderful the April night,
Too faintly sweet the first May flowers,
The stars too gloriously bright,

For me to spend the evening hours,
When fields are fresh and streams are leap-
ing,
Weary, exhausted, dully sleeping.

* * *

Let me refer briefly to a type of literature in which there have been many pens
with all the glory going to one man. Dr.
Du Bois is the most variously gifted writer
which the Race has produced. Poet, novelist, sociologist, historian and essayist, he
has produced books in all these branches of
literature—with the exception I believe, of
a formal book of poems,—and being a man
of indomitable courage I have often wondered why,—and gave to each the distinction of his clear and exact thinking, and
of his sensitive imagination and passionate
vision. "The Souls of the Black Folk" was
the book of an era; it was a painful book,
a book of tortured dreams woven into the
fabric of the sociologist's document. In this
book, as well as in many of Dr. DuBois's
essays, is often my personal feeling that
I am witnessing the birth of a poet, phoenix-
like, out of a scholar. Between "The Souls
of the Black Folk" and "Darkwater," published three years ago, Dr. Du Bois has
written a number of books, none more notable, in my opinion, than his novel "The
Quest of the Silver Fleece" in which he
made *cotton* the great protagonist of fate
in the lives of the Southern people, both
white and black. In European literature
nature and her minions have long been
represented in literature as dominating the
destinies of man; but in America I know
of only two conspicuous accomplishments
of this kind,—one, Frank Norris in his
dramatization of the influence of *wheat* and
the other, Dr. Du Bois's in his dramatization of the influence of *cotton.*

Let me again quote a passage from the
afore-mentioned article from *The Independent:*

"The white writer seems to stand baffled
before the enigma and so he expends all
his energies on dialect and in general on the
Negro's minstrel characteristics. . . . We
shall have to look to the Negro himself to
go all the way. It is quite likely that no
white man can do it. It is reasonable to
suppose that his white psychology will
always be in his way. I am not thinking
at all about a Negro novelist who shall
arouse the world to the horror of the deliberate killings by white mobs, to the
wrongs that condemn a free people to political serfdom. I am not thinking at all of
the propaganda novel, although there is

enough horror and enough drama in the
bald statistics of each one of the annual
Moton letters to keep the whole army of
writers busy. But the Negro novelist, if
he ever comes, must reveal to us much
more than what a Negro thinks about when
he is being tied to a stake and the torch
is being applied to his living flesh; much
more than what he feels when he is being
crowded off the sidewalk by a drunken
rowdy who may be his intellectual inferior
by a thousand leagues. Such a writer, to
succeed in a big sense, would have to forget
that there are white readers; he would have
to lose self-consciousness and forget that his
work would be placed before a white jury.
He would have to be careless as to what
the white critic might think of it; he would
need the self-assurance to be his own critic.
He would have to forget for the time being,
at least, that any white man ever attempted
to dissect the soul of a Negro."

What I here quote is both an inquiry and
a challenge! Well informed as the writer
is, he does not seem to detect the forces
which are surely gathering to produce what
he longs for.

The development of fiction among Negro
authors has been, I might almost say, one
of the repressed activities of his literary
life. A fair start was made the last decade of the Nineteenth century when
Chesnutt and Dunbar were turning out both
short stories and novels. In Dunbar's case,
had he lived, I think his literary growth
would have been in the evolution of the
Race novel as indicated in "The Uncalled"
and the "Sport of the Gods." The former
was, I think, the most ambitious literary
effort of Dunbar; the latter was his most
significant; significant because, thrown
against the background of New York City,
it displayed the life of the Race as a unit,
swayed by the currents of existence, of
which it was and was not a part. The story
was touched with that shadow of destiny
which gave to it a purpose more important
than the mere racial machinery of its plot.
In all his fiction, Dunbar dealt with the
same world which gave him the inspiration
for his dialect poems. It was a world he
knew and loved and became the historian
of without any revising influence from the
world which was its political and social
enemies. His contemporary, Charles W.
Chesnutt, was to supply the conflict between
the two worlds and establish with the precision of a true artist, the fiction of the
Color Line.

Charles W. Chesnutt is one of the enigmas
in American literature. There are five vol-

umes to his credit, not including his life of Frederick Douglass for the Beacon Biography Series. From first to last, he revealed himself as a fictional artist of a very high order. The two volumes of short stories, "The Wife of His Youth and Other Stories," and "The Conjure Woman," are exquisite examples of the short story form equal to the best in American literature. Primarily a short story writer, Mr. Chesnutt showed defects in his long novels which were scarcely redeemed by the mastery of style which made them a joy to read. I recall the shock a certain incident in "The House Behind the Cedars" gave me when I first read the book at the time it was published, puzzled that human nature should betray its own most passionate instincts at a moment of the intensest crisis. I realized later, or at least my admiration for Mr. Chesnutt's art, led me to believe that the fault was not so much his art as the problem of the Color Line. This problem, in its most acute details, was woven into the best novel Mr. Chesnutt has written called "The Marrow of Tradition." Certainly he did in that work an epic of riot and lawlessness which has served for mere pictorial detail as a standard example. In 1905 Mr. Chesnutt published "The Colonel's Dream," and thereafter silence fell upon him. I have heard it said that disappointment because his stories failed to win popularity was the cause of his following the classic example of Thomas Hardy by refusing to publish another novel. The cases are not exactly parallel because, while Hardy has refused to write another novel following the publication of "Jude, the Obscure," I have heard it rumored that Mr. Chesnutt has written other stories but will not permit their publication.

From the publication of Chesnutt's last novel until the present year there has been no fiction by the Race of any importance, with the exception of Dr. Du Bois's "The Quest of the Silver Fleece," which was published in 1911. This year of 1924 will have given four new books by writers, which seem to promise the inauguration of an era that is likely to produce the major novelists. Joshua Henry Jones's "By Sanction of Law," is a book that will hold the attention of readers who demand a thrilling story; it designs no new pattern of fiction, produces no new texture of expression. A vigorous narrative, it piles incident upon incident, with dialogue, love and violence.

Mr. Walter White's novel "The Fire in the Flint," is a swift moving story built upon the authentic experience of the author, with the terrors and pities of racial conflict.

Two outstanding achievements in the entire range of fiction are the books by Jessie Redmon Fauset and Jean Toomer. Miss Fauset in her novel "There is Confusion," has created an entirely new milieu in the treatment of the Race in fiction. She has taken a class within the Race, given it an established social standing, tradition, culture, and shown that its predilections are very much like those of any civilized group of human beings. In her story Race fiction emerges from the color line and is incorporated into that general and universal art which detaches itself from prejudice of propaganda and stands out the objective vision of artistic creation. Her beginning is conspicuous; her development may well be surprising.

These rambling remarks on the Negro in literature I may well bring to a close with this public confession that I believe that of all the writers I have mentioned, the one who is most surely touched with genius is Jean Toomer the author of "Cane." I believe this, not only on account of what he has actually accomplished in "Cane," but for something which is partly in the accomplishment and partly in the half articulate sense and impression of his powers. This young man is an artist; the very first artist in his Race who, with all an artist's passion and sympathy for life, its hurts, its sympathies, its desires, its joys, its defeats, and strange yearnings, can write about the Negro without the surrender or compromise of the artist's vision. It's a mere accident that birth or association has thrown him into contact with the life that he has written about. He would write just as well, just as poignantly, just as transmutingly, about the peasants of Russia, or the peasants of Ireland, had experience but given him the knowledge of their existence. "Cane" is a book of gold and bronze, of dusk and flame, of ecstacy and pain, and Jean Toomer is a bright morning star of a new day of the Race in literature!

FALL BOOKS

WALTER WHITE has written in "The Fire in the Flint" a good, stirring story and a strong bit of propaganda against the white Klansman and the black pussyfoot. White knows his Georgia from A to Z. There is not a single incident or a single character in the book which has not its prototype in real life today. All Mr. White's white people are not villains nor are all his Negroes saints, but one gets a thrilling sense of the devilish tangle that involves good and evil in the southern South.

Perhaps most significant however is the fact that a book like this can at last be printed. For years a flood of filth about the Negro has poured out of the South while no northern firm would consider a book telling even temperately the well-known and widely proven facts concerning the Negor. Subtly and slowly the change has come and Mr. White has been among the first to sense it and to persist courageously and doggedly in having his say.

Of course one can criticise any book and particularly a first one. Perhaps on the economic side Mr. White succumbs too easily to the common mistake of piling the blame of southern wickedness on the "poor whites" and absolving the aristocrats and former slave holders. This is, of course, based on the propaganda which the sons and daughters of slave-barons have spread, but it is far from true. On the human and artistic side, with the possible exception of the younger brother, Mr. White's characters do not live and breathe and compel our sympathy. They are more like labeled figures on a chess board. But despite all this, this story goes and the reader goes with it and that is the first business of a story.

"The Southern Oligarchy" by William H. Skaggs is the most important volume that has come out of the white south since the Civil War. Every intelligent Negro should buy it and own it, even if it does cost five dollars. It is an astonishing vindication of our cause. It is written by a white southerner born and bred in Alabama and it traces the history of oligarchical government in the South from the beginning of slavery down to the present time. While the book is in no sense a pro-Negro document (rather it is distinctly a treatise to defend the poor white), nevertheless Mr. Skaggs' incidental defense of the Negro is remarkable. He says for instance: "An epitome of the Negro's history since his emancipation will show conclusively that his civic and industrial progress has been most remarkable. The truth of this assertion can be proven not only by the records which are available to all intelligent people, who are seeking the truth, but also by the testimony of the most intelligent and reputable white men of the Southern States."

He declares in regard to disfranchisement that "the plans of the leaders of the Oligarchy were not primarily to shut out the Negro vote. The Negro had ceased to vote. The first and essential purpose of further encroachment on the liberties of the people was to make the Oligarchy more secure in its control of the Government. Ballot-box stuffing and other forms of corrupt practices had become so common that every branch of State and county administration was notoriously corrupt and, in many places, important official positions were held by corrupt politicians and their incompetent subordinates. Crimes were increasing and the South was prostrated under the rule of a privileged class of spoilsmen whose gain in power was in proportion to the public loss of moral stamina, intelligence, civic virtue and patriotism". Later on he says: "The sins of carpet-bag rule in the South, as shown in a preceding chapter, were not the result of Negro enfranchisement, nor has the Negro been disfranchised to prevent a recurrence of carpet-bag rule. The Negro was disfranchised for the same reason that the poor white man was disfranchised. It was to prevent any united and organized opposition to the corrupt and lawless practices of the Oligarchy which rules in the South without regard to the rights of the white man or the black man."

He quotes the Alabama Education Commission: "We need not refer to conditions before the war except to repeat that even

51

as far back as 1840 there were proportionately fewer illiterates among the white population than there are today. The Constitution of 1868, though enacted by a so-called 'carpet-bag' government, dealt with the subject of education in a manner far more liberal and infinitely better calculated to promote general intelligence than does either the Constitution of 1875 or that of 1901." And he places the blame for this as follows: "These delinquencies of the South are not due to poverty, nor to unusual financial burdens of these States; nor are these conditions the result of indifference on the part of the great mass of the people, white or colored. The cause of backwardness is found in the antiquated social and economic systems, the gross inefficiency, mismanagement and corruption of an Oligarchy that desires neither liberty nor enlightenment for the people."

As to crime he says that the "South may be called the nursery of crimes in America. The migratory criminal population of the United States may be traced from the Southern States to every part of the country. The highest record of defalcations and embezzlements is found in those sections of the South where election frauds, and other corrupt practices, have been notorious. In the same communities, peonage has prevailed in the most aggravated form; lynchings, race riots and the most appalling crimes had occurred in those communities where corrupt practices and vice have been most flagrant."

As to lynching he says: "It has been asserted time and time again that the lynching evil in the South was necessary to protect the women of the South. This base, spiteful libel on the Negro has been proclaimed in Congress, in political campaigns, on the lecture platform, written in books and dramatized. For example, in a speech in the city of Boston, in 1919, former Governor Emmett O'Neal of Alabama, said: 'The lynching evil in the South had its origin in the revolutionary conditions created by Reconstruction.' The assertion quoted from the former Governor of Alabama has been the rallying shibboleth of the leaders of a provincial and lawless Oligarchy for more than half a century, and it is the most wicked and pernicious slander that ever misled the American people. . . ."

Finally, remember that all these statements are backed by page after page of statistics, quotations from official documents and court decisions filling 444 pages of reading matter to which is appended a careful index of 27 pages. A final quotation will give the spirit of the book so far as the black man is concerned: "Racial friction in the Southern States is not the result of economic or moral decline, nor is it due to the vice or lawlessness of the Negro. The Negro in America is not degenerating. He is advancing along all lines that make for a higher and better civilization. Never has there been a race whose leaders, almost without exception, have struggled with more patience and forbearance, or more heroically, than the leaders of the Negroes in the maintenance of peace between two races."

———

Black Verse

By Frank S. Horne

". . . And do not ask the poor man not to sing,
For song is all he has."—ROBERT NATHAN.

FROM the Trinity College Press, Durham, North Carolina, comes an "Anthology of Verse by American Negroes," edited by Newman Ivey White, Ph.D., Professor of English at Trinity College, and Walter Clinton Jackson, Vice President of the North Carolina College of Women, with an introduction by James Hardy Dillard, Ph.D., L.L.D., President of the Jeanes Foundation and the John F. Slater Fund.

We have here something more than just another anthology. It distinguishes itself, on the one side, by coming from the heart of the Southland, by its utter impartiality, and its scholarly completeness; on the other, by its lack of direction in development, absence of personality, and faultiness of viewpoint.

The professors have been most diligent. There is evidence of concentrated application and profound probing into obscure poetical sources. The book is redolent of the South, the schoolroom, and the professorial dictum. The work is scholarly, and the treatment is both critical and sympathetic to some degree. It at least demonstrates that these two southern scholars have looked upon this definite body of literary production, and deemed it worthy of their recognition. But for all that, the anthology is sluggish; it lacks distinction and verve. It possesses neither the vigor and raciness of Professor Talley's folk lore collection, nor the poetical finesse and judgment of James Weldon Johnson's "Book of American Negro Poetry." The book lacks, in a sense, personality. To a student of the subject, the work is undeniably a worthy contribution; but to the reader of verse, it is a volume he can as well get along without.

In an effort to achieve completeness, the authors have included several worthy features. There is a more or less critical and historical general "Introduction"; brief biographies of the authors accompanying the selections; and a mass of "Bibliographical and Critical Notes" at the end. We shall consider them each in turn. The general "Introduction" is truly more historical than critical. The professors, not being poets, lack the poetical judgment and the insight that is so evident in James Weldon Johnson's "Essay on the Negro's Creative Genius" which serves so aptly as an introduction to his own admirable collection. In essence the two viewpoints stand sharply contrasted when it comes to the question of the ultimate contribution of the Negro to American poetry. The professors, after correctly stating that the constant themes of religion and race in, Negro poetry contribute nothing new, go on to say: "There is, however, a kind of Negro humor that deals in a distinctively racial manner with the Negro's love of music, talk, animals, meetings, dancing, loafing and fishing, and is best exemplified in the poems of Dunbar, Allen, and Davis. In this direction, the Negro is perhaps likely to make a purely racial contribution to American poetry. Otherwise, his contribution is apt to be individual and not racial in character." And there you have it! The compilers of this volume appear to believe that the "loud guffaw and the wide grin" are the paramount expressions of Negro aesthetics. At this point, I join the company of Johnson, Braithwaite, and DuBois, and vehemently dissent. The Negro poet has long since forsaken the jester's tatterdemalion. His contribution is more subtle and pregnant; more sensitive to the adventures of his own harassed soul. And in support might be offered such examples as "Self-Determination", by Leslie Pinckney Hill; "When I Die", by Fenton Johnson; "Fifty Years", by James Weldon Johnson; "And What Shall You Say", by Joseph Cotter, Jr.,—I offer you William Stanley Braithwaite, Jessie Redmond Fauset, and Claude McKay—and I offer you the youngest

James Weldon Johnson

Countee P. Cullen

voices, Countee P. Cullen, Gwendolyn B. Bennett, and Langston Hughes. With the work of such as these already significant, the dictum of the professors need not be taken too seriously.

The brief biographies of the authors accompanying the selections are adequate and interesting. The critical and bibliographical notes at the end of the volume are indispensable to the student, and add much to the value and completeness of the volume.

As for the body of the poetry included, there is little new or distinctive. The verse up to the time of Dunbar is below any real critical standard. It is to be marveled at, that in this period of sordid darkness, even voice was found to essay song. Its essence is a whimpering prayer for the Balm of Gilead to ease these mortal wounds. From Dunbar on, slowly but surely, the expression takes on form and virility, growing sophistication, and an enlivened interest in the life to be lived here and now. There comes the realization that the life of the Negro is a many sided adventure, worthy of recording.

The authors note that it was lack of education that impoverished earlier Negro poetry. They go on to say that this same lack of education perhaps accounts for the almost total absence of free verse from the mass of Negro poetry. This statement is open to considerable doubt. In the first place, the Negro is essentially lyrical. And the subtle rhythm of the best free verse, it might be

urged, is not sufficient for the fullness of his song. From the mass of so-called free verse floating about that has been my lot to read, one might be inclined to express little regret if the Negro never gets educated in that direction. A decided and unmistakable progress in Negro verse, however, is graciously admitted as the compilers conclude that the quality of the poetry has depended generally upon the cultural opportunities of the poets. England took three centuries after the Norman Conquest to produce her first great poet; the Negro has been hardly that long out of Africa! Period for period, we have developed as fully and as rapidly. They see no reason, nor do we, why Negro poets will not reach as ultimate a peak of expression as has ever been or will ever be attained.

After much has been said on either side, we can conclude that the book justifies its existence for us, if only because it includes a selection by Countee P. Cullen. This man, though still very, very young, pens lyrics that already sing. Twice, successively in the last two years, his work has gained second place in the Undergraduate Poetry Contest of the Poetry Society of America; most all of the better magazines have included him in their pages; his sonnets have often topped F.P.A.'s "Conning Tower" in the New York *World;* the *American Mercury* will soon carry something

Leslie Pinckney Hill

55

like a hundred and ninety of his lines. He steps with a sure tread, and we expect him to go far.

So set to, makers of black verse. We have already shown that we can write their music, give them their dance, make their money, and play their games. Your task is definite, grand, and fine. You are to sing the attributes of a soul. Be superbly conscious of the many tributaries to our pulsing stream of life. You must articulate what the hidden sting of the slaver's lash leaves re-verberating in its train,—the subtle hates, the burnt desires, sudden hopes, and dark despairs; you must show that the sigh is mother of the laugh they know so well. Sing, so that they might know the eyes of black babes—eyes that so sadly laugh; that they might know that we, too, like Shylock, cry when we are hurt, but with a cry distinctive, and subtly pregnant with overtones, and fraught with hidden associations. Sing, O black poets, for song is all we have!

OUR BOOK SHELF

The Fire in the Flint

By WALTER F. WHITE

Published by Alfred Knopf, New York. Price $2.50.

IT was Joseph Conrad, the incomparable master of the story, who in an essay on Henry James was prompted to say: "Fiction is history, human history, or it is nothing." For the most part, our sources of knowledge about life in the South have been limited to a petulant defense literature. Except for those romances embodying the soft, insubstantial after-glow of its Feudal past, there has been silence. The South's one dominant passion, the race problem(has inhibited both its life and its letters. Of the natural and unrelieved tragedy of the Negro in his new consciousness in the South, there has similarly been nothing until recently. We have here a facet of life bulging with the full score of human emotions with its comedy, certainly, but in its vital phases balked and convulsed into sombre tragedy. In their sensitive setting it has been not merely polite but a necessary measure of self-preservation to keep inviolate the sacred traditions by which they were bound down, and, until the last embers of the Civil War crumble into ashes, to let these millions remain as it is safe to paint them,—dark, insensible shadows, gliding silently and contentedly up and down endless aisles of cotton.

In Walter F. White's "The Fire in the Flint," this tradition is rudely broken. These dumb, ambulant shadows have been transformed into flesh and soul. Born and educated in Georgia, a Negro and a part of its life, it has been possible for him to fashion with complete understanding and from the simplest experiences a story of intense power. How else after all could we get those tremendous undercurrents of subtly tortured feeling, of life within the deep shadows of the "Black Belt," except as revealed by one who has lived through them? Even the magnificent effort of Clement Wood, despite its earnestness, failed to capture the essense so familiar to Negroes, so incomprehensible to others.

The story itself is a compound of incidents, any of which could probably be documented from the records filed away in Mr. White's desk in the offices of the National Association for the Advancement of Colored People. The thread of the plot might have been borrowed from the life of most any well-educated Negro in, let us say, three-fourths of the South's small towns, and probably in any of the small towns of Georgia, where the scene is laid. It concerns principally the vicissitudes of one refined Negro family. Kenneth Harper, a Harvard graduate and physician, comes home to Centerville to practice his profession. He is a tolerant, mannerly, clean-cut figure, and a skillful surgeon, ambitious to conquer the biting prejudices of his home town by ignoring them, and eventually to build a hospital for Negroes. His brother, Bob, a sensitive, impulsive youth, lacked his tolerance and hopefulness though he managed to keep his emotions in leash. His sister, Mamie, blended with her dark rich beauty the delicate loveliness of faint lavender. Jane Phillips, around whom his romance turned, was distinguished by her quick, incisive intelligence, a practical philosophy and restless idealism.

Among the leading white characters there are several who represent the author's attempt at fair depiction. There is Judge Stevenson, a blunt, discordantly fairminded Southerner who spoke of Nigras, a sort of halfvictory over the orthodox appelation nigger; who secretly helped Kenneth draw up plans for the Negro Farmers' Cooperative Society,—a scarred relic of the Civil War, with plenty of courage, but with little influence against the general sentiment of the town. And there is Mrs. Roy Ewing who, it seems, escaped some of the virulence of Anglo-Saxon prejudice by being born of old French stock in South Carolina. Faced with the loss of her daughter from a malady which the less competent white physician, Dr. Bennett, sorrowfully admitted he could not treat, she persuaded her husband to control his prejudice and permit a "nigger doctor", the only surgeon within two hundred miles, to operate. Dr. Bennett, an old school family physician, innocent for the most part of the advance of his science, at first affectedly contemptuous of the upstart from "up No'th" eventually recognized his merit, a triumph quite compatible with his simple honesty. Roy Ewing, pliant to the force of the town's feeling for Negroes, fearful for his business, was in the end converted.

Through the muck of a small town's petty chicaneries and sexual adventure, gossip, Ku Klux parties, the story ran. Kenneth's fight for self-respect was a losing one. Faith in his philosophy bit by bit was worn down. Landlords robbed their Negro tenants and dared them to complain, the "best citizens" including the sheriff were members of the Ku Klux Klan. His organization of farmers to handle their crop was interpreted as dangerous agitation . Calamity trooped down on his family. Mamie was outraged by two of the town's popular young bloods. Bob's restrain broke. In his blinding rage he killed his sister's assailants as they boasted of their frolic to a hilarious group of their friends lounging about Ewing's store, and in turn Bob was killed by a mob. The citizenry aroused, determined to end Kenneth's obnoxious interference in affairs. The chance came as he left the bedside of his white patient in the Ewing home. On the ready assumption that his mission had been sex adventure, they whetted their passions and killed him.   C. S. J.

Few of the grosser evils of the South are omitted; there are two lynchings, the Ku Klux Klan, the consorting of white men with Negro women, tarrings and beatings, peonage, the inescapable orthodoxy about the Negro's place, "Jim Crow" cars, familiar arguments of the "dominant race", the sycophantic trouble maker known among Negroes as "a white folks' nigger". Nor are the salutary influences neglected. The northern missionaries, the southern inter-racial Commissions, the righteous but impotent few who would end the abuses, come in for mention.

"The Fire in the Flint," like Harriet Beecher Stowe's "Uncle Tom's Cabin" or let us say Upton Sinclair's "The Jungle," is a trail blazer, an epoch marker of sociologic interest, and is aided as a novel by its powerfully expository material, but it lacks the charm of style and subtlety which distinguish both of these. There are too many fiction stereotypes,—an inexpert heavy-handedness in description. Probably the absence of that quality which we feel is in the power of Mr. White to give is accounted for in part by the fact that, as he says, the story was written in two weeks, a prodigious accomplishment, rare even among the most skillful writers. The white mind could be made more intelligible. They are mad men, most of them. Certainly this conduct has some justification in their own minds even if irrational and unsound. It is without apology a tragedy, and as a tragedy, presumably, can register only the intensity of all of these forces in fatal compound. There is yet even more poignant tragedy in the lives of the droning millions who are ground down and broken and who are not permitted even the escape of death.

Remarks by Grant Overton Regarding "The Fire in the Flint"

At Library, November 6, 1924. Typed Manuscript.

[JWJ/MSS/White, W/Misc 106. James Weldon Johnson Collection,

Beinecke Library, Yale University.] [Ellipses appear in the original manuscript]

Taking up a copy of "The Fire in the Flint", Grant Overton said,

"This book is by Walter F. White and I might as well say that the MS was

offered in the office of the publishing house where I have the honor to be. There was a

very decided difference of opinion about it. I read it—or read it in a way in which you

read things under consideration—very hurriedly and I rather wanted to do it. I thought in

fact that it ought to be done. And we thought for many reasons that the book had in it the

possibilities of a very large sale. Well, they disagreed with me and the opinion was so

finely divided that it was very hard to........Where the opinion is not clearly in the majority

for a thing, you think, well, we won't put our money into it. But I said when the book

went away from us that certainly somebody would publish it and I hoped a good

publisher would get it.

As for the book itself, there are so many things about it to be said that I cannot

say them all. I dare say that whatever I said would be judged by some people who would

say, "Oh, well, you are not a southerner; have never lived in the South and all that." That

61

1

is true. On the other hand, when I was about twenty-two years old, I spent almost five months on a deep sea ship and of the crew, eight of us were white and..........and in that passage, insofar as I had any friends (and we weren't very friendly) I can truthfully say that the Negroes were as good friends as I had.

This story is written by a man who has spent some years collecting facts and figures about racial relations in the South. Everything in it is documented, as they say. I don't think there is a thing in it which is not a matter of fact somewhere and at some time and from those things he has selected the ones he needed to make his story. He has written the story of an educated Negro, etc. (tells part of story)

The story moves through incidents of increasing power but ones of very serious tragedy. It is a terribly bitter book. That was one of the arguments considered when we had it under discussion. My answer was that there had been many books published, or at least one that I could think of by Thomas Dixon years ago which was bitter and I thought this book was privileged by the fact that that one had been published. Anyway, I believe personally in letting all those things out.

Of course, this book will not sell through the South except as it may sell through Negroes in the South who may know it though I don't know whether they may even know of it. It will, I think, sell fairly well in the North.

2

Now the question comes up—is it a good book? Not too good. It is not too well done. It is not the work of a born(?) novelist and what I consider a disqualification for any narrative, it more or less preaches and I don't think that is a good thing for any story to do, I don't care what it is—it ought not to preach. You see, if one wants to preach, one wants to deliver a sermon or perhaps write an essay or an article but the purpose of a story is to reach people who cannot be reached by sermons or by essays. The purpose of a story is to show you a thing as it happens and to arouse your feeling about it. For instance, I see some very terrible thing happen in real life or some very beautiful thing. This makes me feel tremendously...

When you feel that way, you want to share it with somebody else. If you want to share it with most people, you probably write a play or a novel and, if you do it well, you don't tell what you felt but you tell what you saw in such a way that they will feel that you knew it(?). Well, there are not any rules for doing it. There are methods by which it can be done..

Now, this book ("A Passage to India") is a very closely observed, very carefully written study of racial contacts in India. I don't know of any book which is so accurately pictured. I think that this is practically more detailed, more exact, and sometimes more humorous than Kipling. You see the whole picture. It is not a good novel in every way.

3

There is not much of a story. The little story there is is not made plausible. You know when something happens in real life, no matter how incredible it is, why you have to believe that it happened but if you take that thing from real life—and this may be one of the defects of this book perhaps—they always think, "Oh, nonsense, that doesn't ring true" but the difference is that life can compel you to believe anything you want to but the novel has got to persuade you. He has got to make it seem plausible. The central episode is not very plausible. The conversation is so handled that half the time I was unable to tell who was talking. "he said, she said". He said what?

I said that I would talk about the fall books. There is a new novel by John Masefield. He is a poet, of course. He has done one or two novels.......(Here followed a resume of the fall books).

Someone questioned Mr. Overton as to what he meant when he said that "The Fire in the Flint" 'preached'.

Yes, I do not know if I am fair to him in that. I do not believe that he preaches but, of course, the novel is in a sense propaganda. I understand the artistic way was to put what the author had seen so as the readers would feel the same thing. Yes, I agree with you. I would like to qualify what I said about that. I think that it does, but I know it makes

4

you feel what the author felt. I suppose my remark arises from the feeling that the thing, after all, is not typical. I think that probably the major part of it is tytical. [sic] It is awfully hard to think about a book of that kind. It is a little bit like "Three Soldiers" and a little bit like "What Price Glory", the play. Three Soldiers", of course, was attacked by people who said, "This is not a true picture of the life in the army. The question is, did the author mean it to be—and I don't think he did. Three rather unusual types of men and he studied them very faithfully. I do not think he was under any obligations to write of typical live [sic] in the army. In "What Price Glory" Stallings and .... have done practically the same thing. They have written the story of a struggle between two....and in that struggle, you have drama, you have clash, you have the grip of a play. It may not be generally representative but then there is no compulsion upon anybody to select a background of a setting for a story that everybody else is using any more than it is compulsory to wear a dress of the color or a hat of a particular design.

I do think awfully well of this book (looks through it again) I think that the ending is good too. It ends with a newspaper clipping.

I don't suppose it will do a bit of good but then there is a great question as to what *will* do any good. I don't think that anything of that sort can do any good. I think that the only good that can come is a matter of personal behavior. It is an individual thing and when there gets to be enough individuality for the Negro to behave with self respect and general decency toward each other, things will work all right and in fact, that

5

condition as far as we can have it, I guess does exist very largely throughout the North here but in the South, well, I know nothing about it I suppose but I should say that perhaps it never would come about. I think probably that the only thing to do is to go away from that kind of country.

James Weldon Johnson: Don't you think the remarkable fact that a Negro would write a book would do some good?

Well, I don't know. Would it be more effective if it were written by a white man?..............

JWJ: I cannot conceive of a Negro writing against his own race so well that it will convince a great many people of........

Yes. Although that does not surprise me so much because men like Dr. DuBoise.......

So far as the southern mind goes, it is closed; it is shut; sealed. It may be opened some day like the tomb of King Tutankhamen three thousand years hence and with as much ceremony and difficulty but at present, I think that the southern mind is—well, as

6

ıne southerner, a white man, said to me, "Of course you appreciate it that the southern ʋhite man would not be found dead with this book in the house."

Why (from all directions)

Because of the set mind.

Mr. Bagnall: I believe that your southern friend was posing from some experiences that I have had. The magazine, "The Crisis" is one about which he probably would have said the same thing and yet in the little town of Uniontown, Alabama, the judge, and the banker and the mayor and the members of the Board of Aldermen, and the superintendent of schools asiduously bought The Crisis every month from the colored woman who was selling it that their servants might read it and the servants interviewed said that they never got a chance to look at it...

That is interesting. (Mr. Bagnall added something re the autobiography of Mark Twain which had been discussed by Mr. Overton)

I am awfully interested. (Mention was made of Stallings having been lambasted in The Macon Telegraph.) All I can say is I wouldn't stay in a place like that among people who had minds of that order.

7

Mr. Young and Mr. Overton had a lengthy discussion about the Negro's coming North, Mr. Young preferring to have them stay South and fight.

A white woman asked a question as to whether or not "The Fire in the Flint" would not influence public opinion in the North so as to force the South to change like "Uncle Tom's Cabin" did.

We had "Uncle Tom's Cabin" and then we had the Civil War. Now, I don't want to see "The Fire in the Flint" followed by a civil war.

The white woman: You say those conditions cannot be changed. They can be changed from what I know of them. I am from the South and I have changed. I own "The Fire in the Flint" but the reason you would not find it in the South is because it is too busy circulating among other southern hands.

8

Reflections on O'Neill's Plays

By PAUL ROBESON

Paul Robeson

ALL this seems so very strange to me—writing about the theatre. If, three years ago, someone had told me that I would be telling of my reactions as an actor I would have laughed indulgently. Even now the whole chain of events has a distinct dream-like quality. To have had the opportunity to appear in two of the finest plays of America's most distinguished playwright is a good fortune that to me seems hardly credible. Of course I am very, very happy. And with these things there has come a great love of the theatre, which I am sure will always hold me fast.

In retrospect all the excitement about "All God's Chillun" seems rather amusing, but at the time of the play's production, it caused many an anxious moment. All concerned were absolutely amazed at the ridiculous critical reaction. The play meant anything and everything from segregated schools to various phases of intermarriage.

To me the most important pre-production development, was an opportunity to play the "Emperor Jones," due to an enforced postponment. This is undoubtedly one of *"the* great plays"— a true classic of the drama, American or otherwise. I recall how marvelously it was played by Mr. Gilpin some years back. And the greatest praise I could have received was the expression of some that my performance was in some wise comparable to Mr. Gilpin's.

And what a great part is "Brutus Jones." His is the exultant tragedy of the disintegration of a human soul. How we suffer as we see him in the depths of the forest re-living all the sins of his past—experiencing all the woes and wrongs of his people—throwing off one by one the layers of civilization until he returns to the primitive soil from which he (racially) came. And yet we exult when we realize that here was a man who

Jungle Scene from the American Production of "The Emperor Jones"

(Courtesy of
Theatre Arts)

*Palace Scene
from
the French
Production
L'Empereur
Jones*

(Courtesy
Theater Arts

in the midst of all his trouble fought to the end and finally died in the "'eighth of style anyway."

In "All God's Chillun" we have the struggle of a man and woman, both fine struggling human beings, against forces they could not control,—indeed, scarcely comprehend—accentuated by the almost Christ-like spiritual force of the Negro husband,—a play of great strength and beautiful spirit, mocking all petty prejudice, emphasizing the humanness, and in Mr. O'Neill's words, "the oneness" of mankind.

I now come to perhaps the main point of my discussion. Any number of people have said to me: "I trust that now you will get a truly heroic and noble role, one portraying the finest type of Negro." I honestly believe that perhaps never will I portray a nobler type than "Jim Harris" or a more heroically tragic figure than "Brutus Jones, Emperor," not excepting "Othello."

The Negro is only a medium in the creation of a work of the greatest artistic merit. The fact that he is a Negro Pullman Porter is of little moment. How else account for the success of the play in Paris, Berlin, Copenhagen, Moscow and other places on the Continent. Those people never heard of a Negro porter. Jones's emotions are not primarily Negro, but human.

Objections to "All God's Chillun" are rather well known. Most of them have been so foolish that to attempt to answer them is to waste time. The best answer is that audiences that came to scoff went away in tears, moved by a sincere and terrifically tragic drama.

The reactions to these two plays among Negroes but point out one of the most serious drawbacks to the development of a true Negro dramatic literature. We are too self-conscious, too afraid of showing all phases of our life,—especially those phases which are of greatest dramatic value. The

great mass of our group discourage any member who has the courage to fight these petty prejudices.

I am still being damned all over the place for playing in "All God's Chillun." It annoys me very little when I realize that those who object most strenuously know mostly nothing of the play and who in any event know little of the theatre and have no right to judge a playwright of O'Neill's talents.

I have met and talked with Mr. O'Neill. If ever there was a broad, liberal-minded man, he is

*Paul Robeson as "The Emperor Jones"
Drawn from life by Clement Wilenchik*

one. He has had Negro friends and appreciated them for their true worth. He would be the last to cast any slur on the colored people.

Of course I have just begun. I do feel there is a great future on the serious dramatic stage. Direction and training will do much to guide any natural ability one may possess. At Provincetown I was privileged to be under the direction of Mr. James Light. I'm sure even he thought I was rather hopeless at first. I know I did. But he was patient and painstaking, and any success I may have achieved I owe in great measure to Mr. Light. I sincerely hope I shall have the benefit of his splendid guidance in the future.

What lies ahead I do not know. I am sure that there will come Negro playwrights of great power and I trust I shall have some part in interpreting that most interesting and much needed addition to the drama of America.

Some Books of 1924

Mr. Arnold Mulder, in an article in the *Independent,* in which he voices a hope that out of the vast, rich depths of Negro life would come forth a novelist to tell the world "something vital" about this race, makes the observation, quite incidentally, but with ample warrant, that a "magazine nowadays without a Negro story is hardly living up to its opportunities." If he had been talking about science or sociology, or economics or politics rather than fiction his comment would have been no less pertinent. Nothing more powerfully expresses the changing attitude of this generation on the Negro than the amount and type of discussion which has centered about him during the past year. In a static society discussion is needless. Only when the seeds of restlessness and unbelief begin to sprout do we get in print the doubts which assail men's consciences,—the explosion of their fears and desires; solutions, palliatives, analysis, and, perhaps what is most hopeful, a general curiosity for some approximation to truth through it all. A candid reviewer in the *Springfield Republican* caught and expressed the note of this new interest at the very beginning of the year in his comment on the anthology of verse by Negro poets prepared by Dr. Robert E. Kerlin under the title "Negro Poets and their Poems." "He is to be thanked," this writer declares, "for giving us something which all too few of us know anything about, let alone enough."

From North Carolina came another anthology of Negro verse prepared by Dr. N. I. White, Professor of English at Trinity College, and W. C. Jackson, Vice President of North Carolina College for Women, with unusual care and judgment. The *American Mercury* precipitated a mild furore when it published "All God's Chillun Got Wings" by Eugene O'Neill, the tragedy of a mixed marriage. It was produced on the stage and published in book form amid fearful warnings of riot and conflict which, strangely enough, never came. Ronald Firbank's "Prancing Nigger" was an ultra-sophisticated novel based on Negro life in the West Indies, "obliquely visual, seen with aloof, yet discerningly selective eyes," says the *New York Times.* Two English writers, Llewelyn Powys and F. Brett Young, did

EUGENE O'NEILL
Author of "All God's Chillun Got Wings"
(From a Drawing by Francis W. Holbrook)

WALTER F. WHITE
Author of "The Fire in the Flint"
(From a drawing by Francis W. Holbrook)

much during the year to re-make Africa for us into something a bit more real than the long tradition of the imperialists, missionaries and European ethnologists. "Black Laughter" a second book on Africa by Powys is filled with "biting realistic sketches which stick close to the concrete truth, and yet have artistry enough to bring out all the color and exotic glamor of the jungle." "Woodsmoke." by Young, shows the possibility of Africa as a background for fiction. Another volume of striking merit is "African Clearings," by J. K. Mackenzie From France came the "The Long Walk of Samba Deouf," by Jerome and Jean Tharaud, a story of life among the Senegalese in West Africa, which the *New York Times* calls "as much of an anthropological study as a novel." Two novels involving the more or less intimate contact of white and black appeared in England: "Gone Native" by Asterisk author of "Isles of Illusion," and "God's Step Children" by Sarah Gertrude Millin. The first is an excellent English counterpart of "The White Cargo" now in its second year of stage production in New York. The English reviews think it "very touching, whimsical and depressing," the American reviewers that it brings clearly to the surface all the nastiness hidden under the beauty of the South Sea "Isles of Illusion." "God's Step Children" is a (race) problem-novel and quite comes up to expectation in being "pathetic, tragic and unreal."

Most significant among the year's offering are the books by Negroes themselves. Jessie Redmond Fauset's novel, "There is Confusion," is probably the first full fledged novel by a Negro woman. I

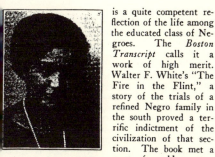

JESSIE REDMOND FAUSETT

is a quite competent reflection of the life among the educated class of Negroes. The *Boston Transcript* calls it a work of high merit. Walter F. White's "The Fire in the Flint," a story of the trials of a refined Negro family in the south proved a terrific indictment of the civilization of that section. The book met a most favorable reception among the critics above the "line" and in at least one case was responsible for the disinheriting of a liberal Georgia critic living in New York who said Mr. White was substantially right on his facts. Henry Joshua Jones, living in Boston, released his novel of the race problem which he called "By Sanction of Law." Another book by W. E. B. DuBois, "The Gift of Black Folk," which is both history and art, adds sturdiness and charm to the year's contribution by Negroes. A new edition of William Picken's "Bursting Bonds" appeared. In the field of history the valuable work of the Association for the Study of Negro History, directed by Carter G. Woodson, begins to flower. Through the Associated Publishers, appeared in 1924 "The Negro in South Carolina During Reconstruction" by A. A. Taylor, a revealing account; "The Everlasting Stain" by Kelly Miller, a writer whose trenchant decisive style is remembered from his "Race Adjustment" and "Out of the House of Bondage" (in this is a splendid introduction by Alain Locke); and a third edition of "The Negro in Our History" by Carter G. Woodson, revised and enlarged.

Out of the South have come books which are a quiet revolution in themselves. Julia Peterkin's "Green Thursday" is one of them. A refined South Carolina woman, isolated on a plantation, she writes about the Negroes around her with a penetrating sympathy. Her characters are neither crap-shooters nor hilarious clowns, but field hands, —black men, women and children faced with problems of life, love and death. A ponderous tome, "The Negro from Africa to America," is another such unusual book from the pen of W. D. Weathrford. "Harrowing, instructive, interesting," it is called by the *Boston Transcript*. Between the extremes of criticism by Hershell Brickell of the *New York Evening Post* that it "leaves little to be learned" and that of Dr. DuBois that it is "poorly balanced" it will be found to be a significant contribution during the year. The success of Negro stories probably prompted the Gullah tales from South Carolina. "With Aesop Along the Black Border" and "The Captain: Stories of the Black Border" by A. E. Gonzales, while amusing, are heavily freighted with the tradition of the plantation, a sort of dead past.

"The Southern Oligarchy" by William H. Skaggs, a white Alabamian, smashes many cherished myths about the Negro's chicanery by telling with calm, scholarly assurance supported by documents more of the facts about the rest of the South. Frank Tannenbaum arrives at something of the same results in his "Darker Phases of the South," a vivid analysis of certain economic and social problems through the fabric of which the Negro is interwoven. Probably because he suspected that he would not be believed, he documented his statements heavily.

We may credit religious bodies with at least four serious and eminently worth while contributions to the science of race relations during 1924. The editor of the *International Review of Missions*, J. H. Oldham, attempted the difficult task of convincing our Christian nation that racial antipathy "is not instinctive or inborn." His "Christianity and the Race Problem" is an admirable study. So also is the English attempt at the same thing, "The Clash of Color, a Study in the Problem of Race," by Basil Matthews, published by the Missionary Education Movement. Robert H. Speer makes a plea for the spirit of Christianity in his "Of One Blood" which carries its argument in its title. The Council of Women for Home Missions is responsible for this volume, and the Christian Way of Life movement for that most unusual collection of stimulating incidents and experiences published under the title "And Who Is My Neighbor?"

More than Lafcadio Hearn's delightful "Creole Sketches" came near the close of the year, posthumously published; and another volume by R. E. Kennedy, "Black Cameos" added much rollicking humor for those who like to laugh at the antics of those Negroes whom Mr. Kennedy says he knows and loves so completely. And for the further delight of those interested in this admittedly distorted but popularly entertaining comedy we may add to the list Robert McBlair's "Mister Fish Kelly" and Octavius Roy Cohen's "Come Seven."

As a much needed antidote for Charles Conant Josey's "Race and National Solidarity" and Lothrop Stoddard's further hysterical utterings in his "Racial Realities in Europe", another edition of Jean Finot's "Race Prejudice" appeared. Two books on the Ku Klux Klan also have a place among the books of interest on the race question. One of these, by Miss S. L. Davis, was a rather belated justification of the first hooded order, the second a more scholarly discussion of the causes back of the development of the present invisible empire by J. M. Mecklen.

This does not pretend to be a statistically complete list. But it covers the high spots and, as must be evident, reveals the extent and diversity of interest now current on our much dissected race question.   C. S. J.

The Significance of Jean Toomer

By Gorham B. Munson

THERE CAN be no question of Jean Toomer's skill as a literary craftsman. A writer who can combine vowels and liquids to form a cadence like "she was as innocently lovely as a November cotton flower" has a subtle command of word-music. And a writer who can break the boundaries of the sentences, interrupt the placement of a fact with a lyrical cry, and yet hold both his fact and his exclamation to a single welded meaning as in the expression: "A single room held down to earth. . . O fly away to Jesus. . . by a leaning chimney . . .", is assuredly at home in the language and therefore is assuredly free to experiment and invent. Toomer has found his own speech, now swift and clipped for violent narrative action, now languorous and dragging for specific characterizing purposes, and now lean and sinuous for the exposition of ideas, but always cadenced to accord with an unusually sensitive ear.

It is interesting to know that Toomer, before he began to write, thought of becoming a composer. One might have guessed it from the fact that the early sketches in *Cane* (1923) depend fully as much upon a musical unity as upon a literary unity. *Karintha*, for example, opens with a song, presents a theme, breaks into song, develops the theme, sings again, drops back into prose, and dies away in a song. But in it certain narrative functions—one might mention that lying back of the bald statement, "This interest of the male, who wishes to ripen a growing thing too soon, could mean no good to her"—are left undeveloped. Were it not for the songs, the piece could scarcely exist.

But electing to write, Toomer was too canny to try to carry literature further into music than this. *Cane* is, from one point of view, the record of his search for suitable literary forms. We can see him seeking guidance and in several of the stories, notably *Fern* and *Avey*, it is the hand of Sherwood Anderson that he takes hold. But Anderson leads toward formlessness and Toomer shakes him off for Waldo Frank in such pieces as *Theatre* where the design becomes clear and the parts are held in a vital esthetic union. Finally, he breaks through in a free dramatic form of his own, the play *Kabnis* which still awaits production by an American theatre that cries for good native drama and yet lacks the wit to perceive the talent of Toomer.

The form of *Kabnis* is a steep slope downward. In the first scene Ralph Kabnis, a neurotic educated Negro who has returned to Georgia from the North, stands on the top of the

slope and delivers a monologue, which reveals his character as that of a frustrated lyricist. In Scene Two he begins to fall in the direction of his weaknesses, in scene three there occurs an opportunity to check his descent, but his momentum carries him straight past it, and in the remaining scenes he lands in a cellar of debauchery. The action of the play then is linear, but what Kabnis falls through is a rich milieu composed of a symbolic ancient Negro who has experienced slavery, an honest craft-loving wheelwright, a bourgeois school supervisor, a clear headed forceful radical black, a couple of prostitutes, a church audience, a minister, and little Carrie K., fresh symbol of a possible future. Toomer's formal achievement is just this: to utilize a milieu and a character, the first as a dense living slope, the second as a swiftly descending point tracing out a line of action upon the first.

It is necessary and important that an artist should be in command of his tools, but if we feel that craftsmanship is only a means to an end, we must proceed to inquire what end Toomer's skill was designed to suit.

b.

Cane is the projection of a vivid personality. What the fundamental motives were that impelled this projection we cannot say, but we can pick out a few probably subsidiary motives that will perhaps indicate Toomer's status at the moment he completed *Cane*. Clearly, he desired to make contact with his hereditary roots in the Southland. One of the poems in *Cane* is an unmistakable recognition of this desire.

"'O land and soil, red soil and sweet-gum tree, So scant of grass, so profligate of pines, Now just before an epoch's sun declines Thy son, in time, I have returned to thee, Thy son, I have in time returned to thee.''

From this one infers a preceding period of shifting and drifting without settled harborage. Weary of homeless waters, he turns back to the ancestral soil, opens himself to its folk-art and its folk-ways, tries to find his roots, his origins. It is a step toward the definition of himself.

What can we add to this purpose? We can say that Toomer makes a very full response to life, a response that is both robust and sensitive, and we can say, to use the conventional phrase, that he "accepts life." It is plain that he has strong instincts, welling and deep and delicate emotions, and a discriminating and analytical intellect (more fully revealed in his critical work); and these are all keenly aware of life. This life that floods in upon his equipment Toomer finds to be potent and sweet, colorful and singing, interesting and puzzling, pathetic and worthy of respect; he is able to accept it,—perhaps because his survey of it shows it to be beautiful and mysterious. At any rate, the only fully adumbrated attitude in *Cane* is that of the spectatorial artist. But that raises the question, under what circumstances can the artist be a spectator?

c.

To be a spectator one must have a firm and fixed point of vantage. Where can such a point be found today? Our social framework is admittedly unsettled, but it is less generally perceived that culturally we are being blown into chaos. Our heritage came from Judea, Greece and Rome, and to that heritage we have added science. Today, it needs but a glance at the vitality of the early Christians and at the legalism and stupor of the modern church to realize that something basic and essential has passed away from Christianity. From the testimony of the humanists themselves we are entitled to conclude that humanism is in decay. And science, upon which the nineteenth century depended, has turned to inner conflict, uncertainty and groping. In short, the Occidental world now has no one body of common experience, no ancestral faith, no *concensus omnium bonorum*, no principle of unification, put it how you will, to which men everywhere may make appeal and upon which the spectatorial artist might situate himself. The great movement of the last few centuries has been romanticism which has glorified personal uniqueness and universal flux and has driven us all away from any possible center of human experience. Born into such circumstances, what is the artist to do? He must choose to work either toward integration or toward disintegration.

Nietzsche, it should be recalled, looked upon artists as casters of glamor over progression and retrogression alike. That is, by virtue of their magic they could glorify either, they could be their saviors or betrayers. An artist who does not care where the lure and grace that he sheds over the objects led his entranced followers naturally will not inquire very deeply into his purpose for creation. He creates beauty and lets truth and goodness go hang. But an artist who feels that his gifts entail a grave responsibility, who wishes to fight on the side of life abundant rather than for life deficient, must pause and seek the answers to certain questions. What is the function of man? What are the potentials of man and what may he become? What is experience and what is knowledge? What is the world?

d.

The significance of Jean Toomer lies in his strenuous attempt to answer these questions. Shortly after writing *Cane*, he formed two convictions. One was that the modern world is a veritable chaos and the other was that in a disrupted age the first duty of the artist is to unify himself. Having achieved personal wholeness, then perhaps he would possess an attitude that would not be merely a reaction to the circumstances of modernity, merely a reflection of the life about him, but would be an attitude that could act upon modernity, dissolve away the remainder of an old slope of consciousness, and plant the seeds for a new slope.

So he turned to an intensive study of his own psychology. He sifted psycho-analysis for what minute grains of truth it might supply, he underwent the training for "conscious control of the body" prescribed by F. Matthias Alexander, he spent a summer at the Gurdjieff Institute, Fontainebleau, France, where he obtained what he regards as the best method for his quest. We should note that his search is distinguished from that of many other American artists (Sherwood Anderson may be cited as typical) by its positive scientific character. These others work from a disgust or a negation. They cut loose from something they abhor and, unprovided with any method, drift aimlessly in search of a leaven which somewhere, somehow, will heal. Toomer has a method and an aim, and he devotes his whole time and energy to them. In his own words, this is what he is doing: "I am. What I am and what I may become I am trying to find out."

He is a dynamic symbol of what all artists of our time should be doing, if they are to command our trust. He has mastered his craft. Now he seeks a purpose that will convince him that his craft is nobly employed. Obviously, to his search there is no end, but in his search there is bound to occur a fusion of his experience, and it is this fused experience that will give profundity to his later work. His way is not the way of the minor art master, but the way of the major master of art. And that is why his potential literary significance outweighs the actualized literary significance of so many of his contemporaries.

AMERICAN LITERARY TRADITION AND THE NEGRO

BY ALAIN LOCKE

DOUBT if there exists any more valuable record for the study of the social history of the Negro in America than the naïve reflection of American social attitudes and their changes in the literary treatment of Negro life and character. More sensitively, and more truly than the conscious conventions of journalism and public debate, do these relatively unconscious values trace the fundamental attitudes of the American mind. Indeed, very often public professions are at utter variance with actual social practices, and in the matter of the Negro this variance is notably paradoxical. The statement that the North loves the Negro and dislikes Negroes, while the South hates the Negro but loves Negroes, is a crude generalization of the paradox, with just enough truth in it, however, to give us an interesting cue for further analysis. What this essay attempts must necessarily be a cursory preliminary survey: detailed intensive study of American social attitudes toward the Negro, using the changes of the literary tradition as clues, must be seriously undertaken later.

For a cursory survey, a tracing of the attitude toward the Negro as reflected in American letters gives us seven stages or phases, supplying not only an interesting cycle of shifts in public taste and interest, but a rather significant curve for social history. And more interesting perhaps than the attitudes themselves are the underlying issues and reactions of class attitudes and relationships which have been basically responsible for these attitudes. Moreover, instead of a single fixed attitude, sectionally divided and opposed, as the popular presumption goes, it will be seen that American attitudes toward the Negro have changed radically and often, with dramatic turns and with a curious reversal of rôle between the North and the South according to the class consciousness and interests dominant at any given time. With allowances for generalization, so far as literature records it, Negro life has run a gamut of seven notes,—heroics, sentiment, melodrama, comedy, farce, problem-discussion and æsthetic interest—as, in their respective turns, strangeness, domestic familiarity, moral controversy, pity, hatred, bewilderment, and curiosity, have dominated the public mind. Naturally, very few of these atti-

79

tudes have been favorable to anything approaching adequate or even artistic portrayal; the Negro has been shunted from one stereotype into the other, but in this respect has been no more the sufferer than any other subject class, the particular brunt of whose servitude has always seemed to me to consist in the fate of having their psychological traits dictated to them.   Of course, the Negro has been a particularly apt social mimic, and has assumed protective coloration with almost every change—thereby hangs the secret of his rather unusual survival.   But of course a price has been paid, and that is that the Negro, after three hundred years of residence and association, even to himself, is falsely known and little understood.   It becomes all the more interesting, now that we are verging for the first time on conditions admitting anything like true portraiture and self-portrayal to review in retrospect the conditions which have made the Negro traditionally in turn a dreaded primitive, a domestic pet, a moral issue, a ward, a scapegoat, a bogey and pariah, and finally what he has been all along, could he have been seen that way, a flesh and blood human, with nature's chronic but unpatented varieties.

Largely because Negro portraiture has rarely if ever run afoul of literary genius, these changes have rather automatically followed the trend of popular feeling, and fall almost into historical period stages, with very little overlapping.   Roughly we may outline them as a Colonial period attitude (1760-1820), a pre-Abolition period (1820-45), the Abolitionist period (1845-65), the Early Reconstruction period (1870-85), the late Reconstruction period (1885-95), the Industrial period (1895-1920), and the Contemporary period since 1920.   The constant occurrence and recurrence of the Negro, even as a minor figure, throughout this wide range is in itself an indication of the importance of the Negro as a social issue in American life, and of the fact that his values are not to be read by intrinsic but by extrinsic coefficients.   He has dramatized constantly two aspects of white psychology in a projected and naïvely divorced shape—first, the white man's wish for self-justification, whether he be at any given time anti-Negro or pro-Negro, and, second, more subtly registered, an avoidance of the particular type that would raise an embarrassing question for the social conscience of the period; as, for example, the black slave rebel at the time when all efforts were being made after the abatement of the slave trade to domesticate the Negro; or the defeatist fiction types of 1895-1920, when the curve of Negro material progress took such a sharp upward rise.   There is no insinuation that much of this sort of reflection has been as conscious or deliberately propagandist as is often charged and believed; it is really more significant as an expression of "unconscious social wish," for whenever there has been direct and avowed propaganda there has always been awakened a reaction in public attitude and a swift counter-tendency. Except in a few outstanding instances, literature has merely registered rather than moulded public sentiment on this question.

Through the Colonial days and extending as late as 1820, Negro life was treated as strange and distant. The isolated instances treat the Negro almost heroically, with an exotic curiosity that quite gaudily romanticized him. At that time, as in the more familiar romantic treatment of the American Indian, there was registered in the emphasis upon "savage traits" and strange ways a revulsion to his social assimilation. The typical figure of the period is a pure blood, often represented as a "noble captive," a type neither fully domesticated nor understood, and shows that far from being a familiar the Negro was rather a dreaded curiosity. Incidentally, this undoubtedly was a period of close association between the more domesticated Indian tribes and the Negroes—an almost forgotten chapter in the history of race relations in America which the heavy admixture of Indian blood in the Negro strain silently attests; so the association of the two in the public mind may have had more than casual grounds. Two of the most interesting features of this period are the frank concession of ancestry and lineage to the Negro at a time before the serious onset of miscegenation, and the hectic insistence upon Christian virtues and qualities in the Negro at a time when the Negro masses could not have been the model Christians they were represented to be, and which they did in fact become later. As James Oneal has pointed out in an earlier article, the notion of the boon of Christianity placated the bad conscience of the slave traders, and additionally at that time there was reason at least in the feeling of insecurity to sense that it was good social insurance to stress it.

By 1820 or 1825 the Negro was completely domesticated, and patriarchal relations had set in. The strange savage had become a sentimentally humored peasant. The South was beginning to develop its "aristocratic tradition," and the slave figure was the necessary foil of its romanticism. According to F. P. Gaines, "the plantation makes its first important appearance in American literature in John Pendleton Kennedy's *Swallow Barn* (1832) and William Carruther's *The Cavaliers of Virginia* (1834)." As one would expect, the really important figures of the régime are discreetly ignored,— the mulatto house servant concubine and her children; the faithful male body-servant, paradoxically enough, came in for a compensating publicity. In fact, the South was rapidly developing feudal intricacies and their strange, oft-repeated loyalties, and was actually on the verge of a golden age of romance when the shadow of scandal from Northern criticism darkened the high-lights of the whole régime and put the South on the defensive. It is a very significant fact that between 1845 and 1855 there should have appeared nearly a score of plays and novels on the subject of the quadroon girl and her tragic mystery, culminating in William Wells Brown's bold exposè *Clothel; or, The President's Daughter* (1853), as the caption of the unexpurgated English edition of this black Abolitionist's novel read. Southern romance was chilled to the marrow, and did not resume the genial sentimental approach to race characters for over a generation.

With the political issues of slave and free territory looming, and the moral issues of the Abolitionist controversy coming on, Negro life took on in literature the aspects of melodrama. The portraiture which had started was hastily dropped for exaggerated types representing polemical issues. The exaggerated tone was oddly enough set by the Negro himself, for long before *Uncle Tom's Cabin* (1852) the lurid slave narratives had set the pattern of Job-like suffering and melodramatic incident. Apart from its detailed dependence on Josiah Henson's actual story, Mrs. Stowe's novel simply capitalized a pattern of story and character already definitely outlined 1845-50, and in some exceptional anticipations ten years previous. Of course, with this period the vital portrayal of the Negro passed temporarily out of the hands of the South and became dominantly an expression of Northern interest and sentiment. In its controversial literature, naturally the South responded vehemently to the Abolitionist's challenge with the other side of the melodramatic picture,— the Negro as a brute and villain. But the formal retaliations of Reconstruction fiction were notably absent; except for a slight shift to the more docile type of Negro and peasant life further removed from the life of the "big house," G. P. James and others continued the mildly propagandist fiction of the patriarchal tradition,—an interesting indication of how the impending danger of the slave régime was minimized in the mass mind of the South. *Uncle Tom's*

Cabin, of course, passes as the acme of the literature of the Abolitionist period, and it is in relation to its influence upon the issues
involved. But as far as literary values go, *Clothel* by Wells Brown
and *The Garies and Their Friends* by Frank J. Webb were closer
studies both of Negro character and of the Negro situation. Their
daring realism required them to be published abroad, and they are
to be reckoned like the Paris school of Russian fiction as the fore-
runners of the native work of several generations later. Especially
Webb's book, with its narrative of a sophisticated and cultured group
of free Negroes, was in its day a bold departure from prevailing conventions. Either of these books would have been greater still had
it consciously protested against the melodramatic stereotypes then in
public favor; but the temptation to cater to the vogue of *Uncle
Tom's Cabin* was perhaps too great. The sensational popularity of
the latter, and its influence upon the public mind, is only another
instance of the effect of a great social issue to sustain melodrama
as classic as long as the issue lives. The artistic costs of all revolu-
tions and moral reforms is high.

The Early Reconstruction period supplied the inevitable sentimental reaction to the tension of the war period. The change to
sentimental genre is quite understandable. If the South could have
resumed the portrayal of its life at the point where controversy had
broken in, there would be a notable Southern literature today. But
the South was especially prone to sugar-coat the slave régime in a
protective reaction against the exposures of the Abolitionist literature. Northern fiction in works like the novels of Albion Tourgee
continued its incriminations, and Southern literature became more
and more propagandist. At first it was only in a secondary sense
derogatory of the Negro; the primary aim was self-justification and
romantic day-dreaming about the past. In the effort to glorfy the
lost tradition and balm the South's inferiority complex after the
defeat, Uncle Tom was borrowed back as counter-propaganda, refur-
bished as the devoted, dependent, happy, care-free Negro, whom the
South had always loved and protected, and whom it knew "better
than he knew himself." The protective devices of this fiction, the
accumulative hysteria of self-delusion associated with its promulga-
tion, as well as the comparatively universal acceptance of so obvious
a myth, form one of the most interesting chapters in the entire
history of social mind. There is no denying the effectiveness of the
Page-Cable school of fiction as Southern propaganda. In terms of

popular feeling it almost recouped the reverses of the war. The North, having been fed only on stereotypes, came to ignore the Negro in any intimate or critical way through the deceptive influence of those very stereotypes. At least, these figures Southern fiction painted were more convincingly human and real, which in my judgment accounted in large part for the extraordinary ease with which the Southern version of the Negro came to be accepted by the Northern reading public, along· with the dictum that the South knows the Negro.

But the false values in the situation spoiled the whole otherwise promising school—Chandler Harris excepted—as a contrast of the later work of Cable or Page with their earlier work will convincingly show. Beginning with good genre drawing that had the promise of something, they ended in mediocre chromographic romanticism. Though the genteel tradition never fully curdled into hatred, more and more hostilely it focussed upon the Negro as the scapegoat of the situation. And then came a flood of flagrantly derogatory literature as the sudden rise of figures like Thomas Dixon, paralleling the Vardamans and Tillmans of political life, marked the assumption of the master-class tradition by the mass psychology of the "poor-whites." Reconstruction fiction thus completed the swing made quite inevitable by the extreme arc of Abolitionist literature; the crudities and animus of the one merely countered the bathos and bias of the other. In both periods the treatment of Negro life was artistically unsatisfactory, and subject to the distortions of sentiment, propaganda, and controversy. The heavy artillery of this late Reconstruction attack has shambled its own guns; but the lighter fussilade of farce still holds out and still harasses those who stand guard over the old controversial issues. But the advance front of creative effort and attack has moved two stages further on.

As a result of the discussion of the Late Reconstruction period "White Supremacy" had become more than a slogan of the Southern chauvinists; it became a mild general social hysteria, which gave an almost biological significance to the race problem. It is interesting to note how suddenly the "problem of miscegenation" became important at a time when there was less of it than at any period within a century and a quarter, and how the mulatto, the skeleton in the family closet, suddenly was trotted out for attention and scrutiny. From 1895 or so on, this problem was for over a decade a veritable obsession; and from William Dean Howells' *Imperative Duty* to

Stribling's *Birthright* the typical and dominant figure of literary interest is the mulatto as a symbol of social encroachment, and the fear of some "atavism of blood" through him wreaking vengeance for slavery. While serious literature was discussing the mulatto and his problem, less serious literature was in a sub-conscious way no less seriously occupied with the negative side of the same problem;—namely, extolling the unambitious, servile, and "racially characteristic" Negro who in addition to presenting diverting humor represented no serious social competition or encroachment. The public mind of the whole period was concentrated on the Negro "in" and "out of his place"; and the pseudo-scientific popularizations of evolutionism added their belabored corollaries. But the real basic proposition underlying it all was the sensing for the first time of the serious competition and rivalry of the Negro's social effort and the failure of his social handicaps to effectively thwart it.

Many will be speculating shortly upon the reasons for the literary and artistic emancipation of the Negro, at a time when his theme seemed most hopelessly in the double grip of social prejudice and moral Victorianism. Of course, realism had its share in the matter; the general reaction away from types was bound to reach even the stock Negro stereotypes. Again, the local color fad and the naturally exotic tendencies of conscious ætheticism gave the untouched field of Negro life an attractive lure. The gradual assertion of Negro artists trying at first to counteract the false drawing and values of popular writers, but eventually in the few finer talents motivated by the more truly artistic motives of self-expression, played its additional part. But in my judgment the really basic factor in the sharp and astonishing break in the literary tradition and attitude toward the Negro came in the revolt against Puritanism. This seems to me to explain why current literature and art are for the moment so preoccupied with the primitive and pagan and emotional aspects of Negro life and character; and why suddenly something almost amounting to infatuation has invested the Negro subject with interest and fascination. The release which almost everyone had thought must come about through a change in moral evaluation, a reform of opinion, has actually and suddenly come about merely as a shift of interest, a revolution of taste. From it there looms the imminent possibility not only of a true literature of the Negro but of a Negro Literature as such. It becomes especially interesting to watch whether the artistic possibilities of these are to be realized, since thrice before this social issues have scotched the artistic potentialities of Negro life, and American literature is thereby poorer in the fields of the historical romance, the period novel, and great problem-drama than it should be. But the work of Waldo Frank, Jean Toomer, Walter White, Rudolph Fisher, and Du Bose Heyward promises greatly; and if we call up the most analogous case as a basis of forecast,—the tortuous way by which the peasant came into Russian literature and the brilliant sudden transformation his advent eventually effected, we may predict, for both subject and its creative exponents, the Great Age of this particular section of American life and strand in the American experience.

◇ ◇ ◇

The Roving Critic

By Carl Van Doren

The Negro Renaissance

Those white Americans who for sixty years have been insisting that the black American must keep in his place have generally been the sort who in another breath could insist that America is the home of opportunity for all men. If now they are disturbed at seeing that the negro's place is no longer what it was, perhaps they can be consoled by thinking that the opportunity was even greater than they realized. It was, after all, too much to expect that the colored tenth of the population, whatever its racial handicap, would not be touched by the gospel of progress which the other nine tenths swore by. That tenth has been touched. It has, in fact, learned its lesson so well that certain of its members decline to remain soil-bound peasants or obliging body-servants or even punctual artisans or melodious entertainers, and manage to become experts, capitalists, even scholars and poets. And in doing this they have done, in the face of American expectation, precisely what Americans at large have done during the past century and a half in the face of European expectation. On the eve of the Revolution the Rev. Andrew Burnaby, a fairly well disposed Briton, had announced that "America is formed for happiness, but not for empire." As late as 1844 a British journalist, less well disposed, announced that "as yet the American is horn-handed and pig-headed, hard, persevering, unscrupulous, carnivorous . . . with an incredible genius for lying." If the whole of the nation could so disappoint prophecy, a part of it could hardly lag entirely behind.

The negroes, though delayed by slavery, have not lagged. In the symposium called "The New Negro," [1] a group of them have undertaken to present their cause after two generations of freedom and to exhibit the best fruits of their achievement. The information of the work is extensive, the reasoning sensible, the temper all that could be desired. Compared with what the white Americans could have exhibited a century ago, when the total population of the United States was roughly equal to that of the colored Americans to-day, the book does not suffer. The fiction may not equal the best of Irving and Cooper, but the verse is higher in workmanship and poetical quality than the verse generally being written in 1826, and the prose discussions put to shame the vexed and feverish provincialism with which Americans then argued their case against Europe. If any evidence is needed, the volume is evidence

[1] "The New Negro." Edited by Alain Locke. Albert and Charles Boni.

635

that the new negro is a civilized and accomplished being, who not only has given to the nation its most joyous dances, which may have a barbaric strain in them, and its most characteristic music, which may be only a folk-art, but who has learned how to write lucid, cogent, and charming prose, which is one of the unmistakable signs of an advanced civilization.

It is no doubt true that the current enthusiasm for negro life and art is in some degree a fad which cannot stay at the high pitch of the past few months. But when the fad has passed it will leave behind such solid documents by white writers as Dorothy Scarborough's "On the Trail of Negro Folk-Songs" (Harvard University) and Howard W. Odum and Guy B. Johnson's "The Negro and His Songs" (University of North Carolina) and R. Emmet Kennedy's "Mellows: Negro Work Songs" (A. & C. Boni) and such sensitive fiction as Du Bose Heyward's "Porgy" (Doran), to say nothing of such veracious contributions by colored writers as "The New Negro" and James Weldon Johnson and J. Rosamond Johnson's "The Book of American Negro Spirituals" (Viking) and Countee Cullen's "Color" (Harper) and Langston Hughes's "The Weary Blues" (Knopf). Something has been poured into the stream of native culture which cannot soon cease to tinge it. Something has been uttered to enlarge the imaginative sympathy between the races which is an absolute essential of any decent solution of the color problem in America.

Fads, of course, do not come without a reason. If the whites have been hospitable to negro themes and modes of expression, it is because there was something for them to be hospitable

to. It is probable that the historian of the episode will trace its roots to Harlem. So long as the negroes continued to be in the main a peasant race, they had little opportunity to make themselves heard. To the white governing class they seemed to be primarily comic or, at best, tuneful. With that gift of theirs which is at once discretion and courtesy, they kept to themselves the genuine impulses stirring within them. They developed a folk-lore and a folk-art which was little conditioned by the industrial system of the country as a whole. Then suddenly a greater number of negroes than had ever before been gathered into any city found themselves in Harlem. They had to struggle against serious difficulties still, but New York was at least cosmopolitan enough to leave them more or less to themselves and to permit them to form as complete a community as they could. A generation before, and the thing might have come too early. Oppressively aware of being freedmen, they might have made a successful effort to lose the traits which could remind them of their former slavery, and might have sunk into a drab, limping uniformity. Whether they might or might not have done this once, they did not do it in the twentieth century. The new generation had outgrown the earlier habit of self-depreciation, and some of them were outgrowing the later, and healthier, habit of self-assertion. They had the courage to cherish certain picturesque racial elements in their natures and customs. They moved from the point at which they were bound together by a common condition, in Mr. Locke's phrase, to the point at which they were bound together by a common consciousness.

And they swiftly flowered into utterance, much as New England, in the early part of the nineteenth century, flowered into Transcendentalism. The scale is obviously not yet the same as it was in New England. No mature Emerson, Hawthorne, Melville, or Thoreau enriches the pages of "The New Negro," although the poetry of Countee Cullen is as good as has been written by any American in his teens or early twenties, and the prose stories of Jean Toomer have exquisite promise. But there was no New-Englander in 1826 who could have produced a better survey of an international complication than Mr. Du Bois has produced in "The Negro Mind Reaches Out," or a better analysis of national conditions than appears in "The New Frontage on American Life" by Charles S. Johnson, or who could have shown himself more learned in various aspects of Americanism than Mr. Locke shows himself in various aspects of Afro-Americanism. In fact, the most striking impression of this book is that the negro is better as analyst than as artist. Perhaps this is because his greatest artistic endowment lies in the direction of dancing and music, which cannot easily be represented in print. But it is none the less true that he has a remarkable skill in stating his case, a skill which, it may be guessed, has come from a prolonged and bitter knowledge of it. At any rate, the art of the new negro in America has now a chance to be built upon a very firm critical foundation.

There is bound, however, to be on this plane of art something of the same conflict between white and black as there has always been in the United States between the majority and any minority whatever. A profound national impulse drives the hundred millions steadily toward uniformity. How can the negro resist the impulse, when the main pattern of life is marked out for him by white institutions, and when, indeed, he can prosper at all only by adjusting himself at most economic, social, and moral points to the prevailing scheme? He cannot mark himself off by special costumes, by a distinctive dialect, by different industries or laws or religions. The best he can do, probably, is to have the courage of certain inherited sentiments and to feel sustained in them by racial consciousness. But this may be a factor of great importance in shaping his future. It may enable him to keep his religion rich and dramatic, instead of thin and formulistic; to permit his public ceremonies, as he does now, to be as gorgeous as he knows how to make them; to prefer, in his daily manners, variety rather than monotony, high color rather than low color, spontaneous rhythms rather than tight, regimented motions, full laughter rather than guarded snickers, metaphor rather than logical demonstration, comfortable song rather than uncomfortable silence. If the negro can by some miracle preserve these generous qualities for a century or so, he may become as fertile a soil for all the arts as for dancing and singing. Yet miracles do not happen. The negro will do a great deal for himself if he carries out a small part of this program which his friends predict for him. And he will thereby do a great deal for American culture generally. If these things happen, 1925 will be marked in the history of the nation as a memorable year, and as the beginning of a new epoch for the African race.

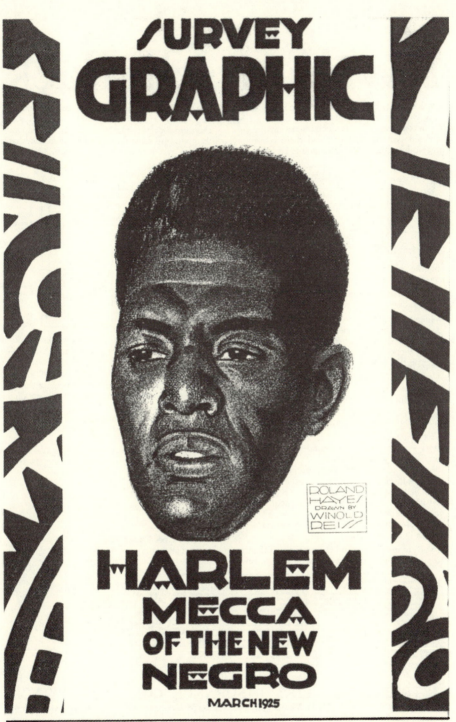

/URVEY GRAPHIC

HARLEM
MECCA
OF THE NEW
NEGRO

MARCH 1925

ROLAND
HAYE/
DRAWN BY
WINOLD
REI//

SURVEY GRAPHIC, published monthly and copyright 1925 by SURVEY ASSOCIATES, Inc., 112 East 19th Street, New York. Price: this copy (March, 1925; Vol. VI, No. 6) 50 cts.; $3 a year; foreign postage, 50 cts. extra; Canadian 30 cts. Changes of address should be mailed us two weeks in advance. When payment is by check a receipt will be sent only upon request. Entered as second-class matter, November 25, 1921, at the post office, New York, N. Y., under the Act of March 3; 1879. Acceptance or mailing at a special rate of postage provided for in Section 1103, Act of October 3, 1917, authorized December 21, 1921. Pres., Robert W. de Forest. Sec'y, Ann Reed Brenner.   Treas., Arthur Kellogg.   Reprinted 1980 by Black Classic Press, P.O. Box 13414, Balto. Md. 21203. Additional copies $6 each plus $1 postage & handling.

Pay Yourself Back

ARE you tired? It is getting close to the time of year when people talk of feeling "all tired out" and there is much discussion of spring tonics. If you are fatigued and there is nothing organically wrong, the tonic you need and prob-

rest. If hard physical work is making you feel "all in" you may require more hours of sleep than usual even though this may mean temporarily giving up some form of amusement. Perhaps you are not eating the right amount of energy-

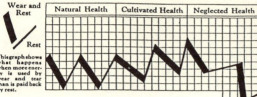

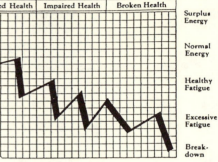

Wear and Rest | Natural Health | Cultivated Health | Neglected Health | Impaired Health | Broken Health

Surplus Energy

Normal Energy

This graph shows what happens when more energy is used by wear and tear than is paid back by rest.

Healthy Fatigue

ably the only one you need is the right kind of rest to restore your energy.

To one person, rest may mean sleep; to another, physical exercise; to a third, recreation.

While it is true that few of us work up to our full capacity, and much so-called fatigue is imagined or just pure laziness—yet it is also true that many people work far beyond their strength without realizing the danger.

A certain amount of fatigue after exertion is natural, but excessive fatigue is Nature's safety-device for warning that rest is needed. When you are over-tired, your powers of resistance are lowered and you are more susceptible to disease.

What brings about excessive fatigue? Usually over-strain—either physical or mental—and insufficient rest. Because your activity is both of the body and the mind, and one reacts on the other, your fatigue is a close interlacing of physical and mental weariness. Neither can be relieved separately. Emotional disturbances—worry, fear, resentment, discontent and depression also cause fatigue. The tired man is often a worried man, and the worried man is usually a tired man.

If you are over-tired, find the reason and then try to plan your time so that you will have sufficient

Excessive Fatigue

Break-down

making food. If you are a mental worker the kind of rest you probably need is exercise in fresh air. If excessive emotion is making you tired, the right kind of recreation probably will help you.

Remember that excessive fatigue is not a thing to be lightly shrugged away. There is often a direct connection between the first neglected signs of fatigue and a serious breakdown from which recovery is a slow, disheartening process. If you tire too easily and if rest does not put you back in good condition, it is more than likely that your health is affected and needs attention.

Workers—take warning! Pay back the energy that you take out of yourself. As the years mount up, longer and longer periods of rest are necessary to make restoration. The "spring tonic" that you need most likely is just a rearrangement of your hours of work, play and rest, and not medicine.

Employers of labor are coming to find that excessive, unnecessary fatigue is a great source of industrial and economic waste. It entails loss of production and loss of earning power. It is said to be a factor in the occurrence of work accidents and is closely related to the cause or aggravation of most cases of severe sickness.

Many large organizations have learned that physical fatigue can be minimized by careful control of working conditions. An increasingly large number of employees are now working only a reasonable number of hours each week. Machines, tables,

benches, and seating facilities are being constructed to serve the needs and comfort of those who use them. Adequate, proper lighting and good ventilation have been found to be important factors in the battle against the serious consequences of abnormal fatigue.

Tests have shown that in connection with certain occupations output can be increased and fatigue decreased by arranging rest periods. Here in the Home Office of the Metropolitan Life Insurance Company, our more than 9000 employees have two rest periods, one in the morning

and one in the afternoon. These periods of relaxation have a beneficial effect on both the work and worker.

There are many hours of the day when men and women do not work. The good use of these hours is as important to health as is the right use of working hours. The Metropolitan has published a booklet, "What Would You Do With 36,000,000 Minutes (70 years of life)!" and another on "Industrial Hygiene." Either or both, of these booklets, will be mailed free to those who ask for them.

HALEY FISKE, President.

Published by

METROPOLITAN LIFE INSURANCE COMPANY—NEW YORK

Biggest in the World, More Assets. More Policyholders. More Insurance in force, More new Insurance each year

The National Urban League

ORGANIZED 1910   INCORPORATED 1913

127 East 23rd Street, New York City

The National Urban League is an organization which seeks to improve the relations between the races in America. It strives to improve the living and working conditions of the Negro.

Its special field of operation embraces cities where Negroes reside in large numbers.

The Executive Boards of the national and of the forty local organizations are made up of white and colored people who have caught the vision of social work and believe in justice and fair play in the dealings of men with each other.

THE LEAGUE'S PROGRAM

1. It makes thorough investigations of social conditions as bases for practical social work.

2. As rapidly as practicable committees are organized to further the recommendations growing out of such studies and especially to stimulate existing social welfare agencies to take on work for Negroes or to enlarge their activities in behalf of their Negro constituents. Occasionally special work for Negroes is organized where existing agencies are not willing to assume work for Negroes, or where there are no available facilities for meeting these needs. Its program embraces definite social service activities where it is not expedient to establish a new agency to meet the need.

3. The League furthers the training of colored social workers through providing fellowships for colored students at schools of social work and providing apprenticeships in the League's field activities for prospective social workers.

It conducts programs of education among colored and white people for the purpose of stimulating greater interest on the part of the general public in social service work for colored people.

It publishes "Opportunity"—a monthly Journal of Negro Life which presents results of scientific research and surveys of social conditions.

We are now trying to launch a new National Industrial Department at a cost of about $9,000 per year for a three year experimental period, the purposes being:

1. To standardize and coordinate the local employment agencies of the League

so that exchange of information and more regular correspondence between them can assure applicants for work more efficient and helpful service and employers of labor a more efficient group of employees.

2. To work directly with large industrial plants both in cities where the League is established and the communities removed from such centers to procure larger opportunity for work and for advancement on the job for Negro workers; and to stimulate Negro workers to a fresh determination to "make good" on the job so that their future place in industry may be assured;

3. To help thru available channels of information to ascertain points at which there is need of Negro labor and points at which there is an oversupply of Negro labor and to use existing agencies of publicity and placement to direct Negro labor, including migrants, to those points where they are most needed and where their families will more easily become adjusted;

4. To help develop a social program by which Negro families may more easily become adjusted to the requirements for good living in the districts to which they go. This program will include, of course, advising these workers at the earliest possible moment after arriving in a new community to connect themselves with some church so that the religious life to which most of the Negro migrants have been accustomed may be continued.

In this connection, it might be well also to mention the fact that it will be our desire to see better relations between white and colored workers—this to be accomplished not through activities involving force, but through the orderly development of a feeling of good fellowship and comradeship.

(In answering this advertisement please mention THE SURVEY. *It helps us, it identifies you.)*

622

NATIONAL URBAN LEAGUE

FOR SOCIAL SERVICE AMONG NEGROES

127 EAST 23RD STREET ROOMS 31-33-34 NEW YORK CITY

TELEPHONE: GRAMERCY 3976

EUGENE KINCKLE JONES
EXECUTIVE SECRETARY

March 1, 1925.

Dear Survey Reader:-

The National Urban League seeks to improve the living conditions of Negroes in cities, making a specialty of opening new avenues of employment to Negroes and encouraging them in their efforts to become more efficient.

There are forty Urban Leagues, twenty-six with offices and staffs. Eighteen are included in community chests, receiving the endorsement that this connection entails. Colored social workers are trained through fellowships provided by the League at leading schools of social work. All League Boards, national and local, are composed of leading white and colored citizens, thus guaranteeing the best inter-racial thought on our common community problems growing out of race contacts.

Our Department of Research makes careful surveys of social conditions preparatory to launching programs of improvement. We provide facts on the Negro for lecturers, writers and students. We publish "OPPORTUNITY" magazine - a journal of Negro life, and our local organizations conduct programs in health, housing, recreation or general community welfare in accordance with the local need and demand.

Our budget for 1925 is $57,000, including $9,000 for the new Industrial Department which we hope will help take the color line out of industry. We invite you to $10 membership in the League or a contribution towards the $1,500 balance needed to complete our special industrial budget.

Sincerely yours,

EKJ/PWJ

Eugene Kinckle Jones
Executive Secretary.

ENDORSED BY NATIONAL INFORMATION BUREAU

(In answering this advertisement please mention THE SURVEY. *It helps us, it identifies you.)*

623

Social Studies

Conducted by
Joseph K. Hart

What Shall We Do with the Facts?

THIS is no easy matter. The old white overseer of a Southern plantation took the employer's son to town with him one August day. He stopped at the grocery to get some provisions. When the grocer had taken down the order he suggested that the overseer take the small boy down to the ice plant to see them make ice. After protesting that the grocer must be "fooling," since anybody knew there "couldn't be ice in August," he reluctantly consented to the adventure. The two of them arrived at the plant just in time to see the workers turning out a number of great transparent cakes, which were undeniably ice. The overseer gazed in terror for a few moments; then seizing the boy by the hand, he ran down the steps and down the street for several blocks before he stopped. Out of breath at last, he turned and, shaking his finger in the small boy's face until he had recovered his breath, he finally said:

"It aint so; and if it is so, it aint right, and I'm going to have the preacher preach agin it next Sunday."

Here, also, are facts. What's to be done about them? Well, it must be confessed that America is, on the whole, in little mood for facts, just now. We prefer fancies more than facts; and we like our fancies to be tinged with fearsomeness.

It cheers us mightily to be afeared. It makes us appreciate our homes and schools and churches. The fate of the Child Labor Amendment shows America at our saddest and best. Facts are dull things. Bed-time stories, with bears growling in the woods and lions under the beds, make our beds feel wonderfully downy and comforting. We are going to take care of our own children: we are not going to let some ogre state, probably taking its cues from Russia, tell us what to do with our children. When we have eaten fearsome fancies long enough we shall become noble; perhaps even become handsome.

There are scientists who say, with that folly that is so characteristic of the scientist: "You'd best be careful how you fool with facts—they are sometimes loaded!" But that sort of talk is just the professional salesman trying to dispose of his own wares. Facts can be evaded—out of hand. We can legislate evolution out of existence. We can turn the scientist out of his chair and restore our old fanciful traditions. We can feed our minds on folly—and grow fat—of mind.

What shall we do with facts? Some people face them—but that gets them into trouble. Perhaps we'd best continue to do as we have always done, praise them and ignore them!

Analytic Index of This Issue

625

A Glimpse Ahead!

KIPLING gave us the high road of India in "Kim." Sinclair Lewis set down America on "Main Street." But that contrast is not the whole story of East and West.

We have no hesitancy in saying that here in the Northern cities of the United States, of which New York is arch type, is going forward something which will take its place in the great pageant of humanity.

But Harlem does not tell the whole story of the Negro in America. It is a fresh approach to an old story. It is a coat cut of city cloth—with the seams of social problems which underlie it, the cultural pattern which surfaces it. In the months ahead Survey Graphic will bring out articles which will throw light on other factors in race relations.

Hampton, Tuskegee and Points North

DR. ROBERT R. MOTON, *Principal, Tuskegee Institute.*

Thousands of countrysides have felt the yeast of the leadership of Armstrong and Frissell, Washington and Moton. Now comes the northward migration. How are the values which have been wrought out in an educational program, which is slowly revolutionizing the economy of the cotton states, to be conserved in the new situation?

A Southern Negro's Impression of Harlem

JOHN HOPE, *President, Morehouse College, Atlanta.*

President Hope, who is throwing open the sciences as never before to the youth of his race, will give his keen and outspoken observations of the Harlem scene.

The School of the Home-Acres

ROSSA B. COOLEY, *Principal, Penn School, St. Helena Island, South Carolina.*

Here on a sea island off South Carolina is carried forward what Professor Hart has called the most interesting experiment in elementary education in the United States today; where the farms have been brought

---

THE Survey Graphic is maintained mutually by 1700 reader-members of Survey Associates to engage in just such pieces of social interpretation as this.

If you are a professional man or woman and want to know of the living contributions of other professions where they overlap yours in the realm of the common welfare; if you are a lawyer who wants to know of the big advances in health, a physician alive to the cross-fires of psychology and education—a business man aware of the upward thrust of labor—

If you want to know Who and How and Whither—the Survey Graphic is for you.

SURVEY ASSOCIATES.
112 East 19th Street, New York.

Put me down for a six-months trial subscription to Survey Graphic, monthly, beginning with the current issue and send me a bill for $1.00 (one year $3.00)

Name ....

Address ....

SG-3-25

---

to school, and then the school spread out on the Island until school and community are coterminous.

Southern Experience in Its Bearing on the Northern City

WILL W. ALEXANDER, *Director, Commission on Inter-racial Cooperation, Atlanta.*

In many Southern communities a new method which has promise has come in with the rise and spread of the inter-racial councils. When the human history of the South is written this movement may come to be looked back upon as ushering in a new epoch. What has this constructive Southern experience to offer the North?

Where East Africa Borders the Future

JAMES H. DILLARD, *President, The Slater Fund, Char-lottesville, Va.*

We would have to go back to Stanley if not to Marco Polo to find a counterpart of the educational expeditions sent out by the Phelps Stokes Fund. Dr. Dillard was a member of the East African Commission which reports this spring.

The Regional Community

IN late April a world conference on Town City and Regional Planning will be held in New York. As their special contribution to the exchange of ideas which will then take place, a small imaginative group of planners who call themselves the Regional Planning Association of America have collaborated with the editors of The Survey in gathering for our May Graphic a series of articles, maps, diagrams and sketches which will throw a fresh light on the enormous quandary in which city-dwellers and city-planners find themselves and on the promise of a new approach to the city, with the region as a base. Among those collaborating:

Governor Alfred E. Smith	Alexander M. Bing
Clarence E. Stein	Benton Mackaye
Lewis Mumford	Stuart Chase
Art Young	Henry Wright
Frederick L. Ackerman	Joseph K. Hart
Frederick Bigger	Robert W. Bruére

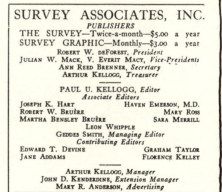

SURVEY ASSOCIATES, INC.
PUBLISHERS

THE SURVEY—Twice-a-month—$5.00 a year
SURVEY GRAPHIC—Monthly—$3.00 a year

ROBERT W. DEFOREST, *President*
JULIAN W. MACK, V. EVERIT MACY, *Vice-Presidents*
ANN REED BRENNER, *Secretary*
ARTHUR KELLOGG, *Treasurer*

PAUL U. KELLOGG, *Editor*
Associate Editors

JOSEPH K. HART	HAVEN EMERSON, M.D.
ROBERT W. BRUÈRE	MARY ROSS
MARTHA BENSLEY BRUÈRE	SARA MERRILL

LEON WHIPPLE
GEDDES SMITH, *Managing Editor*
Contributing Editors

EDWARD T. DEVINE	GRAHAM TAYLOR
JANE ADDAMS	FLORENCE KELLEY

ARTHUR KELLOGG, *Manager*
JOHN D. KENDERDINE, *Extension Manager*
MARY R. ANDERSON, *Advertising*

112 East 19 Street, New York

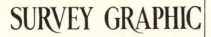

SURVEY GRAPHIC

Vol. VI, No. 6   March, 1925

CONTENTS

The Gist of It

THE Survey is seeking, month by month and year by year to follow the subtle traces of race growth and interaction through the shifting outline of social organization and by the flickering light of individual achievement. There are times when these forces that work so slowly and so delicately seem suddenly to flower—and we become aware that the curtain has lifted on a new act in the drama of part or all of us. Such, we believe, was the case with Ireland on the threshold of political emancipation, and the New Ireland spoke for itself in our issue of November 1921; with the New Russia which was to some degree interpreted in March 1923; and with the newly awakened Mexico, in May 1924. If The Survey reads the signs aright, such a dramatic flowering of a new race-spirit is taking place close at home—among American Negroes, and the stage of that new episode is Harlem.

FOR the concept of this issue, for painstaking collaboration in its preparation, for the full-length study of The New Negro (p. 631) and for many smaller pieces in the mosaic of this number, The Survey is indebted to Alain Locke, a graduate of Harvard, Oxford and Berlin, now professor of philosophy at Harvard University, and himself a brilliant exemplar of that poise and insight which are happy omens for the Negro's future.

THE Making of Harlem is recounted by James Weldon Johnson (p. 635). This journalist, editor, poet, publicist is executive secretary of the National Association for the Advancement of Colored People, editor of the Book of American Negro Poetry, and author of Fifty Years and After, and The Autobiography of an Ex-Colored Man.

CHARLES S. JOHNSON, who studies Black Workers and the City (p. 641) is director of publicity and research for the National Urban League and the editor of its organ, Opportunity; a Journal of Negro Life. A social survey expert, he was assistant secretary of the Chicago Commission on Race Relations. Rudolph Fisher, who sketches some Southern strains in the city (p. 644) is a young short-story writer of distinctive achievement. A West Indian, a journalist and author, W. A. Domingo writes of The Tropics in New York (p. 648).

WINOLD REISS'S studies of Mexican types will be vividly remembered by readers of the Mexican Number.

THE versatile editor of The Crisis, author of Souls of Black Folk, Darkwater, The Gift of Black Folk W. E. B. DuBois presents the Negro bringing gifts (p. 655). For the courtesy of permitting the republication of a number of poems, in addition to those here published for the first time, The Survey's thanks go to the authors and publishers mentioned. J. A. Rogers, who characterizes Jazz at Home (p. 665) is the author of From Superman to Man.

WHAT the Negro's creative temperament may mean to America (p. 668) is the theme of Albert C. Barnes, a connoisseur whose galleries at Merion, Pennsylvania, house a distinguished collection. Arthur A. Schomburg (The Negro Digs Up His Past, p. 670), is a member of the American Negro Academy.

TURNING from art expression to sociological fact and social problem—Melville J. Herskovits, an anthropologist engaged in an extended study of the problem of variability under racial crossing, opens the third section of the issue with a study of The Dilemma of Social Pattern, to which Konrad Bercovici, with the intuitive vigor which characterized his Around the World in New York, offers an intriguing companion-piece in The Rhythm of Harlem.

WALTER F. WHITE, whose The Fire in the Flint was an outstanding novel of 1924, is assistant secretary of the National Association for the Advancement of Colored People. He studies the personal effects of prejudice in Color Lines (p. 680), while Dean Kelly Miller of the Junior College of Howard University, a leader in the Negro Sanhedrin, discusses its social aspects (p. 682). A further sidelight on segregation is carried by Eunice Hunton's Breaking Through (p. 684). Miss Hunton, a recent Smith graduate, is a social worker and writer.

A vocational expert, social worker, leader in women's work, recently appointed assistant principal of Public School No. 89, in Harlem, Mrs. McDougald tells of the double task of Negro women (p. 689). The grim facts of exploitation which must be reckoned with in Harlem are tersely summarized by Winthrop D. Lane (p. 692) a contributing editor of The Survey.

GEORGE E. HAYNES, secretary of the Commission on Church and Race Relations of the Federal Council of Churches of Christ in America, tells of the churches in Harlem (p. 695).

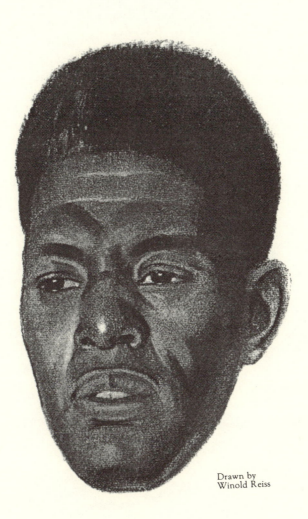

Drawn by
Winold Reiss

ROLAND HAYES

Whose achievement as a singer symbolizes the promise of the younger generation

SURVEY GRAPHIC

MARCH
1925

Volume VI
No. 6

Harlem

IF we were to offer a symbol of what Harlem has come to mean in the short span of twenty years it would be another statue of liberty on the landward side of New York. It stands for a folk-movement which in human significance can be compared only with the pushing back of the western frontier in the first half of the last century, or the waves of immigration which have swept in from overseas in the last half. Numerically far smaller than either of these movements, the volume of migration is such none the less that Harlem has become the greatest Negro community the world has known—without counterpart in the South or in Africa. But beyond this, Harlem represents the Negro's latest thrust towards Democracy.

The special significance that today stamps it as the sign and center of the renaissance of a people lies, however, layers deep under the Harlem that many know but few have begun to understand. Physically Harlem is little more than a note of sharper color in the kaleidoscope of New York. The metropolis pays little heed to the shifting crystallizations of its own heterogeneous millions. Never having experienced permanence, it has watched, without emotion or even curiosity, Irish, Jew, Italian, Negro, a score of other races drift in and out of the same colorless tenements.

So Harlem has come into being and grasped its destiny with little heed from New York. And to the herded thousands who shoot beneath it twice a day on the subway, or the comparatively few whose daily travel takes them within sight of its fringes or down its main arteries, it is a black belt and nothing more. The pattern of delicatessen store and cigar shop and restaurant and undertaker's shop which repeats itself a thousand times on each of New York's long avenues is unbroken through Harlem. Its apartments, churches and storefronts antedated the Negroes and, for all New York knows, may outlast them there. For most of New York, Harlem is merely a rough rectangle of commonplace city blocks, lying between and to east and west of Lenox and Seventh Avenues, stretching nearly a mile north and south—and unaccountably full of Negroes.

Another Harlem is savored by the few—a Harlem of racy music and racier dancing, of cabarets famous or notorious according to their kind, of amusement in which abandon and sophistication are cheek by jowl—a Harlem which draws the connoisseur in diversion as well as the undiscriminating sightseer. This Harlem is the fertile source of the "shufflin' " and "rollin' " and "runnin' wild" revues that establish themselves season after season in "downtown" theaters. It is part of the exotic fringe of the metropolis.

Beneath this lies again the Harlem of the newspapers—a Harlem of monster parades and political flummery, a Harlem swept by revolutionary oratory or draped about the mysterious figures of Negro "millionaires," a Harlem preoccupied with naive adjustments to a white world—a Harlem, in short, grotesque with the distortions of journalism.

YET in final analysis, Harlem is neither slum, ghetto, resort or colony, though it is in part all of them. It is—or promises at least to be—a race capital. Europe seething in a dozen centers with emergent nationalities, Palestine full of a renascent Judaism—these are no more alive with the spirit of a racial awakening than Harlem; culturally and spiritually it focuses a people. Negro life is not only founding new centers, but finding a new soul. The tide of Negro migration, northward and city-ward, is not to be fully explained as a blind flood started by the demands of war industry coupled with the shutting off of foreign migration, or by the pressure of poor crops coupled with increased social terrorism in certain sections of the South and Southwest. Neither labor demand, the boll-weevil nor the Ku Klux Klan is a basic factor, however contributory any or all of them may have been. The wash and rush of this human tide on the beach line of the northern city centers is to be explained primarily in terms of a new vision of opportunity, of social and economic freedom, of a spirit to seize, even in the face of an extortionate and heavy toll, a chance for the improvement of conditions. With each successive wave of it, the movement of the Negro

629

migrant becomes more and more like that of the European waves at their crests, a mass movement toward the larger and the more democratic chance—in the Negro's case a deliberate flight not only from countryside to city, but from mediaeval America to modern.

The secret lies close to what distinguishes Harlem from the ghettos with which it is sometimes compared. The ghetto picture is that of a slowly dissolving mass, bound by ties of custom and culture and association, in the midst of a freer and more varied society. From the racial standpoint, our Harlems are themselves crucibles. Here in Manhattan is not merely the largest Negro community in the world, but the first concentration in history of so many diverse elements of Negro life. It has attracted the African, the West Indian, the Negro American; has brought together the Negro of the North and the Negro of the South; the man from the city and the man from the town and village; the peasant, the student, the business man, the professional man, artist, poet, musician, adventurer and worker, preacher and criminal, exploiter and social outcast. Each group has come with its own separate motives and for its own special ends, but their greatest experience has been the finding of one another. Proscription and prejudice have thrown these dissimilar elements into a common area of contact and interaction. Within this area, race sympathy and unity have determined a further fusing of sentiment and experience. So what began in terms of segregation becomes more and more, as its elements mix and react, the laboratory of a great race-welding. Hitherto, it must be admitted that American Negroes have been a race more in name than in fact, or to be exact, more in sentiment than in experience. The chief bond between them has been that of a common condition rather than a common consciousness; a problem in common rather than a life in common. In Harlem, Negro life is seizing upon its first chances for group expression and self-determination. That is why our comparison is taken with those nascent centers of folk-expression and self-determination which are playing a creative part in the world today. Without pretense to their political significance, Harlem has the same role to play for the New Negro as Dublin has had for the New Ireland or Prague for the New Czechoslovakia.

It is true the formidable centers of our race life, educational, industrial, financial, are not in Harlem, yet here, nevertheless, are the forces that make a group known and felt in the world. The reformers, the fighting advocates, the inner spokesmen, the poets, artists and social prophets are here, and pouring in toward them are the fluid ambitious youth and pressing in upon them are the migrant masses. The professional observers, and the enveloping communities as well, are conscious of the physics of this stir and movement, of the cruder and more obvious facts of a ferment and a migration. But they are as yet largely unaware of the psychology of it, of the galvanizing shocks and reactions, which mark the social awakening and internal reorganization which are making a race out of its own disunited elements.

A railroad ticket and a suitcase, like a Bagdad carpet, transport the Negro peasant from the cotton-field and farm to the heart of the most complex urban civilization. Here, in the mass, he must and does survive a jump of two generations in social economy and of a century and more in civilization. Meanwhile the Negro poet, student, artist, thinker, by the very move that normally would take him off at a tangent from the masses, finds himself in their midst,

in a situation concentrating the racial side of his experience and heightening his race-consciousness. These moving, half-awakened newcomers provide an exceptional seed-bed for the germinating contacts of the enlightened minority. And that is why statistics are out of joint with fact in Harlem, and will be for a generation or so.

HARLEM, I grant you, isn't typical—but it is significant, it is prophetic. No sane observer, however sympathetic to the new trend, would contend that the great masses are articulate as yet, but they stir, they move, they are more than physically restless. The challenge of the new intellectuals among them is clear enough—the "race radicals" and realists who have broken with the old epoch of philanthropic guidance, sentimental appeal and protest. But are we after all only reading into the stirrings of a sleeping giant the dreams of an agitator? The answer is in the migrating peasant. It is the "man farthest down" who is most active in getting up. One of the most characteristic symptoms of this is the professional man himself migrating to recapture his constituency after a vain effort to maintain in some Southern corner what for years back seemed an established living and clientele. The clergyman following his errant flock, the physician or lawyer trailing his clients, supply the true clues. In a real sense it is the rank and file who are leading, and the leaders who are following. A transformed and transforming psychology permeates the masses.

When the racial leaders of twenty years ago spoke of developing race-pride and stimulating race-consciousness, and of the desirability of race solidarity, they could not in any accurate degree have anticipated the abrupt feeling that has surged up and now pervades the awakened centers. Some of the recognized Negro leaders and a powerful section of white opinion identified with "race work" of the older order have indeed attempted to discount this feeling as a "passing phase," an attack of "race nerves," so to speak, an "aftermath of the war," and the like. It has not abated, however, if we are to gage by the present tone and temper of the Negro press, or by the shift in popular support from the officially recognized and orthodox spokesmen to those of the independent, popular, and often radical type who are unmistakable symptoms of a new order. It is a social disservice to blunt the fact that the Negro of the Northern centers has reached a stage where tutelage, even of the most interested and well-intentioned sort, must give place to new relationships, where positive self-direction must be reckoned with in ever increasing measure.

As a service to this new understanding, the contributors to this Harlem number have been asked, not merely to describe Harlem as a city of migrants and as a race center, but to voice these new aspirations of a people, to read the clear message of the new conditions, and to discuss some of the new relationships and contacts they involve. First, we shall look at Harlem, with its kindred centers in the Northern and Mid-Western cities, as the way mark of a momentous folk movement; then as the center of a gripping struggle for an industrial and urban foothold. But more significant than either of these, we shall also view it as the stage of the pageant of contemporary Negro life. In the drama of its new and progressive aspects, we may be witnessing the resurgence of a race; with our eyes focussed on the Harlem scene we may dramatically glimpse the New Negro.   A. L.

Enter the New Negro

By ALAIN LOCKE

IN the last decade something beyond the watch and guard of statistics has happened in the life of the American Negro and the three norns who have traditionally presided over the Negro problem have a changeling in their laps. The Sociologist, The Philanthropist, the Race-leader are not unaware of the New Negro, but they are at a loss to account for him. He simply cannot be swathed in their formulae. For the younger generation is vibrant with a new psychology; the new spirit is awake in the masses, and under the very eyes of the professional observers is transforming what has been a perennial problem into the progressive phases of contemporary Negro life.

Could such a metamorphosis have taken place as suddenly as it has appeared to? The answer is no; not because the New Negro is not here, but because the Old Negro had long become more of a myth than a man. The Old Negro, we must remember, was a creature of moral debate and historical controversy. His has been a stock figure perpetuated as an historical fiction partly in innocent sentimentalism, partly in deliberate reactionism. The Negro himself has contributed his share to this through a sort of protective social mimicry forced upon him by the adverse circumstances of dependence. So for generations in the mind of America, the Negro has been more of a formula than a human being —a something to be argued about, condemned or defended, to be "kept down," or "in his place," or "helped up," to be worried with or worried over, harassed or patronized, a social bogey or a social burden. The thinking Negro even has been induced to share this same general attitude, to focus his attention on controversial issues, to see himself in the distorted perspective of a social problem. His shadow, so to speak, has been more real to him than his personality. Through having had to appeal from the unjust stereotypes of his oppressors and traducers to those of his liberators, friends and benefactors he has subscribed to the traditional positions from which his case has been viewed. Little true social or self-understanding has or could come from such a situation.

But while the minds of most of us, black and white, have thus burrowed in the trenches of the Civil War and Reconstruction, the actual march of development has simply flanked these positions, necessitating a sudden reorientation of view. We have not been watching in the right direction; set North and South on a sectional axis, we have not noticed the East till the sun has us blinking.

Recall how suddenly the Negro spirituals revealed themselves; suppressed for generations under the stereotypes of Wesleyan hymn harmony, secretive, half-ashamed, until the courage of being natural brought them out—and behold, there was folk-music. Similarly the mind of the Negro seems suddenly to have slipped from under the tyranny of social intimidation and to be shaking off the psychology of imitation and implied inferiority. By shedding the old chrysalis of the Negro problem we are achieving something like a spiritual emancipation. Until recently, lacking self-understanding, we have been almost as much of a problem to ourselves as we still are to others. But the decade that found us with a problem has left us with only a task. The multitude perhaps feels as yet only a strange relief and a new vague urge, but the thinking few know that in the reaction the vital inner grip of prejudice has been broken.

With this renewed self-respect and self-dependence, the life of the Negro community is bound to enter a new dynamic phase, the buoyancy from within compensating for whatever pressure there may be of conditions from without. The migrant masses, shifting from countryside to city, hurdle several generations of experience at a leap, but more important, the same thing happens spiritually in the life-attitudes and self-expression of the Young Negro, in his poetry, his art, his education and his new outlook, with the additional advantage, of course, of the poise and greater certainty of knowing what it is all about. From this comes the promise and warrant of a new leadership. As one of them has discerningly put it:

> We have tomorrow   Yesterday, a night-gone thing
> Bright before us   A sun-down name.
> Like a flame.
>
> And dawn today
> Broad arch above the road we came.
> We march!

This is what, even more than any "most creditable record of fifty years of freedom," requires that the Negro of today be seen through other than the dusty spectacles of past controversy. The day of "aunties," "uncles" and "mammies" is equally gone. Uncle Tom and Sambo have passed on, and even the "Colonel" and "George" play barnstorm roles from which they escape with relief when the public spotlight is off. The popular melodrama has about played itself out, and it is time to scrap the fictions, garret the bogeys and settle down to a realistic facing of facts.

FIRST we must observe some of the changes which since the traditional lines of opinion were drawn have rendered these quite obsolete. A main change has been, of course, that shifting of the Negro population which has made the Negro problem no longer exclusively or even predominantly Southern. Why should our minds remain sectionalized, when the problem itself no longer is? Then the trend of migration has not only been toward the North and the Central Midwest, but city-ward and to the great centers of industry—the problems of adjustment are new, practical, local and not peculiarly racial. Rather they are an integral part of the large industrial and social problems of our present-day democracy. And finally, with the Negro rapidly in process of class differentiation, if it ever was warrantable to regard and treat the Negro en masse it is becoming with every day less possible, more unjust and more ridiculous.

The Negro too, for his part, has idols of the tribe to

631

smash. If on the one hand the white man has erred in making the Negro appear to be that which would excuse or extenuate his treatment of him, the Negro, in turn, has too often unnecessarily excused himself because of the way he has been treated. The intelligent Negro of today is resolved not to make discrimination an extenuation for his shortcomings in performance, individual or collective; he is trying to hold himself at par, neither inflated by sentimental allowances nor depreciated by current social discounts. For this he must know himself and be known for precisely what he is, and for that reason he welcomes the new scientific rather than the old sentimental interest. Sentimental interest in the Negro has ebbed. We used to lament this as the falling off of our friends; now we rejoice and pray to be delivered both from self-pity and condescension. The mind of each racial group has had a bitter weaning, apathy or hatred on one side matching disillusionment or resentment on the other; but they face each other today with the possibility at least of entirely new mutual attitudes.

It does not follow that if the Negro were better known, he would be better liked or better treated. But mutual understanding is basic for any subsequent cooperation and adjustment. The effort toward this will at least have the effect of remedying in large part what has been the most unsatisfactory feature of our present stage of race relationships in America, namely the fact that the more intelligent and representative elements of the two race groups have at so many points got quite out of vital touch with one another.

The fiction is that the life of the races is separate, and increasingly so. The fact is that they have touched too closely at the unfavorable and too lightly at the favorable levels.

While inter-racial councils have sprung up in the South, drawing on forward elements of both races, in the Northern cities manual laborers may brush elbows in their everyday work, but the community and business leaders have experienced no such interplay or far too little of it. These segments must achieve contact or the race situation in America becomes desperate. Fortunately this is happening. There is a growing realization that in social effort the cooperative basis must supplant long-distance philanthropy, and that the only safeguard for mass relations in the future must be provided in the carefully maintained contacts of the enlightened minorities of both race groups. In the intellectual realm a renewed and keen curiosity is replacing the recent apathy; the Negro is being carefully studied, not just talked about and discussed. In art and letters, instead of being wholly caricatured, he is being seriously portrayed and painted.

To all of this the New Negro is keenly responsive as an augury of a new democracy in American culture. He is contributing his share to the new social understanding. But the desire to be understood would never in itself have been sufficient to have opened so completely the protectively closed portals of the thinking Negro's mind. There is still too much possibility of being snubbed or patronized for that. It was rather the necessity for fuller, truer, self-expression, the realization of the unwisdom of allowing social discrimination to segregate him mentally, and a counter-attitude to cramp and fetter his own living—and so the "spite-wall" that the intellectuals built over the "color-line" has happily been taken down. Much of this reopening of intellectual contacts has centered in New York and has been richly

fruitful not merely in the enlarging of personal experience, but in the definite enrichment of American art and letters and in the clarifying of our common vision of the social tasks ahead.

The particular significance in the reestablishment of contact between the more advanced and representative classes is that it promises to offset some of the unfavorable reactions of the past, or at least to re-surface race contacts somewhat for the future. Subtly the conditions that are moulding a New Negro are moulding a new American attitude.

However, this new phase of things is delicate; it will call for less charity but more justice; less help, but infinitely closer understanding. This is indeed a critical stage of race relationships because of the likelihood, if the new temper is not understood, of engendering sharp group antagonism and a second crop of more calculated prejudice. In some quarters, it has already done so. Having weaned the Negro, public opinion cannot continue to paternalize. The Negro today is inevitably moving forward under the control largely of his own objectives. What are these objectives? Those of his outer life are happily already well and finally formulated, for they are none other than the ideals of American institutions and democracy. Those of his inner life are yet in process of formation, for the new psychology at present is more of a consensus of feeling than of opinion, of attitude rather than of program. Still some points seem to have crystallized.

UP to the present one may adequately describe the Negro's "inner objectives" as an attempt to repair a damaged group psychology and reshape a warped social perspective. Their realization has required a new mentality for the American Negro. And as it matures we begin to see its effects; at first, negative, iconoclastic, and then positive and constructive. In this new group psychology we note the lapse of sentimental appeal, then the development of a more positive self-respect and self-reliance; the repudiation of social dependence, and then the gradual recovery from hyper-sensitiveness and "touchy" nerves, the repudiation of the double standard of judgment with its special philanthropic allowances and then the sturdier desire for objective and scientific appraisal; and finally the rise from social disillusionment to race pride, from the sense of social debt to the responsibilities of social contribution, and offsetting the necessary working and commonsense acceptance of restricted conditions, the belief in ultimate esteem and recognition. Therefore the Negro today wishes to be known for what he is, even in his faults and shortcomings, and scorns a craven and precarious survival at the price of seeming to be what he is not. He resents being spoken for as a social ward or minor, even by his own, and to being regarded a chronic patient for the sociological clinic, the sick man of American Democracy. For the same reasons, he himself is through with those social nostrums and panaceas, the so-called "solutions" of his "problem," with which he and the country have been so liberally dosed in the past. Religion, freedom, education, money—in turn, he has ardently hoped for and peculiarly trusted these things; he still believes in them, but not in blind trust that they alone will solve his life-problem.

Each generation, however, will have its creed and that of the present is the belief in the efficacy of collective effort, in race cooperation. This deep feeling of race is at present the mainspring of Negro life. It seems to be the outcome of the reaction to proscription and prejudice; an attempt, fairly successful on the whole, to convert a defensive into an offensive position, a handicap into an incentive. It is radical in tone, but not in purpose and only the most stupid forms of opposition, misunderstanding or persecution could make it otherwise. Of course, the thinking Negro has shifted a little toward the left with the world-trend, and there is an increasing group who affiliate with radical and liberal movements. But fundamentally for the present the Negro is radical on race matters, conservative on others, in other words, a "forced radical," a social protestant rather than a genuine radical. Yet under further pressure and injustice iconoclastic thought and motives will inevitably increase. Harlem's quixotic radicalisms call for their ounce of democracy today lest tomorrow they be beyond cure.

The Negro mind reaches out as yet to nothing but American wants, American ideas. But this forced attempt to build his Americanism on race values is a unique social experiment, and its ultimate success is impossible except through the fullest sharing of American culture and institutions. There should be no delusion about this. American nerves in sections unstrung with race hysteria are often fed the opiate that the trend of Negro advance is wholly separatist, and that the effect of its operation will be to encyst the Negro as a benign foreign body in the body politic. This cannot be—even if it were desirable. The racialism of the Negro is no limitation or reservation with respect to American life; it is only a constructive effort to build the obstructions in the stream of his progress into an efficient dam of social energy and power. Democracy itself is obstructed and stagnated to the extent that any of its channels are closed. Indeed they cannot be selectively closed. So the choice is not between one way for the Negro and another way for the rest, but between American institutions frustrated on the one hand and American ideals progressively fulfilled and realized on the other.

There is, of course, a warrantably comfortable feeling in being on the right side of the country's professed ideals. We realize that we cannot be undone without America's undoing. It is within the gamut of this attitude that the thinking Negro faces America, but the variations of mood in connection with it are if anything more significant than the attitude itself. Sometimes we have it taken with the defiant ironic challenge of McKay:

Mine is the future grinding down today
Like a great landslip moving to the sea,
Bearing its freight of debris far away
Where the green hungry waters restlessly
Heave mammoth pyramids and break and roar
Their eerie challenge to the crumbling shore.

Sometimes, perhaps more frequently as yet, in the fervent and almost filial appeal and counsel of Weldon Johnson's:

O Southland, dear Southland!
Then why do you still cling
To an idle age and a musty page,
To a dead and useless thing.

But between defiance and appeal, midway almost between cynicism and hope, the prevailing mind stands in the mood of the same author's To America, an attitude of sober query and stoical challenge:

How would you have us, as we are?
Or sinking 'neath the load we bear,

Our eyes fixed forward on a star,
Or gazing empty at despair?

Rising or falling? Men or things?
With dragging pace or footsteps fleet?
Strong, willing sinews in your wings,
Or tightening chains about your feet?

More and more, however, an intelligent realization of the great discrepancy between the American social creed and the American social practice forces upon the Negro the taking of the moral advantage that is his. Only the steadying and sobering effect of a truly characteristic gentleness of spirit prevents the rapid rise of a definite cynicism and counter-hate and a defiant superiority feeling. Human as this reaction would be, the majority still deprecate its advent, and would gladly see it forestalled by the speedy amelioration of its causes. We wish our race pride to be a healthier, more positive achievement than a feeling based upon a realization of the shortcomings of others. But all paths toward the attainment of a sound social attitude have been difficult; only a relatively few enlightened minds have been able as the phrase puts it "to rise above" prejudice. The ordinary man has had until recently only a hard choice between the alternatives of supine and humiliating submission and stimulating but hurtful counter-prejudice. Fortunately from some inner, desperate resourcefulness has recently sprung up the simple expedient of fighting prejudice by mental passive resistance, in other words by trying to ignore it. For the few, this manna may perhaps be effective, but the masses cannot thrive on it.

FORTUNATELY there are constructive channels opening out into which the balked social feelings of the American Negro can flow freely.

Without them there would be much more pressure and danger than there is. These compensating interests are racial but in a new and enlarged way. One is the consciousness of acting as the advance-guard of the African peoples in their contact with Twentieth Century civilization; the other, the sense of a mission of rehabilitating the race in world esteem from that loss of prestige for which the fate and conditions of slavery have so largely been responsible. Harlem, as we shall see, is the center of both these movements; she is the home of the Negro's "Zionism." The pulse of the Negro world has begun to beat in Harlem. A Negro newspaper carrying news material in English, French and Spanish, gathered from all quarters of America, the West Indies and Africa has maintained itself in Harlem for over five years. Two important magazines, both edited from New York, maintain their news and circulation consistently on a cosmopolitan scale. Under American auspices and backing, three pan-African congresses have been held abroad for the discussion of common interests, colonial questions and the future cooperative development of Africa. In terms of the race question as a world problem, the Negro mind has leapt, so to speak, upon the parapets of prejudice and extended its cramped horizons. In so doing it has linked up with the growing group consciousness of the dark-peoples and is gradually learning their common interests. As one of our writers has recently put it: "It is imperative that we understand the white world in its relations to the non-white world." As with the Jew, persecution is making the Negro international.

As a world phenomenon this wider race consciousness is

a different thing from the much asserted rising tide of color. Its inevitable causes are not of our making. The consequences are not necessarily damaging to the best interests of civilization. Whether it actually brings into being new Armadas of conflict or argosies of cultural exchange and enlightenment can only be decided by the attitude of the dominant races in an era of critical change. With the American Negro his new internationalism is primarily an effort to recapture contact with the scattered peoples of African derivation. Garveyism may be a transient, if spectacular, phenomenon, but the possible role of the American Negro in the future development of Africa is one of the most constructive and universally helpful missions that any modern people can lay claim to.

Constructive participation in such causes cannot help giving the Negro valuable group incentives, as well as increased prestige at home and abroad. Our greatest rehabilitation may possibly come through such channels, but for the present, more immediate hope rests in the revaluation by white and black alike of the Negro in terms of his artistic endowments and cultural contributions, past and prospective. It must be increasingly recognized that the Negro has already made very substantial contributions, not only in his folk-art, music especially, which has always found appreciation, but in larger, though humbler and less acknowledged ways. For generations the Negro has been the peasant matrix of that section of America which has most undervalued him, and here he has contributed not only materially in labor and in social patience, but spiritually as well. The South has unconsciously absorbed the gift of his folk-temperament. In less than half a generation it will be easier to recognize this, but the fact remains that a leaven of humor, sentiment, imagination and tropic nonchalance has gone into the making of the South from a humble, unacknowledged source. A second crop of the Negro's gifts promises still more largely. He now becomes a conscious contributor and lays aside the status of a beneficiary and ward for that of a collaborator and participant in American civilization. The great social gain in this is the releasing of our talented group from the arid fields of controversy and debate to the productive fields of creative expression. The especially cultural recognition they win should in turn prove the key to that revaluation of the Negro which must precede or accompany any considerable further betterment of race relationships. But whatever the general effect, the present generation will have added the motives of self-expression and spiritual development to the old and still unfinished task of making material headway and progress. No one who understandingly faces the situation with its substantial accomplishment or views the new scene with its still more abundant promise can be entirely without hope. And certainly, if in our lifetime the Negro should not be able to celebrate his full initiation into American democracy, he can at least, on the warrant of these things, celebrate the attainment of a significant and satisfying new phase of group development, and with it a spiritual Coming of Age.

Drawn by Walter Von Ruckteschell

YOUNG AFRICA

The Making of Harlem

By JAMES WELDON JOHNSON

I N the history of New York, the significance of the name Harlem has changed from Dutch to Irish to Jewish to Negro. Of these changes, the last has come most swiftly. Throughout colored America, from Massachusetts to Mississippi, and across the continent to Los Angeles and Seattle, its name, which as late as fifteen years ago had scarcely been heard, now stands for the Negro metropolis. Harlem is indeed the great Mecca for the sight-seer, the pleasure-seeker, the curious, the adventurous, the enterprising, the ambitious and the talented of the whole Negro world; for the lure of it has reached down to every island of the Carib Sea and has penetrated even into Africa.

In the make-up of New York, Harlem is not merely a Negro colony or community, it is a city within a city, the greatest Negro city in the world. It is not a slum or a fringe, it is located in the heart of Manhattan and occupies one of the most beautiful and healthful sections of the city. It is not a "quarter" of dilapidated tenements, but is made up of new-law apartments and handsome dwellings, with well-paved and well-lighted streets. It has its own churches, social and civic centers, shops, theatres and other places of amusement. And it contains more Negroes to the square mile than any other spot on earth. A stranger who rides up magnificent Seventh Avenue on a bus or in an automobile must be struck with surprise at the transformation which takes place after he crosses One Hundred and Twenty-fifth Street. Beginning there, the population suddenly darkens and he rides through twenty-five solid blocks where the passers-by, the shoppers, those sitting in restaurants, coming out of theatres, standing in doorways and looking out of windows are practically all Negroes; and then he emerges where the population as suddenly becomes white again. There is nothing just like it in any other city in the country, for there is no preparation for it; no change in the character of the houses and streets; no change, indeed, in the appearance of the people, except their color.

N EGRO Harlem is practically a development of the past decade, but the story behind it goes back a long way. There have always been colored people in New York. In the middle of the last century they lived in the vicinity of Lispenard, Broome and Spring Streets. When Washington Square and lower Fifth Avenue was the center of aristocratic life, the colored people, whose chief occupation was domestic service in the homes of the rich, lived in a fringe and were scattered in nests to the south, east and west of the square. As late as the 80's the major part of the colored population lived in Sullivan, Thompson, Bleecker, Grove, Minetta Lane and adjacent streets. It is curious to note that some of these nests still persist. In a number of the blocks of Greenwich Village and Little Italy may be found small groups of Negroes who have never lived in any other section of the city. By about 1890 the center of colored population had shifted to the upper Twenties and lower Thirties west of Sixth Avenue. Ten years later another considerable shift northward had been made to West Fifty-third Street.

The West Fifty-third Street settlement deserves some special mention because it ushered in a new phase of life among colored New Yorkers. Three rather well appointed hotels were opened in the street and they quickly became the centers of a sort of fashionable life that hitherto had not existed. On Sunday evenings these hotels served dinner to music and attracted crowds of well-dressed diners. One of these hotels, The Marshall, became famous as the headquarters of Negro talent. There gathered the actors, the musicians, the composers, the writers, the singers, dancers and vaudevillians. There one went to get a close-up of Williams and Walker, Cole and Johnson, Ernest Hogan, Will Marion Cook, Jim Europe, Aida Overton, and of others equally and less known. Paul Laurence Dunbar was frequently there whenever he was in New York. Numbers of those who love to shine by the light reflected from celebrities were always to be found. The first modern jazz band ever heard in New York, or, perhaps anywhere, was organized at The Marshall. It was a playing-singing-dancing orchestra, making the first dominant use of banjos, saxophones, clarinets and trap drums in combination, and was called The Memphis Students. Jim Europe was a member of that band, and out of it grew the famous Clef Club, of which he was the noted leader, and which for a long time monopolized the business of "entertaining" private parties and furnishing music for the new dance craze. Also in the Clef Club was "Buddy" Gilmore who originated trap drumming as it is now practiced, and set hundreds of white men to juggling their sticks and doing acrobatic stunts while they manipulated a dozen other noise-making devices aside from their drums. A good many well-known white performers frequented The Marshall and for seven or eight years the place was one of the sights of New York.

T HE move to Fifty-third Street was the result of the opportunity to get into newer and better houses. About 1900 the move to Harlem began, and for the same reason. Harlem had been overbuilt with large, new-law apartment houses, but rapid transportation to that section was very inadequate—the Lenox Avenue Subway had not yet been built—and landlords were finding difficulty in keeping houses on the east side of the section filled. Residents along and near Seventh Avenue were fairly well served by the Eighth Avenue Elevated. A colored man, in the real estate business at this time, Philip A. Payton, approached several of these landlords with the proposition that he would fill their empty or partially empty houses with steady colored tenants. The suggestion was accepted, and one or two houses on One Hundred and Thirty-fourth Street east of Lenox Avenue were taken over. Gradually other houses were filled. The whites paid little attention to the movement until it began to spread west of Lenox Avenue; they then took steps to check it. They proposed through a financial organ-

635

ization, the Hudson Realty Company, to buy in all properties occupied by colored people and evict the tenants. The Negroes countered by similar methods. Payton formed the Afro-American Realty Company, a Negro corporation organized for the purpose of buying and leasing houses for occupancy by colored people. Under this counter stroke the opposition subsided for several years.

But the continually increasing pressure of colored people to the west over the Lenox Avenue dead line caused the opposition to break out again, but in a new and more menacing form. Several white men undertook to organize all the white people of the community for the purpose of inducing financial institutions not to lend money or renew mortgages on properties occupied by colored people. In this effort they had considerable success, and created a situation which has not yet been completely overcome, a situation which is one of the hardest and most unjustifiable the Negro property owner in Harlem has to contend with. The Afro-American Realty Company was now defunct, but two or three colored men of means stepped into the breach. Philip A. Payton and J. C. Thomas bought two five-story apartments, dispossessed the white tenants and put in colored. J. B. Nail bought a row of five apartments and did the same thing. St. Philip's Church bought a row of thirteen apartment houses on One Hundred and Thirty-fifth Street, running from Seventh Avenue almost to Lenox.

The situation now resolved itself into an actual contest. Negroes not only continued to occupy available apartment houses, but began to purchase private dwellings between Lenox and Seventh Avenues. Then the whole movement, in the eyes of the whites, took on the aspect of an "invasion"; they became panic stricken and began fleeing as from a plague. The presence of one colored family in a block, no matter how well bred and orderly, was sufficient to precipitate a flight. House after house and block after block was actually deserted. It was a great demonstration of human beings running amuck. None of them stopped to reason why they were doing it or what would happen if they didn't. The banks and lending companies holding mortgages on these deserted houses were compelled to take them over. For some time they held these houses vacant, preferring to do that and carry the charges than to rent or sell them to colored people. But values dropped and continued to drop until at the outbreak of the war in Europe property in the northern part of Harlem had reached the nadir.

IN the meantime the Negro colony was becoming more stable; the churches were being moved from the lower part of the city; social and civic centers were being formed; and gradually a community was being evolved. Following the outbreak of the war in Europe Negro Harlem received a new and tremendous impetus. Because of the war thousands of aliens in the United States rushed back to their native lands to join the colors and immigration practically ceased. The result was a critical shortage in labor. This shortage was rapidly increased as the United States went more and more largely into the business of furnishing munitions and supplies to the warring countries. To help meet this shortage of common labor Negroes were brought up from the South. The government itself took the first steps, following the practice in vogue in Germany of shifting labor according to the supply and demand in various parts of the country. The example of the government was promptly taken up by the big industrial concerns, which sent hundreds, perhaps thousands, of labor agents into the South who recruited Negroes by wholesale. I was in Jacksonville, Fla., for a while at that time, and I sat one day and watched the stream of migrants passing to take the train. For hours they passed steadily, carrying flimsy suit cases,

Photograph by Paul Thompson

Rush hour at the corner of 135th Street and Lenox Avenue, the subway station in the heart of Harlem. Though the original settlement of Negroes in Harlem came about indirectly because of lack of transit facilities, it is now served by the best New York has to offer, including a branch of the Fifth Avenue bus lines

ew and shiny, rusty old ones, bursting at the seams,
oxes and bundles and impedimenta of all sorts, in-
luding banjos, guitars, birds in cages and what not.
imilar scenes were being enacted in cities and towns
ll over that region. The first wave of the great
xodus of Negroes from the South was on. Great
umbers of these migrants headed for New York or
ventually got there, and naturally the majority
vent up into Harlem. But the Negro population
f Harlem was not swollen by migrants from the
outh alone; the opportunity for Negro labor ex-
rted its pull upon the Negroes of the West Indies,
nd those islanders in the course of time poured into
Harlem to the number of twenty-five thousand or
nore.

These new-comers did not have to look for work;
vork looked for them, and at wages of which they
ad never even dreamed. And here is where the
nlooked for, the unprecedented, the miraculous hap-
ened. According to all preconceived notions, these
Negroes suddenly earning large sums of money for
he first time in their lives should have had their heads
urned; they should have squandered it in the most
illy and absurd manners imaginable. Later, after
he United States had entered the war and even
Negroes in the South were making money fast, many
tories in accord with the tradition came out of that
ection. There was the one about the colored man
vho went into a general store and on hearing a
honograph for the first time promptly ordered six
f them, one for each child in the house. I shall
ot stop to discuss whether Negroes in the South

Photograph by Paul Thompson

*Sadly as Harlem lacks space to play outdoors, there
is no lack of the play spirit either inside Harlem's
crowded homes or on the broad avenues that cut
through it. Parades are almost of daily occurrence
—whether the occasion be the arrival of a vaudeville
troupe, the patriotic enthusiasm of a new organization, or a funeral*

lid that sort of thing or
ot, but I do know that
hose who got to New
'ork didn't. The Negroes
f Harlem, for the greater
part, worked and saved
heir money. N o b o d y
new how much they had
aved until congestion
nade expansion necessary
or tenants and ownership
rofitable for landlords,
nd they began to buy
roperty. Persons who
vould never be suspected
f having money bought
roperty. The Rev. W.
V. Brown, pastor of the
Metropolitan B a p t i s t
Church, repeatedly made
"Buy propery" the text
f his sermons. A large
art of his congregation
arried out the injunc-
ion. The church itself
et an example by pur-
hasing a magnificent
rown stone church build-
ng on Seventh Avenue
rom a white congrega-
ion. Buying property be-

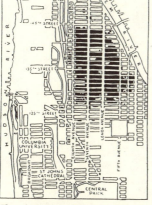

*This sketch map shows approximately
where Negroes live in Harlem, according
to a housing survey made in 1924 by the
New York Urban League. The fringe
of houses in which both Negro and white
tenants live is not indicated. The first
houses occupied by Negroes were on
134th Street east of Lenox Avenue*

came a fever. At the height of this activity, that
is, 1920-21, it was not an uncommon thing for a
colored washerwoman or cook to go into a real
estate office and lay down from one thousand to
five thousand dollars on a house. "Pig Foot Mary"
is a character in Harlem. Everybody who knows
the corner of Lenox Avenue and One Hundred and
Thirty-fifth Street knows "Mary" and her stand
and has been tempted by the smell of her pigsfeet,
fried chicken and hot corn, even if he has not been
a customer. "Mary," whose real name is Mrs.
Mary Dean, bought the five-story apartment house
at the corner of Seventh Avenue and One Hundred
and Thirty-seventh Street at a price of $42,000.
Later she sold it to the Y. W. C. A. for dormitory
purposes. The Y. W. C. A. sold it recently to
Adolph Howell, a leading colored undertaker, the
price given being $72,000. Often companies of a
half dozen men combined to buy a house—these
combinations were and still are generally made up
of West Indians—and would produce five or ten
thousand dollars to put through the deal.

When the buying activity began to make itself

felt, the lending companies that had been holding vacant the handsome dwellings on and abutting Seventh Avenue decided to put them on the market. The values on these houses had dropped to the lowest mark possible and they were put up at astonishingly low prices. Houses that had been bought at from $15,000 to $20,000 were sold at one-third those figures. They were quickly gobbled up. The Equitable Life Assurance Company held 106 model private houses that were designed by Stanford White. They are built with courts running straight through the block and closed off by wrought iron gates. Every one of these houses was sold within eleven months at an aggregate price of about two million dollars. Today they are probably worth about 100 per cent more. And not only have private dwellings and similar apartments been bought but big elevator apartments have been taken over. Corporations have been organized for this purpose. Two of these, The Antillian Realty Company, composed of West Indian Negroes, and the Sphinx Securities Company, composed of American and West Indian Negroes, represent holdings amounting to approximately $750,000. Individual Negroes and companies in the South have invested in Harlem real estate. About two years ago a Negro institution of Savannah, Ga., bought a parcel for $115,000 which it sold a month or so ago at a profit of $110,000.

I am informed by John E. Nail, a successful colored real estate dealer of Harlem and a reliable authority, that the total value of property in Harlem owned and controlled by colored people would at a conservative estimate amount to more than sixty million dollars. These figures are amazing, especially when we take into account the short time in which they have been piled up. Twenty years ago Negroes were begging for the privilege of renting a flat in

Gateway and court in the block designed as a unit by Stanford White before the Negroes moved to Harlem—a block which has few rivals in the city for distinction of line and mass and its air of quiet dignity

Harlem. Fifteen years ago barely a half dozen colored men owned real property in all Manhattan. And down to ten years ago the amount that had been acquired in Harlem was comparatively negligible. Today Negro Harlem is practically owned by Negroes.

The question naturally arises, "Are the Negroes going to be able to hold Harlem?" If they have been steadily driven northward for the past hundred years and out of less desirable sections, can they hold this choice bit of Manhattan Island? It is hardly probable that Negroes will hold Harlem indefinitely, but when they are forced out it will not be for the same reasons that forced them out of former quarters in New York City. The situation is entirely different and without precedent. When colored people do leave Harlem, their homes, their churches, their investments and their businesses, it will be because the land has become so valuable they can no longer afford to live on it. But the date of another move northward is very far in the future. What will Harlem be and become in the meantime? Is there danger that the Negro may lose his economic status in New York and be unable to hold his property? Will Harlem become merely a famous ghetto or will it be a center of intellectual cultural and economic forces exerting an influence throughout the world, especially upon Negro peoples? Will it become a point of friction between the races in New York?

Drawn by M. Gray Johnson

The back of the houses on "Strivers' Row," as the de luxe block on West 139th St. between Seventh and Eighth Avenues is called by dwellers in less beautiful streets

I think there is less danger to the Negroes of New York of losing out economically and industrially than to the Negroes of any large city in the North. In most of the big industrial centers Negroes are engaged in gang labor. They are employed by thousands in the stock yards in Chicago, by thousands in the automobile plants in Detroit; and in those cities they are likely to be the first to be let go, and in thousands, with every business depression. In New York there is hardly such a thing as gang labor among Negroes, except among the longshoremen, and it is in the long shoremen's unions, above all others, that Negroes stand on an equal footing. Employment among Negroes in New York is highly diversified; in the main they are employed more as individuals than as non-integral parts of a gang. Furthermore, Harlem is gradually becoming more and more a self-supporting community. Negroes there are steadily branching out into new businesses and enterprises in which Negroes are employed. So the danger of great numbers of Negroes being thrown out of work at once, with a resulting economic crisis among them, is less in New York than in most of the large cities of the North to which Southern migrants have come.

These facts have an effect which goes beyond the economic and industrial situation. They have a direct bearing on the future character of Harlem and on the question as to whether Harlem will be a point of friction between

he races in New York. It is true
hat Harlem is a Negro community,
vell defined and stable; anchored to
:s fixed homes, churches, institutions,
usiness and amusement places; hav-
ng its own working, business and pro-
essional classes. It is experiencing a
onstant growth of group conscious-
ess and community feeling. Harlem
s therefore, in many respects, typical-
y Negro. It has many unique char-
cteristics. It has movement, color,
aiety, singing, dancing, boisterous
aughter and loud talk. One of its
utstanding features is brass band
arades. Hardly a Sunday passes but
hat there are several of these parades
f which many are gorgeous with
egalia and insignia. Almost any ex-
use will do—the death of an humble
ember of the Elks, the laying of a
orner stone, the
turning out" of

Looking toward the Lafayette theatre on Seventh Avenue

he order of this or
hat. In many of
hese characterist-
:s it is similar to
he Italian colony.
3ut withal, Har-
em grows more
netropolitan and
nore a part of
Jew York all the
vhile. Why is it
h e n t h a t its
endency is not to
ecome a m e r e
quarter"?

I s h a l l give
hree reasons that
eem to me to be
mportant in their
rder. First, the
anguage of Har-
em is not alien; it
s not Italian or

Harlem doorway

iddish; it is English. Harlem talks American, reads
merican, thinks American. Second, Harlem is not phy-
ically a "quarter." It is not a section cut off. It is merely
zone through which four main arteries of the city run.
'hird, the fact that there is little or no gang labor
ives Harlem Negroes the opportunity for individ-
al expansion and individual contacts with the life
nd spirit of New York. A thousand Negroes from
Aississippi put to work as a gang in a Pittsburgh steel
ill will for a long time remain a thousand Negroes from
Aississippi. Under the conditions that prevail in New
'ork they would all within six months become New York-
rs. The rapidity with which Negroes become good New
'orkers is one of the marvels to observers.

These three reasons form a single reason why there is
nall probability that Harlem will ever be a point of race
riction between the races in New York. One of the prin-

cipal factors in the race riot in Chicago in 1919 was the
fact that at that time there were 12,000 Negroes employed
in gangs in the stock yards. There was considerable race
feeling in Harlem at the time of the hegira of white residents due to the "invasion," but that feeling, of course, is
no more. Indeed, a number of the old white residents
who didn't go or could not get away before the housing
shortage struck New York are now living peacefully side
by side with colored residents. In fact, in some cases white
and colored tenants occupy apartments in the same house.
Many white merchants still do business in thickest Harlem.
On the whole, I know of no place in the country where the
feeling between the races is so cordial and at the same time
so matter-of-fact and taken for granted. One of the surest
safeguards against an outbreak in New York such as took
place in so many Northern cities in the summer of 1919 is
the large proportion of Negro police on duty in Harlem.

To my mind, Harlem is more than a Negro community;
it is a large scale laboratory experiment in the race problem. The statement has often been made that if Negroes
were transported to the North in large numbers the race
problem with all of its acuteness and with new aspects would
be transferred with them. Well, 175,000 Negroes live closely
together in Harlem, in the heart of New York, 75,000 more
than live in any Southern city, and do so without any race
friction. Nor is there any unusual record of crime. I
once heard a captain of the 38th Police Precinct (the
Harlem precinct) say that on the whole it was the most
law-abiding precinct in the city. New York guarantees its
Negro citizens the fundamental rights of American citizenship and protects them in the exercise of those rights. In
return the Negro loves New York and is proud of it, and
contributes in his way to its greatness. He still meets with
discriminations, but possessing the basic rights, he knows
that these discriminations will be abolished.

I believe that the Negro's advantages and opportunities are
greater in Harlem than in any other place in the country,
and that Harlem will become the intellectual, the cultural
and the financial center for Negroes of the United States,
and will exert a vital influence upon all Negro peoples.

111

Drawn by Mahonri Young

THE LABORER

Black Workers and the City

By CHARLES S. JOHNSON

THE glamorous city is draining the open spaces; it draws upon the human opulence of Europe; it reatens now to drain the black lt of the South. It makes no fference that New York is fast coming unlivable, a "great op in which people barter and ll, get rich quick and die early" there are millions of others eager to offer themselves. The ll monotony of rural life, the high wages, the gaiety, the oppressive anonymity, the prestige of the city with its owds and exitement set in motion years ago a trek to New ork which knew no color line. How has the Negro fared this drift to the city?

It is a strange fact that in the cities of the North, the native rn Negro population, as if in biological revolt against its vironment, barely perpetuates itself. For whatever reason, ere is lacking that lusty vigor of increase which has nearly bled the Negro population as a whole. Within the past ty years the natural increase of this old Northern stock apart from migrations—has been negligible. And its tus has been shifting. Time was when that small clus- r of descendants of the benevolent old Dutch masters and the free Negroes moved with freedom and complacent portance about the intimate fringe of the city's active life. hese Negroes were the barbers, caterers, bakers, restauran- urs, coachmen—all highly elaborated personal service po- ions. The crafts permitted them wide freedom: they were illed artisans. They owned businesses which were inde- ndent of Negro patronage. This group is passing, its endor shorn. The rapid evolution of business, blind to e amenities on which they flourished, has devoured their tablishments, unsupported and weak in capital resources; e incoming hordes of Europeans have edged them out of eir inheritance of personal service businesses, clashed with em in competition for the rough muscle jobs and driven em back into the obscurity of individual personal service. For forty years, moreover, there have been dribbling in om the South, the West Indies and South America, small crements of population which through imperceptible gra- tions have changed the whole complexion and outlook of the Negro New Yorker. New blood and diverse cultures ese brought—and each a separate problem of assimilation. s the years passed the old migrants have "rubbed off the een," adopted the slang and sophistication of the city, ingled and married, and their children are now the native- rn New Yorkers. For fifty years scattered families have en uniting in the hectic metropolis from every state in the ion and every province of the West Indies. There have ways been undigested colonies—the Sons and Daughters North Carolina, the Virginia Society, the Southern Bene-

From bayou and island and Southern hamlet they have come—the black mas- ses, beckoned by that "new Statue of Liberty on the landward side of New York." What strain and stress of adjust- ment have they met? What have they found to do in the shifting life of the city? What handicaps reappear? What new opportunities have they won?

ficial League—these are surviv- als of self-conscious, intimate bodies. But the mass is in the melting pot of the city.

There were in New York City in 1920, by the census count, 152,467 Negroes. Of these 39,233 are reported as born in New York State, 30,436 in foreign countries, principally the West Indies, and 78,242 in other states, principally the South. Since 1920 about 50,000 more Southerners have been added to the population, bulging the narrow strip of Harlem in which it had lived and spilling over the old boundaries. There are no less than 25,000 Virginians in New York City, more than 20,000 North and South Carolinians, and 10,000 Georgians. Every Southern state has contributed its quota to a heterogeneity which matches that of cosmo- politan New York. If the present Negro New Yorker were analyzed he would be found to be composed of one part native, one part West Indian and about three parts Southern. If the tests of the army psychologists could work with the precision and certainty with which they are accredited, the Negroes who make up the present popula- tion of New York City would be declared to represent dif- ferent races, for the differences between South and North by actual measurement are greater than the differences between whites and Negroes.

II

THE city creates its own types. The Jew, for example, is by every aptitude and economic attachment a city dweller. Modern students of human behavior are dis- covering in his neurotic constitution, now assumed as a clearly recognizable racial characteristic, a definite connec- tion not only with the emotional strain of peculiar racial status but also with the terrific pressure of city life.

The Negro by tradition, and probably by temperament, represents the exact contrast. His metier is agriculture. To this economy his mental and social habits have been adjusted. No elaborate equipment is necessary for the work of the farm. Life is organized on a simple plan looking to a mini- mum of wants and a rigid economy of means. The incom- plex gestures of unskilled manual labor and even domestic service; the broad, dully sensitive touch of body and hands trained to groom and nurse the soil, develop distinctive phy- sical habits and a musculature appropriate to simple proces- ses. Add to this groundwork of occupational habits the social structure in which the Southern rural Negro is cast, his inhibitions, repressions and cultural poverty, and the present city Negro becomes more intelligible. It is a motley group which is now in the ascendency in the city. The pic- turesqueness of the South, the memory of pain, the warped lives, the ghostly shadows of fear, crudeness, ignorance and

641

unsophistication, are laid upon the surface of the city in a curious pattern.

The students of human behavior who with such quick comprehension attribute the nervousness of the Jew and the growing nervous disorders of city dwellers in general to the tension of city life overlook the play of tremendous factors in the life of the Negroes who are transplanted from one culture to another.

The city Negro is only now in evolution. In the change old moorings have been abandoned, personal relations, in which "individuals are in contact at practically all points of their lives" are replaced by group relations "in which they are in contact at only one or two points of their lives." The old controls no longer operate. Whether it is apparent or not, the newcomers are forced to reorganize their lives—to enter a new status and adjust to it that eager restlessness which prompted them to leave home. It is not inconceivable that the conduct of these individuals which seems so strange and at times so primitive and reckless, is the result of just this disorientation. And the conduct so often construed as unbearable arrogance is definitely nothing more than a compensation for the lack of self-respect, which fate through the medium of the social system of the South has denied them. The naive reaction of a migrant, as expressed in a letter to his friend in the South, illustrates the point:

Dear Partner: ... I am all fixed now and living well. I don't have to work hard. Don't have to mister every little boy comes along. I haven't heard a white man call a colored a nigger you know how—since I been here. I can ride in the street or steam car anywhere I get a seat. I don't care to mix with white what I mean I am not crazy about being with white folks, but if I have to pay the same fare I have learn to want the same acomidation and as first in a place here shoping you don't have to wait till all the white folks get thro tradeing yet amid all this I love the good old south and am praying that God may give every well wisher a chance to be a man regardless of his color....

If the Negroes in Harlem show at times less courtesy toward white visitors than is required by the canons of good taste, this is bad, but understandable. It was remarked shortly after the first migration that the newcomers on boarding street cars invariably strode to the front even if there were seats in the rear. This is, perhaps, a mild example of tendencies expressed more strikingly in other directions, for with but few exceptions they are forced to sit in the rear of street cars throughout the South.

The dislocation shows itself in other ways. In the South one dominant agency of social control is the church. It is the center for "face-to-face" relations. The pastor is the leader. The role of the pastor and the social utility of church are obvious in this letter sent home:

Dear pastor: I find it my duty to write you my whereabouts, also family.... I shall send my church money in a few days. I am trying to influence our members here to do the same. I received notice printed in a R. R. car (Get right with God) O, I had nothing so striking as the above mottoe. Let me no how is our church I am so anxious to no. My wife always talking about her seat in the church want to no who occupying it. Yours in Christ.

Religion affords an outlet for the emotional energies thwarted in other directions. The psychologists will find rich material for speculation on the emotional nature of some of the Negroes set into the New York pattern in this confession:

I got here in time to attend one of the greatest revivals in the history of my life—over 500 people join the church. W had a Holy Ghost shower. You know I like to have run wild

In the new environment there are many and varied sub stitutes which answer more or less directly the myriad desire indiscriminately comprehended by the church. The com plaint of the ministers that these "emancipated" souls "stra away from God" when they reach the city is perhaps war ranted on the basis of the fixed status of the church in th South, but it is not an accurate interpretation of what ha happened. When the old ties are broken new satisfaction are sought. Sometimes the Young Mens' Christian Assc ciation functions. This has in some cities made rivalry be tween the churches and the Associations. More often th demands of the young exceed the "sterilized" amusemen of Christian organizations. It is not uncommon to fin groups who faithfully attend church Sunday evenings and a as faithfully seek further stimulation in a cabaret afterward Many have been helped to find themselves, no doubt, b having their old churches and pastors reappear in the ne home and resume control. But too often, as with Europea immigrants, the family loses control over the children wh become assimilated more rapidly than their parents. Trag evidences of this appear coldly detailed in the records o delinquency.

Living in the city means more than mental adjustmen Harlem is one of the most densely peopled spots in the worlc The narrow strip between 114th and 145th Streets, Fif and Eighth Avenues, which once held 50,000 Negroes an was regarded as crowded, now pretends to accomoda nearer 150,000. Some of the consequences of this painfu overcrowding are presented in other pages of this numbe Not the least important is its effect on health. The physic environment of the city registered a disconcerting toll i deaths and disease until the social agencies forsook the ol dogma of the racial scientists that the physical constitutio of the Negro was inherently weak, and set about controllin it. Notable advances have been made, but the glam of the city still casts grim shadows.

III

CITIES have personalities. Their chief industries a likely to determine not only respective characters, b the type of persons they attract and hold. Detroit manufa tures automobiles, Chicago slaughters cattle, Pittsbur smelts iron and steel—these three communities draw diffe ent types of workers whose industrial habits are interlace with correspondingly different cultural backgrounds. Or might look to this factor as having significance in the sele tion of Negro workers and indeed in the relations of t Negro population with the community. The technical i tricacy of the automobile industry, like the army intelligen tests, sifts out the heavy-handed worker who fits admirab into the economy of the steel industries where 80 pe cent of the operations are unskilled. A temperament equipment easily adapted to the knife-play and stench of kill ing and preserving cattle is not readily interchangeable eith with the elaborated technique of the factory or the shee muscle play and endurance required by the mill. The communities draw different types of workers. Perhaps these subtle shades of difference may be attributed— least in part—this fact: Chicago's industries drew from tl current of northward migration a Negro increase of 154 p cent and out of the consequent fermentation grew a race ri which took a terrific toll in life and property. Detroit's industries, just a short space removed, drew an increase of 11.3 per cent, and nothing has happened to break the rhythm of working and living relations. Moreover, in both cities the Negro population by the increase became precisely 4.1 per cent of the whole.

Similar differences between cities account for the curiously varied types of Negroes who manage to maintain themselves in New York. They defy racial classification. The Negro worker can no more become a fixed racial concept than can the white worker. Conceived in terms either of capacity or opportunity, the employment of Negroes gives rise to the most perplexing paradoxes. If it is a question of what a Negro is mentally and physically able to do, there are as many affirmations of competence as denials of it. Employers disagree. Some find Negroes equal to whites, some find them slow and stodgy; some regard them as temperamental and 'snippy," some find them genial and loyal. What has not been taken into account is the difference between the Negro groups already referred to and between the stages of their orientation.

The Negro worker facing a job confronts the cankered traditions of centuries built upon racial dogma, founded upon beliefs long upset. Racial orthodoxy seems to demand that the respective status of the white and Negro races be maintained as nearly intact as the interests of industry will permit. Study the distribution of Negro workers in New York City: they are by all odds the most available class for personal service positions—"blind alley" jobs which lead to nothing beyond the merit of long and faithful service. They are porters, waiters, messengers, elevator tenders, chauffeurs and janitors. In these jobs 24,528 Negro men, by the last census count, found employment. And this number represented nearly half of all the Negro men at work in New York. The work is not difficult, the pay is fair and in lieu of anything better they drift into it. On the other hand employers know that with the normal outlets blocked for superior Negro workers, the chances favor their getting better Negro workers than white for the wages paid. None of the Horatio Alger ascensions from messenger to manager or from porter to president need be counted into the labor turnover where Negroes are concerned. Once a porter, barring the phenomenal, always a porter.

We might take another aspect of this economic picture: Negro workers, it will be found, are freely employed in certain jobs requiring strength and bodily agility, but little skill. A good example of this is longshore work. This is irregular and fitful, combining long periods of rest with sudden and sustained physical exertion. Employment of this type also leads nowhere but to worn bodies and retirement to less arduous tasks. The largest single group of Negro workers are longshoremen. There were 5,387 in 1920: 14 per cent of all the longshoremen in the city and 9 per cent of all the Negro men at work.

Negro women are freely employed as laundresses and servants. Though they are in fierce competition with the women of other races, 24,438 or 60 per cent of all the Negro women working in New York are either laundresses or servants.

In work requiring a period of apprenticeship Negroes are rarely employed. This limits the skilled workers and the number of Negroes eligible on this basis for membership in certain trade unions. There were only 56 Negro ap-

prentices in the 9,561 counted in the census of 1920.

In work requiring contact with the public in the capacity of salesman or representative, Negroes are infrequently employed (if they are known to be Negroes) except in Negro businesses.

In work requiring supervision over white workers they are rarely employed, though there are a few striking exceptions.

In skilled work requiring membership in unions they are employed only in small numbers, and membership is rarely encouraged unless the union is threatened. Since the apprentice-recruits for these jobs are discouraged, and the numbers sparse, the safety of the union is rarely threatened by an unorganized Negro minority. In certain responsible skilled positions, such as locomotive engineers, street car and subway motormen, Negroes are never employed.

The distinctions are irrational. A Negro worker may not be a street or subway conductor because of the possibility of public objection to contact—but he may be a ticket chopper. He may not be a money changer in a subway station because honesty is required—yet he may be entrusted, as a messenger, with thousands of dollars daily. He may not sell goods over a counter—but he may deliver the goods after they have been sold. He may be a porter in charge of a sleeping car without a conductor, but never a conductor; he may be a policeman but not a fireman; a linotyper, but not a motion picture operator; a glass annealer, but not a glass blower; a deck hand, but not a sailor. The list could be continued indefinitely.

For those who might think, however, that this reflects the range of the Negroes' industrial capacity, it is recorded that of 321 specific occupations in New York City listed in the 1920 Census, there were one or more Negroes in 316 of them. In 175 of these occupations over 50 Negroes were employed. This wide range of employment is one of the surface indications of a deeper revolution. The sudden thinning out of recruits for the bottom places in industry following the declaration of war and the restricted immigration of South European laborers, has broken during the past ten years many of the traditions which held the Negro workers with their faces to the wall. New positions in industry have been opened up and gradually Negro men, at least, are abandoning personal service for the greater pay of industrial work.

This can be illustrated by a few significant increases. Shortly after labor unions became active throughout the country Negro artisans threatened to disappear. In 1910 there were but 268 Negro carpenters in New York City. But in 1920 in New York the number had increased to 737. Chauffeurs who numbered 490 in 1910 were 2,195 in 1920. Ten years ago there were no known clothing workers, but now there are over 6,000. The same applies to workers in textile industries who numbered at the last count 2,685. Electricians, machinists and musicians have advanced over a hundred per cent. The number of shoemakers jumped from 14 to 581, stationery firemen from 249 to 1,076, mechanics from practically none to 462 and real estate agents from 89 to 247.

One feels tempted to inquire of the "workers' friend," the unions, why those trades in which these unions are well organized have not shown equivalent increases in Negro workers. Ten years added but 18 brick masons, 81 painters, 16 plasterers and 42 plumbers.

The number of elevator   (Continued on page 718)

The South Lingers On

By RUDOLPH FISHER

and finally their parents, loath to leave their shepherd and their dear, decrepit shacks, but dependent and without choice. "Whyn't y' come to New York?" old Deacon Gassoway had insisted. "Martin and Eli and Jim Lee and his fambly's all up da' now an' doin' fine. We'll all git together an' start a chu'ch of our own, an' you'll still be pastor an' it'll be jes' same as 'twas hyeh." Full of that hope, he had come. But where were they? He had captained his little ship till it sank; he had clung to a splint and been tossed ashore; but the shore was cold, gray, hard and rock-strewn. He had been in barren places before but God had been there too. Was Harlem then past hope? Was the connection between this place and heaven broken, so that the servant of God went hungry while little children ridiculed? Into his mind, like a reply, crept an old familiar hymn, and he found himself humming it softly:

> The Lord will provide,
> The Lord will provide,
> In some way or 'nother,
> The Lord will provide.
> It may not be in your way,
> It may not be in mine,
> But yet in His own way
> The Lord will provide.

ZEKIEL TAYLOR, preacher of the gospel of Jesus Christ, walked slowly along One Hundred and Thirty-Third Street, conspicuously alien. He was little and old and bent. A short, bushy white beard framed his shiny black face and his tieless celluloid collar. A long, greasy, green-black Prince Albert, with lapels frayed and buttons worn through to their metal hung loosely from his shoulders. His trousers were big and baggy and limp, yet not enough so to hide the dejected bend of his knees.

A little boy noted the beard and gibed, "Hey, Santa Claus! 'Tain't Chris'mas yet!" And the little boy's playmates chorused, "Haw, haw! Lookit the colored Santa Claus!"

"For of such is the kingdom of heaven," mused Ezekiel Taylor. No. The kingdom of Harlem. Children turned into mockers. Satan in the hearts of infants. Harlem—city of the devil—outpost of hell.

Darkness settled, like the gloom in the old preacher's heart; darkness an hour late, for these sinners even tinkered with God's time, substituting their "daylight-saving." Wicked, yes. But sad too, as though they were desperately warding off the inescapable night of sorrow in which they must suffer for their sins. Harlem. What a field! What numberless souls to save!—These very taunting children who knew not even the simplest of the commandments—

But he was old and alone and defeated. The world had called to his best. It had offered money, and they had gone; first the young men whom he had fathered, whom he had brought up from infancy in his little Southern church; then their wives and children, whom they eventually sent for;

Then suddenly, astonished, he stopped, listening. He had not been singing alone—a chorus of voices somewhere near had caught up his hymn. Its volume was gradually increasing. He looked about for a church. There was none. He covered his deaf ear so that it might not handicap his good one. The song seemed to issue from one of the private houses a little way down the street.

He approached with eager apprehension and stood wonderingly before a long flight of brownstone steps leading to an open entrance. The high first floor of the house, that to which the steps led, was brightly lighted, and the three front windows had their panes covered with colored tissue-paper designed to resemble church windows. Strongly, cheerily the song came out to the listener:

> The Lord will provide,
> The Lord will provide,
> In some way or 'nother,
> The Lord will provide.

Ezekiel Taylor hesitated an incredulous moment, then smiling, he mounted the steps and went in.

The Reverend Shackleton Ealey had been inspired to preach the gospel by the draft laws of 1917. He remained in the profession not out of gratitude to its having kept him out of war, but because he found it a far less precarious mode of living than that devoted to poker, blackjack and dice. He was stocky and flat-faced and yellow, with many black freckles and the eyes of a dogfish. And he was clever enough not to conceal his origin, but to make capital out of his conversion from gambler to preacher and to confine himself to those less enlightened groups that thoroughly believed in the possibility of so sudden and complete a transformation.

The inflow of rural folk from the South was therefore

644

fortune, and Reverend Shackleton Ealey spent hours in Pennsylvania station greeting newly arrived migrants, urging them to visit his meeting-place and promising them the satisfaction of "that old-time religion." Many had come—and contributed.

This was prayer-meeting night. Reverend Ealey had his seat on a low platform at the distant end of the double room originally designed for a "parlor." From behind a pulpit-stand improvised out of soap-boxes and covered with calico he counted his congregation and estimated his profit.

A stranger entered uncertainly, looked about a moment, and took a seat near the door. Reverend Shackleton Ealey appraised him: a little bent-over old man with a bushy white beard and a long Prince Albert coat. Perfect type—fertile soil. He must greet this stranger at the close of the meeting and effusively make him welcome.

But Sister Gassoway was already by the stranger's side, shaking his hand vigorously and with unmistakable joy; and during the next hymn she came over to old man Gassoway and whispered in his ear, whereupon he jumped up wide-eyed, looked around, and made broadly smiling toward the newcomer. Others turned to see, and many, on seeing, began to whisper excitedly into their neighbor's ear and turned to see again. The stranger was occasioning altogether too great a stir. Reverend Ealey decided to pray.

His prayer was a masterpiece. It besought of God protection for His people in a strange and wicked land; it called down His damnation upon those dens of iniquity, the dance halls, the theatres, the cabarets; it berated the poker-sharp, the blackjack player, the dice-roller; it denounced the drunkard, the bootlegger, the dope-peddler; and it ended in a sweeping tirade against the wolf-in-sheep's-clothing, whatever his motive might be.

Another hymn and the meeting came to a close. The stranger was surrounded before Reverend Ealey could reach him. When finally he approached the old preacher with extended hand and hollow-hearted smile, old man Gassoway was saying:

"Yas, suh, Rev'n Taylor, dass jes' whut we goin' do. Start makin' 'rangements tomorrer. Martin an' Jim Lee's over to Ebeneezer, but dey doan like it 'tall. Says hit's too hifalutin for 'em, de way dese Harlem cullud folks wushup; Ain' got no Holy Ghos' in 'em, dass whut. Jes' come in an' set down an' git up an' go out. Never moans, never shouts, never even says 'amen.' Most of us is hyeh, an' we gonna git together an' start us a ch'ch of our own, wid you f' pastor, like we said. Yas, suh. Hyeh's Brother Ealey now. Brother Ealey, dis hyeh's our old preacher Rev'n Taylor. We was jes' tellin him—"

The Reverend Shackleton Ealey had at last a genuine revelation—that the better-yielding half of his flock was on the wing. An old oath of frustration leaped to his lips—"God—" but he managed to bite it in the middle—"bless you, my brother," he growled.

II

"WHAT makes you think you can cook?"
"Why, brother, I been in the neighborhood o' grub all my life!"
"Humph! Fly bird, you are."
"Pretty near all birds fly, friend."
"Yes—even black birds."
The applicant for the cook's job lost his joviality. "All

right. I'm a black bird. You're a half-yaller hound. Step out in the air an' I'll fly down your dam' throat, so I can see if your insides is yaller, too!"

The clerk grinned. "You must do your cooking on the top of your head. Turn around and fly out that door there and see if the Hundred and Thirty-Fifth Street breeze won't cool you off some. We want a fireless cooker."

With an unmistakable suggestion as to how the clerk might dispose of his job the applicant rolled cloudily out of the employment office. The clerk called "Next!" and Jake Crinshaw, still convulsed with astonishment, nearly lost his turn.

"What kind of work are you looking for, buddy?"
"No purtickler kin', suh. Jes' work, dass all."
"Well, what can you do?"
"Mos' anything, I reckon."
"Drive a car?"
"No suh. Never done dat."
"Wait table?"
"Well, I never is."
"Run elevator?"
"No, suh."
"What have you been doing?"
"Farmin'."
"Farming? Where?"
"Jennin's Landin', Virginia. 'At's wha' all my folks is fum."
"How long you been here?"
"Ain' been hyeh a week yit. Still huntin' work." Jake answered rather apologetically. The question had been almost hostile.

"Oh—migrant." In the clerk's tone were patronization, some contempt, a little cynical amusement and complete comprehension. "Migrant" meant nothing to Jake; to the clerk it explained everything.

"M-hm. Did you try the office up above—between here and Seventh Avenue? They wanted two dozen laborers for a railroad camp upstate—pay your transportation, board and everything."

"Yas, suh—up there yestiddy, but de man say dey had all dey need. Tole me to try y'all down hyeh."

"M-hm. Well, I'm sorry, but we haven't anything for you this morning. Come in later in the week. Something may turn up."

"Yas, suh. Thank y' suh."

Jake made his discouraged way to the sidewalk and stood contemplating. His blue jumpers were clean and spotless—they had been his Sunday-go-to-meeting ones at home. He wore big, broad, yellow shoes and a shapeless tan felt hat, beneath whose brim the hair was close cut, the neck shaved bare. He was very much dressed up.

The applicant who had preceded him approached. "What'd that yaller dog tell you, bud?"

"Tole me come in later."

"Huh! That's what they all say. Only way for a guy with guts to get anything in this town is to be a bigger crook 'n the next one." He pointed to two well-dressed young men idling on the curb. "See them two? They used to wait on a job where I was chef. Now look at 'em —prosperous! An' how 'd they get that way? Hmph! That one's a pimp an' th' other's a pickpocket. Take your choice." And the cynic departed.

But Jake had greater faith in Harlem. Its praises had been sounded too highly—there must be something.

He turned and looked at the signboard that had led him to enter the employment office. It was a wooden blackboard, on which was written in chalk: "Help wanted. All sorts of jobs. If we haven't it, leave your name and we'll find it." The clerk hadn't asked Jake *his* name.

A clanging, shrieking fire engine appeared from nowhere and swept terrifyingly past. It frightened Jake like the first locomotive he had seen as a child. He shrank back against the building. Another engine passed. No more. He felt better. No one minded the engines. No one noticed that he did. Harlem itself was a fire engine.

Jake could read the signs on the buildings across the street: "Harlem Commercial and Savings Bank"—"Hale and Clark, Real Estate"—"Restaurant and Delicatessen, J. W. Jackson, proprietor"—"The Music Shop"—"John Gilmore, Tonsorial Parlor." He looked up at the buildings. They were menacingly big and tall and close. There were no trees. No ground for trees to grow from. Sidewalks overflowing with children. Streets crammed full of street-cars and automobiles. Noise, hurry, bustle—fire engines.

Jake looked again at the signboard. Help wanted—all sorts. After a while he heaved a great sigh, turned slowly, and slouched wearily on, hoping to catch sight of another employment office with a signboard out front.

III

IT was eleven o'clock at night. Majutah knew that Harry would be waiting on the doorstep downstairs. He knew better than to ring the bell so late—she had warned him. And there was no telephone. Grandmother wouldn't consent to having a telephone in the flat—she thought it would draw lightning. As if every other flat in the house didn't have one, as if lightning would strike all the others and leave theirs unharmed! Grandmother was such a nuisance with her old fogeyisms. If it weren't for her down-home ideas there'd be no trouble getting out now to go to the cabaret with Harry. As it was, Majutah would have to steal down the hall past Grandmother's room in the hope that she would be asleep.

Majutah looked to her attire. The bright red sandals and scarlet stockings, she fancied, made her feet look smaller and her legs bigger. This was desirable, since her black crepe dress, losing in width what style had added to its length, would not permit her to sit comfortably and cross her knees without occasioning ample display of everything below them. Her vanity-case mirror revealed how exactly the long pendant earrings matched her red coral beads and how perfectly becoming the new close bob was, and assured her for the tenth time that Egyptian rouge made her skin look lighter. She was ready.

Into the narrow hallways she tipped, steadying herself against the walls, and slowly approached the outside door at the end. Grandmother's room was the last off the hallway. Majutah reached it, slipped successfully past, and started silently to open the door to freedom.

"Jutie?"

How she hated to be called Jutie! Why couldn't the meddlesome old thing say Madge like everyone else?

"Ma'am?"

"Wha' you goin' dis time o' night?"

"Just downstairs to mail a letter."

"You easin' out mighty quiet, if dat's all you goin' do. Come 'eh. Lemme look at you."

Majutah slipped off her pendants and beads and laid them on the floor. She entered her grandmother's room, standing where the foot of the bed would hide her gay shoes and stockings. Useless precautions. The shrewd old woman inspected her grandaughter a minute in disapproving silence, then asked:

"Well, wha's de letter?"

"Hello, Madge," said Harry. "What held you up? You look mad enough to bite bricks."

"I am. Grandmother, of course. She's a pest. Always nosing and meddling. I'm grown, and the money I make supports both of us, and I'm sick of acting like a kid just to please her."

"How'd you manage?"

"I didn't manage. I just gave her a piece of my mind and came on out."

"Mustn't hurt the old lady's feelings. It's just her way of looking out for you."

"I don't need any looking out for—or advice either!"

"Excuse me. Which way—Happy's or Edmonds'?"

"Edmonds'—darn it!"

"Right."

It was two o'clock in the morning. Majutah's grandmother closed her Bible and turned down the oil lamp by which she preferred to read it. For a long time she sat thinking of Jutie—and of Harlem, this city of Satan. It was Harlem that had changed Jutie—this great, noisy, heartless, crowded place where you lived under the same roof with a hundred people you never knew; where night was alive and morning dead. It was Harlem—those brazen women with whom Jutie sewed, who swore and shimmied and laughed at the suggestion of going to church. Jutie wore red stockings. Jutie wore dresses that looked like nightgowns. Jutie painted her face and straightened her hair, instead of leaving it as God intended. Jutie—lied—often.

And while Madge laughed at a wanton song, her grandmother knelt by her bed and through the sinful babel of the airshaft, through her own silent tears, prayed to God in heaven for Jutie's lost soul.

IV

"TOO much learnin' ain' good f' nobody. When I was her age I couldn' write my own name."

"You can't write much mo' 'n that now. Too much learnin'! Whoever heard o' sich a thing!"

Anna's father, disregarding experience in arguing with his wife, pressed his point. "Sho they's sich a thing as too much learnin'! 'At gal's gittin' so she don't b'lieve nuthin'!"

"Hmph! Didn't she jes' tell me las' night she didn' b'lieve they ever was any Adam an' Eve?"

"Well, I ain' so sho they ever was any myself! An' one thing is certain: If that gal o' mine wants to keep on studyin' an' go up there to that City College an' learn how to teach school an' be somebody, I'll work my fingers to the bone to help her do it! Now!"

"That ain' what I'm takin' 'bout. You ain' worked no harder 'n I is to help her git this far. Hyeh she is ready to graduate from high school. Think of it—high school! When we come along they didn' even *have* no high schools. Fus' thing y' know she be so far above us we can't reach her with a fence-rail. Then you'll wish you'd a listened to me. What I says is, she done gone far enough."

"Ain' no sich thing as far enough when you wants to go farther. 'Tain' as if it was gonna cost a whole lot. That's the trouble with you cullud folks now. Git so far an' stop—set down—through—don't want no mo'." Her disgust was boundless. "Y' got too much cotton field in you, that's what!"

The father grinned. "They sho' ain' no cotton field in yo' mouth, honey."

"No they ain't. An' they ain' no need o' all this arguin' either, 'cause all that gal's got to do is come in hyeh right now an' put her arms 'roun' yo' neck, an' you'd send her to Europe if she wanted to go!"

"Well, all I says is, when dey gits to denyin' de Bible hit's time to stop 'em."

"Well all I says is, if Cousin Sukie an' yo' no 'count brother, Jonathan, can send their gal all the way from Athens to them Howard's an' pay car-fare an' boa'd an' ev'ything, we can send our gal—"

She broke off as a door slammed. There was a rush, a delightful squeal, and both parents were being smothered in a cyclone of embraces by a wildly jubilant daughter.

"Mummy! Daddy! I won it! I won it!"

"What under the sun—?"

"The scholarship, Mummy! The scholarship!"

"No!"

"Yes I did! I can go to Columbia! I can go to Teacher's College! Isn't it great?"

Anna's mother turned triumphantly to her husband; but he was beaming at his daughter.

"You sho' is yo' daddy's chile. Teacher's College! Why that's wha' I been wantin' you to go all along!"

V

RARE sight in a close-built, topheavy city—space. A wide open lot, extending along One Hundred and Thirty-Eighth Street almost from Lenox to Seventh Avenue; baring the mangy backs of a long row of One Hundred and Thirty-Ninth Street houses; disclosing their gaping, gasping windows, their shameless strings of half-laundered rags, which gulp up what little air the windows seek to inhale. Occupying the Lenox Avenue end of the lot, the so-called Garvey tabernacle, wide, low, squat, with its stingy little entrance; occupying the other, the church tent where summer camp meetings are held.

Pete and his buddy, Lucky, left their head-to-head game of coon-can as darkness came on. Time to go out—had to save gas. Pete went to the window and looked down at the tent across the street.

"Looks like the side show of a circus. Ever been in?"

"Not me. I'm a preacher's son—got enough o' that stuff when I was a kid and couldn't protect myself."

"Ought to be a pretty good show when some o' them old-time sisters get happy. Too early for the cabarets; let's go in a while, just for the hell of it."

"You sure are hard up for somethin' to do."

"Aw, come on. Somethin' funny's bound to happen. You might even get religion, you dam' bootlegger."

Luck grinned. "Might meet some o' my customers, you mean."

Through the thick, musty heat imprisoned by the canvas shelter a man's voice rose, leading a spiritual. Other voices chimed eagerly in, some high, clear, sweet; some low, mellow, full,—all swelling, rounding out the refrain till it filled the place, so that it seemed the flimsy walls and roof must soon be torn from their moorings and swept aloft with the song:

Where you running, sinner?
Where you running, I say?
Running from the fire—
You can't cross here!

The preacher stood waiting for the song to melt away. There was a moment of abysmal silence, into which the thousand blasphemies filtering in from outside dropped unheeded.

The preacher was talking in deep, impressive tones. One old patriarch was already supplementing each statement with a matter-of-fact "amen!" of approval.

The preacher was describing hell. He was enumerating without exception the horrors that befall the damned: maddening thirst for the drunkard; for the gambler, insatiable flame, his own greed devouring his soul. The preacher's voice no longer talked—it sang; mournfully at first, monotonously up and down, up and down—a chant in minor mode; then more intensely, more excitedly; now fairly strident.

The amens of approval were no longer matter-of-fact, perfunctory. They were quick, spontaneous, escaping the lips of their own accord; they were frequent and loud and began to come from the edges of the assembly instead of just the front rows. The old men cried, "Help him, Lord!" "Preach the word!" "Glory!" taking no apparent heed of the awfulness of the description, and the old women continuously moaned aloud, nodding their bonneted heads, or swaying rhythmically forward and back in their seats.

Suddenly the preacher stopped, leaving the old men and old women still noisy with spiritual momentum. He stood motionless till the last echo of approbation subsided, then repeated the text from which his discourse had taken origin; repeated it in a whisper, lugubrious, hoarse, almost inaudible; " ' In—hell—' "—paused, then without warning wildly shrieked, " ' *In hell—* ' " stopped—returned to his hoarse whisper—" ' he lifted up his eyes. . . .' "

"What the hell you want to leave for?" Pete complained when he and Lucky reached the sidewalk. That old bird would 'a' coughed up his gizzard in two more minutes. What's the idea?"

"Aw hell—I don't know.—You think that stuff's funny. You laugh at it. I don't, that's all." Lucky hesitated. The urge to speak outweighed the fear of being ridiculed. "Dam' 'f I know what it is—maybe because it makes me think of the old folks or somethin'—but—hell—it just sorter—gets me—"

Lucky turned abruptly away and started off. Pete watched him for a moment with a look that should have been astonished, outraged, incredulous—but wasn't. He overtook him, put an arm about his shoulders, and because he had to say something as they walked on, muttered reassuringly:

"Well—if you ain't the damnedest fool—"

The Tropics in New York

By W. A. DOMINGO

ITHIN Harlem's seventy or eighty blocks, for the first time in their lives, colored people of Spanish, French, Dutch, Arabian, Danish, Portuguese, British and native African ancestry or nationality meet and move together.

A dusky tribe of destiny seekers, these brown and black and yellow folk, eyes filled with visions of their heritage—palm fringed sea shores, murmuring streams, luxuriant hills and vales—have made their epical march from the far corners of the earth to Harlem. They bring with them vestiges of their folk life—their lean, sunburnt faces, their quiet, halting speech, fortified by a graceful insouciance, their light, loose-fitting clothes of ancient cut telling the story of a dogged, romantic pilgrimage to the El Dorado of their dreams.

Here they have their first contact with each other, with large numbers of American Negroes, and with the American brand of race prejudice. Divided by tradition, culture, historical background and group perspective, these diverse peoples are gradually hammered into a loose unit by the impersonal force of congested residential segregation. Unlike others of the foreign-born, black immigrants find it impossible to segregate themselves into colonies; too dark of complexion to pose as Cubans or some other Negroid but alien-tongued foreigners, they are inevitably swallowed up in black Harlem. Their situation requires an adjustment unlike that of any other class of the immigrant population; and but for the assistance of their kinsfolk they would be capsized almost on the very shores of their haven.

According to the census for 1920 there were in the United States 73,803 foreign-born Negroes; of that number 36,613, or approximately 50 per cent lived in New York City, 28,184 of them in the Borough of Manhattan. They formed slightly less than 20 per cent of the total Negro population of New York.

From 1920 to 1923 the foreign-born Negro population

The Tropics in New York
By CLAUDE McKAY

Bananas ripe and green, and ginger root,
Cocoa in pods and alligator pears,
And tangerines and mangoes and grape fruit,
Fit for the highest prize at parish fairs.

Set in the window, bringing memories
Of fruit-trees laden by low-singing rills,
And dewy dawns, and mystical blue skies
In benediction over nun-like hills.

My eyes grew dim, and I could no more gaze;
A wave of longing through my body swept,
And, hungry for the old familiar ways,
I turned aside and bowed my head and wept.
—*From Harlem Shadows, Harcourt, Brace & Co.*

---

of the United States was increased nearly 40 per cent through the entry of 30,849 Africans (black). In 1921 the high-water mark of 9,873 was registered. This increase was not permanent, for in 1923 there was an exit of 1,525 against an entry of 7,554. If the 20 per cent that left that year is an index of the proportion leaving annually, it is safe to estimate a net increase of about 24,000 between 1920 and 1923. If the newcomers are distributed throughout the country in the same proportion as their predecessors, the present foreign-born Negro population of Harlem is about 35,000. These people are, therefore, a formidable minority whose presence cannot be ignored or discounted. It is this large body of foreign born who contribute those qualities that make New York so unlike Pittsburgh, Washington, Chicago and other cities with large aggregations of American Negroes.

The largest number came from the British West Indies and were attracted to New York by purely economic reasons. The next largest group consists of Spanish-speaking Negroes from Latin America. Distinct because of their language, and sufficiently numerous to maintain themselves as a cultural unit, the Spanish element has but little contact with the English speaking majority. For the most part they keep to themselves and follow in the main certain definite occupational lines. A smaller group, French-speaking, have emigrated from Haiti and the French West Indies. There are also a few Africans, a batch of voluntary pilgrims over the old track of the slave-traders.

Among the English-speaking West Indian population of Harlem are some 8,000 natives of the American Virgin Islands. A considerable part of these people were forced to migrate to the mainland as a consequence of the operation of the Volstead Act which destroyed the lucrative rum industry and helped to reduce the number of foreign vessels that used to call at the former free port of Charlotte Amelia for various stores. Despite their long Danish connection these people are culturally and linguistically English, rather than Danish. Unlike the British Negroes in New York, the Virgin Islanders take an intelligent and aggressive interest in the affairs of their former home and are organized to cooperate with their brothers there who are valiantly struggling to substitute civil government for the present naval administration of the islands.

To the average American Negro all English-speaking black foreigners are West Indians, and by that is usually meant British subjects. There is a general assumption that there is everything in common among West Indians, though nothing can be further from the truth. West Indians regard themselves as Antiguans or Jamaicans as the case might be, and a glance at the map will quickly reveal the physical obstacles that militate against homogeneity of population; separations of many sorts, geographical, political and cultural tend everywhere to make and crystallize local characteristics.

This undiscriminating attitude on the part of native Negroes, as well as the friction generated from contact between the two groups, has created an artificial and defensive unity among the islanders which reveals itself in an instinctive closing of their ranks when attacked by outsiders; but among themselves organization along insular lines is the general rule. Their social grouping, however, does not follow insular precedents. Social gradation is determined in the islands by family connections, education, wealth and position. As each island is a complete society in itself, Negroes occupy from the lowliest to the most exalted positions. The barrier separating the colored aristocrat from the laboring class of the same color is as difficult to surmount as a similar barrier between Englishmen. Most of the islanders in New York are from the middle, artisan and laboring classes. Arriving in a country whose every influence is calculated to democratize their race and destroy the distinctions they had been accustomed to, even those West Indians whose stations in life have been of the lowest soon lose whatever servility they brought with them. In its place they substitute all of the self-assertiveness of the classes they formerly paid deference to.

West Indians have been coming to the United States for over a century. The part they have played in Negro progress is conceded to be important. As early as 1827 a Jamaican, John Brown Russwurm, one of the founders of Liberia, was the first colored man to be graduated from an American college and to publish a newspaper in this country; sixteen years later his fellow countryman, Peter Ogden, organized in New York City the first Odd-Fellows Lodge for Negroes. Prior to the Civil War, West Indian contribution to American Negro life was so great that Dr. W. E. B. DuBois, in his Souls of Black Folk, credits them with main responsibility for the manhood program presented by the race in the early decades of the last century. Indicative of their tendency to blaze new paths is the achievement of John W. A. Shaw of Antigua who, in the early 90's of the last century, passed the civil service tests and became deputy commissioner of taxes for the County of Queens.

It is probably not realized, indeed, to what extent West Indian Negroes have contributed to the wealth, power and prestige of the United States. Major-General Goethals, chief engineer and builder of the Panama Canal, has testified in glowing language to the fact that when all other labor was tried and failed it was the black men of the Caribbean whose intelligence, skill, muscle and endurance made the union of the Pacific and the Atlantic a reality.

Coming to the United States from countries in which they had experienced no legalized social or occupational disabilities, West Indians very naturally have found it difficult to adapt themselves to the tasks that are, by custom, reserved for Negroes in the North. Skilled at various trades and having a contempt for body service and menial work, many of the immigrants apply for positions that the average American Negro has been schooled to regard as restricted to white men only with the result that through their persistence and doggedness in fighting white labor, West Indians have in many cases been pioneers and shock troops to open a way for Negroes into new fields of employment.

This freedom from spiritual inertia characterizes the women no less than the men, for it is largely through them that the occupational field has been broadened for colored women in New York. By their determination, sometimes reinforced by a dexterous use of their hatpins, these women have made it possible for members of their race to enter the needle trades freely.

It is safe to say that West Indian representation in the skilled trades is relatively large; this is also true of the professions, especially medicine and dentistry. Like the Jew, they are forever launching out in business, and such retail businesses as are in the hands of Negroes in Harlem are largely in the control of the foreign-born. While American Negroes predominate in forms of business like barber shops and pool rooms in which there is no competition from white men, West Indians turn their efforts almost invariably to fields like grocery stores, tailor shops, jewelry stores and fruit vending in which they meet the fiercest kind of competition. In some of these fields they are the pioneers or the only surviving competitors of white business concerns. In more ambitious business enterprises like real estate and insurance they are relatively numerous. The only Casino and moving picture theatre operated by Negroes in Harlem is in the hands of a native of one of the small islands. On Seventh Avenue a West Indian woman conducts a millinery store that would be a credit to Fifth Avenue.

The analogy between the West Indian and the Jew may be carried farther; they are both ambitious, eager for education, willing to engage in business, argumentative, aggressive and possessed of great proselytizing zeal for any cause they espouse. West Indians are great contenders for their rights and because of their respect for law are inclined to be litigious. In addition, they are, as a whole, home-loving, hard-working and frugal. Like their English exemplars they are fond of sport, lack a sense of humor (yet the greatest black comedian of America, Bert Williams, was from the Bahamas) and are very serious and intense in their attitude toward life. Always mindful of their folk in the homeland, they save their earnings and are an important factor in the establishment of the record that the Money Order and Postal Savings Departments of College Station Post Office have for being among the busiest in the country.

Ten years ago it was possible to distinguish the West Indian in Harlem especially during the summer months. Accustomed to wearing cool, light-colored garments in the tropics,

Subway Wind
By CLAUDE McKAY

Far down, down through the city's great, gaunt gut
    The gray train rushing bears the weary wind;
In the packed cars the fans the crowd's breath cut,
    Leaving the sick and heavy air behind.
And pale-cheeked children seek the upper door
    To give their summer jackets to the breeze;
Their laugh is swallowed in the deafening roar
    Of captive wind that moans for fields and seas;
Seas cooling warm where native schooners drift
    Through sleepy waters, while gulls wheel and sweep,
Waiting for windy waves the keels to lift
    Lightly among the islands of the deep;
Islands of lofty palm trees blooming white
    That lend their perfume to the tropic sea,
Where fields lie idle in the dew drenched night,
    And the Trades float above them fresh and free.

—From Harlem Shadows, Harcourt, Brace & Co.

he would stroll along Lenox Avenue on a hot day resplendent in white shoes and flannel pants, the butt of many a jest from his American brothers who, today, have adopted the styles that they formerly derided. This trait of non-conformity manifested by the foreign-born has irritated American Negroes, who resent the implied self-sufficiency, and as a result there is a considerable amount of prejudice against West Indians. It is claimed that they are proud and arrogant; that they think themselves superior to the natives. And although educated Negroes of New York are loudest · in publicly decrying the hostility between the two groups, it is nevertheless true that feelings against West Indians is strongest among members of that class. This is explainable on the ground of professional jealousy and competition for leadership. As the islanders press forward and upward they meet the same kind of opposition from the native Negro that the Jew and other ambitious white aliens receive from white Americans. Naturalized West Indians have found from experience that American Negroes are reluctant to concede them the right to political leadership even when qualified intellectually. Unlike their American brothers the islanders are free from those traditions that bind them to any party and, as a consequence are independent to the point of being radical. Indeed, it is they who largely compose the few political and economic radicals in Harlem; without them the genuinely radical movement among New York Negroes would be unworthy of attention.

There is a diametrical difference between American and West Indian Negroes in their worship. While large sections of the former are inclined to indulge in displays of emotionalism that border on hysteria, the latter, in their Wesleyan Methodist and Baptist churches maintain in the face of the assumption that people from the tropics are necessarily emotional, all the punctilious emotional restraint characteristic of their English background. In religious radicalism the foreign-born are again pioneers and propagandists. The only modernist church among the thousands of Negroes in New York (and perhaps the country) is led by a West Indian, Rev. E. Ethelred Brown, an ordained Unitarian minister, and is largely supported by his fellow-islanders.

In facing the problem of race prejudice, foreign born Negroes, and West Indians in particular, are forced to undergo considerable adjustment. Forming a racial majority in their own countries and not being accustomed to discrimination expressly felt as racial, they rebel against the "color line" as they find it in America. For while color and caste lines tend to converge in the islands, it is nevertheless true that because of the ratio of population, historical background and traditions of rebellions before and since their emancipation, West Indians of color do not have their activities, social, occupational and otherwise, determined by their race. Color plays a part but it is not the prime determinant of advancement; hence, the deep feeling of resentment when the "color line," legal or customary, is met and found to be a barrier to individual progress. For this reason the West Indian has thrown himself whole-heartedly into the fight against lynching, discrimination and the other disabilities from which Negroes in America suffer.

It must be remembered that the foreign-born black men and women, more so even than other groups of immigrants, are the hardiest and most venturesome of their folk. They were dissatisfied at home, and it is to be expected that they

would not be altogether satisfied with limitation of opportunity here when they have staked so much to gain enlargement of opportunity. They do not suffer from the local anesthesia of custom and pride which makes otherwise intolerable situations bearable for the home-staying majorities.

Just as the West Indian has been a sort of leaven in the American loaf, so the American Negro is beginning to play a reciprocal role in the life of the foreign Negro communities, as for instance, the recent championing of the rights of Haiti and Liberia and the Virgin Islands, as well as the growing resentment at the treatment of natives in the African colonial dependencies. This world-wide reaction of the darker races to their common as well as local grievances is one of the most significant facts of recent development. Exchange of views and extension of race organization beyond American boundaries is likely to develop on a considerable scale in the near future, in terms principally of educational and economical projects. Former ties have been almost solely the medium of church missionary enterprises.

It has been asserted that the movement headed by the most-advertised of all West Indians, Marcus Garvey, absentee "president" of the continent of Africa, represents the attempt of West Indian peasants to solve the American race problem. This is no more true than it would be to say that the editorial attitude of The Crisis during the war reflected the spirit of American Negroes respecting their grievances or that the late Booker T. Washington successfully delimited the educational aspirations of his people. The support given Garvey by a certain type of his countrymen is partly explained by their group reaction to attacks made upon him because of his nationality. On the other hand the earliest and most persistent exposures of Garvey's multitudinous schemes were initiated by West Indians in New York like Cyril Briggs and the writer.

Prejudice against West Indians is in direct ratio to their number; hence its strength in New York where they are heavily concentrated. It is not unlike the hostility between Englishmen and Americans of the same racial stock. It is to be expected that the feeling will always be more or less present between the immigrant and the native born. However it does not extend to the children of the two groups, as they are subject to the same environment and develop identity of speech and psychology. Then, too, there has been an appreciable amount of intermarriage, especially between foreign born men and native women. Not to be ignored is the fact that congestion in Harlem has forced both groups to be less discriminating in accepting lodgers, thus making for reconciling contacts.

The outstanding contribution of West Indians to American Negro life is the insistent assertion of their manhood in an environment that demands too much servility and protesting acquiescence from men of African blood. This unwillingness to conform and be standardized, to accept tamely an inferior status and abdicate their humanity, finds an open expression in the activities of the foreign-born Negro in America.

Their dominant characteristic is that of blazing new paths, breaking the bonds that would fetter the feet of a virile people—a spirit eloquently expressed in the defiant lines of the Jamaican poet, Claude McKay:

> Like men we'll face the murderous, cowardly pack,
> Pressed to the wall, dying, but fighting back.

Congo: a familiar of the New York studios

Harlem Types

PORTRAITS BY WINOLD REISS

HERE and elsewhere throughout this number, Winold Reiss presents us a graphic interpretation of Negro life, freshly conceived after its own patterns. Concretely in his portrait sketches, abstractly in his symbolic designs, he has aimed to portray the soul and spirit of a people. And by the simple but rare process of not setting up petty canons in the face of nature's own creative artistry, Winold Reiss has achieved what amounts to a revealing discovery of the significance, human and artistic, of one of the great dialects of human physiognomy, of some of the little understood but powerful idioms of nature's speech. Harlem, or any Negro community, spreads a rich and novel palette for the serious artist. It needs but enlightenment of mind and eye to make its intriguing problems and promising resources available for the stimulation and enrichment of American art.

123

Mother and child

CONVENTIONS stand doubly in the way of artistic portrayal of Negro folk; certain narrowly arbitrary conventions of physical beauty, and as well, that inevitable inscrutability of things seen but not understood. Caricature has put upon the countenance of the Negro the mask of the comic and the grotesque, whereas in deeper truth and comprehension, nature or experience have put there the stamp of the very opposite, the serious, the tragic, the wistful. At times, too, there is a quality of soul that can only be called brooding and mystical. Here they are to be seen as we know them to be in fact. While it is a revealing interpretation for all, for the Negro artist, still for the most part confronting timidly his own material, there is certainly a particular stimulus and inspiration in this redeeming vision. Through it in all likelihood must come his best development in the field of the pictorial arts, for his capacity to express beauty depends vitally upon the capacity to see it in his own life and to generate it out of his own experience.

Young America: native-born

652

124

WINOLD REISS, son of Fritz Reiss, the landscape painter, pupil of Franz von Stuck of Munich, has become a master delineator of folk character by wide experience and definite specialization. With ever-ripening skill, he has studied and drawn the folk-types of Sweden, Holland, of the Black Forest and his own native Tyrol, and in America, the Black Foot Indians, the Pueblo people, the Mexicans, and now, the American Negro. His art owes its peculiar success as much to the philosophy of his approach as to his technical skill. He is a folk-lorist of the brush and palette, seeking always the folk character back of the individual, the psychology behind the physiognomy. In design also he looks not merely for decorative elements, but for the pattern of the culture from which it sprang. Without loss of naturalistic accuracy and individuality, he somehow subtly expresses the type, and without being any the less human, captures the racial and local. What Gauguin and his followers have done for the Far East, and the work of Ufer and Blumenschein and the Taos school for the Pueblo and Indian, seems about to be done for the Negro and Africa: in short, painting, the most local of arts, in terms of its own limitations even, is achieving universality.

A Boy Scout

A woman lawyer

Girl in the white blouse

653

125

A college lad

The Black Man Brings His Gifts

By W. E. BURGHARDT DU BOIS

WE'VE got a pretty fine town out here in middle Indiana. We claim fifty thousand inhabitants although the census cheats us out of nearly half. You can't depend on those guys in Washington. The new Pennsylvania station has just gone up and looks big and clean although a bit empty on account of the new anti-loafing ordinance. There is a White Way extending down through the business section which makes us quite gay at night. Of course, we have Rotary, Kiwanis, the Chamber of Commerce and the Federation of Women's Clubs. There are six churches, not counting the colored folks.

Well, last year somebody suggested we have an America's Making pageant just like New York. You see, we need something to sort of bring us together after the war. We had a lot of Germans here and near-Germans and we had to pull them up pretty stiff. In all, we had seven or eight races or nations, not counting the colored people. We salute the flag and many of us can sing The Star Spangled Banner without books. But we really need Americanization; a sort of wholesome getting together.

So, as I have said, last year the Federation of Women's Clubs started the matter and got a committee appointed. They appointed me and Birdie; Mrs. Cadwalader Lee (who is an awfully aristocratic Southern lady); Bill Graves, who runs the biggest store; the editor of the daily paper and the Methodist preacher, who has the biggest church. They made me secretary but Birdie suggested that we needed an impartial chairman who knew something about the subject, for, says she, "What with the Germans, Poles, Scandinavians and Italians, everybody will claim so much that there'll be nothing left for the real Americans." We met and considered the idea favorably and wrote to the state university. They sent us down a professor with a funny name and any number of degrees. It seems that he taught sociology and "applied ethics," whatever that may be.

"I'll bet he's a Jew," said Birdie as soon as she looked at him. "I've got nothing against Jews but I just don't like them. They're too pushing."

First thing off the bat, this professor, who wore a cloak and spoke exceedingly proper and too low for anybody to hear unless they were listening, asked if the colored people ought not to be represented. That took us a bit by surprise as we hadn't thought of them at all. Mrs. Cadwalader Lee said she thought it might be best to have a small auxiliary colored committee and that she would ask her cook to get one up.

"**W**ELL," says I, after we had gotten nicely settled for our first real meeting, "what is the first thing that's gone to making America and who did it?" I had my own mind on music and painting and I know that Birdie is daft on architecture; but before we either of us could speak, Bill Graves grinned and said, "hard work." The chairman nodded and said, "Quite true, labor."

I didn't know just what to say but I whispered to Birdie that it seemed to me that we ought to stress some of the higher things. The chairman must have heard me because he said that all higher things rested on the foundation of human toil.

"But, whose labor?" asked the editor. "Since we are all descended from working people, isn't labor a sort of common contribution which, as it comes from everybody, need not be counted?"

"I should hardly consent to that statement," said Mrs. Cadwalader Lee, who is said to be descended from a governor and a lord.

"At any rate," said the chairman, "the Negroes were America's first great labor force."

"Negroes!" shrilled Birdie, "but we can't have them!"

"I should think," said Mrs. Cadwalader Lee, softly, "that we might have a very interesting darky scene. Negroes hoeing cotton and that sort of thing." We all were thankful to Mrs. Lee and immediately saw that that would be rather good; Mrs. Lee again said she would consult her cook, a very intelligent and exemplary person.

"Next," I said firmly, "comes music."

"Folk songs," said the Methodist preacher.

"Yes," I continued. "There would be Italian and German and—"

"But I thought this was to be American," said the chairman.

"Sure," I answered, "German-American and Italian-American and so forth."

"There ain't no such animal," says Birdie, but Mrs. Cadwalader Lee reminded us of Foster's work and thought we might have a chorus to sing Old Folks at Home, Old Kentucky Home and Nelly Was a Lady. Here the editor pulled out a book on American folk songs by Krehbiel or some such German name and read an extract. (I had to copy it for the minutes.) It said:

The only considerable body of songs which has come into existence in the territory now compassed by the United States, I might even say in North America, excepting the primitive songs of the Indians (which present an entirely different aspect), are the songs of the former black slaves. In Canada the songs of the people, or that portion of the people that can be said still to sing from impulse, are predominantly French, not only in language but in subject. They were for the greater part transferred to this continent with the bodily integrity which they now possess. Only a small portion show an admixture of Indian elements; but the songs of the black slaves of the South are original and native products. They contain idioms which were transplanted from Africa, but as songs they are the product of American institutions; of the social, political and geographical environment within which their creators were placed in America; of the influences to which they were subjected in America; of the joys, sorrows and experiences which fell to their lot in America. Nowhere save on the plantations of the South could the emotional life which is essential to the development of true folksong be developed; nowhere else was there the necessary meeting of the spiritual cause and the simple agent and vehicle. The white inhabitants of the continent have never been in the state of cultural ingenuousness which prompts spontaneous emotional utterances in music.

This rather took our breath and the chairman suggested that the auxiliary colored committee might attend to this. Mrs. Cadwalader Lee was very nice about it. (She has such lovely manners and gets her dresses direct from New York.) She said that she was sure it could all be worked out satisfactorily. We would need a number of servants and helpers. Well, under the leadership of that gifted cook, we'd have a cotton-hoeing scene to represent labor and while hoeing they would sing Negro ditties; afterward they could serve the food and clean up.

That was fine, but I didn't propose to be sidetracked. "But," I says, "we don't want to confine ourselves to folk songs. There is a lot of splendid American music like that of Victor Herbert and Irving Berlin."

The editor grinned. But the chairman was real nice and he mentioned several folks I never heard of—Paine, Buck, Chadwick and DeKoven. And, of course, I know of Nevin and McDowell. Still that editor grinned and said, "Yes, and Harry Burleigh and W. C. Handy and Nathaniel Dett."

Here the preacher spoke up. "I especially like that man, Dett. Our choir sang his Listen to the Lambs last Christmas."

"Oh, yes," said Mrs. Cadwalader Lee, "and Burleigh's Young Warrior was one of the greatest of our war songs."

"I am sure," said the Methodist preacher, "that our choir will be glad to furnish the music."

"But are they colored?" asked the chairman, who had been silent.

"Colored?" we gasped.

"Well, you see, each race was to furnish its own contribution."

"Yes," we chorused, "but this is white American music."

"Not on your life," said the editor, who is awfully slangy. "Of course you know Burleigh and Dett and Handy are all Negroes."

"I think you're mistaken," said Mrs. Cadwalader Lee, getting a bit red in the face.

But sure enough, the chairman said they were and we did not dare dispute him. He even said that Foster's melodies were based on Negro musical themes.

"Well," said the preacher, "I am sure there are no Negroes in town who could sing Listen to the Lambs," and the editor added, "And I hardly think your choir could render The Memphis Blues just as it ought to be." We looked at each other dubiously and I saw right then and there that America's Making had a small chance of being put on in our town. Somebody said that there was a choir in one of the colored churches that could sing this music, but Mrs. Cadwalader Lee reminded us that there would be insuperable difficulties if we tried to bring in obstreperous and high-brow Negroes who demanded social equality. It seems that one of these churches had hired a new social worker—a most objectionable colored person who complained when Mrs. Lee called her by her first name.

"THAT editor is just lugging the Negroes in," said I to Birdie.

"The Negroes seem to be lugging us in," she replied, and she launched us into architecture. From architecture we went to painting. There were Sargent and Whistler and Abbey. Birdie had seen Tanner's Raising of Lazarus in the Luxembourg and suggested a tableau.

"We might get him to help," said the editor. "He's having an exhibit in New York." We were thrilled, all except Mrs. Lee. "I understand he has Negro blood," she said coldly, "and besides, I do not think much of his work." We dropped that and hurried to inventions.

Here, of course, America is preeminent and we must pick and choose. First the preacher asked what kinds of inventions we ought to stress since America was so very inventive. Bill Graves wanted to stress those which had made big money, while the preacher wanted to emphasize those which had "made for righteousness." Birdie said she was strong for those which were really helpful and the chairman suggested the telephone, things that had helped travel, labor-saving devices, etc.

Well, we named over a number of things and especially stressed the telephone. The editor mentioned Granville Wood as one who had helped to perfect the telephone but we didn't listen. I'm sure he was a Negro. But in spite of all, the chairman spoke up again.

"Shoes," he said.

"Well," said I, "I didn't know we invented shoes. I thought they were pretty common before America was discovered."

"But American shoes are the best in the world," said the editor, and then the chairman told us of the United Shoe Machinery Company and how they made shoes.

"And," he added, "that lasting machine which is at the bottom of their success was invented by a Negro."

"I don't believe it," said Birdie flatly, looking at Mrs. Cadwalader Lee. Mrs. Lee got pale this time.

"Of course," she said, "if you are just going to drag in the Negro by the ears—"

"Still," said the editor, "we are after the truth, ain't we? And it is certainly true that Matzeliger invented the lasting machine and you wouldn't want your sister to marry Matzeliger, now would you?"

"Ain't he dead?" asked Birdie, and Mrs. Cadwalader Lee doubted if we ought to be interested in anything as common as shoes.

"I should think automobiles and locomotives would express our genius better."

"Only, we didn't invent them," said the editor.

"But we did invent a method of oiling them while in motion," said the chairman.

"And I'll bet a colored man did that," said Birdie.

"Quite true," answered the chairman. "His name was Elijah McCoy. He is still living in Detroit and I talked with him the other day."

"MIGHT I ask," said Mrs. Cadwalader Lee, looking the chairman full in the face, "if you yourself are of pure white blood?" We all started and we looked the chairman over. He was of dark complexion and his hair was none too straight. He had big black eyes that did not smile much; and yet there couldn't be any doubt about his being white. Wasn't he a professor in the state university and would they hire a colored man no matter how much he knew? The chairman answered.

"I do not know about the purity of my blood although I have usually been called white. Still, one never knows," and he looked solemnly at Mrs. Cadwalader Lee.

Of course, I rushed in, angels being afraid, and cried.

"Dancing—we haven't provided for dancing and we ought to have a lot of that."

"Lovely," says Birdie, "I know a Mexican girl who can do a tango and we could have folk-dancing for the Irish and Scotch."

"The Negroes invented the tango as well as the cake walk and the whole modern dance craze is theirs," said the editor.

This time the preacher saved us. "I'm afraid," said he, "that I could not countenance public dancing. I am aware that our church has changed its traditional attitude somewhat, but I am old-fashioned. If you are to have dancing—" We hastened to reassure him unanimously. We would have no dancing. We dropped it then and there.

Mrs. Lee now spoke up. "It seems to me," she said, "that the real greatness of America lies in her literature. Not only the great writers like Poe and Lanier but in our folk-lore. There are the lovely legends of the mountain whites and, of course, the Uncle Remus tales. I sometimes used to recite them and would not be unwilling to give my services to this pageant.

"Negro dialect, aren't they?" asked the editor, with vast innocence.

"Yes," said Mrs. Lee, "but I am quite familiar with the dialect."

"But oughtn't they to be given by a Negro?" persisted the editor.

"Certainly not; they were written by a white man, Joel Chandler Harris."

"Yes," added the chairman, "he set them down, but the Negroes originated them—they are thoroughly African."

Mrs. Cadwalader Lee actually sniffed. "I am sorry," she said, "but it seems to me that this matter has taken a turn quite different from our original purpose and I'm afraid I may not be able to take part." This would kill the thing, to my mind, but Birdie was not sure.

"Oh, I don't know," she whispered, "she is too high-brow anyway and this thing ought to be a matter of the common people. I don't mind having a few colored people take part so long as they don't want to sit and eat with us; but I do draw the line on Jews."

Well, we took up education next and before we got through, in popped Booker T. Washington. And then came democracy and it looked like everybody had had a hand in that, even the Germans and Italians. The chairman also said that two hundred thousand Negroes had fought for their own liberty in the Civil War and in the war to make the world safe for democracy. But that didn't impress Mrs. Lee or any of the rest of us and we concluded to leave the Negro out of democracy.

"First thing you know you'll have us eating with Negroes," said Birdie, and the chairman said that he'd eaten with Republicans and sinners. I suppose he meant to slur Democrats and Socialists but it was a funny way to do it. Somehow I couldn't just figure out that chairman. I kept watching him.

Then up pops that editor with a lot of notes and papers. "What about exploration?" he asks. Well, we had forgotten that, but naturally the Italians could stage a good stunt with Columbus.

"And the French and Spanish," said Birdie, "only there are none of them in town, thank God!"

"But there are colored folk!" said that chairman. I just gave him a withering look.

"Were they Columbus' cooks?" I asked.

"Probably," said the chairman, "but the one I have in mind discovered New Mexico and Arizona. But I'm afraid," he added slowly, "that we're getting nowhere."

"We've already got there," said Birdie. But the chairman continued: "How could we when we're talking for people and not letting them express themselves?"

"But aren't we the committee?" I asked.

"Yes, and by our own appointment."

"But we represent all the races," I insisted, "except, well —except the Negroes."

"Just so," replied the chairman, "and while I may seem to you to be unduly stressing the work of Negroes, that is simply because they are not represented here. I promise to say nothing further on the matter if you will indulge me a few minutes. In the next room, a colored woman is waiting. She is that social worker at the colored church and she is here by my invitation, I had hoped to have her invited to sit on this committee. As that does not seem possible, may she say just a word?"

He looked at me. I looked at Birdie and Birdie stared at Mrs. Cadwalader Lee. Mrs. Lee arose.

"Certainly—oh, certainly," she said sweetly. "Don't let me interfere. But, of course, you will understand that we Lees must draw the line somewhere," and out she sailed.

I KNEW the whole thing was dead as a door nail and I was just about to tell Birdie so when in marched that Negro before we'd had a chance to talk about her. She had on a tailor-made gown that cost fifty dollars if a cent, a smart toque and (would you believe it?) she was a graduate of the University of Chicago! If there's anything I hate it's a college woman. And here was a black one at that. I didn't know just how to treat her so I sort of half turned my shoulder to her and looked out the window. She began with an essay. It had a lot of long words which sounded right even if they weren't. What she seemed to be driving at was this:

Who made this big country? Not the millionaires, the ministers and the "know-alls," but laborers and drudges and slaves. And she said that we had no business to forget this and pretend that we were all descended from the nobility and gentry and college graduates. She even went so far as to say that cranks and prostitutes and plain fools had a hand in making this republic, and that the real glory of America was what it proved as to the possibilities of commonplace people and that the hope of the future lay right in these every-day people.

It was the truth and I knew it and so did all of us, but, of course, we didn't dare to let on to each other, much less to her. So I just kept staring out the window and she laid aside her essay and began to talk. She handed to the Negro, music, painting, sculpture, drama, dancing, poetry and letters. She named a lot of people I never heard of; and others like Dunbar and Braithwaite and Chesnutt, but I had always thought they were white. She reminded us of Bert Williams and told us of some fellows named Aldridge and Gilpin.

And then she got on our nerves. She said all this writing and doing beautiful things hurt. That it was born of suffering. That sometimes the pain blurred the message, but that the blood and crying (Continued on page 710)

By *Winold Reiss*

PAUL   ROBESON

130

Youth Speaks

E might know the future but for our chronic tendency to turn to age rather than to youth for the forecast. And when youth speaks, the future listens, however the present may shut its ears. Here we have Negro youth, foretelling in the mirror of art what we must see and recognize in the streets of reality tomorrow.

Primarily, of course, it is youth that speaks in the voice of Negro youth, but the overtones are distinctive; Negro youth speaks out of an unique experience and with a particular representativeness. All classes of a people under social pressure are permeated with a common experience; they are emotionally welded as others cannot be. With them, even ordinary living has epic depth and lyric intensity, and this, their material handicap, is their spiritual advantage. So, in a day when art has run to classes, cliques and coteries, and life lacks more and more a vital common background, the Negro artist, out of the depths of his group and personal experience, has to his hand almost the conditions of a classical art.

Negro genius today relies upon the race-gift as a vast spiritual endowment from which our best developments have come and must come. Racial expression as a conscious motive, it is true, is fading out of our latest art, but just as surely the age of truer, finer group expression is coming in—for race expression does not need to be deliberate to be vital. Indeed at its best it never is. This was the case with our instinctive and quite matchless folk-art, and begins to be the same again as we approach cultural maturity in a phase of art that promises now to be fully representative. The interval between has been an awkward age, where from the anxious desire and attempt to be representative much that was really unrepresentative has come; we have lately had an art that was stiltedly self-conscious, and racially rhetorical rather than racially expressive. Our poets have now stopped speaking for the Negro—they speak as Negroes. Where formerly they spoke to others and tried to interpret, they now speak to their own and try to express. They have stopped posing, being nearer to the attainment of poise.

The younger generation has thus achieved an objective attitude toward life. Race for them is but an idiom of experience, a sort of added enriching adventure and discipline, giving subtler overtones to life, making it more beautiful and interesting, even if more poignantly so. So experienced, it affords a deepening rather than a narrowing of social vision. The artistic problem of the Young Negro has not been so much that of acquiring the outer mastery of form and technique as that of achieving an inner mastery of mood and spirit. That accomplished, there has come the happy release from self-consciousness, rhetoric, bombast, and the hampering habit of setting artistic values with primary regard for moral effect—all those pathetic over-compensations of a group inferiority complex which our social dilemmas inflicted upon several unhappy generations. Our poets no

longer have the hard choice between an over-assertive and appealing attitude. By the same effort, they have shaken themselves free from the minstrel tradition and the fowling-nets of dialect, and through acquiring ease and simplicity in serious expression, have carried the folk-gift to the altitudes of art. There they seek and find art's intrinsic values and satisfactions—and if America were deaf, they would still sing.

But America listens—perhaps in curiosity at first; later, we may be sure, in understanding. But—a moment of patience. The generation now in the artistic vanguard inherits the fine and dearly bought achievement of another generation of creative workmen who have been pioneers and path-breakers in the cultural development and recognition of the Negro in the arts. Though still in their prime, as veterans of a hard struggle, they must have the praise and gratitude that is due them. We have had, in fiction, Chestnutt and Burghardt Du Bois; in drama, Du Bois again and Angelina Grimke; in poetry Dunbar, James Weldon Johnson, Fenton and Charles Bertram Johnson, Everett Hawkins, Lucien Watkins, Cotter, Jameson; and in another file of poets, Miss Grimke, Anne Spencer, and Georgia Douglas Johnson; in criticism and *belles lettres*, Braithwaite and Dr. Du Bois; in painting, Tanner and Scott; in sculpture, Meta Warrick and May Jackson; in acting Gilpin and Robeson; in music, Burleigh. Nor must the fine collaboration of white American artists be omitted; the work of Ridgeley Torrence and Eugene O'Neill in drama, of Stribling, and Shands and Clement Wood in fiction, all of which has helped in the bringing of the materials of Negro life out of the shambles of conventional polemics, cheap romance and journalism into the domain of pure and unbiassed art. Then, rich in this legacy, but richer still, I think, in their own endowment of talent, comes the youngest generation of our Afro-American culture: in music, Diton, Dett, Grant Still, and Roland Hayes; in fiction, Jessie Fauset, Walter White, Claude McKay (a forthcoming book); in drama, Willis Richardson; in the field of the short story, Jean Toomer, Eric Walrond, Rudolf Fisher; and finally a vivid galaxy of young Negro poets, McKay, Jean Toomer, Langston Hughes and Countée Cullen.

These constitute a new generation not because of years only, but because of a new aesthetic and a new philosophy of life. They have all swung above the horizon in the last three years, and we can say without disparagement of the past that in that short space of time they have gained collectively from publishers, editors, critics and the general public more recognition than has ever before come to Negro creative artists in an entire working lifetime. First novels of unquestioned distinction, first acceptances by premier journals whose pages are the ambition of veteran craftsmen, international acclaim, the conquest for us of new provinces of art, the development for the first time among us of literary coteries and channels for the contact of creative

659

minds, and most important of all, a spiritual quickening and racial leavening such as no generation has yet felt and known. It has been their achievement also to bring the artistic advance of the Negro sharply into stepping alignment with contemporary artistic thought, mood and style. They are thoroughly modern, some of them ultra-modern, and Negro thoughts now wear the uniform of the age.

But for all that, the heart beats a little differently. Toomer gives a folk-lilt and ecstasy to the prose of the American modernists. McKay adds Aesop and irony to the social novel and a peasant clarity and naïveté to lyric thought, Fisher adds Uncle Remus to the art of Maupassant and O. Henry. Hughes puts Biblical fervor into free verse, Hayes carries the gush and depth of folk-song to the old masters, Cullen blends the simple with the sophisticated and puts the vineyards themselves into his crystal goblets. There is in all the marriage of a fresh emotional endowment with the finest niceties of art. Here for the enrichment of American and modern art, among our contemporaries, in a people who still have the ancient key, are some of the things we thought culture had forever lost. Art cannot disdain the gift of a natural irony, of a transfiguring imagination, of rhapsodic Biblical speech, of dynamic musical swing, of cosmic emotion such as only the gifted pagans knew, of a return to nature, not by way of the forced and worn formula of Romanticism, but through the closeness of an imagination that has never broken kinship with nature. Art must accept such gifts, and revaluate the giver.

Not all the new art is in the field of pure art values.

There is poetry of sturdy social protest, and fiction of calm, dispassionate social analysis. But reason and realism have cured us of sentimentality: instead of the wail and appeal, there is challenge and indictment. Satire is just beneath the surface of our latest prose, and tonic irony has come into our poetic wells. These are good medicines for the common mind, for us they are necessary antidotes against social poison. Their influence means that at least for us the worst symptoms of the social distemper are passing. And so the social promise of our recent art is as great as the artistic. It has brought with it, first of all, that wholesome, welcome virtue of finding beauty in oneself; the younger generation can no longer be twitted as "cultural nondescripts" or accused of "being out of love with their own nativity." They have instinctive love and pride of race, and, spiritually compensating for the present lacks of America, ardent respect and love for Africa, the motherland. Gradually too under some spiritualizing reaction, the brands and wounds of social persecution are becoming the proud stigmata of spiritual immunity and moral victory. Already enough progress has been made in this direction so that it is no longer true that the Negro mind is too engulfed in its own social dilemmas for control of the necessary perspective of art, or too depressed to attain the full horizons of self and social criticism. Indeed, by the evidence and promise of the cultured few, we are at last spiritually free, and offer through art an emancipating vision to America. But it is a presumption to speak further for those who have spoken and can speak so adequately for themselves.

A. L.

Harlem Life

Seven Poems by COUNTEE CULLEN

Harlem Wine

This is not water running here,
These thick rebellious streams
That hurtle flesh and bone past fear
Down alleyways of dreams.

This is a wine that must flow on
Not caring how or where,
So it has ways to flow upon
Where song is in the air.

So it can woo an artful flute
With loose, elastic lips,
Its measurement of joy compute
With blithe, ecstatic hips.

To a Brown Girl

What if his glance is bold and free,
His mouth the lash of whips?
So should the eyes of lovers be,
And so a lovers lips.

What if no puritanic strain
Confines him to the nice?
He will not pass this way again
Nor hunger for you twice.

Since in the end consort together
Magdalen and Mary,
Youth is the time for careless weather;
Later, lass, be wary.

Tableau

Locked arm in arm they cross the way,
The black boy and the white,
The golden splendor of the day,
The sable pride of night.

From lowered blinds the dark folk stare
And here the fair folk talk,
Indignant that these two should dare
In unison to walk.

Oblivious to look and word
They pass, and see no wonder
That lightning brilliant as a sword
Should blaze the path of thunder.

To a Brown Boy

That brown girl's swagger gives a twitch
To beauty like a queen;
Lad, never dam your body's itch
When loveliness is seen.

For there is ample room for bliss
In pride in clean, brown limbs,
And lips know better how to kiss
Than how to raise white hymns.

And when your body's death gives birth
To soil for spring to crown,
Men will not ask if that rare earth
Was white flesh once, or brown.

—From *The Bookman*

She of the Dancing Feet Sings

And what would I do in heaven, pray,
Me with my dancing feet,
And limbs like apple boughs that sway
When the gusty rain winds beat?

And how would I thrive in a perfect place
Where dancing would be sin,
With not a man to love my face,
Nor an arm to hold me in?

The seraphs and the cherubim
Would be too proud to bend
To sing the faery tunes that brim
My heart from end to end.

The wistful angels down in hell
Will smile to see my face,
And understand, because they fell
From that all-perfect place.

In Memory of Col. Charles Young

Along the shore the tall, thin grass
That fringes that dark river,
While sinuously soft feet pass,
Begins to bleed and quiver.

The great dark voice breaks with a sob
Across the womb of night;
Above your grave the tom-toms throb,
And the hills are weird with light.

The great dark heart is like a well
Drained bitter by the sky,
And all the honeyed lies they tell
Come there to thirst and die.
No lie is strong enough to kill
The roots that work below;
From your rich dust and slaughtered will
A tree with tongues will grow.

A Brown Girl Dead

With two white roses on her breasts,
White candles at head and feet,
Dark Madonna of the grave she rests;
Lord Death has found her sweet.

Her mother pawned her wedding ring
To lay her out in white;
he'd be so proud she'd dance and sing
To see herself tonight.

Lady, Lady

By ANNE SPENCER

Lady, Lady, I saw your face,
Dark as night withholding a star. . .
The chisel fell, or it might have been
You had borne so long the yoke of men.
Lady, Lady, I saw your hands,
Twisted, awry, like crumpled roots,
Bleached poor white in a sudsy tub,
Wrinkled and drawn from your rub-a-dub.
Lady, Lady I saw your heart,
And altared there in its darksome place
Were the tongues of flame the ancients knew,
Where the good God sits to spangle through.

The Black Finger

By ANGELINA GRIMKE

I have just seen a most beautiful thing
Slim and still,
Against a gold, gold sky,
A straight black cypress,
Sensitive,
Exquisite,
A black finger
Pointing upwards.
Why, beautiful still finger, are you black?
And why are you pointing upwards?
—From Opportunity

133

Poems

By CLAUDE McKAY

Like a Strong Tree

Like a strong tree that in the virgin earth
Sends far its roots through rock and loam and clay,
And proudly thrives in rain or time of dearth,
When the dry waves scare rainy sprites away;
Like a strong tree that reaches down, deep, deep,
For sunken water, fluid underground,
Where the great-ringed unsightly blind worms creep,
And queer things of the nether world abound:

So would I live in rich imperial growth,
Touching the surface and the depth of things,
Instinctively responsive unto both,
Tasting the sweets of being and the stings,
Sensing the subtle spell of changing forms,
Like a strong tree against a thousand storms.

Russian Cathedral

Bow down my soul in worship very low
And in the holy silences be lost.
Bow down before the marble man of woe,
Bow down before the singing angel host.
What jewelled glory fills my spirit's eye!
What golden grandeur moves the depths of me!
The soaring arches lift me up on high
Taking my breath with their rare symmetry.

Bow down my soul and let the wondrous light
Of Beauty bathe thee from her lofty throne
Bow down before the wonder of man's might.
Bow down in worship, humble and alone;
Bow lowly down before the sacred sight
Of man's divinity alive in stone.

White Houses

Your door is shut against my tightened face,
And I am sharp as steel with discontent;
But I possess the courage and the grace
To bear my anger proudly and unbent.
The pavement slabs burn loose beneath my feet,
A chafing savage, down the decent street,
And passion rends my vitals as I pass,
Where boldly shines your shuttered door of glass.
Oh I must search for wisdom every hour,
Deep in my wrathful bosom sore and raw,
And find in it the superhuman power
To hold me to the letter of your law!
Oh I must keep my heart inviolate
Against the potent poison of your hate.

Song of the Son

By JEAN TOOMER

Pour, O pour that parting soul in song,
O pour it in the saw-dust glow of night,
Into the velvet pine-smoke air tonight,
And let the valley carry it along,
And let the valley carry it along.
O land and soil, red soil and sweet-gum tree,
So scant of grass, so profligate of pines,
Now just before an epoch's sun declines
Thy son, I have in time returned to thee,
Thy son, I have in time returned to thee.
In time, although the sun is setting on
A song-lit race of slaves, it has not set;
Though late, O soil, it is not too late yet
To catch thy plaintive soul, leaving, soon gone,
Leaving, to catch thy plaintive soul soon gone.
O Negro slaves, dark purple ripened plums,
Squeezed, and bursting in the pine-wood air,
Passing, before they strip the old tree bare
One plum was saved for me, one seed becomes
An everlasting song, a singing tree,
Caroling softly souls of slavery,
What they were, and what they are to me,
Caroling softly souls of slavery.

—*From "Cane", Boni and Liveright*

662

134

Poems

By LANGSTON HUGHES

Poem

We have to-morrow
Bright before us
Like a flame

Yesterday, a night-gone thing
A sun-down name

And dawn to-day
Broad arch above the road we came,
We march.

—From The Crisis

Song

Lovely, dark, and lonely one
Bare your bosom to the sun
Do not be afraid of light
You who are a child of night.

Open wide your arms to life
Whirl in the wind of pain and strife
Face the wall with the dark closed gate
Beat with bare, brown fists
And wait.

Dream Variation

To fling my arms wide
In some place of the sun,
To whirl and to dance
Till the bright day is done.
Then rest at cool evening
Beneath a tall tree
While night comes gently
Dark like me.
That is my dream.
To fling my arms wide
In the face of the sun.
Dance! Whirl! Whirl!
Till the quick day is done.
Rest at pale evening,
A tall, slim tree,
Night coming tenderly
Black like me.

The Dream Keeper

Bring me all of your dreams
You dreamers.
Bring me all of your
Heart melodies.
That I may wrap them
In a blue cloud-cloth
Away from the too rough fingers
Of the world.

Poem

Being walkers with the dawn and morning,
Walkers with the sun and morning,
We are not afraid of night,
Nor days of gloom,
Nor darkness,
Being walkers with the sun and morning.

Sea Charm

Sea charm
The sea's own children
Do not understand.
They know
But that the sea is strong
Like God's hand.
They know
But that sea wind is sweet
Like God's breath
And that the sea holds
A wide, deep death.

An Earth Song

It's an earth song,—
And I've been waiting long for an earth song.
It's a spring song,—
And I've been waiting long for a spring song.
   Strong as the shoots of a new plant
   Strong as the bursting of new buds
   Strong as the coming of the first child from its mother's
      womb.
It's an earth song,
A body-song,
A spring-song,
I have been waiting long for this spring song.

DAWN IN HARLEM

A phantasy by Winold Reiss

Jazz at Home

By J. A. ROGERS

JAZZ is a marvel of paradox: too fundamentally human, at least as modern humanity goes, to be typically racial, too international to be characteristically national, too much abroad in the world to have a special home. And yet jazz in spite of it all is one part American and three parts American Negro, and was originally the nobody's child of the levee and the city slum. Transplanted exotic—a rather hardy one, we admit—of the mundane world capitals, sport of the sophisticated, it is really at home in its humble native soil wherever the modern unsophisticated Negro feels happy and sings and dances to his mood. It follows that jazz is more at home in Harlem than in Paris, though from the look and sound of certain quarters of Paris one would hardly think so. It is just the epidemic contagiousness of jazz that makes it, like the measles, sweep the block. But somebody had to have it first: that was the Negro.

What after all is this taking new thing, that, condemned in certain quarters, enthusiastically welcomed in others, has nonchalantly gone on until it ranks with the movie and the dollar as the foremost exponent of modern Americanism? Jazz isn't music merely, it is a spirit that can express itself in almost anything. The true spirit of jazz is a joyous revolt from convention, custom, authority, boredom, even sorrow—from everything that would confine the soul of man and hinder its riding free on the air. The Negroes who invented it called their songs the "Blues," and they weren't capable of satire or deception. Jazz was their explosive attempt to cast off the blues and be happy, carefree happy even in the midst of sordidness and sorrow. And that is why it has been such a balm for modern ennui, and has become a safety valve for modern machine-ridden and convention-bound society. It is the revolt of the emotions against repression.

The story is told of the clever group of "jazz-specialists" who, originating dear knows in what scattered places, had found themselves and the frills of the art in New York and had been drawn to the gay Bohemias of Paris. In a little cabaret of Montmartre they had just "entertained" into the wee small hours fascinated society and royalty; and, of course, had been paid royally for it. Then, the entertainment over and the guests away, the "entertainers" entertained themselves with their very best, which is always impromptu, for the sheer joy of it. That is jazz.

In its elementals, jazz has always existed. It is in the Indian war-dance, the Highland fling, the Irish jig, the Cossack dance, the Spanish fandango, the Brazilian *maxixe,* the dance of the whirling dervish, the hula hula of the South Seas, the *danse du ventre* of the Orient, the *carmagnole* of the French Revolution, the strains of Gypsy music, and the ragtime of the Negro. Jazz proper, however, is something more than all these. It is a release of all the suppressed emotions at once, a blowing off of the lid, as it were. It is hilarity expressing itself through pandemonium; musical fireworks.

The direct predecessor of jazz is ragtime. That both are atavistically African there is little doubt, but to what extent it is difficult to determine. In its barbaric rhythm and exuberance there is something óf the bamboula, a wild, abandoned dance of the West African and the Haytian Negro, so stirringly described by the anonymous author of Untrodden Fields of Anthropology, or of the *ganza* ceremony so brilliantly depicted in Maran's Batouala. But jazz time is faster and more complex than African music. With its cowbells, auto horns, calliopes, rattles, dinner gongs, kitchen utensils, cymbals, screams, crashes, clankings and monotonous rhythm it bears all the marks of a nerve-strung, strident, mechanized civilization. It is a thing of the jungles—modern man-made jungles.

The earliest jazz-makers were the itinerant piano players who would wander up and down the Mississippi from saloon to saloon, from dive to dive. Seated at the piano with a carefree air that a king might envy, their box-back coats flowing over the stool, their Stetsons pulled well over their eyes, and cigars at an angle of forty-five degrees, they would "whip the ivories" to marvellous chords and hidden racy, joyous meanings, evoking the intense delight of their hearers who would smother them at the close with huzzas and whiskey. Often wholly illiterate, these humble troubadours knowing nothing of written music or composition, but with minds like cameras, would listen to the rude improvisations of the dock laborers and the railroad gangs and reproduce them, reflecting perfectly the sentiments and the longings of these humble folk. The improvised bands at Negro dances in the South, or the little boys with their harmonicas and jews-harps each one putting his own individuality into the air, played also no inconsiderable part in its evolution. "Poverty," says J. A. Jackson of the Billboard, "compelled improvised instruments. Bones, tambourines, make-shift string instruments, tin can and hollow wood effects, all now utilized as musical novelties, were among early Negroes the product of necessity. When these were not available 'patting juba' prevailed. Present day 'Charleston' is but a variation of this. Its early expression was the 'patting' for the buck dance."

Jazzonia

By LANGSTON HUGHES

O, silver tree!
Oh, shining rivers of the soul!

In a Harlem cabaret
Six long-headed jazzers play.
A dancing girl whose eyes are bold
Lifts high a dress of silken gold.

Oh, singing tree!
Oh, shining rivers of the soul!

Were Eve's eyes
In the first garden
Just a bit too bold?
Was Cleopatra gorgeous
In a gown of gold?

Oh, shining tree!
Oh, silver rivers of the soul!

In a whirling cabaret
Six long-headed jazzers play.
—*From The Crisis*

665

The origin of the present jazz craze is interesting. More cities claim its birthplace than claimed Homer dead. New Orleans, San Francisco, Memphis, Chicago, all assert the honor is theirs. Jazz, as it is today, seems to have come into being this way, however: W. C. Handy, a Negro, having digested the airs of the itinerant musicians referred to, evolved the first classic, the Memphis Blues. Then came Jasbo Brown, a reckless musician of a Negro cabaret in Chicago, who played this and other blues, blowing his own extravagant moods and risqué interpretations into them, while hilarious with gin. To give further meanings to his veiled allusions he would make the trombone "talk" by putting a derby hat and later a tin can at its mouth. The delighted patrons would shout, "More, Jasbo. More, Jas, more." And so the name originated.

As to the jazz dance itself: at this time Shelton Brooks, a Negro comedian, invented a new "strut," called Walkin' the Dog. Jasbo's anarchic airs found in this strut a soul mate. Then as a result of their union came The Texas Tommy, the highest point of brilliant, acrobatic execution and nifty footwork so far evolved in jazz dancing. The latest of these dances is the Charleston, which has brought something really new to the dance step. The Charleston calls for activity of the whole body. One characteristic is a fantastic fling of the legs from the hip downwards. The dance ends in what is known as the "camel-walk"—in reality a gorilla-like shamble—and finishes with a peculiar hop like that of the Indian war dance. Imagine one suffering from a fit

Two Drawings by Winold Reiss

of rhythmic ague and you have the effect precisely.

The cleverest Charleston dancers perhaps are urchins of five and six who may be seen any time on the streets of Harlem, keeping time with their hands, and surrounded by admiring crowds. But put it on a well-set stage, danced by a bobbed-hair chorus, and you have an effect that reminds you of the abandon of the Furies. And so Broadway studies Harlem. Not all of the visitors of the twenty or more well-attended cabarets of Harlem are idle pleasure seekers or underworld devotees. Many are serious artists, actors and producers seeking something new, some suggestion to be taken, too often in pallid imitation, to Broadway's lights and stars.

This makes it difficult to say whether jazz is more characteristic of the Negro or of contemporary America. As was shown, it is of Negro origin plus the influence of the American environment. It is Negro-American. Jazz proper however is in idiom—rhythmic, musical and pantomimic— thoroughly American Negro; it is his spiritual picture on that lighter comedy side, just as the spirituals are the picture on the tragedy side. The two are poles apart, but the former is by no means to be despised and it is just as characteristically the product of the peculiar and unique experi-

ence of the Negro in this country. The African Negro hasn't it, and the Caucasian never could have invented it Once achieved, it is common property, and jazz has absorbed the national spirit, that tremendous spirit of go, the nervous ness, lack of conventionality and boisterous good-nature characteristic of the American, white or black, as compared with the more rigid formal natures of the Englishman or German.

But there still remains something elusive about jazz tha few, if any, of the white artists, have been able to capture The Negro is admittedly its best expositor. That elusiv something, for lack of a better name, I'll call Negr rhythm. The average Negro, particularly of the lowe classes, puts rhythm into whatever he does, whether it be shining shoes or carrying a basket on the head to marke as the Jamaican women do. Some years ago while wander ing in Cincinnati I happened upon a Negro revival meeting at its height. The majority present were women, a goodl few of whom were white. Under the influence of the "spirit" the sisters would come forward and strut—much o jazz enters where it would be least expected. The Negr women had the perfect jazz abandon, while the white ones moved lamely and woodenly. This same lack of spontaneity

Interpretations of Harlem Jazz

Jazz has come to stay because it is an expression of the times, of the breathless, energetic, superactive times in which we are living, it is useless to fight against it. Already its new vigor, its new vitality is beginning to manifest itself. . . . America's contribution to the music of the past will have the same revivifying effect as the injection of new, and in the larger sense, vulgar blood into dying aristocracy. Music will then be vulgarized in the best sense of the word, and enter more and more into the daily lives of people. . . . The Negro musicians of America are playing a great part in this change. They have an open mind, and unbiassed outlook. They are not hampered by conventions or traditions, and with their new ideas, their constant experiment, they are causing new blood to flow in the veins of music. The jazz players make their instruments do entirely new things, things finished musicians are taught to avoid. They are pathfinders into new realms.

And thus it has come about that serious modernistic music and musicians, most notably and avowedly in the work of the French modernists Auric, Satie and Darius Milhaud, have become the confessed debtors of American Negro jazz. With the same nonchalance and impudence with which it left the levee and the dive to stride like an upstart conqueror, almost overnight, into the grand salon, jazz now begins its conquest of musical Parnassus.

Whatever the ultimate result of the attempt to raise jazz from the mob-level upon which it originated, its true home is still its original cradle, the none too respectable cabaret. And here we have the seamy side to the story. Here we have some of the charm of Bohemia, but much more of the demoralization of vice. Its rash spirit is in Grey's popular song,

is evident to a degree in the cultivated and inhibited Negro. Musically jazz has a great future. It is rapidly being sublimated. In the more famous jazz orchestras like those of Will Marion Cook, Paul Whiteman, Sissle and Blake, Sam Stewart, Fletcher Henderson, Vincent Lopez and the Clef Club units, there are none of the vulgarities and crudities of the lowly origin or the only too prevalent cheap imitations. The pioneer work in the artistic development of jazz was done by Negro artists; it was the lead of the so-called "syncopated orchestras" of Tyers and Will Marion Cook, the former playing for the Castles of dancing fame, and the latter touring as a concertizing orchestra in the great American centers and abroad. Because of the difficulties of financial backing, these expert combinations have had to yield ground to white orchestras of the type of the Paul Whiteman and Vincent Lopez organizations that are now demonstrating the finer possibilities of jazz music. "Jazz," says Serge Koussevitzy, the new conductor of the Boston Symphony, "is an important contribution to modern musical literature. It has an epochal significance—it is not superficial, it is fundamental. Jazz comes from the soil, where all music has its beginning." And Stokowski says more extendedly of it:

Runnin' Wild:

Runnin' wild; lost control
Runnin' wild; mighty bold,
Feelin' gay and reckless too
Carefree all the time; never blue
Always goin' I don't know where
Always showin' that I don't care
Don' love nobody, it ain't worth while
All alone; runnin' wild.

Jazz reached the height of its vogue at a time when minds were reacting from the horrors and strain of war. Humanity welcomed it because in its fresh joyousness men found a temporary forgetfulness, infinitely less harmful than drugs or alcohol. It is partly for some such reasons that it dominates the amusement life of America today. No one can sensibly condone its excesses or minimize its social danger if uncontrolled; all culture is built upon inhibitions and control. But it is doubtful whether the "jazz-hounds" of high and low estate would use their time to better advantage. In all probability their tastes would find some equally morbid, mischievous vent. Jazz, it is needless to say, will remain a recreation for the industrious and a dissipator of energy for the frivolous, a tonic for the strong and a poison for the weak. (*Continued on page* 712)

Negro Art and America

By ALBERT C. BARNES

THAT there should have developed a distinctively Negro art in America was natural and inevitable. A primitive race, transported into an Anglo-Saxon environment and held in subjection to that fundamentally alien influence, was bound to undergo the soul-stirring experiences which always find their expression in great art. The contributions of the American Negro to art are representative because they come from the hearts of the masses of a people held together by like yearnings and stirred by the same causes. It is a sound art because it comes from a primitive nature upon which a white man's education has never been harnessed. It is a great art because it embodies the Negroes' individual traits and reflects their suffering, aspirations and joys during a long period of acute oppression and distress.

The most important element to be considered is the psychological complexion of the Negro as he inherited it from his primitive ancestors and which he maintains to this day. The outstanding characteristics are his tremendous emotional endowment, his luxuriant and free imagination and a truly great power of individual expression. He has in superlative measure that fire and light which, coming from within, bathes his whole world, colors his images and impels him to expression. The Negro is a poet by birth. In the masses, that poetry expresses itself in religion which acquires a distinction by extraordinary fervor, by simple and picturesque rituals and by a surrender to emotion so complete that ecstasy, amounting to automatisms, is the rule when he worships in groups. The outburst may be started by any unlettered person provided with the average Negro's normal endowment of eloquence and vivid imagery. It begins with a song or a wail which spreads like fire and soon becomes a spectacle of a harmony of rhythmic movement and rhythmic sound unequalled in the ceremonies of any other race. Poetry is religion brought down to earth and it is of the essence of the Negro soul. He carries it with him always and everywhere; he lives it in the field, the shop, the factory. His daily habits of thought, speech and movement are flavored with the picturesque, the rhythmic, the euphonious.

The white man in the mass cannot compete with the Negro in spiritual endowment. Many centuries of civilization have attenuated his original gifts and have made his mind dominate his spirit. He has wandered too far from the elementary human needs and their easy means of natural satisfaction. The deep and satisfying harmony which the soul requires no longer arises from the incidents of daily life. The requirements for practical efficiency in a world alien to his spirit have worn thin his religion and devitalized his art. His art and his life are no longer one and the same as they were in primitive man. Art has become exotic, a thing apart, an indulgence, a something to be possessed. When art is real and vital it effects the harmony between ourselves and nature which means happiness. Modern life has forced art into being a mere adherent upon the practical affairs of life which offer it no sustenance. The result has been that hopeless confusion of values which mistakes sentimentalism and irrational day-dreaming for art.

The Negro has kept nearer to the ideal of man's harmony with nature and that, his blessing, has made him a vagrant in our arid, practical American life. But his art is so deeply rooted in his nature that it has thrived in a foreign soil where the traditions and practices tend to stamp out and starve out both the plant and its flowers. It has lived because it was an achievement, not an indulgence. It has been his happiness through that mere self-expression which is its own immediate and rich reward. Its power converted adverse material conditions into nutriment for his soul and it made a new world in which his soul has been free. Adversity has always been his lot but he converted it into a thing of beauty in his songs. When he was the abject, down-trodden slave, he burst forth into songs which constitute America's only great music—the spirituals. These wild chants are the natural, naive, untutored, spontaneous utterance of the suffering, yearning, prayerful human soul. In their mighty roll there is a nobility truly superb. Idea and emotion are fused in an art which ranks with the Psalms and the songs of Zion in their compelling, universal appeal.

The emancipation of the Negro slave in America gave him only a nominal freedom. Like all other human beings he is a creature of habits which tie him to his past; equally set are his white brothers' habits toward him. The relationship of master and slave has changed but little in sixty years of freedom. He is still a slave to the ignorance, the prejudice, the cruelty which were the fate of his forefathers. Today he has not yet found a place of equality in the social, educational or industrial world of the white man. But he has the same singing soul as the ancestors who created the single form of great art which America can claim as her own. Of the tremendous growth and prosperity achieved by America since emancipation day, the Negro has had scarcely a pittance. The changed times did, however, give him an opportunity to develop and strengthen the native, indomitable courage and the keen powers of mind which were not suspected during the days of slavery. The character of his song changed under the new civilization and his mental and moral stature now stands measurement with those of the white man of equal educational and civilizing opportunities. That growth he owes chiefly to his own efforts; the attendant strife has left unspoiled his native gift of song. We have in his poetry and music a true, infallible record of what the struggle has meant to his inner life. It is art of which America can well be proud.

The renascence of Negro art is one of the events of our age which no seeker for beauty can afford to overlook. It is as characteristically Negro as are the primitive African sculptures. As art forms, each bears comparison with the great art expressions of any race or civilization. In both ancient and modern Negro art we find a faithful expression of a people and of an epoch in the world's evolution.

668

The Negro renascence dates from about 1895 when two men, Paul Laurence Dunbar and Booker T. Washington, began to attract the world's attention. Dunbar was a poet, Washington an educator in the practical business of life. They lived in widely-distant parts of America, each working independently of the other. The leavening power of each upon the Negro spirit was tremendous; each fitted into and reinforced the other; their combined influences brought to birth a new epoch for the American Negro. Washington showed that by a new kind of education the Negro could attain to an economic condition that enables him to preserve his identity, free his soul and make himself an important factor in American life. Dunbar revealed the virgin field which the Negro's own talents and conditions of life offered for creating new forms of beauty. The race became self-conscious and pride of race supplanted the bitter wail of unjust persecution. The Negro saw and followed the path that was to lead him out of the wilderness and back to his own heritage through the means of his own endowments. Many new poets were discovered, while education had a tremendous quickening. The yield to art was a new expression of Negro genius in a form of poetry which connoisseurs place in the class reserved for the disciplined art of all races. Intellect and culture of a high order became the goals for which they fought, and with a marked degree of success.

Only through bitter and long travail has Negro poetry attained to its present high level as an art form and the struggle has produced much writing which, while less perfect in form, is no less important as poetry. We find nursery rhymes, dances, love-songs, paeans of joy, lamentations, all revealing unerringly the spirit of the race in its varied contacts with life. There has grown a fine tradition which is fundamentally Negro in character. Every phase of that growth in alien surroundings is marked with reflections of the multitudinous vicissitudes that cumbered the path from slavery to culture. Each record is loaded with feeling, powerfully expressed in uniquely Negro forms. The old chants, known as spirituals, were pure soul, their sadness untouched by vindictiveness. After the release from slavery, bitterness crept into their songs. Later, as times changed, we find self-assertion, lofty aspirations and only a scattered cry for vengeance. As he grew in culture, there came expressions of the deep consolation of resignation which is born of the wisdom that the Negro race is its own, all-sufficient justification. Naturally, sadness is the note most often struck; but the frequently-expressed joy, blithesome, carefree, overflowing joy, reveals what an enviable creature the Negro is in his happy moods. No less evident is that native understanding and wisdom which—from the homely and crude expressions of their slaves, to the scholarly and cultured contributions of today—we know go with the Negro's endowment. The black scholar, seer, sage, prophet sings his message; that explains why the Negro tradition is so rich and is so firmly implanted in the soul of the race.

The Negro tradition has been slow in forming but it rests upon the firmest of foundations. Their great men and women of the past—Wheatley, Sojourner Truth, Douglass, Dunbar, Washington—have each laid a personal and imperishable stone in that foundation. A host of living Negroes, better educated and unalterably faithful to their race, are still building, and each with some human value which is an added guarantee that the tradition will be strengthened and made serviceable for the new era that is sure to come when more of the principles of humanity and rationality become the white man's guides. Many living Negroes—Du Bois, Cotter, Grimke, Braithwaite, Burleigh, the Johnsons, Mackay, Dett, Locke, Hayes, and many others —know the Negro soul and lead it to richer fields by their own ideals of culture, art and citizenship. It is a healthy development, free from that pseudo-culture which stifles the soul and misses rational happiness as the goal of human life. Through the compelling powers of his poetry and music the American Negro is revealing to the rest of the world the essential oneness of all human beings.

The cultured white race owes to the soul-expressions of its black brother too many moments of happiness not to acknowledge ungrudgingly the significant fact that what the Negro has achieved is of tremendous civilizing value. We see that in certain qualities of soul essential to happiness our own endowment is comparatively deficient. We have to acknowledge not only that our civilization has done practically nothing to help the Negro create his art but that our unjust oppression has been powerless to prevent the black man from realizing in a rich measure the expressions of his own rare gifts. We have begun to imagine that a better education and a greater social and economic equality for the Negro might produce something of true importance for a richer and fuller American life. The unlettered black singers have taught us to live music that rakes our souls and gives us moments of exquisite joy. The later Negro has made us feel the majesty of Nature, the ineffable peace of the woods and the great open spaces. He has shown us that the events of our every-day American life contain for him a poetry, rhythm and charm which we ourselves had never discovered. Through him we have seen the pathos, comedy, affection, joy of his own daily life, unified into humorous dialect verse or perfected sonnet that is a work of exquisite art. He has taught us to respect the sheer manly greatness of the fibre which has kept his inward light burning with an effulgence that shines through the darkness in which we have tried to keep him. All these visions, and more, he has revealed to us. His insight into realities has been given to us in vivid images loaded with poignancy and passion. His message has been lyrical, rhythmic, colorful. In short, the elements of beauty he has controlled to the ends of art.

THIS mystic whom we have treated as a vagrant has proved his possession of a power to create out of his own soul and our own America, moving beauty of an individual character whose existence we never knew. We are beginning to recognize that what the Negro singers and sages have said is only what the ordinary Negro feels and thinks, in his own measure, every day of his life. We have paid more attention to that every-day Negro and have been surprised to learn that nearly all of his activities are shot through and through with music and poetry. When we take to heart the obvious fact that what our prosaic civilization needs most is precisely the poetry which the average Negro actually lives, it is incredible that we should not offer the consideration which we have consistently denied to him. If at that time, he is the simple, ingenuous, forgiving, good-natured, wise and obliging person that he has been in the past, he may consent to form a working alliance with us for the development of a richer American civilization to which he will contribute his full share.

The Negro Digs Up His Past

By ARTHUR A. SCHOMBURG

HE American Negro must remake his past in order to make his future. Though it is orthodox to think of America as the one country where it is unnecessary to have a past, what is a luxury for the nation as a whole becomes a prime social necessity for the Negro. For him, a group tradition must supply compensation for persecution, and pride of race the antidote for prejudice. History must restore what slavery took away, for it is the social damage of slavery that the present generations must repair and offset. So among the rising democratic millions we find the Negro thinking more collectively, more retrospectively than the rest, and apt out of the very pressure of the present to become the most enthusiastic antiquarian of them all.

Vindicating evidences of individual achievement have as a matter of fact been gathered and treasured for over a century: Abbé Gregoire's liberal-minded book on Negro notables in 1808 was the pioneer effort; it has been followed at intervals by less-known and often less discriminating compendiums of exceptional men and women of African stock, But this sort of thing was on the whole pathetically over-corrective, ridiculously over-laudatory; it was apologetics turned into biography. A true historical sense develops slowly and with difficulty under such circumstances. But today, even if for the ultimate purpose of group justification, history has become less a matter of argument and more a matter of record. There is the definite desire and determination to have a history, well documented, widely known at least within race circles, and administered as a stimulating and inspiring tradition for the coming generations.

Gradually as the study of the Negro's past has come out of the vagaries of rhetoric and propaganda and become systematic and scientific, three outstanding conclusions have been established:

First, that the Negro has been throughout the centuries of controversy an active collaborator, and often a pioneer, in the struggle for his own freedom and advancement. This is true to a degree which makes it the more surprising that it has not been recognized earlier.

Second, that by virtue of their being regarded as something "exceptional," even by friends and well-wishers, Negroes of attainment and genius have been unfairly disassociated from the group, and group credit lost accordingly.

Third, that the remote racial origins of the Negro, far from being what the race and the world have been given to understand, offer a record of creditable group achievement when scientifically viewed, and more important still, that they are of vital general interest because of their bearing upon the beginnings and early development of culture.

With such crucial truths to document and establish, an ounce of fact is worth a pound of controversy. So the Negro historian today digs under the spot where his predecessor stood and argued. Not long ago, the Public Library of Harlem housed a special exhibition of books, pamphlets, prints and old engravings, that simply said, to sceptic and believer alike, to scholar and school-child, to proud black and astonished white, "Here is the evidence." Assembled from the rapidly growing collections of the leading Negro book-collectors and research societies, there were in these cases, materials not only for the first true writing of Negro history, but for the rewriting of many important paragraphs of our common Amer-

From the Schomburg Collection, some of the documentary evidences of early scholarship, progressive group organization, and pioneer social reform

670

can history. Slow though it be, historical truth is no exception to the proverb.

Here among the rarities of early Negro Americana was Jupiter Hammon's Address to the Negroes of the State of New York, edition of 1787, with the first American Negro poet's famous "If we should ever get to Heaven, we shall find nobody to reproach us for being black, or for being slaves." Here was Phillis Wheatley's Mss. poem of 1767 addressed to the students of Harvard, her spirited encomiums upon George Washington and the Revolutionary Cause, and John Marrant's St. John's Day eulogy to the 'Brothers of African Lodge No. 459' delivered at Boston in 1784. Here too were Lemuel Haynes' Vermont commentaries on the American Revolution and his learned sermons to his white congregation in Rutland, Vermont, and the sermons of the year 1808 by the Rev. Absalom Jones of St. Thomas Church, Philadelphia, and Peter Williams of St. Philip's, New York, pioneer Episcopal rectors who spoke out in daring and influential ways on the Abolition of the Slave Trade. Such things and many others are more than mere items of curiosity: they educate any receptive mind.

Reinforcing these were still rarer items of Africana and foreign Negro interest, the volumes of Juan Latino, the best Latinist of Spain in the reign of Philip V, incumbent of the chair of Poetry at the University of Granada, and author of Poems printed Granatae 1573 and a book on the Escurial published 1576; the Latin and Dutch treatises of Jacobus Eliza Capitein, a native of West Coast Africa and graduate of the University of Leyden, Gustavus Vassa's celebrated autobiography that supplied so much of the evidence in 1796 for Granville Sharpe's attack on slavery in the British colonies, Julien Raymond's Paris exposé of the disabilities of the free people of color in the then (1791) French colony of Hayti, and Baron de Vastey's Cry of the Fatherland, the famous polemic by the secretary of Christophe that precipitated the Haytian struggle for independence. The cumulative effect of such evidences of scholarship and moral prowess is too weighty to be dismissed as exceptional.

But weightier surely than any evidence of individual talent and

scholarship could ever be, is the evidence of important collaboration and significant pioneer initiative in social service and reform, in the efforts toward race emancipation, colonization and race betterment. From neglected and rust-spotted pages comes testimony to the black men and women who stood shoulder to shoulder in courage and zeal, and often on a parity of intelligence and public talent, with their notable white benefactors. There was the already cited work of Vassa that aided so materially the efforts of Granville Sharpe, the record of Paul Cuffee, the Negro colonization pioneer, associated so importantly with the establishment of Sierra Leone as a British colony for the occupancy of free people of color in West Africa; the dramatic and history-making exposé of John Baptist Phillips, African graduate of Edinburgh, who compelled through Lord Bathurst in 1824 the enforcement of the articles of capitulation guaranteeing freedom to the blacks of Trinidad. There is the record of the pioneer colonization project of Rev. Daniel Coker in conducting a voyage of ninety expatriates to West Africa in 1820, of the missionary efforts of Samuel Crowther in Sierra Leone, first Anglican bishop of his diocese, and that of the work of John Russwurm, a leader in the work and foundation of the American Colonization Society.

When we consider the facts, certain chapters of American history will have to be reopened. Just as black men were influential factors in the campaign against the slave trade, so they were among the earliest instigators of the abolition movement. Indeed there was a dangerous calm between the agitation for the suppression of the slave trade and the beginning of the campaign for emancipation. During that interval colored men were very influential in arousing the attention of public men who in turn aroused the conscience of the country. Continuously between 1808 and 1845, men like Prince Saunders, Peter Williams, Absalom Jones, Nathaniel Paul, and Bishops Varick and Richard Allen, the founders of the two wings of African Methodism, spoke out with force and initiative, and men like Denmark Vesey (1822), David Walker (1828) and Nat Turner (1831) advocated and organized schemes for direct action. This culminated in the gener-

Marrant's Sermon to the first
Lodge of Negro Masons in 1787

Crummell's early plea for higher education:
"Provide you manlier diet"

The ex-slave turned emancipator:
a not unusual role

ally ignored but important conventions of Free People of Color in New York, Philadelphia and other centers, whose platforms and efforts are to the Negro of as great significance as the nationally cherished memories of Faneuil and Independence Halls. Then with Abolition comes the better documented and more recognized collaboration of Samuel R. Ward, William Wells Brown, Henry Highland Garnett, Martin Delaney, Harriet Tubman, Sojourner Truth, and Frederick Douglass with their great colleagues, Tappan, Phillips, Sumner, Mott, Stowe and Garrison.

But even this latter group who came within the limelight of national and international notice, and thus into open comparison with the best minds of their generation, the public too often regards as a group of inspired illiterates, eloquent echoes of their Abolitionist sponsors. For a true estimate of their ability and scholarship, however, one must go with the antiquarian to the files of the Anglo-African Magazine, where page by page comparisons may be made. Their writings show Douglass, McCune Smith, Wells Brown, Delaney, Wilmot Blyden and Alexander Crummell to have been as scholarly and versatile as any of the noted publicists with whom they were associated. All of them labored internationally in the cause of their fellows; to Scotland, England, France, Germany and Africa, they carried their brilliant offensive of debate and propaganda, and with this came instance upon instance of signal foreign recognition, from academic, scientific, public and official sources. Delaney's Principia of Ethnology won public reception from learned societies, Penington's discourses an honorary doctorate from Heidelberg, Wells Brown's three years mission the entree of the salons of London and Paris, and Douglass' tours receptions second only to Henry Ward Beecher's.

After this great era of public interest and discussion, it was Alexander Crummell, who, with the reaction already setting in, first organized Negro brains defensively through the founding of the American Negro Academy in 1874 at Washington. A New York boy whose zeal for education had suffered a rude shock when refused admission to the Episcopal Seminary by Bishop Onderdonk, he had been befriended by John Jay and sent to Cambridge University, England, for his education and ordination. On his return, he was beset with the idea of promoting race scholarship, and the Academy was the final result. It has continued ever since to be one of the bulwarks of our intellectual life, though unfortunately its members have had to spend too much of their energy and effort answering detractors and disproving popular fallacies. Only gradually have the men of this group been able to work toward pure scholarship. Taking a slightly different start, The Negro Society for Historical Research was later organized in New York, and has succeeded in stimulating the collection from all parts of the world of books and documents dealing with the Negro. It has also brought together for the first time cooperatively in a single society African, West Indian and Afro-American scholars. Direct offshoots of this same effort are the extensive private collections of Henry P. Slaughter of Washington, the Rev. Charles D. Martin of Harlem, of Arthur Schomburg of Brooklyn, and of the late John E. Bruce, who was the enthusiastic and far-seeing pioneer of this movement. Finally and more recently, the Association for the Study of Negro Life and History has extended these efforts into a scientific research project of great achievement and promise. Under the direction of Dr. Carter G. Woodson, it has con-

tinuously maintained for nine years the publication of the learned quarterly, The Journal of Negro History, and with the assistance and recognition of two large educational foundations has maintained research and published valuable monographs in Negro history. Almost keeping pace with the work of scholarship has been the effort to popularize the results, and to place before Negro youth in the schools the true story of race vicissitude, struggle and accomplishment. So that quite largely now the ambition of Negro youth can be nourished on its own milk.

Such work is a far cry from the puerile controversy and petty braggadocio with which the effort for race history first started. But a general as well as a racial lesson has been learned. We seem lately to have come at last to realize what the truly scientific attitude requires, and to see that the race issue has been a plague on both our historical houses, and that history cannot be properly written with either bias or counter-bias. The blatant Caucasian racialist with his theories and assumptions of race superiority and dominance has in turn bred his Ethiopian counterpart—the rash and rabid amateur who has glibly tried to prove half of the world's geniuses to have been Negroes and to trace the pedigree of nineteenth century Americans from the Queen of Sheba. But fortunately today there is on both sides of a really common cause less of the sand of controversy and more of the dust of digging.

Of course, a racial motive remains—legitimately compatible with scientific method and aim. The work our race students now regard as important, they undertake very naturally to overcome in part certain handicaps of disparagement and omission too well-known to particularize. But they do so not merely that we may not wrongfully be deprived of the spiritual nourishment of our cultural past, but also that the full story of human collaboration and interdependence may be told and realized. Especially is this likely to be the effect of the latest and most fascinating of all of the attempts to open up the closed Negro past, namely the important study of African cultural origins and sources. The bigotry of civilization which is the taproot of intellectual prejudice begins far back and must be corrected at its source. Fundamentally it has come about from that depreciation of Africa which has sprung up from ignorance of her true role and position in human history and the early development of culture. The Negro has been a man without a history because he has been considered a man without a worthy culture. But a new notion of the cultural attainment and potentialities of the African stocks has recently come about partly through the corrective influence of the more scientific study of African institutions and early cultural history, partly through growing appreciation of the skill and beauty and in many cases the historical priority of the African native crafts, and finally through the signal recognition which first in France and Germany, but now very generally the astonishing art of the African sculptures has received. Into these fascinating new vistas, with limited horizons lifting in all directions, the mind of the Negro has leapt forward faster than the slow clearings of scholarship will yet safely permit. But there is no doubt that here is a field full of the most intriguing and inspiring possibilities. Already the Negro sees himself against a reclaimed background, in a perspective that will give pride and self-respect ample scope, and make history yield for him the same values that the treasured past of any people affords.

The Art of the Ancestors

FROM one of the best extant collections of African art, that of the Barnes Foundation of Merion, Pennsylvania, come these exemplars of the art of the ancestors. Primitive African wood and bronze sculpture is now universally recognized as "a notable instance of plastic representation." Long after it was known as ethnological material, it was artistically "discovered" and has exerted an important influence upon modernist art, both in France and Germany. Attested influences are to be found in the work of Matisse, Picasso, Modigliani, Archipenko, Lipschitz, Lembruch and others, and in Paris centering around Paul Guillaume, one of its pioneer exponents, a coterie profoundly influenced by the aesthetic of this art has developed.

Masterful over its material, in a powerful simplicity of conception, design and effect, it is evidence of an aesthetic endowment of the highest order. The Negro in his American environment has turned predominantly to the arts of music, the dance, and poetry, an emphasis quite different from that of African culture. But beyond this as evidence of a fundamental artistic bent and versatility, there comes from the consideration of this ancient plastic art another modern and practical possibility and hope, that it may exert upon the artistic development of the American Negro the influence that it has already had upon modern European artists. It may very well be taken as the basis for a characteristic school of expression in the plastic and pictorial arts, and give to us again a renewed mastery of them, a mine of fresh motifs, and a lesson in simplicity and originality of expression. Surely this art, once known and appreciated, can scarcely have less influence upon the blood descendants than upon those who inherit by tradition only. And at the very least, even for those not especially interested in art, it should definitely establish the enlightening fact that the Negro is not a cultural foundling without an inheritance.   A. L.

Dahomey (Bronze)

Soudan-Niger   *Baoule*

Yabouba

145

Heritage

By COUNTÉE CULLEN

WHAT is Africa to me:
Copper sun, a scarlet sea,
Jungle star and jungle track,
Strong bronzed men and regal black
Women from whose loins I sprang
When the birds of Eden sang?
One three centuries removed
From the scenes his fathers loved
Spicy grove and banyan tree,
What is Africa to me?

Africa? A book one thumbs
Listlessly till slumber comes.
Unremembered are her bats
Circling through the night, her cats
Crouching in the river reeds
Stalking gentle food that feeds
By the river brink; no more
Does the bugle-throated roar
Cry that monarch claws have leapt
From the scabbards where they slept.
Silver snakes that once a year
Doff the lovely coats you wear
Seek no covert in your fear
Lest a mortal eye should see:
What's your nakedness to me?

Bushongo

African sculpture

All day long and all night through
One thing only 'I must do
Quench my pride and cool my blood,
Lest I perish in their flood,
Lest a hidden ember set
Timber that I thought was wet
Burning like the dryest flax,
Melting like the merest wax,
Lest the grave restore its dead.
Stubborn heart and rebel head.
Have you not yet realized
You and I are civilized?

So I lie and all day long
Want no sound except the song
Sung by wild barbaric birds
Goading massive jungle herds,
Juggernauts of flesh that pass
Trampling tall defiant grass
Where young forest lovers lie
Plighting troth beneath the sky.

674

146

Ivory Coast—ceremonial mask

My conversion came high-priced.
I belong to Jesus Christ,
Preacher of humility:
Heathen gods are naught to me—
Quaint, outlandish heathen gods
Black men fashion out of rods,
Clay and brittle bits of stone,
In a likeness like their own.

"Father, Son and Holy Ghost"
Do I make an idle boast,
Jesus of the twice turned cheek,
Lamb of God, although I speak
With my mouth, thus, in my heart
Do I not play a double part?
Ever at thy glowing altar
Must my heart grow sick and falter
Wishing He I served were black.
Thinking then it would not lack
Precedent of pain to guide it
Let who would or might deride it;
Surely then this flesh would know
Yours had borne a kindred woe.
Lord, I fashion dark gods, too,
Daring even to give to You
Dark, despairing features where
Crowned with dark rebellious hair,
Patience wavers just so much as
Mortal grief compels, while touches
Faint and slow, of anger, rise
To smitten cheek and weary eyes.

Lord, forgive me if my need
Sometimes shapes a human creed.

So I lie, who always hear
Though I cram against my ear
Both my thumbs, and keep them there,
Great drums beating through the air.
So I lie, whose fount of pride,
Dear distress, and joy allied,
Is my sombre flesh and skin
With the dark blood dammed within.
Thus I lie, and find no peace
Night or day, no slight release
From the unremittant beat
Made by cruel padded feet,
Walking through my body's street.
Up and down they go, and back
Treading out a jungle track.
So I lie, who never quite
Safely sleep from rain at night
While its primal measures drip
Through my body, crying, "Strip!
Doff this new exuberance,
Come and dance the Lover's Dance."
In an old remembered way
Rain works on me night and day.
Though three centuries removed
From the scenes my fathers loved.

Zouenouia

675

147

The Dilemma of Social Pattern

By MELVILLE J. HERSKOVITS

LIMPSES of the whirring cycle of life in Harlem leave the visitor bewildered at its complexity. There is constantly before one the tempting invitation to compare and contrast the life there with that of other communities one has had the opportunity of observing. Should I not find there, if anywhere, the distinctiveness of the Negro, of which I had heard so much? Should I not be able to discover there his ability, of which we are so often told, to produce unique cultural traits, which might be added to the prevailing white culture, and, as well, to note his equally well-advertised inability to grasp the complex civilization of which he constitutes a part?

And so I went, and what I found was churches and schools, club-houses and lodge meeting-places, the library and the newspaper offices and the Y. M. C. A. and busy 135th Street and the hospitals and the social service agencies. I met persons who were lawyers and doctors and editors and writers, who were chauffeurs and peddlers and longshoremen and real estate brokers and capitalists, teachers and nurses and students and waiters and cooks. And all Negroes. Cabarets and theaters, drugstores and restaurants just like those everywhere else. And finally, after a time, it occurred to me that what I was seeing was a community just like any other American community. The same pattern, only a different shade!

Where, then, is the "peculiar" community of which I had heard so much? Is the cultural genius of the Negro, which is supposed to have produced jazz and the spiritual, the West African wood-carving and Bantu legalism, non-existent in this country, after all? To what extent, if any, has this genius developed a culture peculiar to it in America? I did not find it in the great teeming center of Negro life in Harlem, where, if anywhere, it should be found. May it not then be true that the Negro has become acculturated to the prevailing white culture and has developed the patterns of culture typical of American life?

Let us first view the matter historically. In the days after the liberation of the Negroes from slavery, what was more natural than that they should strive to maintain, as nearly as possible, the standards set up by those whom they had been taught to look up to as arbiters—the white group? And we see, on their part, a strong conscious effort to do just this. They went into business and tried to make

Looked at in its externals, Negro life, as reflected in Harlem registers a ready—almost a feverishly rapid—assimilation of American patterns, what Mr. Herskovits calls "complete acculturation." It speaks well both for the Negro and for American standards of living that this is so. Internally, perhaps it is another matter. Does democracy require uniformity? If so, it threatens to be safe, but dull. Social standards must be more or less uniform, but social expressions may be different. Old folkways may not persist, but they may leave a mental trace, subtly recorded in emotional temper and coloring social reactions. In the article which follows this Mr. Bercovici tells of finding, by intuition rather than research, something "unique" in Harlem—back of the external conformity, a race-soul striving for social utterance

sold hair-straightening devices and medicines are a matter of record.

In Harlem we have today, essentially, a typical American community. You may look at the Negroes on the street. As to dress and deportment, do you find any vast difference between them and the whites among whom they carry on their lives? Notice them as they go about their work—they do almost all of the things the whites do, and in much the same way. The popular newspapers in Harlem are not the Negro papers—there is even no Negro daily—but the city newspapers which everyone reads. And there is the same gossipy reason why the Harlemites read their own weeklies as that which causes the inhabitants of Chelsea, of the Bronx, of Putnam, Connecticut, or of West Liberty, Ohio, to read theirs. When we come to the student groups in Harlem, we find that the same process occurs—the general culture-pattern has taken them horse, foot and artillery. Do the whites organize Greek-letter fraternities and sororities in colleges, with pearl-studded pins and "houses"? You will find a number of Negro fraternities and sororities with just the same kind of insignia and "houses." Negro community centers are attached to the more prosperous churches just as the same sort of institutions are connected with white churches. And they do the same sort of things there; you can see swimming and gymnasium classes and sewing classes and nutrition talks and open forums and all the rest of it that we all know so well.

When I visit the Business Men's Association, the difference between this gathering and that of my Rotary Club

money as their white fellows did. They already had adopted the white forms of religious faith and practise, and now they began to borrow lodges and other types of organization. Schools sprang up in which they might learn, not the language and technique of their African ancestors, but that of this country, where they lived. The "respected" members of the community were those who lived upright lives such as the "respected" whites lived—they paid their debts, they walked in the paths of sexual morality according to the general pattern of the prevailing Puritanical culture, and they went to church as was right and proper in every American town. The matter went so far that they attempted to alter their hair to conform to the general style, and the fortunes made by those who

is imperceptible. And on the other end of the economic scale that equally applies to Negro and white, and which prevails all over the country, we find the Socialist and labor groups. True, once in a while an element peculiarly Negro does manifest itself; thus I remember vividly the bitter complaints of one group of motion picture operators at the prejudices which prevent them from enjoying the benefits of the white union. And, of course, you will meet with this sort of thing whenever the stream of Negro life conflicts with the more general pattern of the "color line." But even here I noticed that the *form* of the organization of these men was that assumed by their white fellow-workers, and similarly when I attended a Socialist street-meeting in Harlem, I found that the general economic motif comes in for much more attention than the problems which are of interest to the Negro per se.

Perhaps the most striking example of complete acceptance of the general pattern is in the field of sex relations. I shall never forget the storm of indignation which I aroused among a group of Negro men and women with whom I chanced to be talking on one occasion, when, *a propos* of the question of the treatment of the Negro woman in literature, I inadvertently remarked that even if the sexual looseness generally attributed to her were true, it was nothing of which to be essentially ashamed, since such a refusal to accept the Puritanical modes of procedure generally considered right and proper might contribute a welcome leaven to the conventionality of current sex *mores*. The reaction, prompt and violent, was such as to show with tremendous clarity the complete acculturation of these men and women to the accepted standards of sex behavior. There was not even a shade of doubt but that sexual rigidity is the ultimate ideal of relations between men and women, and certainly there was no more indication of a leaning toward the customs to be found in ancestral Africa than would be found among a group of whites.

Or, let us consider the position of the Negro intellectuals, the writers and artists. The proudest boast of the modern young Negro writer is that he writes of humans, not of Negroes. His literary ideals are not the African folk-tale and conundrum, but the vivid expressionistic style of the day—he seeks to be a writer, not a Negro writer. It was this point, indeed, which was especially stressed at a dinner recently given in New York City for a group of young Negro writers on the occasion of the publication of a novel by one of their number. Member after member of the group stated his position as his own—not Negro as such, but human—another striking example of the process of acculturation.

The problem then may be presented with greater clarity. Does not the Negro have a mode of life that is essentially similar to that of the general community of which he is a part? Or can it be maintained that he possesses a distinctive, inborn cultural genius which manifests itself even in America? To answer this, we must answer an even more basic question: what is cultural genius? For the Negro came to America endowed, as all people are endowed, with a culture, which had been developed by him through long ages in Africa. Was it innate? Or has it been sloughed off, forgotten, in the generations since he was brought into our culture?

To understand the problem with which we are presented, it may be well to consider what this thing, culture, is, and

the extent to which we can say that it falls into patterns. By the word culture, I do not mean the refinements of our particular civilization which the word has come to connote, but simply those elements of the environment which are the handiwork of man himself. Thus, among ourselves, we might consider a spinning machine, or the democratic theory of society, or a fork, or the alphabet as much a cultural fact as a symphonic tone-poem, a novel, or an oil painting.

We may best come to an understanding of culture through a consideration of some of the phases of primitive life, where the forces at work are not overshadowed by the great imponderable fact of dense masses of population. As we look over the world, we see that there is no group of men, however simply they may live their lives, without the thing we call culture. And, what is more important, the culture they possess as the result of their own historical background— is an adult affair, developed through long centuries of trial and error, and something constantly changing. Man, it has been said, is a culture-building animal. And he is nowhere without the particular culture which his group have built. It is true that the kinds of culture which he builds are bewilderingly different—to compare the civilization of the Eskimo, the Australian, the Chinese, the African, and of ourselves leaves the student with a keener sense of their differences, both as to form and complexity, rather than with any feeling of resemblances among them. But one thing they do have in common: the cultures, when viewed from the outside, are stable. In their main elements they go along much as they always have gone, unless some great historical accident (like the discovery of the steam engine in our culture or the intrusion of the Western culture on that of the Japanese or the transplanting of Negro slaves from Africa to America) occurs to upset the trend and to direct the development of the culture along new paths. To the persons within the cultures, however, they seem even more than just stable. They seem fixed, rigid, all-enduring—indeed, they are so taken for granted that, until comparatively recent times, they were never studied at all.

But what is it that makes cultures different? There are those, of course, who will maintain that it is the racial factor. They will say that the bewildering differences between the cultures of the Englishman, the Chinaman, the Bantu and the Maya, for example, are the result of differences in innate racial endowment, and that every race has evolved a culture peculiarly fitted to it. All this sounds very convincing until one tries to define the term "race." Certain anthropologists are trying, even now, to discover criteria which will scientifically define the term "Negro." One of the most distinguished of these, Professor T. Wingate Todd, has been working steadily for some years in the attempt and the net results are certain hypotheses which he himself calls tentative. The efforts of numerous psychological testers to establish racial norms for intelligence are vitiated by the two facts that first, as many of them will admit, it is doubtful just what it is they are testing, and, in the second place, that races are mixed. This is particularly true in the case of the Negroes; in New York City, less than 2 per cent of the group from whom I obtained genealogical material claimed pure Negro ancestry, and while this percentage is undoubtedly low, the fact remains that the vast majority of Negroes in America are of mixed ancestry.

If ability to successfully live in one culture were restricted to persons of one race, how could we account for the fact that we see persons of the most diverse races living together, for example, in this country, quite as though they were naturally endowed with the ability to meet the problems of living here, while again we witness an entire alien people adopting our civilization, to use the Japanese again for illustration?

OUR civilization is what it is because of certain historic events which occurred in the course of its development. So we can also say for the civilization of the African, of the Eskimo, of the Australian. And the people who lived in these civilizations like ourselves, view the things they do—as a result of living in them—not as inbred, but as inborn. To the Negro in Africa, it would be incomprehensible for a man to work at a machine all day for a few bits of paper to be given him at the end of his work-day, and in the same way, the white traveler stigmatizes the African as lazy because he will not see the necessity for entering on a gruelling forced march so as to reach a certain point in a given time. And when we turn to our civilization, we find that it has many culture-patterns, as we may term these methods of behavior. They are ingrained in us through long habituation, and their violation evokes a strong emotional response in us, no matter what our racial background. Thus for a person to eat with a knife in place of a fork, or to go about the streets hatless, or for a woman to wear short dresses when long ones are in fashion, are all violations of the patterns we have been brought up to feel right and proper, and we react violently to them. More serious, for a young man not to "settle down" and make as much money as he can is regarded as bordering on the immoral, while, in the régime of sex, the rigid patterns have been remarked upon, as has been the unmitigated condemnation which the breaking of these taboos calls forth. The examples which I have given above of the reaction of the Negro to the general cultural patterns of this country might be multiplied to include almost as many social facts as are observable, and yet, wherever we might go, we would find the Negro reacting to the same situations in much the same fashion as his white brother.

What, then, is the particular Negro genius for culture? Is there such a thing? Can he contribute something of his vivid, and yet at the same time softly gracious personality to the general culture in which he lives? What there is today in Harlem distinct from the white culture which surrounds it, is, as far as I am able to see, merely a remnant from the peasant days in the South. Of the African culture, not a trace. Even the spirituals are an expression of the emotion of the Negro playing through the typical religious pattern of white America. But from that emotional quality in the Negro, which is to be sensed rather than measured, comes the feeling that, though strongly acculturated to the prevalent pattern of behavior, the Negroes may, at the same time, influence it somewhat eventually through the appeal of that quality.

THAT they have absorbed the culture of America is too obvious, almost, to be mentioned. They have absorbed it as all great racial and social groups in this country have absorbed it. And they face much the same problems as these groups face. The social ostracism to which they are subjected is only different in extent from that to which the Jew is subjected. The fierce reaction of race-pride is quite the same in both groups. But, whether in Negro or in Jew, the protest avails nothing, apparently. All racial and social elements in our population who live here long enough become acculturated, Americanized in the truest sense of the word, eventually. They learn our culture and react according to its patterns, against which all the protestations of the possession of, or of hot desire for, a peculiar culture mean nothing.

As we turn to Harlem we see its social and economic and political makeup a part of the larger whole of the city—separate from it, it is true, but still essentially not different from any other American community in which the modes of life and of action are determined by the great dicta of "what is done." In other words, it represents, as do all American communities which it resembles, a case of complete acculturation. And so, I return again to my reaction on first seeing this center of Negro activity, as the complete description of it: "Why, it's the same pattern, only a different shade!"

Our Land

By LANGSTON HUGHES

Drawings by Winold Reiss

We should have a land of sun,
Of gorgeous sun,
And a land of fragrant water
Where the twilight is a soft bandanna handkerchief
Of rose and gold,
And not this land
Where life is cold.

We should have a land of trees,
Of tall thick trees,
Bowed down with chattering parrots
Brilliant as the day,
And not this land where birds are gray.

Ah, we should have a land of joy,
Of love and joy and wine and song,
And not this land where joy is wrong.

—From *Opportunity*

The Rhythm of Harlem

By KONRAD BERCOVICI

WHEN, in the course of my study of New York City, I visited Harlem, a white and a colored man put the very same question to me, in exactly the same words. They have branded themselves in my memory:

"Why do you go to Harlem? For material?"

And what they meant was: "Would you have developed such an enthusiasm if you did not have to write—or want to write—about Negroes?"

That Harlem was a revelation to me; that I enjoyed its colorfulness and vividness of life as much as I have enjoyed anything in this country, would not have been enough of an answer for either of my interrogators. The colored people did not believe my friendship. The white ones suspected it. The question put to me was the quintessence of the colored man's attitude toward the white man and the white man's attitude toward another white man who shows an interest in the life of the colored people.

I am now, perhaps, better fitted to understand a good many things that happened to me in Harlem. I have been through Louisiana and Tennessee. . . . I understand better the gaze in the eyes of my Negro friends, and the drooping corners of the mouths of the white ones, one sniffing and the other sneering at my interest. It is this suspicion which lives in Harlem, fostered by the years of slavery. It has raised a second wall to surmount; thicker even than the wall the white man has raised between himself and the colored population. Culture, friendship may after all be unable to break these walls down.

The white man does not believe that the Christian Negro, praying in a Christian church, to the Christian God, is entitled to do so. Does he believe that his God is listening to the Negroes' prayers? The colored man thinks that praying in a Christian church to a Christian God in a Christian language entitles him to the white God's mercy and to equality. I wondered and still wonder why the colored people have not evolved a religion of their own, a church of their own and a God of their own.

AN awakened consciousness of race stirs Harlem. Backs are straightened out and heads are raised. Eyes look to their own level when they seek those of other people. The feeling is still one of being better than thou, but underneath that, it seemed to me, there was a striving for another culture that was not an imitative one. Surely greater difficulties beset this undercurrent than one would casually think. The greatest of them all is the one of language. For in the same word-figures one limits himself to the same thought as the others using similar word-figures. At bottom, the white man's feeling of superiority is based on the fact that the Negroes have no language of their own. Had they preserved their African tongue it would have been different. "We are as good and as bad as the white man, neither better nor worse" is the feeling of Harlem. It is not the winning attitude for a people so different! Different from

the whites would be the right starting point for a new culture. For the few hundred thousand Negroes in Harlem will ultimately be to the colored race living in the United States the intellectual center from which its culture will emanate. To pile up wealth as the white man has done will not further them. To pile up industrial organizations, institutions, universities, charities and armies will not do it. A different culture, a different music, a different art, of which the Negroes are capable and which should be like a gift to the races they live with, will do it.

They are not inferiors. They do not have to strive for equality. They are different. Emphasizing that difference in their lives, in their culture, is what will give them and what should give them their value. They should take a leaf out of the race life of the Jews. The Jews have maintained their racial entity by being different. Where and when they have ceased to do so, they have ceased to exist as such without in any way changing the attitude of their neighbors. Quite the opposite. The non-Jew is less friendly to the unorthodox than to the orthodox Jew.

I LISTENED to the preachers in the churches of Harlem. I understood the language. But was there not something unsaid in the preachment? Was the preacher, the minister, not fashioning another God for himself and for his congregation while he spoke? It seemed impossible that they should all be serving the same one.

I went to the theater. Colored actors were playing a play of colored people. And there, too, the whole thing seemed to me a translation from an unspoken language lying dormant in the souls of the people, which they had forgotten and yet translated from. The color of the voice, the tone, the rhythm, the music of the phrase was something peculiarly their own. Beautiful? Yes. But different. The words never meant anything to me. There was another medium of communication. Words of another language should have gone with that music, with that rhythm, with that cadence. The thought process that animated them was so different it required another medium than the one used.

I have heard their music and I have seen their dances. Beautiful? Yes. But how totally unlike the music of the rest of the people, and the dance of the rest of the people. I was a stranger to it. It was a stranger to me. We remained strangers.

I have heard Harlem men planning business, planning politics, speaking of life and death. And in all of this, though the surface was clear and understandable, there was another element under the surface, hardly hinted at in the words spoken.

Long after the white people have ceased, if they ever do cease, to have any feeling of superiority toward the colored race, there will still remain that feeling of essential difference. It is up to the colored people to direct their creative thought into such channels as will give them a distinctive superiority. Only then will one's friendship be neither suspected nor reproached.

Color Lines

By WALTER F. WHITE

HE hushed tense-ness within the theatre was brok-en only by the excited chattering between the scenes which served as oases of relief. One reassured himself by touching his neighbor or gripping the edge of the bench as a magnificently proportioned Negro on the tiny Provincetown Theatre stage, with a voice of marvelous power and with a finished artistry enacted Eugene O'Neill's epic of human terror, The Emperor Jones. For years I had nourished the conceit that nothing in or of the theatre could thrill me—I was sure my years of theatre-going had made me immune to the tricks and the trappings which managers and actors use to get their tears and smiles and laughs. A few seasons ago my shell of conceit was cracked a little—in that third act of Karel Capek's R. U. R. when Rossum's automatons swarmed over the parapet to wipe out the last human being. But the chills that chased each other up and down my spine then were only pleasurable tingles compared to the sympathetic terror evoked by Paul Robeson as he fled blindly through the impenetrable forest of the "West Indian island not yet self-determined by white marines."

Nor was I alone. When, after remaining in darkness from the second through the eighth and final scene, the house was flooded with light, a concerted sigh of relief welled up from all over the theatre. With real joy we heard the reassuring roar of taxicabs and muffled street noises of Greenwich Village and knew we were safe in New York. Wave after wave of applause, almost hysterical with relief, brought Paul Robeson time and time again before the curtain to receive the acclaim his art had merited. Almost shyly he bowed again and again as the storm of handclapping and bravos surged and broke upon the tiny stage. His color—his race—all, all were forgotten by those he had stirred so deeply with his art.

Outside in narrow, noisy Macdougal Street the four of us stood. Mrs. Robeson, alert, intelligent, merry, an expert chemist for years in one of New York's leading hospitals; Paul Robeson, clad now in conventional tweeds in place of the ornate, gold-laced trappings of the Emperor Jones; my wife and I. We wanted supper and a place to talk. All about us blinked invitingly the lights of restaurants and inns of New York's Bohemia. Place after place was suggested and discarded. Here a colored man and his companion had been made to wait interminably until, disgusted, they had left. There a party of four colored people,

The color line, we say—but there are many color lines. One bars the man but not the artist; another the man who looks black but not the man who looks white, regardless of race; another divides the black from the mulatto. Some cross the lines, and some refuse to do so. Mr. White explores these tangled inhibitions and their bearing on the human spirit—the personal aspects of race and color prejudice. In the succeeding article Dean Miller studies the mass effects of prejudice, viewing it dispassionately as a factor in social development

whose art had brought homage to his feet from sophisticated New York could not enter even the cheapest of the eating places of lower New York with the assurance that some unpleasantness might not come to him before he left.

What does race prejudice do to the inner man of him who is the victim of that prejudice? What is the feeling within the breast of the Paul Robesons, the Roland Hayes's, the Harry Burleighs, as they listen to the applause of those whose kind receive them as artists but refuse to accept them as men? It is of this inner conflict of the black man in America—or, more specifically in New York City, I shall try to speak.

I approach my task with reluctance—it is no easy matter to picture that effect which race or color prejudice has on the Negro of fineness of soul who is its victim. Of wounds to the flesh it is easy to speak. It is not difficult to tell of lynchings and injustices and race proscription. Of wounds to the spirit which are a thousand times more deadly and cruel it is impossible to tell in entirety. On the one hand lies the Scylla of bathos and on the other the Charybdis of insensivity to subtler shadings of the spirit. If I can evoke in your mind a picture of what results proscription has brought, I am content.

With its population made up of peoples from every corner of the earth, New York City is, without doubt, more free from ordinary manifestations of prejudice than any other city in the United States. Its Jewish, Italian, German, French, Greek, Czechoslovakian, Irish, Hungarian quarters with their teeming thousands and hundreds of thousands form so great a percentage that "white, Gentile, Protestant" Nordics have but little opportunity to develop their prejudices as they do, for example, in Mississippi or the District of Columbia. It was no idle joke when some forgotten wit remarked, "The Jews own New York, the Irish run it and the Negroes enjoy it."

New York's polyglot population which causes such distress

all university graduates, had been told flatly by the proprietress, late of North Carolina, she did not serve "niggers." At another, other colored people had been stared at so rudely they had bolted their food and left in confusion. The Civil Rights Act of New York would have protected us—but we were too much under the spell of the theatre we had just quitted to want to insist on the rights the law gave us. So we mounted a bus and rode seven miles or more to colored Harlem where we could be served with food without fear of insult or contumely. The man to the Lothrop Stoddards and the Madison Grants, by a curious anomaly, has created more nearly than any other section that democracy which is the proud boast but rarely practiced accomplishment of these United States. The Ku Klux Klan has made but little headway in New York City for the very simple reason that the proscribed outnumber the proscribers. Thus race prejudice cannot work its will upon Jew or Catholic—or Negro, as in other more genuinely American centers. This combined with the fact that most people in New York are so busy they haven't time to spend in hating other people, makes New York as nearly ideal a place for colored people as exists in America.

Despite these alleviating causes, however, New York is in the United States where prejudice appears to be indigenous. Its population includes many Southern whites who have brought North with them their hatreds. There are here many whites who are not Southern but whose minds have indelibly fixed upon them the stereotype of a Negro who is either a buffoon or a degenerate beast or a subservient lackey. From these the Negro knows he is ever in danger of insult or injury. This situation creates various attitudes of mind among those who are its victims. Upon most the acquisition of education and culture, of wealth and sensitiveness causes a figurative and literal withdrawal, as far as is humanly possible or as necessity permits, from all contacts with the outside world where unpleasant situations may arise. This naturally means the development of an intensive Negro culture and a definitely bounded city within a city. Doubtless there are some advantages, but it is certain that such voluntary segregation works a greater loss upon those within and those without the circle.

Upon those within, it cuts off to a large extent the world of music, of the theatre, of most of those contacts which mean growth and development and which denied, mean stagnation and spiritual atrophy. It develops as well a tendency towards self-pity, towards a fatal conviction that they of all peoples are most oppressed. The harmful effects of such reactions are too obvious to need elaboration.

Upon those without, the results are equally mischievous. First these is the loss of that deep spirituality, that gift of song and art, that indefinable thing which perhaps can best be termed the over-soul of the Negro, which has given America the only genuinely artistic things which the world recognizes as distinctive American contributions to the arts.

More conventional notions as Thomas Dixon and Octavus Roy Cohen and Irvin Cobb have falsely painted them, of what the Negro is and does and thinks continue to persist, while those who represent more truly the real Negro avoid all contact with other races.

There are, however, many other ways of avoidance of proscription and prejudice. Of these one of no small importance is that popularly known as "passing," that

is, those whose skin is of such color that they can pass as white may do so. This is not difficult; there are so many swarthy races represented in New York's population that even colored people who could easily be distinguished by their own race as Negroes, pass as French or Spanish or Cuban with ease. Of these there are two classes. First are those who for various reasons disappear entirely and go over the line to become white in business, social and all other relationships. The number of these is very large—much larger that is commonly suspected. To my personal knowledge one of the prominent surgeons of New York City who has an elaborately furnished suite of offices in an exclusive neighborhood, whose fees run often into four figures, who moves with his family in society of such standing that the names of its members appear frequently in the society columns of the metropolitan press, is a colored man from a Southern city. There he grew tired of the proscribed life he was forced to lead, decided to move North and forget he was a colored man. He met with success, married well and he and his wife and their children form as happy a family circle as one could hope to see. O'Neill's All God's Chillun Got Wings to the contrary, his wife loves him but the more for his courage in telling her of his race when first they met and loved.

This doctor's case is not an exception. Colored people know many of their own who have done likewise. In New York there is at least one man high in the field of journalism, a certain famous singer, several prominent figures of the stage, in fact, in almost any field that could be mentioned there are those who are colored but who have left their race for wider opportunity and for freedom from race prejudice. Just a few days before this article is being written I received a note from a woman whose name is far from being obscure in the world of the arts. The night before, she wrote me, there had been a party at her studio. Among the guests were three Southern whites who, in a confidential mood, had told her of a plan the Ku Klux Klan was devising for capitalizing in New York prejudice against the Negro. When I asked her why she had given me the information she told me her father, resident at the time of her birth in a Southern state, was a Negro.

The other group is made up of the many others who "pass" only occasionally. Some of these do so for business reasons, others when they go out to dine or to the theatre.

If a personal reference may be forgiven, I have had the unique experience within the past seven years of investigating some thirty-seven lynchings and eight race riots by the simple method of not telling those whom I was investigating of the Negro blood within my veins.

Large as is the number of those who have crossed the line, they form but a small percentage of those who might follow such an example but who do not. The

Baptism

By CLAUDE McKAY

Into the furnace let me go alone;
Stay you without in terror of the heat.

I will go naked in—for thus 'tis sweet—
Into the wierd depths of the hottest zone.
I will not quiver in the frailest bone,
You will not note a flicker of defeat;
My heart shall tremble not its fate to meet,
Nor mouth give utterance to any moan.
The yawning oven spits forth fiery spears;
Red aspish tongues shout wordlessly my name.
Desire destroys, consumes my mortal fears,
Transforming me into a shape of flame.

I will come out, back to your world of tears,
A stronger soul within a finer frame.

—From Harlem Shadows, Harcourt, Brace & Co.

153

constant hammering of three hundred years of oppression has resulted in a race consciousness among the Negroes of the United States which is amazing to those who know how powerful it is. In America, as is well known, all persons with any discernible percentage of Negro blood are classed as Negroes, subject therefore to all of the manifestations of prejudice. They are never allowed to forget their race. By prejudice ranging from the more violent forms like lynching and other forms of physical violence down to more subtle but none the less effective methods, Negroes of the United States have been welded into a homogeneity of thought and a commonness of purpose in combatting a common foe. These external and internal forces have gradually created a state of mind among Negroes which is rapidly becoming more pronounced where they realize that just so long as one Negro can be made the victim of prejudice because he *is* a Negro, no other Negro is safe from that same oppression. This applies geographically, as is seen in the support given by colored people in cities like Boston, New York and Chicago to those who oppose lynching of Negroes in the South, and it applies to that large element of colored people whose skins are lighter who realize that their cause is common with that of all Negroes regardless of color.

Unfortunately, however, color prejudice creates certain attitudes of mind on the part of some colored people which form color lines within the color line. Living in an atmosphere where swarthiness of skin brings, almost automatically, denial of opportunity, it is as inevitable as it is regrettable that there should grow up among Negroes themselves distinctions based on skin color and hair texture. There are many places where this pernicious custom is more powerful than in New York—for example, there are cities where only mulattoes attend certain churches while those whose skins are dark brown or black attend others. Marriages between colored men and women whose skins differ markedly in color, and indeed, less intimate relations are frowned upon. Since those of lighter color could more often secure the better jobs an even wider chasm has come between them, as those with economic and cultural opportunity have pr·gressed more rapidly than those whose skin denied them opportunity.

Thus, even among intelligent Negroes there has come into being the fallacious belief that black Negroes are less able to achieve success. Naturally such a condition had led to jealousy and suspicion on the part of darker Negroes, chafing at their bonds and resentful of the patronizing attitude of those of lighter color.

In New York City this feeling between black and mulatto has been accentuated by the presence of some 40,000 Negroes from the West Indies, and particularly by the propaganda of Marcus Garvey and his Universal Negro Improvement Association. In contrast to the division between white and colored peoples in the United States, there is in the West Indies, as has been pointed out by Josiah Royce and others, a tri-partite problem of race relations with whites, blacks and mulattoes. The latter mingle freely with whites in business and other relations and even socially. But neither white nor mulatto has any extensive contact on an equal plane with the blacks. It is this system which has enabled the English whites in the islands to rule and exploit though they as rulers are vastly inferior numerically to blacks and mulattoes.

The psychology thus created is visible among many of the West Indian Negroes in New York. It was the same background of the English brand of race prejudice which actuated Garvey in preaching that only those who were of unmixed Negro blood were Negroes. It is true beyond doubt that such a doctrine created for a time greater antagonisms among colored people, but an inevitable reaction has set in which, in time, will probably bring about a greater unity than before among Negroes in the United States.

We have therefore in Harlem this strange mixture of reaction not only to prejudice from without but to equally potent prejudices from within. Many are the comedies and many are the tragedies which these artificial lines of demarcation have created. Yet with all these forces and counter forces at work, there can be seen emerging some definite and hopeful signs of racial unity. Though it hearkens back to the middle ages, this is essential in the creation of a united front against that race and color prejudice with which the Negro, educated or illiterate, rich or poor, native or foreign-born, mulatto, octaroon, quadroon, or black, must strive continuously.

The Harvest of Race Prejudice

By KELLY MILLER

PREJUDICE is a state of mind. Some affect to believe that it is an innate passion parallel with instinct, and is therefore unalterable. Others maintain that it is a stimulated animosity modifiable by time, place and condition, and is on the same footing with other shallow obliterative feelings. But whatever the basis of race prejudice, whether natural or acquired, we do know certainly that it is a pressing, persistent fact, easily stimulated and appeased with difficulty. It forms a barrier between the races which is as real as the seas and as apparent as the mountains.

Like a two-edged sword, race prejudice cuts both ways. It weakens the energies and paralyzes the moral muscle of the white race; it stultifies the conscience and frustrates the normal workings of democracy and Christianity. It fosters a double standard of ethics, and leads to lawlessness, lynching, and all manner of national disgrace. The elements of the white race that are most thoroughly obsessed by this passion show the lowest average of intellectual, moral and spiritual achievement. The Ku Klux Klan spreads its virus through our democracy; Nordicism carries it to the ends of the earth. Its effects are nationally and internationally threatening, and the American people and the Nordic civilization of which they are a part must stop to consider whether in this evil fruit they are not nurturing the fatal seeds of world dissension and catastrophe.

But our present concern is mainly to describe prejudice as

it affects the Negro. Here the harvest of prejudice is ripe for the sociologist's gleaning. The outstanding and all-inclusive effect of race prejudice on the Negro can be summed up in one word, *segregation*. This is but the outer embodiment of the inner feeling of the white race. Whatever the nature and origin of this attitude, it is well nigh universal in the scope of its operation. The watch word is "miscegenation"; the rallying cry is "social equality." The cunning propagandist knows how to play upon these alarms and to adjust their appeal to the varying moods of popular passion and prejudice as a skilled musician plays upon his favorite instrument. Until recently the Negro has been the victim, with little capacity to resist.

This attitude of the white race has decreed residential segregation. Several municipalities have sought to embody this feeling in restrictive ordinances. In their too hasty zeal they over-rode the reaches of the constitution and the law; Negroes, through the National Association for the Advancement of Colored People, contested the constitutionality of these ordinances and won a unanimous decision from the Supreme Court. Yet the legal victory merely modified the details of procedure; it had little effect upon the actual fact of segregation, which operates as effectively without the law as within it, except as to the finality of its boundaries.

The most gigantic instance of racial segregation in the United States is seen in Harlem. There is no local law prescribing it. There does not have to be. And yet, under the normal operation of race prejudice, we find 200,000 Negroes shut in segregated areas as sharply marked as the aisles of a church. This is but an example of what it taking place in every city and center where the Negro resorts in great numbers. The recent tide of Northern migration greatly emphasized this tendency. In Boston, New York, Philadelphia, Baltimore, Washington, Pittsburgh, Detroit, Indianapolis and Chicago, the Negro contingent lives in wards and sections of wards which the politician and the real estate dealer know as well as the mariners know the depths and shallows of the seas.

We may then take Harlem as a fair specimen of the harvest of race prejudice throughout the United States. Here we have the largest Negro community in the world. It is a city within a city, a part of, and yet apart from the general life of greater New York. We need not stop here to dilate upon the inhumanity, the cruelty or the hardships of race prejudice. The outstanding fact and the consequences immediately flowing from it suffice for the present purpose.

These Negro communities are everywhere extending their boundaries without tending to any fixed limits we can now set. In Chicago the rapidly expanding boundary of the black belt precipitated the lamentable race riot. The issue is still the cause of race agitation in milder form in all parts

of the country. The whites are trying to keep back the rising tide of black invasion into residential areas previously regarded as exclusively theirs. The Negroes are pushing over the boundaries of racial restriction in quest of more room and better facilities. We may expect this minor border warfare to continue until the matter settles itself by custom, understanding and acceptance. Thus it is that the sharp accentuation of race consciousness on the part of the white race is developing a counter-tendency on the part of the Negro. This is the first fruit of segregation.

If Negroes were indiscriminately interspersed among the white population of New York, race consciousness would weaken to the point of disappearance. Three hundred thousand Negroes intermingled among six million whites would be unnoticeable. But when segregated in two or three centers the African contingent becomes not only apparent, but impressive. Whenever p e o p l e are thrown together they begin to think of their common interests. A common consciousness emerges which shortly expresses itself in organized endeavor. The Negro race as a whole has hitherto had a somewhat vague and indefinite collective consciousness stimulated in large part by stress of outside compulsion. But the race is too numerous, too widespread in territory and too diverse in interests to give this conscious edge. Harlem furnishes the needed pressure. The Garvey movement furnishes the most extreme focussing of this feeling. Marcus Garvey found in Harlem not only a mass of Negroes surrounded and overshadowed by whites, but also a considerable group of West Indians, who, in many ways, felt themselves isolated and circumscribed by the native Afro-Americans. Shrewdly enough he seized upon this group as the basis of his focal operation. He preached the impossibility of racial entente on the same soil and under the same political and social régime, and urged a racial hegira. His philosophy does not in this connection interest us. But he has shown to the world the possibility of focussing the racial mind, and of mobilizing racial resources about a formulated ideal.

Another fruit of prejudice is the direction which race effort and organization has been impelled to take; until recently the Negro has been thrown quite too much on the defensive. The National Association for the Advancement of Colored People arose to cope with this situation on the basis of fight and protest. Their fundamental philosophy is based upon the belief that race prejudice is medicable by legal and judicial process. Their method is militant; their mood is optimistic. Equality is their goal; the elimination of prejudice their objective. The Urban League, on the other hand, represents the ameliorative method which hopes that in the long run smooth working relations will be effected on the basis of mutual forbearance and good will. Its main attack is local, urban (*Continued on page 711*)

I, Too

By LANGSTON HUGHES

I, too, sing America.

I am the darker brother.
They send me to eat in the kitchen
When company comes.
But I laugh,
And eat well,
And grow strong.

Tomorrow
I'll sit at the table
When company comes
Nobody 'll dare
Say to me,
"Eat in the kitchen"
Then.

Besides, they'll see how beautiful I am
And be ashamed,—

I, too, am America.

Breaking Through

By EUNICE ROBERTA HUNTON

ARLEM is a modern ghetto. True, that is a contradiction in terms, but prejudice has ringed this group around with invisible lines and bars. Within the bars you will find a small city, self-sufficient, complete in itself— a riot of color and personality, a medley of song and tears, a canvas of browns and golds and flaming reds. And yet bound.

In it are some who year in and year out never leave the narrow confines of Harlem. There are those who make rare excursions into the larger shopping districts and rarer still to the theatrical center. There are those whose work takes them down to New York's factories, office buildings, hotels, restaurants and places of amusement, but they know these places only in working hours; their life is the life of Harlem. There are those who, still ghetto-bound mentally, have been pressed through the bars of the cage, but they have been caught up and placed in tiny ghettos of their own in other sections of Manhattan, Brooklyn, the Bronx and on Long Island. Their lives too are race-bound. But there is another group, which is not Harlem bound, whose contacts are many, whose sphere of activity is wide and ever widening. Theirs is New York in its entirety; theirs is the opportunity of giving Harlem to New York and New York to Harlem.

Education is the way out of the ghetto. Age submits, but youth—even though the door be barred—revolts. In many instances age contributes to the burden by pressing youth into the beaten paths of experience, by insisting upon teaching, preaching and medicine as the appropriate professional goals. Now youth is revolting and getting away from the compromise so often expressed in words like these: "Well, I'll take it up any way, even if I cannot practice it, perhaps I can teach it." Youth is escaping into business, art and the technical professions. A few even are escaping into the broad freedom of the leisure class.

In sharp contrast with these rebels of success who are seeking to work out their own destiny, these individualists who often appear in the first instance to be deserting the race, are the conscious pathbreakers—those who protest at proscription. We find them of varied ardors and enthusiasms, often misguided, from those who won't go to a colored church or who will break into a white block to those who organize some definite assault on occupational proscription. Whereas many who break the bonds are actuated solely by the desire to get the best for themselves in spite of proscription, a few realize that they are blazing a trail that others of the race may follow. This kind of thing is instanced by the young man who about seven years ago succeeded in becoming the first interne known to be of Negro extraction in a New York city hospital, or by the older surgeon who a little while ago became the first of his race to be permitted to conduct operations in one of the city's large hospitals. This being "first" means a great deal in the life of the racial group. There is a constant struggle among young men and women to be the "first" to do a certain thing, for the pioneer in any thing significant occupies, if only for a little while, an exalted position while a large portion of the race indulges in a mild form of hero worship. These achievements are the pride of the race; this business of reaching new heights is taken very seriously by the ghetto bound, for each is a milestone on the road of progress which leads to the goal of unrestricted opportunity.

These achievements have not always been regarded as breaking paths for others to follow. There was a time, in fact, when they were truly exceptional, when there was a first and never a second, when the proud possessor of such a record was even jealous and fearful lest some one rob him of his uniqueness. Now among leaders and youth there is prevalent the relay spirit which seeks to "keep openings open."

THERE is also some tugging from without at the ropes that bind the ghetto. It is the result of the efforts of the whites because of curiosity, self-interest, a spasm of self-righteousness or—very rarely—genuine interest, to establish a contact with those within the ghetto. It takes the form of the establishment of various organizations within the ghetto and organizations outside the ghetto to "help" those inside. We see it in the Christian societies, in the numerous clinics, health organizations and social service bureaus which are operating in Harlem, in the rapidly increasing group of whites who are attending civic and social affairs there and for varied reasons attempting to establish understanding and friendship with those within.

In many cases this is no conscious attempt to break the ghetto bonds; indeed it may be a deliberate attempt to go in and satisfy the needs of the inhabitants to prevent their leaving the ghetto. Sometimes the ruse is successful but more often, in the long run, it defeats its own end, for it sets an example of broadness that the ghetto-bound spirit eagerly seizes upon. Having secured a taste of the world outside, the ghetto youth is eager to get more of it and the determination to grow strong and break through increases.

There is another side of the picture; it is a tale of long dark years of dismal failure, of brave struggles to rise above mediocrity, of bitter fights for existence, a tale twisted with heartaches and heartbreaks, a tale drenched in sweat and blood, but still shot through with flashes of sunlight upon pure gold. It takes rare courage to fight a fight that more often than not ends in death, poverty or prostitution of genius. But it is to these who make this fight despite the tremendous odds, despite the deterring pessimism of those who see in the tangle of prejudice that surround the ghetto a hopeless barrier, that we must look for the breaking of the bonds now linked together by ignorance and misunderstanding.

684

Four Portraits of Negro Women

Drawn by Winold Reiss

A Woman from the Virgin Islands

The Librarian

Two Public School Teachers

ELISE JOHNSON McDOUGALD

The Double Task

The Struggle of Negro Women for Sex and Race Emancipation

By ELISE JOHNSON McDOUGALD

HROUGHOUT the long years of history, woman has been the weather-vane, the indicator, showing in which direction the wind of destiny blows. Her status and development have augured now calm and stability, now swift currents of progress. What then is to be said of the Negro woman today?

In Harlem, more than anywhere else, the Negro woman is free from the cruder handicaps of primitive household hardships and the grosser forms of sex and race subjugation. Here she has considerable opportunity to measure her powers in the intellectual and industrial fields of the great city. Here the questions naturally arise: "What are her problems?" and "How is she solving them?"

To answer these questions, one must have in mind not any one Negro woman, but rather a colorful pageant of individuals, each differently endowed. Like the red and yellow of the tiger-lily, the skin of one is brilliant against the star-lit darkness of a racial sister. From grace to strength, they vary in infinite degree, with traces of the race's history left in physical and mental outline on each. With a discerning mind, one catches the multiform charm, beauty and character of Negro women; and grasps the fact that their problem cannot be thought of in mass.

Because only a few have caught this vision, the attitude of mind of most New Yorkers causes the Negro woman serious difficulty. She is conscious that what is left of chivalry is not directed toward her. She realizes that what ideals of beauty, built up in the fine arts, exclude her almost entirely. Instead, the grotesque Aunt Jemimas of the street-car advertisements proclaim only an ability to serve, without grace or loveliness. Nor does the drama catch her finest spirit. She is most often used to provoke the mirthless laugh of ridicule; or to portray feminine viciousness or vulgarity not peculiar to Negroes. This is the shadow over her. To a race naturally sunny comes the twilight of self-doubt and a sense of personal inferiority. It cannot be denied that these are potent and detrimental influences, though not generally recognized because they are in the realm of the mental and spiritual. More apparent are the economic handicaps which follow her recent entrance into industry. It is conceded that she has special difficulties because of the poor working conditions and low wages of her men. It is not surprising that only the determined women forge ahead to results other than mere survival. The few who do prove their mettle stimulate one to a closer study of how this achievement is won in Harlem.

Better to visualize the Negro woman at her job, our vision of a host of individuals must once more resolve itself into groups on the basis of activity. First, comes a very small leisure group—the wives and daughters of men who are in business, in the professions and in a few well-paid

personal service occupations. Second, a most active and progressive group, the women in business and the professions. Third, the many women in the trades and industry. Fourth, a group weighty in numbers struggling on in domestic service, with an even less fortunate fringe of casual workers, fluctuating with the economic temper of the times.

The first is a pleasing group to see. It is picked for outward beauty by Negro men with much the same feeling as other Americans of the same economic class. Keeping their women free to preside over the family, these women are affected by the problems of every wife and mother, but touched only faintly by their race's hardships. They do share acutely in the prevailing difficulty of finding competent household help. Negro wives find Negro maids unwilling generally to work in their own neighborhoods, for various reasons. They do not wish to work where there is a possibility of acquaintances coming into contact with them while they serve and they still harbor the misconception that Negroes of any station are unable to pay as much as persons of the other race. It is in these homes of comparative ease that we find the polite activities of social exclusiveness. The luxuries of well-appointed homes, modest motors, tennis, golf and country clubs, trips to Europe and California, make for social standing. The problem confronting the refined Negro family is to know others of the same achievement. The search for kindred spirits gradually grows less difficult; in the past it led to the custom of visiting all the large cities in order to know similar groups of cultured Negro people.

A spirit of stress and struggle characterizes the second two groups. These women of business, profession and trade are the hub of the wheel of progress. Their burden is twofold. Many are wives and mothers whose husbands are insufficiently paid, or who have succumbed to social maladjustment and have abandoned their families. An appalling number are widows. They face the great problem of leaving home each day and at the same time trying to rear children in their spare time—this too in neighborhoods where rents are large, standards of dress and recreation high and costly, and social danger on the increase.

The great commercial life of New York City is only slightly touched by the Negro woman of our second group. Negro business men offer her most of their work, but their number is limited. Outside of this field, custom is once more against her and competition is keen for all. However, Negro girls are training and some are holding exceptional jobs. One of the professors in a New York college has had a young colored woman as secretary for the past three years. Another holds the head clerical position in an organization where reliable handling of detail and a sense of business ethics are essential. For four years she has steadily advanced. Quietly these women prove their worth, so that when a vacancy exists and there is a call, it is difficult to find even one competent colored secretary who is not employed. As a result of opportunity in clerical work in the educational system of New York City a number have qualified for such positions, one being appointed within the year to the office work of a high school. In other departments the civil service in New York City is no longer free from discrimination. The casual personal interview, that tenacious and retrogressive practice introduced in the Federal administration during the World War has spread and often nullifies the Negro woman's success in written tests. The successful young woman just cited above was three times "turned down" as undesirable on the basis of the personal interview. In the great mercantile houses, the many young Negro girls who might be well suited to salesmanship are barred from all but the menial positions. Even so, one Negro woman, beginning as a uniformed maid, has pulled herself up to the position of "head of stock."

Again, the telephone and insurance companies which receive considerable patronage from Negroes deny them proportionate employment. Fortunately, this is an era of changing customs. There is hope that a less selfish racial attitude will prevail. It is a heartening fact that there is an increasing number of Americans who will lend a hand in the game fight of the worthy.

In the less crowded professional vocations, the outlook is more cheerful. In these fields, the Negro woman is dependent largely upon herself and her own race for work. In the legal, dental, medical and nursing professions, successful women practitioners have usually worked their way through college and are "managing" on the small fees that can be received from an underpaid public. Social conditions in America are hardest upon the Negro because he is lowest in the economic scale. This gives rise to a demand for trained college women in the profession of social work. It has met with a response from young college women, anxious to devote their education and lives to the needs of the submerged classes. In New York City, some fifty-odd women are engaged in social work, other than nursing. In the latter profession there are over two hundred and fifty. Much of the social work has been pioneer in nature: the pay has been small with little possibility of advancement. For even in work among Negroes, the better paying positions are reserved for whites. The Negro college woman is doing her bit in this field at a sacrifice, along such lines as these: in the correctional departments of the city, as probation officers, investigators, and police women; as Big Sisters attached to the Childrens' Court; as field workers and visitors for relief organizations and missions; as secretaries for travelers-aid and mission societies; as visiting teachers and vocational guides for the schools of the city; and, in the many branches of public health nursing, in schools, organizations devoted to preventive and educational medicine, in hospitals and in private nursing.

In New York City, nearly three hundred Negro women share the good conditions in the teaching profession. They measure up to the high pedagogical requirements of the city and state law and are increasingly, leaders in the community. Here too the Negro woman finds evidence of the white workers' fear of competition. The need for teachers is still so strong that little friction exists. When it does seem to be imminent, it is smoothed away, as it recently

was at a meeting of school principals. From the floor, a discussion began with: "What are we going to do about this problem of the increasing number of Negro teachers coming into our schools?" It ended promptly through the suggestion of another principal: "Send all you get and don't want over to my school. I have two now and I'll match their work to any two of your best whom you name." One might go on to such interesting and more unusual professions as journalism, chiropody, bacteriology, pharmacy, etc., and find that, though the number in any one may be small, the Negro woman is creditably represented in practically every one. According to individual ability she is meeting with success.

Closing the door on the home anxieties, the woman engaged in trades and in industry faces equally serious difficulty in competition in the open working field. Custom is against her in all but a few trade and industrial occupations. She has, however been established long in the dressmaking trade among the helpers and finishers, and more recently among the drapers and fitters in some of the best establishments. Several Negro women are themselves proprietors of shops in the country's greatest fashion district. Each of them has, against great odds, convinced skeptical employers of her business value; and, at the same time, has educated fellow workers of other races, doing much to show the oneness of interest of all workers. In millinery, power sewing-machine operating on cloth, straw and leather, there are few Negro women. The laissez-faire attitude of practically all trade unions makes the Negro woman an unwilling menace to the cause of labor.

In trade cookery, the Negro woman's talent and past experience is recognized. Her problem here is to find employers who will let her work her way to managerial positions, in tea-rooms, candy shops and institutions. One such employer became convinced that the managing cook, a young colored graduate of Pratt Institute, would continue to build up a business that had been failing. She offered her a partnership. As in the cases of a number of such women, her barrier was lack of capital. No matter how highly trained, nor how much speed and business acumen has been acquired, the Negro's credit is held in doubt. An exception in this matter of capital will serve to prove the rule. Thirty years ago, a young Negro girl began learning all branches of the fur trade. She is now in business for herself, employing three women of her race and one Jewish man. She has made fur experts of still another half-dozen colored girls. Such instances as these justify the prediction that the foothold gained in the trade world will, year by year, become more secure.

Because of the limited fields for workers in this group, many of the unsuccessful drift into the fourth social grade, the domestic and casual workers. These drifters increase the difficulties of the Negro woman suited to housework. New standards of household management are forming and the problem of the Negro woman is to meet these new business-like ideals. The constant influx of workers unfamiliar with household conditions in New York keeps the situation one of turmoil. The Negro woman, moreover, is revolting against residential domestic service. It is a last stand in her fight to maintain a semblance of family life. For this reason, principally, the number of day or casual workers is on the increase. Happiness is almost impossible under the strain of these conditions. Health and morale suffer, but how else can her children, loose all afternoon, be gathered together at night-fall? Through it all she manages to give satisfactory service and the Negro woman is sought after for this unpopular work largely because her honesty, loyalty and cleanliness have stood the test of time. Through her drudgery, the women of other groups find leisure time for progress. This is one of her contributions to America.

IT is apparent from what has been said, that even in New York City, Negro women are of a race which is free neither economically, socially nor spiritually. Like women in general, but more particularly like those of other oppressed minorities, the Negro woman has been forced to submit to over-powering conditions. Pressure has been exerted upon her, both from without and within her group. Her emotional and sex life is a reflex of her economic station. The women of the working class will react, emotionally and sexually, similarly to the working-class women of other races. The Negro woman does not maintain any moral standard which may be assigned chiefly to qualities of race, any more than a white woman does. Yet she has been singled out and advertised as having lower sex standards. Superficial critics who have had contact only with the lower grades of Negro women, claim that they are more immoral than other groups of women. This I deny. This is the sort of criticism which predicates of one race, to its detriment, that which is common to all races. Sex irregularities are not a matter of race, but of socio-economic conditions. Research shows that most of the African tribes from which the Negro sprang had strict codes for sex relations. There is no proof of inherent weakness in the ethnic group.

Gradually overcoming the habitual limits imposed upon her by slave masters, she increasingly seeks legal sanction for the consummation and dissolution of sex contracts. Contrary to popular belief, illegitimacy among Negroes is cause for shame and grief. When economic, social and biological forces combined bring about unwed motherhood, the reaction is much the same as in families of other racial groups. Secrecy is maintained if possible. Generally the married aunt, or even the mother, claims that the illegitimate child is her own. The foundling asylum is seldom sought. Schooled in this kind of suffering in the days of slavery, Negro women often temper scorn with sympathy for weakness. Stigma does fall upon the unmarried mother, but perhaps in this matter the Negroes' attitude is nearer the modern enlightened ideal for the social treatment of the unfortunate. May this not be considered another contribution to America?

With all these forces at work, true sex equality has not been approximated. The ratio of opportunity in the sex, social, economic and political spheres is about that which exists between white men and women. In the large, I would say that the Negro woman is the cultural equal of her man because she is generally kept in school longer. Negro boys, like white boys, are usually put to work to subsidize the family income. The growing economic independence of Negro working women is causing her to rebel against the domineering family attitude of the cruder working-class Negro man. The masses of Negro men are engaged in menial occupations throughout the working day. Their baffled and suppressed desires to determine their economic life are manifested in over-bearing domination at home. Working mothers are unable to instill different ideals in their sons. Conditions change slowly. Nevertheless, education and opportunity are

modifying the spirit of the younger Negro men. Trained in modern schools of thought, they begin to show a wholesome attitude of fellowship and freedom for their women. The challenge to young Negro womanhood is to see clearly this trend and grasp the proferred comradeship with sincerity. In this matter of sex equality, Negro women have contributed few outstanding militants. Their feminist efforts are directed chiefly toward the realization of the equality of the races, the sex struggle assuming a subordinate place.

OBSESSED with difficulties that might well compel individualism, the Negro woman has engaged in a considerable amount of organized action to meet group needs. She has evolved a federation of her clubs, embracing between eight and ten thousand women, throughout the state of New York. Its chief function is to crystallize programs, prevent duplication of effort, and to sustain a member organization whose cause might otherwise fail. It is now firmly established, and is about to strive for conspicuous goals. In New York City, one association makes child welfare its name and special concern. Others, like the Utility Club, Utopia Neighborhood, Debutante's League, Sempre Fidelius, etc., raise money for old folks' homes, a shelter for delinquent girls and fresh air camps for children. The Colored Branch of the Y. W. C. A. and the womens' organizations in the many churches, as well as in the beneficial lodges and associations, care for the needs of their members.

On the other hand, the educational welfare of the coming generation, has become the chief concern of the national sororities of Negro college women. The first to be organized in the country, Alpha Kappa Alpha, has a systematized and continuous program of educational and vocational guidance for students of the high schools and colleges. The work of Lambda Chapter, which covers New York City and its suburbs, is outstanding. Its recent campaign gathered together nearly one hundred and fifty such students at a meeting to gain inspiration from the life-stories of successful Negro women in eight fields of endeavor. From the trained nurse, who began in the same schools as they, these girls drank in the tale of her rise to the executive position in the Harlem Health Information Bureau. A commercial artist showed how real talent had overcome the color line. The graduate physician was a living example of the modern opportunities in the newer fields of medicine open to women. The vocations as outlets for the creative instinct became attractive under the persuasion of the musician, the dressmaker and the decorator. Similarly, Alpha Beta Chapter of the national Delta Sigma Theta Sorority recently devoted a week to work along similar lines. In such ways as these are the progressive and privileged groups of Negro women expressing their community and race consciousness.

We find the Negro woman, figuratively, struck in the face daily by contempt from the world about her. Within her soul, she knows little of peace and happiness. Through it all, she is courageously standing erect, developing within herself the moral strength to rise above and conquer false attitudes. She is maintaining her natural beauty and charm and improving her mind and opportunity. She is measuring up to the needs and demands of her family, community and race, and radiating from Harlem a hope that is cherished by her sisters in less propitious circumstances throughout the land. The wind of the race's destiny stirs more briskly because of her striving.

Ambushed in the City

The Grim Side of Harlem

By WINTHROP D. LANE

N unkempt woman, with hair graying, shoulders rounded and eyes rimmed with thick glasses, reads a newspaper on a subway car in New York City. She is colored. Her skirt is in rags, one toe shows through a shoe, an elbow pushes the lining of her sleeve into sight; perhaps she has just left her mop and pail in some downtown office building. Turning the pages hastily, she seems to be hunting for a particular place. At last she stops. Her forefinger runs up and down the columns. She is looking at the financial page. Finding an item, she gazes closely at it for a moment, and then throws the paper on-to the seat beside her. She has a dejected look. Apparently she is through with the paper.

She has been looking for "the numbers." The numbers she wanted were the day's totals of bank exchanges and bank balances—announced each day by the Clearing House and published by the newspapers. On these she has been gambling. Suppose the exchanges were $793,482,450 and the balances $86,453,624. She is then interested in the number 936, because that is made up of the seventh and eighth digits, reading from the right, of the first, and the seventh digit of the second. She and many others are playing this game—a species of policy. If she has put her money, which may be only a few pennies, on 936 that day, she wins. Each day she looks forward to discovering what this combina-tion is. It is the bright spot for her.

The stakes are high if she wins. She reaps 600 times what she wagers. If she wagers a nickel, she wins thirty dollars; if she wagers a quarter, she wins $150; a deposit of fifty cents will bring her $300. These stakes have lure; they are a king's stakes. They will make her rich for the moment. She does not consider the chances against her. She does not consider that she has never won and that only once did she ever hear of anybody winning. The bare possibility of capturing so much money makes her heart beat faster.

Since there are 999 numbers of three digits, or 1000 if we include 000, she seems to have about one chance in a thousand of winning. By the law of averages, she might play the same number daily for three years without a strike. The banker pays 600 times the sum wagered. He, therefore, seems to have a sure thing; barring lucky wins by large gamblers, he can't lose in the long run. That does not interest her, either.

All Harlem is ablaze with "the numbers." People play it everywhere, in tenements, on street corners, in the backs of shops. "Bankers" organize it, promote it, encourage it. They send their runners into flats and stores. You give the runner the money you are betting, write your number on a slip of paper, and wait. If the number you chose is the one that wins next day, you get your money. Runners round up new business, stake off territory and canvass all the people they can reach. A person living in an apartment

house may be the agent for that house. The names of these bankers are known in the neighborhood. One rides around in a $12,000 limousine and has a liveried chauffeur. Minor bankers abound; men and women, getting $200 capital, start in the "numbers" business. Recently, it is said, white men have been trying to wrest the control of the game from blacks; a Jew who formerly used his talents in the hooch business is spoken of as the leader in this effort.

"Always out first with the bank clearing numbers" reads a placard advertising the New York Sun in Harlem. Inspira-tion for lucky numbers is got from every source. People get their numbers from dream books; fifteen or twenty cents will buy a dream book, and a dream about any topic listed in it has an appropriate number. Or two people exchange street addresses. "Ah'm gonna play it! Ah'm gonna play it!" says one, as he takes down the address of the other. They get their numbers from the numbers of hymns given out in church, from subway cars, from telephone numbers, from dates, from baseball scores, from the prices they pay for purchased articles, from the license tags of passing auto-mobiles. By combining or rearranging these, or using them unchanged, they tempt fortune.

One trouble is, of course, that they don't always get what they win. Many a banker, finding that large sums have been won from him, avoids payment; his victim has no recourse, since the whole transaction is outside the law. The streets of Harlem are being walked by people looking for those who owe them money won at "the numbers." The New York Age, a colored weekly, published a story about one banker who skipped to Cuba with $100,000 taken from the Negroes of Harlem; it is common to win $12, $18 and $30 and not get it. This is only an exasperation of the extortion. The whole game, as it is staged, smells of exploitation.

G REAT number of Negroes have recently swarmed up from the South to swell the Negro colonies of Northern cities. Many of them are unfamiliar with city ways. They have become an invitation to the exploiter and the fakir—the gambling promoter, the necromancer, the fortune teller, the fake druggist, the quack doctor, and even more deliberate cheaters, such as the rent gouger. Living compactly in restricted areas, they supply a fertile field. Density of population is the fakir's paradise; it is the cheater's fairest opportunity for secrecy and success. There he can strike and hide, or be continuously lost in the moving mass of his fellow beings. And, credulous and child-like, the Negro peasant migrant has provided fresh opportunities in Northern cities for many forms of exploitation.

Black art flourishes in Harlem—and elsewhere in New York. Egyptian seers uncover hidden knowledge, Indian fortune-tellers reveal the future, sorcerers perform their mysteries. Feats of witchcraft are done daily. A towel for turban and a smart manner are enough to transform any

Harlem colored man into a dispenser of magic to his profit. Come with me into any little stationery store on Lenox or Seventh Avenues—the two main business thoroughfares of the district—and peep into the dream and mystery books there offered for sale. Some of these can be bought, as said, for fifteen or twenty cents; others cost a dollar. Here is one called Albertus Magnus. It is described as the "approved, verified, sympathetic and natural Egyptian secrets, or White and Black Art for Man and Beast, revealing the Forbidden Knowledge and Mysteries of Ancient Philosophers." Another is Napoleon's own Oraculum and Book of Fate, containing the explanations of dreams and other mysteries consulted on every occasion by Napoleon himself.

Stop in front of a well-known drug store on Lenox Avenue. Here roots, herbs and barks are displayed in the window. "Devil's Shoestring" one of these is called; others are "Jim Shanks," "John Conqueror," "Rattlesnake Master," "Sacred Bark" and "Jesuits' Bark." In curled forms, in powders, in spirally bunches, in thick little knots, they lie there; they are sold as cures for various forms of illness. I was interested in knowing just what these were; so I asked the druggist. He showed me the United States Dispensatory. Some of the names in his window are local and folk names for plants growing in various parts of this country and elsewhere, and these plants are mentioned in the Dispensatory as being credited with cathartic, diaphoretic and other medicinal qualities. That is all very well; it does not mean that taking these roots and leaves home and boiling them and then drinking the water enables you to obtain the benefit of those qualities. The plants have other qualities which come out in the water as well as those you want, and you get the essence of the whole, which may have quite other effects than those you anticipate. Again, no one can tell whether these plants are really what they are represented to be or not. Their sale is under no supervision; they may be roots of saplings dug in the Bronx, or bark from cherry trees disguised.

In these matters the Negro is, in large measure, his own enemy. He is bringing his own simplicity to the help of those who would take advantage of him. No good can come from blinking the fact that the Negro is, by and large, the great exploitable race of the Western world. Many Negroes find it so easy to expect something wonderful to happen; eager for pleasure, they are sanguinely expectant that it awaits them around every corner. They have the child's love of phantasy, too; they would escape from the harsh realities of a world in which they are not treated very well.

In addition to all this, many of the uneducated majority have a deeply imbedded trust in the white man—a holdover from slavery. This lies at the root of much exploitation. The Negro comes to our Northern cities, and we think that he is ready to cope with the complexity of St. Louis, Chicago and New York City. He is not. To transplant him from Georgia to Lenox Avenue is not to change him on the train; often he is still the simple and innocent child of his Southern life.

I am not blithely cataloging the Negro here as the possessor of a "child-mind." That is the pet formula of pseudo-scientific race detractors. The Negro has sufficiently proved —and this number of Survey Graphic is only further proof— that, given opportunities, he can rise to any heights. The simplicity, innocence and child-like qualities of some Negroes are due in large part to lack of education and to the lack

of certain kinds of experiences. They have not been invited to play an aggressive role, or even to create beautiful things. They have been kept under the thumb of the whites. Their innocence is the sort that you will find among rural whites and "green" foreign immigrants; it is "peasant-mindedness" in part.

Neither the facts, nor the explanations of the facts, however, justify members of his own race, or whites, in taking advantage of the simplicity that lies around them.

THERE are ways in which the Negro is more deliberately exploited in Harlem than in other Northern cities. He is subject to being fleeced in rent. This is not a rhetorical flourish. It is cold fact. I am not here referring merely to high rents, to "what the traffic will bear." I am referring to extortion.

The Negro is gouged. Because he is a Negro, because he can be taken advantage of, because his racial position makes it possible to gouge him, he is gouged.

Hear John R. Davies, judge in the Municipal Court in Harlem, who sees colored tenants pass in streams before him, seeking relief: "It is common for colored tenants in Harlem to pay twice as much as white tenants for the same apartments."

Hear Lillian Grant, acting chairman of the Mayor's Committee on Rent Profiteering, also white, who looks at the whole city and sees Harlem in the perspective of comparison: "Negroes pay exorbitant rents. Their situation is terrible."

Let us come to particulars. Sophie Ellerbee is a colored tenant worth knowing. She came into court the other day and told the judge that the white family preceding her in the apartment into which she had just moved had paid $50 a month; the corporation owning it was asking her to pay $75 now. This increase she thought excessive. Her attorney requested that the owner be brought into court and required to divulge its income, expenses and investment (as it could be compelled to do under the law), and thus to show whether the rent was justified. The jury awarded Mrs. Ellerbee a $20 reduction from the sum asked. When the verdict was announced, the attorney for the owner, who was a colored lawyer, moved to have it set aside. "This rent is justified," he said. "The colored district is crowded. These Negroes cannot go anywhere else. If they attempt to move into houses formerly occupied by whites, they should pay what the landlords ask. It is the law of supply and demand."

The judge, Jacob Panken, flamed at him. Judge Panken had seen many colored tenants come into court with tales similar to that of Mrs. Ellerbee, and he said:

"I agree that the verdict should be set aside, but for the purpose of securing Mrs. Ellerbee a still greater reduction in rent. Your own client has admitted that it is making $10,000 a year on a $30,000 investment. That is excessive. This rent is too large. And you, as a colored attorney, ought to be ashamed of yourself. You as a lawyer are helping colored and white landlords to prey on your own."

As the attorney left the court, embarrassed, cries of "Shame!" came to him from the Negro spectators in the room.

Other colored tenants were in court the same day. Through the services of a white lawyer twenty-one of these secured reductions varying from $10 to $23 below the rents asked. "It is pretty good evidence that the landlord knows he is charging excessive rents if he accepts a reduction voluntarily, without going to trial," said the attorney. The calendar of the Municipal Court in Harlem is crowded with the cases of colored tenants seeking relief. The white lawyer who acts as attorney for the West Harlem Tenants' League, an organization befriending tenants in that neighborhood, had 15 cases set down for trial on one day, 41 on another, 37 on another and 32 on another.

The National Urban League is an organization of white and colored social workers and others. It is interested in the welfare of city Negroes. The New York branch of the league studied rents paid by both white and colored people in blocks accomodating both in the spring of 1924. "We found that Negroes paid from 40 to 60 per cent higher rents than white people did for the same class of apartments," said Mr. Hubert, secretary of the Harlem office.

Through the courts, under the emergency New York state rent laws, relief can be secured. It is the families that do not go to court that continue to pay the unduly high rents. Unfortunately these are the vast majority. For every Mrs. Ellerbee there are many other colored tenants who, through ignorance, inertia or the congestion of the court calendar, do not get relief. Obviously individual trials cannot be given every tenant who is charged too high rent in Harlem; the court of justice is not the remedy for an extensive economic practice.

Let us look for a moment at the growth of this situation. Fifteen years ago Harlem as it is today did not exist; the colored population then was much smaller than it is now. It has grown continuously, swollen by additions from without. As the colored area grew, it has pressed against contiguous white territories. Block after block gave way. Stubbornly each block yielded. White people did not want to see their neighborhoods turn black. First one street was set as the "dead line" (in the white parlance) of the Negro advance, and then another. Always there were outposts, colored families breaking over the bounds and invading territory hitherto exclusively white.

This situation is the paradise of the ruthless landlord, or rent charger. If you own an apartment house in Harlem, if you do not live in it, and if you want the largest profits you can get, you will open it to those tenants who will pay you most. These are the tenants who are most in need of it. The whites do not have to have it. They can go elsewhere— to other parts of the city, to the suburbs, or they can just keep ahead of the Negro invasion and move a few blocks away. The Negro cannot; he will not be given an apartment elsewhere, he cannot be easily accomodated. He can live only in a limited area, and that area grows only bit by bit. So he will pay what you ask—or, rather, he will agree to pay what you ask and then he will pay it if he can. The profiteering is not all done by white landlords. There are men of both races who have a reputation for fairness. There are colored operators who have performed a public service to their race in addressing themselves to the extreme problem of shelter, but there are colored owners of houses who charge just as high rents as do white owners. Investigation shows that taking advantage of the colored people, or making money out of them, is not a white monopoly.

How, it will be asked, do Negroes find money to pay these rents? By strategy, and taking their own part. They do it by going without other things. They cut down on fun,

food and clothing, and stretch what money they have to cover the rent. But they have other tricks. One is the "rent party." This is a popular form of diversion in Harlem. It goes by the name of the "social parlor." A person invites friends in for the evening, to dance and have a good time, and charges them twenty-five cents a couple; that is one way of getting help to meet the monthly rent bill. Another is to take in lodgers. Lodgers are legion in Harlem. The State Housing Commission told of one apartment properly accomodating about ten persons that was occupied by forty-four. Harlem has gone to the extreme of the double shift. One room is not infrequently let out to two people, one of whom occupies it at night and the other during the day.

THE moment one begins to inquire about exploitation in Harlem, he hears about cabarets. In Harlem there are cabarets to which both white and colored people are admitted. There are cabarets where white and colored sit at the same table, dance together, talk together, drink together, leave together. Many flashy young people of both colors come to these and get riotously or near riotously merry; some less flashy people come; and some sober and sedate folk sit at the tables. All told there are about fifteen cabarets in Harlem. A few cater only to the well-behaved, others to the less well-behaved, and some to roughnecks. Two or three of the better places are now the resorts of downtown specialists in the latest places of interest.

No doubt people are fleeced a bit in paying for their entertainment, no doubt some people are swept along pretty rapidly on a current of erotic pleasure, a current of uncertain direction and ambiguous goal. But they come there of their own accord; they seek the cabaret. As an instrument of exploitation the cabaret does not touch many people. Its scope is the scope of a retreat for devotees.

Another subject often mentioned in connection with exploitation is prostitution. I am aware of no way of proving that the Negro is sexually more or less moral than other people. If there is any exceptional organized assault upon the continence of Negro women, I do not know of it.

LET us turn now to the gentle subject of hooch. Harlem is hooch-ridden. He is a bold man who will undertake to say what part of a city like New York, with its many congested foreign and native quarters, is the wettest. The wash of the booze sea has not left Harlem out; that district may well claim a deeper inundation than any other.

Those syndicates, or firms, or companies, or combinations, that set you up in business as a druggist, equipping you with the white jars and other colorful stock of a druggist's shelves, in order that behind your counters you may run a hooch dispensary, have lined Lenox and Seventh Avenues with such fake establishments. These sell rivers of bad booze to the colored residents of Harlem. There are excellent drug stores in Harlem, but these are drug stores only in name. They have small stocks and cannot fill prescriptions adequately. They specialize in synthetic gin and bad whiskey. Practically all of these places are owned by white people.

There are syndicates also that fit you out with the window displays and front rooms of delicatessen stores.

"A Negro clerk who works in a drug store on Lenox Avenue came running in to me the other day," a competent colored pharmacist in Harlem said (Continued on page 713)

The Church and the Negro Spirit

By GEORGE E. HAYNES

HE last Sunday of September, 1924, was a dramatic day in Harlem. The Salem Methodist Episcopal Church, a congregation of Negroes, took possession of the church building, parish house and parsonage of the Metropolitan Methodist Episcopal Church, a body of white communicants. The white congregation had assembled in large numbers for the last service they were to hold in their accustomed place of worship. Just a few blocks away there was an unusual attendance of the Negro congregation at the building—two converted apartment houses with the partition walls removed—they had used for fourteen years, beginning with the days when the church was a mission. At a designated hour, the Negro congregation marched quietly and in an orderly manner out of their old structure and up Seventh Avenue toward the Metropolitan Methodist Episcopal church house. The doors of the Metropolitan Church opened wide; the white pastor and his people arose to receive the Negro pastor and his people. There were Negro and white visitors from their common denomination to witness and participate in this historic event. The Negro pastor and the president of his board of trustees were welcomed to the pulpit by the white pastor and the president of his board. After appropriate songs and addresses, the keys of the church property were presented by the white trustees of the outgoing congregation to the Negro trustees of the incoming congregation. The benediction was pronounced amid expressions of joy and fellowship not unmixed with tears.

The taking over of church property by Negroes is a frequent occurrence in Harlem, as it is in the other rapidly growing Negro centers in the cities of the North. About eight years ago the Metropolitan Baptist Church bought from a white congregation an imposing stone building at Seventh Avenue and 128th Street and moved into it. Three years ago the Williams Institutional Church of the Colored Methodist Episcopal denomination purchased an excellent plant—once a flourishing Jewish synagogue—in 130th Street.

Such a transfer of white church property not infrequently accompanies a shifting of population. Within the past three years the Negro population of Harlem has pushed forward as the white population has moved westward across Eighth Avenue to St. Nicholas Park and up beyond 145th Street almost to the boundary of the Polo Grounds, and south of 125th Street, between Eighth and Lenox Avenues. During that time the fine building of a Swedish congregation west of

Eighth Avenue has been taken over by a body of Negro Congregationalists, the Grace Congregational Church of Harlem. The imposing structure of a Lutheran Church at Edgecombe Avenue and 140th Street has been bought and occupied by the Calvary Independent Methodist Church. According to a recent announcement, the Mt. Olivet Baptist Church, one of the oldest and largest Negro congregations in the city, after worshipping for many years in a church house in 53rd Street, has purchased for $450,000 the beautiful Adventist Temple, built of white Indiana limestone, at 120th Street.

Quite as interesting as these acquisitions of existing edifices has been the success of Negro congregations in erecting new church structures in the face of the high cost of land and building construction in Manhattan. About fifteen years ago St. Philip's Protestant Episcopal Church sold its property in the Pennsylvania Station zone for a large sum and used a part of the proceeds to erect, under the supervision of a Negro architect, an attractive and very serviceable brick church building and parish house on lots extending from 133rd to 134th Streets. The Abyssinian Baptist Church sold its property in 40th Street and built, on 138th Street, a church building and community house at a cost of about $325,000. In plan and program, like many of the churches named here it is a thing of beauty and an instrument of service. "Mother Zion" Church, of the African Methodist Episcopal Zion connection, found about twenty years ago that its constituency was becoming too far removed from its location in Bleecker Street. A fine structure therefore was erected in 86th Street where its leaders thought a Negro neighborhood would develop, but the subway opened up and carried Negroes farther north. About twelve years ago "Mother Zion" moved again and erected a building in 136th Street. To accommodate its growing institutional activities a new addition to the structure is now completed on a plot which runs through to 137th Street. In a triangle near 138th Street, St. Mark's Methodist Episcopal Church, now in the mid-town district, is erecting an institutional structure to cost a half million dollars.

In the purchase of buildings from white congregations and in the erection of new structures, the development in Negro church equipment in New York is typical of what has happened on smaller scale in such cities as Baltimore, Chicago, Cleveland, Saint Louis. Also in a few smaller cities churches have made commendable efforts to meet the growing demands of these people. In Saint Louis during the observance of Race Relations Sunday this winter

St. Philip's P. E. Church

695

167

delegations from white congregations that had sold their structures to Negro congregations returned for services on that day to their former churches to worship with the present occupants. St. John's Congregational Church in Springfield, Mass., Bethel African Methodist Episcopal Church of Chicago, the Sharp Street Methodist Church of Baltimore, Olivet Baptist Church in Chicago, "the largest Protestant church in the world," with nearly 11,000 members, and the Second ·Baptist Church of Detroit are outstanding examples of a broad and vigorous institutional service.

THE Negro church is at once the most resourceful and the most characteristic organized force in the life of the Negroes of the Northern cities as it was in the Southern communities from which they come. Some of its main problems may be summarized in a four-fold statement:

1. To provide adequate buildings and other physical equipment for attracting and serving the rapidly increasing populations.
2. To give fellowship to newcomers who have been connected with the church of the same faith and order in their former homes.
3. To have adequate personnel and organization for rendering social service in the housing, health, recreational and other needs of a large proportion of the masses in the community.
4. To meet with understanding and wisdom the increasing throng of intelligent people, who know little of serfdom, and who feel the urge of their vigorous years in the turmoil of the city.

We have spoken of typical solutions of the first of these; let us now consider the others.

So recently have men of all races come to dwell in cities that their churches often have the organization and equipment typical of the small town and rural district. This is especially the case with the Negro church because only in the past sixty years have its constituents been moving with the population stream from the rural districts to urban centers. Only within the last twenty years have the numbers assumed large proportions in most of the communities that have grown up around the industrial plants of the Northern cities. As Negroes moved North they have

brought their church with them. Individuals and groups, mainly of Baptists and Methodists, have transferred their relationships from the little churches of their Southern communities to the "watch-care" or to full membership of churches of the "same faith and order" in Northern communities. In a few cases whole congregations from Southern communities have moved North together and brought their pastors with them. In other cases Negro churches in Northern cities, which before the heavy migration of the last ten years had small struggling congregations, have increased their membership to large numbers and have become powerful in resources. Many of them have able ministers who, like the physicians, lawyers, editors, and business men who followed in the wake of the wage-earners, have come from the South to answer the Northern call.

Back in the Southern communities the little rural church, conspicuous for its bell tower, rests among the trees beside the road. It is the natural meeting place of the people once or twice a month when the non-resident minister comes to preach, and when the weather does not make the roads unfit for travel. Often the people come as far as ten or fifteen miles. Frequently they bring baskets of food and remain all day. Between the enthusiastic and extended services and amid the social amenities of meal time, they exchange the gossip of the countryside, the wisdom and experience of the cropping season, and the prospects, hopes and fears of the future.

In the typical Southern town or small city one or two churches of each of the more popular denominations, particularly of Baptists and the four principal Methodist denominations, have a resident minister. The church building is better built than those of the churches in the open country and the services are held usually every Sunday with Sunday School for the children. The church enters considerably, too, into the leisure time and recreational life of the people by an occasional sociable or picnic, stereopticon exhibition and, on ·rare occasions, a traveling moving picture show. Around the church revolve the interests of family life. The churches in the larger cities such as Atlanta, Memphis, Louisville or Richmond, in architectural design, physical facilities, and personnel compare reasonably with other favorable phases of Negro life. In Norfolk one of the lead-

"Mother Zion", A. M. E. Zion Church   Mt. Olivet Baptist Church   Abyssinian Baptist Church

ing Baptist churches, under the guidance of a young college-trained man, has a community program including extension classes for boys and girls, day nursery, playground and other social features.

From these communities of the South—rural districts, towns and cities—thousands of Negroes have moved to Northern cities. With the rapid increase of colored populations in the Northern cities, church facilities have not been adequate either in seating space for the assembly of worshippers, in arrangements for religious education, still in its infancy among white groups, or in sufficient personnel to give the service of social ministry to the thousands that come. For example, in 1920 the estimated seating capacity of Negro churches in Greater New York was about 24,000. In 1924 with the increase that has been made by taking over additional churches from white congregations and the erection of commodious buildings, the estimated seating capacity of twenty-seven Negro churches and sixteen missions in Harlem alone is about 21,000. There are thirteen churches with estimated seating capacity from 500 to 2,500 each; the others range from 200 to 400.

The thirst of the people for the cooling water brooks of religion is shown in the way they crowd the buildings that are available. Examples are many. The seats of the large auditorium of the Abyssinian Baptist Church are filled when the hour of service arrives and often standing room is at a premium. St. Philip's Protestant Episcopal Church, with a service of high church type, is often crowded to the doors on Sunday morning. Mother Zion African Methodist Episcopal Church and Metropolitan Baptist Church often have larger numbers than they can comfortably seat. Frequently some of these churches have overflow services.

Besides the large self-supporting congregations with well-appointed buildings, there are nearly a score of "house-front" and "mission" churches. The "mission" churches are those that receive a part of their support from denominational missionary or extension societies which are stirred to action by the teeming unchurched masses of the district. These societies subsidize salaries of ministers, assist in the purchase of buildings or in other ways help to extend denominational effort to evangelize and serve the people of this region. The "house-front" churches are started usually when some individual who has felt the call to the ministry has gathered about himself a little flock, or when several persons join together and ask a minister to lead them. The purchase of an equity in a private house is usually made. The double parlors on the first floor are used for church purposes while the upper floors serve as a residence for the minister or for other tenants.

THE organization, support and operation of Negro churches have become increasingly independent of white people. Negroes have thus had valuable experience and group training in standing upon their own legs and in going forward to achieve ends mapped out by themselves. The Negro churches are almost exclusively racial both in their membership and in their administration. Even congregations that belong to denominations made up of a majority of white communicants, such as the Protestant Episcopal, Methodist Episcopal and the Congregational Churches, are for all practical purposes autonomous, exercising great independence in government and being controlled only to a nominal extent by the general organization.

In no place, perhaps, is the independent, voluntary character of the Negro church better illustrated than in Harlem. One of the strongest Baptist churches in this area has been developed during the past fifteen years under the guidance of a minister of striking power, who once remarked that "a leader is a fellow who has some followers." In about ten years his preaching and work have enlarged a handful of members into a host. With money largely raised by themselves, they moved from a dingy brick basement to one of Harlem's best stone church edifices. St. Philip's Protestant Episcopal Church is widely known for its financial resources; it purchased, more than ten years ago, a number of apartment houses in 135th Street. Three of these churches have parish houses, three others have institutional equipment, and two others that are soon to come into the district have announced their plans for developing work along these lines.

With the growth of numbers there has been concentration of Negro communicants in distinctly Negro congregations, and the denominations made up altogether of members of the race have shown especially (Continued on page 708)

Metropolitan Baptist Church   *Williams Institutional C. M. E. Church*   *St. Philip's P. E. Church*

EDITORIALS

HARLEM is a new community. Its social work structure, slight as it is, is probably more effective for that reason; it has been built flexibly and not around a set of fixed ideas.

New as it is, however, Harlem inherited its physical framework. One of its best informed leaders remarks that the Negro in Harlem is like the poor relation who inherits a limousine: he can ill afford to keep it going. Harlem was built for families with incomes well above the average. The Negroes who find themselves masters of it have not, in the mass, attained to that standard. So the mere pressure to win and hold shelter imposes a tax on the wage-earner that leaves little margin for self-improvement, and less for cooperative social activity. Out of Harlem's pinched resources, again, have come surprising sums for church buying and building, as Mr. Haynes testifies. While several of these churches have distinguished themselves by providing institutional facilities and using them for needed social service, most of them have not, so that the wave of church-building has meant that the lion's share of the money Harlem has had to give away has gone into brick and stone.

Harlem's newness affects also the personal resources on which social work must draw. There is a leisure class in Harlem, but it is not a large one, and it is not yet widely diversified. Its money is new money, and much of it has been made, not in the ordinary turnover of varied trades and industries, but in the more picturesque enterprises—cabarets, the stage, sports, sumptuary establishments. Rich as Harlem is in personal good-will and neighborly helpfulness, it is not such money as this that makes good "prospects" for social work financing.

Nor is the community as a whole, in spite of its apparent cohesiveness, knit closely together. It has been recruited too quickly from elements too diverse. It has been hammered together by segregation, to be sure, but the unity that results is different in kind from that which grows slowly among people who live together and in a particular place by their own full choice. Harlem is probably no more factional or parochial than the typical American city of 150,000 or 200,000 souls, but it is not safe to argue from the accident of color that it is less so.

The leaders in Harlem social work are sensitive to these facts. They recognize the comparative inexperience of the Negro in organized social effort, and welcome the technical aid and advice of the maturer organizations of New York. Whether those organizations have been fully aware of their responsibility to the rapidly growing Negro community is a fair question. A recent conference on delinquency, for instance, revealed an almost total lack of attention to the underprivileged Negro boy. A thorough-going social survey of Harlem—had New York any cooperative body capable of making one—would no doubt uncover so many unmet and ill-met needs that the "downtown" agencies would be spurred to more adequate and more imaginative cooperation with those groups among the Negroes which are already struggling with their own difficult problems with growing initiative and self reliance.

Granting the handicaps to community organization, it is true that Harlem has exceptional resources in the service of professional volunteers—notably such physicians as those who compose the North Harlem Medical Association. Henry Street nurses testify to the unusually cordial cooperation of local doctors with their work; the eagerness with which the services of the New York Tuberculosis Committee were received and used, and the long association of Negro physicians with the local work of the Charity Organization Society, are cases in point. Negro dentists not only give their time for clinical service but have clubbed together to buy equipment for their clinic.

WHAT agencies has Harlem for social work? The list is a long one, and to answer the question fully here is clearly impossible. Only a handful can be mentioned. The work of the churches, for example, is presented elsewhere in this issue: here it may be said in passing that they are doing yeoman service in meeting one of Harlem's most pressing needs—that for day nursery care for the children of thousands of employed women, many of whom work the long hours of the domestic servant.

Harlem is fortunate above other communities of its size in having one generalized community agency. While the New York Urban League has a specific program of its own, its significance is that it links up the social and civic work to be done with the potential workers in the community. It pioneers in its own right, and it organizes lines of communication after it has shown the way. It has had a hand in the beginning of a number of enterprises which, once begun, it has left free to develop. It has recently formed a continuing committee of one hundred women representing the whole community. Subcommittees deal with special phases of the Urban League program, but the group as whole is in readiness for any call and limits itself by no fixed objectives. The staff of the League, which of course is Negro, has called together a luncheon conference of fourteen local executives from social, health and educational agencies who meet periodically for common counsel. It serves as a clearing-house for newcomers in New York, and for specialized workers. It functions, in other words, a little like a nascent community council.

The range of its own activities may be imagined from the article on another page by Mr. Johnson of the National Urban League. Like the national body, it is controlled by

170

a board of white and Negro directors, with the Quaker tradition strong among them; like the national body, it devotes much attention to the special problems of the Negro in industry. It studies and promotes vocational opportunities; it seeks to adjust the Negro in industry to his employer and the unions; in some fields it does individual placement work. In housing it acts as a medium between tenants and owners; in recreation it has labored with but a remote hope of success—for public outdoor playgrounds, of which there is but one, and that on the western fringe, in all Harlem. In health it is centering its efforts now on the problem of convalescence, and on the annual health week. Some indication of its standing in Harlem may be seen in the fact that its income from local membership has increased more than sixfold in five years.

It is the Urban League, too, which has provided the nucleus for a central social service building. It shares the dwelling-house which it now owns (and which is soon to be enlarged) with the Henry Street Visiting Nurse service and with the Harlem Tuberculosis Committee of the New York Tuberculosis Association.

The Henry Street Nurses do their customary work, and place special emphasis on a prenatal clinic. The Tuberculosis Committee comes near to being a general public health agency. Its chairman, a Negro physician, is a member of the board of directors of the New York Tuberculosis Association. Its program, shaped by a group made up about equally of Negro physicians and laymen and white social workers, and in the hands of a Negro staff, is a broad and flexible interpretation of the anti-tuberculosis campaign. Beginning with health talks in the churches and schools, it has come to include school nutrition classes; summer institutes at which local physicians have an opportunity to study the best technique in the handling of tuberculosis—an opportunity which is the more valuable because even in New York the limitations on hospital experience hinder the training of Negroes in medicine; medical examinations; a health club for mothers; and a free dental clinic organized at the behest of local dentists, with a volunteer staff of thirteen. It served as the gathering point for the Harlem Health Conference and each year gives the executive service necessary for carrying on Health Week in behalf of this conference.

Other agencies too are building up their community contacts. For example, during the past year the district secretary of the Charity Organization Society has been released from casework in order to develop community-wide relationships. A special committee on Negro problems, organized some years ago on the initiative of Negroes, has by a gradual and natural process been merged with the district committee, which thus becomes interracial, and there has been growing local support for the Negro case-worker on the district staff. The A. I. C. P., and other city-wide organizations, render their usual services in Harlem under central office direction.

THE Young Men's and Young Women's Christian Associations, both directed and officered entirely by Negroes, both housed in handsome new buildings in central locations, provide two much-used social centers for Harlem. The Y. M. C. A. serves about a thousand members with a dormitory, games, religious, athletic and social group activities, an employment office, a swimming pool and gymnasium, and, this year for the first time, with a summer camp. Thanks to a productive plant it is very nearly self-supporting. By way of community service, it keeps a well-informed secretary on duty all night to direct and help newcomers in New York (sent often by the Negro red-caps at the stations); maintains a rooming-house directory; opens its pool one morning a week through the summer to all boys of the neighborhood; and was the first association in the city to institute "splash week," during which every boy in the local schools— white or black—who does not know how to swim is given free instruction.

The Young Women's Christian Association, with a nominal fee, has two thousand members. For the time being it is without dormitory facilities, but it too maintains an all-night service and refers girls and women to suitable rooms, not to mention more difficult social adjustments, and its cafeteria is much used by both men and women. Emphasis is placed on a wide range of trade training courses. The index of the educational department's booklet is intriguing: Bible, Bookkeeping, Business English, Charm School, Children's Sewing, Citizenship, Crochet Beading, Dennison Craft, Dressmaking and Designing, English, Eyebrow-Eyelash Culture, Facial Massage, Filing. . . . A valued community service is given by the association merely by opening its meeting-rooms to various outside groups—groups which have made themselves so much at home that they often schedule their meetings without consulting their host! And no one can doubt that the agreeably-furnished lobby where girls and their friends of both sexes are welcome adds greatly to the amenities of huddled Harlem.

THE branch of the New York Public Library which stands on the main cross thoroughfare of Harlem, 135th Street, seeks to be what the Carnegie Corporation would call an intelligence center. Its staff includes both white and Negro librarians. It has held exhibitions of Negro art and readings of Negro literature. On March 1 it will open a loan exhibition of the original portraits and drawings by Winold Reiss which are reproduced in this number, together with a number of others made at the same time, some of which will appear in future issues of The Survey.

The library is now beginning to build up a special students' collection of Negro literature. Although there is rich and varied material by and about Negroes, it is so widely scattered in homes, in bookshops, in great reference libraries where it is a small part of the whole, and in private collections that it is comparatively unknown to most white people and to a large proportion of Negroes themselves. The library will set apart a special floor where such a collection may be easily available, with a competent colored librarian in charge, and has already formed a permanent organization of men and women to lend it support and to preserve and stabilize its policies. Much of the material sought for this collection consists of rare, out-of-print or costly books. It is hoped that many such now lost to the public in garrets or second-hand shops will find their way to a collection so well-founded and so safeguarded for public use. Much material usually regarded as ephemeral will be considered an essential part:

photographs, broadsides, prints, newspaper articles, autographed letters, and the like. Survey readers who can help in gathering such material are invited to do so and should communicate with Ernestine Rose, branch librarian, 103 West 135th Street, New York.

THE Canadian Industrial Disputes Investigation Act was on January 20 declared *ultra vires,* or as we should say, unconstitutional, by the Lords of the Judicial Committee of the Privy Council. The purpose of the act was to enable the Dominion Government to appoint anywhere in Canada a board of conciliation and investigation to which the dispute between an employer and his employes might be referred. Among other things it made it unlawful for an employer to lock-out or for a workman to strike, on account of the dispute, prior to or during the reference, and imposed an obligation on employes and employers to give thirty day's notice of any intended change affecting wages and hours.

The powers of the Dominion Government, conferred upon it by the Imperial Parliament, are defined in the British North America Act. Under a section of this act, the Dominion Parliament has a general power to make laws for Canada as a whole; but these laws are not to relate to classes of subjects assigned to the provinces, unless their enactment falls under heads specifically enumerated in the act. Exceptions to this rule might arise in case of war and of emergencies affecting the entire dominion such as the outbreak and spread of epidemic disease. The Supreme Court of Ontario had upheld the Disputes Act on the ground that a strike might conceivably spread from province to province and so create a menace to the dominion as a whole. It rested its argument largely upon an earlier decision of the Judicial Committee of the Privy Council that it was within the competence of the Dominion Parliament to establish a uniform system for prohibiting the liquor traffic throughout Canada excepting under restrictive conditions. The Judicial Committee finds that this decision is not applicable to the case of the Industrial Disputes Act, on the ground that at the period of the passing of the Canada Temperance Act an emergency affecting Canada as a whole must be assumed to have existed, whereas neither in 1907 when the Disputes Act was passed nor since that time has a strike or lockout constituted such an emergency.

The final court of appeal in the British Empire therefore finds that in passing the Industrial Disputes Investigation Act, the Dominion Parliament exceeded its powers and after eighteen years of the law's operation declares it invalid.

IN a report which celebrated its semi-centennial, the Board of Health of Michigan tells of the remote days of the seventies and eighties when people had hardly heard of germs. One visitor, gazing through a microscope, asked how long those germs were, and learned with visible relief that 20,000 of them, laid in a row, would measure approximately one inch. "Oh," she said, "I'm not afraid of them little fel-

lers." Within the past three months, however, some of them little fellers, and the belief of the public in their unseen powers, has laid low an industry which involves millions of dollars annually. As some hundreds of cases of typhoid fever, with scores of deaths, have been numbered in New York, Chicago and other cities which draw their supplies of oysters from the Atlantic beds, such a state of public panic has been created that oystermen from the Chesapeake northward are out of work; their season is almost over and their oysters have had no sale. Though some branches of the oyster industry have persisted in an unfortunate policy of shilly-shally, pointing accusing fingers at lettuce or celery as the source of the epidemic, the bulk of the group of producers have accepted sensibly the inescapable inference that there has been some pollution of oysters somewhere. They are ready to do almost anything to restore public confidence, but what? A Vigilance Committee of the producers centering in New York pledge their word of honor that only oysters of the most impeccable quality are admitted to the New York markets; other groups are crying for government investigation and certification. The Secretary of Commerce has asked Congress to appropriate $25,000 for a survey into the oyster industry to remove conditions which might cause typhoid or other disease, to be administered in all probability by the United States Public Health Service, which conducted a series of similar studies before the war. Whether the oyster industry succeeds in cleaning its own house, or we shall be obliged to bring in the government broom, it, and any other industry which observe its pitiful and generally undeserved plight, have had an impressive lesson in the sensitiveness of the popular mind to the germ theory, in the economies of prevention over cure and in the fact that an industry, like a chain, is judged by its weakest link.

THE dismissal of the notorious suit to test the constitutionality of California's minimum wage law (see The Survey, Feb. 15, 1925) leaves the question of the constitutionality of the law, so far as the California state courts are concerned, where it was before.

In Wisconsin Federal Judge Claude Z. Luse has made permanent the preliminary injunction restraining the Industrial Commission from enforcing the provisions of the minimum wage law relative to adult women workers in the plant of the Folding Furniture Works. In his ruling Judge Luse stated that "this case involves no attack upon that part of the minimum wage law which applies to the wages of minors. This court is bound to apply the principle of the Adkins case to the one at bar, and it is therefore held that the Wisconsin Act, so far as it affects the plaintiff in employing adult women, is invalid."

In view of the fact that the members' of the Industrial Welfare Commission of California, as defendants in the suit against the state minimum wage law, while accepting the decision of the United States Supreme Court in the Adkins case, leaned heavily upon the contention that that decision did not properly apply in the differing environment and circumstances surrounding the state's minimum wage laws, this ruling of Judge Luse in the Folding Furniture case gives occasion for serious apprehension. Doubt with respect to the future status of minimum wage legislation is increased by the similar action of the Supreme Court of Porto Rico. Because of the decision of the United States Supreme Court that the minimum wage law of the District of Columbia was not a health measure and was unconstitutional, the Supreme Court of Porto Rico has reversed its earlier favorable decision and has declared the Minimum Wage Act of 1919 unconstitutional.

WHEN the American delegation entered gallantly into the opium affray at Geneva it had three main propositions: to "pull up the poppy," that is, to limit the production of raw opium; to abolish the smoking of opium in the East through a ten years' period of progressive restriction; and to establish a Central Board of Control to list and check the amount of opium needed in each country for manufacture for home use or export, and control shipments from one country to another. The poppy is not to be pulled up, at least for the present; the abolition of opium smoking is shoved off almost indefinitely; but the Central Board of Control has been salvaged out of the confusion of crossed interests, and apparently the United States and Germany are to be asked to appoint representatives to sit with the Council of the League in the election of its members.

The first opium conference, which was convened last November, met to consider the question of opium smoking in the East. The tangible result of that conference is the convention abolishing the "farm system," with an attached protocol. This convention removes opium from the field of private sale and profit, and makes its distribution a government monopoly—an essential stage in the process of government regulation. The protocol, embodying a British suggestion, would limit smoking opium through a period of fifteen years, to start *after* an impartial commission has decided that the time is ripe for it—that is, in effect, when smuggling has been stopped, when China has established internal control which will afford some check on the appalling recrudescence of opium growing in her provinces, and when the force of public opinion in the other eastern states will permit more drastic regulation than their representatives now declare possible. The policy of registering and rationing opium addicts was affirmed as a declaration of principle. In the meantime all the states are to use all possible means to check the practice. This is a disappointing application of the principle in Article 6 of the Opium Convention that 'The Contracting Powers shall take measures for the gradual and effective suppression of the manufacture of, internal trade in, and use of, prepared opium."

The second conference, of powers which produce opium and other products from which narcotic drugs are manufactured, has set up the Central Board of Control practically according to the American plan. This board is to consist of eight persons, not government employes, chosen to inspire general confidence by reason of their technical competence, impartiality and disinterestedness. It will receive estimates from the various governments stating in advance their probable requirements of opium for medical and scientific uses. Every three months it will receive and publish estimates of the current imports and exports of opium. The discrepancy between the amount necessary for medicinal purposes and the amount actually imported in each instance will give a continuous indication of the quantities diverted to illegitimate uses. If an undue amount is shipped to any one point, the board can call the attention of the nations to the phenomenon, and request that shipments be suspended pending investigation. It has no administrative except publicity. What the effect—or whether there will be an effect—of this new machinery can be determined only by actual trial of it. It certainly will show where the raw opium is going, and how much of the manufactured product is accounted for in legitimate export or home use; moreover it offers the inspiring precedent of an international body met to consider the world's supply and distribution of one raw material on the basis of national needs. Supported by vigorous public opinion that principle might go far.

ASIDE from their administrative achievements, the two conferences have accomplished a piece of public education of enormous magnitude, though many of their revelations have been negative. They have shown the tremendous complexities which beset the carrying out of any straightforward policy in the control of the world's supply of opium. Before that can be assured, China must put down her civil wars; Persia and Turkey, which produce opium for export, say that they must have loans and other help to enable them to change the custom of centuries and adapt other crops to the regions where opium now is grown; Jugo-Slavia must provide for her opium farmers; India, which alone eats opium, must discontinue the practice by domestic legislation, or yield the principle, hitherto guarded jealously, that her habits are subject to international agreement; the colonies of the western powers in the Orient must find a substitute for the opium revenue and some method other than the keeping of opium dens, to attract Chinese coolie labor; and a network of smuggling, spread over the East, the Philippines, linked even to the Occident, must be broken. Ideally the logical method to cut under all these difficulties would have been to stop excess cultivation of the poppy, and nip opium in the bud. Since the largest producer, China, has apparently no power to enforce such policy on her subjects, and the other countries have at present no intention or desire to do so (if the ability) the actual achievement of the conferences—the Central Board— must be accepted as important in its potentialities, and as a present tool for focussing and bringing into action that part of the world's public opinion which believes that opium must and shall go.

JUST a year afer The Survey's Giant Power number went to press, its forecasts of the social consequences reasonably to be anticipated from the rapid extension of large scale electrical development are sustained and reenforced by the scholarly and illuminating report of Pennsylvania's Giant Power Survey Board. The authenticity of The Survey's forecasts was largely due to the generous cooperation of Morris Llewellyn Cooke, director of the work of the Board whose findings and recommendations

Governor Pinchot laid before Pennsylvania's General Assembly on February 17.

On the basis of intensive research carried on under his direction during the past pear by an expert corps of engineers and economists, Mr. Cooke reaffirms our conclusion that electrical development, and especially the art of transmitting current in large volume over great distances practically without loss, has brought us to the threshold of momentous changes in our industrial, home and farm management, and transportation technique which will vitally affect conditions of life in both urban and rural areas. These changes are already in process on a gigantic scale. It is only a matter of months before electric generating and distributing companies will be interconnected from Chicago to the Gulf, from the Atlantic Coast to the Great Plains, from the state of Washington to and across the Mexican border. The quantity of electric energy now used for heat, light and power is such that in view of the present trend toward tying together the generating, transmitting and distribution systems, unprecedented economies are within reach. "This," says Mr. Cooke, "makes possible not only a widespread distribution but a revolutionary increase in the use of electricity in factory and in home, on the farm and in transportation."

These social advantages will not accrue to the great masses of our people unless they bring to bear upon the electrical industry the control of an enlightened public opinion. "No one," says Governor Pinchot in his message of transmittal, "who studies the electrical developments already achieved and those planned for the immediate future can doubt that a unified electrical monopoly extending into every part of this nation is inevitable in the very near future." It is impossible, he affirms, to imagine the force and intimacy with which such a monopoly will touch and affect, for good or evil, the life of every cititzen. "The time is fully in sight when every household operation from heating and cooking to sweeping and sewing will be performed by the aid of electrical power; when every article on the average man's breakfast table, every item of clothing, every piece of his furniture, every tool of his trade, will have been manufactured or transported by electric power; when the home, the farm and the factory will be electrically lighted, heated and operated; when from morning to night, from the cradle to the grave, electric service will enter at every moment and from every direction into the daily life of every man, woman and child in America." The question before us, he adds, is not whether there shall be such a monopoly, but whether we as a people shall control it or shall permit it to control us—whether we shall respect the human wastes and tragedies which were the by-products of the steam revolution, or whether by taking counsel of that experience we shall make the new giant more the servant than the master of our common life.

The report of Pennsylvania's Giant Power Survey Board is not only a great state paper but such a treasure house of information arranged and simply interpreted for the use of the laymen as has never before been available on the supremely important subject with which it deals, and which is of direct concern to men and women in every branch of social activity—industry, education, health and family casework. Readers who were interested in The Survey's Giant Power number will be glad to know that a limited number of copies are available upon application to the Giant Power Survey Board in Harrisburg.

702

The Negro in Print

A Selected List of Magazines and Books By and About Negroes

THE whole trend of literature about the Negro has turned from the controversial to the informational within the last ten years, and a culling of the most outstanding recent literature has been made for Survey readers. Except for purposes of historical record, whole libraries of controversial "problem literature" are now obsolete, and the primary requirements of the new situation are a fresh start and an open mind. In the general literature of the subject there are now available comprehensive and well-documented histories of the Negro, both in relation to America and to the African origins, with a marked tendency to take the whole question out of the context of debate and controversy and set it in terms of factual evidence in an accurate historical background and perspective. Even in relation to Southern conditions, the economic and sociological interpretation has eventually prevailed, and bias and special pleading are fading out of the literature. The following list is selected for general reading.

I—General Reading

A SOCIAL HISTORY OF THE AMERICAN NEGRO, by *Benjamin Brawley*. Macmillan. Price $4.00.
THE NEGRO IN OUR HISTORY, by *Carter G. Woodson*. Third Edition. Associated Publishers. Price $2.50.
THE NEGRO, by *W. E. B. Du Bois*. (Home University Library) Henry Holt. Price $1.00.
THE GIFT OF BLACK FOLK, by *W. E. B. Du Bois*. The Stratford Co.
THE NEGRO FACES AMERICA, by *Herbert J. Seligmann*. Harper & Co. Price $2.50.
THE NEGRO FROM AFRICA TO AMERICA, by *W. D. Weatherford*. Doran. Price $5.00.
CHRISTIANITY AND THE RACE PROBLEM, by *J. H. Oldham*, Doran. Price $1.75.
RACE ADJUSTMENT, by *Kelly Miller*. Neale Publishing Co.
THE EVERLASTING STAIN, by *Kelly Miller*. Associated Publishing Co. $2.50.

More representative still of the modern scientific attitude and approach, is the marked growth of special studies of the Negro, not only of the academic type, and of the practical scientific study, but also of the reliable popular compendium of detailed information, the latter especially in connection with details of current developments within the Negro group. Quite noteworthy are the increasing evidences of liberalism of view on the part of Southern investigators and of the tendency to go to the Negro himself for that information which can only come reliably from inside the group life. A list has been made of the best available sources of detailed scientific and sociological information.

II—Sociological and Special Studies

A CENTURY OF NEGRO MIGRATION, by *Carter G. Woodson*. Associated Publishing Co. Price $2.00.
NEGRO MIGRATION, by *Thomas J. Woofter*. W. D. Gray Co.
THE EDUCATION OF THE NEGRO PRIOR TO 1861, by *Carter G. Woodson*. Associated Publishing Co.
THE NEGRO IN CHICAGO, Chicago Inter-Racial Commission, University of Chicago Press.
DARKER PHASES OF THE SOUTH, by *Frank J. Tannenbaum*. Putnam. Price $2.00.
THE SOUTHERN OLIGARCHY, by *William H. Skaggs*. Devin-Adair Co. Price $5.00.

WHY HAVE LYNCHINGS
DECREASED

FROM 60 A YEAR TO 16 IN 1924?

THE NATIONAL ASSOCIATION FOR THE ADVANCEMENT OF COLORED PEOPLE OFFERS IN EVIDENCE THE FACTS BELOW:

1. The N.A.A.C.P., beginning 1916, has SPENT MORE THAN $50,000 in the first and only organized, persistent, intensive campaign of fact and education against lynching in America.

2. The N.A.A.C.P. has HELD MORE THAN 4,000 PUBLIC MEETINGS and has distributed MILLIONS OF PIECES OF LITERATURE.

3. The N.A.A.C.P. has INVESTIGATED 44 LYNCHINGS ON THE SPOT, often at risk of life of the investigators, and has spread the facts obtained throughout the civilized world.

4. The N.A.A.C.P. FORCED THE DYER ANTI-LYNCHING BILL THROUGH THE HOUSE OF REPRESENTATIVES by a vote of 230 to 119, making that measure a national issue.

5. The N.A.A.C.P. published "Thirty Years of Lynching," a 105-page book, the ONLY AUTHENTIC RECORD OF LYNCHING IN AMERICA.

6. The N.A.A.C.P. HELD THE FIRST NATIONAL ANTI-LYNCHING CONFERENCE in New York, in 1919. Among those attending were Charles Evans Hughes, Governor O'Neill of Alabama, and Moorfield Storey. This Conference issued an ADDRESS TO THE NATION signed by 4 attorneys-general, 7 governors, 20 leading Southerners, and others.

7. The N.A.A.C.P. SPENT $6,980 in reaching 5 million people through "THE SHAME OF AMERICA," a full-page advertisement in leading dailies throughout the country, setting forth the plain facts about lynching.

8. The N.A.A.C.P. sent a MEMORIAL TO THE SENATE urging enactment of the Dyer Bill, the signers including 24 STATE GOVERNORS, 39 MAYORS, 88 BISHOPS AND CHURCHMEN, 29 COLLEGE PRESIDENTS AND PROFESSORS, 30 PROMINENT EDITORS, and many other influential persons.

9. COMMENT OF THE JUDICIARY COMMITTEE OF THE HOUSE OF REPRESENTATIVES (1924): "We believe that the decrease (in lynching) is due to the publicity given this crime, and the fear of a law by the United States, providing for punishment for those who participate and are responsible for lynchings. The American people generally have been for the first time told the truth regarding lynchings, and that they are not caused by the commission of heinous crimes, except in a small part of the total number lynched."

BUT LYNCHING IS NOT YET ABOLISHED—THE DYER BILL MUST PASS

IN ADDITION

177

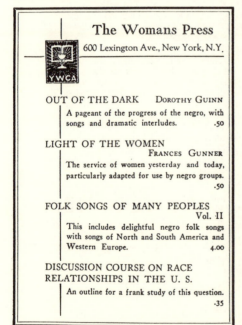
178

AFRICAN CLEARINGS, by *Jean K. Mackenzie*. Houghton, Mifflin. Price $2.50.
THE QUAINT COMPANIONS, by *Leonard Merrick*. Dutton. Price $1.90.
GOD'S STEPCHILDREN, by *Sarah G. Millin*. Boni & Liveright. Price $2.00.
THE LONG WALK OF SAMBA DIOUF, by *Jerome and Jean Tharaud*. Duffield. Price $1.75.

Negro Culture

AFRO-AMERICAN FOLKSONGS, by *H. E. Krehbiel*.
SONGS AND TALKS FROM THE DARK CONTINENT, by *Natalie Burlin Curtis*. Schirmer. Price $4.00.
NEGRO CULTURE IN WEST AFRICA, by *George W. Ellis*. Neale Publishing Co. Price $2.00.
PRIMITIVE NEGRO SCULPTURE, by *Paul Guillaume and T. Munro*. (on press) Barnes Foundation.
African Art Issue of OPPORTUNITY, May 1924.

Sharing increasing contact with the general world of letters, and speaking with a new cultural emphasis and breadth, Negro authors are collaborating in giving an artistically conceived version of Negro life and feeling to the world.

V—Negro Belles Lettres

Poetry

AMERICAN NEGRO POETRY, *compiled by James Weldon Johnson*. Harcourt, Brace & Co. Price $1.75.
AN ANTHOLOGY OF AMERICAN NEGRO VERSE, *compiled by N. I. White and C. A. Jackson*. Trinity College Press, Durham, N. C. Price $2.00.
FIFTY YEARS AND AFTER, by *James Weldon Johnson*. Cornhill. Price $1.25.
THE HOUSE OF FALLING LEAVES, by *Wm. Stanley Braithwaite*. Luce. Price $1.00.
SANDY GEE AND OTHER POEMS, by *Wm. Stanley Braithwaite*.
THE HEART OF A WOMAN & OTHER POEMS, by *Georgia Douglas Johnson*. Cornhill. Price $1.25.
BRONZE, by *Georgia Douglas Johnson*.
HARLEM SHADOWS, by *Claude McKaye*. Harcourt, Brace & Co. Price $1.35.
THE COLLECTED POEMS OF PAUL LAURENCE DUNBAR. Dodd Mead & Co. Price $2.50.

Drama

RACHEL, by *Angelina Grimke*.

Fiction

SPORT OF THE GODS, by *Paul Laurence Dunbar*. Dodd Mead. Price $1.50.
THE UNCALLED, by *Paul Laurence Dunbar*.
THE MARROW OF TRADITION, by *Charles W. Chesnutt*. Houghton Mifflin. Price $1.50.
THE HOUSE BEHIND THE CEDARS, by *Charles W. Chesnutt*. Houghton Mifflin. Price $1.50.
THE WIFE OF HIS YOUTH AND OTHER STORIES, by *Charles W. Chesnutt*. Houghton Mifflin. Price $1.50.
THE CONJURE WOMAN, by *Charles W. Chesnutt*. Houghton Mifflin. Price $1.25.
THE QUEST OF THE SILVER FLEECE, by *W. E. B. Du Bois*. McClurg. Price $1.20.
BATOUALA, by *René Maran*. Seltzer. Price $1.25.
CANE, by *Jean Toomer*. Boni & Liveright.
THERE IS CONFUSION, by *Jessie Fauset*. Boni & Liveright. Price $2.00.
THE FIRE IN THE FLINT, by *Walter F. White*. Knopf. Price $2.50.

General

THE SOULS OF BLACK FOLK, by *W. E. B. Du Bois*. McClurg. Price $1.35.
DARKWATER, by *W. E. B. Du Bois*. Harcourt, Brace. Price $2.25.
THE POETIC YEAR, by *Wm. Stanley Braithwaite*. Small, Maynard. Price $2.00.
UP FROM SLAVERY, by *Booker T. Washington*. Houghton Mifflin.
AUTOBIOGRAPHY, *Frederick Douglass*. A. L.

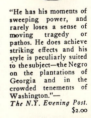
707

179

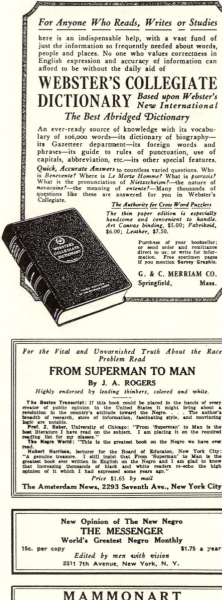
THE CHURCH AND THE NEGRO SPIRIT
(_Continued from page 697_)

the vigor and power of numbers. In the independent Negro denominations there are more than 35,000 churches with over four million members enrolled and church property valued at over seventy million dollars. In the mixed religious bodies there are over 6,000 Negro churches, nearly three quarter million Negro members enrolled and over seventeen millions in church property.*

There is a strong racial tie between Negro churches, both of the independent group and of mixed denominations. Recently churches of the several denominations of Harlem joined forces in a league, affiliated with the New York Church Federation and employed an executive secretary. Denominational differences are no problem with these churches as there are frequent visits of delegations from one congregation to another and frequent ministerial fellowship and exchange of pulpits.

The Negro ministry has been making gradual gains in intelligence and social vision. The facilities for training of Negro religious leaders, however, are not commensurate with the provision for training in other lines. A recent survey of theological education showed how inadequate are the curriculum and the personnel of institutions for theological training of Negro youth. In New York, of course, all avenues of religious and theological education are open to Negro leaders, but most of the ministers lived during their years of training in sections where such facilities were not open to them. Negroes trained in social work have been on the scene in small numbers the past twelve or fifteen years, but social plans and programs are yet uncertain and have not fully engaged the churches. The Negro churches of Harlem, however, are developing along these lines. Six churches have trained staff assistants for religious education and social service. The great demand is for trained helpers for ministers to foster programs in these churches which will meet the larger needs of worship, religious education and social service.

A WHITE visitor to the morning services of a popular Harlem church remarked, "These people are taking their religion with intense earnestness. A white congregation is usually so restrained in their services that they seem to measure the transaction they are carrying on with God." The spirit of the Negro people is shown in the fleeting hours of their amusement and play, in the furtive expression of their appreciation of things beautiful, and in outpourings of personality and emotion as they gather in their places of worship, and as they render the many personal services the one to the other in the routine of daily life. Free self-expression in these directions is often limited in America by economic and social discriminations. Emotional experience and the personal experience of service, however, find large objective opportunity through the Negro church. The churches of the Negro people are channels of their spiritual life blood. They are less restricted, probably, than any other group organization. Especially in the South, from which the majority of the Negroes in New York, Philadelphia, Chicago and

* See Negro Yearbook, 1921-22, pp. 202-3.

other Northern cities have come in the last twenty years, the church is the most effective community agency for emotional, intellectual and other group expression. "The pillars of the church" are usually the leaders of the community. The social and cultural life of the group is largely influenced by these leaders; and the new environment puts this leadership to new tests.

RESIDENCE in northern cities brings to Negroes several advantages, such as greater freedom of movement, freedom of speech and assembly, that give play to increased group expression and intra-group intercourse. Lack of restrictions on street cars and railroad trains removes irritation of mind and body. The greater attraction of the paved and lighted streets, the parks, playgrounds and water fronts offer allurements to the young folk. Greater access to libraries, moving picture shows, theatres, dance halls, and other means of self-expression set up keen competition with the churches.

The throngs of the present generation have come up through public and private schools which although inadequate have given them a point of view based on modern knowledge. Negro illiteracy has been reduced from 90 to 22 per cent in sixty years. Thousands have been awakened in rural communities through such means as visiting lectures and the war drives. They are no longer satisfied with the older types of church service. These must therefore be pitched upon a plane of intelligence with an emotional appeal which holds its own in competition with those other channels of knowledge and emotional enthusiasm.

Nearly all the Harlem churches are led by men who sense this situation. Athletic and social clubs for young people are promoted. Musical and literary organizations which meet both on weekdays and Sundays attract large numbers. The Sunday afternoon lyceum or forum is on the program of many churches. Week day religious instruction and vacation Bible schools have also been fostered. The regular religious services for the adult congregation in most instances are conducted with dignity and order, with intelligent sermons to meet the personal and group problems with which these people wrestle. These church forces have been the principal power against the evils of the district which are always present.

The Negro churches of Harlem are visible evidence of the struggle of an aspiring people to express the best of life within them. Either in structures purchased from white congregations or in those they themselves build, they are organizing and developing personnel and membership to conserve the spiritual and ethical values of the race. They are struggling, often against great odds, to provide an avenue of self-expression to a people that is seeking to serve and to walk humbly with God.

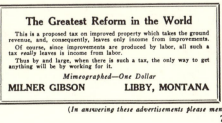
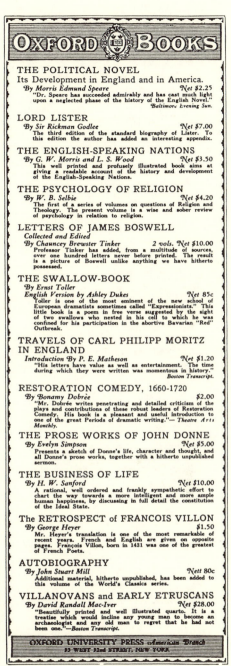

THE BLACK MAN BRINGS HIS GIFTS
(Continued from page 657)

lurked beneath. And at last she took out a little thin black book and read.

She read about this country not belonging to white folks any more than it did to black folks and that the black folks got here before the pilgrims. I couldn't help stepping on Birdie's toes because she says her people came in on some boat named after a flower so long ago she's forgot their names. The black girl said that the story of the Negro could be found on every page of the story of America. This made me sick and I turned and glared right at her. But she looked right through me and went on. She said Negroes had been soldiers in all our wars, had nursed the babies, cooked the food and sung and danced besides working so hard that "working like a nigger" was about the hardest work you could picture.

And she asked us if America could have been America without Negroes.

She had me up a tree, I must admit. And I reckon the rest felt as I did—all except that editor.

The chairman looked at us with owl-like eyes; then he shoved a paper at me and read it aloud as he did:

"Timeo Nigros et dona ferentes"

Nobody knows what he meant and nobody gave him the satisfaction of asking.

WELL, we just sat and stared until she left. Then we went on talking but we didn't touch the real question; and that was, could we have America's Making without Mrs. Cadwalader Lee and with the Negroes?

We couldn't make up our minds and before we had courage to say so openly we went smash on religion.

We might possibly have had some sort of an America's Making pageant if we hadn't discussed religion. You see, the editor who is downright malicious and hates the Federation of Women's Clubs because they start things, got us all wrong by trying to get a definition of religion. He was strong on meekness and humility and turning the other cheek and that sort of thing and I know he didn't mean a word of it.

"I suppose," said Birdie, "that you'll be saying that the Negroes have given us all our religion because they're cowards and allowed themselves to be slaves and take insult today meekly."

"I must admit," said the preacher, "that if the meek inherit the earth, the American Negro will get a large share."

"But will the meek inherit the earth?" I asked.

"I think so," said the chairman calmly.

Birdie jumped up and reached for her cloak. "I believe you're a Jew and a pacifist," she said.

"I am both," he answered.

"And I suppose," said I, getting my hat on straight, "that when somebody slaps you over, you turn the other cheek."

"I did," said he.

"Well, you're a fool," I answered, reaching for my coat. And Birdie yelled, 'And what did they do to you after you turned the other cheek? Answer me that."

"They crucified me," said the chairman.

THE HARVEST OF RACE PREJUDICE
(*Continued from page* 683)

urban and industrial. The Negro Sanhedrin, the most recent attempt at race organization, seeks to understand the nature and extend of race prejudice, and to work on the basis of this understanding. If it should turn out that race prejudice cannot be overcome by direct attack and opposition, it may possibly be circumvented by building independently where independence is necessary, and by cooperation where cooperation is possible. It would at least garner the harvest of prejudice to the best advantage of the race. The Negro Sanhedrin seeks to find the common denominator of racial ills, and would federate into one effective effort the scattered energies which are so largely wasted by friction and cross purpose. As a matter of fact, the race as a whole had never hitherto seriously essayed collective handling of the racial situation as a whole. There have been innumerable attempts at dealing with special features along local, religious, political and economic lines. But the integration of the race mind and the focalization of endeavor still await the fuller unfoldment of the workings of some such comprehensive movement as the Negro Sanhedrin. The twelve millions scattered throughout the length and breadth of the land are treated by a single formula so far as the white race is concerned. And yet the Negro has had to rely upon local and scattered effort to offset the solid line of racial exclusiveness with which he is confronted. He must seek concerted action to confront difficulties that are nationwide and race-deep.

Every minority and suppressed group seeks self-expression. Woodrow Wilson let off the lid of a new Pandora's box when he so eloquently preached this doctrine as the shibboleth of the war. The Negro seeks self-determination also. In Harlem he seeks political self-expression. He wants men of his own race to represent him in the city council, in the state legislature and in the national Congress. Wherever a political area is numerically dominated by members of the race, they will naturally seek a voice in political councils. Here again segregation is basic. If the Negro were thinly scattered throughout greater New York, he would be politically negligible. In Chicago, in the recent election, Negro candidates were successful for state Senate, Assembly and the municipal Bench, and the whole race rejoices. What is it that twelve million Negroes in jubilation over such successes but the uniting force of race prejudice?

Business is the last place in which prejudice shows itself, and it is in this field that its harvest is least manifest. Scattered throughout Harlem on practically every street corner are Jewish stores catering to the vast Negro constituency. The Jew makes the most acceptable merchant among Negroes because he knows how to reduce race prejudice to a minimum. In Harlem, as in every other large city, the Negro proprietor conducts mainly sumptuary establishments such as eating-houses, barber-shops, beauty parlors, pool rooms, and such places as cater immediately to the appetite or to the taste. The more substantial stores which require a larger exercise of the imagination, such as those dealing in dry goods, shoes, furniture, hardware and groceries, are usually in the hands of whites. Race prejudice will sooner or later lead to race patronage in business as it has already

done in the professions; but it awaits the time when the Negro shall have developed the business aptitude to compete with the white dealer, who is shrewd enough to hold prejudice in restraint for the sake of trade.

The final outcome of race prejudice operating to establish and maintain Negro sections in New York and elsewhere must evidently be a self-sufficient Negro community, competent to cater to its own needs and necessities as well as to contribute its quota to the general industrial and economic life of the city as a whole. What then will be the form of race adjustment? Will the relationship of the two be characterized by amity or by enmity? We approach the issue with a mixed feeling of hopes and fears, but with our hopes triumphant over our fears. However bitter the fruit of the tree of prejudice may be, the Negro will eat thereof and thrive by the eating.

JAZZ AT HOME
(*Continued from page* 667)

For the Negro himself, jazz is both more and less dangerous than for the white—less in that, he is nervously more in tune with it; more, in that at his average level of economic development his amusement life is more open to the forces of social vice. The cabaret of better type provides a certain Bohemianism for the Negro intellectual, the artist and the well-to-do. But the average thing is too much the substitute for the saloon and the wayside inn. The tired longshoreman, the porter, the housemaid and the poor elevator boy in search of recreation, seeking in jazz the tonic for weary nerves and muscles, are only too apt to find the bootlegger, the gambler and the demi-monde who have come there for victims and to escape the eyes of the police.

Yet in spite of its present vices and vulgarizations, its sex informalities, its morally anarchic spirit, jazz has a popular mission to perform. Joy, after all, has a physical basis. Those who laugh and dance and sing are better off even in their vices than those who do not. Moreover jazz with its mocking disregard for formality is a leveler and makes for democracy. The jazz spirit, being primitive, demands more frankness and sincerity. Just as it already has done in art and music, so eventually in human relations and social manners, it will no doubt have the effect of putting more reality in life by taking some of the needless artificiality out. . . . Naturalness finds the artificial in conduct ridiculous. "Cervantes smiled Spain's chivalry away," said Byron. And so this new spirit of joy and spontaneity may itself play the role of reformer. Where at present it vulgarizes, with more wholesome growth in the future, it may on the contrary truly democratize. At all events jazz is rejuvenation, a recharging of the batteries of civilization with primitive new vigor. It has come to stay, and they are wise, who instead of protesting against it, try to lift and divert it into nobler channels.

AMBUSHED IN THE CITY
(Continued from page 694)

to me. "He said: 'A friend of mine brought this prescription into my store. I can't fill it. You fill it for me. If he'd been a stranger, I'd have given him something. But I don't want to hand out to a friend that stuff we have on our shelves.' He didn't bother much with prescriptions, he confessed. Sometimes he put in substitute ingredients; sometimes he left out something that was called for. 'You leave your label off this and I'll put ours on' he said."

The Negro pharmacist continued:

"Some of these drug stores certainly are fakes. Why, they don't keep enough drugs on hand to fill simple prescriptions. Not long ago I sent three prescriptions out to fifteen of 'em—easy prescriptions; I just wanted to make a little experiment. I didn't bother with those drug stores over on Lenox Avenue—I knew what I'd be gettin' into there. I just stuck to Seventh Avenue.

"Well, you should have seen the collection that came back. One prescription called for a nerve sedative, a compound of chloral hydrate, tincture canabis and some other things. Two druggists put elixir of lactated pepsin—for indigestion!—into the prescription, instead of the elixir triple bromides I called for. And you should have seen those bottles! Some were half choked with gelatinous substances that had no business there; others had sediment. They were every color from yellow to dark brown. Why, those druggists just put in any old thing. Another prescription called for a seven-grain capsule. The capsules came back weighed all the way from three grains to ten; the average was about four. They couldn't even get the quantity right! Those stores are a crime. 'Anything's good enough for niggers!' say the people who run them."

There are other forms of hooch joints—cigar stores, small restaurants, saloon-like shops, delicatessen stores and the like. The drinks they sell are very bad; it is commonly declared that the worst of the illegal booze is worked off on the Negro. These places have been exposed. Their addresses have been published time and again. The owner of The New York Age, Fred R. Moore, already referred to, is a fighting Negro. He is educated and intelligent. He believes in protecting his people from exploitation. Every week for months he has been publishing in his weekly a list of addresses; over it he puts the headline: Old and New Hooch Joints in Harlem. I know of no publication of a similar list of addresses elsewhere. Sometimes Mr. Moore puts his list on the front page; it runs to about a hundred addresses. Here is part of the list on one street, taken from the issue of October 25, 1924: 404, 414, 419, 434, 448, 452, 481, 476, 477, 486, 488a—eleven within a single hundred numbers. Mr. Moore has never been the defendant in a libel action for characterizing these places as illegally engaged in selling liquor, and that fact is pretty good evidence that they are really what he calls them.

THE Negro in Harlem, like Negroes in many other places, is prey for poorly-trained white doctors and for unmistakable quacks. Some of these come to Harlem because they know that here quackery is easy; they fatten on the credulity of the Negro, and on his faith in the white man. Many of these doctors are prominent members of the community; a population of 200,000 spreads out before them, offering a lucrative field, and they take advantage of it.

Not long ago a white doctor in Harlem dismissed a colored patient, telling him that he had "spider cancer" at the base of his spine, and that it was incurable. Now, there is no such thing as spider cancer. The man had come to the doctor because he had hurt his back in a fall. The doctor applied dressing after dressing and plaster after plaster, and finally produced a creased, web-like spot on the man's back; it was

═AMALGAMATED BANK═
OF NEW YORK

FIRST LABOR BANK IN NEW YORK

103 East 14th St.   Cor. 4th Avenue at Union Square

Our Second Birthday

APRIL 14th, 1925

We have reached

Over 5 Million Dollars

in total assets

Check Accounts	Thrift
Foreign Remittances	Accounts!
Steamship Tickets	Our Interest Dept. Pays **4%**
Letters of Credit	Compounded Quarterly

325 Banks Use Our Foreign Department

These banks recognize our excellent connections and avail themselves of our prompt, dependable and efficient service. Many thousands of individuals as well as organizations also send their remittances through our Foreign Department. We deliver U. S. Dollars to all parts of the world, including Soviet Russia.

Open an Account

in the

Amalgamated Bank
of New York

Member Federal Reserve System

Conveniently Located—Convenient Banking Hours

103 East 14th St.   Cor. 4th Avenue at Union Square

Banking Hours

Mon., 9 A. M.-8 P. M.   Sat., 9 A. M.-5 P. M.

Other Days, 9 A. M.-6 P. M.

(In answering this advertisement please mention THE SURVEY. *It helps us, it identifies you.)*

713

185

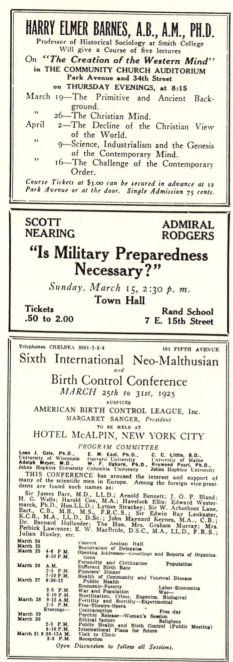

this that he called "spider cancer." The poor fellow received proper treatment only when he went to a trained colored physician in the neighborhood.

"We know some of our white colleagues by their trails," said a colored physician, attached to the out-patient department of Harlem Hospital, to me. He was unwilling to be quoted if the names of these doctors were to be used, and so I have substituted letters for their names. "There's Doctor X, for instance. He is known by the plasters he leaves behind him. Whenever a patient has a pain, X puts a plaster over it. If you raise the shirt of a patient and find a plaster of mole skin adhesive there, you can say, 'Oh, I see you've been to Doctor X.' He always uses mole skin adhesive.

"Then there's Doctor Y. He uses pills, rotating them by color. 'What color did I give you last time?' he asks his patients, and then changes to another. It's easy to follow Doctor Y; just look at the mantlepiece and if his pills are there, you know what your patient has been up against.

"Doctor Z flops down on his knees and prays and prays with his patients. Though white, he knows his colored people, or a certain class of them. He will blare out in fine style his appeals to the Lord to help the treatment he has just given. I guess prayer is often necessary.

"Then there's Doctor A. 'What!' exclaimed Doctor A. 'Read medical books! I haven't read a medical book for ten years. I don't have to read 'em to practice on niggers!'

"They charge some of these colored people pretty high fees, too. The other day a white doctor charged $600 for drawing the water off a patient who had pleurisy—aspirating, it is called. This is ordinarily done by a physician in the course of a routine call. This doctor called it 'a major operation' and collected $600. They play on the Negro's ignorance of what is being done to him, and rob him."

ALL this, it can readily be imagined, has none too good an effect upon the Negro's health.

Any improvement that the race makes is made despite great obstacles. We all have heard that the Negro is not a healthy race. In a measure, this is true. Tuberculosis is the great enemy of the Negro. In the long run it kills one out of every six; few races show a greater tuberculosis deathrate. The incidence of rickets, a disease of malnutrition among children, is also high with the Negro. Chronic degenerative diseases, such as cerebral hemorrhage and organic diseases of the heart, are strong among Negroes. Cancer and diabetes carry off large numbers of them. The deathrate for the race as a whole is high, especially in cities.

In 1921 the deathrate among Negroes in the rural parts of registration states was 13.8 per 1,000; it was 10.8 for whites. In the cities it was 19.7 for Negroes, 11.8 for whites. Mortality among Negroes, 30 per cent higher than that among whites in the rural parts, was 67 per cent higher in the cities. In New York City the deathrate for Negroes in 1923 was 20.85, for whites 11.25. It looks as if the Negro were paying an unnecessarily heavy toll to the city by being unadapted to climatic conditions, or to prevailing industries, or to the housing available, or to all.

But what has the Negro been doing about this? He has been showing the world how a race can improve in health. His record is amazing. It is as if the Negro had said, "Come, we will be a bigger, better and physically more perfect race," and then had achieved it. Not long ago, Louis I. Dublin, statistician of the Metropolitan Life Insurance Company, published facts concerning health among the two million colored policyholders of that company; here is a group large enough to be representative and they live chiefly in towns and cities. From 1911 to 1923—twelve years—the deathrate for tuberculosis among these policyholders fell from 418 per 100,000 to 246, a startling improvement. In this same period the deathrate from typhoid was reduced 77.5 per cent. Who will say that

714

186

the Negro is not improving in health? The four communicable diseases of childhood—measles, scarlet fever, whooping-cough and diphtheria—together show a decline of 33 per cent; there was a drop of more than 50 per cent in the mortality rates from diarrhea and enteritis among young colored children. The mortality rate for colored children under fifteen years was 10.1 per 1,000 in 1911; in 1923 it was only 5.5. "Colored mothers," writes Mr. Dublin, "have not been slow to learn how to care for and feed their babies in accordance with the best practice of the day.

Translate these figures into terms of life expectancy. In 1911 the Negro in this country—considering the Metropolitan figures as representative—was enjoying an average expectation of life of slightly more than forty-one years. In 1923 he was enjoying an expectation of nearly forty-seven years. In the short space of twelve years the Negro added six years to the length of time he had reason to expect to live, an astounding improvement.

The Negro's life expectancy to-day is just about that of the white people of the United States thirty or forty years ago; he is only a generation behind. He is where a number of European countries were just before the Great War. The mortality rate from tuberculosis is beginning to look like that among whites only twenty years ago, when the anti-tuberculosis campaign was begun. A race still living under primitive conditions in many places and often from hand to mouth has done this. "The Negro in America has proved himself thoroughly capable of profiting from the public health campaign," says Mr. Dublin.

All the more disheartening, then, are the difficulties to which attention has been called. The Negro in the Northern city lives in restricted areas of great congestion; he is elbowed and crowded by people of his own and the white color; he knows the evils of bad housing and often of bad sanitation and even squalor; he is set upon by quacks, tricked by fake druggists, fed every form of vile nostrum and vicious patent remedy concocted by man. "Anything is good enough for niggers" is the motto of too many white doctors, druggists, dentists, practitioners of all sorts who infest the colored districts and who have deliberately flocked thither as the colored population has grown.

The Negro has come to the Northern city and the exploiter, the conscienceless sucker of other people's welfare, has risen in his midst.

May it be as a result of these conditions that the improvement just noted has already suffered a set-back in some cities? In Chicago in 1923 the mortality rate was 27 per cent higher than in 1921; in Detroit it was 23 per cent higher. Has the Negro found that in health the Northern city is inhospitable? Have congestion and other difficulties reached a point at which they are beginning to take toll? The effect of the Northern city upon the Negro will bear watching.

Send for a Bundle

Copies for your friends, your fellow workers, your minister, any one who is or ought to be interested in this

Harlem Issue
of Survey Graphic

Price: 1 copy   50 cents
       10 copies $4.00
       25 copies $8.75
      100 copies $30.00
in a bundle mailed to one address.

Survey Associates

112 East 19 Street   New York City

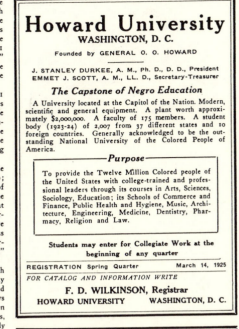

Howard University
WASHINGTON, D. C.
Founded by GENERAL O. O. HOWARD

J. STANLEY DURKEE, A. M., Ph. D., D. D., President
EMMET J. SCOTT, A. M., LL. D., Secretary-Treasurer

The Capstone of Negro Education

A University located at the Capitol of the Nation. Modern, scientific and general equipment. A plant worth approximately $2,000,000. A faculty of 175 members. A student body (1923-24) of 2,007 from 37 different states and 10 foreign countries. Generally acknowledged to be the outstanding National University of the Colored People of America.

―Purpose―

To provide the Twelve Million Colored people of the United States with college-trained and professional leaders through its courses in Arts, Sciences, Sociology, Education; its Schools of Commerce and Finance, Public Health and Hygiene, Music, Architecture, Engineering, Medicine, Dentistry, Pharmacy, Religion and Law.

Students may enter for Collegiate Work at the beginning of any quarter

REGISTRATION Spring Quarter   March 14, 1925

FOR CATALOG AND INFORMATION WRITE

F. D. WILKINSON, Registrar
HOWARD UNIVERSITY   WASHINGTON, D. C.

The NEW YORK URBAN LEAGUE is located at 202-204 West 136th Street in the heart of Harlem. t seeks to make the Negro in New York City economically self-supporting by promoting programs of better Health, Housing, Industry and Recreation. It works to secure more and better jobs for Negro workers, especially in the skilled trades.

The budget of the League for 1925 is $30,639.96. The League also seeks funds to complete payments on buildings recently purchased and to be remodeled as a Center for Welfare Agencies working among Negroes in New York.

Officers of the League are:

ARTHUR C. HOLDEN, Chairman
JOHN E. NAIL, Vice-Chairman
A. S. FRISSEL, Treasurer
EVA D. BOWLES, Secretary
JAMES H. HUBERT, Executive Secretary

The League is supported by volunteer contributions.

715

187

Swift Memorial College

Swift Memorial College, Rogersville, Tennessee, is an institution for the Christian and higher education of Negro youth, and is under the auspices of the Presbyterian Church, U. S. A.

It is directly under the supervision of the National Board of Missions for Colored People, Pittsburgh, Pa.

It carries an English, Normal, Scientific, Teachers, and College Courses.

Its students have been recognized by the leading colleges and Universities of the U. S. A.

It is painstaking in the selection of its teachers, careful in the government of its students and thorough in instruction and training. No mistake will be made in going to Swift Memorial College.

All necessary information can be had by addressing,

W. H. FRANKLIN, PRESIDENT,

Swift Memorial College,
Rogersville, Tenn.

To the

NEW NEGRO

Greetings
from

WILEY COLLEGE

Marshall, Texas

M. W. Dogan, President

A Class "A" College for Future Leaders. Makes a Specialty of the Study of Race Problems

---

State of New Jersey

Manual Training and Industrial School

at

BORDENTOWN

Maintained for the vocational training of colored youth, with admission open to all residents of New Jersey.

Academic training for all students.

Stress is laid on all round development of students, physical and social as well as mental.

"Bordentown trains for life by giving the students a taste of life."

———

W. R. Valentine . . . . **Principal**

The

Atlanta School

of

Social Work

Trains Colored Social Workers for the South

Courses offered in

Social Case Work

Community Organization and Social Research

Field Work with Social Agencies

For further information address:

E. FRANKLIN FRAZIER, A. M.

36 Chestnut Street
Atlanta, Georgia

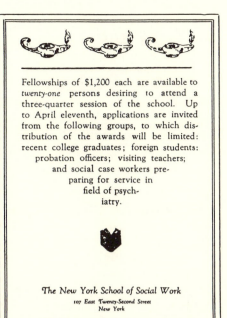
189

HARTFORD

W. Douglas Mackenzie, President

Theological Seminary
Dean, M. W. Jacobus

School of Religious Pedagogy
Dean, E. H. Knight

Kennedy School of Missions
Dean, E. W. Capen

Through these associated schools Hartford offers full training for:

1. The Christian ministry.
2. Religious education and social service.
3. The foreign field.

Each school has its independent faculty and its own institutional life, and together they form one interdenominational institution with the unity of common aim and spirit.

Hartford Seminary Foundation, Hartford, Conn.

Spring Quarter Begins March 30th

1925 Summer Quarter

First Term, June 22—July 29
Second Term, July 30—September 4

Courses leading to the degree of A.M. and Ph.D. A limited number of fellowships and scholarships available for the academic year 1925-26. Special arrangements for undergraduate and unclassified students with adequate experience in social work. For Announcements, apply to Box 55, Faculty Exchange, The University of Chicago.

The Johns Hopkins University Courses in Social Economics

Courses offered: History and Development of Social Work, Family Case Work, Child Welfare, Health and Preventable Disease, Social Medicine, Community Problems and Organization, Social Law, Immigrant Peoples, Home Economics, Social Legislation, Delinquency and Probation, Social Statistics, Administration, Publicity and Finance of a Social Organization.

Field work training under professional executives. Psychiatric and General Medical Social Service training given in conjunction with the Social Service Department of the Johns Hopkins Hospital.

College graduates eligible for M.A. degree after completing the two years' course.

For circulars address Miss Theo Jacobs, The Johns Hopkins University, Baltimore, Maryland.

THE UNPRINTABLE TEXT BOOK
A handy pamphlet reprint of a stimulating article by Prof. Joseph K. Hart, Editor of The Survey's Education Department. Free to teachers on request. To others, .10 cents. The Survey, 112 East 19th Street, New York City.

BLACK WORKERS AND THE CITY
(Continued from page 643)

tenders and teamsters decreased absolutely in the last decade. Aside from the clothing industry, the range of work remained about the same. Nearly 5,000 new women entered domestic service. The gross numbers of Negro men go into unskilled labor. There was an increase of only 57 male servants during the ten years and just 301 janitors. The solid concentration in personal service is being broken, and the workers scattered, but the skilled trades in such centers as New York still remain virtually locked to Negroes. The increases—where they occur—are striking, but this can be attributed to the low base from which these increases must be computed.

One may look to the character of New York's industries for another peculiar handicap. While offering a diversity of employment, the city has no such basic industries as may be found, for example, in the automobile plants of Detroit, or the iron and steel works and gigantic meat slaughtering industries of Chicago. In Chicago there is diversified employment, to be sure, but there is a significantly heavier concentration in the basic industries; more that that, there are gradations of work from unskilled to skilled. In certain plants skilled workers increased from 3.5 per cent of the Negro working population in 1910 to 13.5 per cent in 1920 in Chicago. In the slaughtering houses there are actually more semi-skilled Negro workers than laborers. The number of iron molders increased from 31 in 1910 to 520 in 1920 and this latter number represents 10 per cent of all the iron molders.

In the working age groups of New York there are more women than men. For every hundred Negro men there are 110 Negro women. This is abnormal and would be a distinct anomaly in an industrial center. The surplus women are doubtless the residue from the general wash and ebb of migrants who found a demand for their services. The city actually attracts more women than men. But surplus women bring on other problems, as the social agencies will testify. "Where women preponderate in large numbers there is proportionate increase in immorality because women are cheap." . . . The situation does not permit normal relations. What is most likely to happen, and does happen, is that women soon find it an added personal attraction to contribute to the support of a man. Demoralization may follow this—and does. Moreover, the proportion of Negro women at work in Manhattan (60.6) is twice that of any corresponding group, and one of the highest proportions registered anywhere.

The nature of the work of at least 40 per cent of the men suggests a relationship, even if indirectly, with the tensely active night life by which Harlem is known. The dull, unarduous routine of a porter's job or that of an elevator tender, does not provide enough stimulation to consume the normal supply of nervous energy. It is unthinkable that the restlessness which drove these migrants to New York from dull small towns would allow them to be content with the same dullness in the new environment, when so rich a supply of garish exitements is available.

IV

WITH all the "front" of pretending to live, the aspect of complacent wantlessness, it is clear that the Negroes are in a predicament. The moment holds tolerance but no great promise. Just as the wave of immigration once swept these Negroes out of old strongholds, a change of circumstances may disrupt them again. The slow moving black masses, with their assorted heritages and old loyalties, face the same stern barriers in the new environment. They are the black workers.

Entering gradually an era of industrial contact and competition with white workers of greater experience and numerical superiority, antagonisms loom up. Emotions have a way of reenforcing themselves. The fierce economic fears of men in competition can supplement or be supplemented by the sentiments engendered by racial difference. Beneath the disastrous East St. Louis conflict was a boiling anger toward Southern Negroes coming in to "take white men's jobs." The antagonisms between the Negroes and the Irish in New York, which even now survive, were first provoked sixty years ago when these workers met and clashed over jobs. The hostile spirit was dominant in the draft riots of New York during the Civil War and flared again in the shameful battle of "San Juan Hill" in the Columbus Hill District. These outbreaks were distinctly more economic than racial.

Herein lies one of the points of highest tension in race relations. Negro workers potentially menace organized labor and the leaders of the movement recognize this. But racial sentiments are not easily destroyed by abstract principles. The white workers have not, except in few instances, conquered the antagonisms founded on race to the extent of accepting the rights of Negro workers to privileges which they enjoy. While denying them admission to their crafts they grow furious over their dangerous borings from the outside. "The Negroes are scabs!" "They hold down the living standards of workers by cutting under!" "Negroes are professional strike breakers!" These sentiments are a good nucleus for elaboration into the most furious fears and hatreds.

It is believed variously that Negro workers are as a matter of policy opposed to unions or as a matter of ignorance incapable of appreciating them. From some unions they are definitely barred; some insist on separate Negro locals; some limit them to qualified membership; some accept them freely with white workers. The situation of the Negroes, on the surface, is to say the least compromising. Their shorter industrial experience and almost complete isolation from the educative influence of organized trade unions contribute to some of the inertia encountered in organizing them. Their traditional positions have been those of personal loyalty, and this has aided the habit of individual bargaining for jobs in industry. They have been, as was pointed out, under the comprehensive leadership of the church in practically all aspects of their lives including their labor. No effective new leadership has developed to supplant this old leadership. The attitude of white workers has sternly opposed the use of Negroes as apprentices through fear of subsequent competition in the skilled trades. This has limited the number of skilled Negroes trained on the job. But despite this denial, Negroes have gained skill.

This disposition violently to protest the employment of Negroes in certain lines because they are not members of the union and the equally violent protest against the admission of Negroes to the unions, created in the Negroes, desperate for work, an attitude of indifference to abstract pleas. In 1910 they were used to break the teamster's strike and six years later they were organized. In 1919 they were used in a strike of the building trades. Strained feelings resulted, but they were finally included in the unions of this trade. During the outlaw strike of the railway and steamship clerks, freight handlers, expressmen and station employes, they were used to replace the striking whites and were given preference over the men whose places they had taken. During the shopmen's strike they were promoted into new positions and thus made themselves eligible for skilled jobs as machinists. In fact, their most definite gains have been at the hands of employers and over the tactics of labor union exclusionists.

Where the crafts are freely open to them they have joined with the general movement of the workers. Of the 5,386 Negro longshoremen, about 5,000 are organized. Of the 735 Negro carpenters, 400 are members of the United Brotherhood of Carpenters and Joiners. Of the 2,275 semi-skilled clothing workers practically all are members of the International Ladies Garment Workers Union. The musicians are 50 per cent organized. The difficulty is that the great preponderance

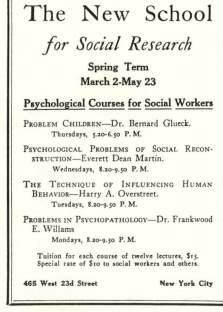

AMERICAN BIRTH CONTROL LEAGUE—President, Margaret Sanger, 104 Fifth Avenue, New York City. Objects: To educate American people in the various aspects of the dangers of uncontrolled procreation; to establish centers where married persons may receive contraceptive advice from duly licensed physicians. Life membership $1.00; Birth Control Review (monthly magazine) $2.00 per year.

AMERICAN CHILD HEALTH ASSOCIATION—Headquarters, 532 17th St., N.W., Washington, D. C.; Administrative Offices, 370 7th Avenue, New York. Herbert Hoover, President; L. Emmett Holt, M.D.;* Livingston Farrand, M.D.; Thomas D. Wood, M.D.; Mrs. Maud Wood Park, 1st, 2nd, 3rd, 4th Vice-Presidents respectively; Corcoran Thom, Treasurer; Philip Van Ingen, M.D., Secretary; Edward M. Flesh, Comptroller. To promote health among children from conception to maturity—this to be accomplished through cooperation with parents, doctors, nurses, teachers, and other health workers; by dissemination of scientific information and teaching methods in schools, through conferences, addresses, pamphlets, publicity material, and a monthly magazine, "Child Health Magazine."

* Deceased.

AMERICAN COUNTRY LIFE ASSOCIATION—K. L. Butterfield, president; Henry Israel, executive secretary. Room 1849, Grand Central Terminal Bldg., New York City. Emphasizes the human aspect of country life. Annual membership $5.00 includes "Rural America" (monthly bulletin) and Annual Conference Proceedings.

AMERICAN FEDERATION OF ORGANIZATIONS FOR THE HARD OF HEARING—Promotes the cause of the hard of hearing; assists in forming organizations. Pres., Dr. Gordon Berry; Field Secretary, Miss Betty Wright, 1601 35th St. N.W., Washington, D. C.

AMERICAN HEART ASSOCIATION—Dr. Lewis A. Connor, president. Miss M. L. Woughter, acting executive secretary, 370 Seventh Avenue, New York. Organized for the purpose of promoting the prevention of heart disease and the care of those with damaged hearts in the United States and Canada.

AMERICAN HOME ECONOMICS ASSOCIATION—Leta Bane, executive secretary, Grace Dodge Hotel, Washington, D. C. Organized for betterment of conditions in home, school, institution and community. Publishes monthly Journal of Home Economics: office of editor, Grace Dodge Hotel, Washington, D. C.; of business manager, 1211 Cathedral St., Baltimore, Md.

AMERICAN PEACE SOCIETY—Founded 1828, labors for an international peace of justice. Its official organ is the Advocate of Peace, $2.00 a year. Arthur Deerin Call, secretary and editor, 612-614 Colorado Building, Washington, D. C.

AMERICAN SOCIETY FOR THE CONTROL OF CANCER—Frank J. Osborne, executive secretary; 370 Seventh Ave., New York. To disseminate knowledge concerning symptoms, diagnosis, treatment and prevention. Publication free on request. Annual membership dues, $5.00.

AMERICAN SOCIAL HYGIENE ASSOCIATION—370 Seventh Ave., New York. To promote a better understanding of the social hygiene movement; to advance sound sex education; to combat prostitution and sex delinquency; to aid public authorities in the campaign against the venereal diseases; to advise in organization of state and local social-hygiene programs. Annual membership dues $2.00 including monthly journal.

COMMUNITY SERVICE—315 Fourth Ave., New York City. A national civic movement for promoting citizenship through right use of leisure. It will, on request, help local communities work out leisure time programs. H. S. Braucher, secretary.

COUNCIL OF WOMEN FOR HOME MISSIONS—156 Fifth Avenue, New York. Organized in 1908; 20 constituent Protestant national women's mission boards. Florence E. Quinlan, exec. sec'y. Committee on Farm and Cannery Migrants, Summer Service for College Students, Laura H. Parker, exec. supervisor.

FEDERAL COUNCIL OF THE CHURCHES OF CHRIST IN AMERICA—Constituted by 28 Protestant communions. Rev. C. S. Macfarland and Rev. S. M. Cavert, Gen. Sec's: 105 E. 22d St., N.Y.C. Dept. of Research and Education, Rev. F. E. Johnson, Sec'y. Commissions: Church and Social Service, Rev. W. M. Tippy, Sec'y; International Justice and Goodwill: Rev. S. L. Gulick, Sec'y; Church and Race Relations: Dr. G. E. Haynes, Sec'y.

HAMPTON INSTITUTE—Trains Negro and Indian youth for community service. Advanced courses: agriculture, builders, business, home-economics, normal. Publishes "Southern Workman" and free material on Negro problems. J. E. Gregg, principal.

INTERNATIONAL MIGRATION SERVICE—To assemble data on international social problems and through work with individual cases to develop methods of international social service. Headquarters, London. Viscountess Gladstone, chairman; Gilbert Murray, treasurer; Ruth Larned, executive. Address all inquiries to American bureau, 1 Madison Avenue, New York City. Director, Mary E. Hurlbutt.

JOINT COMMITTEE ON METHODS OF PREVENTING DELINQUENCY—Graham Romeyn Taylor, executive director, 50 East 42nd Street, New York. To promote the adoption of sound methods in this field, with particular reference to psychiatric clinics, visiting teacher work, and training for these and similar services; to conduct related studies, education and publication; and to interpret the work of the Commonwealth Fund Program for the Prevention of Delinquency.

NATIONAL BOARD OF THE YOUNG WOMEN'S CHRISTIAN ASSOCIATIONS—Mrs. Robert E. Speer, president; Miss Mabel Cratty, general secretary, 600 Lexington Avenue, New York City. This organization maintains a staff of executive and traveling secretaries to cover work in the United States in 1,034 local Y. W. C. A.'s on behalf of the industrial, business, student, foreign born, Indian, Colored and younger girls. It has 159 American secretaries at work in 49 centers in the Orient, Latin America and Europe.

NATIONAL CHILD LABOR COMMITTEE—Owen R. Lovejoy, general secretary, 215 Fourth Avenue, New York. Industrial, agricultural investigations. Works for improved laws and administration, children's codes. Studies child labor, health, schools, recreation, dependency, delinquency, etc. Annual membership, $2, $5, $10, $25 and $100 includes monthly publication, "The American Child."

NATIONAL CHILD WELFARE ASSOCIATION, INC. (est. 1911, incorp. 1914), 70 Fifth Ave., N. Y. (tel. Chelsea 8774). Promotes as its chief object the building of character in the children of America through the harmonious development of their bodies, minds, and spirits. Its method is, in co-operation with other organizations, to originate and disseminate educational material in the form of posters, books, bulletins, charts, slides, and insignia. Through its "Knighthood of Youth" it provides homes, schools and church schools with a method of character training through actual practice. Officers: Dr. John H. Finley, Pres.; Amos L. Prescott, Treas.; Charles F. Powlison, Gen. Sec'y.

THE NATIONAL COMMITTEE FOR MENTAL HYGIENE, INC.—Dr. William H. Welch, honorary president; Dr. Charles P. Emerson, president; Dr. Frankwood E. Williams, medical director; Dr. Clarence J. D'Alton, executive assistant; Clifford W. Beers, secretary; 370 Seventh Avenue, New York. Pamphlets on mental hygiene, mental and nervous disorders, feeblemindedness, epilepsy, inebriety, delinquency, and other mental problems in human behavior, education, industry, psychiatric social service, etc. "Mental Hygiene," quarterly, $3.00 a year; "Mental Hygiene Bulletin," monthly, $ .50 a year.

NATIONAL COMMITTEE FOR THE PREVENTION OF BLINDNESS—Lewis H. Carris, managing director; Mrs. Winifred Hathaway, secretary; 130 East 22nd Street, New York. Objects: To furnish information, exhibits, lantern slides, lectures, personal service for local organizations and legislation, publish literature of movement—samples free, quantities at cost. Includes New York State Committee.

NATIONAL CONFERENCE OF SOCIAL WORK—Wm. J. Norton, president, Detroit, Michigan; W. H. Parker, Secretary, 25 East Ninth Street, Cincinnati, Ohio. The Conference is an organization to discuss the principles of humanitarian effort and to increase the efficiency of social service agencies. Each year it holds an annual meeting, publishes in permanent form the Proceedings of the meeting, and issues a quarterly Bulletin. The fifty-second annual meeting of the Conference will be held in Denver, Colorado, June 10th to 17th, 1925. Proceedings are sent free of charge to all members upon payment of a membership fee of five dollars.

NATIONAL COUNCIL OF JEWISH WOMEN—2109 Broadway, New York. Miss Rose Brenner, pres.; Mrs. Estelle M. Sternberger, ex. sec'y. Promotes civic cooperation, education, religion and social welfare in the United States, Canada, Cuba, Europe. Department of Immigrant Aid—799 Broadway, Miss Florina Lasker, chairman. For the protection and education of immigrant women and girls. Department of Farm and Rural Work—Mrs. Leo H. Herz, chairman, 5 Columbus Circle, New York City.

THE NATIONAL COUNCIL OF THE YOUNG MEN'S CHRISTIAN ASSOCIATIONS OF THE UNITED STATES OF AMERICA—347 Madison Avenue, New York City (Telephone, Vanderbilt 1200). Composed of 344 business and professional men, representing 1,540 Associations in 48 states, Hawaii, and the Canal Zone, and 388 Associations in 32 Foreign Lands. Officers: F. W. Ramsey, Cleveland, O., President; Adrian Lyon, Chairman of the General Board; John R. Mott, New York, General Secretary.

NATIONAL LEAGUE OF GIRLS' CLUBS—Mrs. Fannie M. Pollak, president; Mary L. Ely, Educational Secretary. Non-sectarian and self-governing organization of working women's clubs for recreation and promotion of program in Adult Education. Vacation Camps. 472 West 24th St., New York City.

NATIONAL ORGANIZATION FOR PUBLIC HEALTH NURSING—Member, National Health Council—Anne A. Stevens, R.N., director, 370 Seventh Avenue, New York. For development and standardization of public health nursing. Maintains library and educational service. Official Magazine, "Public Health Nurse."

NATIONAL PHYSICAL EDUCATION SERVICE—315 Fourth Ave., New York, N. Y. To obtain progressive legislation for physical education. Established at the request of a committee created by the United States Bureau of Education; 35 national organizations cooperating. Maintained by the Playground and Recreation Association of America.

of Negro jobs is in lines which are not organized. The porters, laundresses (outside of laundries) and servants have no organization. The Negroes listed as painters are not in the painters' union, many of them being merely whitewashers. The tailors are in large part cleaners and pressers. The waiters, elevator tenders (except females) are poorly organized.

The end of the Negro's troubles, however, does not come with organization. There is still the question of employers, for it is a certain fact that preference is frequently given white workers when they can be secured, if high wages are to be paid. A vicious circle indeed! The editors of The Messenger have suggested a United Negro Trades Union built on the plan of the United Hebrew Trades and the Italian Chamber of Labor. The unions are lethargic; the Negroes skeptical, untrained and individualistic. Meanwhile they drift, a disordered mass, self-conscious, but with their aims unrationalized, into the face of new problems.

V

WITH the shift toward industry now beginning, and a subsequent new status already foreshadowed, some sounder economic policy is imperative. The traditional hold of domestic service vocations is already broken: witness the sudden halt in the increase of Negro male servants and elevator men. The enormous growth of certain New York industries has been out of proportion to the normal native production of workers. The immigration on which these formerly depended has been cut down and the prospects are that this curtailment will continue. For the first time, as a result of promotion, retirement and death, gaps are appearing which the limited recruits cannot fill. Note the clothing industry, one of the largest in New York. There is a persistent lament that the second generation of immigrants do not continue in the trade. Already Negro workers have been sought to supplement the deficiencies in the first generation recruits. This sort of thing will certainly be felt in other lines. The black masses are on the verge of induction from their unenviable status as servants to the forces of the industrial workers, a more arduous, but less dependent rank. They require a new leadership, training in the principles of collective action, a new orientation with their white fellow workers for the sake of future peace, a reorganization of the physical and mental habits which are a legacy of their old experiences, and deliberate training for the new work to come. It is this recreation of the worker that the Urban Leagues have tried to accomplish, accompanying this effort with a campaign against the barriers to the entrance of Negro workers into industry. Conceiving these workers as inherently capable of an infinite range of employment this organization insists merely upon an openness which permits opportunity, an objective experiment uncluttered by old theories of racial incompetence and racial dogmas.

The workers of the South and the West Indies who have come to this city with vagrant desires and impulses, their endowments of skill and strength, their repressions and the telltale marks of backward cultures, with all the human wastes of the process, have directed shafts of their native energy into the city's life and growth. They are becoming a part of it. The restive spirit which brought them to the city has been neither all absorbed nor wasted. Over two-thirds of all the businesses operated by Negroes in New York are conducted by migrant Negroes. They are in the schools—they are the radicals and this is hopeful. The city Negro—an unpredictable mixture of all possible temperaments—is yet in evolution.

But a common purpose is integrating these energies and once leashed to a purposeful objective, it is not improbable that in industry and in the life of the city the black workers will compensate in utility and progressiveness for what they lack in numbers and traditions.

CLASSIFIED ADVERTISEMENTS

WORKERS WANTED

SUPERVISING MATRON (white) for an institution of 300 children with an opportunity for working out the problem of the colored child along advanced lines. 5079 SURVEY.

WOMAN WORKER WANTED: Jewish, assistant and secretary to Superintendent small institution for unmarried mothers on Staten Island. Must have social service experience. 5034 SURVEY.

EMPLOYMENT office worker, college graduate with case work or employment experience preferred. Protestant, young, able to use typewriter. $1200.00-$1500.00. Apply to Carol W. Adams, 1545 Glenarm St., Denver, Colorado.

WANTED in a Philadelphia Hospital, a Social Case Worker, College Graduate with at least one year of Social Case Work Experience. Hospital Experience not necessary. 4996 SURVEY.

WANTED: Girls Club Leader, Eastern Settlement, State education, experience and references. 5063 SURVEY.

WANTED: Trained nurse and social worker to take charge of small mining community situated about forty miles from New York City. No. 5069 THE SURVEY.

SEVERAL financial secretaries for permanent positions are required by philanthropic institution. 5091 SURVEY.

WANTED: Family Case Worker for small Family Case Agency. Preferably one with experience and good theoretical training. Must speak Yiddish. 5096 SURVEY.

The Ad.

Wanted, for October 1st, home for little girl of four. Business mother travels part time. Desires complete care for child during absence from city. Child attends play school 9 to 12. Vicinity thirteenth street, west. 4890 Survey.

The Result

"I want you to know how effective the 'ad' proved which I placed in The Survey. I received only three answers but each one was from exactly the right sort of person. At the same time I advertised in the New York Times on Sunday. I received five times as many replies as from The Survey ad but not one of these answers was even worth looking into. These people entirely disregarded the points I made.

"4890 Survey."

WORKERS WANTED

NURSES, DOCTORS, TECHNICIANS of all kinds assisted in securing better places and better help. Hospitals, Schools and Industrial plants furnished with efficient nurses. We usually recommend only one applicant, never more than two or three. HUGHES PROFESSIONAL EXCHANGE, 603 Scarritt Building, Kansas City, Mo.

WANTED: Man to act as Boy's Supervisor and wife to act as babies caretaker. Children's Home located near city in country and modern congregate plan. Man should be active with boys and able to work with boys. Wife should be able to substitute in other lines such as ironing, seamstress and allied work if necessary. 5099 SURVEY.

COOPERATIVE PLACEMENT SERVICE. Social workers, secretaries, superintendents, matrons, housekeepers, dietitians, cafeteria managers. The Richards Bureau, 68 Barnes Street, Providence, R. I.

GRADUATE NURSES, dietitians, laboratory technicians for hospital positions everywhere. Write for free book now. Aznoe's Central Registry for Nurses, 30 N. Michigan Ave., Chicago, Illinois.

WANTED: Refined married couple to take charge of cottage unit, thirty boys, small school near New York. Preferably one or both should be qualified for class room instruction, grammar grades. Apply by letter only. A. E. Wakeman, 72 Schermerhorn Street, Brooklyn, N. Y.

TEACHERS WANTED

TEACHERS wanted for public and private schools, colleges and universities. Education Service, Steger Building, Chicago; Southern Building, Washington; 1254 Amsterdam Ave., New York.

WOMAN TEACHER for lower primary grades; also young man teacher, unmarried, for manual training and elementary agriculture; at boys' training school of non-military type where home atmosphere is emphasized, situated in Ohio. Attractive compensation depending upon experience. Position open in September. 5094 SURVEY.

FOR THE HOME

Tea Room Management

In our new home-study course, "COOKING FOR PROFIT." Booklet on request.
Am. School of Home Economics, 840 E. 58th St., Chicago

EXECUTIVE with years of intensive experience organizing and conducting institutions and other works of social character in connection with dependent. delinquent and problem boys desires position as Superintendent of large Orphanage or Industrial School. Rural community and cottage plan preferred. References from those with national reputation as authorities. 5068 SURVEY.

Young couple, Jewish, thoroughly experienced SUPERINTENDENT and MATRON, who have satisfactorily filled previous positions eleven years, desire affiliation with Institution, highest references. 5088 SURVEY.

TRAINED AND EXPERIENCED social workers supplied for high-class positions. SOCIAL SERVICE DEPARTMENT, EXECUTIVE SERVICE CORPORATION, 1515 Pershing Square Building, N. Y. C.

YOUNG WOMAN, 30, Protestant, college graduate, desires travel Europe this summer as amanuensis to author, or governess-companion; German and French. 5087 SURVEY.

POSITION wanted by a trained and experienced social worker. 5098 SURVEY.

SCHOOL EXECUTIVE, 33, now public school superintendent Connecticut town, specialist educational and vocational guidance and social studies desires executive position or department headship in a New School. Begin September. 5060 SURVEY.

YOUNG MAN, experienced in institutional work for blind children wishes a position as superintendent or principal of a school for handicapped children. Prefers to build up a small school. 5092 SURVEY.

HOUSEMOTHER or superintendent in school or institution for boys or girls. Excellent qualifications. 4994 SURVEY.

JEWISH social worker, male, 38, fourteen years experience in executive capacity now employed, is seeking a new connection. Write to 5084 SURVEY.

EXECUTIVE Public Health Nurse desires position as Director of Health Center, Visiting Nurse Association, or County Health Work. 5082 SURVEY.

YOUNG MAN, 30, Jewish, with executive experience in public schools and private institutions desires work in executive or semi-executive capacity. Can assist in publicity as a speaker or writer. 5061 SURVEY.

EXPERIENCED New York man seeks position where his knowledge of publicity, motion pictures, exhibit and poster planning, editorial supervision and booklet writing may be used. Moderate salary. 5097 SURVEY.

COLLEGE trained, experienced, well recommended woman, seeks position with child-caring institution, in or near New York City. 5095 SURVEY.

SUPERINTENDENT of home for delinquent boys desires to make a change about May first. Good references. Age 49. Protestant. 5093 SURVEY.

Here and Now

Don't read Survey Graphic over somebody's shoulder in a streetcar. It annoys him, it aggravates you to have only a glimpse of what is going on in social work and social thought. Here's the place and now is the time to have your own copy, monthly, fresh from the press, with articles in early issues by

Alain Locke
Robert R. Moton
James H. Dillard
Will W. Alexander
John Hope
Rossa B. Cooley
Gov. Alfred E. Smith
Francis K. Hackett
S. K. Radcliffe
Jacob Billikopf
Arthur Ruhl
Edward T. Devine
Patrick Geddes

And others

Survey Graphic, 112 East 19 Street, New York City

Gentlemen: Enter my subscription for Survey Graphic for 6 months' trial trip $1 (or full year $3) for which I enclose $......

Name ....

Address x

THE CENTER OF DISTINGUISHED SOCIAL LIFE

The Mayflower

WASHINGTON D.C.

THE NEWEST AND MOST LUXURIOUSLY APPOINTED HOTEL IN THE NATIONAL CAPITAL

CONNECTICUT AVENUE
MIDWAY BETWEEN THE WHITE HOUSE & DUPONT CIRCLE

THE PELHAM TOURS

"MOTORING IN EUROPE"

From Naples to Paris by Automobile

From a Diary, The Pelham Tours . . . Extract No. 6.

Stratford-on-Avon, July 30th: We crossed to England by the Hook of Holland. I had heard so much about the English Channel that I was really uneasy but I went to bed as soon as we got on the boat and knew nothing more until we were at Harwich in the morning. So much for the Channel. We were in London a week and the longer I was there the more I liked it. It is so absolutely different from anything else we have seen; so grey and misty where Paris is all sparkling light; so solid and British, so matter-of-fact and at the same time so full of a poetic beauty. The wonderful facades of the Houses of Parliament, seen from Lambeth Bridge, with Westminster Abbey in the distance, all veiled by the pale blue haze that often hangs over the Thames, are a lovely sight. I have stood on London Bridge and it did not fall down; I have seen the Tower of London and marvelled at the Crown Jewels and no less at the Beef-Eaters in their mediaeval costumes, standing guard over them. Somehow when an Englishman wears a mediaeval costume he looks as if he were "dressing up," whereas an Italian is an un-selfconscious as a child. One day we went up the Thames to Windsor Castle and it was most beautiful. We lunched at Richmond on the River and on the way home we passed any number of little boats, or punts, tied to the bank, while the occupants drank their afternoon tea as calmly as you please. Nothing interferes with that important function in England. The London shops were quite wonderful and the literary landmarks of more interest to me here than at any other place; probably because I know a bit more about English literature. We visited The Old Curiosity Shop and Dr. Johnson's old tavern, "The Cheshire Cheese." It was a never-failing source of delight to me to prowl about in these narrow lanes and by-ways leading off from the Strand; to wander up through Drury Lane and into Covent Garden or take the bus for a long ride over to Cheapside and hear English spoken by Cockneys so that it seemed as unintelligible to me as a foreign tongue.

We have had one day at Stratford-on-Avon. It is a delightful place of thatched cottages and half-timbered houses. The home of Shakespeare is most interesting and the cottage of Ann Hathaway across the fields at Shottery, most enchanting. It would be easy to fall in love there.

Tomorrow we go to Oxford and then on to Salisbury. Then home. It has been a wonderful summer, every minute of it and I am sorry it is almost over.

For information concerning these tours, write to "The Pelham Tours,"
Room 1514, 100 East 42nd Street, New York City

(In answering these advertisements please mention THE SURVEY. *It helps us, it identifies you.)*

Give us Telephones

Following the war, when business and social life surged again into normal channels, there came the cry from homes, hospitals, schools, mills, offices—"Give us telephones." No one in the telephone company will ever forget those days. Doctors, nurses and those who were sick had to be given telephones first. New buildings, delayed by war emergency, had to be constructed, switchboards built and installed, cables made and laid, lines run and telephones attached.

The telephone shortage is never far away. If for a few years the telephone company was unable to build ahead, if it neglected to push into the markets for capital and materials for the future's need, there would be a recurrence of the dearth of telephones. No one could dread that eventuality so much as the 350,000 telephone workers.

Bell System engineers measure and forecast the growth of communities; cables, conduits, switchboards and buildings are planned and developed years ahead of the need, that facilities may be provided in advance of telephone want. Population or business requirement added to a community must find the telephone ready, waiting.

AMERICAN TELEPHONE AND TELEGRAPH COMPANY
AND ASSOCIATED COMPANIES
BELL SYSTEM
One Policy, One System, Universal Service

198

Prologue

Anatole Longfellow, alias the Scarlet Creeper,[1] strutted aimfully down the east side of Seventh Avenue. He wore a tight-fitting suit of shepherd's plaid which thoroughly revealed his lithe, sinewy figure to all who gazed upon him, and all gazed. A great diamond, or some less valuable stone which aped a diamond, glistened in his fuchsia cravat. The uppers of his highly polished tan boots were dove-coloured suède and the buttons were pale blue. His black hair was sleek under his straw hat, set at a jaunty angle. When he saluted a friend—and his acquaintanceship seemed to be wide—two rows of pearly teeth gleamed from his seal-brown countenance.

It was the hour when promenading was popular— about eleven o'clock in the evening. The air was warm, balmy for June, and not too humid. Over the broad avenue, up and down which multi-hued taxicabs rolled, hung a canopy of indigo sky, spangled with bright stars. The shops, still open, were brilliantly illuminated. Slouching under the protecting walls of the buildings, in front of show-windows, or under the trees, groups of young men

---

[1] The reader will find, at the end of this volume, a glossary of the unusual Negro words and phrases employed in this novel.

[3]

congregated, chattering and laughing. Women, in pairs, or with male escorts, strolled up and down the ample sidewalk.

Hello, 'Toly! A stalwart black man accosted the Creeper.

Hello, Ed. How you been?

Po'ly, thank you. How *you* been?

No complaints. Nummer come out. Drew sixty-seven bucks.

Holy Kerist!

Yeh. Anatole displayed his teeth.

What nummer?

Seven-Nine-Eight.

Whah you found et?

Off'n a gal's fron' do'.

Comin' out?

Goin' in. Ah went out duh back winder. Her daddy done come home widout writin'.

Hush mah mouf!

Ah doan mean mebbe.

As Anatole walked on, his self-esteem flowered. Unbuttoning his coat, he expanded his chest, dangerously stretching the gold watch-chain which extended from pocket to pocket across his muscular belly.

Howdy.

Howdy.

He greeted in passing Leanshanks Pescod, a mulatto lightweight who, in successive Saturday

[4]

sessions at the Commonwealth Club, had defeated two white comers.

Is you enjoyin' de air, Mr. Longfellow?

'Deed, Ah is, Mrs. Guckeen. How you been? The Creeper's manner became slightly flirtatious.

Thank you, Mr. Longfellow, an' pretty well.

Mrs. Imogene Guckeen was the proprietor of a popular beauty parlour further up the avenue. It was Anatole's custom to indulge in a manicure at this parlour every afternoon around five. As a wide circle of admiring women was cognizant of this habit, five was the rush hour at Mrs. Guckeen's establishment. She was fully aware of the important rôle this customer played in her affairs and, as a consequence, made no effort to collect his always considerable bill. Occasionally, moreover, the Creeper would slip her five or ten dollars on account, adding a chuck under her drooping chin and a devastating smile.

Turning about at One hundred and twenty-seventh Street, Anatole faced north and resumed his leisurely promenade. Now, however, despite the apparently careless flipping and twisting of his ebony cane, tipped with a ball of ivory, his air was more serious. He peered into the faces of the women he encountered with an expression that was almost anxious. Once, so eagerly did he seek a pair of eyes which obstinately refused to return his stare, he bumped into an elderly black man with a

[5]

long white beard, who limped, supported by a cane. Anatole caught the old fellow only in time to prevent his falling.

Ah sartainly beg yo' pahdon, he said with his most enchanting smile.

The octogenarian returned the smile.

'Pears to me, he squeaked, dat you's mos' unnacherly perlite fo' dis street at dis hour.

The Creeper's breast expanded a full two inches, causing his watch-chain, stretched to capacity, to drag a ring of jangling keys from his waistcoat pocket. Replacing the keys, he reflected that he could afford to be agreeable, even magnanimous, to harmless old gentlemen. Was there another sheik in Harlem who possessed one-tenth his attraction for the female sex? Was there another of whose muscles the brick-pressers, ordinarily quite free with their audible, unflattering comments about passers-by, were more afraid? As he meditated in this wise, his pride received an unexpected jolt. Under the bright lights in front of the Lafayette Theatre, he discerned a pompous figure whose presence obliterated the smug cheerfulness from his heart.

A few years earlier Randolph Pettijohn had made his start in Harlem as a merchant of hot-dogs. His little one-storey shop, hugged between two towering buildings, had rapidly become popular. His frankfurters were excellent; his buns were fresh; his mustard beyond reproach. In a short time Pettijohn's business was so successful, the over-

[6]

head expense so light—he was his own cook and he personally served his customers over the counter— that he had saved a sufficient sum of money to invest in real-estate, an investment which increased in value over-night. Next, with the proceeds of a few judicious sales, he opened a cabaret which shortly became the favourite resort in Harlem. Now, his Bolito game had made him so rich that his powerfully exerted influence began to be felt in political circles.

Unreasoningly, Anatole hated him. He had never inimically crossed the Creeper's path, but somehow, subconsciously, Anatole was aware that such an eventuality was by no means impossible. Besides, it irked the Creeper to realize that any one else possessed power of whatever kind. The feeling was not reciprocated. Anatole was frequently a spectacular figure at the Winter Palace, Pettijohn's cabaret, where he was welcome because he was known to be a particular favourite with jig-chasers from below the line.

How you been, 'Toly? The Bolito King greeted the Creeper warmly, even affectionately.

Hello, Ran.

Lookin' 'em over?

Ah'm takin' 'em in. The Creeper was reticent.

You sartainly are one dressin' up fool, Creeper, one of the King's companions inserted.

Heavy lover, too, another added.

The King offered his accolade: Nobody like

[7]

203

duh Creeper fo' close an' women, nobody a-tall.

Anatole exposed his pearls. Bottle et, he suggested.

Come in an' see me, Pettijohn invited. Mah Winter Palace is open winter an' summer.

Completely at his ease again, the Creeper strutted on, swinging his cane, expanding his chest, and humming to himself:

> Mah man's got teeth lak a lighthouse on duh sea,
> An' when he smiles he throws dem lights on me.

Howdy, 'Toly!

As Anatole looked into the unwelcome eyes of a high yellow boy whose suit was shiny and whose boots were patched, his manner became a trifle patronizing.

How you been, Duke?

Not so good, 'Toly. Duh show done went broke.

Dere'll be annudder.

Sho'. How's Ah gwine live till den?

The Creeper proffered no advice.

You lookin' mighty lucky, 'Toly. The Duke's tone was one of whining admiration.

The Creeper preserved his discreet silence.

Ah nebber did see no sheik what had yo' gif' fo' dressin'.

The Creeper's chest was the thermometer of the effect of this compliment.

Ah's hungry, 'Toly. Hones'. Gimme duh price of a dog.

[8]

Nigger Heaven

Drawing a handful of loose change from his trouser-pocket, with great deliberation the Creeper selected a quarter from this heap and passed it to his indigent acquaintance.

Heah you is, Duke. . . . He had the air of a munificent benefactor. . . . Now why ain' you git mo' providen'?

Ah is, 'Toly, when Ah gits duh chance. 'T'ain' mah fault duh show done went broke. Inserting the quarter in his mouth, the boy made a sudden dash down a side-street.

Han' full o' gimme, mouf full o' much oblige, mused the Creeper.

At the corner of One hundred and thirty-seventh Street, surrounded by a numerous group of spectators, many of whom clapped their hands rhythmically, a crowd of urchins executed the Charleston. Apparently without intent, Anatole joined these pleasure-seekers. His eyes, however, quickly shifted from the dancers and stole around the ring of onlookers, in hasty but accurate inspection. Suddenly he found that for which he had been searching.

She was a golden-brown and her skin was clear, as soft as velvet. As pretty a piece, he reflected, as he had seen around these parts for some time, and he had not happened to see her before. Her slender body was encased in coral silk, the skirt sufficiently short to expose her trim legs in golden-brown stockings. A turquoise-blue cloche all but covered her straight black shingled hair. Her soft, brown eyes

[9]

seemed to be begging. Withdrawing his own gaze almost immediately, so swift had been his satisfactory appraisal, he was nevertheless aware that she was contriving, without appearing to do so, without, indeed, appearing to look at him at all, to edge nearer to him. Never once, while she carried out her design, did her hands refrain from the rhythmic clapping which accompanied the juvenile dancers. When at last, she stood by his side, so close that he might touch her, she continued to pretend that she was only interested in the intricate steps of the Charleston. Anatole, outwardly, gave no sign whatever that he was aware of her presence.

After they had played this game of mutual duplicity for some time, she, losing patience or acquiring courage, accosted him.

Hello, 'Toly.

He turned, without a smile, and stared at her.

Ah doan seem to recerllec' dat Ah got duh honour o' yo' acquaintance.

You ain', Mr. 'Toly, an' dat's a fac'. Mah name's Ruby.

He did not encourage her to proceed.

Ruby Silver, she completed.

He remained silent. Presently, in an offhand way, he began to clap his hands. A particularly agile lad of six was executing some pretty capers. Hey! Hey! Do that thing!

[10]

Everybody knows who you is, Mr. 'Toly, *everybody!* Her voice implored his attention.

The Creeper continued to clap.

Ah been jes' nacherly crazy to meet you.

The Creeper was stern. What fo'? he shot out.

You knows, Mr. 'Toly. I guess you knows.

He drew her a little apart from the ring.

How much you got?

Oh, Ah been full o' prosperity dis evenin'. Ah met an ofay wanted to change his luck. He gimme a tenner.

The Creeper appeared to be taking the matter under consideration. Ah met a gal las' night dat offer me fifteen, he countered. Nevertheless, it could be seen that he was weakening.

Ah got annuder five in mah lef' stockin', an' Ah'll show you lovin' such as you never seen.

The Creeper became more affable. Ah do seem to remember yo' face, Miss Silver, he averred. Will you do me duh favour to cling to mah arm.

As they strolled, their bodies touching, down a dark side-street, his hand freely explored her flesh, soft and warm under the thin covering of coral silk.

Wanna dance? he demanded.

Luvvit, she replied.

Come across.

She stooped to fumble in her stockings, first the right, then the left. Presently she handed him two

[11]

bills which he stuffed into his waistcoat pocket without the formality of examination.

Winter Palace? she inquired.

A nasty shadow flitted across Anatole's face.

Naw, he retorted. Too many ofays an' jig-chasers.

Bowie Wilcox's is dicty.

Too many monks.

Atlantic City Joe's?

Too many pink-chasers an' bulldikers.

Where den?

Duh Black Venus.

A few moments later they were swallowed by an entrance on Lenox Avenue, flanked by two revolving green lights. Arm in arm, they descended the stairs to the basement. As they walked down the long hallway which led to the dance-floor, the sensual blare of jazz, slow, wailing jazz, stroked their ears. At the door three waiters in evening clothes greeted the Creeper with enthusiasm.

Why, dat's sartainly Mr. 'Toly.

Good evenin'.

Gwine sit at mah table?

Mine?

Mine, Mr. 'Toly?

Expanding his chest, Anatole gazed down the length of the hall. Couples were dancing in such close proximity that their bodies melted together as they swayed and rocked to the tormented howling of the brass, the barbaric beating of the drum. Across

[12]

each woman's back, clasped tight against her shoulder blades, the black hands of her partner were flattened. Blues, smokes, dinges, charcoals, chocolate browns, shines, and jigs.

Le's hoof, Ruby urged.

Le's set down, Anatole commanded. Passing his straw hat to the hat-check girl, he followed a waiter to an empty table, pushing Ruby ahead of him.

Hello, 'Toly! A friend hailed him from an adjoining table.

Hello, Licey.

A pint, the Creeper ordered.

The waiter Charlestoned down the floor to the intoxicating rhythm, twirling his tray on palm held high overhead.

Put ashes in sweet papa's bed so as he can' slip out, moaned Licey in the Creeper's ear. Ah knows a lady what'll be singing, Wonder whah mah easy rider's gone!

Bottle et.

Licey chuckled. Hush mah mouf ef Ah doan!

The waiter came back, like a cat, shuffling ingeniously from one side of the room to the other, in and out of the throng of dancers. Charleston! Charleston! Do that thing! Oh boy!

On his tray were two glasses, two splits of ginger ale, and a bowl of cracked ice. From his hippocket he extracted a bottle containing a transparent liquid. He poured out the ginger ale. Anatole poured out the gin.

[13]

Tea fo' two! he toasted his companion, almost jovially.

She gulped her glassful in one swallow, and then giggled, 'Toly, you's mah sho' 'nough daddy an' Ah sho' does love you wid all mah h'aht.

Everybody loves mah baby, tooted the cornet.

But mah baby doan love nobody but me, Ruby chimed in. She tentatively touched the Creeper's arm. As he did not appear to object to this attention, she stroked it tenderly.

Jes' once 'roun', she pleaded.

He humoured her. Embracing her closely, he rocked her slowly around the hall. Their heels shuffled along the floor. Their knees clicked amorously. On all sides of the swaying couple, bodies in picturesque costumes rocked, black bodies, brown bodies, high yellows, a kaleidoscope of colour transfigured by the amber searchlight. Scarves of bottle green, cerise, amethyst, vermilion, lemon. The drummer in complete abandon tossed his sticks in the air while he shook his head like a wild animal. The saxophone player drew a dilapidated derby over the bowl of his instrument, smothering the din. The banjos planked deliriously. The band snored and snorted and whistled and laughed like a hyena. This music reminded the Creeper of the days when he worked as a bootblack in a Memphis barbershop. Hugged closely together, the bodies rocked and swayed, rocked and swayed. Sometimes a

[14]

rolling-eyed couple, caught in the whirlpool of aching sound, would scarcely move from one spot. Then the floor-manager would cry, Git off dat dime!

Unexpectedly it was over. The saxophone player substituted the stub of a black cigar for the tube of his instrument. As if they had been released from some subtle enchantment the dancing couples broke apart, dazed, and lumbered towards their tables. Now that music was lacking their bodies had lost the secret of the magic rhythm. Normal illumination. A new mood. Laughter and chatter. A woman shrieked hysterically. The Creeper drew the bottle from his hip-pocket and poured out two more drinks.

Again Ruby drained her portion at one gulp. This time she had repudiated the ginger ale. Again she caressed her companion's arm. Again she sought his eyes, his great brown eyes, like a doe's.

Ah sho' will show you some lovin', daddy, she promised.

The Creeper grunted his approval.

Does you know what Ah calls dis? she continued rapturously.

Calls what?

Dis place, where Ah met you—Harlem. Ah calls et, specherly tonight, Ah calls et Nigger Heaven! I jes' nacherly think dis heah is Nigger Heaven!

[15]

Nigger Heaven

On the floor a scrawny yellow girl in pink silk,
embroidered with bronze sequins in floral designs,
began to sing:

> Mah daddy rocks me with one steady roll;
> Dere ain' no slippin' when he once takes hol' . . .

The Creeper sipped his gin meditatively.

[16]

Opportunity Literary Contest

TO STIMULATE creative expression among Negroes and to direct attention to the rich and unexploited sources of materials for literature in Negro life, OPPORTUNITY will offer prizes for short stories, poetry, plays, essays, and personal experience sketches to the amount of

FIVE HUNDRED DOLLARS

There will be three awards for each division. Further particulars about this contest and an announcement of the judges will appear in the September issue of this magazine. If you can write, this is your *Opportunity*.

* * *

Vol. 2   SEPTEMBER, 1924   No. 21

EDITORIALS

An Opportunity for Negro Writers

A NEW period in creative expression among Negroes is foreshadowed in the notable, even if fugitive and disconnected successes of certain of the generation of Negro writers now emerging. The body of experience and public opinion seem ripe for the development of some new and perhaps distinctive contribution to art, literature, and life. But these contributions demand incentives. The random and obviously inadequate methods of casual inquiry have already disclosed an unexpected amount and degree of writing ability among Negroes which gives promise of further development on a large scale. The ability of these scattered writers has become known largely by the accident of locality. There are undoubtedly others to be discovered. The question of markets has been an agent of inertia in this regard. Even for those of acknowledged competence an almost insuperable discouragement has been the unpopularity of those themes with which Negro writers have been most familiar. This is changing now. The judgment of some of the foremost students of American literature offers encouragement for the future of imaginative writing by Negroes.

There is an extreme usefulness for the cause of inter-racial good-will as well as racial culture and American literature in interpreting the life and longings and emotional experiences of the Negro people to their shrinking and spiritually alien neighbors; of flushing old festers of hate and disgruntlement by becoming triumphantly articulate; of forcing the interest and kindred feeling of the rest of the world by sheer force of the humanness and beauty of one's own story. The old romantic Negro characters of fiction are admittedly *passe*. Negroes have been swept along, even if at the rear of the procession, with the forward movement of the rest of the world. There is an opportunity now for Negroes themselves to replace their out-worn representations in fiction faithfully and incidentally to make themselves better understood.

The purpose, then, of OPPORTUNITY's literary contest can thus be stated in brief: It hopes to stimulate and encourage creative literary effort among Negroes; to locate and orient Negro writers of ability; to stimulate and encourage interest in the serious development of a body of literature about Negro life, drawing deeply upon these tremendously rich sources; to encourage the reading of literature both by Negro authors and about Negro life, not merely because they are Negro authors but because what they write is literature and because the literature is interesting; to foster a market for Negro writers and for literature by and about Negroes; to bring these writers into contact with the general world of letters to which they have been for the most part timid and inarticulate strangers; to stimulate and foster a type of writing by Negroes which shakes itself free of deliberate propaganda and protest.

• • •

Opportunity's Literary Prize Contest Awards

THE CONTEST will include first, second, and third prizes for the following types of writing:

Short Story—First Prize $100.00
Second Prize 40.00
Third Prize 15.00
Poetry—First Prize $40.00
Second Prize 15.00
Third Prize 5.00
Play—First Prize $60.00
Second Prize 35.00
Third Prize 15.00
Essay—First Prize $50.00
Second Prize 30.00
Third Prize 10.00
Personal Experience Sketch—
First Prize $30.00
Second Prize 20.00
Third Prize 5.00

For the next ten best stories, poems, plays, and essays there will be free criticism by competent authorities in each field of letters.

The winning stories will be published.

Prize winners will be formally announced at a special meeting in New York.

RULES OF THE CONTEST

This contest is designed to stimulate creative effort among Negroes and quite without any notion of discrimination is confined to Negro contestants.

SHORT STORIES

The stories must deal with some phase of Negro life, either directly or indirectly; otherwise there are no restrictions. They may be romantic, realistic, humorous, and will be judged upon their quality as a good short story.

These stories must not exceed 5000 words.

POETRY

No restrictions are placed upon the themes of the poems.

PLAYS

The plays must deal with some phase of Negro life, either directly or indirectly; otherwise there are no restrictions. They may be romantic, realistic, humorous, and will be judged upon their quality as a good play.

ESSAYS

The object here is simply to bid for a much abused type of literary expression, in the hope of finding some examples of recognizable literary merit. The contestant will strive for clarity of diction, forcefulness, and originality of ideas, logical structure, deft and effective employment of language, accuracy of data, and economy of words. The subject may be of the contestant's selection but must relate directly or indirectly to Negro life and contacts, or situations in which Negroes have a conspicuous interest.

These essays are limited to 3000 words.

PERSONAL EXPERIENCE SKETCHES

These sketches must be an actual experience and relate to some incident or situation or circumstance of personal life which makes it possible to understand how one feels and acts in the presence of a particular life problem. The contestant will strive for complete frankness and self-scrutiny, truthfulness, and clarity of expression.

These will be limited to 2000 words.

Any story, poem, play, essay, or personal experience sketch that has already been published is ineligible for this contest.

The contest will close December 31, 1924.

This contest reserves the right to reject all manuscripts in any division if the contributions are deemed below a reasonable standard of quality or insufficient in number.

A complete list of the judges will be published in a later issue. Some of the acceptances are quoted for their expressed interest in the future of creative expression among Negroes. They include the sentiments of leaders of American letters.

John Farrar, Editor, THE BOOKMAN, says:
"I shall be very happy to act as judge in the poetry contest and am honored that you want me to do so. As you know, I am much interested in work of all young writers, and perhaps even more in that of the Negro race."

Carl Van Doren, Editor, CENTURY MAGAZINE, author, writes:
"I shall be glad to serve as one of the judges of your prize contest for short stories by Negro writers if you want me to. Though I have lately declined every other such invitation, on the score of overwork, this one has not caused me a moment's hesitation."

Clement Wood, author, contributor of poems, articles and short stories to magazines, replies:
"I am delighted to serve as one of the judges of OPPORTUNITY's poetry contest for the younger Negro writers."

John Macy, author and editor, says:
"I shall be very glad to act as one of the judges in your contest and to help your work in any way that I can."

Montgomery Gregory, Director, Department of Dramatics, Howard University, states:
"I want to congratulate you upon having taken a step that should do more than anything in the past toward the development of the younger Negro writers. It has been my dream: it is your splendid realization.

"I shall be delighted to serve as one of the judges for plays and I shall, therefore, await further instructions from you. I note that you have made an unusually happy choice of persons to serve as judges."

Robert Hobart Davis, dramatist, Editor, MUNSEY'S, responds as follows:
"I am interested in . . . the work of the Negro writers in this country. I would like to do whatever I can to encourage them in their development."

Dorothy Scarborough, author, book reviewer and short story critic, contributor of short stories, articles and verse to newspapers and magazines, writes:
"I am very much interested in the development of

(Continued on page 279)

Opportunity's Literary Prize Contest
(Continued from page 277)

the talents, artistic and otherwise, of the Negroes. and I shall be happy to serve as a judge in the short story contest. I think the plan excellent for arousing interest."

Zona Gale, author, contributor to magazines, says:
"I am very much honored by your invitation to act as one of the judges in the Negro writers' contest. Thank you for thinking of me, and I accept with pleasure."

Edna Worthley Underwood, writer, linguist, author of "The Passion Flower," "The Penitent," writes:
"I am just in receipt of your favor relative to OPPORTUNITY's $500 prize contest. I think it is a splendid plan which you outline to me in your letter and I shall be most happy to serve as one of the judges."

Blanche Colton Williams, editor, author, instructor, Columbia University, accepts as follows:
"Your request honors me and I take pleasure in saying I will gladly serve as judge in connection with the $500 offer of OPPORTUNITY . . .

"The award that OPPORTUNITY will make in this contest seems to me a happy idea and one that cannot but be helpful to more than one young man and woman."

217

revealing an altogether admirable group of new writers.

These facts should be remembered: *The stories, plays, and essays must deal directly or indirectly with some phase of Negro life; the poetry is unrestricted; the personal experience sketches must be true stories. No limit is placed upon the number of manuscripts which any person may submit, or upon the kinds of writing contributed. The contest opened September 1 and closes December 31. It would facilitate the handling of manuscripts if they are sent in before the very end of the contest.*

Since this journal is our surest medium for communicating information concerning the progress of this contest, it is advisable that those interested arrange to secure issues regularly.

Opportunity's Prize Contest

NINETEEN judges, all of whom are crowded with their own literary duties, have consented promptly and eagerly to pass upon the merits of the contributions by Negroes to OPPORTUNITY's contest. Their consent is both a gesture of friendliness toward a long submerged and virtually inarticulate group, and a recognition of the rich stores of material in Negro life to be exploited in the interest of American literature generally. Since the last issue acceptances have come in from Fannie Hurst, one of America's foremost short story writers; Robert C. Benchley, dramatic critic and editor of *Life;* Witter Bynner, poet and anthologist; Alexander Woollcott, dramatic critic of the New York *Sun;* Henry Goddard Leach, editor of the *Forum;* Van Wyck Brooks, an essayist of distinction and formerly editor of the *Freeman;* Dorothy Canfield Fisher, novelist; and James Weldon Johnson, one of the best known of the Negro writers and anthologists.

With the attention and real interest of those whose judgments and advice can contribute so materially to the orientation of new writers and old ones to the world of letters, it would be inexcusable if an adequate response failed to develop from this opportunity,—worse we fear: it would be disillusioning. The numerous inquiries, however, which followed the first announcement offer abundant hope, and the quality of some of the manuscripts already submitted gives promise of

The Last Warning **O**PPORTUNITY'S Literary Contest closes December thirty-first. As we go to press, one month and a half before the final date, 231 manuscripts have been entered. Stories, poems, plays, a sparkling colorful miscellany,—from the sophisticated centers of culture, from the rich veins of Negro life in the South, from tiny towns with unfamiliar postmarks, from the wide stretches of the West, from Panama and the Virgin Islands. About them all is a passionate earnestness; and out of this surprising concourse of themes and aspirations we have confidence will emerge a group of creative artists who have caught the furtive soul of their people.

Negro life is the one unexplored sector of American life. It has been for the most part, so long and so carefully protected by the incrustations of taboo and misrepresentation that it emerges now upon a world jaded and bored, with all the flaring revelations of a new country. *Harper's Magazine* for October allowed Konrad Bercovici to discover Harlem, which he did interestingly even if his contact with life there was as fleeting as "the kiss of two billiard balls." The *Forum Magazine's* winning story, selected out of 600 entries and published in November, was a Negro story. During the same month *Theatre Arts* published *"The No-Count Boy,"* a bewitchingly romantic play with a theme woven around three Negro characters, and Countee Cullen's poems appeared simultaneously in four literary journals. Walter White's *"The Fire in the Flint"* has drawn the approbation of a wide circle of critics. Jessie Fauset's *"There Is Confusion"* is passing through its third printing and a translation. No less than fifteen books, exclusive of scientific publications, have appeared this year on Africa; more than fifty books have appeared this year dealing directly or indirectly with Negro life and problems.

There is a curiosity about this life as well as about the power of those who know it best to write about it.

The contest aims to bring these new voices into tune with the larger world of letters,—to help them discover themselves. It could have no other purpose. Once before we quoted Robert H. Davis, Editor of the Munsey publications, who expressed a hope which is general: that the Contest will reveal "some rare first note" worthy of development and of free incorporation into the stream of American letters. Upon this hope we rest until the judges decide.

OPPORTUNITY

Editorials  *May 1925*
Vol. 3 No. 29

The Contest WE announce in this issue the winning contestants in OP-PORTUNITY's Literary Contest. Because this has been an experiment,—a frank search throughout the country for Negro writers of ability and promise, extraordinary measures have been taken to give to each contestant a fair hearing. The twenty-four judges of the Contest, all busy persons, have contributed generously of their time and energies to encompass a task greatly in excess of the usual demands of judges. Theirs has been a large and valuable contribution. The result has been thoroughly encouraging. For those of the 732 entries who failed to receive one of the fifteen prizes, there should be some satisfaction in the knowledge that the average quality of the manuscripts was high in all divisions of the Contest. Judgment did not come easily.

On the quality of the manuscripts the judges have commented in terms of surprised delight. Witter Bynner, a poet, poetry critic and founder of the Annual Intercollegiate Poetry Contest, expressed himself enthusiastically upon the quality evoked in the best of the poems and "countless signs among the manuscripts of vitality and skill." Clement Wood, another poetry judge and author of a recent volume on Contemporary American Poetry, thought that "the general standard of the contributions was higher than such Contests usually bring out." Referring to one of the prize winning poems, he characterized it as "exquisitely rhymed—the choice of words never *outre* and never hackneyed—the outlook broader than any one race, in message and technique magnificent." James Weldon Johnson says of the poem, "The Weary Blues" which took first prize, that it "shows a revolting and breaking away from worn out forms . . . is devoid of cliches, and has the added value of being characteristic." John Farrar, editor of the *Bookman*, felt that "the poems of the entire contest are of singularly pleasing quality."

In the field of short story there was a most intense interest, probably, because the creative ability of Negroes has not often been expressed through this medium. Here there were eight judges, an unusual number. But from all of them came a profound appreciation of the deeply moving pictures of Negro life presented by these writers. Robert H. Davis, editor of the *Munsey* fiction publications, noted that most of the stories

displayed "extraordinary imaginative gifts" and added: "I have no hesitation about saying that these stories show that the American Negro has found articulation and out of it will arise benefits of incalculable value." Dr. Blanche Colton Williams, who has written many books on the short story, in observing that the whole series was "remarkably good," said: "I liked the writers' sticking to their people, to the subjects about which they should be familiar, the straightforward manner of presenting the stories and in some instances the professional quality revealed through the style or through the story technique or both." Zona Gale felt that the stories "revealed great treasure." Edna Worthley Underwood made this significant comment: "I fancy the stories mark an epoch in the history of American letters—the entrance into the domain of art of a new race, differently dowered, but with something we can not well do without. In the future we must learn to look—more and more—to the black races for art, because joy—its mainspring—is dying so rapidly now in the Great Caucasian Race. Without joy, art can not be. The stories, too, are revelation to the whites—through the intensified vision of creative mind—of the soul of the black man. They give to him the seal of a new equality—sometimes with a disturbing inclination to go as our Spanish neighbors to the south would say—*sobre la cima*. Art should be—and undoubtedly will be—the powerful and compelling liaison officer between nations and races. You will probably recall that it was the art of Heinrich Heine that tore up the Treaties of Vienna and moved the boundaries of France to the Rhine. Success in it carries along—as a kind of by-product—the indisputable cachet of domination, and of constantly widening boundaries."

The comments of the other judges of the short stories are equally interesting.

The significance of the plays may be sensed when one considers that the plays about Negro life available in this country may be counted on the fingers of one hand. The Contest brought to light about sixty-five, many of which have a distinct merit and are producible.

In the division of essays, there was at first some concern. The grist, however, revealed writings of exceptional charm. Speaking generally of these one of the judges remarked upon the "amount of

220

close thinking which is being done by the Negro about the problems of the race."

The personal experience sketches came like a passionate outburst. These sketches are slices from real life and in the telling these are given a vital significance.

From the point of view of the subject matter the Contest has been a success. From the angle of this journal's interest in uncovering writers of ability and promise the results have been pleasing beyond expectation. For the benefit of those who desire to read for their own entertainment and profit the offerings of the most promising of these writers we shall carry, after the prize winning manuscripts, certain of those which acheived honorable mention, and which were in competition for the place of highest rank. The work of the contest is just beginning. We advise those of our contestants who are interested in this whole developing movement to *stand by.*

emotions of the Negroes was beginning to mount; when the polite barriers erected by the magazine editors and publishers were beginning to crumble softly. And for the most part, they have come to this field not so much because they are interested in Negroes as because the field itself is interesting to literature and scarcly touched. In one of Dr. Henry Seidel Canby's essays in contemporary criticism (Americans in Fiction), he does not hesitate to point out as an exception to the outworn or unutilizable subjects for American literature, the Negro "whose literature is just beginning." "Special circumstances," he continues, "make him more at home in America than the rest of racial aliens and yet keep him further apart. He has appeared in our literature as propaganda, as folk lore, as comic relief, and as sentiment. His nature is rich. . . . As material for American literature, he is the least worked, but not the easiest. *Probably the literature of the American Negro can be written only by himself."* (The italics are ours.)

This is precisely the keynote of this new awakening among the present generation of Negroes, which OPPORTUNITY is attempting to encourage. It explains the limitation of the Contest to subjects pertaining directly or indirectly to the Negro. It explains also the amazingly interesting stories about real Negroes, which have come to light, revealing pictures, compelling in their sheer charm and underlying humanity.

We expect of literature, nowadays, to reveal with some measure of faithfulness something of the life of a people; something of those subtle forces which sustain their hopes and joys, stiffens them in sorrow. A start in this direction has already been made in certain of the recently published works by Negro writers. Jean Tooner's "Cane" is an outstanding example of the wealth of color, exoticism and poetry possible. Walter White's "The Fire in the Flint" and Jessie Fauset's "There is Confusion," suggest the materials. That there is more in the making the work of those new writers represented in OPPORTUNITY's Contest will show. They and others like them will be heard, and what they have to say, we are courageous enough to believe, will make the pictures by which Negroes of all strata of this society will hereafter be known.

Out of the Shadow   A CRITICISM of Negro efforts at artistic expression well merited has been that the members of this group with a background of deep toned and gorgeously colorful experience all their own, have, with the characteristic self consciousness of the parvenu, strained desperately to avoid or deny it.

In avoiding their own life, they have been no different from the early American writers who looked to England for their patterns and with these patterns took much of their subject matter. In denying it, they have been no different from the Southern writers who produced at least sixty-five novels in answer to "Uncle Tom's Cabin," offering pictures of a precisely opposite but sweetly unrealistic state of affairs. Even the names of the novels of rebuttal are forgotten.

Since that period, however, the American writers have discovered themselves and their country and are already looking for other words to conquer. The Negro writers, in large part, following the same path of evolution, have spent the greater portion of their freedom protesting against the dialect which they know perfectly well the illiterate ones of their own group used, snubbing the spirituals, genuflecting themselves before remote and wholly irrelevant Egyptian altars, or painting white heroes black and black villains white. Not that this sort of thing is wholly wrong or unexampled even in the history of Americans. The point is that in bending all efforts to prove that they are just like other people, they have ignored perhaps the only vital differences that can give prestige, which is, incidentally, the very object of most of the effort.

The first significant exploitation of the materials of Negro life has come not from Negro but white writers. But Stribling, Shands and Clement Wood, the first of the moderns, have merely hinted at the vastness and deep moving interest of this field of material. They heaved into print at a time when public curiosity over the inner thoughts and

Contest Awards

The winning manuscripts selected from 732 entries in the five divisions of OPPORTUNITY's Literary Contest, as announced at the special meeting in New York City on the evening of May 1st, are given below:

The Short Story

First Prize of $100.00 to FOG, by John Matheus, of Institute, West Virginia.

Second Prize of $35.00 to SPUNK, by Zora Neale Hurston, of Jacksonville, Florida.

Third Prize of $15.00 to THE VOODOO'S REVENGE, by Eric D. Walrond, of New York City.

For Honorable Mention

1. THE BOLL WEEVIL STARTS NORTH, by N. B. Young, of St. Louis, Mo.
2. THE HANDS, by Marieta Bonner.
3. BLACK DEATH, by Zora Neale Hurston, of Jacksonville, Florida.
4. A SOUL GOES WEST ON THE B. & O., by Frank Horne, of Brooklyn.
5. ANTE BELLUM, by John Davis, of Lewiston, Me.
6. ALL GOD'S CHILLUN GOT SHOES, by N. B. Young, of St. Louis, Mo.
7. THE EXAMINATION, by Eugene F. Gordon, of Boston, Mass.
8. A CHRISTMAS JOURNEL, by Louis L. Redding, of Atlanta, Georgia.

Judges for Short Stories

Dr. Blanche Colton Williams, Chairman of Committee, Columbia University and Hunter College, Author.
Carl Van Doren, Literary Editor of the Century Magazine.
Zona Gale, Novelist and Playwright.
Fannie Hurst, Short Story Writer.
Robert Hobart Davis, Editor, Munsey's Magazine.
Dorothy Canfield Fisher, Novelist.
Edna Worthley Underwood, Novelist.
Alain Locke, Howard University, Writer.
Dorothy Scarborough, Novelist, Columbia University.

Poetry

First Prize of $40.00 to THE WEARY BLUES, by Langston Hughes, of Washington, D. C.

Second Prize of $15.00 TO ONE WHO SAID ME NAY, by Countee Cullen, of New York City.

Third Place. For the third place there was a tie between the winners of the first and second prizes: A SONG OF SOUR GRAPES, by Countee Cullen, and AMERICA, by Langston Hughes, receiving the same number of votes. The Judges decided to award the honor to both and the cash prize to the two contestants receiving Fourth Place.

Cash Price of $5.00 to SOLACE, by Clarissa Scott, of Washington, D. C.

Cash Price of $5.00 to THE WAYSIDE WELL, by Joseph S. Cotter, of Louisville, Kentucky.

For Honorable Mention

1. WORDS TO MY LOVE, by Countee Cullen.
2. SYMPHONIES, by Esther Popel, of Washington, D. C.

3. THE JESTER, by Langston Hughes.
4. SONGS TO A DARK VIRGIN, by Langston Hughes.
5. PREFERENCE, by Dora Lawrence Houston, of Washington, D. C.
6. MY LOVE, by Carrie B. McWatt, of St. Paul, Minnesota.
7. A BABE IS A BABE, by Joseph S. Catter.
8. A TREE AT NIGHT, by Helene Johnson.
9. BROTHERS, by Carrie W. Clifford, of Washington, D. C.
10. FALL OF MAN, by Joseph Bennett, of New York City.
11. LINES TO A SHY WOMAN, by Robert Tard, of Columbus, Ohio.

Judges for Poetry

Clement Wood, Chairman of Committee.
Witter Bynner, Poet.
John Farrar, Editor of the Bookman.
James Weldon Johnson, Poet, Anthologist.

Essays

First Prize of $50.00 to SOCIAL EQUALITY AND THE NEGRO, by E. Franklin Frazier, of Atlanta, Ga.

Second Prize of $30.00 to ROLAND HAYES by Sterling Brown of Lynchburg, Va.

Third Prize of $10.00 to THE NEGRO POET, by Laura D. Wheatley, of Baltimore, Md.

For Honorable Mention

1. PERSISTENT DEVELOPMENT OF A MENACING SITUATION, by Lucius Scott of Washington, D. C.
2. A QUESTION OF SINCERITY, by G. A. Stewart, of Columbus, Ohio.
3. THE NEGRO AND EXPEDIENCY, by Lionel B. Fraser, of Hampton, Va.
4. THE NECESSITY FOR MIGRATION, by H. M. Bond, of Langston, Okla.
5. THE DEVELOPMENT OF NEGRO EDUCATION IN THE SOUTH, by Charles Cooper, Hampton, Va.

Judges for Essays

Henry Goddard Leach, Editor of The Forum, Chairman of Committee.
Van Wyck Brooks, Author, formerly Editor of The Freeman.
L. Hollingsworth Wood.
John Macy.

Plays

First Prize of $60.00 to FRANCES, by G. D. Lipscomb.

Second Prize of $35.00 to
HUMBLE INSTRUMENT, by Warren A. MacDonald, of Philadelphia, Pa., and
COLOR STRUCK, by Zora Neale Hurston, of Jacksonville, Fla.

Third Prize of $15.00 to THE BOG GUIDE, by Jean Ray, of Baltimore, Md.

For Honorable Mention
1. COOPED UP, by Eloise Bibb Thompson, of Los Angeles, Calif.
2. FALL OF THE CONJURER, by Willis Richardson, of Washington, D. C.
3. SPEARS, by Zora Neale Hurston, of Jacksonville, Fla.

Judges for Plays

Montgomery Gregory, formerly Instructor in Dramatics, Howard University, Chairman of Committee.
Alexander Woollcott, Dramatic Critic.
Robert C. Benchley, Dramatic Critic and Editor of Life.
Edith Isaacs, Editor, Theatre Arts Magazine.

Personal Experience Sketches

First Prize of $30.00 to MY FELLOW TRAVELER, by G. A. Steward of Columbus, Ohio.

Second Prize of $20.00 to AN EXPERIENCE, by Fidelia Ripley, of Boston, Mass.

Third Prize to PERSONAL EXPERIENCE by J. C. Stubbs, of Detroit, Mich.

For Honorable Mention—
1. CAT AND THE SAXOPHONE, by Esther Popel, of Washington, D. C.
2. ANOTHER ANGEL UNAWARE, by Palice Matox, of Hillsboro, Ohio.
3. A FLORIDA SUNDAY, by Louis L. Redding, of Atlanta, Ga.

Judges for Sketches

Eugene Kinckle Jones, Chairman of Committee.
Lillian A. Alexander.
Rev. Frank Lorimer.

The Weary Blues

By LANGSTON HUGHES

Awarded First Prize

Droning a drowsy syncopated tune,
Rocking back and forth to a mellow croon,
    I heard a Negro play.
Down on Lenox Avenue the other night
By the pale dull pallor of an old gas light
    He did a lazy sway . . .
    He did a lazy sway . . .
To the tune o' those Weary Blues.
With his ebony hands on each ivory key
He made that poor piano moan with melody.
    O Blues!
Swaying to and fro on his rickety stool
He played that sad raggy tune like a musical fool.
    Sweet Blues!
Coming from a black man's soul.
    O Blues!
In a deep song voice with a melancholy tone

I heard that Negro sing, that old piano moan—
    "Ain't got nobody in all this world,
    Ain't got nobody but ma self.
    I's gwine to quit ma frownin'
    And put ma troubles on the shelf."
Thump, thump, thump, went his foot on the floor.
He played a few chords then sang some more—
    "I got the Weary Blues
    And I can't be satisfied.
    Got the Weary Blues
    And can't be satisfied—
    I ain't happy no mo'
    And I wish that I had died."
And far into the night he crooned that tune.
The stars went out and so did the moon.
The singer stopped playing and went to bed
While the Weary Blues echoed through his head.
He slept like a rock or a man that's dead.

To One Who Said Me Nay

By COUNTEE CULLEN

Awarded Second Prize

This much the gods vouchsafe today:
That we two lie in the clover,
Watching the heavens dip and sway,
With galleons sailing over.

This much is granted for an hour:
That we are young and tender,
That I am bee and you are flower,
Honey-mouthed and swaying slender.

This sweet of sweets is ours now:
To wander through the land,
Plucking an apple from its bough
To toss from hand to hand.

No thing is certain, joy nor sorrow,
Except the hour we know it;
Oh, wear my heart today; tomorrow
Who knows where the winds will blow it?

Fog

By John Matheus

Awarded First Prize—Short Story Section

THE stir of life echoed. On the bridge between Ohio and West Virginia was the rumble of heavy trucks, the purr of high power engines in Cadillacs and Paiges, the rattle of Fords. A string of loaded freight cars pounded along on the C. & P. tracks, making a thunderous, if tedious way to Mingo. A steamboat's hoarse whistle boomed forth between the swish, swish, chug, chug of a mammoth stern paddle wheel with the asthmatic poppings of the pistons. The raucous shouts of smutty speaking street boys, the noises of a steam laundry, the clank and clatter of a pottery, the godless voices of women from Water Street houses of ill fame, all these blended in a sort of modern babel, common to all the towers of destruction erected by modern civilization.

These sounds were stirring when the clock sounded six on top of the Court House, that citadel of Law and Order, with the statue of Justice looming out of an alcove above the imposing stone entrance, blindfolded and in her right hand the scales of Judgment. Even so early in the evening the centers from which issued these inharmonious notes were scarcely visible. This sinister cloak of a late November twilight Ohio Valley fog had stealthily spread from somewhere beneath the sombre river bed, down from somewhere in the lowering West Virginia hills. This fog extended its tenacles over city and river, gradually obliterating traces of familiar landscapes. At five-thirty the old Panhandle bridge, supported by massive sandstone pillars, stalwart, as when erected fifty years before to serve a generation now passed behind the portals of life, this *old* bridge had become a spectral outline against the sky as the toll keepers of the *new* bridge looked northward up the Ohio River.

Now at six o'clock the fog no longer distorted; it blotted out, annihilated. One by one the street lights came on, giving an uncertain glare in spots, enabling peeved citizens to tread their way homeward without recognizing their neighbor ten feet ahead, whether he might be Jew or Gentile, Negro or Pole, Slav, Crotian, Italian or one hundred per cent American.

An impatient crowd of tired workers peered vainly through the gloom to see if the headlights of the interurban car were visible through the thickening haze. The car was due at Sixth and Market at six-ten and was scheduled to leave at six-fifteen for many little towns on the West Virginia side.

At the same time as these uneasy toilers were waiting, on the opposite side of the river the car had stopped to permit some passengers to descend and disappear in the fog. The motorman, flagged and jaded by the monotony of many stopping and starting waited mechanically for the conductor's bell to signal, "Go ahead."

The fog was thicker, more impenetrable. It smothered the headlight. Inside the car in the smoker, that part of the seats nearest the motorman's box, partitioned from the rest, the lights were struggling bravely against a fog of tobacco smoke, almost as opaque as the dull grey blanket of mist outside. A group of red, rough men, sprawled along the two opposite bench-formed seats, parallel to the sides of the car, were talking to one another in the thin, flat colorless English of their mountain state, embellished with the homely idioms of the coal mine, the oil field, the gas well.

"When does this here meetin' start, Bill?"

"That air notice read half after seven."

"What's time now?"

"Damned 'f I know. Hey, Lee, what time's that pocket clock of yourn's got?"

"Two past six."

There was the sound of a match scratching against the sole of a rough shoe.

"Gimme a light, Lafe."

In attempting to reach for the burning match before its flame was extinguished, the man stepped forward and stumbled over a cheap suitcase of imitation leather. A vile looking stogie fell in the aisle.

"God! Your fee're bigger'n Bills's."

The crowd laughed uproariously. The butt of this joke grinned and showed a set of dirty nicotine stained teeth. He recovered his balance in time to save the flaring match. He was a tremendous man, slightly stooped, with taffy colored, straggling hair and little pig eyes.

Between initial puffs he drawled: "Now you're barkin' up the wrong tree. I only wear elevens."

"Git off'n me, Lee Cromarty," growled Bill. "You hadn't ought to be rumlin' of *my* feathers the wrong way—and you a-plannin' to ride the goat."

Lake, a consumptive appearing, undersized, bovine eyed individual, spat out the remark: "Naow, there! You had better be kereful. Men have been nailed to the cross for less than that."

"Ha! ha!—ho! ho! ho!"

There was a joke to arouse the temper of the crowd.

A baby began to cry lustily in the rear and more commodious end of the car reserved for nonsmokers. His infantine wailing smote in sharp contrast upon the ears of the hilarious joshers, filling the silence that followed the subsidence of the laughter.

"Taci, bimba. Non aver paura!"

Nobody understood the musical words of the patient, Madonna eyed Italian mother, not even the baby, for it continued its yelling. She opened her gay colored shirt waist and pressed the child to her bosom. He was quieted.

"She can't speak United States, but I bet her Tony Spaghetti votes the same as you an' me. The young 'un 'll have more to say about the future of these Nunited States that your children an' mine unless we carry forward the word such as we are going to accomplish tonight."

"Yeh, you're damned right," answered the scowling companion of the lynx-eyed citizen in kahki clothes, who had thus commented upon the foreign woman's offspring.

"They breed like cats. They'll outnumber us, unless——"

A smell of garlic stifled his speech. Nich and Mike Axaminter, late for the night shift at the La Belle, bent over the irate American deluging him with the odor of garlic and voluble, gutteral explosions of a Slavak tongue.

"What t' hell! Git them buckets out o' my face, you hunkies, you!"

Confused and apologetic the two men moved forward.

"Isn't this an awful fog, Barney," piped a gay, girlish voice.

"I'll tell the world it is," replied her red-haired companion, flinging a half smoked cigarette away in the darkness as he assisted the girl to the platform.

They made their way to a vacant seat in the end of the car opposite the smoker, pausing for a moment respectfully to make the sign of the cross before two Sisters of Charity, whose flowing black robes and ebon headdress contrasted strikingly with the pale whiteness of their faces. The nuns raised their eyes, slightly smiled and continued their orisons on dark decades of rosaries with pendant crosses of ivory.

"Let's sit here," whispered the girl. "I don't want to be by those niggers."

In a few seconds they were settled. There were cooings of sweet words, limpid-eyed soul glances. They forgot all others. The car was theirs alone.

"Say, boy, ain't this some fog. Yuh can't see the old berg."

"'Sthat so. I hadn't noticed."

Two Negro youths thus exchanged words. They were well dressed and sporty.

"Well, it don't matter, as long as it don't interfere with the dance."

"I hope Daisy will be there. She's some stunnin' high brown an' I don't mean maybe."

"O boy!"

Thereupon one began to hum "Daddy, O Daddy" and the other whistled softly the popular air from "Shuffle Along" entitled "Old-Fashioned Love."

"Oi, oi! Ven I say vill dis car shtart. Ve must mek dot train fur Pittsburgh."

"Ach, Ish ka bibble. They can't do a thing without us, Laban."

They settled down in their seats to finish the discussions in Yiddish, emphasizing the conversation with shrugs of the shoulder and throaty interjections.

In a seat apart to themselves, for two seats in front and behind were unoccupied, sat an old Negro man and a Negro woman, evidently his wife. Crowded between them was a girl of fourteen or fifteen.

"This heah is suah cu'us weather," complained the old man.

"We all nevah had no sich fog in Oklahoma."

The girl's hair was bobbed and had been straightened by "Poro" treatment, giving her an Egyptian cast of features.

"Gran'pappy," said the girl, "yo' cain't see ovah yander."

"Ain't it de troot, chile."

"Ne' min', sugah," assured the old woman. "Ah done paid dat 'ployment man an' he sayed yo' bound tuh lak de place. Dis here lady what's hirin yo' is no po' trash an' she wants a likely gal lak yo' tuh ten' huh baby."

Now these series of conversations did not transpire in chronological order. They were uttered more or less simultaneously during the interval that the little conductor stood on tiptoe in an effort to keep one hand on the signal rope, craning his neck in a vain and dissatisfied endeavor to pierce the miasma of the fog. The motorman chafed in his box, thinking of the drudging lot of the laboring man. He registered discontent.

The garrulous group in the smoker were smouldering cauldrons of discontent. In truth their dissatisfaction ran the gamut of hate. It was stretching out to join hands with an unknown and clandestine host to plot, preserve, defend their dwarfted and twisted ideals.

The two foreign intruders in the smoker squirmed under the merciless, half articulate antipathy. They asked nothing but a job to make some money. In exchange for that magic English word job, they endured the terror that walked by day, the boss. They grinned stupidly at profanity, dirt, disease, disaster. Yet they were helping to make America.

Three groups in the car on this foggy evening were united under the sacred mantle of a common religion. Within its folds they sensed vaguely a something of happiness. The Italian mother radiated the joy of her child. Perhaps in honor of her and in reverence the two nuns with downcast eyes, trying so hard to forget the world, were counting off the rosary of the blessed Virgin—"Ave, Maria," "Hail, Mary, full of grace, the Lord is with thee; blessed art thou among women."

The youth and his girl in their tiny circle of mutual attraction and affection could not as in Edwin Markham's poem widen the circle to include all or even to embrace that small circumscribed area of humanity within the car.

And the Negroes? Surely there was no hate in their minds. The gay youths were rather indifferent. The trio from the South, journeying far for a greater freedom of self expression philosophically accepted the inevitable "slings and arrows of outrageous fortune."

The Jews were certainly enveloped in a racial consciousness, unerringly fixed on control and domination of money, America's most potent factor in respectability.

The purplish haze of fog contracted. Its damp presence slipped into the car and every passenger shivered and peered forth to see. Their eyes were as the eyes of the blind!

At last the signal bell rang out staccato. The car suddenly lurched forward, shaking from side to side the passengers in their seats. The wheels scraped and began to turn. Almost at once a more chilling wetness filtered in from the river. In the invisibility of the fog it seemed that one was traveling through space, in an aeroplane perhaps, going nobody knew where.

The murmur of voices buzzed in the smoker, interrupted by the boisterous outbursts of laughter. A red glare tinted the fog for a second and disappeared. La Belle was "shooting" the furnaces. Then a denser darkness and the fog.

The car lurched, scintillating sparks flashed from the trolley wire, a terrific crash—silence. The lights went out. Before anybody could think or scream, there came a falling sensation, such as one experiences when dropped unexpectedly in an elevator or when diving through the scenic railways of the city amusements parks, or more exactly when one has nightmare and dreams of falling, falling, falling.

"The bridge has given way. God! The muddy water! The fog! Darkness. Death."

These thoughts flashed spontaneously in the consciousness of the rough ignorant fellows, choking in the fumes of their strong tobacco, came to the garlic scented "hunkies", to the Italian Madonna, to the sisters of Charity, to the lover boy and his lover girl, to the Negro youths, to the Jews thinking in Yiddish idioms, to the old Negro man and his wife and the Egyptian-faced girl, with the straightened African hair, even to the bored motorman and the weary conductor.

To drown, to strangle, to suffocate, to die! In the dread silence the words screamed like exploding shells within the beating temples of terror-stricken passengers and crew.

Then protest, wild, mad, tumultuous, frantic protest. Life at bay and bellowing furiously against its ancient arch-enemy and antithesis—Death. An oath, screams,—dull, paralyzing, vomit—stirring nausea. Holy, unexpressed intimacies, deeply rooted prejudices were roughly shaken from their smug moorings. The Known to be changed for an Unknown, the ever expected, yet unexpected, Death. No! No! Not that.

Lee Cromarty saw things in that darkness. A plain, one-story frame house, a slattern woman on the porch, an overgrown, large hipped girl with his face. Then the woman's whining, scolding voice and the girl's bashful confidences. What was dimming that picture? What cataract was blurring his vision? Was it the fog?

To Lafe, leader of the crowd, crouched in his seat, his fingers clawing the air for a grasping place,

came a vision of a hill-side grave,—his wife's—and he saw again how she looked in her coffin—then the fog.

"I'll not report at the mine," thought Bill. "Wonder what old Bunner will say to that."

The mine foreman's grizzled face dangled for a second before him and was swallowed in the fog.

Hoarse, gasping exhalations. Men, old men, young men, sobbing. "Pietà! Madre mia!—Mercy, Virgin Mary! My child!"

No thoughts of fear or pain on the threshold of death, that shadow from whence all children flow, but all the Mother Love focused to save the child.

"Memorare, remember, O most gracious Virgin Mary, that never was it known that any one who fled to thy protection, implored thy help and sought thy intercession was left unaided."

The fingers sped over the beads of the rosary. But looming up, unerasable, shuttled the kaleidoscope of youth, love, betrayal, renunciation, the vows. *Miserere, Jesu!*

"Life is ever lord of Death
And Love can never lose its own."

The girl was hysterical, weeping, screaming, laughing. Did the poet dream an idle dream, a false mirage? Death is master. Death is stealing Love away. How could a silly girl believe or know the calm of poesie?

The boy crumbled. His swagger and bravado melted. The passionate call of sex became a blur. He was not himself, yet he was looking at himself, a confusion in space, in night, in Fog. And who was she hanging limp upon his arm?

That dance? The jazz dance? Ah, the dance! The dance of Life was ending. The orchestra was playing a dirge and Death was leading the Grand March. Fog! Impenetrable fog!

All the unheeded, forgotten warnings of ranting preachers, all the prayers of simple black mothers, the Mercy-Seat, the Revival, too late. Terror could give no articulate expression to these muffled feelings. They came to the surface of a blunted consciousness, incoherent.

Was there a God in Israel? Laban remembered Russia and the pogrom. He had looked into the eyes of Fate that day and watched God die with his mother and sisters. Here he was facing Fate again. There was no answer. He was silent.

His companion sputtered, fumed, screeched. He clung to Laban in pieces.

Laban remembered the pogrom. The old Negro couple remembered another horror. They had been through the riots in Tulsa. There they had lost their son and his wife, the Egyptian-faced girl's father and mother. They had heard the whine of bullets, the hiss of flame, the howling of human wolves, killing in the most excruciating manner. The water was silent. The water was merciful.

The old woman began to sing in a high quavering minor key:

"Lawdy, won't yo' ketch mah groan,
O Lawdy, Lawdy, won't yo' ketch mah groan."

The old man cried out: "Judgment! Judgment!"

The Egyptian-faced girl wept. She was sore afraid, sore afraid. And the fog was round about them.

Time is a relative term. The philosophers are right for once. What happened inside the heads of these men and women seemed to them to have consumed hours instead of seconds. The conductor mechanically grabbed for the trolley rope, the motorman threw on the brakes.

The reaction came. Fear may become inarticulate and paralyzed. Then again it may become belligerent and self-protective, striking blindly in the maze. Darkness did not destroy completely the sense of direction.

"The door! The exit!"

A mad rush to get out, not to be trapped without a chance, like rats in a trap.

"Out of my way! Damn you—out of my way!"

Somebody yelled: "Sit still!"

Somebody hissed: "Brutes! Beasts!"

Another concussion, accompanied by the grinding of steel. The car stopped, lurched backward, swayed, and again stood still. Excited shouts re-echoed from the ends of the bridge. Automobile horns tooted. An age seemed to pass, but the great splash did not come. There was still time—maybe. The car was emptied.

"Run for the Ohio end!" someone screamed.

The fog shut off every man from his neighbor. The sound of scurrying feet reverberated, of the Italian woman and her baby, of the boy carrying his girl, of the Negro youths, of the old man and his wife, half dragging the Egyptian-faced girl, of the sisters of Charity, of the miners. Flitting like wraiths in Homer's Hades, seeking life.

In five minutes all were safe on Ohio soil. The bridge still stood. A street light gave a ghastly glare through the fog. The whore houses on Water Street brooded evily in the shadows. Dogs barked, the Egyptian-faced girl had fainted. The old Negro woman panted, "Mah Jesus! Mah Jesus!"

The occupants of the deserted car looked at one another. The icy touch of the Grave began to thaw. There was a generous intermingling. Everybody talked at once, inquiring, congratulating.

"Look after the girl," shouted Lee Cromarty.

"Help the old woman, boys."

Bells began to ring. People came running. The ambulance arrived. The colored girl had recovered. Then everybody shouted again. Profane miners, used to catastrophe, were strangely moved. The white boy and girl held hands.

"Sing us a song, old woman," drawled Lafe.

"He's heard mah groan. He done heard it," burst forth the old woman in a song flood of triumph.

    "Yes, he conquered Death and Hell,
    An' He never said a mumblin' word,
    Not a word, not a word."

"How you feelin', Mike," said Bill to the garlic eater.

"Me fine. Me fine."

The news of the event spread like wildfire. The street was now crowded. The police arrived. A bridge official appeared, announcing the probable cause of the accident, a slipping of certain supports. The girders fortunately had held. A terrible tragedy had been prevented.

"I'm a wash-foot Baptist an' I don't believe in Popery," said Lake, "but, fellers, let's ask them ladies in them air mournin' robes to say a prayer of thanksgiving for the bunch."

The Sisters of Charity did say a prayer, not an audible petition for the ears of men, but a whispered prayer for the ears of God, the Benediction of Thanksgiving, uttered by the Catholic Church through many years, in many tongues and places.

"De profundis," added the silently moving lips of the white-faced nuns. "Out of the depths have we cried unto Thee, O Lord. And Thou hast heard our cries."

The motorman was no longer dissatisfied. The conductor's strength had been renewed like the eagle's.

"Boys," drawled Lake, "I'll be damned if I'm goin' to that meetin' tonight."

"Nor me," affirmed Lee Comarty.

"Nor me," repeated all the others.

The fog still crept from under the bed of the river and down from the lowering hills of West Virginia—dense, tenacious, stealthy, chilling, but from about the hearts and minds of some rough, unlettered men another fog had begun to life.

Trees at Night

By HELENE JOHNSON

Given Honorable Mention

Slim Sentinels
Stretching lacy arms
About a slumbrous moon;
Black quivering
Silhouettes,
Tremulous,
Stencilled on the petal
Of a bluebell;
Ink spluttered
On a robin's breast;
The jagged rent
Of mountains
Reflected in a
Stilly sleeping lake;
Fragile pinnacles
Of fairy castles;
Torn webs of shadows;
And
Printed 'gainst the sky—
The trembling beauty
Of an urgent pine.

Frances—A Play in One Act

By G. D. Lipscomb

Awarded First Prize—Play Section

PERSONS OF THE PLAY

Frances
Abram, the uncle of Frances
George Mannus, a teacher
Charles Thawson, a planter

Time—Winter, about eight o'clock in the evening.

Place—In the Yazoo Delta of Mississippi.

Scene: The poor but neat room of a typical shot-gun house. In the left-center can be seen a bed, next to it a fireplace, and in the middle of the room, a table. In the middle of the back-wall, above the mantel, is an old-fashioned weight-clock that strikes every hour. Back-stage, to the right, is a door that opens on the little front porch. In the left-center is a door leading to the rear part of the house.

Scene discovers Frances, a neat and intelligent girl of about nineteen, seated near the bed sewing, with a book lying open before her on the bed. Abram, the grizzled and swarthy old uncle, is coming in through the door with an armful of wood.

ABRAM (throwing the wood down before the fire). Frances, I shot de back do' an' got de key in my pocket so's if anybody come while I'm gone dey got to come in dis front way. An' don't let nobody git back in dat kitchen while I'm gone. . . . You gwine to be heah while I'm gone? Cause a heap o' dese niggahs 'u'd run an' tell Mistah John dat I'm makin' gosh. (As the old man talks he leans forward away from Frances, swinging suddenly around so as to peep into her face when he wants to drive his points home.)

FRANCES. Yes, uncle. Where you going?

ABRAM. I got to step down across de ditchbank to ole man Humphrey's to speak to him 'bout gittin' his drag. We goin' to drag back ez fur ez de school tomorrow. . . . By de way—de County ain't gwine to fix dat road up pas' de school like dey had 'cided.

FRANCES. Why?

ABRAM. I reckon dat school's in about broke up. Jes' like I tole you—jes' like I tole you—dat niggah done broke his own neck wid his smaht talk.

FRANCES. Professor Mannus has lost . . .

ABRAM. No. he ain't 'zactly los' de school. De County Sup'intender say he won't fiah him, but dey refuse to give him any mo' of his back pay. But de Sup'intender say he'll move him to anotheh fiel' 'fo' he'll let him go intiahly, cause he's sech a good teachah. Well, I 'spect, when it comes right down to teachin', he's de bes' dey evah had 'roun' heah—Dey say he runs ovah some dese white teachahs.

FRANCES. Oh, isn't that too bad! I was afraid of that. I told Professor Mannus to be careful.

ABRAM. Now, don't you have nothin' 'tall to do wid hit now, cause hit's bes' dat he goes on off somewheahs else. Dis way he's got—goin' 'roun' heah tellin' dese niggahs what dey ought an' oughten' to stan' fur is hurtin' us mo' den anything else.

FRANCES. Well, is he going away?

ABRAM. I dunno—if he is I glad of it. Well, I got to go. You take keer o' things while I'm gone, you heah?

FRANCES. Yes, uncle. (Exit Abram).

FRANCES. My God! I was afraid of this! I told George—but he knew. (Reflectingly) There's something else behind this. That wretch called me today! (jumping up) I wonder where I can find him. (Goes to the window, looks out, sighs with despondency, comes back to her seat, sits down, and resumes her work. After an interval there is a knock at the door. Frances goes to the door.)

Who is it?

VOICE FROM WITHOUT. Mannus. (Frances opens the door, and George appears with a suitcase in his hand.)

FRANCES. O George! I'm so glad you came.

GEORGE (a tall, brown man, well-formed and intelligent; plainly dressed in clothes that have been well worn. There is a sad and cynical expression on the man's youthful, but drawn face; but he tries to smile when he sees Frances). I'm glad you are, Frances. Is your uncle home?

FRANCES. No. We can have a few minutes to ourselves. Rest your hat and coat.

GEORGE (putting his hat on the table) No, Frances, I won't rest my coat—I can't stay that long.

FRANCES. Sit down. I was just thinking about you; what has happened? Tell me. (Seeing the suitcase) O George! is it really true?

GEORGE (still standing). That was your uncle I saw going out across the bridge?

FRANCES. Yes. What is all of this about the school?

GEORGE. What have you heard?

FRANCES. That they're not going to have the school any longer.

GEORGE. Oh, I suppose they'll continue the school—the good people in the county won't see it go entirely out of existence. But I'm not to have it any longer.

FRANCES. Why?

GEORGE. The planters say that I've been causing dissatisfaction among the tenants and they're closing the school and holding up my pay.

FRANCES. What planters?

GEORGE. Oh, it's that click. That Charles Thawson is at the bottom of it all—and the insulting things he said to me I don't intend to take from any man. I simply can't stand it any longer. Frances . . .

FRANCES. But George, you have friends here. . . .

GEORGE. I know that. But they can't do anything until we have a trial and investigation. You know what that means. They say they can do nothing. They advise me to leave if I care to live twenty-four hours longer.

FRANCES. George!

GEORGE. Yes, Mr. Coleman talked to the sheriff, and he said he would do what he could to protect me, if I would go to him and give myself up; but that the charges . . .

FRANCES. What charges?

GEORGE. You know as much about it as I do.

FRANCES. That beast Thawson—Mister Charley!

GEORGE. Yes, it is he and I for it, I suppose. He came into the classroom yesterday and insulted me. I might have taken a personal insult, but when he mentioned you I struck him.

FRANCES. George!

GEORGE. So he's got his bunch together and they threaten to get me before tomorrow night.

FRANCES. George, get away from here as soon as you can! Take uncle's gun. (She starts for it.)

GEORGE. Frances, Frances, I don't want any gun. I'm going to get out of his way. I'm going to Chicago tonight. And, Frances, I'm going to take you with me. (Frances is silent.) Madge has gone to get my trunk now; we'll leave his house at nine. He'll drive us over to Boyle in time to catch the *Cannon Ball* to Memphis. By tomorrow night we'll be in Chicago.

FRANCES. George, I hate to see you go, but you must . . .

GEORGE. You're going with me, Frances, see, I brought this bag. You put all the things you need into it and we'll get away before your uncle returns.

FRANCES. No, George.

GEORGE. Why?

FRANCES. I can't—this is my home—all the home I have. I must stay here. And my uncle needs me.

GEORGE. What on earth does he need you for? to drag your young life down into the the servile slime and ignorance of his own? What has he done for you? tried to make you anything but decent, and what you are, you are in spite of him—against his protest.

FRANCES. Don't George, it. hurts: you don't understand my position. Too, you must

remember, I am indebted to my uncle. He has tried to carry out the wish of my mother. He has even borrowed money from Thawson to send me to school, and what little education I have I must thank him for.

GEORGE. What good is it, Frances, to have an education and not be free? Why did Thawson let him have the money for your schooling? And why did he compel you to come back here from Meridian to eke out your existence in this ignorance? That money for your schooling only sold you further into bondage.

FRANCES. George, please don't—don't hurt me. I can't go.

GEORGE (drawing her to him and looking into her eyes). Frances, it is for you that I am going: but. for you I'd stay here and face that mob. I'd send him to hell to answer to the devil for his lies. I'd fight this thing out to the bitter end. I'd stick to the resolve I had when I came here, of raising this mass from ignorance and depravity at any cost. But I know it is all foolhardy now. I have abandoned that hope. Now my only hope is to snatch you from eternal degredation. Maybe I am selfish, but to win you means more than to atone for my lost ideal. Come, Frances, I offer you my life for happiness, come. (Frances stares at the floor and shakes her head). Are you coming, Frances?

FRANCES (chokingly). I can't.

GEORGE. (Slowly kisses her on the forehead, then turns suddenly, gets his hat, and starts toward the door). Well then I hope that I may see you again before tomorrow night, but I'm afraid I shan't. I've got to go before your uncle comes.

FRANCES. Don't, George, don't go! (catch him him by the lapels of his coat). Do you really think that it would be right for me to go?

GEORGE. Frances, have I ever asked you to do anything that wasn't right?

FRANCES. George, would my life really mean anything to you in the North?

GEORGE. I love you and want you with me eternally; without you my life is nothing.

FRANCES. I love you, George. (George kisses her. Then, without another word, Frances takes the bag and goes into her chamber. George paces the floor and looks out of the window as if watching. He takes an automatic from his pocket. Examines it, and puts it back again; then he stands with his arms folded and stares into the fire. Frances returns with the bag.)

GEORGE. Are you ready, Frances?

FRANCES. I've got everything in here that I need.

GEORGE (taking the bag). Well, get your coat and hat and we'll go.

FRANCES. No. you take the bag and go ahead, George; I'll come later.

GEORGE. What!

FRANCES. You say you'll be ready to leave at nine?

GEORGE. Yes.

FRANCES. Then go ahead; I'll meet you there at nine. You see, if I leave now—my uncle isn't in yet—you know he's always suspicious if I go out at night without letting him know where I'm going, and he'll look for me. But if I stay here until he comes in, I can go out after he goes to sleep. He'll go to sleep long before nine o'clock, and I can get out all right.

GEORGE. Frances, I don't want to take that chance. Suppose he doesn't go to sleep— you don't know whether you can get out at nine or not.

FRANCES. Oh, I'm sure he'll be asleep by eight-thirty. But to be sure, you send the little boy Andy down for me if I'm not there by ten minutes of nine. He always comes for me when Aunt Lucy is sick. Just tell him to say that Aunt Lucy wants me to rub her back.

GEORGE. Well, all right.

FRANCES (looking out of the window). Hurry, George, there comes Abram now.

GEORGE. Frances, I'll be waiting at Madge's house.

FRANCES. Yes.

(After a quick embrace George goes out. Frances shuts the door and stands against it for a moment, then she runs and falls across the bed, burying her head in the pillow. Then, as if remembering that she has a game to play, she sits up in her chair and resumes her work. In a few minutes Abram is heard at the front entrance scraping and stamping his feet while saying good-bye to a friend outside. (Enter Abram.)

ABRAM. Ole man Shivers is got hisse'f two noo mules an' narry one of 'em is ez peert ez dat ole brood sow o' mine out dere in de lot: deir years draps down ovah deir eyes jes' like tossuls, an' dey's might'night shaggy ez Newfoundlan' dogs. (He takes off his coat, seats himself before the fire, takes off his boots, then his hat, takes his pipe and lights it.)

FRANCES. How is the weather out there, uncle?

ABRAM. Hit's jes' a leetle bit wahmah. De win' is shiftin' to de South. Dey gwine to be mo' weathah; my knee bin talkin' to me all day. Ho, ho, hum. Lawdy mussy, I show it tiuhd. (He rears back in his chair, cocking his feet up in another, and remains silent for a while, evidently lost in cunning and mischievous meditation, leaning slightly forward now and then to spit in the fire. At length he speaks as if finally assured that he has struck upon the proper way of beginning a touchy subject.) Frances, when is you seed Mistah Chahles?

FRANCES. I saw him today, uncle.

ABRAM. You did, wheah?

FRANCES. He was down at Uncle Lish's where they're dragging the road. When I was bringing the clothes home from Mrs. Millock's I saw him.

ABRAM. Did he say anything 'tall to you?

FRANCES. No, sir.

ABRAM. Nothin' 'tall?

FRANCES. Oh, he hollud. But I was an eighth of a mile off and so I kept on going.

ABRAM. What he say?

FRANCES. He called me. I kept on going.

ABRAM (rousing himself and leaning forward). You didn't say nothin' 'tall to him? You's actin' mighty stange heah lately. You bettah be keerful how you does—you heah me!

FRANCES. I hear you uncle.

ABRAM. I know you heah me—dat ain't all, dat ain't all; you bettah go on an' treat Cap with respect ez you has bin doin'. You know Mistah Chahles has done a powahful lot fo' us. 'Twon't bin fo' him we wouldn't have dis leetle fahm—an' you knows well ez I does it ain't paid fo' yet, 'tain't cleah' yet; dey's a mo'gige on it an' he hol's de mo'gige. Now heah I is night an' day scufflin' an' tryin' to git in de cleah an' git a leetle laid up fo' us when I gits too ole to work. Now you oughter undahstan' an' 'preciate what I'm tryin' to do an' he'p me out dat much.

FRANCES. O Uncle, you know I want to help you all I can in an honorable way, but I won't be a slave to dat devil.

ABRAM. Tek heah! ain't no body axin' you to be no slave! You knows bettah'n dat. 'T ain't gwine hurt you to treat Cap with respect an' keep him feelin' good 'til we gits in de cleah. You got to do a heap o' things dat don't jes' please you 'till you kin git independent of folks. When you gits ez ole ez I is—dog-bite-my-cat— bin kicked eroun' ez much, you'll learn bettah.

FRANCES. But, Uncle.

ABRAM. N'mine now, I know what's ailin' you. You was goin' 'long jes' nice an' was he'pin' me all you could an' Mistah Chahles was feelin' good 'til dat dat Geo'ge Mannus come down f'om de Nawth an' filled yo' haid wid a lot o' foolishness.

FRANCES. George is a . . .

ABRAM. N'mine now, you le' me talk! I knows dat Geo'ge is a nice edgicated coluhd man he means well—but you mus' remembah, you mus'. undahstan', he's f'om de Nawth wheah he's used to doin' ez he please. He don't know nothin' 'tall 'bout how we folks does to git along down heah.

FRANCES (in an undertone). And I hope to be with him some day in the North.

ABRAM. Hish up! Hish up! You don't know what you talkin' 'bout. Now why kain't you go long an' keep Mistah Chahles in good humah 'til we gits in de cleah an' gits ouah nose off de grin'stone? Now, why kain't you do dat? why kain't you, fo' yo' sake an' fo' mine?

FRANCES. I can't!

ABRAM. Why kain't you!

FRANCES. O Uncle Abram! you pretend not to understand no matter how reasonable I try to be.

ABRAM. Oh, I undahstan' all right: it's jes' some o' dat nonsince dat nawthe'n dahky put in yo' haid. He ain't got nothin' but his han's. You bettah let him go on 'bout his business an' look out fo' yo'se'f.

FRANCES. Stop, Uncle Abram, please!

ABRAM. What you mean wid dat "stop"? Ain't I advisin' you fo' yo' own good? You bettah listen to me an' not git Mistah Chahles down on you.

Now, Mistah Chahles gwine to be heah aftah while an' I wants you to look peaht an' sweet—'t ain't gwine hurt you.

FRANCES. Oh, is he coming here tonight! I can't stand it—I won't.

ABRAM. Look aheah, you imp'dent heafah, you dare to sassy me! you got to stan' it!

FRANCES (rising) I won't stand it! There was a time when I didn't know any better—I didn't think—that time has passed. I am a changed woman. George has come into my life. Until I met him I believed that I was doing the right thing to make the sacrifice and be a slave to that brute—obligate myself to him— I did not think. I took his money. Now I feel no obligation. No, I won't have a thing to do with him! If you insist, I'll leave home—I'll go away wtih George. He wants me to live right and honest.

ABRAM. Fool! fool! heah me! If you leaves dis house you'll regret it to yo' las' day—to yo' ve'y las'. Dis dahky don't keer nothin' 't all 'bout you. Wheah kin he tek you? what is he got? Pleg-on de niggah's hide! I wish he'd nevah seed you.

FRANCES. You call him a nigger because he has race pride and is a gentleman. You're the nigger, you and your type—you're the cause. . . . Oh, it's just as George says: we're still slaves. Oh, I wish I was free. I wish I was away from this place. I want to be a free woman. It's as George says—you've tried to make me a concubine of this white man. You've tried to sell me body and soul for a scrap of paper and a two-faced grin. What does he care about me? got a wife and family in Memphis!

ABRAM. How you know dat?

FRANCES. Anybody with three grains of sense would know it.

ABRAM. Poot! poot! dat ain't nothin' an' I don't b'lieve it nohow.

FRANCES. No, I know you don't think that is anything: that's just how little you know about decency. And I know you don't believe a lot of things that I could tell you—that George could tell you if you would only listen to him. You think we're getting this farm paid for, don't you? you think we have a deed to this forty . . . (There is the sound of a machine outside.)

ABRAM. Sh-sh Lawd, dare's Mistah Chahles now! (Knocking at the door). Open de do', Frances.

FRANCES (going to the door, then backing against the wall). Open it yourself.

ABRAM (shuffles to the door, opens it, and bows low). Good ev'nin', Mistah Chahles—Good ev'nin'. Come right in. (Enter Charles.)

CHARLES. Howdy, Uncle Abram, how you feelin'?

ABRAM. Oh, I ain't much, Mistah Chahles, my back's bin hurtin' me; mus' be mo' weathah comin'. Sit down.

CHARLES. I can't stay ve'y long, Unc' Abram. Where's Frances?

(Frances still stands with her back to the wall looking blankly into space. As Charles asks this question he sweeps the room with his glance and sees her standing there.)

You got the backache too, Frances?

ABRAM. D'ain't nothin' 't all mattah wid huh, Cap, but lonesome. Bin quahlin' all ev'nin' heah wid me; thought you had done fo'got huh. You show punished huh by not comin' roun' dooin' o' de pas' mont. (To Frances) . You little ole big-eyed, good-lookin' rascal, you knows you wants to be right in Mistah Chahles' ahms.

FRANCES. How dare you stand there and tell such a lie!

ABRAM. Hish up! you good-lookin' wench—you knows you's bin cryin' you' eye-balls mighty nigh out to git me to go ovah an' see what had done happen' to Mistah Chahles.

CHARLES. I know what's t'mattah with Frances: she just thought I was likin' Sally Jones, because she seen me down there talkin' to ole Lish and kinda' hangin' aroun'. (To Frances) Th' ain't nothin' 't all to it, Frances, I like you jus' the same. But what makes me so confounded mad, you hang aroun' that Mannus nigger. I know he's been talkin' to you an' puttin' a lot of Yankee lies in your head; he's been goin' aroun' talkin' about me; but I seen him today and shook my fist all up in his face and give him just till tomorrow night to get his hide out of these parts, that's what I did. An' if he's caught aroun' here after tomorrow night he gets a rope aroun' his neck. By golly, I'm a good guy an' I think a lot of my nigger frien', but I'll be damned if I'm goin' to have a northern nigger aroun' poisenin' their min's.

FRANCES. Oh, you dirty . . .

ABRAM (threatening her). Hish up 'fo' you say somethin' you don't mean!

CHARLES. Frances, come here (she ignores him). You're not comin'? What's the matter with you? (To Abram) Say Abe, you got anything stimulatin'?

ABRAM. Yassuh, Cap. (He goes out toward the kitchen.)

CHARLES. Let's have some. I'm goin' to stay here tonight. (He takes off his coat and seats himself before the fire. Abram returns with whiskey and glasses. They drink. In the meantime Frances retires stealthily from the room.) Say, Abram, what the devil's got into Frances' head lately? d'you s'pose she's really takin' up with that nigger?

ABRAM. Now, nawsah, Cap.

CHARLES. Look ahere, don't you lie to me; you know she's been gettin' with him—look how she cuts me up.

ABRAM. I swear 'fo' God, Cap, she don't keer nothin' 'bout dat niggah—jes' poutin'—(he calls) Frances! Wheah'd she go? (Frances comes from antechamber with hat and coat). Wheah you gwine? (both Frances and Abram make a dash toward the door; Abram reaches it first, locks it and puts the key in his pocket). Put dat hat an' coat right back wheah you got 'em. I be-dog-bite-my-cat if you goes out'n dis house tonight. Put dem clothes right back wheah you got 'em an' go an' pay some repect to Mistah Chahles who done come all the way ovah heah jes' to see you.

(Frances flops herself down despondently in a chair and stares at the floor.)

CHARLES (standing with a glass of whisky half raised to his lips). Here, take a little of this, it'll do you good. (He goes toward Frances and tries to put his arm around her.)

FRANCES (retreating). Don't come near me!

CHARLES (following her aways to apply the glass and embrace her).

FRANCES (fighting him off). Get away, don't touch me! (She strikes with her hand, hitting the glass and spilling the brandy over Charles).

CHARLES. What in the hell is the matter with you, woman!!

ABRAM (whipping out his bandana handkerchief, starts to wipe the whiskey from Charles). Look heah what you done done! ain't you 'shamed o' yo'se'f—git right down an' axt Mistah Chahles' pahdon.

FRANCES. I told him to keep away from me. I didn't mean to spill the whiskey on him but it serves him right.

CHARLES. You little nigger wench! what do you mean by all of this? I see there's somethin' in you and I'm goin' to have it out right here. (To Abram) Bring me them deeds, the deeds to this forty. (Abram goes for the deeds). I know what's the matter with you all right—that Mannus has fed you a lot of stuff. You're gettin' beside yourself. But I'm goin' to put you right where you belong tonight.

ABRAM (returning without the papers). Mistah Chahles, I don't zactly amembah wheah I put 'em. (He is very uneasy).

CHRLES (sarcastically). Maybe I can help you—look up there in that ole clock; I think I see 'em up there. (Abram obeys, bringing the papers forth from the clock, above the mantel). You mem'ry's gettin' kinda short on some things, ain't it. (taking the deeds) But you needn't worry much about these. Now, Miss Frances, since you have got so beside yourself here lately,

I want to jus' show you where you are—these deeds ain't never been recorded. This property is mine. I've been acceptin' payments from your uncle, but I didn't intend that she should buy it with anything but you. You're my woman!

FRANCES. Oh no. I was foolish, but, thank God, I'll never be your woman.

CHARLES. So you've turned on me for a little jackleg nigger professor, eh?

FRANCES. Call him jackleg if you want to, but I love him and hate you. I hate you! I despise you, as I despise dirt—I hate you and all your kind, and I love him more than I hate you.

CHARLES. Well, if this lover of yours is caught aroun' here after tomorrow night his hide will be roastin' in front of the court-house an' you can come up an' get a few of his ashes so you can have somethin' to remember him by. And be mighty damn careful how you talk to me too— to think that I'm goin' to stan' any of your sass after all I've done for you. An' before this argument goes any further I jus' want to tell both of you that you can get out of my house tonight!

ABRAM. Lawd, Mistah Chahles, you mean to tell me dat I bin workin' all dese yeahs mekin' payments on dis prop'ty, an' heah when I thought I had in about paid fo', you mean to tell me dat dem deeds ain't nevah been recohded? Mistah Thawson, I always has believed in you, but I don't b'lieve you's tellin' me de trouth now.

CHARLES. Why, you ignorant ole cuss, you thought you'd doublecross me; you thought you'd fool me into lettin' you have this property in your name, then you'd turn dog. You an' your niece here have insulted me, she has insulted me for the last six months. Im goin' to show you right where you stand tonight! (He starts to tear the papers).

ABRAM (who has fallen at Charles' feet—clasping him by the feet). Lawd, Mistah Chahles, please don't teah dem papahs!

FRANCES. Yes, George is right! That's the "Mistah Charles" you've been worshipping. Let him have his farm. . . .

ABRAM (grovelling on the floor in mental agony). Lawd! Lawd! Lawd! I ain't got no mo' confidence in dis worl'. To think a frien' I done worked fo' an' trusted would fool me all dese yeahs an' now when I'm ole an' gray 'uld take de onliest thing I has in dis worl'! (Rising slowly, becoming more and more frantic, curving his fingers and fiercely gnashing his teeth). To think how I done worked fo' you—Life ain't wuhth livin' no mo'. You's a damned two-faced devil! (now standing, his clawlike fingers quivering menacingly in Charles' face, while the latter is calmly tearing the paper into fine bits) I won't stan' it! I won't see you live! (He leaps onto Charles, who is borne to the floor. They grapple in a terrific struggle.

(*Frances screams and rushes toward the door, calling George. She pounds on the door with her fists. Then there is the report of a revolver from the scene of the scuffle. Abram rolls over and remains still. Charles struggles to his knees and crouches over Abram with one hand on his pistol, the other hand is still clutching Abram's collar. Charles' clothes are torn and he is bleeding about the face and throat. At the sound of the shooting Frances rushes from the door to the scene of the late action.*)

FRANCES. My God! My Uncle! (*She falls on him and tears frantically at his breast, then looks up at Charles, who is crouched and ready with his gun as he looks in the direction of the door. It is ten minutes of nine. There is knocking at the door.*) You have shot him! Shot my Uncle! *Charles pays Frances no heed*).

(*Frances gathers all her strength and snatches at the pistol with both hands, jerking it away from Charles and gaining her feet before he can be upon her. Abram is showing signs of life. Charles is up and seizes the girl before she can make any disposition of the gun. He seizes the arm of the hand that holds the gun, and, rushing her against a table, turns that wrist until she shrieks with* pain. Abram, just behind them on the floor, is making desperate efforts to rise. The knocking ceases at the sound of Frances' screaming. Frances, writhing in pain, slowly releases her hold on the pistol until it drops to the floor near Abram, who seizes it immediately. Charles, uttering an oath, throws the girl from him and turns to pick up his revolver, but stops short in this movement when he sees the gun in Abram's hand and pointed deliberately at him.

ABRAM (*groggy, but stiffening himself*). De Lawd has puhserved me fo' dis one pu'pose. (*He shoots and sinks back to the floor. Charles falls dead across the table*).

(*Frances, from where she has fallen on the floor, gazes in bewilderment at the spectacle, then jumps up and, running to her Uncle, seizes his head in her arms and buries her face in his wooly hair. There is silence for a minute, then the clock over the mantel strikes out nine times. Frances looks up at the clock, then returns to her attitude over her Uncle.*)

CURTAIN

My Fellow Traveller

By Gustavus Adolphus Stewart

Awarded First Prize—Personal Experience Sketch

THE train from St. Louis to Kansas City was rapidly filling. By dint of a little running and much good luck I had secured a seat in the day coach. In the murky distance, the entrance gates were enshrouded in a maze of smoke and steam and leaden air. Leaning out of the window, I could see against this dingy background a surging melange of pale and drab objects which, as their owners emerged from the turbulent mass, gradually assumed shape as hands and faces, hats and bags. The crowd slowly funneled itself on to the platform along the track, subdividing into scurrying humans in the process. Finally passed through the gate a young man in a wheelchair pushed by a hurrying, puffing Negro station attendant. As they came beneath my window, I was struck by the cadaverous physique of the man in the chair. At the car steps, the black porter helped his charge from the chair and up the steps, part of the time supporting him with one arm and adding the strength of his own sturdy legs to the tottering limbs of his patient, and part of the time all but bearing him in his arms. As they entered the door, the pair became the one commanding focal point of sentiment, interest, curiosity and comment in the car. With the other passengers, I turned to watch their progress through the rear door of the coach. Leaning with all his wasted weight upon the Negro, the man was barely able to get along. His step was weak and uncertain like that of a child just learning to walk. His entire presence was ghost-like. The skin of his face resembled nothing so much as water-soaked, discolored waxed paper. It was drawn so tautly that his sharply protruding cheekbones appeared to be striving impatiently to break through the faintly resisting integument so feebly imprisoning them. They had already achieved a startling degree of visibility, and only the man's unnaturally bright eyes, abnormally sunk into their unhealthy deep sockets, and his thin, quivering, expanded nostrils, saved him from being a veritable death's head.

After a totally exhausting effort, which consumed an unprecedented amount of time and vitality, considering the short distance traversed, the sick man subsided into a seat immediately behind me, relieved, panting and sweating. The Negro attendant, with agile tenderness, made him comfortable with pillow and shawl and hastened out. This matter accomplished to the entire satisfaction and immense emotional easement of all in the car, I with the others prepared to resume that fidgety attitude which seems to possess passengers seated and waiting for the train to move.

Scarcely had the porter left, however, when a fit of the most distressing coughing racked the man. It was terrible to hear. It was a raucous, hollow, yet a wrenching and destructive sound. It seemed to spring from some remote cavernous recess of his frame, welling up from the most vital depths, tearing its devastating way through his body with indescribable wheezings, raspings and rattlings, exploding with a fury that all but annihilated its victim. That cough unnerved me. I felt a singularly distracting malaise, akin to nausea, while I was overcome with compassion for the young man. I wanted so badly to do something, anything to stop that cough.

Suddenly the coughing ceased. Between gasps, a far-away, weakly-agitated voice, resembling slightly a ventriloquist's faking, murmured: "Ah f'got to mail mah muthah's lettah. Ah'm goin' to Colorado, an' Ah mail huh a lettah ev'ry day." I never knew whom he was addressing. Perhaps me, perhaps no one. I rather imagine that he was merely thinking aloud. At any rate, I was about to offer to mail his letter for him, at the risk of losing my seat and perhaps missing the train, when the Negro train porter, concluding those final preparations which signalize the almost immediate departure of the train, entered the car. He took the letter. He had only moments for his errand, and consequently was obliged to run the entire length of the platform to the mail-box inside the gate and back. Yet I was happy in the thought that surely he didn't mind doing it, that an anxious mother would get her expected daily letter from her invalid son.

The train had started. Another attack of that dreadful coughing overwhelmed the man as it jolted along. The lady, who had unfortunately not obtained a seat, returned from the forward end of the coach, stopped beside me, looked at the unoccupied half of my seat, gave me a swift glance, hesitated, passed by, saw the vacant space next the consumptive and flopped into it. I was glad. I took pleasure in the fact that I was colored, for if noticeably "colored," one is almost always assured of a comfortable seat alone even in the most uncomfortably crowded Northern trains, provided, of course, one has been lucky enough to find a seat on entering. But I was glad also for the man. He would now have a seat-mate to share the monotony of the journey. A well person finds a long, day-trip alone on the train somewhat irksome. It must be an exceedingly trying experience for a sick man. What a comfort it would therefore be to this sufferer to have an agreeable companion beside him, and particularly a woman, to whom he might talk about "muthah"! These were my thoughts.

The two became acquainted. Talk began. The effort to sustain the conversation may have been too great a strain on the man's almost negligible lung power. At any rate, a spasm of coughing seized him, a violent, relentless convulsion, which threatened to rip his very lungs from his body. I was appalled by the utter hopelessness of it, and was turning in my seat, again about to rise to offer any possible assistance, when the coughing once more suddenly stopped. Almost at once I heard these numbing words from the lips of this near-corpse. They were emitted in a sort of two-syllabled rhythm, each pair of sounds requiring his entire short and labored expiration, and seemed thereby to be drenched in icy contempt: "Ah see—niggahs—ride

in—cahs with—white fo'ks—up hyeah. — In mah state — they don't —allow 'em." The words were gasped in an anguish of shortened breath, and I imagined him looking at my brown neck as I sank again into my seat, the impulse to help dead within me and a seething hate rapidly filling my every fibre. I don't know what else was said, never knew. My heart, which had been swelling with sorrow for this sorely afflicted man, suddenly contracted, expelling sympathy as though it were a vile and venomous thing. Pity froze within me. Diabolical madness leaped into my soul, while little, persistent, clamoring, persuasive devils urged me to mount the emaciated form of the speaker, with my hands clutch his scrawny throat in a death-producing grasp, and furiously clamp it until those eyes, reposing now so far back in their hollow pockets, should slowly but steadily move forward on to his bony cheek, until their preternatural brilliancy became dull, ashen, gleamless. These murderous devils at last desisted, and I joyously nursed my new-born, raging hate with the wish that this disease which was making pulp of his lungs and a bubble of his heart, might choke him to death long before he reached Colorado.

"NIGGAHS!" "Niggahs" had ministered to him as gently as to a babe when placing him aboard the train, had eagerly served him by mailing his almost forgotten letter, and for aught I knew had "birthed," fed and reared him! Betrayed by his speech, he was surely from that South, land of the famous "black mammy," who was midwife, cook, laundress, child nurse, housemaid and family counsellor, all in one—that South where a young man able to travel for his health to Colorado very likely had numerous underpaid black servants to dance attendance upon him. Indeed, considering "black mammy's" all embracing ability, it was very probable that he had lived and had his sickly, short-lived being solely because of the recurring service of "niggahs." How I hated him then, this dying man, who was only a day's journey from the grave, yet was arrogantly certain of his superiority, as strong and assertive in his contempt for the "niggahs" who had so recently befriended him as his poor, sputtering flame of life would let him be! I was glad he wouldn't live much longer to disseminate his noxious notions.

But that cough! If it had never begun again I might have continued blissfully and indefinitely my delirious hate-jag. Even if I had heard that disquieting agony for but an hour, I might have indulged myself limitlessly in the most wildly homicidal designs upon his moribund, racially biased Southerner. But a whole day of it was unbearable. Its torture was atonement. I melted in warm gushes of sympathy. I knew its victim could never escape its ever tightening grip, that Colorado could perform no miracles, yet as I boarded the street car at the Kansas City station, I could not prevent myself from hoping that "muthah" would get that daily letter—at least for a little while longer.

Spunk

By Zora Neale Hurston

Awarded Second Prize

A GIANT of a brown skinned man sauntered up the one street of the Village and out into the palmetto thickets with a small pretty woman clinging lovingly to his arm.

"Looka theah, folkses!" cried Elijah Mosley, slapping his leg gleefully. "Theah they go, big as life an' brassy as tacks."

All the loungers in the store tried to walk to the door with an air of nonchalance but with small success.

"Now pee-cople!" Walter Thomas gasped, "Will you look at 'em!"

"But that's one thing Ah likes about Spunk Banks—he ain't skeered of nothin' on God's green footstool—*nothin'!* He rides that log down at saw-mill jus' like he struts 'round wid another man's wife—jus' don't give a kitty. When Tes' Miller got cut to giblets on that circle-saw, Spunk steps right up and starts ridin'. The rest of us was skeered to go near it."

A round shouldered figure in overalls much too large, came nervously in the door and the talking ceased. The men looked at each other and winked.

"Gimme some soda-water. Sass'prilla Ah reckon," the new-comer ordered, and stood far down the counter near the open pickled pig-feet tub to drink it.

Elijah nudged Walter and turned with mock gravity to the new-comer.

"Say Joe, how's everything up yo' way? How's yo' wife?"

Joe started and all but dropped the bottle he held in his hands. He swallowed several times painfully and his lips trembled.

"Aw 'Lige, you oughtn't to do nothin' like that," Walter grumbled. Elijah ignored him.

"She jus' passed heah a few minutes ago goin' thata way," with a wave of his hand in the direction of the woods.

Now Joe knew his wife had passed that way. He knew that the men lounging in the general store had seen her, moreover, he knew that the men knew *he* knew. He stood there silent for a long moment staring blankly, with his Adam's apple twitching nervously up and down his throat. One could actually *see* the pain he was suffering, his eyes, his face, his hands and even the dejected slump of his shoulders. He set the bottle down upon the counter. He didn't bang it, just eased it out of his hand silently and fiddled with his suspender buckle.

"Well, Ah'm goin' after her today. Ah'm goin' an' fetch her back. Spunk's done gone too fur."

He reached deep down into his trouser pocket and drew out a hollow ground razor, large and shiny, and passed his moistened thumb back and forth over the edge.

"Talkin' like a man, Joe. Course that's *yo'* fambly affairs, but Ah like to see grit in anybody."

Joe Kanty laid down a nickel and stumbled out into the street.

Dusk crept in from the woods. Ike Clarke lit the swinging oil lamp that was almost immediately surrounded by candle-flies. The men laughed boisterously behind Joe's back as they watched him shamble woodward.

"You oughtn't to said whut you did to him, Lige, —look how it worked him up," Walter chided.

"And Ah hope it did work him up. Tain't even decent for a man to take and take like he do."

"Spunk will sho' kill him."

"Aw, Ah doan't know. You never kin tell. He might turn him up an' spank him fur gettin' in the way, but Spunk wouldn't shoot no unarmed man. Dat razor he carried outa heah ain't gonna run Spunk down an' cut him, an' Joe ain't got the nerve to go up to Spunk with it knowing he totes that Army 45. He makes that break outa heah to bluff us. He's gonna hide that razor behind the first likely palmetto root an' sneak back home to bed. Don't tell me nothin' 'bout that rabbit-foot colored man. Didn't he meet Spunk an' Lena face to face one day las' week an' mumble sumthin' to Spunk 'bout lettin' his wife alone?"

"What did Spunk say?" Walter broke in—"Ah like him fine but tain't right the way he carries on wid Lena Kanty, jus' cause Joe's timid 'bout fightin'"."

"You wrong theah, Walter. 'Tain't cause Joe's timid at all, it's cause Spunk wants Lena. If Joe was a passle of wile cats Spunk would tackle the job just the same. He'd go after *anything* he wanted the same way. As Ah wuz sayin' a minute ago, he tole Joe right to his face that Lena was his. 'Call her,' he says to Joe. 'Call her and see if she'll come. A woman knows her boss an' she answers when he calls.' 'Lena, ain't I yo' husband?' Joe sorter whines out. Lena looked at him real disgusted but she don't answer and she don't move outa her tracks. Then Spunk reaches out an' takes hold of her arm an' says: 'Lena, youse mine. From now on Ah works for you an' fights for you an' Ah never wants you to look to nobody for a crumb of bread, a stitch of close or a shingle to go over yo' head, but *me* long as Ah live. Ah'll git the lumber foh owah house tomorrow. Go home an' git yo' things together!'"

"'Thass mah house' Lena speaks up. 'Papa gimme that.'

"Well," says Spunk, "doan give up whut's yours, but when youse inside don't forgit youse mine, an' let no other man git outa his place wid you!"

"Lena looked up at him with her eyes so full of love that they wuz runnin' over an' Spunk seen it an' Joe seen it too, and his lip started to tremblin' and his Adam's apple was galloping up and down his neck like a race horse. Ah bet he's wore out half a dozen Adam's apples since Spunk's been on the job with Lena. That's all he'll do. He'll be back heah after while swallowin' an' workin' his lips like he wants to say somethin' an' can't."

"But didn't he do *nothin'* to stop 'em?"

"Nope, not a frazzlin' thing—jus' stood there. Spunk took Lena's arm and walked off jus' like nothin' ain't happened and he stood there gazin' after them till they was outa sight. Now you know a woman don't want no man like that. I'm jus' waitin' to see whut he's goin' to say when he gits back."

II

But Joe Kanty never came back, never. The men in the store heard the sharp report of a pistol somewhere distant in the palmetto thicket and soon Spunk came walking leisurely, with his big black Stetson set at the same rakish angle and Lena clinging to his arm, came walking right into the general store. Lena wept in a frightened manner.

"Well," Spunk announced calmly, "Joe come out there wid a meatax an' made me kill him."

He sent Lena home and led the men back to Joe—Joe crumple and limp with his right hand still clutching his razor.

"See mah back? Mah cloes cut clear through. He sneaked up an' tried to kill me from the back, but Ah got him, an' got him good, first shot," Spunk said.

The men glared at Elijah, accusingly.

"Take him up an' plant him in 'Stoney lonesome'," Spunk said in a careless voice. "Ah didn't wanna shoot him but he made me do it. He's a dirty coward, jumpin' on a man from behind."

Spunk turned on his heel and sauntered away to where he knew his love wept in fear for him and no man stopped him. At the general store later on, they all talked of locking him up until the sheriff should come from Orlando, but no one did anything but talk.

A clear case of self-defense, the trial was a short one, and Spunk walked out of the court house to freedom again. He could work again, ride the dangerous log-carriage that fed the singing, snarling, biting, circle-saw; he could stroll the soft dark lanes with his guitar. He was free to roam the woods again; he was free to return to Lena. He did all of these things.

III

"Whut you reckon, Walt?" Elijah asked one night later. "Spunk's gittin' ready to marry Lena!"

"Naw! Why Joe ain't had time to git cold yit. Nohow Ah didn't figger Spunk was the marryin' kind."

"Well, he is," rejoined Elijah. "He done moved most of Lena's t'ings—and her along wid 'em—over to the Bradley house. He's buying it. Jus'

like Ah told yo' all right in heah the night Joe wuz kilt. Spunk's crazy 'bout Lena. He don't want folks to keep on talkin' 'bout her—thass reason he's rushin' so. Funny thing 'bout that bob-cat, wan't it?"

"Whut bob-cat, 'Lige? Ah ain't heered 'bout none."

"Ain't cher? Well, night befo' las' was the fust night Spunk an' Lena moved together an' jus' as they was goin' to bed, a big black bob-cat, black all over, you hear me, *black*, walked round and round that house and howled like forty, an' when Spunk got his gun an' went to the winder to shoot it, he says it stood right still an' looked him in the eye, an' howled right at him. The thing got Spunk so nervoused up he couldn't shoot. But Spunk says twan't no bob-cat nohow. He says it was Joe done sneaked back from Hell!"

"Humph!" sniffed Walter, "he oughter be nervous after what he done. Ah reckon Joe come back to dare him to marry Lena, or to come out an' fight. Ah bet he'll be back time and agin, too. Know what Ah think? Joe wuz a braver man than Spunk."

There was a general shout of derision from the group.

"Thass a fact," went on Walter. "Lookit whut he done; took a razor an' went out to fight a man he knowed toted a gun an' wuz a crack shot, too; 'nother thing Joe wuz skeered of Spunk, skeered plumb stiff! But he went jes' the same. It took him a long time to get his nerve up. 'Tain't nothin' for Spunk to fight when he ain't skeered of nothin'. Now, Joe's done come back to have it out wid the man that's got all he ever had. Y'll know Joe ain't never had nothin' nor wanted nothin' besides Lena. It musta been a h'ant cause ain' nobody never seen no black bob-cat."

" 'Nother thing," cut in one of the men, "Spunk waz cussin' a blue streak today 'cause he 'lowed dat saw wuz wobblin'—almos' got 'im once. The machinist come, looked it over an' said it wuz alright. Spunk musta been leanin' t'wards it some. Den he claimed somebody pushed 'im but 'twant nobody close to 'im. Ah wuz glad when knockin' off time come. I'm skeered of dat man when he gits hot. He'd beat you full of button holes as quick as he's look atcher."

IV

The men gathered the next evening in a different mood, no laughter. No badinage this time.

"Look 'Lige, you goin' to set up wid Spunk?"

"Naw, Ah reckon not, Walter. Tell yuh the truth, Ah'm a lil bit skittish. Spunk died too wicket—died cussin' he did. You know he thought he wuz done outa life."

"Good Lawd, who'd he think done it?"

"Joe."

"Joe Kanty? How come?"

"Walter, Ah b'leeve Ah will walk up thata way an' set. Lena would like it Ah reckon."

"But whut did he say, 'Lige?"

Elijah did not answer until they had left the lighted store and were strolling down the dark street.

"Ah wuz loadin' a wagon wid scantlin' right near the saw when Spunk fell on the carriage but 'fore Ah could git to him the saw got him in the body—awful sight. Me an' Skint Miller got him off but it was too late. Anybody could see that. The fust thing he said wuz: 'He pushed me, Lige—the dirty hound pushed me in the back!'—He was spittin' blood at ev'ry breath. We laid him on the sawdust pile with his face to the East so's he could die easy. He helt mah han' till the last, Walter, and said: 'It was Joe, 'Lige—the dirty sneak shoved me . . . he didn't dare come to mah face . . . but Ah'll git the son-of-a-wood louse soon's Ah get there an' make hell too hot for him. . . . Ah felt him shove me. . . .!' Thass how he died."

"If spirits kin fight, there's a powerful tussle goin' on somewhere ovah Jordan 'cause Ah b'leeve Joe's ready for Spunk an' ain't skeered anymore—yas, Ah b'leeve Joe pushed 'im mahself."

They had arrived at the house. Lena's lamentations were deep and loud. She had filled the room with magnolia blossoms that gave off a heavy sweet odor. The keepers of the wake tipped about whispering in frightened tones. Everyone in the Village was there, even old Jeff Kanty, Joe's father, who a few hours before would have been afraid to come within ten feet of him, stood leering triumphantly down upon the fallen giant as if his fingers had been the teeth of steel that laid him low.

The cooling board consisted of three sixteen-inch boards on saw horses, a dingy sheet was his shroud. The women ate heartily of the funeral baked meats and wondered who would be Lena's next. The men whispered coarse conjectures between guzzles of whiskey.

Roland Hayes

By STERLING BROWN

Awarded Second Prize

A WALL of faces fronts the sprawling platform of the old hall. On one side, extending from beneath one basket-ball goal, and to the place where gawky youngsters jump center,—whites. They twist a bit uneasily on seats, hard seats befitting surrounding shabbiness. Curiosity and their inalienable right to patronize overcome natural distaste at hard seats, and being grouped side by side with, instead of in front of Negroes —a thing by all laws inevitable.

On the other side, from the center mark of the basket-ball hall, to the other basket, sit Roland's own. They too, are divided into two aisles. But the distance between aisles two and three is infinitely wider than between one and two, or three and four. Yet the distance is actually the same. What is it I mean, I wonder?

On one side, kindly, curious contempt. More kindly to Roland, who has succeeded "white folks' way," and is the exception. On the other, self-conscious hostility to neighbors, curiosity, shy arrogation, half envy of Roland. And a feeling of difference to him.

A flurry of handclaps. One gazes instantly at the stage. A dapper fellow nervously—not self-consciously—perhaps the word should be nerveful,—tense, dynamic,—steps quickly to the only artistic thing in the hall, a beautiful Steinway, crudely surrounded by hothouse palms. He is made to look taller by his dress suit—yet the impression is still of tininess. Not puniness, as in a lounging suit, but tininess, coupled with a confident dignity and grace.

Another enters with him, accomplished in his way, but not finished. His slight jerkiness accentuates the smoothness of—"what, is that Roland Hayes?"

Silence, and then an outburst of pure beauty. Flawless, energetic, enrapturing beauty. Handel himself could not have grudged this interpreter. Poignant, passionate tones, vibrant, colorful. Roland Hayes gives himself to ecstatic despair, as if it were a long familiar thing. The beauty of it is troubled, and those who have not plumbed the deeps whence such beauty rises, even they are vaguely disturbed.

Then, as he could easily have learned from studying the ways of his folk, he turns from tragedy to lightness, from Angelo to Fragonard. The whites applaud the perky "Would You Gain the Tender Creature." Strange thing, this, their love of lilting artificial bric-a-brac. . . .

The applause is stentorian. There has been nothing like this in this truly Southern city. The flashes that another of ours, Anne Spencer, can see piercing the slovenliness are hidden from most. But here are vistas of beauty open to all—to nearly all.

A few more, some of the so-called "classics" by which people mean easily followed harmony, not ragtime—but music. They are right in its not being ragtime. Hayes sings all superbly, a consummate artist in pleasing all.

His white teeth flash from his dark brown face —he strides swiftly off, followed by a smiling youngster.

Emotion has gripped the faces and the hands obey its dictates. The noise startles the blackness of Main Street, more than a flaming cross born by ghostlike creatures ever startled.

Roland Hayes reappears, and finally returns to sing.

A genius inspired hearer has requested as the encore a startling melody of Dvorak.

Roland sings. . . .

By the waters of Babylon—

The whites start at the wild summoning of beautiful distress. Why is there arranging of them in a cantor's song—sung by a Negro? What histrionic ability in this man to so feign passionate despair!

We sat down and wept
Yea we wept
When we remembered Zion.

The Negroes brood; are stirred by something deep within, something as far away as all antiquity, as old as human wrong, as tragical as loss of worlds. What does he mean—and why are we so stirred—

. . . required of us a song
And they that wasted us
Required of us mirth.

And a thousand of our girls prostitute their voices singing jazz for a decadent white and black craving, and a number of lyricists turn off cheap little well-made bits of musical bric-a-brac, and Mose, having trundled a white man's fertilizer, walks wearily home, strumming a guitar. And a street car conductor jogs a black bricklayer to hear a comic monologue.

How shall we sing the Lord's song in a strange land?

Roland Hayes is singing with eyes closed, and head thrown back:

If I forget thee, O Jerusalem
If I forget thee, O Jerusalem
Let my right hand forget her cunning.

What is it that he sees, this mystic seer clutched by the ferocity of the final phrases. . . . What is it that is denied to us. . . . that frightens us, nay, appals?

This is no pose, this tense attitude, this head flung haughtily back, these closed eyes. . . .

Many did not notice that he had left the stage. The applause is not terrific. The whites do not understand, will not, cannot. They only know that they have caught distant glimpses from lofty perilous places. The Negroes feel somehow rebuked—

. . . required of us mirth
How shall we sing the Lord's song
My tongue cleave to the roof of my mouth
If I forget thee.

Roland has not forgotten.

Cognizant of Shakespeare's craft—of Reynold's —of Dickens; Hayes ushers in to dispel the impression of *katharsis* a few inescapable spirituals, one definitely comic, one an amusing but sympathetic portrayal of our primitive beliefs—and one a tender picture of a Lynchburg (why not) mammy, whose heaven is where at last she will

Sit down.

All of her ironic seizure on religion, her personal claiming of Jesus—her naive belief in heaven as a rocking chair, is so tenderly, comically sung —the whites feel their hearts go out to their near-human watchdog—Annie or Lizzie or Maggie or Sue, and resolve that if they can so manage she will have ten more minutes in which she may

Sit down.

Then, the dynamic, syncopated

Everytime I feel de Spirit

and the wierd

You hear de Lambs a-cryin'

and then the quiet consummation—renunciation, Negroid faith in another better world where one can

Steal away to Jesus.

But one must steal away, or he will be suddenly blocked even from there. Whites to Front. Colored to Rear.

Why need mention ever be made of the cheap dance that followed, to which our elite stole away—or the brask braying of a dancer that he was pretty good, but that 'for huhself she'd rather hear Jonnie steppin' on it, as would most others, but he was pretty good.'

Why need mention be made of the whites, their stealing away? Half uplifted, changed, and half insistent on his being an exception and all the way desirous of not brushing elbows on the stairs, they silently crept out—and draped the upholstery of their cars about them, and sank down to whitefolks' dreams. . . .

Roland Hayes sings. And as he sings, things drop away, the uglier apparel of manhood slinks off, and the inescapable oneness of all becomes perceptible. Roland Hayes sings, and no centuries of fostered belief can change the brotherhood of white and black. Roland Hayes sings, and boundaries are but figments of imagination, and prejudice but insane mutterings. And what is real is a great fellowship of all in pain, a fellowship in hope. Roland Hayes sings, and for that singing moment, however brief, the world forgets its tyranny and its submissive.iess.

By the waters of Babylon, we sat down
and wept,

Yea, we wept, when we remembered Zion.

America

Awarded Third Place

Little dark baby,
Little Jew baby,
Little outcast,
America is seeking the stars,
America is seeking tomorrow.
You are America.
I am America
America—the dream,
America—the vision.
America—the star-seeking I.
Out of yesterday
The chains of slavery;
Out of yesterday,
The ghettos of Europe;
Out of yesterday,
The poverty and pain of the old, old world,
The building and struggle of this new one,
We come
You and I,
Seeking the stars.
You and I,
You of the blue eyes
And the blond hair,
I of the dark eyes
And the crinkly hair.
You and I
Offering hands
Being brothers,
Being one,
Being America.
You and I.
And I?

Who am I?
You know me:
I am Crispus Attucks at the Boston Tea Party;
Jimmy Jones in the ranks of the last black troops
    marching for democracy.
I am Sojourner Truth preaching and praying
    for the goodness of this wide, wide land;
Today's black mother bearing tomorrow's Amer-
    ica.
Who am I?
You know me,
Dream of my dreams,
I am America.
I am America seeking the stars.
America—
Hoping, praying,
Fighting, dreaming.
Knowing
There are stains
On the beauty of my democracy,
I want to be clean.
I want to grovel
No longer in the mire.
I want to reach always
After stars.
Who am I?
I am the ghetto child,
I am the dark baby,
I am you
And the blond tomorrow
And yet
I am my one sole self,
America seeking the stars.

By Langston Hughes

Solace

Awarded Fourth Place

My window opens out into the trees
And in that small space
Of branches and of sky
I see the seasons pass
Behold the tender green
Give way to darker heavier leaves.
The glory of the autumn comes
When steeped in mellow sunlight
The fragile, golden leaves
Against a clear blue sky
Linger in the magic of the afternoon
And then reluctantly break off
And filter down to pave
A street with gold.
Then bare, gray branches
Lift themselves against the
Cold December sky
Sometimes weaving a web
Across the rose and dusk of late sunset
Sometimes against a frail new moon
And one bright star riding
A sky of that dark, living blue
Which comes before the heaviness

Of night descends, or the stars
Have powdered the heavens.
Winds beat against these trees;
The cold, but gentle rain of spring
Touches them lightly
The summer torrents strive
To lash them into a fury
And seek to break them—
But they stand.
My life is fevered
And a restlessness at times
An agony—again a vague
And baffling discontent
Possesses me.
I am thankful for my bit of sky
And trees, and for the shifting
Pageant of the seasons.
Such beauty lays upon the heart
A quiet,
Such eternal change and permanence
Take meaning from all turmoil
And leave serenity
Which knows no pain.

By CLARISSA M. SCOTT.

241

The Opportunity Dinner

Sketches made at the Meeting by FRANCIS HOLBROOK

"*A novel sight, that dinner—white critics, whom 'everybody' knows, Negro writers, whom 'nobody' knew—meeting on common ground.*" *From an editorial in the "The New York Herald-Tribune.*" So it was. Three hundred and sixteen persons —youthful prize winners, friends of Negro writers, critics and creators of American letters, editors, publishers, free lances, poets, novelists— a magnificent assemblage came to hear the Awards in OPPORTUNITY's first literary contest; to the formal expression of what this same editorial quoted above referred to as the "Negro Renaissance."

There was a program. The editor spoke briefly. In the presence of that gathering he saw the augury of a generous fund of interest which offered a surer foundation for the expressed objectives of OPPORTUNITY, its supporters, and of that vigorous new group now making its first passionate confessions of life, and longings and of beauty. This he said in welcoming them, and turned the meeting over to the Chairman, Mr. John Erskine, Professor of English, Columbia University, President of the Poetry Society of America, co-editor of the "Cambridge History of American Literature." Mr. Erskine saw in the approach of these new writers to American literature, the play of the same human emotions in a new field. A keen appreciation of beauty is theirs, he told them. Yes, they have a contribution to make.

JOHN ERSKINE

For each of the five sections of the Contest, there was a chairman, who commented critically upon manuscripts passed to the judges, explained the method of determining the ratings and announced the winners.

Clement Wood, poet, novelist, and critic, as chairman of the Poetry Section, sketched the contribution of Negro poets to the poetry of America and speculated upon their future contributions. While there is as yet perhaps no Negro poet of the magnitude of the ten greatest American poets, the extraordinary work of such young writers as Cullen, Hughes, Mackay, threatens to invade this rank. The Negro poet has a natural gift of song; the "hot, pelting passion of the jungle." He read "The Weary Blues." A rich, bold ringing voice he has, and a rare sensiness to the tripping melody of the poem by Langston Hughes, which captured the first prize. He read Countée Cullen's exquisite lyric, "To One Who Said Me Nay," and Clarissa Scott's "Solace."

DR. BLANCH C. WILLIAMS

Dr. Blanche Colton Williams was the chairman of the Short Story Section. The writers, she thought, showed a remarkable skill in selecting and handling vital story material. She reviewed the three prize stories, all of widely different themes, differently handled, but each having distinctive merit.

Montgomery Gregory was chairman of the Plays Section. Here is a field, he said, in which the skill of a few Negro actors has outstripped the playwrights. Gilpin and Robeson, to mention but two of the most recent of our talented actors, are without vehicles. A really practical w l come greets plays of Negro life. He sketched hastily the history of the Negro in the field of the drama. It developed that the winner of the third prize, "The Bog Guide" announced as Jean Ray was Miss Mae Miller, daughter of Kelly Miller of Howard University.

MONTGOMERY GREGORY

L. HOLLINGS-WORTH WOOD

Henry Goddard Leach, editor of the FORUM, chairman of the Essay Section, was called away from the meeting. L. Hollingsworth Wood, one of the judges of the Section, commented upon the essays and announced the winners.

Eugene Kinckle Jones spoke for the Personal Experience Sketches, of their ringing intensity, their sociological as well as literary value.

L. Hollingsworth Wood presented the awards amid a lusty cheering, and the interest of the Contestants was made a bit more manifest. For many of them were present from distant cities: John Matheus of Institute, West Virginia; Langston Hughes and Clarissa Scott, of Washington, D. C.; Mae Miller of Baltimore; and E. Franklin Frazier of Atlanta.

CLEMENT WOOD

Alain Locke of Howard University, who with Paul Kellogg produced the amazing Harlem Numbers of the SURVEY GRAPHIC, a restlessly active interpreter of the new awakening among the young

Negro writers, compressed into a few significant sentences the new departure of this group of writers. He spoke for the movement.

James Weldon Johnson, whom Clement Wood ranked in the foremost group of the Negro poets, a judge of the Poetry Section, versatile, urbane and always interesting, was the last speaker. There were both hope and warning in his words: "No race can ever become great that has not produced a literature."

JAMES WELDON JOHNSON

Now here is the significant part of the meeting. It was not a spasm of emotion. It was intended as the beginning of something and so it was. The meeting was ended with three announcements, all of which bound this initial effort to the future. A lover of poetry, who wished to remain anonymous, out of consideration for the excellence of the poetry entries, and wishing to equalize the awards, presented his check which doubled the sums offered as prizes for poetry, making the first prize $80.00 instead of $40.00 and the second $30.00 instead of $15.00. The second announcement was of the offer of criticism by Clement Wood to any of the Negro poets who wanted it as an aid to the mastery of technique. This offer was made through OPPORTUNITY and without charge. The third announcement was in the form of a letter and check for $500.00 from a New York Negro merchant. The letter was read and is reproduced here:

My dear Mr. Johnson:

Having been all my life a firm and enthusiastic believer in the creative genius of the Black Race, to which I humbly belong, OPPORTUNITY'S Prize Contest to foster artistic expression among Negroes has been a source of breathless interest to me. I honestly think it will go far towards consolidating the interests of, and bridging the gap between, the black and white races in the United States today, and particularly will it encourage among our gifted youth the ambition to scale the empyrean heights of art and literature.

It is, therefore, with a heart bursting with joy and appreciation for what you have so nobly and unselfishly undertaken that I take this opportunity to present to you my check for $500.00 (Five Hundred Dollars) in order that you may be able to conduct during the coming year (1926) another Literary Prize Contest which I am sure will prove just as productive of desirous results as this one has undoubtedly proven to be.

With assurances of my deepest interest in the far-reaching effects of the great work you are doing, I beg to remain,

Yours sincerely,

(Signed) CASPER HOLSTEIN

The meeting, aside from a pre-arranged program, was not stiffly formal. There was an opportunity for many of the Contestants to meet in person many of those who are making American literature and who came out to encourage and welcome them. Carl Van Doren, an ardent friend of these aspirants, with Irita Van Doren, was there; Robert H. Davis, editor of the *Munsey* Magazine, Fannie Hurst and Walter Drey of *Forbes* Magazine, flanked the extreme rear of the room. There was a *Survey* table at which Paul and Arthur Kellogg, Alain Locke and about six others sat. The Scribblers Club of Baltimore, an enthusiastic group of writers, was represented with about eight members; Arthur Ruhl, just back from Haiti, Charles Edward Russell and Mrs. Russell, who arrived the same morning from a year's visit in Europe; Jean Toomer, Poet and Short Story writer, author of "Cane," with his friend Gorham B. Munson; Rudolph Fisher, Edna Worthley Underwood, Mr. Henry Goddard Leach of the *Forum* and Mrs. Leach who contributed the first $500.00 for the prizes; Paul Robeson, the incomparable "Emperor Jones," L. Hollingsworth Wood, and his bride of one week, the erstwhile Miss Martha T. Speakman, Mary White Ovington and

CARL VAN DOREN

JEAN TOOMER

EUGENE KINC KLE JONES

WINOLD REISS

Miss Anna Nathan Meyer, Jessie Fauset, who distinguished herself last year with the novel "There is Confusion," Winold Reiss, the artist and Hans Reiss, May Freud Dickinson, Herman Hershin, Dr. and Mrs. E. P. Roberts, good patrons of the arts, Lester Walton, Georgia Douglass Johnson, one of whose poems Clement Wood used to open his discourse on the Negro Poetry, Lawrence Brown, doing for Negro music what these writers are trying to do for Negro life, Eric Walrond whom Zona Gale called "the natural stylist, moving in the air of literature unconditioned." Eugene F. Gordon and George Margetson came down from Boston; Carol Carson, Dean Lucy Slowe, Mary Burrell and Rudolph Fisher, a new luminary, came up from Washington. Carl Van Vechten, lover of the exotic, Burton Ruscoe, Countee Cullen, C. C. Spaulding of Durham, Grace Nail Johnson and Elsie McDougald and Arthur Schomburg. There were, as we said in the beginning 316 guests and for their inclusion it would take more space than we have.

The Prize Winners

John Matheus, of Institute, W. Va. Awarded First Prize for Short Story "Fog".

Langston Hughes, of Washington, D. C. Awarded First Prize for Poem "The Weary Blues" Tied for third place with poem "America"

E. Franklin Frazier, af Atlanta, Ga. Awarded First Prize for Essay "Social Equality and the Negro."

G. D. Lipscomb, Marshall, Texas. Awarded First Prize for play "Frances".

G. A. Steward, of Columbus, Ohio. Awarded First Prize for Personal Experience Sketch "My Fellow Traveller."

Zora Neale Hurston of Jacksonville, Fla. Awarded Second Prize for Short Story "Spunk" Awarded Second Prize for play "Color Struck."

Eric Walrond of New York City. Awarded Third Prize for Short Story "The Voodoo's Revenge."

Countée Cullen of New York City. Awarded Second Prize for poem "To One who Said Me Nay". Tied for the third place with poem "A Song of Sour Grapes."

Clarissa M. Scott of Washington. Tied for the fourth place for poem "Solace"

Laura D. Wheatley of Baltimore, Md. Awarded Third Prize for essay "The Negro Poet."

May Miller, of Baltimore, Md. Awarded Third Prize for play "The Bog Guide."

Joseph S. Cotter, of Louisville, Ky. Tied for fourth place for poem, "The Wayside Well.

Pot-Pourri

A Negro Renaissance

THE dinner given a few nights ago in honor of the prize winners in the literary contest conducted my the Negro magazine OPPORTUNITY was only a somewhat more conclusive indication of a phenomenon of which there have been many symptoms—of the fact that the American Negro is finding his artistic voice and that we are on the edge, if not already in the midst, of what might not improperly be called a Negro renaissance.

Negro actors appear in serious dramas, like "The Emperor Jones" and "All God's Chillun Got Wings." A Negro tenor, singing with equal ease, apparently, in his native "spirituals," or the most polished French, gathers a white audience that packs Carnegie Hall from pit to dome. Greenwich Village is quite démodé by the Negro cabarets of Harlem, and the average New Yorker (if there is such a bird!) suddenly discovers that in that part of his town a new Negro city, with theatres and restaurants, doctors, lawyers, merchants, priests, has sprung up, so to say, over night. The Survey Graphic, a magazine devoted to the consideration of significant social phenomena, gives a whole issue to this new Negro metropolis, described as the Mecca of the "new Negro." People read poems in white magazines by one Countée Cullen, and little dream that the writer, who decidedly seems to "have it in him," is a Negro undergraduate in a New York university.

The significant thing in all this, at any rate in that part of it represented by the dinner of the other night, is not that people with more or less Negro blood can write—Dumas was the grandson of a Negro—but that these American Negroes are expressing for the most part essentially Negro feelings and standing squarely on their racial inheritance. The prize winning poem—the judges of the contest were well known critics and professors of English—was called "The Weary Blues." The clash in the prize play was between an "old" Negro, quite willing to be subservient to the white owner of his little farm, even to sacrificing his daughter, and the new generation represented by the educated daughter and her Negro school-teacher lover. Some of the titles of stories submitted were "The Voodoo's Revenge," "A Soul Goes West on the B. and O.," "Color Struck," "Black Death," "A Florida Sunday," "The Boll Weevil Starts North," "Cat and the Saxophone."

These young people—and youth was another striking thing about this gathering—were not trying to imitate the white man nor repeating the professional white story-teller's dreary stencils of the "darkey." They were expressing their own feelings, frankly and unabashed, even if it took them back to the jungle. When rain threshes on the roofs of their Harlem flats they do not try to imagine what Wordsworth might have said about it. They stuff their fingers in their ears to shut out the sudden maddening memory of the sound of rain on banana leaves, of dances in the moonlight, and the tom-toms throbbing through the breathless tropic night!

A novel sight, that dinner—white critics, whom "everybody" knows, Negro writers, whom "nobody" knew—meeting on common ground. The movement behind it doubtless means something to the race problem in general; certainly it means something to American literature. The African, with his love of color, warmth, rhythm and the whole sensuous life, might, if emotionally liberated, do interesting things to a "Nordic" stock, so bustling and busy, so preoccupied with "doing things" in the external world, as almost to forget, sometimes, that it has any senses. And it would be one of fate's quaint but by no means impossible revenges if the Negro's real contribution to American life should be in the field of art.—New York *Herald-Tribune.*

A Point of View

(An Opportunity Dinner Reaction)

By Brenda Ray Moryck

IRVIN COBB and Octavus Roy Cohen, — recognized experts in the field of the short story of ebony hue and chocolate flavor? Why, I thought they were white men!''

"I thought so too."

"But they can't be!"

"Why not?"

"Because they write Negro stories."

"Well,—suppose they do."

"Then they must be Negroes themselves. We are told that people can only write very well of their own race because they know that race best."

"Indeed."

The foregoing bit of conversation was recently overheard in a Southern city.

And there you have it,—the Caucasian, with his facile pen, sketching life, wherever he finds it, excelling in any field to which he turns his art, while he recommends with sincerest sophistry that his darker brother keep within the narrow and prescribed area of his own racial precincts.

A paradox,—a white man may be an expert in his treatment of a theme on black folk, but a colored man, and I say "colored" advisedly, is not to be encouraged to emulate his example by reciprocation. Strange, too, when colored people always have known, and always will know, as long as white people continue to depend upon them for the most intimate personal services one human being can render another, far more about them individually and collectively than they will ever know about the black race.

Yet one of the most popular arguments advanced by modern critics, to convince the Negro writer of the wisdom of curtailing whatever free play he might care to allow his imagination in the treatment of any and all themes is the one which states that he knows best about his own people. Granted that he does, is it not possible that in the range of his varied experiences he may not, through intimate contact with other peoples, come to know them equally as well, even as Thomas Nelson Page, Ruth McEnery Stuart, Joel Chandler Harris and others, not omitting the estimable Messrs. Cobb and Cohen, have come to know and understand a certain type of Negro? I venture to say that a Negro writer living North could excel some of his present peers in the handling of an Irish or Jewish or Italian or Polish or even upper-class Caucasian theme if he were to try, for living and attending school for the most part, as he does, among the heterogeneous type of Americans, native, or foreign-born, contemptuously classed as "poor white trash," and either working for or with,—no matter which, so the daily contact is there, —better class Caucasians from clerks to royalty, he runs the gamut of the social scale in his daily existence and may be presumed to have direct knowledge of all classes of white people.

Then, too, his schooling, whether little or much, if academic training is as valuable as it is purported to be, should have contributed vastly to his understanding of white people. Whether or not the Negro writer has attended mixed schools or colored schools, been tutored by white or colored instructors, or by both, is of scant importance. The essential point is that his entire history and literature courses have been built up almost exclusively about the geneology, character, growth, development and achievements of the Caucasian race. Where more than a passing reference to Negroes or Mongolians has been made in a school text, it has been by way of some dry-as-dust anthropological treatise intended to draw the attention of an esoteric few. The daily newspapers with exception of those few Afro-American sheets which recently became so popular with both blacks and whites, are journals of Caucasian customs, manners, habits, pursuits, enterprises and engagements. The intelligent Negro lives in a white world perforce, for since he is outnumbered ten to one according to the census count, he can not ward off this daily enlightenment as to how the other nine-tenths live, even if he would. He begins the a b c of knowledge of the white race with his first academic studies, and does not take his final degree in "Caucasianology" until the hour of his death, frequently being ministered to by a white physician during his passing, by which time he merits every award given for high attainment and proficiency in a prescribed course. His natural endowment of curiosity renders him an apt pupil in the school of life.

If then, familiarity with the subject is the first requisite for intelligent writing about it, the educated Negro possesses the proper basic material in a pre-eminent degree. Pause but a moment and think of the beautiful and appealing love lyrics of the Negro poet,—on his haunting and wistful nature poems, so devoid of any reference to color,—so charmingly free of all race consciousness. Consider "Fog," as a prose example, the story which took first prize in a recent literary contest inaugurated to discover Negro talent. With a masterly and impersonal stroke, the author has handled varied classes, types and races of people,—the Negro element in his theme, sketched in evidently to make it conform to the rules of competition, being the weakest part. The Negro poet has long since discarded the bonds of Negro dialect as the sole vehicle of his expression and gloriously transcended themes purely subjective in character. His fancy wanders where it lists. Why not the Negro writer of fiction?

I am not, however, advocating that he direct his talent to delineating Caucasian character to the utter exclusion of his interest in his own race. My intention is merely to point out his ability to write freely on any subject, should he elect to do so, contrary to the advice of his wellwishers and critics.

There is a danger, it seems to me, in confining a writer to certain limits. His vision is narrowed, his imagination is dwarfed and warped, and his theme is robbed of its universality of appeal if he must forever be bound to the task of depicting racial reactions peculiar to the Negro. The Negro race as a whole now differs from the white race in externals only. "Death and the mysteries of life, the pain and the grief that flesh and souls are heirs to, the eternal problems that address themselves to all generations and races, produce in the soul of the Negro the same reactions as in any other individual," says Robert T. Kerlin in his essay on Contemporary Poetry of the Negro. Granted that intrinsically the Negro of pure African stock is more emotional, has greater depth of feeling, larger capacity for enjoyment, vaster appreciation for sensuous beauty than his white brother. —is essentially more of the artist,—more of the poet,—and also more of the buffoon, still he exhibits his atavistic traits after three hundred years of cultivation and adulteration only in proportion as he is removed from modern civilized culture. The individual differences so avidly hit upon by contemporary writers are found only in a certain type of Negro — a very captivating colorful creature of swiftly changing moods, and unexpected humorous or sad reactions is true, but one type only, nevertheless.

The writer who wishes to confine either his realism or his imagination to the still primitive groups, groups, whose precinct is Seventh Street or Seventh Avenue, Chicago or Alabama, will find an unfailing wealth of marketable material whose novel appeal can not be denied. And the author who would make the prose literature of his race, can not afford to discount the valuable contribution which a study of any people still in the elementary stages of American civilization furnishes. Myra Kelly has given us those charming stories, "Little Citizens" and "Little Aliens," Kathleen Norris, with her delightful gift for portraying Irish humor and

Irish pathos still paints the Americanized descendants of Ireland's emigrants; O. Henry offered us young America of the gutter and the curbstone, and I am told, upon excellent authority that "Little Afro-Americans" is now in the process of being manuscripted.

Further still, the Negro writer must delve into the past and steep himself in all the tragic lore of the South prior to the Civil War, adding to his present invaluable memory-store of slave history and slave legend, those poignant episodes of Negro life so replete with the very essence of reality, and with his native capacity for relishing the dramatic,—the sad as well as the gay, interpret them for the World, as only he can, if he would complete and enrich the racial literature which will some day be held precious.

But when he has finished this task of painting tragic history, albeit history embellished by the imagination,—when he wearies of the grotesque and the humorous in his race, when his pen lags over the delineation of those superstitions and credulous characters once so numerous in the south but now fast disappearing; when he is done with slush and maudlin sentimentality, to what shall he turn his attention?

There still remains a rich unexplored field if he must continue the study of his own race,—the vast domain of the colored *hoi polloi*—the middle class Negro, neither unintelligent nor yet cultured,—and the realm of the highly cultivated few,—few, not in numbers, but by comparison. Jessie Fauset, in "There is Confusion"', has sketched both classes, and Walter White, with another motive than that of pure entertainment, has presented us the problems and difficulties daily faced by the ambitious, educated groups of Negroes in his book "The Fire in the Flint." Other writers may follow their lead with similar works, but such stories, estimable though they are, do not represent purely creative art. They are both, more or less, propaganda novels, conceived for the purpose of presenting to a white audience certain facts and conditions concerning Negroes. They are not the charming impersonal themes so ably handled by many of the best Caucasian writers, and not always the best either, but the most widely read.

Let the young writer try his hand at this sort of writing for the sole purpose of entertaining. He will discover before very long, when he writes of life as he finds it, and so will his audience and his critics, that he is writing not of Negroes but of just people,—people no different in standards, customs, habits and culture from any other enlightened American groups, —merely American people. I say American, because the Negro is now American, thoroughly so,—having through amalgamation of blood,— there is no denying it when one views the ever increasing Nordic features and coloring appearing among the so-called blacks,—through assim-ilation of ideas and ideals, and conscious and unconscious imitation, absorbed every iota of the good and bad in American life.

Undoubtedly, if he had been allowed to remain in his native land, Africa, and his black blood had never known the taint of many nations diffused through it in honorable and dishonorable ways, he would still have been as distinctly different in character as the Mongolian or Jew alienated from other peoples either by physical, political, or racial barriers, and developing in isolation a distinct race consciousness. Or, if, having been brought to America, he had been huddled into a pale or ghetto, there to develop solely among his own kind, we should still see among all classes, traits and characteristics peculiarly individual to him. We should then probably have had a black Tolstoi writing of a dusky Anna Karenina.

But the Negro, for a large part, is no longer a Negro. He is an American, or living abroad, an Englishman, a Frenchman, or a German, according to his present place of abode ,with *sometimes* a dark skin and sometimes a skin not so dark. Contrary to the premise submitted by many so-called scientists that one drop of Negro blood makes a man a Negro, the black blood is not strong, but weak, and when once permeated by the Caucasian complex, the Negro becomes a Caucasian in all but his physique and frequently even in that. He sheds his peculiarly different African heritage with the ease with which a chameleon changes its colors and dons a new garment which, in the fifth and sixth generation of American civilization,—the heritage which many Negroes can now boast, has become his skin.

How long has the Jew or any other immigrant remained racially different once he has become a part of America? Only so long as he has been forced to keep to himself and has not been assimilated in the great melting pot. Once he has acquired money and grappled to himself those advantages which he came seeking, he emerges from racedom, just as an American citizen. Witness the upper class Jew in any community or study the high-born Mongolians numerous in diplomatic circles in Washington or on the Pacific Coast. Seldom, if ever, are their reactions in any way peculiarly racial once they have become Americanized. They differ only as any other people differ according to birth and breeding. That too when both races have carefully preserved their racial integrity.

In any untutored people, we find emotionalism, unrestraint and novel and unexpected responses to the experiences of life, hence the naivete of the masses of Negroes, who have long fascinated the white public and recently have begun to charm their own people. In any peoples just emerging from a long period of subjugation to a dominant group, we find greater depth of feeling, more intense religious fervor, a more serious and challenging outlook on life, than in the chosen few, who are the lords of the earth. The ordinary Negro is but a part of the great human family.

Likewise does he run true to form in the upper strata of society. He has on the one hand, all the airs, graces, superficialities and hypocrisies of the white race; all the shallowness, the meanness, the irreverence for holy things, the insatiable thirst for pleasure, the irritation at restraint, the envy, the jealousy; the contempt for the weak, the repudiation of the idea that he is his brother's keeper and the rejection of the Golden Rule which have ever characterized the over-sophisticated and too successful since the days of Babylon's glory, while on the other hand, he possesses in the same degree as all other representatives of a high degree of civilization,—the tamperng of his white forbears is responsible for the present degree—noble ideals, lofty thought, keen intellect, sane philosophy, sound judgment, hunger for knowledge, and a craving for all that is finest and best in life.

Prejudice against his color, when he shows any, has greatly hampered his progress as far as his material desires are concerned, but in spite of Fate, the mass Negro, the financially successful Negro and the cultured Negro as a whole, parallel their Caucasian complements in all but monetary wealth.

A story of any one of these types can be worked up into a purely Negro theme of course, by depicting the tragedies and disappointments wrought by discrimination, and injustice,—common occurrences in the daily lives of colored people—but at best such works are morbid. Yet any other attempt to portray the normal, ordinary pursuits of the classes of Negroes just described, unless spattered with constantly repeated references to color or to race, becomes at once, simply an account of individuals, not of Negroes as such.

Konrad Bercovici, in a recent article published in the Harlem number of the *Survey Graphic*, argues that the Negro should preserve his racial heritage even as the Jew has held fast to his. The cases are not analogous, even in the instances where Jews are found to be true to the original type. Their ranks were closed against all modifying and assimilating influences of their religion. Now that their orthodoxy is somewhat weakening in this country, even they are becoming more and more like any other Americans. "The Good Provider" an undeniably true picture of prosperous American Jewish life gives patent evidence of that fact. "Humoresque" likewise a gripping portrait of the Jew, represents his gradual change in character in proportion to his contact with the broadening influences of life. The high class young Jews found in private schools and colleges are exactly the prototype of other American youth.

Granted, however, that the Negro should wish to emulate the Jew, in his earlier stages of development in America, it is too late. He was robbed forever of his opportunity of remaining a distinct group people long, long ago by his white ancestors. He is now from one-sixteenth to nine-tenths Caucasian and if he preserves any racial characteristics at all they must be of a Janus nature.

Mr. Bercovici likewise points out that in his study of Negro groups gleaned from intimate Harlem contacts with all classes of colored Americans, he found among them distinct differences of character and thought, peculiarly individual to the Negro.

I beg to differ with his findings.

Because I have discovered so few people whose opinions I value, to agree with me on this subject, and can quote no significant authorities, I must be intensely personal in what follows, offering my own experiences and those of others well known to me to support my contention. I therefore ask my readers' indulgence.

If Mr. Bercovici were to leave off his exquisite word-painting of gypsy and Roumanian life and write a story of his colored friends,—a certain well-known Negro actor and his clever wife, —a chemist of recognized ability in her line,— would he find, I wonder, when that comedian had doffed the robes of the "Emperor Jones" or when Mrs "Emperor Jones" had returned to her tiny New York apartment, or any of the others of the little Harlem group, anything especially different in their habits of life or manner of thought which would be a startling revelation to a jaded world fast learning how the other half lives? I think not.

Yet, not alone, either, are Konrad Bercovici and the other Caucasian critics, in staunchly advocating the idea that a Negro writer must forever write of Negroes, first because he lacks the necessary knowledge for any other sort of writing and second, because portrayal of the Negro character offers something new and refreshing. They are warmly seconded by many of the ablest men of letters of the darker race. At a dinner not so long ago, I heard a prominent Negro, distinguished in a certain field of literature, eloquently argue for this same prescribed idea—he—a man of distinctly Caucasian features, and soft, straight hair, whose only identity with the race is his color and his wish, —whose wife is a highly cultivated young woman, charming and beautiful after the Spanish pattern, whose fair-skinned babies—four of them, two of them fair-haired also, gambol about their inviting play-room, just as any babies do, scrapping, hitting, pounding, banging, crying, only to don quickly their company manners and smile and curtsey adorably or offer a pink-dimpled hand when guests appear, just as

Continued on page 251

(*Continued from page* 249)
any other well-bred infants do the world over, exhibiting in no-wise those peculiarly different characteristics attributed to the Negro and argued for by their father.

For pastime, I recently wrote an intimate study of an eminent Negro author and his lovely wife and submitted it to a number of personal friends for their diversion. Except for the use of names and a passing reference to the color and features of a child, no one recognized it as a "colored story." There was nothing in the scholarly elegance of the man nor in the gracious charm of the woman nor in the cunning capers of the three children to brand them as Negroes, although in reality this couple very ardently and energetically identifies itself with the black race.

These are but a few examples. A panoramic view of cultured American Negro life will reveal many, many others of the same cast all over the country. The colored schools are filled with the children of such parents, the large southern cities abound in their number,—not always with quite the same cultural attainment, as the very privileged few,—but with a background as fitting and an outlook as sane and devoid of emotion as any of their compatriots of the same level of society, whose ancestors have enjoyed some little education and certain additional advantages.

Without stressing the unpleasant and dismal element of race-prejudice and its cursed results, it would be impossible to construct a Negro theme as such, from the daily tragedies and joys and ordinary pursuits of colored people, except of those belonging to the untrained and inexperienced groups, who through continued lack of enlightenment and contact with refining influences have reverted or remained true to the African type, which I frankly and readily admit is peculiarly different from all other race types.

Above that class, the Negro becomes just a person, differing from all other persons in color, according to the amount of Negro blood in his veins,—in dress, tastes and habits, according to the degree of his cultivation, in manner of living, according to wealth. Proof of this fact may be found in the thousands of so-called colored people who yearly sever themselves with such ease from the race to which the laws of Virginia and South Carolina and a few other states, grown hysterical over what they once started and can not now control, have assigned them, to become lost in the milieu of an immigrant crowded white world. If he were inherently different, the peculiar racial characteristics supposedly his would be as apparent in the white-skinned Negro as in the black.

If then, a survey of colored American life reveals the fact that people are people, white or black, the Negro prose writer with safe assurance may invade with his pen, any world he desires, for by merely knowing his own race people, he knows in addition all other people of his country not alone through study and observation but *per se*. Freedom of range of idea, unhampered by race consciousness or smothered by race pride, he as well as the poet must have, if the latent gift of creative art recently uncovered to the public is to reach the ripe fulfilment of its rich promise.

Not only then will he produce a great Negro literature, but beyond that in time, he too, will be added to that list of honored men, which bears the names of the makers of the creative literature of the world.

⁂

OPPORTUNITY

Editorials

October 1925
Vol. 3 No. 34

The Contest

WE announce the Second Annual OPPORTUNITY Contest for Negro writers with increased awards and extended departments. The first experiment in the field of literature netted conspicuous and pleasing results. It located about 800 Negroes scattered through nearly every state in the union, the great majority of whom can express themselves effectively in prose and verse, and some of whom give promise of definite accomplishment in the field of letters. It marked, rather dramatically the awakening of artistic effort among the newer Negroes. The world is hearing more of this sector of American life than it ever thought existed. The contagion of Langston Hughes' "The Weary Blues," which captured first prize, has been unmistakable. And soon his first book of poems under that title will appear. The story, "Fog" has been recommended by Dr. Blanche Colton Williams to the O'Henry Memorial Prize Committee on its sheer merit as a short story, and will appear in the book, *The New Negro,* which Alain Locke is editing for A. & C. Boni. publishers. Zora

Neale Hurston, whose *Spunk* and *Color Struck* received prizes in the Contest will go to Barnard College on a scholarship. She will be its first colored student.

The poems and stories of promising writers remote from literary centers, and hidden away behind their timidities and doubts, have revealed a marvellous comprehension of life, and a facility and charm in expressing themselves. It is not wholly surpising, then, that a writer of distinction, who has followed their work in OPPORTUNITY should be lead to remark: " . . . The recent outburst of Negro genius into literature is positively amazing. The Negro's touch upon trifles is marvellously delicate—coexistent as it is, with the strong handling of the things that make for tragedy and passion.''

Encouraged by the remarkable record of these young writers in their first impassioned effort at self expression, Mr. Casper Holstein, who at our Awards dinner, presented his check for $500.00 to insure the Second Contest, has exactly doubled his original gift, making possible an increase in the awards and further funds for reaching an even greater number of writers. This is a faith and service deserving of more than casual appreciation. A Negro who is by no means a millionaire has faith enough in the future of his own developing race to give of his means to encourage it.

New features are added this year—awards for musical composition, The Alexander Pushkin Poetry Prize and the F. C. W. C. Prizes for constructive journalism. These mark progress, and the projection of other hopes. With the appearance of this issue the Contest is formally opened.

Opportunity's Second Annual Contest for Negro Writers Offers

1000.00 IN PRIZES

—to stimulate and foster creative literary effort among Negroes; to uncover those hidden treasures of artistic materials in Negro life; to locate and aid in orienting Negro writers of ability; to stimulate and encourage interest in the serious development of a body of literature about Negro life.

The Holstein Prizes

CASPER HOLSTEIN

Who has donated $1,000.00 to OPPORTUNITY for the establishment of the HOLSTEIN PRIZES and for the promotion of the Contest among Negro writers.—From a drawing by Francis C. Holbrook.

"Having been all my life a firm and enthusiastic believer in the creative genius of the Black Race, to which I humbly belong, OPPORTUNITY'S Prize Contest to foster artistic expression among Negroes has been a source of breathless interest to me. I honestly think it will go far towards consolidating the interests of, and bridging the gap between the black and white races in the United States today, and particularly will it encourage among our gifted youth the ambition to scale the empyrean heights of art and literature."

Short Stories

First Prize ---------------$100.00
Second Prize -------------- 50.00
Third Prize -------------- 25.00

               $175.00

The stories must deal with some phase of Negro life, either directly or indirectly; otherwise there are no restrictions. They may be romantic, realistic, humorous and each will be judged upon its quality as a good short story . . .

These stories must not exceed 5,000 words.

Poetry

First Prize --------------- $50.00
Second Prize ------------- 35.00
Third Prize ------------- 10.00
Fourth Prize ------------ 5.00

               $100.00

The theme may be the Negro or it may be some national figure or event, some natural symbol, some product of nature; a mood or musings,—anything at all, whether it relates to Negro life or thought or not.

Plays

First Prize	$60.00
Second Prize	35.00
Third Prize	15.00

$110.00

The plays must deal with some phase of Negro life, either directly or indirectly, otherwise, there are no restrictions. They may be romantic, realistic, humorous, and each will be judged upon its quality as a good play.

Personal Experience Sketches

First Prize	$30.00
Second Prize	20.00
Third Prize	10.00

$60.00

These sketches must be an actual experience and relate to some incident or situation or circumstance of personal life which makes it possible to understand how one feels and acts in the presence of a particular life problem. The contestant will strive for complete frankness and self-scrutiny, truthfulness, and clarity of expression.

These will be limited to 2,000 words.

Essays

First Prize	$50.00
Second Prize	30.00
Third Prize	10.00

$90.00

The object here is to bid for a much abused type of literary expression in the hope of finding some examples of recognizable literary merit. The contestant will strive for clarity of diction, forcefulness, and originality of ideas, logical structure, deft and effective employment of language, accuracy of data, and economy of words. The subject may be of the contestant's selection but must relate directly or indirectly to Negro life and contacts, or situations in which Negroes have a conspicuous interest.

The essays are limited to 3,000 words.

Musical Compositions

First Prize	$75.00
Second Prize	50.00
Third Prize	25.00

$150.00

These must be original musical compositions for either instrument or voice. No restriction is placed upon the theme.

All compositions must be written legibly in ink.

No work will be eligible that has been published.

Texts must be in English.

ALEXANDER PUSHKIN POETRY PRIZE. Award of $100.00

(a) This section is expected to call forth the most ambitious and most mature work of the Negro poet, and it is requested that to this section only the best work be sent.

(b) The contest will be open to all Negro poets in this country or elsewhere.

(c) Poems must be original and unpublished, and not more than three may be entered by one poet.

(d) Poems must not exceed three hundred lines in length.

(e) Poems must be in English.

(f) Only one prize of $100.00 will be awarded, but honorable mention will be given to other ranking poems.

THE F. C. W. C. PRIZES FOR CONSTRUCTIVE JOURNALISM

(Presented by the Department of Literature of the New York State Federation of Colored Women's Clubs, through Mrs. Addie W. Hunton, State President.)

I. For the editorial appearing in any Negro weekly newspaper attaining highest literary quality, the theme of which is calculated to effect the greatest good in the interest of inter-racial peace—

A Prize of $100.00

II. For the news story from any Negro weekly newspaper which, from the standpoint of accuracy, style, and public usefulness, is adjudged of highest quality,

A Prize of $50.00

III. For the feature article from any Negro weekly newspaper, which from the point of view of organization of materials, clarity of expression, effectiveness, revealing authentic information adjudged as most important to an understanding of Negro life or character,

A Prize of $50.00

CONDITIONS

(a) Entries to this section may be made by the newspaper itself, or by any reader.

(b) Only articles published between the dates February 1, 1925, and January 30, 1926, will be eligible.

(c) Entries should be specifically labeled for the Contest and bear the name and address of the sender.

(d) Entries made by newspapers should bear the name of the writer of the article.

(e) The full page of the paper should be sent.

GENERAL RULES

Entries submitted in this Contest shall not be submitted the same year for prizes in any other Contest.

Any story, poem, play, essay, or personal experience sketch that has already been published is ineligible for this Contest.

The Contest opens October 1, 1925, and closes January 31, 1926.

This Contest reserves the right to reject all manuscripts in any division if the contributions are deemed below a reasonable standard of quality or insufficient in number.

Entries submitted should bear a nom de plume and in a sealed envelope the real name and address of the contestant.

O PPORTUNITY'S Second Annual Contest for Negro writers closed on January 31st. The volume of entries shows a notable increase over last year, but more important still, the **The Contest** entries, particularly in the poetry and short story sections, are generally of a higher level of craftsmanship. Such success as attended last year's experiment has drawn eager aspirants from every state of the Union in which any considerable number of Negroes live; from Africa, France, England, The West Indies, The Virgin Islands, Panama, and even Spain. It is certain, from an examination of these manuscripts, many of which are throbbing with life and possess a distinctive beauty, that some really distinguished examples of literary creativeness will be revealed when, on May 1st, in New York City, the awards are made.

OPPORTUNITY

L. Hollingsworth Wood
Chairman

Eugene Kinckle Jones
Executive Secretary

Charles S. Johnson
Editor

A JOURNAL OF NEGRO LIFE
Published Monthly by
The Department of Research and Investigations

NATIONAL URBAN LEAGUE
127 EAST 23rd STREET, NEW YORK, N. Y.
Telephone Gramercy 3976

William H. Baldwin
Secretary

Lloyd Garrison
Treasurer

Eric Walrond
Business Manager

Vol. 4   JUNE, 1926   No. 42

Contents

Single Copies, Fifteen Cents—*Yearly Subscriptions*, One Dollar and a Half, Foreign, $1.75.
Entered as second-class matter, October 30, 1923, at the Post Office at New York, New York, under the act of March 3, 1879.

commends the study of Oriental Art as the only approach for the layman to the heart of Asia, to an understanding of the essential harmony of the human mind. The same advice applies to Negro life and its art. For fellowship can be found in beauty of whatever origin and it never fails to reveal something of the inner feeling of one who creates it. This conviction is behind the Opportunity Contests for Negro writers. The hundreds of these writers who responded assume an important, if unconscious task. They are the new interpreters.

Editorials

THIS month's Opportunity is in large part a Contest number. The five prize poems, the first prize short story and play are carried.

A Contest Number Other entries receiving high place in the ratings will follow these. All of them have some features of astonishingly high merit. All of them we submit as the flowering of a brand new skill and of a similarly new outlook on life.

Professor George Sarton in the *Yale Review*

258

neath the light music." James Weldon Johnson found *To a Persistent Phantom* by Frank Horne "an impressionistic poem with a vaguely haunting idea at its center—unmarred by technical faults." Of Countee Cullen's poems Mr. Frost remarked: "He cares and knows how to make you feel he cares. I admire his stroke." The "fantasticality and pithy philosophy" of Wallace Thurman's *God's Edict,* the "macabresque fantasy mingled with living emotion" in Helene Johnson's *Magalu,* the "great beauty of simple expression" in Arna Bontemps' poem, *Golgotha,* "the notable command of versification and smoothness of rhythm" of Claude MacKay's *Desolate,* "the fine lyricism" of Georgia Douglas Johnson's *Song of the Sinner—* these reflect descriptive judgments which may be easily confirmed on a reading of the poems themselves. To Helene Johnson goes the distinction of having produced two of the finest lines of the entries.

The selections this year represent an advance in which both old and new contestants are participating, and only one who is privileged to examine the complete mass of entries can know how deep lying is this artistic awakening.

I T is always difficult for juries to agree. The judges in this contest were asked to read a larger number of manuscripts than is the custom.

The Judges and the Entries Differences in response were frequent and at times rather far apart. But they centered with certainty about a group to which first preferences were given. It would be pleasing to give our readers a full view of the comments from those undoubted authorities in American letters on the technical excellencies and failings of the entries submitted. For reasons apparent that is impracticable. In another section of this issue we carry some of the comments on the entries in each section as a group. But it will be enlightening here to refer to some of the poetry entries in particular. Of *No Images* Mr. Braithwaite said: "It is the most perfect poem in the Contest, a fine conception and strikingly symbolized—it really haunts," and of *Northboun',* "it is a fulfillment of Matthew Arnold's conception of poetry as a 'criticism of life' as applied to dialect currently used." The two, he adds, are poems "in which I would not change a word"! Clement Wood thot *No Images* "an exquisite, successful piece," and William Rose Benet found in it a "true poignance and wistful beauty," although he liked better Gwendolyn Bennett's *Hatred* which he characterized as "almost flawless of its kind" and John Matheus' *The Frost Has Painted Calvary on the Windows of the Churches,*" which "in spite of obvious defects, has a certain wild magic of color and is distinctly moving." Mr. Robert Frost calls Arna Bontemps' *Golgotha Is a Mountain* "the wayward thinking of real poetry—beautiful." Joseph Cotter's *The Tragedy of Pete,* Witter Bynner called "a crisp, cogent and genuine ballad — a vital and valuable poem," and Lucy Ariel

Golgotha Is a Mountain

By Arna Bontemps

Awarded Alexander Pushkin *Poetry Prize*

Golgatha is a mountain, a purple mound
Almost out of sight.
One night they hanged two thieves there,
And another man.
Some women wept heavily that night;
Their tears are flowing still. They have made a
    river;
Once it covered me.
Then the people went away and left Golgotha
Deserted.
Oh, I've seen many mountains:
Pale purple mountains melting in the evening mists
    and blurring on the borders of the sky.
I climbed old Shasta and chilled my hands in its
    summer snows.
I rested in the shadow of Popocatepetl and it
    whispered to me of daring prowess.
I looked upon the Pyranees and felt the zest of
    warm exotic nights.
I slept at the foot of Fujiyama and dreamed of
    legend and of death.
And I've seen other mountains rising from the
    wistful moors like the breasts of a slender
    maiden.
Who knows the mystery of mountains!
Some of them are awful, others are just lonely.

*   *   *

Italy has its Rome and California has San Fran-
    cisco,
All covered with mountains.
Some think these mountains grew
Like ant hills
Or sand dunes.
That might be so—
I wonder what started them all!
Babylon is a mountain
And so is Nineval,
With grass growing on them;
Palaces and hanging gardens started them.
I wonder what is under the hills
In Mexico
And Japan!

There are mountains in Africa too.
Treasure is buried there:
Gold and precious stones
And moulded glory.
Lush grass is growing there
Sinking before the wind.
Black men are bowing.
Naked in that grass
Digging with their fingers.
I am one of them:
Those mountains should be ours.
It would be great
To touch the pieces of glory with our hands.
These mute unhappy hills,
Bowed down with broken backs,
Speak often one to another:
"A day is as a year," they cry,
"And a thousand years as one day."
We watched the caravan
That bore our queen to the courts of Solomon;
And when the first slave traders came
We bowed our heads.
Oh, Brothers, it is not long!
Dust shall yet devour the stones
But we shall be here when they are gone."
Mountains are rising all around me.
Some are so small they are not seen;
Others are large.
All of them get big in time and people forget
What started them at first.
Oh the world is covered with mountains!
Beneath each one there is something buried:
Some pile of wreckage that started it there.
Mountains are lonely and some are awful.

*   *   *

One day I will crumble.
They'll cover my heap with dirt and that will make
    a mountain.
I think it will be Golgotha.

Symphonesque

By ARTHUR HUFF FAUSET

Awarded First Prize—Short Story Section

I

Allegro non troppo

Allegro vivace et caprioso.

THE tiny village of Gum Ridge, Texas, fairly hummed under a sizzling white sun that mounted higher and higher in the gray-blue space lately traversed by the stars. Living creatures fled the exposed valley and sought shelter beneath the leafy branches of giant cottonwoods, pecans and maples that studded the sides of the towering hill which lent its name to the village.

The parched fields lay desolate, looking like huge burnt carcasses, and brittle as dead men's bones. They listened to the dull droning of the dust-ridden atmosphere as it quivered under the murderous lashings of the sun, and occasionally to the sonorous hum-m-m-m-m of a solitary bee that braved the death-dealing rays of heat in quest of some petalled haven.

Far down in the blistered valley, within a wretched log cabin, Cudjo, brown youth of seventeen summers, raised himself drowsily from his torn and tattered couch. In a corner of the cabin, Old Ben lay sound asleep. Cudjo knew he was sound asleep by the noise of his snoring, harmonizing ludicrously with the bzz-bzz-bzz of the giant horse-flies that frisked and frolicked about the old man's mouth and from time to time raised huge lumps on his lips and the top of his bald head.

Cudjo stretched and yawned.

He sat down on the edge of his couch and looked about him. The cabin was littered with filth. Rubbish of all sorts was strewn over the floor. Vermin crawled from the bed clothing, from his clothes, and from the newspapers that adorned the walls. Sleek rats darted occasionally across the floor. The smothering rays of the sun, shimmering through long thin cracks in the roof fell with a dazzling brilliance on the nauseating spectacle.

For a moment Cudjo was filled with loathing. Although he had never known any other kind of existence, something within him was not reconciled to this slovenliness. A curious shiver coursed slowly through his body, starting at the base of his spine and trickling out on his lips. Under that burning roof he felt his teeth chattering.

It took but a moment to put on his few fragments of clothing. Then he crept to the door of the shack and started to open it, but of a sudden shut it, exclaiming,: "Damn hot . . . Baptism today too . . . Niggahs gonna do dere stuff f' sho' in all dis heat . . . Gotta be dere . . . gotta be dere."

In the corner Old Ben continued to snore profoundly. Cudjo observed him intently for an instant.

"Oughta be up an' gittin' to de ribber, sho's yuh bo'n. Dat's his lil' red wagon ah reckon. Spec' ah bettah let 'um sleep an' tek his rest. If he misses baptism though, be jes' too bad."

He reached for an old black hat hanging on a nail in the door. and pulled it far over his face as he emerged from the cabin.

"Wow, but it's hot," he exclaimed as his bare feet trod upon the sandy road that felt like a bake oven. "Twarn't fo' de damn foolishness ah'd git baptize' m'se'f dis hot day . . . . Somepin' mattah wid mah soul right now an' ah knows it . . . Gotta git dis out O'm' system somehow . . . wonder what's eatin' me?"

He passed old Ebenezer Baptist Church. Standing on a small eminence overlooking the surrounding lands it had the appearance of a smoke-gray lighthouse in an ocean of heat-flame. Cudjo laughed cynically as he stepped by.

"All dis 'ligion ain't gittin' nobody nowheah. All it does, mek yo' all feel good. Mek yo' feel like yo' treading' on soft cushions in Gawd's he'b'n. But it ain't gittin' nobody nuffin' ain't gittin' me a damn thing. Dis 'ligion don't keep folks f'um laughin' at me cause ah'm diff'ant f'um dem. Don't kep White Man f'um raisin' hell any time he feelin' dat-a-way. Jes' mek yo' happy dat's all. Mek yo' damn happy. Feel good . . . yea bo'."

He looked into the heavens. The sun was a whirling white streak in a hazy gray-blue pattern. His eyes could not stand the glare.

With hands folded behind him he sauntered along as in a dream, thinking, thinking, unmindful of heat or shade. His eyes seemed to be covered with mist. They were nearly closed. He did not have to see. What were feet for? Did they not have ten eyes, as many noses, and mouths as well? There was nothing which could be perceived by the ordinary senses that these wonderfully trained friends did not discover even more readily. If he was hungry, they led him to patches of wild blackberries and juicy strawberries. When he was tired and sleepy they carried him gently over rocks and stones, avoiding pits, brambles and poisonous snakes. They knew the east from the west; the quiet lanes that led down to the cool, refreshing brook from the steep stony paths which ascended to the crests of those mighty shaggy turrets that people called hills; those hills from whose tops he delighted to look down on the sleepy villages below and pretend that he was God.

God again!

What was all this talk about God? These nig-

gers and their God! Fools, that's all they were,
they and their God.

Did they think that God gave a tinker's damn for
them, they in their dirty shacks that bred scorpions,
bedbugs and rats, and gave forth a stench that
would knock down a polecat! Where was their
God when White Man came along at the end of
the harvest season and told the niggers they hadn't
made enough cotton to pay for their grub to say
nothing of their shelter, their clothing, their
very liberty!

And what was He doing on that hot afternoon
when White Man took Zack Jones and riddled his
body with bullets after he had been strung up to a
big tree for being in the neighborhood when little
"Miss" Dora suddenly took a notion it would be
funny to pretend that some nigger had said naughty
things to her? . . .

He liked to go up on Gum Ridge in the late
afternoon when pale, purple clouds hovered over
the tiny villages like a hen over her brood of
chicks. It was like being in heaven to be there and
hurl a stone high in the air only to watch it fall
on some naked roof in the white section of the village; then with fists clenched and arms raised in
mighty exaltation to exclaim: "Damn yuh, when
ah'm down in de valley yo' all white folks is Gawd.
Yeh. Ain't no mo' Gawd when ah'm down dere.
But when ah gits up in dese pahts ah'm Gawd.
Hyeah me, yo' gawddamned w'ite trash. Yo' all
listen to me. Ah'm Gawd. An' one o' dese days
ah'm gonna baptize yo' all wif fiah an' brimstone!"

He arrived at the bank of the Tugaloo River, the
sluggish, anemic stream that mocking white folks
called Ebenezer's Jordan. No other person was in
sight. Cudjo lifted himself upon the stern of a
small motor launch that lay anchored near the shore,
masterfully perched for witnessing the baptismal
ceremony.

The sickening sun smote him with its sleep-dis-
pensing rays. He began to feel drowsy. A gentle
mist formed over his half-closed eyes; the world
commenced to swim from under him.

Pictures flitted across the space in front of him,
flickering glimpses of the same slim brown girl who
seemed to dance for his pleasure and performed
miraculous gyrations like some whirling pinwheel.
In a half doze he mumbled to himself: "Damn
. . . that's Amber Lee. Sho' is. Amber Lee.
Wonder ef she be hyeh today?"

The slim brown figure whirled round and round
until it appeared as dazzling as the sun. Cudjo
shook himself from sheer dizziness.

"Ah got funny feelin's these days. Don't know
whut's wrong wid me. Ah wants to dance an'
shout. An' raise hell in gen'ral ah' reckons."

His head nodded. Asleep. Awake. Here, then
there, now dead, alive, just enough alive to feel
himself crooning an old melody he had often heard
Old Ben sing:

"Hop right! goin' to see mah baby Lou!
Goin' to walk an' talk wid mah honey!
Goin' to hug an' kiss mah honey . . .
Hop right, mah baby!"

He *hopped right* out of his reverie when a party
of picnickers, breezing by in a small launch yelled
out to him amidst waving of flags and handker-
chiefs: "Hello Cudjo! Hello Crazy Cudjo!"

Cudjo's arm shot out with a jovial fling, but
ended with a stock gesture, the outstretched fingers
of his right hand in close proximity to his nose and
yelled back: "Hope t' Gawd yo' all boat turns
over!"

There was no more chance to dream. The worshippers were coming down to the river; at first
small straggling droves of children; soon after,
clustered crowds of men, women and children.

It was hot. The dank water of the Tugaloo
smelled like a cistern containing an old corpse.
Men and women perspired till the air was filled
with a thick pungent odor like soapy stale salt.
Old people looked on at the gathering crowd and
said little; the young folk laughed and twitted each
other. Ebenezer Baptist was on party display. Her
women were clad in every description of red, yellow, purple, pink, blue. Many of them wore
dresses of brilliant hues woven into Egyptian patterns. They raised gay paper parasols and cotton
umbrellas to ward off the scorching sunshine.
Young men sported wide trousers with gaudy sus-
penders or broad brilliantly colored belts. Their
belt-furrowed coats made of screaming brown and
blue cloth displayed a profusion of buttons some of
them hanging from long tassel-like cords. They
wore large brown and black felt hats and glistening
derbies.

The congregation grew thicker and noisier.
Members found places on odd stacks of lumber
that were piled up here and there on the shore; in
rowboats which they tied together; on the roofs of
sheds and outhouses. Some of the young bucks sat
on the trestle of the railroad bridge that spanned
the river.

Cudjo viewed the gaudy parade with great
glee. He chuckled low to himself and clapped
his hands. "Hotdam," he muttered half aloud,
"gonna be big doin's in dis man's town dis
yere day . . . sho' is . . . Hotdam!"

A loud murmur emanating from the gathering
throng attracted his attention to the bank of the
river. A cry surged through the congregation.
"Uh-uh . . . hyeh dey come . . . hyeh
dey come . . . hyeh dey all come'."

II

Crescendo

Religioso furioso

All eyes focused on the preacher, shepherd of the
flock who appeared leading his baptismal lambs.
He was a tremendous black figure with a large
round stomach that almost bulged out of his dark
blue vest. As he waddled, his corpulent body
seemed like a huge inflated balloon made of thick
rubber swaying upon two large resilient pillars.
He wore a white robe that was neither long

enough to hide the tips of his blue trousers nor wide enough to cover the heavy gold watch-chain that circled his paunch. A hush came over the ever-increasing throng as the preacher and two deacons prepared a passageway to the river for the baptismal candidates. In their stocking feet they waded out in the smutty brown water and drove two long staves about a yard apart into the soft mud. To the ends of these they fastened ropes which they brought back to the shore and attached to hooks that had been driven into some pilings on the river bank.

The converts, dressed in white, were lined up one behind the other on the shore. Most of them were young girls. Their eyes were red with weeping. Now and then one of them sobbed and fell into the arms of a buxom matron who crooned old Baptist hymns in her ears.

The preacher bustled about, imparting final instructions to his deacons while they waited for a tall brown man, clad in white robes, to make his way through the dense crowd. He was the exhorter.

The ceremony began.

The exhorter discarded the white cap that adorned his head and exposed himself to the excruciating heat. He commenced singing in a high quavering voice:

"Run away, run away,
Run away, run away,
Ain't gonna see you any more."

At the third "run away" the entire congregation echoed the song fervidly. The young candidates took this for a signal to shriek and sob. Their voices rent the sizzling air like screaming sirens in the black of a starless night.

The exhorter continued:

"Cry some more, cry some more,
Cry some more, cry some more,
Ain't gonna see you any more."

Some one in the congregation started to sing:

"How many done dead an' gone?
Couldn't have religion I would not be."

The exhorter desiring even more fervor decided that one more song was necessary. Soon the air rang with melody.

"Ain' we some angels of Jesus, some angels
of Jesus, some angels of Jesus,
Surely He died on Calvary,
Calvary, Calvary,
Calvary, Calvary,
Calvary, Calvary,
Surely He died on Calvary."

The singing became hysterical. Men and women cried. Some swayed their bodies from right to left; some leapt into the air; others shook themselves up and down like coarse dancers in a burlesque theatre.

Crescendo, crescendo, crescendo. Mighty roar of an ocean tumult. Thunder. Tumult of song that challenges the listening heavens agape.

(*Continued on page* 198)

Symphonesque

(*Continued from page* 180)

"Calvary, Calvary,
Calvary, Calvary,
Calvary . . . "

As if by signal the torrent of song diminishes in volume and velocity; step by step, pitch by pitch, it diminishes. Nothing remains but a gentle soft crooning that seems like the pattering of raindrops on the leaves after a storm.

The crooning stops abruptly. The soft voice of the big black preacher wafts its way soothingly over the congregation like an evening lullaby. "Come on chillun, da's 'nough now . . . chillun . . . Gawd done hyard yo' all . . . Gawd sho' hyard his white lambs dat time. Now we gwine ha' prayer by Brother Simpson."

Brother Simpson stepped out from the throng. He threw his battered straw hat on the muddy bank and flung his long black arms toward the sun-lit heavens. He spoke slowly at first in low tones that were scarcely audible above the quiet murmuring that wrapped itself around the devout worshippers like a soft blanket. He prays:

"Oh Lawd . . . dis is a prayer to you . . . dis is a prayer to m' father in heb'n, oh Lawdy Jesus . . . yas . . . yas . . . Done turn mah face to de jasper walls so's you kin see de heb'nly sunshine in mah eyes . . . Oh Lawdy Jesus . . . done renounce de flesh an' de debil. . . ."

His prayer grows warmer and warmer. He punctuates each fervent plea with a deep gasp resembling a suffocating man struggling for air.

"Oh, Lawd, Lawdy, u-n-n, hab mercy on dis po' creature of yours, u-n-n, hab mercy on dis thy humble servant, u-n-n oh Lawd, deliber us, u-n-n, f'm de debil's wiles, u-n-n ah holy Lawd Jesus, u-n-n, watch . fo' us, u-n-n an' pray, u-n-n, fo's u-n-n, that we be not led, u-n-n, into de temptation ob de wilderness, u-n-n, and fall beneath de prickly feet of dat wicked debil, u-n-n."

The deacon exhorts. He cajoles and laments. He pants, sings, groans and croons. Great clouds of steam fall from his face.

At first the congregation with heads bowed listen in a rhapsody of terror and exaltation. After a little while they too shout and scream as the deacon denounces the wickedness of the devil and depicts the horrors of hell. From time to time the preacher dips down into the muddy stream with his hands and brings up water to bathe the head of the sweltering deacon and his own as well. After each application he emits a shrill laugh whose fiendish notes resounds on the stifling atmosphere like the midnight cry of a panicky jungle cat. The prayer ended.

The congregation breaks into spontaneous song. Bodies swayed to left and right. Body touched body. A corporate thrill passes through the entire congregation.

Spontaneous song.

"Oh Lord, thy will be done.
Oh Lord, thy will be done.
Our Father which art in heaven,
Hallowed be thy name,
Thy kingdom come,
Thy will be done,
Oh Lord, thy will be done."

No one was more affected than Cudjo. The scoffer could not help himself. Emotion overcame reason. He laughed and shouted. Tears streamed from his eyes. He pranced in the air, slapping his thighs with the palms of his hands, while his lithe body bent and swayed to the rhythm of the songs. He sang with tears in his eyes and throat, as if his heart brimmed over with heavenly moisture. Like a drunken man he was reeling in an orgy of emotional rapture, drowning in a warm, rich, overwhelming flood of sensual experience.

An ominous grin spread over his entire countenance. Again his eyes seemed covered with mist. He scarcely knew where or who he was. Uneasiness crept over the members of the congregation who stood by him.

The preacher called for the candidates. Single file they marched through the passageway that led to the living water.

The first was a tender child of fifteen years. She tugged and fought with the leaders as they led her to the stream. Under the scathing sun energies soon fagged and good humors vanished. The preacher was sorely tried. He calling out constantly to the congregation to restrain their zeal. Finally he looked in the direction of Cudjo and screamed: "If any yo' niggahs cain't behave yo'se'ves hyeh, yuh kin git out right now . . . any you niggahs!"

Water off a duck's back. Cudjo clapped his hands and laughed the more.

Religious frenzy gave strength to the young candidate. It took two deacons and the preacher to immerse her. One took her by the arms while the other two each grasped a struggling ankle. For a moment, the congregation looked on in tense silence. The silence became a dumb shudder. Even the struggling girl, suspended in midair, looked on in dumb wonder as Cudjo rushed down through the surprised throng, and leaping over the ropes made as if to snatch her from the arms of her preceptors. The perspiration gleamed on his face. The muscles of his arms bulged as he tried to tear the girl from the grasp of the amazed preacher.

"You black debil," he shouted to the holy emissary, "you'se a sinner an' a hypocrite. Take yo' orn'ny hands f'um off'n her. De voice ob Gawd speakin' th'oo de clouds f'um he'b'n. Hyeah me, now, hyeah me. John de black Baptis', he hyeah now tellin' me to do all dis. Yo' all baptize wid water but ah baptize . . . " He got no further.

Pandemonium.

Cries of "Lawd Ha' mercy, oh Lawd, Gawd: Save us . . . . Save us, f'um dis debil!"

The candidate still hung suspended in midair, the preacher, two deacons, and Cudjo grasping some part of her. She had fainted and lay lifeless in their hands.

Mad fury swept over the congregation. The baptism was suddenly converted into a scene of near carnage.

"Kill him, kill him, kill the black fool," they all shouted.

Cudjo held on and laughed fiendishly. They swarmed around him and started to crush and pummel him. For a moment he was certain to be killed, but the saner preacher, recovering from his surprise, released the girl and rushed at Cudjo from behind. A dozen stalwart deacons came to his assistance. From the hysterical circle of women and children, flaying him with umbrellas and pelting him with missiles, the outraged deacons bore him clear through the throng out into the open.

Up the banks they ran dragging the interrupter with them. Finally they rushed behind a clump of tall bushes many yards from the scene of the baptism. Like an outcast devil they lifted Cudjo into the air and hurled him as far as they were able. Solemnly they watched him fall in a senseless heap. Then breathless and tired they made their way back to calm the awestruck candidates and to resume the baptism.

III

Agitato

Agitato appasionato

Smorzando et tranquillo

Cudjo landed in a thick patch of dry grass. The sudden impact stunned him but aside from painful bruises, he was none the worse for his wild adventure. The merciless rays of the sun beating down upon him seemed more cruel than the scourging crowd, and he crawled to the clump of bushes, grateful for some shade and shelter. There he sat on the hot grass nursing the muscles of his legs. Down by the river he could hear soft music crooned by the congregation, and the rhythmic tread of feet patting on the ground. Gradually the energy of youth returned. He laughed aloud. He looked at his bare feet, burned almost black by the sun; then at his soiled hands. He clapped them together and kicked his heels as high as his sore calves would permit.

He laughed aloud. He cried; he panted. He crooned to himself as if to soothe his torn soul; half speaking, half singing he consoled himself in words of self-pity and encouragement.

"What's matter, ol' Cudjo?" he said. "Cain't yo' all behave yo'se'f? Yo' all done raise 'nough hell fo' one day!"

The echoes of another song wafted over from the river. He heard the congregation crying and screaming, and listened to their stamping and moaning.

"Take mah Lawd away, Lawd away, Lawd away,
Take mah Lawd away,
Not a mumbelin' word did he say,
Nevah said a mumbelin' word.
Not a word,
Not a word,
Nevah said a mumbelin' word."

Music. Rhythm. Dancing.

Warm bodies swaying like tall sugar cane in an evening breeze. The earth seemed to be swaying beneath him. Unconsciously his own body commenced to sway. A tongue of flame shot from beneath a hidden soul-cloud and set his whole body on fire. Desire possessed his body. He felt an outpouring of white hot desire.

Like a starved beast of the forest who scents game Cudjo sprang erect and poised himself for the leap to the goal of his desire. Savage music tingled in his hot blood. His feet danced away to the mad strains and carried him on and on through the dry grass in long rapid strides.

Gum Ridge lay in the distance. Nearer and nearer his feet took him, then more than half way round, till he could see a cozy green cabin that lay sequestered beneath some maple trees.

Slackening his pace, Cudjo peered intently, while his heart thumped against his chest like angry waters against the shore . . . each thump was a song . . . each song a dance . . . and she who danced . . . was . . . Amber Lee.

Fires within and without.

Cudjo stooped down in some tall bushes that offered protection from the sun. He heard the swarming of insects. He knew they were singing songs to each other. He bent down and listened. And understood.

"I want you. I want you. I'm coming after you my honey. Coming after you and take you. Take you. Hear me my hones. I'm coming to take you. You. You. I'm going to wrap myself around you, all over you, take you, you my honey . . . . take my honey . . . your honey . . I . . . want you . . . I'm going to take you."

He waited for the answer.

"Come and take me. Come and take me. Take me. But you've got to catch me. I want you to take me. But you've got to catch me. Come and take me. Come take me. Come and wrap yourself all around me and over me and take me. Take my honey, come and take. . ."

So this was it!

Cudjo sprang to his feet. He wanted to rush out blindly—to seize her and carry her far off.

The blistering sun brought him back to some realization of earth. He gazed skyward and exclaimed: "Lawd, how come ah nevah know befo' dis? Lawd, ah wants her. Amber Lee dat's what been ailin' me. Lawd, ah wants her. An' Lawd ah gwine to tek her!

He looked in the direction of the cabin. It stood in a veritable forest of shade. At first sun blindness prevented him from seeing. He peered intently into the open space between the cabin and the trees that sheltered it. She was there. Amber Lee. Pale straw face brown. Sad face Amber Lee.

Luscious big brown eyes like swelling bays of tears. Pity. Sadness. Hunger. Warmth. Amber Lee. Two warm golden brown breasts soft like young bird's feathers, flaky, soft. Amber Lee. Pale straw face brown Amber Lee. Limbs full and graceful like apple boughs in spring.

Oh, oh, Amber Lee. Amber, Amber Lee. Why

did God make you so lovely so lovely down there under the tropical sun where hearts whose passions lie asleep wake overnight throbbing with hot desire—where new seed shoots when the old has scarcely taken root?

Cudjo watched her intently. He lay flat on his belly, hidden in the parched grass while the sun beat down upon him like a burning flail. He only felt a burning sensation from within.

His body was a drum; his heart was the drummer. The flames were passion-music.

And why, dear Cudjo, do you lie there on your belly and watch like a wild beast intent on seizing its prey? Is it not the one—your Amber Lee—the only one in fifty miles who ever understood you and your strange fancies and dreams? It is no new experience for you to hold her in your arms. Remember the day you rescued her from the lake? You have been her friend and playmate. You have done her chores for her. She has sat at your feet in the dark shadows of the night and listened to you as you told her your dreams and your fantasies.

Why then do you linger in the tall grass and let the relentless sun smite you while you only devour your treasure with your eyes?

Amber Lee.

Amber Lee feels no presence; she sees no person. She feels only herself, her budding self. It is warm, it is hot, it is smouldering. She is warm, she is hot, she is smouldering.

Her heart sings an inward song. She feels but she does not understand. What is this which thunders like a rumbling polonaise and marches through her tortuous limbs on up to the ruddy tips of her swelling breasts?

She hears the song of nature's creatures and feels its echoes quivering through her limbs and breasts.

"Come and take me. Come and take me. Me. But you've got to catch me. Got to catch me. Come and take me. Come and wrap yourself all around me. And over me and take me. Take my honey, come."

But she cannot understand—

The sun had passed beyond the last high curve in the vaulted heavens. Slowly it retreated into the distant west, the pale whiteness of noon absorbed in a vista that grew more and more rosy.

But Cudjo perceived only Amber Lee. Unnoticed were the softer rays of the receding sun, unnoticed the shade which steadily enveloped the fields where he lay hidden. The outer cool only intensified his inner heat. He lay in the grass like a panting beast, his mouth watering for the distant prey.

He could contain himself no longer. Like a tricky savage he quietly bestirred himself. Like a sneakthief in the night he stole his way towards her. The friend and playmate of Amber Lee, twin to her sorrows and longings, stole his way towards her, gliding through the tall grass and skirting the leafy trees like a sneakthief in the night.

Amber Lee.

Gradually she sensed him, sensed a presence. What was it? What was that rumbling through her limbs, her bosom, that quivering in her breasts? What did she want? Want? Want?

Before she knew, even before he could realize, she was in his arms—in Cudjo's warm perspiring brown arms that throbbed and quivered with passion. She looked into his eyes, ravenous flaming eyes that peered out at her as through a silken shade. A chill came over her as she saw those eyes; she became suddenly cold with fright.

She lay in his arms affrighted, like a startled fawn who after she has been pounced upon by a wild beast cowers in silence and stares with an icy stare. She perceived the message of those eyes: "I want you. I want you, you, you. I want you."

Her own which had been so soft and warm responded with terror. The starved beast has his prize. He feasts upon her with his eyes but as he sees her own stricken with terror he can find in them no answering warmth. He has her. She makes no outcry; she offers no resistance. She is his, all his. But she rests in his arms a poor quivering human leaf, her eyes melting into tears of terror and shame.

The fires that had leaped into bursting flame so suddenly, fled as precipitously back to the dark recesses from which they sprang.

Cudjo's eyes filled with tears. Tears of what? He stroked Amber Lee's face and hair gently. "Me, me," he whispered. "Gawd, Amber Lee, it's me. Yo' all know me. Cudjo, ah wouldn't hurta hair on yo' head. Amber Lee. Amber Lee, m' chile. It's me. Jes' want scare mah lil' Amber Lee, da's all. Lee. Amber, Amber Lee. Un'stan'? Jes' want scare mah lil' Amber Lee."

He placed her gently on the warm grass and did not even kiss her.

She sat upright and looked at him as through a cloud. Limbs quivering, mouth wide open she kept staring at him. All the warm music of her body had ceased; the song in her limbs and breasts had vanished. Once she felt a chill breath steal over her that might have been like death. She quivered.

"Cudjo, Cudjo, you only you. But it wasn't you at first. No, no Cudjo, not you. Only some fierce demon who looked at me with frightful eyes like Satan's. And you rescued me, didn't you Cudjo, just like you saved me in the lake! Oh, Cudjo," she exclaimed, and buried her head in her own bosom.

Cudjo looked down upon her in silence. Far in the west he saw a blood red sun retreating under banks of thick dark cloud. Gum Ridge waned in the distance, a thin shimmering light playing on her crest.

His own body was cool now. The flaming coals of high noon were reduced to barely flickering ashes. His eyelids closed. Without so much as a single look backwards he started towards the towering hill. It seemed far away.

Slowly he mounted its steep sides to the summit. A chill wind had commenced to blow; it was cool there.

He sat on a ledge which jutted out from the very topmost point of the hill and dropped tiny pebbles on the little huts below.

The sinking sun disappeared in the big hollow under the west.

Sugar Cain

By FRANK H. WILSON

Awarded First Prize—Play Section

Characters—Paul, Martha, Sugar Cain, Fred, Howard, Ora.

Scene—Room at the Cain Homestead, Waynesboro, Georgia.

Time—Present.

Curtain Rises Showing—Small room in an old-fashioned frame house, the wall hung with cheap wall paper, some of it hanging down in long strips. The wooden floor is covered with a torn, and dilapidated rug. In the center of the room stands a small wooden table covered with cheap oilcloth. An old oil lamp sits in the center of table, shedding a faint glow throughout the room, two hand-made wooden chairs sit at each end of the table. Back up against the wall center, is an old couch, with broken springs—hanging up on the wall are several religious pictures and mottoes—over on the left side is an old bureau, cheaply covered and with many trinkets and glasses upon it. Down left front is the door leading into the spare room. Up right rear are steps leading up stairs to the rooms above. Down right the door leads out through the kitchen to the back yard. At the foot of the stairs is a small window, with a broken pane of glass in it. Cheap curtains hang from the top of the window. The whole room gives the appearance of honest, but poor people. There is a small cuspidor down along side one of the chairs.

Pause

Sugar enters from spare room. She is a young dark brown skin girl about 23 years old, comely and well built. She closes the door quietly, as if not to disturb someone asleep therein, she then moodily crosses the room, and goes out through the kitchen door.

Paul comes down the stairs as Sugar is crossing the room. He is an old-fashioned Negro, about 62 years old, with grey beard, eyebrows and hair, walks and moves somewhat feeble from hard work. Watches Sugar as she crosses room and goes out through kitchen.

Martha enters from kitchen, wiping her hands on her old apron. (She is a small dark complexioned old lady of about 55 years, with kindly face and disposition.)

MARTHA—Wat yer want Paul?

PAUL—What's de matter wid Sugar?

MARTHA (coming in)—I don aknow, why?

PAUL—She's bin actin mouty funny dese las few days.

MARTHA—Funny—how?

PAUL—Well she's walkin roun hear lak she's in a trance.

MARTHA—Mebbe she's think bout dat Howard Hill.

PAUL (Angrily coming down from stairs)—Doan mention dat black guard's name in mah house. I tole yer'.

MARTHA—Oh, Paul, scuse me. I fergot yo ain't go no use fer him.

PAUL (coming down)—Ain't got no use fer him, nor fer anny buddy fum up North (pause). Dat's wot's de matter wid Sugar. Dat's why she's havin dem quiet spells, case she's worried bout her troubles (going over to chair left of table). All comes o' yo' lettin dat Northern nigger stay hyer. I tole yo I didn't want him in de furst place.

MARTHA (pleadingly—Oh, Paul, please doan go over all dat agin. I admit it was mah mistake, wot mo kin ah do?

PAUL (sitting in chair)—I know, but it makes me mad ebery time I think of it.

MARTHA (timidly)—Goin' ter church ter-night?

PAUL (taking out his pipe)—No.

MARTHA—Why, not?

PAUL—Case I don't feel lak it.

MARTHA—Ye ought ter go ter church mo, Paul. Mebbe yo'd feel better.

PAUL—Feel better nothin. Think I'd go down there among dem ole gossippy an back biten brothers, dey done scandelize our name all over de town.

MARTHA—No dey didn't.

PAUL (lighting his pipe)—Doan tell me ooman. De minnit dat Hill boy started stoppin hyer dey started talkin, en wen he lef an dey heard about Sugar's baby, de talked fer sho den. (*Pause.*) I wish yo had taken mah advice an not let him stay hyer. But you so hard headed. Wouldn't lissen ter me.

MARTHA—Sugar says twarnt him.

PAUL—Sugar lies, who else could it be?

MARTHA (her feelings hurt, goes back into the kitchen).

PAUL (turns, sees that Martha has walked out on him spits in cuspidor and grunts)—Humph.

FRED (enters from kitchen—he is husky young Negro, about 24 years old. He is dressed in soft blue shirt, open at the throat, blue overalls, tan shoes and black felt hat)—Hello, Pop.

PAUL (grunts)—Umph.

FRED (coming in)—Jist met our fren—Lee Drayton.

PAUL—Whar?

FRED—Goin' down de road towards his house, gwine ter pay his mother her usual weekly wisit I reckon. (Pause.) He goes away some time and stays months.

PAUL—I reckon Miss Mary generally knows whar he is.

FRED—No, she don't.

PAUL—How you know?

FRED—She tole me so her sef, she did an'——— (Paul grunts and continues to smoke his pipe.)

FRED—It's queer ter me how a good woman lak Miss Mary kin have sich a son.

PAUL (spits again)—Yo des doan understan him—dat's all.

FRED—Ha ahm goin ter understan him, wen his own mother don't?

PAUL—De boys wile lake all yo youngsters.

FRED—He's mo den wile.

PAUL—I know he's a lil ruff and gruff in his talk.

FRED—An actions.

PAUL—But wot kin yer spec. His ole man befo him was dat away. He ain't no wurse den any of de res ob dese white folks down hyer.

FRED—Oh, yes he is, Pop. Dere's some fine white folks down hyer I know. But Lee Drayton ain't one of em.

PAUL (spits disgustedly)—He may not be alright ter people lak dat Hill boy fum up North—who doan know ha ter act wen he gits in dis part ob de country, but ter we folks down hyer who understans dese white folks—Lee Drayton is alright. (Puffs on his pipe.)

FRED (looks at Paul for a minute)—Pop, yo puts too much faith in dese white folks.
Paul gives him an angry look.

FRED (taking a seat)—Yo's too willin ter believe eberything dey say. Yo seems ter have mo faith in dem den you hab in God.

PAUL (quickly and angrily)—Wot if I has?

FRED—Yer ought ter believe a lil mo in you own race—git a lil mo race pride.

PAUL (spits angrily)—Whard yo git all dat foolishness, fum dat northern nigger—Hill, I reckon.

FRED—No, pop, I didn't git it fum nobody, but since I bin gitten a lil older Ahm trying ter think fer ma sef, these white folks bin thinking fer me long enuf.

PAUL—Yes, and if dey hadn't bin thinkin fer yo, whar would yo be now — running round in Africa half naked, an yo wouldn't knowed B fum Bull frog. (Pause.) Who's got everything down hyer—white folks, ain day?

FRED (reluctantly)—Yes.

PAUL—An who's got nothin'—we has, ain't we?

FRED (shakes his head yes).

PAUL—Alright—now we wants what de white man's got—or some of it.

FRED (quickly)—We wants our share.

PAUL (settling himself back n chair)—Well, ha yo goin ter git it? Take it away fum him, I specs?

FRED (fails to find an answer to this question).

PAUL (spits)—Yo upstart youngsters know so-o-o much an we ole folks dat libed fer years among dese people doan know nothin. (Pause.) If a man's goin ter fight yo and he's gotta gun, and yo ain't got nothin—what you goin ter do?

FRED (quickly)—Fight him.

PAUL—An git killed, dat's wot de Indians done wen de white man come ter dis country—fought him—dat's the reason Indians are so scarce now days.

FRED (anxiously)—But de respec him mo fo it.

PAUL (impatiently)—I ain't lookin fer no respec. (Pause.) I'm lookin fer sumphin dat going ter feed me an my family. (Pause.) Dis house hyer whar yo an Sugar was born an raised—it's mine, ain't it?

FRED (quietly)—Yes, sir.

PAUL—It may not be no palace, but it's MINE jist de same. (Points out window.) So is dat patch ob farmland out dere—all mine. How you reckon I got it, by fightin dese white folks down hyer. Humph—I guess not.

FRED—But dey thinks dey better den we are, Pop.

PAUL (in exasperation)—Wot if dey does. It ain't going ter hurt em ter think is it? (Pointing his pipe at him.) As long as I can fool dese white folks outer dere money an land, by lettin feel dat deys better dan I am, dat's wot ahm goin ter do. (Spits.) Lissen, son—I got money an I got property. I could buy an sell some o dees white folks roun hyer—but I ain't goin ter let dem know it. I could fix dis shack up an live in grand style if I wanted to—but de minnit I did dat dese folks would git curious an wanter say dat I didn't know mah place, an dat I was tryin ter act lak white folks—fus thing you know I'd have a lot ob trouble on mah hans—an I couldn't stay hyer—so I fools em. Ah banks mah money, keeps mah mouth shut, an makes believe ahm a poor ole Nigger, and dat deys de cock o de walk. And I kin git dere shirt. I know em. An I didn't learn dat in no school neither. I ain't bin livin in de southlan all dese years fer nothin.

FRED—But, Pop, do you think dat's right ter—

PAUL (emphatically)—Yes, its right. Yo all talk bout race pride, you'd better get a lil race sense. Dese Niggers round hyer ain't got nothin ter give yo—nothin. (Imitating.) Niggers taik about "aw dey kaint do dat ter us—we kin do dis, and we kin do dat—Niggers kaint do nothin—NOTHIN." White folks got ebery thing—an ahm going ter git some of it.

FRED (rises dispondently, and goes up to window).

PAUL (takes a puff at his pipe)—Yo bin gittin all dese low down notions fum Hill.

FRED (turning quickly)—I ain't got no mo use fer Hill den you has.

PAUL (turning to him)—Stop lyin'.

Pause

FRED (looks at his dad for a minute, and then turns and looks out the window).

PAUL—I know wot yer bin doin, yo bin round town shootin off yo mouth dat you was gittin tired of de souf, dat you wuz goin up North ter live so yo could git a education. Whar else did you git dat but fum Hill.

FRED (looking down at Paul)—Well, I do think I could stand a lil mo learnin'—both me an Sugar.

PAUL (rising)—Well, if you wants learnin' yo'd better git it down hyer, case I ain't got nothin fer up North ter do. Dis is mah home, whar I wuz bred an born, an its whar I wants ter be buried wen I die—I doan care if I never see any buddy fum up North—and if I ever lays mah hans on dat skunk Hill—I'll kill him.

PAUL (stands glaring at Fred).

FRED (does not answer).

PAUL (exits into kitchen).

FRED (takes letter from his pocket, then looks at it).

MARTHA (enters from kitchen)—Fred, yo goin ter church wit me ter nite, ain't yer?

FRED (still looking at letter)—Yessem.

MARTHA—I kaint git yer father to go.

FRED—I wuz jist tellin Pop bout Lee Drayton.

MARTHA—Wots the matter wit him?

FRED—Pop says he's alright.

MARTHA (kindly)—A man wit sich a fine mother lak Miss Mary must hab some good in him. Yo know wot she say de odder day? She say, "Martha, I'm sick an kaint git about so good, an yo all mus come down an see me often. We's all brudders and sisters in de sight ob de Lord. We got ter live tergether in Heaven, so we mought well git used ter it down hyer on earth."

FRED—Yeh, I know Miss Mary's alright, but dat ain't her son.

MARTHA—Oh, he's des young.

FRED—Umph, de oney one dat seems ter think he's low down is me an Hill. (Shows Martha letter in his hand.)

MARTHA—Wot's dat?

FRED—Dat's a letter fum Hill.

MARTHA (surprised)—Howard Hill?

FRED—Yes, I got it yestiddy. He sent it ter me, sayin he wuz comin down hyer ter make a surprise visit, an ter see dat Sugar wuz home.

FRED—I bin holdin it secret, scared ter say anying, yo know how Pop is wid Hill.

MARTHA—Yes Lord, doan let him see dat—wen is he comin?

FRED—Ter day, I think. (Looks at letter). Yes, Sunday.

MARTHA—Mebbe he's comin back ter (hesitates) marry Sugar.

FRED—Do you know, Mom, I ought ter hate dat boy, but I don't.

MARTHA (looking apprehensively toward kitchen)—I lak him, Fred. (Lowers her voice.) He didn't do zactly right by Sugar wen he ran off dat away. But we all makes mistakes.

FRED—I lak him, cas he's got learnin. But I wonder why Sugar protects him?

MARTHA—Case she loves him.

FRED—Wot do you think bout it?

MARTHA—He's de father ob dat chile, alright. But Sugar's afraid ter ammit it, for fear I'll git down on him. She knows her dad's on to him already.

SUGAR (enters trom kitchen door).

MARTHA—Whar's you father?

SUGAR—Sitten out in de yard.

MARTHA—He's kinder cranky dis evening.

SUGAR—He's cranky every evening.

MARTHA—Fred, Son, get dressed fer church.

FRED—Yessem.

            Fred goes upstairs.

MARTHA (looks at Sugar a minute, then speaks) —Fred jist got a letter.

SUGAR—From who?

MARTHA—Howard Hill.

SUGAR (gives a slight start)—Wot does he say?

MARTHA—Fred said dat he wanted it kept fum yo'—but ah reckon I'd better tell you.

SUGAR—Wanted wot kept from me?

MARTHA—The fac dat he wuz comin down hyer.

SUGAR (greatly alarmed)—What?

MARTHA—Yes.

SUGAR—Wot's he comin down hyer fo'.

MARTHA—Ter see yo.

SUGAR (stands as if in a daze).

MARTHA—Ah frightened stiff. Yo father threatened ter kill him on sight, now wot are we gwine ter do?

SUGAR (as if in a daze)—Wen is he comin?

MARTHA—Ter day—or ter nite de letter said. (Calls.) Fred!

SUGAR (quickly)—Doan call him.

FRED—What is it, Mom?

SUGAR (in a whisper)—Doan call him.

MARTHA (looking at Sugar)—Ne'mine gettin ready fer church.

SUGAR—Wot shall I do?

MARTHA—Fergive him, Sugar. I'm sho he'll make you a fine husband.

SUGAR (almost to herself)—I wonder if he'll ever forgive me?

MARTHA—Fergive yo— yo ain't done nothin.

SUGAR—Yes I have.

MARTHA—Wot have yo done!

SUGAR (her voice choking with emotion)—I—I——

FRED (coming down stairs, dressed for church)—Ready for church, Mom?

MARTHA—Yes, an you had better come along, Sugar.

            (Fred goes to window and looks out.)

MARTHA—Whars Ora?

SUGAR (points to door left).

MARTHA—Asleep?

SUGAR—Yessem.

MARTHA—She'll sleep until we get back, come on.

SUGAR—I'm afraid dey church bell might frighten her. When it rings she always wakes up. I'm goin ter stay hyer.

FRED (to Martha)—Did yo tell her?

MARTHA—Yes—I thought it would make her feel kinder glad, but she's a giten scart.

SUGAR—Din yo say dat Pop wuz goin ter kill Howard if he came down hyer?

MARTHA—He'll be glad enuf ter see de man come back if he does de right thing.

SUGAR—I'm goin ter stay hyer an meet him.

FRED—Church time, Mom.

MARTHA—Well, if yo won't go ter church, I'm goin ter pray fer yo both. Yo and yo father's goin ter let people's tongues keep yo outer Heaven. (Starts for door.)

FRED—Goes out kitchen door.

SUGAR (quickly)—Mom.

MARTHA (stopping)—Wot's de matter?

SUGAR—Let Fred go ter church alone. I wanter talk ter ye.

MARTHA (yelling off to Fred)—Fred!

FRED (voice off)—Mam?

MARTHA—Go long ter church. I'll be there presently.

SUGAR (stands looking pitiously at Martha).

MARTHA (coming back)—Talk fas. I doan wanna miss dat Sermon.

SUGAR (goes over, puts her arms about Martha's neck and starts crying).

MARTHA (caressing her)—Wot is it, Sugar?

SUGAR—Howard's comin.

MARTHA—I know dat.

SUGAR (now holding down her head)—But there is something else ye don't know.

MARTHA (pointing towards room)—I know dat's his chile in dere.

SUGAR—No, Mom——

MARTHA—Wot?

SUGAR—Dat ain't his chile.

MARTHA—Yo still sticks ter dat story wen we knows different?

SUGAR—Yo de oney one I can trust, Mom. I've got ter tell yo dis.

MARTHA—Tell me de truf den, dat Howard Hill wuz de man.

SUGAR—No.

MARTHA—Ain't it enuf ter bring disgrace down on your poor ole mother and father?

SUGAR (goes over to chair, sits down and weeps).

MARTHA (her heart softening)—Who's de guilty one, Sugar? Tell me (goes over to her). I laked Howard, an I wuz willin ter stand fer dis, but fum no odder man livin. Tell me who de scamp wuz so I kin put him in jail.

SUGAR (without looking up)—Lee Drayton.

Pause.

MARTHA (stands as if petrified).

SUGAR (sits, afraid to move).

MARTHA—Wot's dat yo said bout Lee Drayton?

(*Continued on page* 201)

Sugar Cain

(*Continued from page* 184)

SUGAR (speaking slowly)—Lee Drayton is the father.

MARTHA (frightened)—Stop, Gal, shut yo mouth——

SUGAR—It's the truth, Mom.

MARTHA—How—wen did it——

SUGAR—Wen yo sent me down there with Miss Mary's clothes——

MARTHA (forcefully)—I doan believe it.

SUGAR—He would'n let me go. He would'n let let me go—he threatened the whole family in case I tole any buddy—he said he'd bring the clan down on us—I feared fer you, Pop an Fred—I did'n dare tell you the truth bout who it wuz.

MARTHA (sinks helplessly in chair)—If you had oney spoken en tole me——

SUGAR—I wuz afraid, I wanted ter tell you dat Howard wuz innocent, but you might question me too close, and fine out the truth——

MARTHA—What could we do——

SUGAR—Fred's so hot headed—Wot am I going ter do—Howards comin——

MARTHA (after thinking a minute)—I doan know—I'm goin ter church, an do the oney thing I kin do—Pray—Yo'd better come along wid us——

PAUL (enters from kitchen, goes toward stairs, stops and looks at them both)—Wot's the matter, you all ain't gwine ter church?

MARTHA—Yes—come on, Sugar.

SUGAR (shakes her head no).

PAUL (gives Sugar a curious glance, then goes upstairs, and off).

MARTHA (looks at Sugar—tries to speak, words failing her, she goes on out).

SUGAR (looks toward bedroom, apparently listening, then comes slowly down and sits in chair).
Pause.

HOWARD (peeks in through window, he looks about room until he spies Sugar, he then smiles and leaves the window quietly).

SUGAR (buries her head in her arms, leans on table and groans).

HOWARD (enters kitchen door quietly; he is a fine looking, well dressed young Negro, about 24 years old, speaks with a clean and pure diction)—He steals softly toward Sugar—his straw hat that accidentaly drops from his hand.

SUGAR (turns to him with a quick start).

HOWARD (stands looking at her, smiling).

SUGAR (rises from the chair and quickly backs around to the other side of the table).

HOWARD—Celia—I wanted to surprise you. I sent word to your brother, Fred.

SUGAR (stands with a frightened look, staring at him).

HOWARD (pause)—Noticing her actions. Aren't you glad to see me?

SUGAR (smiling sickly)—Yes, Howard——

HOWARD—You don't look it——

SUGAR (looks fearfully toward stairs)—Let's go outside (starts toward kitchen door).

HOWARD (unable to restrain himself, takes her in his arms)—Celia, my Celia Cain, called Sugar for Sweet, I told you I'd come back after I graduated. Three years is a long time—but I'm happy now. All I need is your mother and father's consent to our marriage.

SUGAR (struggles free from his grasp)—Please, Howard — don't — (staggers weakly back against table).

HOWARD (astonished)—Celia——

SUGAR (leans heavily against table).
(Church bell is heard tolling nearby.)

SUGAR (a look of fear coming to her face, stares at bedroom).

HOWARD (stands non-plussed).

ORA (voice heard off in bedroom)—"Ma, Ma" —"Ma, Ma."

HOWARD (looks toward bedroom door).

ORA (enters quickly in her night dress; she is a little brown baby, about 2 years old)—"Ma, Ma"—I fraid—(runs to Sugar, holding up her arms to be taken up.)

HOWARD (looks from Sugar to Ora).

SUGAR (frightened, holds baby close to her side).

HOWARD—Who—who is this——

SUGAR (struggling to suppress her emotions, picks Ora up in her arms)—My baby.

HOWARD (stands dazed at this confession).
Pause.

PAUL (comes quietly downstairs—sees Howard— a look of intense hatred comes to his face, his eyes riveted on Howard, he goes stealthily upstairs again).

HOWARD—You—tell me this is your child?

PAUL (comes downstairs quickly, looking at Howard, he has a loaded shot gun in his hand— Yo dirty Varmit (points gun at Howard).

SUGAR (screams and rushes in between them holding Ora in her arms).

PAUL (angrily)—Git one side Gal till I blow this snake ter hell——

SUGAR—No Pop.

PAUL (coming down with gun raised—One side I tell you, you and his brat.

HOWARD (steps out from behind Sugar).

SUGAR (quickly jumps in front of him)—No Pop, you wrong, this aint his, it's Lee Drayton——

PAUL—Wot?——

HOWARD (looks at her at the name of Lee Drayton).

SUGAR—Ora is Lee Drayton's child.

PAUL—Ye lie gal—What are yer tryin' ter do, save him—Come out fum behind there Nigger.

HOWARD—Mr. Cain——

PAUL—Mister nothin'—Sugar move I tell yer.

SUGAR (pleading)—No, Pop—it wuz Lee Drayton I tell yo——

HOWARD (to Sugar)—Do you mean to tell me that this is—is—(points at Ora).

SUGAR—Yes, Howard, I——

HOWARD—I'll get him—(darts quickly out of room).

SUGAR (calling after him)—Howard.

PAUL—Runnin' away, eh—Well, I'll git him fo he gits outer town—

SUGAR—Pop——

PAUL (angrily)—Git outer ma sight, fo I does yo bof harm, yo an Ora—

SUGAR (crying puts Ora in the bed room, fearing Paul in his frenzy might harm them—she locks the door taking the key herself).

PAUL—It aint enuf fer yo ter disgrace me wid dat kid—but yo got dat nigger hangin roun hyer—well, he'll never go north again—I'll— (A shot is heard off toward Drayton's house).

SUGAR (screams)—Howard—Howard, Pop, he's innocent, he's bin killed!

PAUL (lowering his gun)—Hope he has—serves him right—mebbe Fred got him.

HOWARD (enters kitchen door, all out of breath, with a revolver in his hand)—I got him!

PAUL (turning toward Howard)—What?

SUGAR (quickly wrenches gun from Paul).

PAUL—Gimme dat gun gal——.

SUGAR (running toward stairs)—No!

PAUL (comes back to Howard)—Yer got who?

HOWARD—Lee Drayton!

SUGAR and PAUL—Lee Drayton?

HOWARD—Yes—I met him just as he was coming out of the house, he knew I was after him, for the minute he saw me he drew his gun and fired but missed—

SUGAR (prayerfully)—Thank God!

HOWARD—I closed in on him before he could fire again, and we grappled. In the struggle we both fell, he was underneath, his head struck a large rock, he lay motionless. (Quietly) God Almighty placed that rock there to save me from being a murderer.

PAUL—Yo mean ter tell me yo killed Lee Drayton?

HOWARD (starts to speak).

(There is a loud roar from the direction of Drayton's house, of many excited yells, and roars—shouts, and murmurs.)

SUGAR (frenzidly)—There comin' Pop, the mob they are comin' after us—(comes down from stairs.)

PAUL—Gimme mah gun——

HOWARD—Don't give it to him—until I find out why he threatens me.

SUGAR—It's my fault——

(Voices seem to be getting nearer.)

HOWARD (listening)—Mr. Cain, this mob's coming down here after me—and I'm going to fight, are you fighting with me, or against me?

PAUL (angrily)—I'm against yo tooth and toe nail, this gal's lyin ter perteck yo, dats all. She can't fool me—I opened mah door ter yo before, and yo done me dirt—an now yer done come down hyer, an stirred up dese white folks—Git outer mah house!

HOWARD (tensely)—You try and put me out—

PAUL (turning angrily to Sugar)—Gimme dat gun I tole yer.

SUGAR (runs up and throws shot gun out of the window, breaking the glass and tearing down the curtain in doing so—)

PAUL (in a rage)—Yo impudent hussy—— (Noise of crowd is still heard much louder.) (A red glow shines in through the broken window.)

PAUL (rushes up to window to look for gun, sees the reflection of the glow, and looks down towards Drayton's house)—Fire!

SUGAR and HOWARD (look up at window bewildered).

PAUL (still looking out window)—Fire—it's Miss Mary's house.

SUGAR (in alarm)—Miss Mary!

PAUL (looking at Howard)—Yo done this.

MARTHA (comes in hastily)—Paul! Paul!—Miss Mary's house is on fire.

PAUL—I know it——

MARTHA—Fred's gone town ter save Miss Mary——

PAUL and SUGAR—Wot?

MARTHA—We saw the glow fum de church. Fred rushed on down there (crying, crying). Oh, poor Miss Mary, wot can we do?

SUGAR—They'll kill him.

MARTHA—Kill who?

SUGAR—Fred.

MARTHA (looks bewildered).

PAUL (pointing at Howard)—This man killed Lee Drayton.

MARTHA—Good, he——

PAUL (surprised)—Wot——?

FRED (voice off)—Mom! Mom!

SUGAR (somewhat relieved at his voice)—It's Fred——

MARTHA (turns toward door).

FRED (rushes in, his clothes slightly burned, his face scorched, and his hand cut)—Miss Mary's safe—She wasn't hurt a bit—des a lil frightened, some of the folks are teken her to de hospital in dere machines.

MARTHA (sees his hand)—Fred—son, yo's hurt——

FRED—Just a lil cut ah got while smashin' mah way frew de back winder.

HOWARD—What about the mob?

FRED (looking at Howard for the first time)—Oh, hello Hill——

HOWARD—Where's the mob?

FRED—Wot mob?

HOWARD—Wasn't there a gang coming down this way?

FRED (sits in chair)—No——

PAUL—Wot wuz all dat noise?

FRED—Dat wuz de crowd cheerin' when I saved Miss Mary——

PAUL, SUGAR and HOWARD (breath a sigh of relief).

FRED—All I fergot ter tell yer, Lee Drayton is dead——

PAUL—Yes—dis man——(points at Howard—)

FRED—Dey des dragged his body fum de fire.

SUGAR—What——?

FRED—Almos' burned ter a crisp.

MARTHA (in horror)—Oh! dis blow will kill Miss Mary——

HOWARD—Did you say they dragged Lee Drayton's body from the house?

FRED—Yes, saw it wid mah own eyes.

SUGAR—Yo said he fell in de yard, Howard.

HOWARD (speaking to Fred)—I guess he was only stunned; when he fell in the yard, he came to, saw the fire, and rushed in to save his mother—

MARTHA—An wen he got in de house, God punished him fer his sins.

PAUL—Wot sins?

MARTHA—His sins—gainst yo, an me—an Sugar.

PAUL—Den yo believe that he——

MARTHA—Yes—I believe mah Sugar all de time.

FRED—Gee, dis han hurts—must ter burnt me mo den I fought.

MARTHA—Come on in de kitchen, Fred, till I put somfin on it (exits into kitchen).

FRED (rising)—Do yo know, folks, ah feels lak ah done sumfin, savin Miss Mary today— She's a woman wurth savin—(goes out into kitchen).

Pause.

PAUL (goes up by window, and stands looking out in a depressed manner).

HOWARD (stands down right, looking into space, thinking deeply).

SUGAR (stands, looking doubtfully at Howard).

HOWARD (picks up his hat from the floor).

SUGAR (turns her head slowly, sees Paul, goes up to him, weakly lays her hand on his shoulder).

PAUL (without even looking at her, goes dejectedly up stairs).

SUGAR (wavers for a minute by the window, hardly able to stand, and then falls limply on the stairs, sobbing and crying).

Pause.

HOWARD (stands thinking deeply, hearing Sugar's sobs, he turns, looks at her for a minute, then walks up slowly looking down at her, his heart softens. He kneels down beside her, lifts her gently up, and holds her to his bosom, as she sobs and crys broken heartedly).

(The church bell tolls dismally.)

Pause.

(Ora's baby is heard behind the bedroom door crying and beating her little hands upon the door.)

HOWARD (looks toward the door, hearing the child's voice).

(As Howard is looking toward door, Sugar reaches up appealingly, and puts her arms about his neck——.)

HOWARD (turns tearfully to Sugar and holds her to his bosom, as——)

The Curtain Falls.

Northboun'

By Lucy Ariel Williams

Awarded One-half of First and Second Prizes—Poetry Section

O' de wurl' ain't flat,
An' de wurl' ain't roun',
H'its one long strip
Hangin' up an' down—
Jes' Souf an' Norf;
Jes' Norf an' Souf.

O' de wurl' ain't flat,
An' de wurl' ain't roun',
H'its one long strip
Hangin' up an' down—
Jes' Souf an' Norf;
Jes' Norf an' Souf.

Talkin' 'bout sailin' 'roun' de wurl'—
Huh! I'd be so dizzy my head 'ud twurl.
If dis heah earf wuz jes' a ball
You no the people all 'ud fall.

Talkin' 'bout the City whut Saint John saw—
Chile you oughta go to Saginaw;
A nigger's chance is "finest kind,"
An' pretty gals ain't hard to find.

Huh! de wurl' ain't flat
An' de wurl' ain't roun'
Jes' one long strip
Hangin' up an' down.
Since Norf is up,
An' Souf is down,
An' Hebben is up,
I'm upward boun'.

The Kingdom of Art

By John Macy

(Remarks at the Opening of the Opportunity *Awards Meeting by the Chairman)*

Your chairman will detain you only a few minutes, because the imps of influenza have their red-hot pincers on his larynx. So he will promptly pass the buck of oratory to other speakers vocally if not intellectually more competent. It is the duty and privilege of a chairman to rap the intellectual tuning-fork and set the pitch for the evening. Our note tonight will be one of joy, for we are gathered in the name of literature and the other arts. We have no artificial stimulant and we need none. The liquor we drink is the water of the Pierian spring, the fountain of everlasting youth, over which Mr. Volstead and Mr. Wheeler have no control.

Our interest tonight is literature. Literature teaches us, if it teaches anything, to view all the facts of life, and to view them in their true relations, in their proper proportions, with the right emphasis. Let our emphasis be right. We rejoice because *good work* has been done, not that good work has been done by *Negroes*. It is the beauty of the poem that counts, not the fact that it was written by a Negro. I don't want to hear about Roland Hayes, the Negro tenor. The man whose singing charms and thrills us is Roland Hayes, the *tenor*. We must all be individual or we are nothing, but even the youngest poet among you with the egotism and ambition of authorship will learn to value the thing created rather than the person who creates.

We who try to express ourselves belong to a great freemasonry which knows nothing of color, race, and creed, except the cult of beauty and wisdom. It is composed of men and women all over the world, whose language we cannot perhaps understand but whose spirit is akin to ours. It is the most democratic and the most aristocratic society in the world. Title to membership is ability to express something beautiful or wise. And since we are not all gifted with the power to express, there is an associate order of lay brothers composed of those who love and appreciate the expression of others, who are held together by what Tolstoy found to be the essential of all art, the contagion that unites beholders and creators.

Now in apparent, but not essential contradiction to that universality of art, there is this important consideration. We must write intensely of ourselves and our race. In looking over these manuscripts I was struck not only by their literary excellence, but by their frankness, their honesty, their sincerity. The writers took themselves for granted as Negroes, stood up on their own hind legs and said what they had to say and let it go at that. No affectation, no striving after artificial effect. The prevailing attitude was neither apologetic nor hostile but simply self-respecting. All artists in the world must express intensely their race, nation, time, family, personality. This is true of all people who try to be

artists. My learned friend, Dr. Stuart Sherman, and I may imagine ourselves, if the fancy please us, a couple of cute little cherubim sitting on the edge of the moon. We are in fact New England or Middle Western Yankees, and we are fore-doomed to the end of our days to write as Yankees. We cannot write like Russian novelists or French poets. If we try, we shall make a sorry fizzle of it, an even worse fizzle than we sometimes make trying to write as well as we can as Yankees. Every man to his own racial and individual nature and belief and mother tongue. I find myself at variance with two lines in a poem by Countee Cullen, in that perplexed challenge to God. The concluding lines seem to me the only false note in all Mr. Cullen's beautiful work:

Yet do I marvel at this curious thing,
To make a poet black and bid him sing.

Well, why not? What is curious about it? We do not write verses with our skin or sing with our hair. Art belongs to everybody who can make it and enjoy it.

At every gathering of people assembled in the name of literature there is one noble anecdote which ought to be told. In 1870 the German armies were hammering at the walls of Paris. The great French scholar, Gaston Paris, went serenely on with his lectures at the College de France. Some of his pupils were boys who had been wounded and being no longer useful as soldiers were permitted to be students. Gaston Paris had a great respect for the German philologists, and then, as in the war through which we have recently come, German scholarship was discredited because it was German. Gaston Paris made a confession of faith which runs something like this:

"I profess absolutely that common studies pursued with a common purpose make a community of interest above all consideration of race, nation, yes, even religion and morality. These studies form, above restricted, diverse and hostile nationalities, a great country which no war can defile, no conqueror threaten, where souls find the refuge and unity afforded in the old religious times by the *Civitas Dei* of St. Augustine, the City of God."

So, sisters and brothers, though our bodies may be condemned to the earthly perdition of living in Mississippi or New Jersey, our souls and intelligences can live in the city of God, where the muses dwell, and where there are angles of light and song, where God's favorite children have wings. From the wings of the angles a few small but genuine feathers have descended upon this country.

The Awards Dinner

THE Awards Dinner of OPPORTUNITY's Second Contest was held at the Fifth Avenue Restaurant on May 1st. There were four hundred persons present, among whom were: Stuart Sherman, Fannie Hurst, Dr. Blanche Colton Williams, Clement Wood, John Macy, Nathaniel Dett, Gloria Goddard, Mr. and Mrs. Henry Goddard Leach, Jessie Fauset, Emmett Scott, Mr. and Mrs. Walter F. White, Fania Marinoff, Jean Toomer, Prof. Leon Whipple, Mary White Ovington, Dr. and Mrs. Arthur B. Spingarn, Mrs. Joel Spingarn, Mr. and Mrs. Gorham B. Munson, Frederick Allen, Carl Van Vechten, Harry Bloch, Albert Boni, Walter Drey, L. Hollingsworth Wood and Dr. Alain Locke, and many other white and Negro persons interested in letters and in the younger Negro writers whom, to mention, would require more space than we have. They included visitors from Boston, Philadelphia, Baltimore, Washington, and even as far west as Columbus, Ohio.

The meeting was formally opened by Charles S. Johnson, Editor of OPPORTUNITY, and after brief remarks on the general character of the entries, their volume, the spirit of the aspiring contestants and their well wishes, turned the meeting over to the presiding officer selected for the occasion, Mr. John Macy, author of *The Spirit of American Literature* and of the more recent volume, *The Story of the World's Literature*. His address, because of its great beauty and sincerity, is carried in full in this issue.

There were eight sections of the contest comprising the Casper Holstein Awards, each section announcing the awards through its chairman. Dr. Blanche Colton Williams, author of several books on the short story, head of the English Department at Hunter College and a professor of the short story at Columbia University, spoke for short stories. Clement Wood, poet and poetry critic, commented on trends in literature in general and on poetry. Paul Robeson spoke for the plays, Nathaniel Dett for the music, Eugene Kinckle Jones for the personal experience sketches and Henry Goddard Leach for essays. There was a new section this year for prizes for constructive journalism, sponsored by the Empire State Federation of Colored Women's Clubs. Mr. L. Hollingsworth Wood announced the awards for editorials, and Mr. Emmett Scott spoke for feature stories.

The Bordentown Chorus of twenty voices sang about eight Negro spirituals. This group has been trained under the direction of Frederick Work, an outstanding collector of Negro folk songs, and had come eighty miles to appear on the program. Their music served well to enliven the evening and to join, pleasantly, the maturer contributions of Negro music to the beginnings of a new contribution in letters.

277

LUCY ARIEL WILLIAMS   WARING CUNEY   F. H. WILSON   ARNA BONTEMPS

Our Prize Winners and What

LUCY ARIEL WILLIAMS (Awarded one-half of first and second prizes for poem *Northboun'*)—Has achieved an enviable reputation at both Talladega and Fisk for her versatility. She is quite well known as a modiste, poet and a very talented pianist. She has been heard over the radio from Nashville several times this year, each time giving pleasing performances. Her interest in poetry is innate, as her father is an excellent writer of prose and verse.

WARING CUNEY—Whose pseudonym "Ford Kramer" was awarded one-half of first and second prizes for poem *No Images*—Born May 6, 1906, at Washington, D. C.; a graduate of Armstrong High School; at present a student at Lincoln University, Pa.

MILES MARK FISHER—Awarded second prize for essay *Modernism and the Negro Church*.

HALL JOHNSON—Awarded third prize for musical composition *Way Up in Heaven*.

F. H. WILSON—Awarded first prize for play *Sugar Cain*—Born in New York, has spent 12 years in vaudeville as organizer and baritone singer in "The Carolina Comedy Four"; as lead at the Bramhall Playhouse in Butler Davenport's "Justice"; created Joe in Eugene O'Neill's "All God's Chillun Got Wings"; supported both Paul Robeson and Charles Gilpin in "The Emperor Jones"; played the name part in O'Neill's "The Dreamy Kid," and others. Has written sixteen one-act playlets and four three-act plays; has produced eleven of the playlets and one play. Was three years writing "Sugar Cain."

ARNA BONTEMPS (Awarded Alexander Pushkin poetry prize for *Golgotha Is a Mountain*)—As my name indicates, I was born in Louisiana (Alexandria). That was in 1902, and in about three years my parents carried me to California, where I lived until September, 1924. Attended public and private grammar schools in Los Angeles and Glendale; high school at San Fernando; college at University of California (Southern Branch), and Pacific Union College where I received the degree of B.A. in 1923 (with honors—as they say of all students who pass without difficulty). For one season I earned my salt, ice cream, etc., singing with a male quartet, then came to New York where ever since I have taught in the small private school, Harlem Academy. I can think of nothing remarkable to point to—that is, nothing that would do to tell, still I think that I have had a most interesting and unusual life.

ANITA SCOTT COLEMAN—Awarded second prize for personal experience sketch *The Dark Horse*—Place of birth, Guaymas, Mexico; attended school in Silver City; an ex-school teacher; am married; live on a ranch; engaged in raising children and chickens.

WARREN A. McDONALD—Awarded third prize for play *Blood*—As yet I have not accomplished enough to furnish material for even a brief sketch. I am one of those people who do not have any good excuse or reason for scribbling—but who insist upon doing it.

ARTHUR HUFF FAUSET (Awarded first prize for short story *Symphonesque* and first prize for essay *Segregation*)—A Philadelphian, but by accident born in Flemington, N. J. This accident and my failure to make Phi Beta Kappa are my only two great regrets in life.

Achievements—I feel that I have not achieved anything up to the present, and least of all in literature where I have always hoped to make my greatest contribution. "Symphonesque" marked the first milestone in

MILES MARK FISHER   HALL JOHNSON   ANITA SCOTT COLEMAN   WARREN McDONALD

ARTHUR HUFF FAUSET   EDMUND JENKINS   JOHN MATHEUS   WILLIAM KELLY

They Say of Themselves

my literary march, for when I had written that I felt for the first time in my life that I had written something that was truly stirring and from a literary standpoint approaching the beautiful. However, no one realizes more keenly than I how infinitely superior must be the work of those artists who contribute the prize stories of a year or so from now. My heart goes out to the men and women who did not "come through" this year, and I wish simply to say that none should feel discouraged or give up hope of arriving ultimately; for my own meager successes have come only after most bitter experience with the terrible dragons of discouragement, lack of faith, disappointment, and heartaches of every description.

EDMUND JENKINS—Awarded first and second prizes for musical compositions *African War Dance* and *Sonata in A Minor.*

DOROTHY WEST—Awarded one-half second prize for short story *The Typewriter*—As yet I have a simple biography. I was born in Boston—I can never remember the name of the street—eighteen years ago and educated in the public schools, for which, I must confess, I had no great fondness. To be conventional, my favorite author is Dostoevsky, my favorite pastime, the play. I am rather a reticent sort, but I am intensely interested in everything that goes on about me. I love to sit apart and read—as best I can—the souls of my neighbors. I do want here to thank the judges for their choice of "The Typewriter." I haven't written enough to call it my favorite story and, incidentally, it's my first. But I do like it awfully, and I hope your readers will, too. Heavens knows, I am terribly encouraged. I would like to say this likeness is a poor one. But it isn't.

BRENDA MORYCK—Awarded second prize for essay *A Man I Know*—If Someone else were given this task, the resulting account might contain a few lines of interest, but since it is I who must write about myself, I can only say—and not through spurious modesty either, but lest I laud myself too much, that babies are my hobby, writing is my avocation, and teaching my vocation. I have been writing since I was six years old, and have a stack of infantile efforts at story-writing. Writing is a tradition in our family. The Reverend Charles Ray, my great grandfather, was quite a distinguished man of letters. My grandfather was editor of a Boston paper from 1850-1860 and my mother writes. I love writing, and write most of the time just for fun, burdening my friends with unwieldy letters of from 16 to 80 pages. I was educated at home, at St. Vincent's Academy and Barringer High School of Newark, New Jersey, my native city and state, and Wellesley College. I am single—teach English in the Armstrong Technical High School of Washington, D. C.

JOHN MATHEUS—Awarded first prize for personal experience sketch *Sand,* and second prize for play *'Cruiter.*

WILLIAM KELLY—Editor of the *Amsterdam News,* awarded one-half of prize for editorial *On the Road to Sing Sing.*

EUGENE GORDON—Awarded fourth prize for short story *Rootbound.*

JOSEPH S. COTTER—Awarded third prize for poem *The Tragedy of Pete.*

DOROTHY WEST   BRENDA MORYCK   EUGENE GORDON   JOSEPH S. COTTER

IN announcing the Third Annual OPPORTUNITY Contest with the Holstein prizes for literary excellence, we affirm again the faith of this magazine, its supporters, and the donor **The Third Opportunity Contest** of the prizes in the soundness and very real progress of this movement for the artistic self-expression of Negroes. The stories and poetry which have appeared in these pages, and which, indeed, with surprising frequency, have been republished elsewhere, with the stamp of authoritative approval, stand as their own testimony of the strength of this new literary fermentation.

This year it will be the aim of the Contest, not merely to draw in for appraisal, the fugitive work of our scattered writers, but with deliberate care and the best suggestions possible to us, to guide these prodigal energies to the most promising sources of power. Some of the writers do not need this, as the successful entries, for the most part, showed. But in that large body of manuscripts which this year and last, failed to attain recognition, it is evident that a mine of material lies half buried. Our concern now is to stimulate a product that can in larger degree and volume stand without the need of apology; that need not at any point rely upon sheer exoticism for its acceptance. To an extent this is being accomplished in the more recent writing of negroes, and, of course, has been accomplished in the past by some of the emancipated masters of the craft. But a world yet remains to be conquered.

The major defects of our Negro writers, it will be interesting to note, find their exact counterpart in the efforts of the writing public in general. The editors of *Harper's Magazine,* commenting upon the results of its Intercollegiate Literary Contest have observations and advice which apply with equal force to the less impressive work of the Negro writers. And because these reveal weaknesses characteristic of immaturity in general, and thus cannot be construed by the sensitive ones as special advice for Negro writers, it seems appropriate to repeat them here. These editors complain that the stories, and articles received showed a tendency to deal with subjects remote from the personal experience of the writers; to imitate, not only the methods of certain well known authors but to attempt to reproduce the substance of these models; to write about people and conditions concerning which the writer had only second or third-hand evidence— about arch dukes and countesses, gangsters, old men facing death, etc., the result being usually a performance empty of significance. "Many of the contestants," to quote directly, "apparently had not grasped the fact that writing is a form of self-expression; that the promising writer is not he who merely avoids errors of grammar, punctuation, and arrangement, nor even he who is able to produce a respectable imitation of a masterpiece, but he who adapts his gift of language and of form to the presentation of something drawn from his own observation and experience."

Here is sound advice for Negro writers on their own possible contributions. In the re-discovery of the world of Negro life, which has its charm and poignant human qualities, and is, perhaps of all American life, least known, they have a definite advantage over all other Americans. They are best able to portray it for the world and for themselves. For it is their experience.

"Having been all my life a firm and enthusiastic believer in the creative genius of the Negro race, to which I humbly belong, OPPORTUNITY's Contest to foster literary expression among Negroes has been a source of abiding interest to me. I honestly believe that it will go far towards consolidating the interests of and bridging the gap between the black and white races in the United States today. And particularly will it encourage among our gifted youth the ambition to scale the empyrean heights of art and literature."

Casper Holstein

who has again donated $1,000 for the Holstein Prizes in the Third Annual OPPORTUNITY Contest for the fostering of creative literary expression among Negroes.

Opportunity's Third Annual Contest
for Negro Writers Offers
$1000.⁰⁰ in Prizes

—to stimulate and foster creative literary effort among Negroes; to uncover those hidden treasures of artistic materials in Negro life; to locate and aid in orienting Negro writers of ability; to stimulate and encourage interest in the serious development of a body of literature about Negro life.

The Holstein Prizes

Short Stories

First Prize	$100.00
Second Prize	50.00
Third Prize	25.00

$175.00

The stories must deal with some phase of Negro life, either directly or indirectly; otherwise there are no restrictions. They may be romantic, realistic, humorous, and each will be judged upon its quality as a good short story. These stories must not exceed 5,000 words.

Poetry

First Prize	$50.00
Second Prize	35.00
Third Prize	10.00
Fourth Prize	5.00

$100.00

The theme may be the Negro or it may be some national figure or event, some natural symbol, some product of nature; a mood or musings—anything at all, whether it relates to Negro life or thought or not.

Essays

First Prize	$50.00
Second Prize	30.00
Third Prize	10.00

$90.00

The object here is to bid for a much abused type of literary expression in the hope of finding some examples of recognizable literary merit. The contestants will strive for clarity of diction, forcefulness, and originality of ideas, logical structure, deft and effective employment of language, accuracy of data, and economy of words. The subject may be of the contestant's selection, but must relate directly or indirectly to Negro life and contacts, or situations in which Negroes have a conspicuous interest.
The essays are limited to 3,000 words.

Plays

First Prize	$60.00
Second Prize	35.00
Third Prize	15.00

$110.00

The plays must deal with some phase of Negro life, either directly or indirectly, otherwise, there are no restrictions. They may be romantic, realistic, humorous, and each will be judged upon its quality as a good play.

Personal Experience Sketches

First Prize	$30.00
Second Prize	20.00
Third Prize	10.00

$60.00

These sketches must be an actual experience and relate to some incident or situation or circumstance of personal life which makes it possible to understand how one feels and acts in the presence of a particular life problem. The contestant will strive for complete frankness and self-scrutiny, truthfulness, and clarity of expression.
These will be limited to 2,000 words.

Musical Compositions

First Prize	$75.00
Second Prize	50.00
Third Prize	25.00

$150.00

These must be original musical compositions for either instrument or voice. No restriction is placed upon the theme. All compositions must be written legibly in ink. No work will be eligible that has been published. Texts must be in English.

Alexander Pushkin Poetry Prize

AWARD OF $100.00

(a) *This section is expected to call forth the most ambitious and most mature work of the Negro poet, and it is requested that to this section only the best work be sent.*

(b) *The contest will be open to all Negro poets in this country or elsewhere.*

(c) *Poems must be original and unpublished, and not more than three may be entered by one poet.*

(d) *Poems must not exceed three hundred lines in length.*

(e) *Poems must be in English.*

(f) *Only one prize of $100.00 will be awarded, but honorable mention will be given to other ranking poems.*

General Rules

Entries submitted in this contest shall not be submitted the same year for prizes in any other Contest.

Any story, poem, play, essay, or personal experience sketch that has already been published is ineligible for this Contest.

The Contest opens October 1, 1926 and closes February 28, 1927.

This Contest reserves the right to reject all manuscripts in any division if the contributions are deemed below a reasonable standard of quality or insufficient in number.

Additional Prizes to be awarded will be announced in forthcoming issues of OPPORTUNITY.

thentic new voices, acknowledgment should be made
to Mr. Caspar Holstein, whose contribution of a
thousand dollars for this purpose made possible the
offers of awards; to the distinguished jury of writers
and critics who gave graciously and generously of
their time to these manuscripts; and to the other
friends and well-wishers of the new Negro generation whose stimulation has been even more potent
than the hope of monetary award.

T HE Awards in OPPORTUNITY'S Third Annual
     Contest for Negro Writers were made on
May 7th. More new writers of promise and some
                       measure of accomplishment strug-
The   gle to the surface through a vast
Contest   volume of manuscripts. The wide
                       geographical distribution of prize
                       winners points to the developing
interest in creative expression beyond the limits of
the recognized culture centers. This in itself is a useful and encouraging revelation. There is a rich variety, in theme and style; in most of the sections
there was improvement over previous years. There
is yet, however, some distance to go, and one obvious
shortcoming of too hasty work, in certain of the less
successful entries may be overcome by these writers
by beginning now on the careful preparations for
the next year.

The July issue of *Opportunity* will carry the first
group of successful contest entries. Our readers thus,
will have the opportunity to judge for themselves,
the character and thoroness of this "awakening", as
well as the efficacy of our efforts in this direction.

II.

The awards of prizes and honorable mention do
not wholly divide the good from the bad. They indicate an approach to agreement among the judges
on the essential elements in a good story or poem or
essay. They cannot always indicate the degree of
promise in manuscripts still lacking in correctable
faults of technique. This fact so manifest in this last
contest stimulated the offer by George W. Buckner,
a Negro business man of St. Louis, Missouri, of five
additional awards for *conspicuous promise*.

Beyond these is a group of manuscripts which
show a more than ordinary competence. While escaping selection from the group for mention, they
stand as sound evidence of the developing powers of
our young writers, and of the new horizons toward
which they are now plodding.

III.

For such as this latest contest has revealed in au-

Contest Awards

The winning manuscripts in the eight divisions of OP-PORTUNITY'S Third Literary Contest, as announced at the OPPORTUNITY dinner on May 7th, are as wollows:

HOLSTEIN PRIZES

THE SHORT STORY

First and second prizes of $100 and $50 divided be-tween *Game* by Eugene Gordon of Boston, Mass., and *The Flyer* by Cecil Blue of Charlotte, N. C.

For third place two awards of $25 each to *Buzzards* by Eugene Gordon, and to *The Overcoat* by John P. Davis of Cambridge.

Judges in the Short Story section: Theodore Dreiser, Novelist; Wilbur Daniel Steele, Short Story Writer; Eric Walrond, Author and Journalist; Zona Gale, Novelist and Playwright; Irita Van Doren, Editor of *Books* of the *New York Herald-Tribune* and Harry Hansen, critic.

POETRY

In the general section first prize of $50 to *When De Saints Go Ma'chin' Home* by Sterling A. Brown of Jef-ferson City, Mo.; second prize of $35 to *Summer Matures* by Helene Johnson of New York; third prize of $10 to *The Resurrection* by Jonathan H. Brooks of Lexington, Miss., and fourth prize of $5 to *Sonnet To a Negro In Harlem* by Helene Johnson.

Honorable Mention to: 1. *April Is On the Way* by Alice Dunbar Nelson of Wilmington, Del. 2. *Confes-sion* by Donald Jeffrey Hayes of Atlantic City, N. J. 3. *De Jail Blues Song* by Waring Cuney of Boston. 4. *A Garden Cycle* by Arna Bontemps of New York and *Youth* by Frank Horne of Brooklyn. 5 *Song Phantasy* by Dutton Waldonym of Washington, D. C. and *Revival* by John F. Matheus of Institute, West Virginia. 6. *Noc-turne of the Wharves* by Arna Bontemps.

In the Alexander Pushkin Section, the single award of $100 went to *The Return* by Arna Bontemps.

Honorable Mention to: 1. *I Thought It Was Tangiers* by Langston Hughes of Lincoln, Pa. 2. *The Dancer* by Donald Jeffrey Hayes of Atlantic City, N. J. and *A Tradi-tional Marching Song* by Waring Cuney of Boston, Mass. 3. *Dinah Dreams* by William H. A. Moore of Chicago, Ill.

Judges in the Poetry Section: Joseph Auslander, Poet and Critic; William Stanley Braithwaite, Poet and Anthol-ogist; Carl Sandburg, Poet, Biographer and Critic; Maxwell Bodenheim, Poet and Novelist; Ridgely Torrence, Poet, Playwright, and Poetry Editor of *The New Republic;* and Countee Cullen, Poet, and assistant editor of OPPOR-TUNITY.

ESSAYS.

First prize of $50 *Moving Pictures In An Old Song Shop* by Ted (pseudonym, identity as yet unrevealed), second prize of $30 to *On Race Equality* by James H. Young of Philadelphia, Pa.; third prize of $10 divided between *Concerning White People* by Frank Horne of New York and *The Plight of Certain Intellectuals* by Sterling A. Brown of Jefferson City, Mo.

Honorable Mention to: 1. *Teaching Negro History in Schools* by Willis Huggins of New York City. 2. *When A Negro Sings* by Brenda Moryck of Washington, D. C.

Judges in the Essay Section: Henry Goddard Leach, Editor of *The Forum;* Benjamin Brawley, Author and Professor of English at Shaw University; Christopher Morley, Author and Columnist.

PERSONAL EXPERIENCE SKETCHES

First and second awards divided into two prizes of $25 each to *Sasswood* by Mrs. Shadd Jones of Columbus, Ohio, and *Letters* by Idabelle Yeiser of Philadelphia, Pa. The third prize of $10 was divided between *I Am Initiated Into the Negro Race* by Frank Horne of Brooklyn and *Black* by Nellie Bright of Philadelphia, Pa.

Honorable Mention to: 1. *What's In a Name?* by Sid-ney Peterson of Brooklyn. 2. *The Enchanted Garden* by Ruth E. Bowles of Cincinnati, Ohio. 3. *Battlefields* by John Matheus of Institute, West Virginia.

Judges in the Personal Experience Sketch Section: Mary White Ovington, Author; Eugene Kinckle Jones, Executive Secretary of the National Urban League; and L. Hollingsworth Wood, Chairman of the National Urban League.

MUSICAL COMPOSITION

First prize of $50 for a composition of from two to six instruments to *Sonata* by Hall Johnson of New York; second prize of $25 to *Memories of Dixieland* by Mrs. Florence Price of Little Rock, Arkansas; a prize of $50 for a vocal composition for solo to *Fiyer* by Hall Johnson of New York; a prize of $50 for vocal composition for chorus to *Banjo Dance* by Hall Johnson of New York. The prize of $35 for a piano composition in smaller form was divided between *Concert Fugue* by Andrades Lind-say of Brooklyn, New York and *Intermezzo* by Tourgee Du Bose of Talladega, Alabama.

For the arrangement of Negro Spirituals and folk songs, the first prize of $40 went to *All I Want* by J. Bruce. A second award of 15 was given *Nobody Knows De Trouble I've Seen* by Ernest E. Peace of Washington, D. C.

Judges in the Music Section: William Grant Still, Com-poser; Olga Samaroff, Pianist and Music Critic, and Daniel Gregory Mason, Music Lecturer, Author and Composer.

PICTORIAL AWARDS

A first award of $75 to a drawing by Aaron Douglas of New York City; two second awards of $25 each to *November* by Allan Freelon of Philadelphia, Pa., and *Reservoir Road* by Antonio Jarvis of St. Thomas, Virgin Islands.

Honorable Mention to entries by Allan Freelon, Aaron Douglas and Richard Bruce.

Judges in the Art Section: Winold Reiss, Artist; Dr. Alain Locke, Author and Art Collector, and Miss Grace Hatheway, Art Editor of *The Survey.*

PLAYS

First prize of $60 to *Plumes* by Georgia Douglas John-son of Washington, D. C.; second prize of $25 to *The Hunch* by Eulalie Spence of Brooklyn, New York; third prize, of $15 divided between *Four Eleven* by William Jack-son of Montclair, New Jersey, and *The Starter* by Eulalie Spence.

Honorable Mention to *Bleeding Hearts* by Randolph Edmonds of Baltimore, Md.

Judges in the Play Section: Paul Green, Playwright and Professor of Philosophy at the University of North Caro-lina; Lula Vollmer, Playwright; Edith Isaacs, Editor of *Theatre Arts Monthly* and Paul Robeson, Actor and Con-cert Artist.

SPECIAL BUCKNER AWARDS

Through the generosity of George W. Buckner of St. Louis, Mo., *Opportunity* has been enabled to offer five prizes of ten dollars each to entries that showed con-spicuous promise. The awards are as follows: 1. To Blanche Taylor Dickinson of Sewickley, Pa. for her poem *A Sonnet and A Rondeau.* 2. To Dorothy West of New York City for her story *An Unimportant Man.* 3. To Emily May Harper of Nashville, Tenn. for her story *Ma Kilpatrick, Boss.* 4. To Frank Horne of Brooklyn, N. Y. for his essay *Concerning White People.* 5. To Sterling A. Brown of Jefferson City, Mo. for his essay *The Plight of Certain Intellectuals.*

The Return

By ARNA BONTEMPS

Awarded the Alexander Pushkin Prize

I

ONCE more, listening to the wind and rain,
　Once more, you and I, and above the hurting sound
Of these comes back the throbbing of remembered rain,
Treasured rain falling on dark ground.
Once more, huddling birds upon the leaves
And summer trembling on a withered vine.
And once more, returning out of pain,
The friendly ghost that was your love and mine.

II

THE throb of rain is the throb of muffled drums;
　Darkness brings the jungle to our room.
Darkness hangs our room with pendelums
Of vine and in the gathering gloom
Our walls recede into a denseness of
Surrounding trees.　This is a night of love
Retained from those lost nights our fathers slept
In huts; this is a night that cannot die.
Let us keep the dance of rain our fathers kept
And tread our dreams beneath the jungle sky.

III

THE downpour ceases.
　Let us go back, you and I, and dance
Once more upon the glimmering leaves
And as the throbbing of drums increases
Shake the grass and the dripping boughs of trees.
A dry wind stirs the palm; the old tree grieves.
Time has charged the years and they have returned.
Then let us dance by metal waters burned
With gold of moon, let us dance
With naked feet beneath the young spice trees.
What was that light, that radiance
On your face?—something I saw when first
You passed beneath the jungle tapestries?
A moment we pause to quench our thirst
Kneeling at the water's edge, the gleam
Upon your face is plain; you have wanted this.
Oh let us go back and search the tangled dream
And as the muffled drum-beats throb and miss
Remember again how early darkness comes
To dreams and silence to the drums.

IV

LET us go back into the dusk again,
　Slow and sad-like following the track
Of blown leaves and cool white rain
Into the old grey dreams; let us go back.
Our walls close about us, we lie and listen
To the noise of the street, the storm and the driven birds.
A question shapes your lips, your eyes glisten
Retaining tears, but there are no more words.

When De Saints Go Ma'ching Home

By Sterling A. Brown

Awarded First Prize—Holstein Poetry Section

(To Big Boy Davis, Friend) *In Memories of Days Before He Was Chased Out of Town for Vagrancy.*

1

HE'D play, after the bawdy songs and blues,
After the weary plaints
Of "Trouble, Trouble deep down in muh soul,"
Always one song in which he'd lose the role
Of entertainer to the boys. He'd say
"My mother's favorite." And we knew
That what was coming was his chant of saints
"When de Saints go ma'chin home . . ."
And that would end his concert for the day.

Carefully as an old maid over needlework,
Oh, as some black deacon, over his Bible, lovingly,
He'd tune up specially for this. There'd be
No chatter now, no patting of the feet.
After a few slow chords, knelling and sweet—
Oh when de saints go ma'chin home
Oh when de sayaints goa ma'chin home   . . .
He would forget
The quieted bunch, his dimming cigarette
Stuck into a splintered edge of the guitar.
Sorrow deep hidden in his voice, a far
And soft light in his strange brown eyes;
Alone with his masterchords, his memories . . .
Lawd I wanna be one in nummer
When de saints go ma'chin home.
Deep the bass would rumble while the treble scat-
tered high
For all the world like heavy feet a trompin' toward
the sky.
With shrillvoiced women getting 'happy'
All to celestial tunes.
The chap's few speeches helped me understand
The reason why he gazed so fixedly
Upon the burnished strings.
For he would see
A gorgeous procession to 'de Beulah Land'
Of Saints—his friends—'a climbin' fo' deir wings.'
Oh when de saints go ma'chin home
Lawd I wanna be one o' dat nummer
When de saints goa ma'chin home   . . .

THERE'D BE—so ran his dream
"Old Deacon Zachary
With de asthmy in his chest
A puffin' an' a wheezin'
Up de golden stair
Wid de badges of his lodges
Strung acrost his heavin' breast
An' de hoggrease jest shinin'
In his coal black hair   . . .

An' ole Sis Joe
In huh big straw hat
An' huh wrapper flappin'
Flappin' in de heavenly win'
An' huh thinsoled easy walkers

Goin' pitty pitty pat
Lawd she'd have to ease her corns
When she got in!"
Oh when de saints go ma'chin home.
"Ole Elder Peter Johnson
Wid his corncob jes a puffin'
And de smoke a rollin'
Like stormclouds out behin'
Crossin' de cloud mountains
Widout slowin' up fo' nuffin'
Steamin' up de grade
Lak Wes' bound No. 9.

An' de little brownskinned chillen
Wid deir skinny legs a dancin'
Jes' a kickin' up ridic'lous
To de heavenly band
Lookin' at de Great Drum Major
On a white hoss jes' a prancin'
Wid and gold and silver drumstick
A waggin' in his han'.
Oh when de sun refuse to shine
Oh when de mo-on goes down
     In Blood
"Old Maumee Annie
Wid huh washin' done
An' huh las' piece o' laundry
In de renchin' tub,
A wavin' sof' pink han's
To de much obligin' sun
An' her feet a moverin' now
To a swif' rub a dub;
And old Grampa Eli
Wid his wrinkled old haid
A puzzlin' over summut
He ain' understood
Intendin' to ask Peter
Pervidin' he ain't skyaid
'Jes what mought be de meanin'
     Of de moon in blood? . . .
Wen de saints go ma'chin home   . . .

3

WHUFFOLKS, *he dreams, will have to stay outside*
     Being so onery.' But what is he to do
With that red brakeman who once let him ride
An empty, going home? Or with that kindfaced man
Who paid his songs with board and drink and bed?
Or with the Yankee Cap'n who left a leg
At Vicksburg? *'Mought be a place, he said*
Mought be another mansion for' white saints
A smaller one than hisn'   . . . not so gran'
As for the rest   . . .   oh let them howl and beg.
Hell would be good enough, if big enough
Widout no shade trees, lawd, widout no rain
Whuffolks sho to bring nigger out behin'
Excep'—wen de saints go ma'chin home.

4.

Sportin' Legs would not be there—nor lucky Sam
Nor Smitty, nor Hambone, nor Hardrock Gene
An' not too many guzzlin', cuttin' shines
Nor bootleggers to keep his pockets clean.
An' Sophie wid de sof' smile on her face,
Her foolin' voice, her strappin' body, brown
Lak coffee doused wid milk—she had been good
To him, wid lovin', money and wid food.—
But saints and heaven didn't seem to fit
Jes rite wid Sophy's Beauty—nary bit—
She mought stir trouble, somehow, in dat peaceful
    place
Mought be some dressed up dudes in dat fair town.

5

He sees

I SE got a dear ole modder
She is in hebben I know

Mammy
L'il mammy—wrinkled face
Her brown eyes, quick to tears—to joy
With such happy pride in her
Guitar plunkin' boy.
Oh kain't I be one in nummer?

Mammy
With deep religion defeating the grief
Life piled so closely about her
Ise so glad trouble doan last 'alway'
And her dogged belief
That some fine day
She'd go a ma'chin
When de saints go ma'chin home.
He sees her ma'chin home, ma'chin along,
Her perky joy shining in her furrowed face,
Her weak and quavering voice singing her
    song—
The best chair set apart for her worn out body
In that restful place . . .
I pray to de Lawd I'll meet her
When de saints go ma'chin home.

6.

H E'D shuffle off from us, always, at that,—
His face a brown study beneath his torn
    brimmed hat
His broad shoulders slouching, his old box strung
Around his neck;—he'd go where we
Never could follow him—to Sophie probably,
Or to his dances-in old Tinbridge flat.

Summer Matures

By HELENE JOHNSON.

Awarded Second Prize—Holstein Poetry Section

Summer matures. Brilliant Scorpion
Appears. The pelican's thick pouch
Hangs heavily with perch and slugs.
The brilliant-bellied newt flashes
Its crimson crest in the white water.
In the lush meadow, by the river,
The yellow-freckled toad laughs
With a toothless gurgle at the white-necked stork
Standing asleep on one red reedy leg.
And here Pan dreams of slim stalks clean for piping,
And of a nightingale gone mad with freedom.
Come. I shall weave a bed of reeds
And willow limbs and pale night flowers.
I shall strip the roses of their petals,
And the white down from the swan's neck.
Come. Night is here. The air is drunk
With wild grape and sweet clover.
And by the sacred fount of Aganippe
Euterpe sings of love. Ah, the woodland creatures,
The doves in pairs, the wild sow and her shoats,
The stag searching the forest for a mate,
Know more of love than you, my callous Phaon.
The young moon is a curved white scimitar
Pierced through the swooning night.
Sweet Phaon. With Sappho sleep like the stars at
　　　dawn.
This night was born for love, my Phaon.
Come.

Plumes

A ONE ACT PLAY

By GEORGIA DOUGLAS JOHNSON

Awarded First Prize—Play Section.

CAST OF CHARACTERS

CHARITY BROWN .... The Mother
EMMERLINE BROWN .... The Daughter
TILDY .... The Friend
DR. SCOTT .... Physician

SCENE: *The kitchen of a two-room cottage. A window overlooking the street. A door leading to street, one leading to the back yard, and one to the inner room. A stove, a table with shelf over it, a wash tub. A rocking chair, a cane bottom chair. Needle, thread, scissors, etc., on table.*
A groaning is heard from the inner room. Scene opens with Charity Brown heating a poultice over the stove.

CHARITY—Yes, honey, mamma is fixing somethin' to do you good. Yes, my baby, jus' you wait— I'm a coming.
(*Knock is heard at door. It is gently pushed open and Tildy comes in cautiously.*)
TILDY (*whispering*)—How is she?
CHARITY—Poorly, poorly. Didn't rest last night none hardly. Move that dress and set in th' rocker. I been trying to snatch a minute to finish it but don't seem like I can.. She won't have nothing to wear if she—she——
TILDY—I understands. How near done is it?
CHARITY—Ain't so much more to do.
TILDY (*takes up dress from chair, looks at it*)—I'll do some on it.
CHARITY—Thank you, sister Tildy. Whip that torshon on and turn down the hem in the skirt.
TILDY (*measuring dress against herself*)—How deep?
CHARITY—Let me see now (*Studies a minute with finger against lip*)—I tell you—jus' baste it, cause, you see—she wears 'em short, but—it might be—— (*stops*)
TILDY (*bowing her head comprehendingly*)— Eughhu (*meaning yes*) I see exzackly (*sighs*) You'd want it long—over her feet—then.
CHARITY—That's it, sister Tildy. (*Listening*) She's some easy now. (*Stirring poultice*) Jest can't get this poltis hot enough somehow this morning.
TILDY—Put some red pepper in it. Got any?
CHARITY—Yes.. There ought to be some in one of them boxes on the shelf there. (*Points*)
TILDY (*Goes to shelf, looks about and gets the pepper*)—Here, put a plenty of this in.
CHARITY (*Groans are heard from the next room*)— Good Lord, them pains got her again. She suffers so, when she's wake.
TILDY—Poor little thing. How old is she now, sister Charity?
CHARITY—Turning fourteen this coming July.
TILDY (*Shaking her head dubiously*)—I sho hope she'll be mended by then.
CHARITY—It don't look much like it but I trusts so——

(*looking worried*) That doctor's mighty late this morning.
TILDY—I expects he'll be long in no time. Doctors is mighty onconcerned here lately.
CHARITY (*Going toward inner room with poultice*) —They surely is and I don't have too much confidence in none of 'em. (*You can hear her soothing sick girl*)
TILDY (*listening*)—Want me to help you put it on, sister Charity?
CHARITY (*from inner room*)—No, I can fix it. (*Coming back from sick room shaking her head rather dejectedly*).
TILDY—How's she restin' now?
CHARITY—Mighty feeble. Gone back to sleep. My poor little baby. (*Bracing herself*) I'm going to put on some coffee now.
TILDY—I'm sho glad. I feel kinder low spirited.
CHARITY—It's me that's low sperited. The doctor said last time he was here he might have to oparate—said she *might* have a chance then. But I tell you the truth, I've got no faith at all in 'em. They takes all your money for nothing.
TILDY—They sho do, and don't leave a thing for putting you away.
CHARITY—That's jest it. They takes every cent you got and then you dies jest the same. It ain't like they was sure.
TILDY—No, they ain't sure. That's it exzactly. But they takes your money jest the same, and leaves you flat.
CHARITY—I been thinking 'bout Zeke these last few days—how he was put away——
TILDY—I wouldn't worry 'bout him now; he's out of his troubles now.
CHARITY—I know . . . But it worries me when I think about how he was put away . . . that ugly pine coffin, jest one shabby old hack and nothing else to show—to show—we thought somethin' about him.
TILDY—Shoo . . . hush, sister, don't you worry over him. He's happy now anyhow.
CHARITY—I can't help it . . . then little Bessie.

. . . . We all jest scrouged in one hack and took her little coffin in our lap all the way to the graveyard. (*Breaks out crying*).

TILDY—Do hush, sister Charity. You done the best you could. Poor folks have to make the best of it. The Lord understands.

CHARITY—Yes. I know . . . but I made up my mind when little Bessie went that the next one of us what died would have a sho nuff fun'ral—plumes! So I saved and saved and now —this doctor——

TILDY—All they think about is cuttin' and killing and taking your money. I got nothin' to put 'em doing.

CHARITY (*Goes over to wash tub and rubs on clothes*)—Me neither. Now here's these clothes got to get out. I needs every cent.

TILDY—How much that washing bring you?

CHARITY—Dollar and a half. It's worth a whole lot more. But what can you do?

TILDY—You can't do nothing—— Look, sister Charity, ain't that coffee boiling?

CHARITY (*wipes her hands on apron and goes to stove*)—Yes, it's boiling good fashioned—come on, let's drink it.

TILDY—There ain't nothing I'd rather have than a good strong cup of coffee. (*Charity pours Tildy's cup*).

TILDY (*sweetening and stirring hers*)—Pour you some. (*Charity pours her own cup*). I'd been dead too long if it hadn't been for my coffee.

CHARITY—I love it but it don't love me, gives me the shortness of breath.

TILDY (*finishing her cup, taking up sugar with spoon*)—Don't hurt me. I could drink a barrel.

CHARITY (*drinking more slowly, reaching for coffee pot*)—Here, drink another cup.

TILDY—I shore will. That cup done me a lot of good.

CHARITY (*looking into her empty cup thoughtfully*) —I wish Dinah Morris would drop in now. I'd ask her what these grounds mean.

TILDY—I can read 'em a little myself.

CHARITY—You can? Well, for the Lord's sake look here and tell me what this cup says.

(*Offers cup to Tildy. Tildy wards it off*).

TILDY—You got to turn it round in your saucer three times first.

CHARITY—Yes, that's right, I forgot. (*Turns cup round counting*) One, two, three. (*Starts to pick it up*).

TILDY—Eughn nhu (*meaning no*) Let it set a minute. It might be watery. (*After a minute while she finishes her own cup*) Now let me see? (*Takes cup and examines it very scrutinizingly*).

CHARITY—What you see?

TILDY (*hesitatingly*)—I ain't seen a cup like this one for many a year. Not since—not since——

CHARITY—When?

TILDY—Not since jest before ma died. I looked in the cup then and saw things and . . .I stopped looking . . .

CHARITY—Tell me what you see, I want to know..

TILDY—I don't like to tell no bad news——

CHARITY—Go on. I can stan' any kind of news after all I been thru.

TILDY—Since you're bound to know I'll tell you. (*Charity draws nearer*) I sees a big gethering!

CHARITY—Gethering, you say?

TILDY—Yes, a big gethering—people all crowded together. Then I see 'em going one by one and two by two. Long lines stretching out and out and out!

CHARITY (*softly*)—What you think it is?

TILDY (*awed like*)—Looks like (*hesitates*) a possession.

CHARITY—You think it is?

TILDY—I know it is.

(*Just then the toll of a church bell is heard and then the steady and slow tramp, tramp of horses' hoofs. Both women look at each other*).

TILDY (*in a hushed voice*)—That must be Bell Gibson's funeral coming way from Mt. Zion (*gets up and goes to window*) Yes, it sho is.

CHARITY (*looking out of window also*)—Poor Bell suffered many a year; she's out of her pain now.

TILDY—Look, here comes the hearse by!

CHARITY—My Lord, ain't it grand. Look at them horses—look at their heads—plumes—how they shake 'em! Land O'mighty! Ain't it a fine sight?

TILDY—That must be Jeremiah in that first carriage, bending over like, he shorely is putting her away grand.

CHARITY—No mistake about it. That's Pickett's best funeral turnout he got.

TILDY—I bet it cost a lot.

CHARITY—Fifty dollars, so Matilda Jenkins told me. She had it for Bud. The plumes is what cost.

TILDY—Look at the hacks (*counts*) I believe to my soul there's eight.

CHARITY—Got somebody in all of 'em, too—and flowers—— She shore got a lot of 'em. (*Both women's eyes follow the tail end of the procession, horses' hoofs die away as they turn away from window*).

(*The two women look at each other significantly*).

TILDY (*significantly*)—Well——

TILDY (*significantly*)—Well—— (*They look at each other without speaking for a minute*). (*Charity goes to the wash tub*)—Want these cups washed up?

CHARITY—No, don't mind 'em. I rather you get that dress done. I got to get these clothes out.

TILDY (*picking up dress*)—Shore, there ain't so much more to do on it now.

(*Knock is heard on the door. Charity answers knock and admits Doctor*).

DR. SCOTT—Good morning—how's my patient today?

CHARITY—Not so good, doctor. When she ain't asleep she suffers so, but she sleeps mostly.

DR. SCOTT—Well, let's see—let's see. Just hand me a pan of warm water and I'll soon find out just what's what. (*Continued on page 217*)

Plumes

(Continued From Page 201)

CHARITY—All right, doctor, I'll bring it to you right away. (*Bustles about fixing water*).
(*Looking toward dress Tildy is working on*) Poor little Emmerline's been wanting a white dress trimmed with torshon a long time—now she's got it and it looks like—well——

TILDY—Don't take on so, sister Charity—The Lord giveth and the Lord taketh.

CHARITY—I know—but it's hard—hard—— (*Goes to inner door with water. You can hear her talking with the doctor after a minute and the doctor expostulating with her—in a minute she appears at the door, being led from the room by the doctor*).

DR. SCOTT—No, my dear Mrs. Brown. It will be much better for you to remain outside.

CHARITY—But, doctor——

DR. SCOTT—No. You stay outside and get your mind on something else. You can't possibly be of any service. Now be calm, will you?

CHARITY—I'll try, doctor.

TILDY—The doctor s'right. You can't do no good in there.

CHARITY—I knows, but I thought I could hold the pan or somethin'. (*Lowering her voice*) Says he got to see if her heart is all right or somethin'. I tell you——

CHARITY (*softly to Tildy*)—Hope he won't come out here saying he got to oparate. (*Goes to wash tub*).

TILDY—I hope so, too. Wont' it cost a lot?

CHARITY—That's jest it. It would take all I got saved up.

TILDY—Of couse if he's goin' to get her up—but I don't believe——

CHARITY—He didn't promise tho—even if he did, he said maybe it wouldn't do any good.

TILDY—I'd think a long time before I'd let him oparate on my chile. Taking all your money, promising nothing and ten to one killing her to boot.

CHARITY—This is a hard world.

TILDY—Don't you trust him. Coffee grounds don't lie!

CHARITY—I don't trust him. I jest want to do what's right by her. I ought to put these clothes on the line while you're settin' in here, but I hate to go out doors while he's in there.

TILDY—(getting up)—I'll hang 'em out. You stay here. Where your clothes pins at?

CHARITY—Hanging right there by the back door in the bag. They ought to dry before dark and then I can iron tonight.

TILDY (picking up tub)—They ought to blow dry in no time. (Goes toward back door).

CHARITY—Then I can shore rub 'em over tonight. Say, sister Tildy—hist 'em up with that long saplin' prop leaning in the fence corner.

TILDY (going out)—All right.

CHARITY (standing by table beating nervously on it with her fingers—listens—and then starts to bustling about the kitchen). (Enter doctor from inner room).

DR. SCOTT—Well, Mrs. Brown, I decided on the operation——

CHARITY—My Lord, doctor—don't say that!

DR. SCOTT—It's her only chance.

CHARITY—You mean she'll get well if you do?

DR. SCOTT—No, I can't say that. It's just a chance —a last chance. And I'll do just what I said, too, cut the price of the operation down to fifty dollars. I'm willing to do that for you.

CHARITY—Doctor, I was so in hopes you wouldn't operate—I—I—— And you say you ain't a bit sure she'll get well—even then?

DR. SCOTT—No, I'm not sure. You'll have to take the chance. But I'm sure you want to do everything——

CHARITY—Sure, doctor, I do want to—do—everything I can do to—to—— Doctor, look at this cup. (Picks up fortune cup and shows doctor). My fortune's been told this very morning—look at these grounds—they says—(softly)—it ain't no use, no use a tall.

DR. SCOTT—Why, my good woman, don't you believe in such senseless things. That cup of grounds can't show you anything. Wash them out and forget it.

CHARITY—I can't forget it, doctor—I feel like it ain't no use. I'd jest be spendin' the money that I needs—for nothing—nothing.

DR. SCOTT—But you won't, tho—— You'll have a clear conscience. You'd know that you did everything you could.

CHARITY—I know that, doctor. But there's things you don't know 'bout—there's other things I got to think about. If she goes . . . If she must go . . . I had plans . . . I had been getting ready . . . now . . Oh, doctor, I

jest can't see how I can have this oparation— you say you can't promise—nothing!

DR. SCOTT—I didn't think you'd hesitate about it— I imagined your love for your child——

CHARITY (breaking in)—I do love my child. My God, I do love my child. You don't understand . . . but . . . can't I have a little time to think about it, doctor . . . it means so much —to her—and—me!

DR. SCOTT—I tell you. I'll go on over to the office and as soon as you make up your mind get one of the neighbors to run over there and tell me. I'll come right back. But don't waste any time now, every minute counts.

CHARITY—Thank you, doctor. Thank you. I'll shore send you word as soon as I can. I'm so upset and worried I'm half crazy.

DR. SCOTT—I know you are . . . but don't make it too long . . . say within an hour at longest. Remember—it may save her. (Doctor exits).

CHARITY (goes to door of sick room, looks inside for a few minutes, then starts walking up and down the little kitchen first holding a hand up to her head and then wringing them). (Enter Tildy from yard with tub under her arm).

TILDY—Well, they're all out, sister Charity—what's the matter?

CHARITY—The doctor wants to oparate.

TILDY (softly)—Where he—gone?

CHARITY—Yes—he's gone, but he's coming back— if I send for him.

TILDY—You going to? (puts down tub and picks up white dress and begins sewing)

CHARITY—I don't know—I got to think.

TILDY—I can't see what's the use myself—he can't save her with no oparation—coffee grounds don't lie.

CHARITY—It would take all the money I got for the oparation and then—he can't save her—I know he can't—I feel it . . . I feel it . . .

TILDY—It's in the air . . .
(Both women sit tense in the silence. Just then a strange strangling noise comes from the inner room).

TILDY—What's that . . .

CHARITY (running toward and into the inner room) —Oh, my God!
(Tildy starts toward inner room. Stops. Sighs, and then walks slowly back to chair).
(Charity it heard moaning softly in the next room, then she appears at doorway. Leans against jam of door).

CHARITY—Rip the hem out, sister Tildy.
(Curtain)

Arna Bontemps   *Georgia Douglas Johnson*   *Hall Johnson*   *Eugene Gordon*

The Contest Spotlight

ARNA BONTEMPS (awarded the Alexander Pushkin prize for his poem, *The Return*) writes: "The trouble with me is that at present I am getting fat and the thing worries me. I should be doing road work rather than writing poetry. That, I think, is my true sorrow.

"I have lived in Louisiana, California, and New York. And I have just gone back to school again, after four years, to do post-graduate work.

"My thanks to the judges for giving me the Pushkin award again. At least it would seem that matrimony and fatherhood do not especially shorten one's luck."

GEORGIA DOUGLAS JOHNSON (awarded first prize for her play, *Plumes*) writes from her home in Washington: "I sing because I love to sing—runs the lines of a popular song; even so, I might say, I write because I love to write, for this is indeed true. If I might ask of some fairy godmother special favors, one would sure be for a clearing space, elbow room in which to think and write and live beyond the reach of the Wolf's fingers. However, much that we do and write about comes just because of this daily struggle for bread and breath—so, perhaps it's just as well. Long years ago when the world was new for me, I dreamed of being a composer—wrote songs, many of them. The words took fire and the music smouldered and so, following the lead of friends and critics, I turned my face toward poetry and put my songs away for a while. Into my poems I poured the longing for music. Then came drama. I was persuaded to try it and found it a living avenue and yet—the thing left most unfinished, less exploited, first relinquished, is still nearest my heart and most dear."

HALL JOHNSON (awarded first prize for his composition, *Sonata*, first prize for his vocal solo composition, *Fiyer*, and first prize for his vocal chorus composition, *Banjo Dance*) is at present living in New York, where, for the past ten years, he has led an active musical life. He is the organizer and director of the Hall Johnson singers, a chorus group which aims at the perpetuation of Negro folk tunes and of the work of Negro composers. His operetta *Goophered*, for which Langston Hughes has done several of the lyrics, is scheduled for fall publication.

EUGENE GORDON (awarded one-half of first and second prizes for his short story, *Game*, also third prize for his story *Buzzards*) imparts the following information and convictions: "I was born colored in Oviedo, Florida, and have remained more or less so since. I honestly admit that I am not proud of being known everywhere I go and by everything I do as a colored man. I find myself less annoyed in this respect, however, in Massachusetts than was the case in Washington, D. C., or Oviedo, or New Orleans.

"I abominate Negro literature because of the limited scope of its appeal; I like literature which takes cognizance of the Negro's place in the national life because it is usually freshly original and is universal in appeal. The short story, in my opinion, is the most highly developed form of expression in prose fiction, but too few of our talented colored writers pay enough attention to its technique. They agree that a so-called born musician must study music before he becomes a master, but they cannot understand why a so-called born writer must study just as hard before he becomes a master."

Tourgee DeBose   *Eulalie Spence*   *Idabelle Yeiser*   *Allan Freelon*

William Jackson   *Florence Price*   *Ernest E. Peace*   *James H. Young*

TOURGEE DEBOSE (awarded one half the prize for a piano composition for his manuscript *Intermezzo*) writes from Talladega, Ala.: "Born in Gainesville, Florida, in the nineties. Sixteen years later achieved an intoxicating fame in a nearby town by organizing and leading the school band. Graduated from Fisk University and the Oberlin Conservatory of Music. At the latter institution we shortened the life of Dr. Andrews, when he fain would have taught us to score a choral or write reasonable variations even upon a theme of our own. Subsequently wrote fugues which did *not* put to flight our teacher, Dr. Goetschius.

"At present Director of Music at Talladega College, where we indulge in Chorus, orchestra, piano teaching and piano recitals."

EULALIE SPENCE (awarded second prize for her play *The Hunch* and one-half the third prize for her play *The Starter*) says: "The theatre will always possess a great attraction for me. Acting, play production, writing of plays —it is indeed hard to say which holds the greater lure. I studied dramatic art and playwriting at Columbia University. There I was advised by an instructor to take up Elocution professionally. I took her advice and am now teaching Elocution in the Eastern District High School in Brooklyn. In May, The Krigwa Little Negro Theatre produced a one act play of mine, *Fool's Errand*, in the Belasco Little Theatre Tournament in which seventeen little theatres throughout the country competed. The play, much to my surprise, was given one of the two Samuel French Awards of $200 for an unpublished manuscript. This play, in booklet form, is now being published by Samuel French."

IDABELLE YEISER (awarded one-half of first and second prizes for her personal experience sketch *Letters*) writes: "After finishing the Montclair, New Jersey, State Normal, I have been teaching and specializing in languages —I studied and traveled abroad during the year 1925-1926 —studying French and Spanish."

"As to my career, I love writing, but up to now it has been my avocation rather than my vocation. I do it rather spasmodically, but hope eventually to make it my vocation. At present I'm teaching in Philadelphia."

ALLAN R. FREELON (awarded a second prize for his painting *November*) writes of himself: "I was born in Philadelphia and educated in the Public Schools, in local Art Schools, and the University of Pennsylvania. While still in school I exhibited a landscape at the Albright Art Gallery in Buffalo, and was listed in 'Who's Who in American Art.' At present I am an assistant to the Director of Art Education in the Philadelphia Public Schools."

WILLIAM JACKSON of Montclair, N. J. (awarded one half the third prize for his play *Four Eleven*) writes: "As yet, there is nothing much of importance in my career. My college years were divided among Howard, Lincoln and Columbia Universities. At Howard, I was a member of the Stylus; at Lincoln, I represented the University in intercollegiate debating; at Columbia I received a 'C' for football, and my A. B. degree.

"I am interested in building: building themes for plays, as well as building small houses for people. I favor the latter just now for material gain, and the former as a means of expressing life as it reacts on me, and as I react to it." *(Continued on page 213)*

Shad Jones   *Blanche Taylor Dickinson*   *Emily May Harper*   *Frank Horne*

The Contest Spotlight

(*Continued From Page 205*)

FLORENCE PRICE (awarded second prize in music for her composition *Memories of Dixieland*) is a graduate of the New England Conservatory of Music, as Miss Florence Beatrice Smith. She is the daughter of the late Dr. and Mrs. J. H. Smith, the wife of Thomas J. Price of Little Rock, and the mother of two little musical daughters, Florence L. Price, age 10 years, and Edith C. Price, age 6 years.

ERNEST EVERETT PEACE (awarded second prize for his arrangement of the Negro Spiritual *Nobody Knows De Trouble I've Seen*) was born in Henderson, North Carolina, December 16, 1890. He moved to Washington, D. C., in 1898, where he made his home. In 1908 he was graduated from the M Street High School, entering Howard University the following year. In 1912 he was graduated from the Teachers' College of Howard University, taking two degrees, Bachelor of Arts and Bachelor of Pedagogy. He is now an employee in the Office of the Chief of Staff, War Department, at Washington.

JAMES H. YOUNG (awarded second prize for his essay *On Race Equality*) sends the following biography: Educated in Philadelphia Public Schools, Germantown High School, 1923; Philadelphia Normal School, 1925; since February, 1925, a teacher in Philadelphia Public Schools; studying at University of Pennsylvania.

He writes: "I feel certain that the time is not far distant when all civilization will be rocked by an explosion that will awaken the Negro race from its lethargy into a group determined to create powerful and beautiful things."

SHAD JONES (awarded one-half of first and second prizes for his personal experience sketch *Sasswood*) writes from Columbus, Ohio: "Born in Lynchburg, Virginia; came to Boston with my parents at age of five, was educated in public schools of Boston and Sangus, Massachusetts. Graduated from Sangus High School in 1900 and entered Harvard College that year at age of 16. Spent one year at Harvard and later entered Sheffield Scientific School (Yale University) in class of 1911, (Mining Engineering). Taught Psysics and Chemistry at Tuskegee in 1911 and 1912. Was appointed head of Engineering and Science Department at Western University, Kansas, 1912-1916. Appointed Engineer to Liberian Government in 1916. Remained in Liberia, 1916-1920; appointed Director of Engineering at Wilberforce University, 1921. Served there until 1924. Accepted position with Industrial Branch, Y. M. C. A., Columbus, Ohio, in 1924, and am still in that position."

BLANCHE TAYLOR DICKINSON (awarded a special Buckner prize for her poem *A Sonnet and a Rondeau*) sends the following information from her home in Sewickley, Penna.: "As far back as I can remember I have had the urge to write poetry and stories. My mother says that her youthful dreams were based on the same idea and perhaps she gave it to me as a pre-natal gift. I do write a salable story once in a while and an acceptable poem a little oftener. *The American Anthology,*, Unicorn Press, just released, contains three of my poems. I am intensely interested in all the Younger Negro writers and try to keep in touch with them through the Negro press."

EMILY MAY HARPER (awarded a special Buckner prize for her short story *Ma Kilpatrick, Boss*) writes from Nashville, Tennessee: "I am a Bachelor of Science graduate of Howard University and have always intended to study medicine. I am here teaching Mathematics at Walden College. I admit that does not sound like the background of a short story writer, but I have done some 'scribbling' ever since I was admitted to the Stylus at Howard. In the course of being a Y. W. C. A. secretary, an insurance agent, and a teacher of almost every subject in the high school curriculum, I have written and produced one play and three pageants, many little verses, one novel and several short stories.

"Some day I hope to find the leisure to write more systematically. If I have any contribution to make to the field of Negro literature I feel that it is not in newness of style but of material. I have lived among and seen many a romance among what we call 'the natives' in Oklahoma."

FRANK HORNE (awarded one-half the third prize plus a special Buckner award for his essay *Concerning White People*, also one half the third prize for his personal experience sketch, *I Am Initiated Into the Negro Race*) writes from Fort Valley, Georgia: "Here you have me down in the Georgia 'sticks,' where I have spent the winter at the Fort Valley High and Industrial School. I've been doing publicity work, teaching a little and mainly recovering my health. It seems I had to come way down here to have any luck in your contest. I have been trying to write as long as I can well remember. I am addicted, however, to the extremely lazy practice of composing in my head. I usualy think that I have the composition complete in my mind, both in idea and form, before I put the pen on the paper, and then, strange to relate, when it gets down, it's apparently very different—sometimes very discouraging. It is my earnest desire to write good prose but my only recognition has resulted from my attempts at poetry, a form of expression in whose adequacy I haven't much faith."

The Opportunity Dinner: An Impression

By EUGENE GORDON

Prize Winner, Twice-Over, in the Short Story Section.

WHEN we arrived at the Fifth Avenue Restaurant, the scene of Opportunity's third annual dinner, we found the doors already open and a number of persons scattered throughout the expansive white and gold and mirrored dining room. Mrs. Charles S. Johnson, petite, serious-faced and luminous-eyed, stood near the door; she welcomed us, and I felt a thrill of pleasure that she remembered me from last year. We checked our coats and hats in the cloak room, then went out to see whether we knew anyone among the early arrivals. The first acquaintances we met from home were the Misses Alvira Hazzard and Florence Harmon, members of the Saturday Evening Quill Club, of Boston, who stood somewhat hesitantly near a table set for ten, and which bore in its center a white card with a red border and the inscription, "Reserved for the Quill Club." . . .

Even at this early hour there is noticeable an air of tenseness, of suppressed expectancy. The Misses Hazzard and Harmon are making their first visit, and I suspect that there are many others similarly experiencing a new emotion. The observant can almost unmistakably pick out the contributors from the mere visitors. Here stands a good-looking young woman from out-of-town; she is trying to carry on a lively conversation with another young woman and a man. Her quick, bright-eyed glances all about her, her tense clutching of the cords of her hand-bag, her heightened color, her concert of erratic movements—these all betray a nervousness which for weeks must have been growing upon her. At a table, agitatedly fingering the silverware, sits a small group which laughs and talks immoderately, in order to conceal its deeper feeling; individually they make inane or foolishly flippant remarks, quirking their heads about to observe the newcomers; remark repeatedly on the slowness with which the dinner is getting under way; finger their silverware.

But the tables are gradually being filled. Foreign-looking waiters fill the glasses with water and drop at each plate a chunk of bread—a crusted, brown roll. Then the waiters disappear for a moment behind mirrored columns or pots of tropic palms; presently they return with plates of soup. Repressed excitement begins to pain, for one knows now that the event for which all these persons have waited since February 28, the final date for accepting manuscripts, will soon reach its climax. Now, one by one and two by two, the long table at the end of the room begins to fill.

These are the judges: Harry Hansen, book review editor of the *Morning World*, slides into his place. Over there in the center is Charles S. Johnson. Then there is Professor John Dewey, the list of whose degrees and of the books that he has written overawes; and L. Hollingsworth Wood, head of the National Urban League; and Mrs. Edith R. Isaacs, editor of the *Theatre Arts Magazine;* and Paul Green, who has just received a big prize for the play, *In Abraham's Bosom.* Mrs. Green, admiration for her handsome young husband reflected in her eyes, sits beside him. John Macy, author of *The Story of the World's Literature* and last year's chairman at the awards dinner, sits near Mr. and Mrs. Green. I wish I knew the names of the others, but I don't, and have no way of finding out. I observe also that scores of notable persons are seated with friends here and there all over the dining room.

Someone beside me touches my arm and whispers: "Say, who's that? I've seen his pictures somewhere. Now, who . . ."

"Carl Van Vechten," I reply. "I've never met him, but once you see his picture you know him. Remember that interview in the Boston *Herald* in which he——"

"Who's that rather nice looking young fellow at the same table? I mean the fellow that's lost his necktie—and collar. He's wearing a blue shirt——"

"I can tell you who *he* is. That's Richard Bruce. Didn't you read the first installment of his novel in *Fire?* Say . . ."

The soup plates have disappeared and the table is bare, except for the chunks of bread. I take up mine and on its hard-shellaced surface: "Souvenir. Opportunity Awards Dinner, 1927. Quill Club." Everybody at the table is chattering that the idea is good. It is original. I take up my wife's silken-beaded bag and force the chunk of bread into it; wondering whether I am observed, and, if so, what my observer thinks.

Noah D. Thompson comes and takes me to meet a Mr. Barnett, who represents the Associated Press. With Mr. Barnett is a Japanese young man, publisher of a Japanese newspaper. His name, thrice repeated, is still elusive. Mr. Johnson introduces me to Wilbur Daniel Steele, whose stories appear almost monthly in *Harper's,* and who persistently wins the annual O. Henry Memorial Award prize. I take Mr. Steele to my table and introduce the Quill Club to him. He is a tall, rugged man, with graying hair and a pleasant smile. He replies to a query that he was born in a theological seminary, and that by adoption and training he is a New England yankee. . . .

Dinner has long since started, but only now are the last of the stragglers being seated. As these come to their places the anxiety on the faces of friends, who have been craning in all directions for an hour, disappears. There is much loud laughter everywhere, most of it designed to conceal nervousness, much cheerful and loud chatter, much playful raillery; much teasing speculation. . . . James

Weldon Johnson is bending over Carl Van Vechten and whispering; they are looking toward our table. Now they approach and touch Aaron Douglas' arm. Douglas and Van Vechten shake hands. Johnson and Van Vechten saunter off. Someone suggests in a whisper that Mr. Johnson has been telling Van Vechten about Douglas' drawings in *God's Trombones.*

Another course is placed on the table. It is a full plate of half a broiled spring chicken, peas, and mashed potato. That passes, and then comes the dessert and coffee. In the meantime the judges at the long table are bending this way and that in earnest conversation with one another. I know that everyone is wondering what they are talking about. The buzzing of voices is now a smooth plane of sound; it is broken here and there only by tense laughter. The voices are less raucous than a few minutes ago. The climax . . .

A waiter in the rear of the dining room drops a plate, and its shattering pieces reverberate like a harsh gong; fire engines screech and roar in 24th street. . . . Our waiter places a saucer on the table and clinks a 50-cent piece into it.

"Bait!" someone laughs, and tosses in a dime. "No need to try to bait me; I've got to get back to Boston."

There follows a brief period of clinking sounds. Someone lays a dollar bill upon the small mound of coins and takes up three quarters. The roar of the fire engines outside has now become as the roar of presses in the bowels of a newspaper plant, or that of engines in an ocean liner. We strain our eyes toward the long table; we should like to know what those numberless sheafs of paper contain. Mr. Johnson seems to be distributing them to the chairmen of the various committees. When we look again at our own table it has been cleared. The white card with its inscription and its red border remain, and I pass it around for signatures. We shall frame this and hang it up somewhere. When *are* they going to start? · . . .

Even while we wonder there comes a concerted rush and a roar as, everyone grabbing his chair, we stampede toward the long table. Now we are packed in close;there are row on row of chairs. Some of those who sat with us at the table are left behind. We look back and exchange smiles of sympathy. We

are all near enough to see. So in our new position we look about for celebrities we could not see before. There is Mrs. James Weldon Johnson, a lady of stately carriage and queenly graces. Jessie Fauset, with pensive brown face and sad eyes, is sitting not far away. And there, someone really worth seeing, is the expatriate Mississippian, Maxwell Bodenheim, whose *Ninth Avenue* dares even more than *Nigger Heaven.* Then there is Alain Locke, editor of *The New Negro,* and Eric Walrond of the *Tropic Death* accomplishment, and Alice Dunbar Nelson, whose beautiful poems. . . .

Charles S. Johnson is speaking. It is clear that his talk is extemporaneous, for he reiterates as he goes along: " . . . er . . . er . . . er . . ." He is wholly unconscious of it, and, becoming more and more interested, I, too, am unconscious of it. He has introduced John Dewey. Mr. Dewey introduces the chairmen of the various divisions of the contest. I cannot remember the order of the speakers, and I cannot hear very well what they are saying. It seems that I have been satiated with excitement through fulfilled hopes. Sights, sounds, the pressure of those nearest me, the pall of light descending from the lamps above—these are a crazyquilt of impressions in which I am completely wrapped. I know that Paul Green has just said something about knowing the colored people, mentioning his Pulitzer Prize play in passing; that John Macy, chairman at the awards dinner last year, has emphasized the point that color and hair texture have nothing to do with the producing of art; that there has just been some fine singing from the balcony over on the right and somewhat to the rear, close up under the ceiling; that a former Governor of Colorado named Sweet has said something about how he kept segregation out of the State capital because the good people of Colorado could get along without it, and how, out of the goodness of his expansive heart, he approved the building of a colored Y. M. C. A. at the staggering cost of $85,000; that everything is over now except the shaking of hands, the uttering of platitudes to those who won and to those who did not, and the rushing for coats and hats. . . .

Outside on 24th street some of the crowd stop to watch the fire engines. It is nearly 11 by the Metropolitan tower clock. We move toward Fifth avenue and the Harlem buses.

EDITORIALƒ

T HE literary contest which OPPORTUNITY has held annually for three successive years will be for the coming year suspended, and, in all probability re-opened in 1928. This deci-

The Opportunity Contest

sion was not made without deliberation, and not the least of the arguments for continuing them without interruption was their unquestioned usefulness in keeping alive a measure of the incentive to productive literary effort among Negroes. Out of these contests have come some new voices and new names for the roster of young American writers. And many of these, having found themselves, are carrying on with dignity and a delightful competence. Moreover, it is not now so difficult as formerly for manuscripts by Negroes, when they meet the standard literary requirements, to get acceptance at the hands of publishers of magazines and books.

The OPPORTUNITY contests have aimed to stimulate not merely an interest in Negro life and in the work of the artists of the race, but work of a character which stands firmly and without apology along with that of any other race. The success of its prize entries is satisfying evidence that some of the hopes in this direction have materialized. And for the same reason that these contests to stir Negro writers to their best efforts and give aid in presenting this work to the world, were begun in a field theoretically open but practically barred, we feel it important that the years shall show development, both in better work and new voices, proportionate with the opportunities revealed.

Examination of the mass of manuscripts shows that there has been improvement over the mass of other years, and that in general they are not very much worse than those of other general contests. We have concluded, however, that with the point of the contests known, more time for the deliberate working of manuscripts will yield vastly more valuable results. Most important, this extension of time should allow for our aspiring writers a margin for experimentation with more than one manuscript, in the search for the most effective channels of expression.

In the field of poetry and the short story, undoubtedly, the greatest gains have been made. Plays and essays, however, have offered the most formidable difficulties. And it is an interesting fact to be associated that poetry and short stories are practically the only kinds of literature by Negroes appearing now in the standard literary journals, while the demand for plays and essays goes unfilled. This suggests that the poets and story writers have been longer in training; also that it is practically next to impossible to do a play or an essay interestingly on the inspiration of the moment, or with a single effort fortuitously blending all the required elements of technique.

There has been no flagging of interest on the part of the men and women of letters whose services have been sought on the various juries of the contests. Each year has met a new group of them eagerly willing to lend their aid toward the encouragement of creative expression in a long silent race.

It is, thus, with reasoned judgment, that we announce the suspension of the contests for one year, and urge those who have been interested in making preparations for them, to let this intervening period be not wasted. The channels of communication, meanwhile, will not be closed: there will be sent to those who have submitted manuscripts in the past, occasional memoranda which shall deal more intimately with their problems and materials.

THROUGH the generosity of a reader of *Opportunity*, who desires to remain anonymous, a prize of $100.00 is offered for the best short story **An Opportunity** or essay of Negro life of **Award** 5,000 words or less written by a Negro. The donor is of the opinion that the development of able writers is of vast importance in the improvement of race relations in America and he desires to stimulate the Negro's creative impulse in literature in so far as that is possible.

There can be no question that the written word can penetrate where the spoken word may not be heard. And where once the eloquence of the orator shaped public opinion, today the skillful and persuasive writer has taken his place. The *Opportunity* awards of a few years ago attracted the attention of America's literati to the efforts of Negro writers. And though racial attitudes here as elsewhere tend to handicap and thwart the full expression of Negro genius, there are no barriers which can permanently keep real ability from getting a hearing.

Indeed America's response to the artistic expression of the Negro confounds one by its contradictions. He, who looks apprehensively lest a Negro sit beside him in the concert hall, a minute later leads all the rest in applause as Roland Hayes or Paul Robeson concludes a song. She, who hastily exchanges her seat with her male escort at the approach of a Negro can be seen furtively sniffing when Clarence Muse stands dejected and mute, while the steamer bears his little grandson away to the cold No'th in the motion picture "Hearts in Dixie." A thousand eyes are dabbed nightly by scented kerchiefs in the hands of those who hold only scorn for Negroes as the "Chillun of Isre'l" are about to reach the Promised Land in the current production of "Green Pastures."

It is evident that the emotional responses of white America are not inhibited by race except where proximity compels contact. I is within the power of the creative artist ir literature to evoke these responses. Through distinctive literary achievement the Negro artist might conceivably bring about a change in the attitude of his oppressors. At least it is worth the attempt. For through the ages Orpheus has drawn iron tears down Pluto's cheek. And the Negro should not merely be driven by the urge to create beautiful things but by the knowledge that in so doing he makes it possible for some beauty to find its way into the lives of his people.

We hope that those who believe they can write will take advantage of this prize offer. The contest will close December 31, 1931. Information as to details can be obtained by communicating with the Editor, *Opportunity* Magazine, 1133 Broadway, New York City.

▼ ▼ ▼ ▼ ▼

IN the $100.00 essay and short story con-
test OPPORTUNITY hopes to discover a
new crop of writers who will be able to
write acceptably
The New for magazine pub-
Opportunity Awards lication; not only
for OPPORTUNITY
but for other magazines as well. Throughout the nation young colored men and
women are writing, perhaps, as never before. A number of these unquestionably
are gifted, but for the most part they have
not developed that type of craftmanship
which present day magazines demand.

A study of the manuscripts which come
to OPPORTUNITY reveals certain tendencies
which undoubtedly reflect the methods that
are employed in the departments of English
in our colleges and universities. These manuscripts show a marked inclination to follow the formalism of the English essayists
of the 18th Century or to slavishly follow
the style of the literary elect of the 19th
Century. As a result the writing lacks
spontaneity and vigor or what is popularly
called "punch."

Important as are the models of fine writing of the 18th and 19th Centuries in the
development of appreciation of literature,
they will not serve as absolute criteria for
the present day. The tempo of life has
been vastly accelerated during the 20th
Century. And this tempo has affected the
reading habits of the population. The essayists and novelists of the 18th and 19th
Centuries wrote for an age when the reading class was largely the leisure class for
whom life moved in stately tread. And the
literature of the period conformed to the
manner of life. Just so the literature of this
age marches with the tempo which the machine has made, and if one would write for
reading (and who does not) he must keep
step with his time.

We do not mean that OPPORTUNITY merely wishes to stimulate the adoption of those
cheap devices of the new realism which currently pass for literature, nor the bizarre
technique of some of the so-called modernists. We hope merely to encourage the emu-
lation on the part of some of the younger
Negro writers of the best magazine writing
of the present day.

301

IN the OPPORTUNITY contest which closes on December 31st, we hope that the stories and in so far as possible the essays will in a measure depict

Essays And Stories something of the real spirit which animates the American Negro. From few novels and fewer short stories of Negro life is one able to form an adequate conception of the forces which have sustained the Negro in his struggle for survival in an indifferent if not an hostile world. Writers both black and white have a tendency to see the Negro in a hopeless struggle against conditions which he is powerless to change or overcome. Disappointment gives way to despair, frustration precedes disintegration, and finally the inevitable catastrophe seals a career of futility.

Now this picture of the Negro in the American environment is no more authentic than the portrayal which depicts the Negro as a perpetual buffoon or just a simple-minded servant. The truth is that in not a few instances the Negro has been able to surmount obstacles, to outwit his enemies and to confound his traducers. If this were not true then the Negro would be only a little better off now than during the slave regime. The fact that he has steadily moved forward in industry, in politics, in education indicates that somehow he is conquering the forces arrayed against him.

In one of the once popular "blues" there is a sentiment which expresses the spiritual perspective of the Negro better than most of the stories which purport to reveal something of his soul:

> *The road is rocky*
> *But the rider, he is here.*

So goes the song. In truth it fairly represents the mental attitude of the American Negro. We hope that there will be a recognition of this quality of the Negro in the manuscripts submitted in the contest.

302

OPPORTUNITY is extremely fortunate
in being able to secure three of the
most outstanding individuals in the con-
                        temporary Ameri-
The Judges   can literary scene
                        to act as judges of
the manuscripts submitted in the Short
Story-Essay Contest which comes to an end
on December 31, 1931. It would be difficult to find three persons who might bring
to this task deeper critical insight, greater
knowledge of the requirements of present
day publications and more sensitive appreciation of the Negro as a subject for dis-
sertation and short story than these: Carl
J. Ackerman, dean of the Pulitzer School
of Journalism, Rudolph Fisher, short story
writer and author of *The Walls of Jericho*,
and Edward J. O'Brien, author of *The
Dance of the Machines* and editor of the
Anthology of *Best Short Stories of the Year*.

Editorials

A T midnight on the 31st day of December, 1931, the $100.00 contest for short stories and essays of 5,000 words or less conducted by OPPORTUNITY closed. The editor was a bit surprised and highly elated by the number of manuscripts submitted. One hundred and seventy-five in all were entered from all over America, the West Indies and even as far away as Angola, Portuguese East Africa.

The Contest

The name of the winner and the manuscript which is awarded the prize will be published in OPPORTUNITY as soon as the judges have completed their task of selection. Until that time the editor respectfully asks the indulgence of the contestants.

▼ ▼ ▼ ▼

Editorials

OPPORTUNITY extends its sincere congratulations to Charles W. Cranford, winner of the $100.00 award for his short story, A Plantation Episode, and no less to the one hundred and seventy-five men and women who entered manuscripts in the contest. As has been announced in OPPORTUNITY, the value of the manuscripts from the standpoint of magazine publication was the principal factor upon which the judges based their decision. The contest confirmed the belief that there are a group of young Negroes who can write not only interestingly but brilliantly, that the future of the American Negro in creative literature is definitely assured, and that the depiction of Negro life need not rest solely on the efforts of those who see Negro life through the distorted lens of outworn social dogma.

The Opportunity Award

Charles W. Cranford

Winner of OPPORTUNITY *Award*

THE $100.00 award offered by *Opportunity* Magazine for the best short story or essay of 5000 words has been awarded to Charles W. Cranford of Cassville, West Virginia, for his story, A Plantation Episode. A total of one hundred and seventy-five manuscripts were entered in the contest. They came from nearly every state in the Union, from the West Indies and from Africa.

Charles Cranford was born in Buxton, Iowa, June 25, 1907. For six years he attended the public schools of Degnan, Oklahoma. From Oklahoma his family moved to West Virginia and he completed the grammar school of Harrison County in that State. In 1925 he was graduated from the Kelly Miller High School in Clarksburg, West Virginia, whereupon he entered West Virginia State College, and in 1930 received the degree of Bachelor of Science in Business Administration. Since his graduation he has engaged in various kinds of work—clerical, secretarial, and occasionally he has substituted as a teacher in an elementary school. In the meantime he has done free lance writing for newspapers and magazines. A short story, Coke, was published in *Opportunity* in July, 1929, and recently another one, The Rat, was featured in *Grit*. He plans to study short story writing and magazine editing and looks forward to a career in journalism. He lives with his parents in Cassville, West Virginia, and is unmarried.

Few literary contests have been able to

Charles W. Cranford

command the critical acumen of a more distinguished group than those who consented to act as judges in this contest.

Edward J. O'Brien, now at Oxford, for a number of years has edited an Anthology of the Best Short Stories that have appeared in America and Great Britain. He is the author of many books, including *The Bloody Fool, The Advance of the American Short Story, The Dance of the Machines.*

Rudolph Fisher, whose short stories have appeared in many of America's best magazines, is the author of *The Walls of Jericho.* Although a physician by profession. Dr. Fisher not only has attained high rank as a short story writer but as a critic of novels dealing with Negro life. His book reviews, which have appeared in the New York *Herald Tribune,* have been characterized by a sensitive appreciation of style and a profound knowledge of the vagaries of Negro life in America.

Carl W. Ackerman is the dean of the Pulitzer School of Journalism, Columbia University. He was formerly special correspondent of the *Saturday Evening Post* in Mexico, Spain, France and Switzerland, and has been associated with the New York *Tribune* and New York *Times.* He is the author of *Mexico's Dilemma; Trailing the Bolsheviki; Germany, the Next Republic* and other books.

A Plantation Episode, the story which was awarded the $100.00 prize, will be published in a future issue of *Opportunity.*

THE CRISIS

Vol. 25. No. 1   NOVEMBER, 1922   Whole No. 145

"Not those who inflict most but those who suffer most will conquer."
—*Terrence McSwiney.*

TRUTH AND BEAUTY

IN November, 1910, THE CRISIS was born. With this issue, November, 1922, we are completing our twelfth year and we pause to thank all those who have made our long and fairly successful career possible. We have for the future both promises and apologies.

First, we want to apologize to the large number of people who subscribe indirectly to THE CRISIS and either do not get their subscriptions or have them delayed. It can be easily seen that this is not wholly the fault of THE CRISIS: THE CRISIS cannot fulfil a subscription until it receives it or at least receives notice that it has been paid. On the other hand, many subscriptions are taken in the drives for memberships of the N.A.A.C.P. and this has always been a great and valuable source of support for THE CRISIS. When, however, subscriptions are paid thus indirectly, first to a solicitor, then handed to a captain, then slowly collected by a local secretary, then forwarded to the national secretary, and finally handed to THE CRISIS business manager,—all this involves much delay and several possibilities of mistake. Anyone thus subscribing for THE CRISIS indirectly should always and simultaneously notify THE CRISIS office of the facts. If there is anyone who having thus subscribed has not received THE CRISIS,

we shall be only too glad to learn tne facts and make all reparation.

So much for apology. Now to our muttons. THE CRISIS has always stood for Truth,—for the Truth when it is bitter, because we believe this is the only path to reform; for the Truth when it is sweet, for that heartens all. We shall continue to stand thus for the Truth. In addition to this we want to increase that part of our mission which, while not neglected, has had too little attention in the past, and that is the work of propagating and encouraging Beauty. We Negroes have gone fast forward in economic development, in political and social agitation; and we are likely to forget that the great mission of the Negro to America and the modern world is the development of Art and the appreciation of the Beautiful. The esthetic life of black folk is likely to be choked—not by toil, for they are gifted with that divine laziness that will rest and dream in spite of laws and lash and silly money; but with the over-emphasis of ethics to meet the Puritans round about who conceal their little joys and deny them with crass utilitarianism.

Why even our song — that vivid burst of sorrow burnt with joy—our love of life, the wild and beautiful desire of our women and men for each other—all, all this sinks to being "good" and being "useful" and being "white."

THE CRISIS wishes by picture and drawing, by fiction, essays, poetry, by the organization of a Negro Institute of Literature and Art, to increase, nourish and encourage the Beautiful

307

among Negroes and among Americans. As a beginning of this work for our New Year, we have the honor to announce a Christmas cover by Henry O. Tanner. And as a second step the *Delta Omega* Chapter of the *Alpha Kappa Alpha* Sorority at Virginia Normal and Industrial Institute, Petersburg, Va., offers through THE CRISIS a prize of fifty dollars for the best short story written by a Negro student.

THE PRIZE STORY COMPETITION

THE contest initiated by the Delta Omega Chapter of the Alpha Kappa Alpha Sorority was important to the Editors of the CRISIS in more ways than in the offer and bestowal of a prize. It gave us an opportunity to gain a concept of what the younger generations of colored people are doing and thinking.

I may say at the outset that the stories submitted gave much ground, generally speaking, for disappointment. But before going into this let us consider the ingredients without which a short story—or any sort of story—must fail of success. It is axiomatic that a story have a plot, which shall be clear, well-rounded, and sustained. In addition one expects in greater or less degree imagination, clearness and charm. These last three qualities go to make up that elusive thing called style and the greatest of these is imagination.

Nineteen stories were submitted. Of these twelve were plotless, three possessed a slight plot, two started off with the makings of a good plot which their authors failed to sustain; one possessed a strong, clearly developed plot, and the last, the prize-winner, was built around a plot slightly less strong, but so mingled with the elements of charm, and imagination that the members of the Committee, although they sent in their findings separately, gave it a unanimous first vote. Fifteen of the stories showed absolutely no play of imagination yet we are called an imaginative people. Where does the fault lie?

I have been a teacher so I am rather chary about placing the blame for the shortcomings of pupils on the members of the teaching profession. Yet in this case, since all the entrants were students, and probably representative, I should say that much of the blame must lie with the method of instruction. No matter how much a person desires to write he cannot write unless he has practice. And he cannot practice without models. One does not spring like Minerva from the head of Zeus, full-panoplied into the arena of authordom. Do our colored pupils read the great writers and stylists? Are they ever shown the prose of Shaw, Galsworthy, Mrs. Wharton, DuBois or Conrad, or that old master of exquisite phrase and imaginative incident—Walter Pater? Are they encouraged to develop a critical faculty? Does a teacher tell them this?—"Select a passage which appeals to you, find out why it appeals, and try to write a passage in the same style, but on another sub-ject." Or: "Make up a story which is full of the real but the unusual." Or lastly: "Try to spin a yarn which is obviously unlikely, but none the less fascinating."

The first time this task is set before a pupil he will blench, and so will the teacher when he reads the results. But each successive set of results will be better. I know this. Of course this savors of the bare skeleton of preparation. It would seem to advocate writing by a formula. But all real writing is done that way—by a formula, by a fixed purpose which the writer holds in his brain, perhaps subconsciously, while he is perfecting his task. He wants his readers to feel sorrow, joy, amusement, despair and so he chooses his words, he dresses up his phrases, he picks his incidents to that end.

One's predilection for Writing, as one's predilection for Music or Painting is an inborn thing. One's success in Writing as in Music or Painting is a matter of conscious effort, of unwearying determination. The masterpieces are the compositions which have been worked at, thrown aside, picked up again, despaired over, cut and slashed and mended and sworn at. Until one day their creator finds they are good.

More than ever we need writers who will be able to express our needs, our thoughts, our fancies. The geniuses of course are born, but the shaping of most writers of talent lies in the hands of our teachers.

JESSIE FAUSET.

TO A WILD ROSE
A Prize Story

 卐 卐   OTTIE B. GRAHAM   卐 卐

THIS story has been selected for the prize of fifty dollars offered by the Delta Omega Chapter of the Alpha Kappa Alpha Sorority "for the best short story written by a Negro student". The Committee of Award consisted of Arthur B. Spingarn, Jessie Fauset and W. E. B. DuBois. Their decision was unanimous.

Miss Graham was born in Virginia in 1900, educated in the public schools of Philadelphia and at Howard University, and is now an undergraduate at Columbia University, New York. She is the daughter of the Rev. W. F. Graham of Philadelphia.

The story awarded second place, also by unanimous decision, was submitted by John Howe of Lincoln University and will be published in a future number of THE CRISIS.

OTTIE BEATRICE GRAHAM

"OL' man, ol' man, why you looking at me so?" Tha's what you sayin', son. Tha's what you sayin.' Then you start a-singin' that song agin, an' I reckon I'm starin' agin. I'm just a wonderin', son. I'm just a-wonderin'. How is it you can sing them words to a tune an' still be wantin' for material for a tale? "Georgia Rose". An' you jus' sing the words an' they don't say nothin' to you? Well listen to me, young un, an' write what you hear If you want to. Don't laugh none at all if I hum while I tell it, 'cause maybe I'll forget all about you; but write what you hear if you want to.

Thar's just me in my family, an' I never did know the rest. On one o' them slave plantations 'way down in the South I was a boy. Wan't no slave very long, but know all about it jus' a same. 'Cause I was proud, they all pestered me with names. The white uns called me red nigger boy an' the black uns called me red pore white. I never 'membered no mother—just the mammies 'round the place, so I fought when I had to and kep' my head high without tryin' to explain what I didn't understan'.

Thar was a little girl 'round the house, a ladies' maid. Never was thar angel more heavenly. Flo they called her, an' they said she was a young demon. An' they called her witch, an' said she was too proud. Said she was lak her mother. They said her mother come down from Oroonoka an' Oroonoka was the prince captured out o' Africa. England took the prince in the early days o' slavery, but I reckon we got some o' his kin. That mean we got some o' his pride, young un, that mean we got some o' his pride. Beautiful as was that creature, Flo, she could 'ford bein' proud. She was lak a tree—lak a tall, young tree, an' her skin was lak bronze, an' her hair lak coal. If you look in her eyes they was dreamin', an' if you look another time they was spaklin' lak black diamonds. Just made it occur to you how wonderful it is when somethin' can be so wild an' still so fine lak. "My blood is royal! My blood is African!" Tha's how she used to say. Tha's how her mother taught her. Oroonoka! African pride! Wild blood and fine.

Thar was a fight one day, one day when things was goin' peaceful. They sent down from the big house a great tray of bones from the chicken dinner. Bones for me! Bones for an extra treat! An' the men an' the women an' the girls an' the boys all come round in a ring to get the treat. The

Butler stood in the center, grinnin' an' makin' pretty speeches about the dinner an' the guests up at the big house. An' I cried to myself, "Fool—black fool! Fool—black fool!" An' I started wigglin' through the legs in the crowd till I got up to the center. Then I stood up tall as I could and I hissed at the man, an' the words wouldn't stay down my throat, an' I hollered right out, "Fool—black fool!" An' 'fore he could do anything atall, I kicked over his tray of gravy an' bones. Bones for me! Bones for an extra treat!

The old fellah caught me an' started awackin', but I was young an' tough an' strong, an' I give him the beatin' of his life. Pretty soon come Flo to me. "Come here, Red-boy," she say, an' she soun' like the mistress talkin', only her voice had more music an' was softer. "Come here, Red-boy," she say, "we have to run away. I would not carry the tray out to the quarters, an' you kicked it over. We're big enough for floggin' now, an' they been talkin' about it at the big house. They scared to whip me, 'cause they know I'll kill the one that orders it done first chance I get. But they mean to do somethin', an' they mean to get you good, first thing."

We made little bundles and stole off at supper time when everybody was busy, an' we hid way down in the woods. 'Bout midnight they came almost on us. We knew they would come a-huntin'. The hounds gave 'em 'way with all their barkin,' and the horses gave 'em 'way steppin' on shrubbery. The river was near an' we just stepped in; an' when we see we couldn't move much farther 'less they spot us, we walked waist deep to the falls. Thar we sat hidin' on the rocks, Flo an' me, with the little falls a-tumblin' all over us, an' the search party walkin' up an' down the bank, cussin' an' swearin' that Flo was a witch. thar we sat under the falls lak two water babies, me a-shiverin', an' that girl a-laughin'. Yes, such laughin'! Right then the song rose in my heart tha's been thar ever since. It's a song I could never sing, but tha's been thar all a same. Son, you never seen nothin' lak that. A wild thing lak a flower—lak a spirit—sittin' in the night on a rock, laughin' through the falls, with a laugh that trickled lak the water. Laughin' through the falls at the hunters.

After while they went away an' the night

was still. We got back to the bank to dry, but how we gonna dry when we couldn't make a fire? Then my heart start a-singin' that song again as the light o' the moon come down in splashes on Flo. She begin to dance. Yes suh, dance. An' son, you never seen nothin' lak that. A wild thing lak a flower the wind was a-chasin'—lak a spirit a-chasin' the wind. Dancin' in the woods in the light o' the moon.

"Come Red-boy, you gotta get dry." And we join hands an' whirled round together till we almost drop. Then we eat the food in our little wet bundles—wet bread an' wet meat an' fruit. An' we followed the river all night long, till we come to a little wharf about day break. A Negro overseer hid us away on a small boat. We sailed for two days, an' he kep' us fed in hidin'. When that boat stopped we got on a ferry, an' he give us to a man an' a woman. Free Negroes, he told us, an' left us right quick.

I ain't tellin' you, young un, where it all happen, cause that ain't so particular for your material. We didn't have to hide on the ferry-boat, an' everybody looked at us hard. The lady took Flo an' the man took me, an' we all sat on deck lak human bein's. When we left the ferry we rode in a carriage, an' finally we stopped travellin' for good. Paradise never could a' been sweeter than our new home was for me. They said it was in Pennsylvania. A pretty white house with wild flowers everywhere. An' they went out an' brought back Flo to set 'em off. An' when I'd see her movin' round among 'em, an' I'd ask her if she wasnt happy, she'd throw back that throat o' bronze, an' smile lak all o' Glory. "I knew I'd be free, Red-boy. Tha's what my mother said I'd have to be. My blood is African! My blood is royal!" Then the song come a-singin' itself again in my heart, an' I hush up tight. Wild thing waterin' wild things—wild thing in a garden.

Thar come many things with the years; the passin' o' slavery an' the growin' up o' Flo. Thar wasn't nothin' else much that made any difference. I went to the city to work, but I went to visit Flo an' the people most every fortnight. One time I told her about my love; told her I wanted her to be my wife. An' she threw back her curly head, but she didn't smile her bright smile. She closed her black eyes lak as though she was in pain, an' lak as though the pain come from pity. An' I hurried up an' said I knew I should a-gone to school when they tried to make me, but I could take care o' her all a same. But she said it wasn't that—wasn't that.

"Red-boy," she said, "I couldn't be your wife, 'cause you—you don't know what you are. It wouldn't matter, but *I* am *African* and my blood is *royal!*"

She fell on my shoulder a-weepin', an' I understood. Her mother stamped it in her. Oroonoka! Wild blood and fine.

I went away as far as I could get. I went back to the South, an' I went around the world two years, a-workin' on a ship, an' I saw fine ladies everywhere. I saw fine ladies, son, but I ain't seen none no finer than her. An' the same little song kep' a-singin' itself in my heart. I went to Africa, an' I saw a prince. Pride! Wild blood an' fine.

Thar was somethin' that made me go back where she was. Well, I went an' she was married, an' lived in the city. They told me her husband come from Morocco an' made translations for the gover'ment.

"Morocco," I thought to myself. "That's a man knows what he is. She's keepin' her faith with her mother."

I rented me a cottage. I wanted to wait till she come to visit. They said she'd come. I settled down to wait. Every night I listen to the March wind a-howlin' while I smoked my pipe by the fire. One night I caught sound o' somethin' that wasn't the wind. I went to my door an' I listen, an' I heard a voice 'way off, kind a-moanin' an' kind a-chantin'. I grabbed up my coat an' hat an' a lantern. Thar was a slow, drizzlin' rain, an' I couldn't see so well even with the lantern. I walked through the woods towards where I last heard the voice a-comin'. I walked for a good long time without hearin' anything a-tall. Then thar come all at once, straight ahead o' me, the catchin' o' breath an' sobs, an' I knew it was a woman. I raised my lantern high an' thar was Flo. Her head was back, an'

The Delta Omega Chapter of the Alpha Kappa Alpha Sorority of southeast Virginia. This chapter is a graduate chapter made up of graduates of Howard, Chicago, Illinois, and Rhode Island State Universities. Its headquarters are at the Virginia Normal and Industrial Institute, Petersburg, Va., and these women furnished the fifty dollars for the prize story.

she open an' shut her eyes, an' opened an' shut her eyes, an' sobbed an' caught her breath.

An', spite o' my wonderin' an' bein' almost scaired, that little song started up in me harder than ever. Son, you never seen nothin' lak that. A wild, helpless thing lak a thistle blowed to pieces—a wild, helpless thing lak a spirit chained to earth. Trampin' along in the woods in the night, with the March wind a-blowin' her along. Trampin' along, a-sobbin' out her grief to the night.

Thar wasn't no words for me to say; I just carried her in my arms to the fire in my house. I took off her coat an' her shoes an' put her by the fire, an' I wipe the rain out o' her hair. She was a-clutchin' somethin' in her hand, but I ain't said nothin' yet. I knew she'd tell me. After while she give the thing to me. It was a piece o' silk, very old an' crumpled. A piece of paper was tacked on it. Flo told me to read it. That time when we run away from the plantation she took a little jacket all braided with silk in her bundle. 'Twas the finest jacket her mother used to wear. This dreary night, when Flo come to visit, she start a-ransackin' her old trunk. She come across the jacket and ripped it up; an' she found the paper sewed to the linin'. An' when I read what was on the paper, I knew right off why I found her in the woods, a-running lak mad in the March night wind.

Her mother had a secret, an' she put it down on paper 'cause she couldn't tell it, an' she had to get it out—had to get it out. Thar was tears in every word an' they made tears in my eyes. The blood o' Oroonoka was tainted—tainted by the blood of his captor. The father o' her little girl was not Negro, an' the pride in her bein' was wounded. She was a slave woman, an' she was a beauty, an' she couldn't 'scape her fate. Thar was tears, tears, tears in every word.

I looked at Flo; her head was back. I never did see a time when her head wasn't back. It couldn't droop. She threw it back to laugh, an' she threw it back to sigh. Now she was a-starin' at the fire, an' the fire was a-flarin' at her. Wild thing lak a spirit—lak a scaired bird ready to fly. Oroonoka! Blood o' Oroonoka tainted.

"Red-boy," she said to me, an' she never look away from the fire. "Red-boy, I'm lookin' for a baby. I'm lookin' for a baby in the winter. How am I gonna welcome my baby? Anything else wouldn't matter so much—anything else but white. *That* blood in me—in my baby! Oh, Red-boy, I ain't royal no more!" I couldn't say much, but I took her hand an' I smoothed her hair, an' I led her back to the white house down the way.

Thar in the country she stayed on an' on, an' I stayed on too. Her husband come to see her every week, an' he look proud. He look proud an' happy, an' she look proud an' sad. She wandered in the woods an' she sang a low song. An' she stood at the gate an' she fed the birds. An' she sat on the grass an' she gazed at the sky. Wild thing, still an' proud—wild thing, still an' sad.

An' she stayed on an' on till the winter come. An' the baby come with the winter. She lie in the bed with the baby in her arm. Son, you never see nothin' lak that. A wild thing lak a flowerin' rose—lak a tired spirit. Flower goin', goin'; bud takin' its place. She said somethin' 'fore she died. She look at me an' said it.

"Red-boy, my blood is royal, but it's paled. Don't tell her,—yes tell her. Tell her about the usurpers o' Oroonoka's blood."

But I never did tell her, I went away again an' I stay twenty years. I just find out not long ago where her father went to live. I went to see 'em an' I make myself known. I didn't do so much talkin', so the miss entertain me. She played on the piano and forgot that she was a-playin'. Right then she was her mother. Yes suh, thar sat Flo. Wild thing! Royal blood! Paled, no doubt, but royal all a same.

Then she turned around, an' she wasn't Flo no longer. The brown skin was thar, an' the black, wild eyes, an' the curly dark hair. She spoke soft an' low, but she never did say, "*My* blood is royal! I am *African.*" An' she never did say "Red-boy". Her father had never told her about Oroonoka—that was it. An' I come back too late to tell her.

Well it don't matter no how, I thought, so long as she can hold her head lak that, an' long as she can look so beautiful, an' long as she make her mark in the world with that music. But the little song started a-singin' itself in my heart, an' I could see the flower agin.

Tha's your material boy. 'Member how I told it to you, a-fishin' on the river edge. 'Member how you was a-singin' "Georgia Rose". Thar's your material. Georgia Rose. Oroonoka. A wild, young thing, 'an' a little song in an old man's heart.

THE CRISIS

| Vol. 28. No. 5 | SEPTEMBER, 1924 | Whole No. 167 |

THE AMY SPINGARN PRIZES

"MY husband and I have long had a deep interest and faith in the contribution of the American Negro to American art and literature. It is with the hope of assisting THE CRISIS, that I should like to offer through THE CRISIS a series of prizes for literary and possibly also artistic contributions. I am accordingly enclosing my check for three hundred dollars ($300) for this purpose. The circumstances and conditions under which the prizes are to be awarded should be left entirely to the decision of the Board of Directors of the National Association for the Advancement of Colored People after consultation with the editor of THE CRISIS.

"AMY E. SPINGARN,
"(MRS. J. E. SPINGARN)."

THE CRISIS

| Vol. 28. No. 6 | OCTOBER, 1924 | Whole No. 168 |

THE AMY SPINGARN PRIZES IN LITERATURE AND ART

WE take pleasure in announcing cash prizes aggregating six hundred dollars, in literature and art, the gift of Mrs. Amy Spingarn.

For stories, prizes of $100, $50 and $20.

For plays, prizes of $75, $40 and $10.

For illustrations, prizes of $75, $40 and $10.

For essays, prizes of $50, $30 and $10.

For poems, prizes of $50, $30 and $10.

Free memberships in the Crisis Guild of Writers and Artists (CRIG-WA) will be given all prize-winners and all other writers and artists who show distinct promise. Manuscripts and drawings must be in our hands on or before June first, 1925.

For further details write to the editor.

Mary Effie Lee. Indeed, THE CRISIS has always preferred the strong matter of unknown names, to the platitudes of well-known writers; and by its Education and Children numbers, it has shown faith in the young."

Since 1920 THE CRISIS has had the pleasure of publishing the work of Joseph Cotter, Joseph Cotter, Jr., Claude McKay, C. B. Johnson, Langston Hughes, Maud Cuney Hare, Jean Toomer, Leslie Pinckney Hill, Countee P. Cullen, Walter F. White, Alain Locke, Anne Spencer, E. Franklin Frazier, Ottie B. Graham, Willis Richardson, Edwin Morgan, Gwendolyn Bennett, Julian E. Bagley, Eugene Corbie, Abram Harris and Walter E. Hawkins.

Nevertheless our word of 1920 is still true:

"We have today all too few writers, for the reason that there is small market for their ideas among whites, and their energies are being called to other and more lucrative ways of earning a living Nevertheless, we have literary ability and the race needs it. A renaissance of American Negro literature is due; the material about us in the strange, heart-rending race tangle is rich beyond dream and only we can tell the tale and sing the song from the heart."

Today and suddenly $1,100 **are** offered in prizes to Negro writers and artists. Without either knowing the other's plans or intentions, both THE CRISIS and the magazine published by the Urban League, "Opportunity", have offered a series of prizes. Mrs. Spingarn's offer was made to us in July, but "Opportunity" first gave publicity to its prize offer. In order, therefore, to give young authors every chance we have put the date of our competition well on in the spring so that there will be no unnecessary rivalry and all can have the full benefit of this great generosity and foresight on the part of friends.

TO ENCOURAGE NEGRO ART

HE CRISIS said, editorially, in 1920:

"Since its founding, THE CRISIS has been eager to discover ability among Negroes, especially in literature and art. It remembers with no little pride its covers by Richard Brown, William Scott, William Farrow and Laura Wheeler; and its cartoons by Lorenzo Harris and Albert Smith; it helped to discover the poetry of Roscoe Jamison, Georgia Johnson, Fenton Johnson, Lucian Watkins and Otto Bohanan; and the prose of Jessie Fauset and

The Amy Spingarn Prizes in Literature and Art

As we have already announced, through the kindness of Mrs. Amy B. Spingarn, THE CRISIS is enabled to offer a series of prizes for writing and drawing.

Time.—The manuscripts and drawings must be in THE CRISIS office, 69 Fifth Avenue, on or before APRIL 15, 1925. The names of the prize winners will be announced in the July CRISIS, which will be published June 20, 1925.

Conditions.—These prizes are offered to persons of Negro descent in order to encourage their aptitude for art expression.

Prizes for Writing.—Prizes are offered for fiction, plays, essays and verse as follows: For *Fiction*—$100, $50, $20. The stories should be preferably four to five thousands words in length or five to seven pages of THE CRISIS. In no case must they exceed eight thousand words. For *Plays*—$75, $40, $10. Plays must deal with some phase of Negro history or experience and should occupy from five to seven pages of THE CRISIS in length. For *Essays*—$50, $30, $10. Essays should occupy from one to six pages of THE CRISIS and in no case should they exceed five thousand words. They may deal with personal experience, biography, history, scientific research, art, criticism or any subject. For *Verse*—$50, $30, $10. The specimens submitted may be of any length up to three pages of THE CRISIS and may be on any subject.

All of the manuscripts indicated above should be typewritten or legibly copied by hand on one side of the paper. The pages should be numbered and on the top of the first page, in addition to the subject, should appear the pseudonym under which the author is writing. A sealed envelope should accompany the manuscript; on it should be written the pseudonym and in it should be the real name and address of the author and postage for the return of the manuscript in case it is not used. All manuscripts must be original, never before published in any form, and at the time of entering this contest they must not be in the hands of any other publisher. THE CRISIS will reserve to the author all rights of publication and reproduction in any way except the rights to first serial publication. THE CRISIS shall have the right to return or publish at its regular rates of compensation any of the manuscripts submitted.

Illustrations.—Illustrations may be for covers of THE CRISIS or for decorations of THE CRISIS page, cartoons or general illustrations. The prizes will be $75, $40, $10. The illustrations may be in black and white or in oil or water colors. They should be carefully packed so as not to be broken or spoiled in transit. They should be signed on the back with a pseudonym and a sealed envelope with the real name and address of the artist and return postage should be enclosed. All drawings must be original and never before published and no copies of them must be in the hands of any other periodical at the time of submission to THE CRISIS. THE CRISIS will reserve to the artist all rights of reproduction except the rights to first serial publication in THE CRISIS. THE CRISIS shall have the right to return or publish at its regular rates any of the drawings submitted.

During the years 1925 and 1926 THE CRISIS will publish the prize manuscripts and drawings and such others as have merit. Further announcements concerning the prizes will be as follows: in the DECEMBER CRISIS the names of the judges and an editorial on *short stories* will appear. In the JANUARY CRISIS an editorial on *plays;* in the FEBRUARY CRISIS an editorial on *essays;* and in the MARCH CRISIS an editorial on *verse* will appear. In the APRIL CRISIS the plans of CRIGWA, THE CRISIS Guild of Writers and Artists, will be announced.

The editor will be very glad to answer any letters concerning these prizes.

Answers

1. *Yes, any one may compete for two or more of the prizes.*

2. *No, you must not copy matter; it must be original and composed by you, yourself.*

24

ABOUT THE SHORT STORY

MARK SEYBOLDT

THE Amy E. Spingarn prizes for short-stories which THE CRISIS is offering are three in number, $100, $50 and $20. "The stories should be preferably 4,000 to 5,000 words in length or 5 to 7 pages of THE CRISIS. In no case must they exceed 8,000 words."

I am asked to say a word about the short-story. The writing of fiction is an art. People do not simply "tell a story." They tell it in such a way that the hearer wants to listen and gets some interesting message from the narrative. In rare instances this art of telling may be happened on by chance. Usually it is a matter of careful study and long effort.

First of all, what is a short-story? As has been pointed out by many writers, it is not simply a story that is short, and here everyone must quote that classic dictum by Edgar Allen Poe, one of the greatest of short-story writers. In reviewing Hawthorne's "Tales" in 1842, Poe declared that the highest form of literary genius, in his opinion, lay in the writing of a rhymed poem which would take. about an hour to read. He then continued: "Were I called upon however, to designate that class of composition which, next to such a poem as I have suggested, should best fulfill the demands of high genius—should offer it the most advantageous field of exertion,—I should unhesitatingly speak of the prose tale as Mr. Hawthorne has here exemplified it. I allude to the short prose narrative requiring from a half hour to one or two hours in its perusal. The ordinary novel is objectionable from its length, for reasons already stated in substance. As it cannot be read at one sitting, it deprives itself, of course, of the immense force derivable from totality. Worldly interests intervening during the pauses of perusal, modify, annul, or counter-act in a greater or less degree the impressions of the book. But simple cessation in reading would of itself be sufficient to destroy the true unity. In the brief tale however, the author is enabled to carry out the fulness of his intention be it what it may. During the hour of perusal the soul of the reader is at the writer's control."

Since this time many other statements and definitions with regard to the short-story have been made. Those who wish to read an excellent short treatment of the general subject should look at chapter 12 of Bliss Perrys "Study of Prose Fiction", published by Houghton Mifflin Co. in 1902. Here in 34 pages is an excellent general view. This may be supplemented by chapters 10 and 11 in Clayton Hamilton's "Materials and Methods of Fiction", published by the Baker & Taylor Co. in 1908. The best single volume that the beginner in short-story writing could buy is the little volume by W. P. Atkinson, "The Short-Story". It is published by Allyn & Bacon and has both an excellent introduction on methods and six illustrative stories.

The short-story is, of course, a very old form of art. It occurs among the Egyptians 2,500 years B.C. We note it in the Book of Ruth in the Bible, written 450 B. C.; in the story of Cupid and Psyche of the second century A.D.; in the tales of Boccaccio; and then on down the years. Among the English, Stevenson, Kipling and Rider Haggard are the great modern exponents; among the French, Zola, de Maupassant, Daudet and Paul Marguerite; among the Russians, Tolstoi. The 12 best American short-stories were suggested by the *Critic* in 1897: E. E. Hale's "Man Without a Country"; Bret Harte's "Luck of Roaring Camp"; Nathaniel Hawthorne's "The Great Stone Face"; Edgar Allen Poe's "The Gold Bug" and "The Murders in the Rue Morgue"; Frank R. Stockton's "The Lady or the Tiger"; Washington Irving's "Rip Van Winkle"; Thomas Nelson Page's "Marse Chan"; Thomas Bailey Aldrich's "Marjorie Daw"; and Mary E. Wilkins' "The Revolt of Mother".

The older short-stories can be divided into *myths* like that of the Labors of Hercules, the *legends* like. St. George and the Dragon, *fairy tales* like Cinderella, *allegories* like Addison's "Vision of Mirza", and *parables* like The Prodigal Son. In our day Barrett has distinguished 9 forms of the short-story: the tale, the moral story, the wierd story, the character study, the dialect story, the parable of the times, the story of ingenuity, the humorous story and the dramatic story.

Of course no amount of study and thought is going to make a story writer out of persons who have no gift therefor, but given native talent, then careful study is indispensable for the best results. Two books are especially to be recommended for longer study: Charles E. Barrett's "Short-Story Writing" published by the Baker & Taylor Co. in 1900; or Evelyn M. Albright's "The Short-Story" published by Macmillan in 1907. These authors treat of plots, characters, titles, dialogue, climax, conclusion and other such matters. Atkinson has an interesting plan of a short-story of which this is a modification:

(Small-Maynard & Co.). Mr. O'Brien selects the best short stories each year and it is of interest to us to know that in his selection of 1923 he included Jean Toomer's "Blood-Burning Moon". Mr. O'Brien has also a book on present tendencies, "The Advance of the American Short-Story", published by Dodd, Mead & Co. in 1923.

We are proud to know that among the masters of the short-story in the United States is our own Charles W. Chesnutt, and those who would study the art of short-story writing as applied to the American Negro should by all means read "The Conjure Woman" and "The Wife of His Youth". To this they may add a study of the story whose first part appears in this number of THE CRISIS, "The Marked Tree·".

Finally let me say to all beginners, the

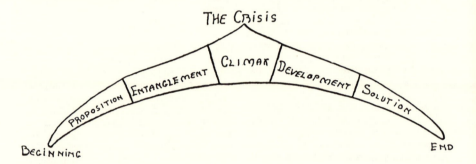

To those who would go more deeply and seriously into art and technique we can recommend H. A. Phillips' "Art in Short-Story Narrative" published by the Stanhope-Dodge Publishing Co.; R. W. Neal's "The Short-Story in the Making", Oxford University Press, 1914; W. B. Pitkin's "How to Write Stories", Harcourt, Brace and Co., 1923, and Glenn Clark's "A Manual of Short-Story Art", Macmillan Co., 1922.

For a clear conception of what the short-story should and can be, naturally nothing is better than reading the best models. Jessup and Canby published in 1912 (Appleton & Co.), an historical collection of short-stories called, "The Book of the Short-Story". Here one may go in 500 pages from 2500 B.C. to modern days and read the best of the world's short-story fiction. For contemporary short-stories one should follow "The Best Short-Stories" published each year by E. J. O'Brien

way to learn to write is to write. These prizes are to encourage writers: those who have written, those who are writing, and those who have always thought they might like to. Let everybody try. Hunt up the old story that is hidden away and furbish it up. Unfold again the story that has been rejected by all the editors, so long as it has not yet been published; or take from the recesses of your mind the story that has long been tingling there and waiting to be born.

_____

(*Mr. Seyboldt will write next month on plays. May we remind our readers that* THE CRISIS *is offering $600 in prizes for writers of Negro descent—$170 for stories; $125 for plays; $90 for essays; $90 for verse; and $125 for illustrations. Manuscripts and drawings must reach us on or before April 15, 1925. Write us for information.*)

PLAY-WRITING

MARK SEYBOLDT

THESE are the books on the subject:

1. William Archer: Playmaking. Small, Maynard & Co., 1912. 419pp.
2. George P. Baker: Dramatic Technique. Houghton Mifflin Co., 1919. 531pp.
3. Brander Matthews: A Study of the Drama. Houghton Mifflin Co., 1910. 320pp.
4. Percival Wilde: The Craftsmanship of the One-Act Play. Little, Brown & Co., 1923. 396pp.
5. Charlton Andrews: The Technique of Play-Writing. Home Correspondence School, 1915. 269pp.
6. Elizabeth R. Hunt: The Play of To-day. Dodd, Mead & Co., 1924. 238pp.
7. Frank Archer: How to Write a Good Play. Sampson, Low, Marston & Co., 1892. 224pp.
8. Fanny Cannon: Do's and Don'ts for the Playwright. T. S. Demson & Co., 1922. 65pp.

THE CRISIS is offering $125 in prizes for plays—$75 for the best, $40 for the second best and $10 for the third. The plays must deal with some phase of Negro history or experience and should occupy from 3 to 7 pages of THE CRISIS.

What now is a play and how may one be written? Of course "dramatists are born, not made" but as Mr. Baker points out most attempts at writing plays fall into two classes—the well-written but trite; the fresh and interesting but badly written. It is the second class which interests THE CRISIS. The birth-born gift is there but only study and experience will develop it.

The art of the drama can best be comprehended by careful reading of books like Baker's, Matthews' and Archer's. Hamilton writes: *"A play is a story devised to be presented by actors on a stage before an audience."* Here then are three things:

1. The audience
2. The actors
3. The story

Our writers may have two quite different audiences in mind:

A. White Americans used to theatre going
B. Colored folk.

While we set no limitations we are mainly interested in the second audience; we want colored folks to add the new diversion of the drama to their lives. We want the dramatic instinct of the masses to find outlet in the seen and spoken drama. It will stimulate and broaden cramped lives; it will bring inspiration, ambition, satisfaction. Hitherto they have had almost nothing but caricature or broad farce. The possibilities can be dimly sensed in the pageant "The Star of Ethiopia" as given some years ago in the east and now to be revived this spring in California.

The actors need not bother our playwright as actual staging of these plays is a matter of the future, and good colored and white actors are procurable. The chief thing is the Story. "There are no rules for writing a play" but there is lots to learn. First of all the writer must have an interesting story; this story must move, develop, come to a climax. "In a well-made modern play in three acts, the line of interest, broken into three pieces, is not likely to vary greatly from this:" (Brander Matthews)

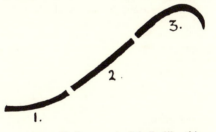

He plots Shakespeare's Othello like this:

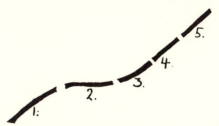

323

All this means Unity; the one who sees a play sees it all and at one sitting with only the drop of a curtain between. He cannot lay it aside like a novel. The play then must move quickly and powerfully. There is no time for long descriptions and speeches, autobiographies and explanations The art of successful play writing, says Pinero, "is nothing else than to achieve that *compression* of life, which the stage undoubtedly demands, without *falsification*".

Moreover the one act play, and that is what THE CRISIS wants—something running to 3 to 7 of its printed pages, is unity and compression to the Nth degree. Wilde says that the one act play is not an abbreviated play. "Unity is its inspiration. Unity is its aim. Unity is its soul." "The swiftness of exposition, the brevity, the homogeneity of effect which insists that every word contribute towards that effect." "A single effect, conveyed powerfully or delicately, or poetically or rudely, or seriously or whimsically, according to the character of the effect itself; an instantaneous arrest of attention, a continued grasp, and relinquishment only after the curtain has fallen; this is the goal and method of the true one act play."

The amateur may use the practical books to advantage: Andrews', Hunt's and Cannon's. Cannon's third part is especially stimulating to beginners:

A. Learn something about the theatre.

B. Remember that the story of your play must be a single episode or plot.

C. Remember that your story must have "action".

D. Make your conclusion logical.

And especially these "don'ts":

Don't { use stories so simple that they are over before they are begun. start to write without a plan. write "high flown" speeches for everyday people. leave us at the end asking what it all means!

Again: there are lynchings in the United States; there is sorrow among black folk; there is poverty, misfortune and sometimes despair; but do not confine yourself to these themes. There are also sunshine and kindness and ambition and hope. Think of these too.

Finally we must append this word by George Barnard Shaw which he has kindly and whimsically sent to THE CRISIS:

"The first lesson a colored (or white) playwright has to learn is never under any circumstances to show his play to another playwright, or to anyone but a manager, before it is produced or published."

"The second lesson is never to read an unperformed or unpublished play, as the inevitable consequence is an accusation of plagiarism, which is quite likely to be well founded, as a born dramatist cannot help assimilating a dramatic idea, consciously or unconsciously."

THE CRISIS

Vol. 30　No. 1　　　　MAY, 1925　　　　Whole No. 175

THE NEW CRISIS

E have assumed, with the Spring, with the beginning of our 30th semi-annual volume, with our 175th number and with the closing of a fateful quarter century, something of a new dress and a certain renewal of spirit.

How long may a CRISIS last? one might ask, sensing between our name and age some contradiction. To which we answer: What is long? 15 or 5000 years? But even in 15 years we see curious and suggestive change. In November, 1910, we wrote:

"The object of this publication is to set forth those facts and arguments which show the danger of race prejudice, particularly as manifested today toward colored people. It takes its name from the fact that the editors believe that this is a critical time in the history of the advancement of men. Catholicity and tolerance, reason and forbearance can today make the world-old dream of human brotherhood approach realization; while bigotry and prejudice em-

phasized race consciousness and force can repeat the awful history of the contact of nations and groups in the past. We strive for this higher and broader vision of Peace and Good Will." ———

Then we set forth the plan to make THE CRISIS (1) a newspaper, (2) a review of opinion, (3) a magazine with "a few short articles".

This initial program has unfolded itself, changed and developed. There is no longer need of a monthly newspaper for colored folk. Colored weeklies have arisen with an efficiency and scope in news-gathering that was not dreamed of in 1910. Our news therefore has transformed itself into a sort of permanent record of a few matters of widespread and historic importance. Our review of opinion continues in both "Opinion" and "Looking Glass", but rather as interpretation than as mere quotation. Particularly has our policy changed as to articles. They have increased in number, length and authority.

And above all, out of the broad vagueness of our general policy have emerged certain definite matters which we shall pursue with increased earnestness. We name them in something like the order in which they appeal to us now:

1. Economic Development

At Philadelphia, the N. A. A. C. P. made a suggestion of alliance among the laboring people of the United States across the color line. The American Federation of Labor has as yet made no active response to our overtures. Meantime, however, we are not waiting and we propose to make a crusade in THE CRISIS covering the next three years and taking up in succession the history and significance of the Labor Movement in the modern world, the present actual relation of Negroes to labor unions and a practical plan of future co-operation.

2. Political Independence

We shall stress as never before political independence. No longer must Negroes be born into the Republican Party. If they vote the Republican ticket or any other ticket it must be because the candidates of that party in any given election make the best promises for the future and show the best record in the past. Above all we shall urge all Negroes, male and female, to register and vote and to study political ethics and machinery.

3. Education and Talent

We shall stress the education of Negro youth and the discovery of Negro talent. Our schools must be emancipated from the secret domination of the Bourbon white South. Teachers, white or black, in Negro schools who cannot receive and treat their pupils as social equals must go. We must develop brains, ambition, efficiency and ideals without limit or circumscription. If our own Southern colleges will not do this, and whether they do it or not, we must continue to force our way into Northern colleges in larger and larger numbers and to club their doors open with our votes. We must provide larger scholarship funds to support Negroes of talent here and abroad.

4. Art

We shall stress Beauty—all Beauty, but especially the beauty of Negro life and character; its music, its dancing, its drawing and painting and the new birth of its literature. This growth which THE CRISIS long since predicted is sprouting and coming to flower. We shall encourage it in every way—by reproduction, by publication, by personal mention—keeping the while a high standard of merit and stooping never to cheap flattery and misspent kindliness.

5. Peace and International Understanding

Through the Pan-African movement we shall press for better knowledge of each other by groups of the peoples of African descent; we shall seek wider understanding with the brown and yellow peoples of the world and thus, by the combined impact of an appeal to decency and humanity from the oppressed and insulted to those fairer races who today accidentally rule the world, we shall seek universal peace by abolishing the rivalries and hatreds and economic competition that lead to organized murder.

6. The Church

We shall recognize and stress the fact that the American Negro church is doing the greatest work in social uplift of any present agency. We criticise our churches bitterly and in these plaints THE CRISIS has often joined. At the same time we know that without the help of the Negro church neither the N. A. A. C. P. nor THE CRISIS could have come into being nor could they for a single day continue to exist. Despite an outworn creed and ancient methods of worship the black church is leading the religious world in real human brotherhood, in personal charity, in social uplift and in economic teaching. No such tremendous force can be neglected or ignored by a journal which seeks to portray and expound the truth. We shall essay, then, the contradictory task of showing month by month the accomplishment of black religious organization in America and at the same time seeking to free the minds of our people from the futile dogma that makes for unreason and intolerance.

7. Self-criticism

THE CRISIS is going to be more frankly critical of the Negro group. In our fight for the sheer crumbs of decent treatment we have become habituated to regarding ourselves as always right and resenting criticism from whites and furiously opposing self-criticism from within. We are seriously crippling Negro art and literature by refusing to contemplate any but handsome heroes, unblemished heroines and flawless defenders; we insist on being always and everywhere all right and often we ruin our cause by claiming too much and admitting no fault. Here THE CRISIS has sinned with its group and it purposes hereafter to examine from time to time judicially the extraordinary number of very human faults among us—both those common to mankind and those born of our extraordinary history and experiences.

8. Criticism

This does not mean that we propose for a single issue to cease playing the gadfly to the Bourbon South and the Copperhead North, to hypocritical Philanthropy and fraudulent Science, to race hate and human degradation. _____

All this, we admit, is an enormous task for a magazine of 52 pages, selling for 15 cents and paying all of its own expenses out of that 15 cents and not out of the bribes of Big Business.

We shall probably fall far short of its well doing but we shall make the attempt in all seriousness and good will. And, Good Reader, what will you do? Write and tell us.

THE CRISIS

Vol. 30   No. 3   JULY, 1925   Whole No. 177

THE AMY SPINGARN PRIZES

E are glad to announce that Mrs. Amy Spingarn has been so pleased with the results of our prize contest that she has already paid over to the treasury of the N. A. A. C. P. another sum of six hundred dollars for the prize contest of 1926. The details of this contest will be announced at the time when the prizes of the 1925 contest are awarded. In the meantime and in the name not only of itself but of the young Negro artists THE CRISIS wishes to express to Mrs. Spingarn its deep appreciation of her thoughtfulness.

KRIGWA

THE award of prizes in the Amy Spingarn Contest in Literature and Art is as follows:

STORIES

Judges—H. G. Wells, Sinclair Lewis, Charles W. Chesnutt, Mary White Ovington.

First Prize—$100, "High Yaller", by "John Chauncey Brown" (Pseudonym), Rudolph Fisher, M. D., Freedmen's Hospital, Washington, D. C.

Second Prize—$50, "There Never Fell A Night So Dark," by "Jean France" (Pseudonym), Mrs. Marie French, 518 North Pine Street, Colorado Springs, Colorado.

Third Prize—$20, "Three Dogs and a Rabbit," by "Elizabeth Stokes" (Pseudonym), Mrs. Anita Scott Coleman, Box 252, Silver City, New Mexico.

ESSAYS

Judges—Edward Bok, J. E. Spingarn, Benjamin Brawley.

First Prize—$50, "On Being Young—A Woman—and Colored," by "Jean Talbot" (Pseudonym), Miss Marietta O. Bonner, 7 Dennison Street, Roxbury, Massachusetts.

Second Prize—$30, "The Fascination of Cities," by "Raif Dickerson" (Pseudonym), Langston Hughes, 1816 Twelfth Street, N. W., Washington, D. C.

Third Prize—10, "Salvation," by "Anthropos" (Pseudonym), G. A. Stewart, 222 North 21st St., Columbus, Ohio.

PLAYS

Judges—Eugene O'Neill, Charles Burroughs, Lester A. Walton.

First Prize—$75, "The Broken Banjo," by Willis Richardson, 2023 Thirteenth Street. N. W., Washington, D. C.

Second Prize—$40, "The Church Fight," by "Auntie" (Pseudonym), Ruth Ada Gaines Shelton, 1523 Good Avenue, St. Louis, Missouri.

Third Prize—$10, "For Unborn Children," Miss Myrtle Athleen Smith, 615 Sixth Street, Greeley, Colorado.

POEMS

Judges—William Stanley Braithwaite, Robert Morss Lovett, Leslie Pinckney Hill.

First Prize—$50, "Two Moods of Love," by "Timothy Tumble" (Pseudonym), Countée Cullen, 2190 Seventh Avenue, New York, N. Y.

Second Prize—$30, "Letters Found Near A Suicide," by "Xavier I" (Pseudonym), Frank Horne, 351 Lenox Avenue, New York, N. Y.

Third Prize—$10, "Poems," by "Ralph Anson" and "Jerry Biera" (Pseudonym), Langston Hughes, 1816 Twelfth Street, N. W., Washington, D. C.

ILLUSTRATIONS

Judges—Walter Jack Duncan, H. Glintenkamp, Winold Reiss.

First Prize—$75, "Outis" (Pseudonym), E. A. Harleston, 118 Calhoun Street, Charleston, South Carolina.

Second Prize—$40, Albert Smith, care American Express Company, 11 Rue Scribe, Paris, France.

Third Prize—$10, H. A. Woodruff, Suite 314, 46 North Penn Street, Indianapolis, Indiana.

The initial sifting of the manuscripts and selection of those of merit was done by the editors of THE CRISIS with the inestimable co-operation of Mary White Ovington, Jean Toomer, Lester Walton, Emmett J. Scott, Jr., Edwin Morgan and Yolande DuBois.

OTHER CONTESTANTS **B**ESIDE the three prize stories there are seven others of sufficient merit for THE CRISIS to publish during the next year. Among these are:

"The Third and Fourth Generations" by Lucille Francis.

"Immolation" by "Albert Gold" (Pseudonym), Mrs. C. F. Cook, Washington.

"Swamp Judgment" by N. B. Young, Jr., St. Louis, Mo.

"The Blue Awning" by Jean A. Stewart, Columbus, Ohio.

"Preacher" by "Le Triste" (Pseudonym).

"The Hedge" by Olive Green

"The Parafine Cover" by Adele Brigham.

Among the essays are four which we shall publish:

"Dunbar, the Poet" by Amy Williams.

"Remarks Upon Three Things as They Are" by Mrs. Anita Scott Coleman, Silver City, New Mexico.

"The Coming of the Black Modernist" by Cassius Van Dyke.

"The Psychology of the Garvey Movement" by "Mbombu" (Pseudonym), E. Franklin Frazier, Atlanta, Georgia.

Among the poems we shall publish:

"A Sketch of Lenox Avenue" by "She" (Pseudonym) and others by Grace P. White and Martin W. Hawkins.

We shall also use a cover contributed by Laura Wheeler.

WORDS OF THE JUDGES **O**UR judges have expressed gratification at the high character of the work submitted to them in THE CRISIS Art contest. Of the stories, H. G. Wells, perhaps the foremost novelist of the world, writes: "'High Yaller' is first-class work. I congratulate Mr. Brown [Pseudonym for Rudolph Fisher] on a good, clear, effective story. He will go far. I put 'Three Dogs and a Rabbit' second on the list. Congratulations to Miss Stokes [Pseudonym for Mrs. Anita Scott Coleman]."

Sinclair Lewis, the most popular contemporary American novelist, adds: "Of these stories, it seems both to me and my wife that 'High Yaller' is incomparably the best, and we have read them all with great care."

Charles W. Chesnutt, our own laureate, says: "'High Yaller', the most ambitious of the four stories, is very well written. Of course an editor reading it with a view to publication could make certain suggestions as to the language and figures of speech here and there. The plot is well worked out, with a heroine and a hero and a villain, and its atmosphere may be a correct reflection of Negro life in Harlem, with which I am not very familiar. But to me at least the theme is not convincing. . . .

"'There Never Fell a Night So Dark' is in my opinion the best of the lot. The theme is human. It is a simple sketch, though with some elements of improbability in the plot. . . .

"If I were grading the stories I should

make 'There Never Fell a Night So Dark' No. 1, 'High Yaller' No. 2, 'Three Dogs and a Rabbit' No. 3, and 'Easy Pickin's' No. 4."

Of the essays Joel E. Spingarn, whom most colored people know as a friend and most white people as a keen student of literary criticism, writes: "Only one of the essays you sent me is an essay in the conventional sense, and that is very conventional indeed. All the others are 'sketches', and all of them are so full of promise that it is very difficult to place them in any formal order of merit. But I like 'On Being Young, a Woman, and Colored' best. The mood of being young in an old world, a woman in a man's world, and colored in a white world is all there—and back of the mood, vistas and vistas. Then I place 'Salvation', if only because the vivid yet clipped and staccato sentences of 'The Fascination of Cities' are at times artificial and trying. But all three are good. They are charged with feeling, personal feeling rooted in race feeling, and the sense of a personal wound is never absent. Personal wounds are an advantage to the artist, I often think—if he can transcend them, that is, make of them a ladder and not a burden,, or (to use the jargon of aesthetics) if his practical personality is sublimated into an artistic personality. To the thinker a personal wound can never be a ladder, but only a burden of which he must divest himself or cease to be a thinker. To make a personal grievance eloquent, that will suffice for orator, reformer, prophet, agitator, literary man and religious teacher; but to the artist that is not enough, and to the thinker that is nothing at all. I see everywhere the artist in the American Negro rising to find expression, and I have faith that the thinker too will find his universal thought."

Edward Bok, former editor of the *Ladies' Home Journal*, writes: "I have been very much impressed with the equal merit of these contributions. There is some excellent writing in them."

The judges of poetry were headed by William Stanley Braithwaite, who writes: "I read the poems yesterday and report the following selections in the order given. That is, I am naming what seems to me the four best poems. They are: first, 'If Love Be Staunch'; second, 'Lament'; third, 'Cross'; fourth, 'To "Chick"'. I have not taken 'Three Moods of Love' as one poem. 'Lament' is very nearly as good as 'If Love Be Staunch', but in two lines the writer makes one slur the accent, and this gives a slight tarnish to the imagery.

"As a disinterested arbiter I could only make my selection on the basis of actual achievement, an important part in which is the adequacy of form; but I do want to speak an appreciative word for 'A Sketch of Lenox Avenue, New York', by 'She'. Whoever this writer is, she has the ore of poetry in her, and it only needs the refining process of technical command to achieve a notable visionary expression. There's power there and a keen assemblage of values."

Robert Morss Lovett, of the *New Republic*, says: "I am glad to have had the opportunity of reading them."

On the plays we quote only the Master, Eugene O'Neill: "I am glad to hear that the judges all agreed on 'The Broken Banjo' and that the play was so successfully staged. Willis Richardson should certainly continue working in this field."

THE 599   AND finally of the five hundred and ninety-nine who tried and received neither word nor prize; we are going to write each one of you and tell you what we think of your effort and what Krigwa advises and how the advice may best be followed.

And in 1926: another $600 in prizes!

THE CRISIS

Vol. 31 No. 1   NOVEMBER, 1925   Whole No. 181

KRIGWA, 1926

WE have printed and mailed to inquiring friends the first bulletin of our plans for Negro Artists and Writers. We will be glad to send this bulletin to all who apply, not forgetting a stamp.

Our program to encourage Negro Art next year is as follows:

From October 1925 to April 1926 we shall publish the prize material of our 1925 contest.

From November 1, 1925, until May 1, 1926, we shall be glad to receive manuscripts, drawings and paintings for the following prizes aggregating $600:

For stories, prizes of $100 and $50.

For plays, prizes of $100 and $50.

For CRISIS covers, prizes of $75 and $25.

For essays, prizes of $75 and $25.

For poems, prizes of $75 and $25.

These manuscripts, etc., must be in THE CRISIS office on or before May 1, 1926. The award of prizes will be announced in October, 1926. The name and address of the author must appear on the first page of the manuscripts. Please keep a copy of all manuscripts as none will be returned. Paintings and drawings will be returned in November, 1926.

KRIGWA 1926

THROUGH the kindness of Mrs. Amy B. Spingarn THE CRISIS is enabled to offer for a second year a series of prizes for writing and drawing.

TIME.—The manuscripts and drawings must be in THE CRISIS office on or before *May 1, 1926*. The names of the prize winners will be announced in the November number published *October 15, 1926*.

CONDITIONS.—These prizes are offered to persons of *Negro* descent in order to encourage their aptitude for art expression.

PRIZES FOR WRITING.—Prizes are offered for *fiction, plays, essays* and *verse* as follows: For *Fiction*—Prizes of $100, $50 and honorable mention. The stories should not exceed *8,000 words*. For *Plays*—Prizes of $100, $50 and honorable mention. For *Essays*—Prizes of $75, $25 and honorable mention. Essays should not exceed *5,000 words*. For *Verse*—Prizes of $75, $25 and honorable mention.

All of the manuscripts should be *typewritten* or legibly copied on one side of the paper. The pages should be numbered and on the *top of the first page* in addition to the subject should appear the *pen name* under which the author is writing. The same name should appear on a *sealed envelope* accompanying the manuscript and in the sealed envelope should be the real name and address of the author. If the author insists upon the return of his manuscript then he must *also* inclose within the sealed envelope an envelope large enough to contain the manuscript, carefully addressed to himself and with sufficient first class postage pasted on this envelope. *We trust, however, that no one will ask for the return of his manuscript.* Always in sending away manuscripts it is best to keep a copy. Manuscripts are liable to loss in mails and the physical labor of returning them is too great for an ordinary office to undertake successfully.

All manuscripts will be *acknowledged by postal-card* when received and may be sent in any time after *October 1, 1925.* They must be plainly addressed to us as follows: *The Crisis Prize Contest, 1926,* care of *The Crisis Magazine, 69 Fifth Avenue, New York City.*

All manuscripts must be original, never before published in any form and at the time of entering this contest they must not be in the hands of any other publisher. THE CRISIS will reserve to the author all rights of publication and reproduction in any way except the rights to first serial publication. THE CRISIS shall have the right to return or publish at its regular rates of compensation any of the manuscripts submitted.

ILLUSTRATIONS.—Illustrations may be for covers of THE CRISIS or for decorations of THE CRISIS page, cartoons or general illustrations. The prizes will be $75, $25 and honorable mention. Especial care should be taken carefully to pack the illustrations so that they will not be broken or spoiled in transit. They should have *permamently attached or written* upon them the real name and address of the artist. *No pen name is necessary.* All drawings must be original, never before reproduced in any way and no copies of them must be in the hands of any other periodical at the time of submission to THE CRISIS. THE CRISIS will reserve to the artist all rights of reproduction except the rights to first serial publication in THE CRISIS. THE CRISIS shall have the right to return or publish at its regular rates any of the drawings submitted. *Send sufficient money to pay for the return of the drawings.*

During the years 1926 and 1927 THE CRISIS will publish the prize manuscripts and drawings and produce the plays.

Further announcements concerning the prizes will be made in successive numbers of THE CRISIS. All persons interested in any form of art expression are invited to enroll with *Krigwa.* Correspondence is invited.

KRIGWA, 1926

WE ARE ALREADY RECEIV-
ING manuscripts for our literary
contest, 1926. There are $600 in
prizes for stories, plays, essays,
poems and covers.

We want especially to stress the
fact that while we believe in Negro
art we do not believe in any art simply for art's sake. We want the
earth beautiful but we are primarily
interested in the earth. We want Negro writers to produce beautiful
things but we stress the things rather
than the beauty. It is Life and
Truth that are important and Beauty
comes to make their importance visible and tolerable. Even this as we
say it is not altogether true.

Write then about things as you
know them; be honest and sincere.
In THE CRISIS at least, you do not
have to confine your writings to the
portrayal of beggars, scoundrels and
prostitutes; you can write about ordinary decent colored people if you
want. On the other hand do not fear
the Truth. Plumb the depths. If you
want to paint Crime and Destitution
and Evil paint it. Do not try to be
simply respectable, smug, conventional. Use propaganda if you want.
Discard it and laugh if you will. But
be true, be sincere, be thorough, and
do a beautiful job.

The contest closes May 1, 1926.

THE CRISIS

Vol. 32 No. 2 | JUNE, 1926 | Whole No. 188

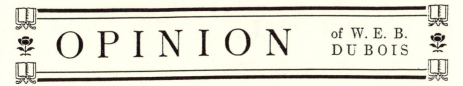

OPINION of W. E. B. DU BOIS

KRIGWA

WE HAVE RECEIVED in the Krigwa competition of 1926, 700 stories, plays, essays and drawings. The prizes, aggregating $600, will be awarded to the successful contestants Friday, October 15, 1926, in the ballroom of International House, Riverside Drive, New York City. At the same time, on the stage, one or more plays will be given by a band of Krigwa players.

There have been formed in the United States a half dozen or more Krigwa bands for the encouragement of Negro art and literature. Several of these are giving plays, especially the Krigwa players of New York City who have started at the 135th Street branch of the New York Public Library a Little Negro Theatre. They gave three plays in May in three performances.

In addition to this a most encouraging movement has come toward book buying. For instance, a few of the St. Louis public school teachers have organized the St. Louis "Book Chat Circle". Their joining fee is a subscription to THE CRISIS and their main purpose the buying of books written by Negroes. The circle is at present pledged to buy annually one book of Negro authorship for each four members.

Service, popularly known as the Garland Fund, will become one of the main agencies for the emancipation of the American Negro. Its work for colored people has not been heralded, but it is of far-reaching importance. First and foremost, it did the square thing by the Negro race by appointing a colored man, James Weldon Johnson, on its Board of Directors. This is more than the General Education Board or even the John F. Slater Board has dared to do, although common justice demands it.

This Fund has helped to secure justice for the Virgin Islands; has contributed toward the trade union movement to organize Negro workers; has appropriated money to the National Urban League to study the relations of Negroes to trade unions; has appropriated money to THE CRISIS to study Negro common school education; and has helped the anti-lynching campaign and the Defense Fund of the National Association for the Advancement of Colored People.

The American Fund received from Charles Garland $901,555.90. It has spent in three years $310,126 and because of the increase in the value of the original gift it still has on hand a principal of $777,094.

THE CRISIS

Vol. 32 No. 6   OCTOBER, 1926   Whole No. 192

OPINION of W. E. B. DU BOIS

PRIZES

ON OCTOBER 25TH in the hall and theatre of International House on Riverside Drive, New York City, THE CRISIS will give a program of plays and readings in honor of those who have entered manuscripts and drawings in THE CRISIS Prize Competition of 1926 and to all friends of these contestants and of the Renaissance of Negro Art. The plays will be interesting, the speeches will be few and short, the prize winners will be announced and presented, and a reception will follow. The price of admission will be one dollar. The public is cordially invited to be present. At this time also we shall announce certain prize competitions for 1926-27.

FOR A PRIZE NOVEL, $1,000

TO THE AUTHOR w h o the judges decide has written the best novel of Negro life, Messrs. Albert & Charles Boni, Inc., will pay outright as a Prize $1,000 in addition to the usual terms of royalty which will be arranged with the author.

Conditions

1. The author must be of Negro descent.

2. The novel must deal with Negro life in the sense that one or more of its leading characters must be of Negro descent and its action must show the influence of this fact.

3. Only manuscripts of unpublished works, submitted to Albert & Charles Boni before September 1, 1926, and accompanied by the declaration of the author that the manuscript is submitted in competition for the Prize will be considered.

4. All manuscripts submitted in competition must be offered to Albert & Charles Boni, Inc., for publication on terms to be arranged between the author and publisher. The successful work shall be chosen from among those manuscripts accepted by Albert & Charles Boni, Inc., for publication and the Prize shall be in addition to and independent of the royalty to be arranged for in the usual way.

5. No manuscript containing less than 30,000 words shall be considered as a novel for the purpose of this competition, and preference will be given in general to works of full novel length.

6. Albert & Charles Boni, Inc., will use all reasonable care to pass promptly on manuscripts submitted in competition for this Prize and to return those found unavailable for publication, but they shall not be responsible for those lost in transit.

7. The judges for the competition will be

Henry Seidel Canby	Edna Kenton
W. E. B. Du Bois	Laurence Stallings
Charles S. Johnson	Irita Van Doren
James Weldon Johnson	

Their decision shall be accepted on all questions of eligibility or interpretation of the rules, and their award shall be final.

8. The award will be made and publicly announced as soon as possible after the close of the competition, and not later than January 2, 1927.

For further information address Albert and Charles Boni, 66 Fifth Avenue, New York, N. Y.

———

A NUMBER OF PRIZES in Negro Literature and Art will be distributed in 1927 through THE CRISIS Magazine.

Prizes will be offered for

1. Plays
2. Short Stories
3. Poetry
4. Essays
5. Covers for THE CRISIS
6. Songs

All manuscripts and illustrations must be in our hands by May 1, 1927. Awards will be announced October 24, 1927.

We find it necessary this year to lay down more stringent rules as to entrants than we have heretofore.

All persons wishing to enter the contest must fill out an entry blank. This blank and the rules of the contest will be ready for mailing January 15, 1927. A stamped self-addressed envelope mailed to THE CRISIS will bring a copy by return mail after that date.

To date over $1000 has been pledged for these prizes.

Krigwa, 1927

THE Editor of THE CRISIS MAGAZINE takes pleasure in announcing prizes in Literature and Art for the year 1927 to the aggregate amount of two thousand and thirty-five dollars ($2035). The money for these prizes has been furnished by the following persons and organizations:

Mrs. Amy E. Spingarn..............$ 600
Mrs. E. R. Mathews 125
Carl Brandt 100
Empire State Federation of Colored
   Women's Clubs 100
Eight Colored Banks 400
Five Colored Insurance Companies... 360
                                   ─────
   Total $1685
The Charles Waddell Chesnutt Hon-
   orarium ....$ 350
                                   ─────
   Grand Total $2035

The sum of $1685 will be distributed for stories, plays, poetry, essays, songs and covers for THE CRISIS under the following conditions:

1. All matter entered for these prizes must be in THE CRISIS office on or before June 15, 1927. The awards will be announced October 24, 1927.

2. All entrants must be of Negro descent. They are urged to become subscribers to THE CRISIS MAGAZINE. Without continuous personal touch with entrants we cannot be sure of their addresses or advise them through our columns.

3. All persons who have received two prizes, first and second, in any one class of entries in CRISIS contests will not compete in this contest but will be placed *hors concour*, becoming automatically members of the Krigwa Academy; they will be asked to serve as judges. The first members of the Krigwa Academy are *Willis Richardson, Washington, D. C.*, who has twice received first prize for plays and *Countée Cullen, New York City*, who has received first and second prizes for poems.

4. All persons who propose to enter the contest must send a stamped addressed envelope for entry blanks.

5. Each manuscript or drawing submitted must be accompanied by an entry blank.

6. No manuscripts will be returned except as follows:
Stories, plays and songs if accompanied by a stamped self-addressed envelope for each manuscript will be returned as soon as practical after the announcement of prizes. Under no circumstances will poems or essays be returned; contestants should therefore keep copies of these. Drawings will be returned after the contest if accompanied by sufficient postage.

7. Each entry upon reception will be acknowledged by post-card.

8. The prizes offered are as follows:

NEGRO BUSINESS PRIZES: $725.

The economic development of the Negro in the last two decades has been phenomenal and it is time that the new development of art and literature among us should be linked up with the economic trend. At the request of THE CRISIS five of the largest and oldest Negro insurance societies and eight of the best banks have consented to head a movement designed to direct the attention of young writers to Negro business.

The following Negro business organizations have united in this effort:

Insurance Companies

The Liberty Life Insurance Company, Chicago, Ill., M. O. Bousfield, President.

The North Carolina Mutual Life Insurance Company, Durham, N. C., C. C. Spaulding, President.

The Northeastern Life Insurance Company, Newark, N. J., H. H. Pace, President.

The Southern Aid Society, Richmond, Va., J. T. Carter, President.

The Supreme Life and Casualty Company, Columbus, O., T. K. Gibson, President.

Banks

The Binga State Bank, Chicago, Ill., Jesse Binga, President.

The Citizens and Southern Bank and Trust Company, Philadelphia, Pa., R. R. Wright, Sr., President.

The Danville Savings Bank, Danville, Va., M. C. Martin, President.

The First Standard Bank, Louisville, Ky., Wilson Lovett, President.

The Peoples Finance Corporation, St. Louis, Mo., G. W. Buckner, Vice-President.

The Prudential Bank, Washington, D. C., J. R. Hawkins, President.

The St. Lukes Penny Savings Bank, Richmond, Va., Mrs. Maggie L. Walker, President.

The Wage Earners Bank, Savannah, Ga., L. E. Williams, President.

The prizes are:

For Short Stories

First Prize $150
Second Prize 100
Third Prize 50

For Essays

First Prize $100
Second Prize 50
Third Prize 25

For Cartoons

First Prize $125
Second Prize 75
Third Prize 50

_____
$725

This amount may be increased later by the entry of other organizations which still have the matter under consideration. If so, the facts will be published.

The object of these prizes is to stimulate general knowledge of banking and insurance in modern life and specific knowledge of what American Negroes are doing in these fields; and to collect facts and impressions concerning Negro workers and their relation to Negro business.

The stories must have literary merit and be real stories and not mere statements, advertisements or sermons. They should not exceed 8000 words in length.

The essays should not exceed 5000 words in length and should be specific rather than general and based on real knowledge and personal experience. Entrants for these prizes should write to and, if possible, visit the insurance companies and banks for first-hand information and should study their cities and neighborhoods for illustrative facts.

The cartoons must be done in black and white (pen, pencil, wash or charcoal) and must be drawn on regular illustration board. They may consist of one picture or a series but in any case they must be of a size so that all may be reduced to appear on a page 9¾ by 13½ inches, with space for title or caption at the bottom. The subject of the cartoons must be banking and insurance among American Negroes. The drawings must be securely wrapped and sent flat, not folded or rolled. They must have an entry blank pasted on the back with full postage for return.

PRIZES IN LITERARY ART AND EXPRESSION
$350

These prizes are offered out of the gift of Mrs. Amy E. Spingarn, who now for the third year is expressing her faith and interest in Negro ability.

In this contest we are offering the following prizes for short stories, plays and essays:

First Prize $200
Second Prize 100
Third Prize 50

_____
$350

Our plan is to ask three sets of judges to choose two stories, two plays and two essays from those submitted; we shall give honorable mention to these. Out of these we shall ask a separate set of judges to select on the basis of literary merit, excellence in the use of the English language, human characterization and personal promise of future growth, first, second and third awards regardless of whether the specimen is fiction, drama or essay. This we think, will avoid awarding mediocre work simply because it is best in its class. Stories must not exceed 8000 words; essays must not exceed 5000 words; plays should be one act in length.

PRIZES FOR POETRY, $225

These prizes are offered by Mr. Carl Brandt and the Empire State Federation of Colored Women's Clubs. We seek here expression and beauty in rhythm and word. The entries may be poems or any other rhythmic form in sermons, speeches, etc. If the poems are a group they must have some central theme or recognizable unity. The prizes offered are:

First Prize $150
Second Prize 50
Third Prize 25

_____
Total $225

PRIZES FOR SONGS, $125

Through the kindness of Mrs. E. R. Mathews we offer these prizes for songs:

First Prize $100
Second Prize 25

_____
Total $125

The songs must be original melodies or musical settings with or without words. If with words, the words may be original or adapted.

COVERS FOR THE CRISIS, $260

First Prize $150
Second Prize 75
Third Prize 25
Fourth Prize 10

_____
Total $260

These prizes are offered from Mrs. Spingarn's gift. The requirements are limited and exact and must be *carefully kept*. The drawings must be in black and white (pen, pencil, wash or charcoal) and must be drawn on regular illustration board. The drawings must have conspicuously at the top the words, THE CRISIS, in bold lettering. They must be of a size to be reduced so as to appear on a page 9¾ by 13½ inches. There must be a space at the bottom for the insertion of month and year on the left and "Fifteen cents a copy" must be written in on the right.

The drawings must be wrapped securely and flat, not rolled or folded. They should have an entry blank pasted on the back with full postage for return. The drawings must have some reference to colored people—that is: they must portray colored faces or suggest allusions to the history, art or experience of colored peoples. Under "colored" is understood black, brown, red and yellow peoples, including Negroes, mulattoes, Chinese, Japanese, Egyptians, Arabs, Indians, etc.

All manuscripts and drawings must be original, never before published in any form and at the time of entering this contest they must not be in the hands of any other publisher. THE CRISIS will reserve to the author all rights of publication and reproduction in any way except the rights to first serial publication. THE CRISIS shall have the right to return or publish at its regular rates of compensation any of the manuscripts or drawings submitted.

The Charles Waddell Chestnutt
Honorarium, $350

In honor of the first and still foremost novelist of Negro descent in America, seven "Friends of THE CRISIS" have offered us the sum of $350 to be paid for the three best contributions published in THE CRISIS during the year 1927. The contributions selected must be written by persons not on the editorial staff and the decision will be taken by vote of the subscribers to THE CRISIS. Coupons for voting will appear in the March CRISIS. The awards are:

Best contribution	$200
Second best contribution	100
Third best contribution	50
	$350

Finally, as we have said before:

"We trust that all entrants will remember that the prizes are the least valuable part of a prize contest. The great object of these contests is to stimulate effort, set a standard of taste and enable persons to discover in themselves capabilities."

KRIGWA, 1927

THE Editors of THE CRISIS, with the aid and suggestion of various authors, artists and experts with whom they consulted, have decided to distribute THE CRISIS prizes as follows:

Prizes in Literary Art and Expression offered out of the gift of Mrs. Amy E. Spingarn, who now for the third year is expressing her faith and interest in Negro ability:

First Prize $200
Miss Marita O. Bonner, Washington, D. C., for:
"The Purple Flower", a fantasy.
"Exit", a play.
"Drab Rambles", a short story.
"The Young Blood Hungers", an essay.

Second Prize $100
Miss Brenda Ray Moryck, Washington, D. C., for:
"Old Days and New", a short story.
"Days", a short story.
"Her Little Brother", a short story.

Third Prize $50
Miss Eulalie Spence, New York City for:
"Hot Stuff", a play.
"Undertow", a play.

Honorable Mention
Mrs. Esther P. Young, Texas.
Hubert A. Brown, Massachusetts.
Julian E. Bagley, California.
Miss Angel Estha Renn, California.
George A. Singleton, Illinois.
Nathan Ben Young, Missouri.
John F. Matheus, West Virginia.
S. Randolph Edmonds, Maryland.

Prizes in Poetry, offered by the Program and Literature Department of the Empire State Federation of Women's Clubs through Mrs. A. W. Hunton ($100), and by Mr. Carl Brandt ($125).

First Prize $150
Miss Mae Cowdery, Philadelphia, Pa., for:
"Longings".
"Lamps".

Second Prize $50
Edward Silvera, Lincoln, Pa., for:
"Song to a Dark Girl".

Third Prize $25
Miss Ethel M. Caution, New York City, for:
"To . . . .".

December, 1927

Honorable Mention
Miss Marguerite A. Low, New York.
George L. Allen, North Carolina.

Prizes for Covers, from Mrs. Spingarn's gift:
First Prize $150
Miss Vivian S. Schuyler, New York City for:
"Lift Every Voice and Sing".

Second Prize $75
Roscoe C. Wright, Roxbury, Mass., for:
"Black Womanhood Unfettered".

Third Prize $25
Cornelius W. Johnson, Chicago, Ill., for:
"A Chicago Chap".

Fourth Prize $10
Allan R. Freelon, Philadelphia, Pa., for:
"A Jungle Nymph".

Honorable Mention
William S. Carter.
Joseph C. Carpenter, Jr., Washington, D. C.
Clifford Chelterham, New York.
Bennie H. Robynson, New York.
George B. Morse, New York.
Cornelius W. Johnson, Illinois.
Solomon W. Griffin, New York.
Handsel G. Bell, Arizona.
Roscoe C. Wright, Massachusetts.
Nathaniel Bailey, New Jersey.
Edwin Smith, New York.
Lucille C. Rogers.
Leon J. Moore, New York.

Prizes for Songs, offered by Mrs. E. R. Mathews:

First Prize $100
Edna Rosalyne Heard, California.

Second Prize $25
Miss Jeannette L. Norman, New York.

Honorable Mention
Miss Velma D. Nutter, Pennsylvania.
J. Harvey Herbron, Pennsylvania.

ECONOMIC PRIZES

WE are having a queer experience with the Economic Prizes offered by Negro banks and insurance societies through THE CRISIS. They were announced first early in 1927; then withdrawn because of lack of response, and announced again in March, 1928. At the close of the Contest, December 31, 1928, only twenty-one entries were received, and of these only six came anywhere near the requirements laid down. These requirements asked "for stories, essays or cartoons which will illustrate or study or tell the story of the economic development of the Negro." We will consider carefully the merits of the six entrants and announce our decision concerning them in the May number of THE CRISIS.

Meantime, however, it seems certain that the young Negro writers and thinkers of today are not applying their minds to the economic problem of their race. And yet that problem is, and, for many generations, must be, the central problem of our existence and survival. How are we going to bring the attention of the young to the importance of that problem? Manifestly prizes for writing are not effective. What will be effective? We shall be glad to learn.

March, 1929

THE DU BOIS LITERARY PRIZE

THE facts are these: Once upon a time I took a long and beautiful journey into Time and Space. I saw again Eisenach beneath the shadow of the Wartbourg, and heard the voices of that merry party—Dora, blue-eyed and black-haired; the red-haired Elsa, the Sonderhofs, the Keims from France and little McMahon of England; and I felt again the stern presence of Oberpharrer Herr Doctor Marbach.

Then I went to Berlin to see its astonishing transformation; then through the North Sea to Russia, that greatest and most startling of modern human experiments; out to the Volga and down through the Ukraine to the Black Sea, and so to the City of Cities, Constantinople.

And, being near the edge of beggary, I wired for a second class cabin, Naples to New York, on the magnificent Duilio. Then I rushed to Italy through Athens and Brindisi, and was informed most politely that all second class accommodations were gone but that they had saved me a lovely cabin in the first class!

There were two objections: First its cost would land me in New York just about penniless, and secondly if there is anything from which I run, it is the kind of American snob that travels first class in a Trans-Atlantic boat. Let humanity take any form but that, and my firm nerve shall never tremble! But I had to take that boat for work called.

On the boat, the ordeal of the dining room was rather well solved: two priests, a nice old couple from the Middle West, and a few silent nonentities. I could eat in peace. Just as matters were settling down to my ocean-going routine of sleeping, eating, writing and dozing, I noted an American and his family of a wife and a daughter. He approached me, appeared to know me, talked and invited me to join the family at tea. With much politeness, I refused for the day and shunted the invitation to a distant future. I was afraid of that usual social triangle where the Colored Person comes as an invited guest and finds other friends of the family present who are surprised and snippy, if not worse.

After a few days, to save my own sense of courtesy, I went over to the group in the beautiful Salon and had tea. And thus began the most interesting of all my twelve voyages across the Atlantic. We talked and walked and sat silently together. We discussed poetry and travel and the world in general. There was one birthday dinner, with champagne, (quite outside the twelve-mile limit!)

The friendship thus begun has continued. The daughter last year married Oliver La Farge of "The Laughing Boy"; and this year, out of a very blue sky, Mrs. Mathews announced her purpose to endow "The Du Bois Literary Prize"!

With a lack of modesty, quite shameless, I hasten to accept and commend, because I have hopes that this substantial prize, as the years go by, will draw the thought and genius of our young writers away from the school of Van Vechten and the later McKay to a more human and truthful portraiture of the American Negro in the 20th Century. I do not want a Prunes and Prism school but I want writers frank and unafraid, daring to produce things that are true and beautiful, and thinking last of all of the wealth which books and poems seldom bring. These are the facts and they please me, as I hope they will you.

The Donor of the Du Bois Literary Prize

An Autobiography

YOUR question, "Who am I?" revives neglected memories. I cannot recall having been asked this question here during thirty years "in residence". New England is undoubtedly a solid background and Boston names useful for introductions, but the rest of the map seems to New York far off and obscure. One soon learns that childhood reminiscences unless abutting on Central Park are not of social interest. It is then, with a sense of relief from my cramped position as an alien, that I answer your question.

My father, John Albee, was a historian and poet. Upon being graduated from Harvard, that university offered him a Chair in Greek. This professorship was of short duration, as with John Fiske and others he was urged to resign, their budding views on evolution being at variance with Agassiz who at this time ruled the University and opposed Darwin's theories with immense vigor. My father's classical downfall was not without retaliation, as he carried off a bride,—the pride of the family.

He began to write following the Transcendental School: "Literary Art", "Goethe's Life and Times", "A Life of Emerson", as well as local histories and books of poetry. He was a warm friend of Emerson and Lincoln and carried on a voluminous correspondence with men of letters all over the world.

His mother, Patty Thayer, had been a flaming Abolitionist. Slaves lucky enough to reach eastern Massachusetts were hidden in her attic. So cleverly had she partitioned and cam-

When Mrs. E. R. Mathews wrote the editor announcing her gift, he replied:

"I cannot express to you my deep appreciation for this splendid offer. There are many reasons why this prize might be named after some one else, but there is one reason for having my name used which overcomes any feeling of modesty on my part. And that is, that I have been striving in recent years to induce the stream of Negro-American literature, especially of our younger writers, to return to a normal, human and truthful channel, rather than to be led astray by considerations of income and sensationalism. I have talked so much about this that I hope that my name in connection with this prize will emphasize my thought and feeling still more.

"Of course, many persons are going to ask us who is Mrs. Mathews? Will you not write me a word about yourself that I can publish?"

Here is the answer.

ouflaged this space that nobody was ever discovered, in spite of repeated search. The dramatic value of Patty's attic ranked with us children, neck and neck with the story of the elder Booth in "Othello" who frequently forgot that he was playing Shakespeare and believed himself the outraged husband and had to be subdued by force and dragged from the stage.

My mother founded in Boston the first non-sectarian hospital in this country, known today, as then, as the Channing Home. This outstanding venture aided by extreme youth and beauty brought her into great prominence. Her virtues were extolled in verse by Lowell and Longfellow, and there was hardly a contemporary prose writer who did not contribute something to her fame. Queen Victoria wrote a charming letter in her own hand, inviting her to visit at Buckingham Palace. She never left her work, however, and caring for the sick contracted consumption of which she died. She named her two younger children Robert Shaw and Loulie Shaw, for the Colonel who led the colored soldiers in the Civil War and his remarkable sister. These were the two members of her family she loved the most.

There is a great deal more that could be said of the generation past, as for the present, "We mention but the facts" as Bill Nye puts it. We grew up on the tip of an island in New Hampshire, in one of the oldest houses in the country, now belonging to the Government, the Jaffrey Mansion.

I married Edward Roscoe Mathews, of Valley Forge, Pa. and have one daughter, Mrs. Oliver La Farge.

I would suggest that in printing my first letter, you print your own reply which has real bearing on the literature of the young Negroes. I agree with you so heartily in hoping that they will express their own original and unique qualities. Of my second letter, take out whatever would be of use to you, remembering always the old motto, "Least said, soonest mended."

Proposed Rules of the Competition

1. THE Du Bois Literary Prize is to be open to any work written in English by a Negro born or naturalized in any country or island of the Western Hemisphere.

2. The word Negro shall be understood in its popular North American significance, that is, a person who traces his descent from a Negroid race of Africa.

3. The prize shall be awarded in successive years in rotation, for fiction, prose non-fiction, and poetry. In the awarding of the prize consideration shall be given to the whole volume of a writer's work during the preceding three years.

In considering works for the prize the judges will give preference in the prose works to books of 50,000 words or more, or to plays sufficient for an entire performance or for two or three shorter plays. In poetry, full volumes rather than single poems will be considered.

4. If in any year no work in the class under consideration seems worthy, the judges may refuse to make an award.

5. The prize shall be awarded, with the consent of the trustee, by a Board of Judges which shall be selected annually by the Nominating Committee. This Board shall consist of three judges, of whom one must be of Negro descent.

6. The Nominating Committee shall consist of five members, of whom the trustee shall be one, and of whom not less than three must be of Negro descent. This Committee shall have the sole power to nominate books for consideration by the judges. The members of the Committee shall serve for a term of five years, and may be re-elected. Upon the first formation of the Committee, its members shall be divided into classes, retiring in one, two, three, four and five years, in such manner that the term of not more than one expires each year. When vacancies occur, they shall be filled by a majority vote of the members of the Com-

consideration of the Nominating Committee. They will be invited to attend the awarding of the prize.

8. Publishers shall be invited to submit titles for the consideration of the Nominating Committee, and the Nominating Committee shall consider such titles, together with those recommended by the Advisory Board, and those recommended by its own members.

9. The Nominating Committee shall submit four titles to the judges and shall accompany these by such recommendations as it may desire to make, including, if it wishes, a recommendation that no award be made. In any case, however, final decision as to the award rests with the judges and the trustee.

10. The money for the prizes is put in the custody of the trustee who will make it available for presentation in accordance with the awards. The trustee will be a member of the Nominating Committee, ex-officio, and will act as representative of the donor.

11. The Pulitzer Prize, having no class and no race limitation, is regarded as having priority over this prize. Nominations, therefore, will not be made by the Nominating Committee until the Pulitzer Awards for the year have been made.

Nominations of works deemed eligible for the prize shall be made by the Nominating Committee not earlier than May 15, and shall include works published prior to January 1 of that same year. These nominations, together with copies of the works nominated, and the recommendations of the Nominating Committee, must be submitted to the Board of Judges not later than July 1. The award must be reported to the trustee not later than September 15. When this award is approved by him, he will cause it to be announced on October 1 following. The prize will be presented to the winner on the earliest convenient date but not later than November 15. These dates may be changed from time to time if it seems necessary.

12. The calendar year shall be used, so that the prize awarded in 1934 will contemplate books published during 1931, 1932 and 1933.

13. All positions mentioned herein as well as all prizes are open to women as well as to men.

14. The Nominating Committee may at any time recommend to the trustee such changes in the time and character of the award as will seem to be best to make the prize in the future calculated to carry out the wishes and plans of the donor.

***

THE attention of publishers is called to the Du Bois Literary Prize of $1,000:

1. Mrs. E. R. Mathews offers an annual prize of $1,000 for published books written by Negroes. The first prize in to be given in the fall of 1932.

2. Only books of fiction published during the calendar years 1929, 1930 and 1931 will be considered for the 1932 prize. Of the books published, certain ones will be chosen by the Nominating Committee between May 15 and July 1, 1932.

The following Advisory Board has kindly assumed the duty of recommending books for the consideration of the Nominating Committee:

Charles W. Chesnutt
Dorothy Canfield Fisher
Du Bose Heywood
Waldo Frank
William Allen White
Eugene O'Neill
Carl van Doren
Sinclair. Lewis
Edna St. Vincent Millay
Mordecai Johnson

3. In 1933, books of non-fiction published in 1930, 1931 and 1932 will be considered, and in 1934, books of poetry published during 1931, 1932 and 1933; and so on in rotation.

4. The books chosen by the Nominating Committee will be submitted to a Board of Judges selected annually by the Committee and the prize volume will be announced on October 1. The presentation of the prize will take place not later than November 15, 1932.

Publishers are invited to submit copies of books for the consideration of the Nominating Committee. The following Nominating Committee will consider such books, together with such books as are recommended by the Advisory Board:

Oliver La Farge, Trustee.
William Stanley Braithwaite
Lewis Gannett
James Weldon Johnson
W. E. B. Du Bois

Persons or publishers who have books which they wish considered by the Nominating Committee may send them at any time to the Du Bois Literary Prize, 69 Fifth Avenue, New York.

THE DU BOIS LITERARY PRIZE

IT is the feeling of the Nominating Committee of the W. E. B. Du Bois Literary Prize that the first award made should be to the author of a work of such indisputable literary merit that insofar as is humanly possible a serious reception of the award by critics and the general public will be assured. It is their opinion that to commence with what might be called a weak or makeshift award of this important prize would be construed in some quarters almost as a confession that in the field of competition, work of first rate importance could not be found; and would tend to discredit further awards in succeeding years, even when they were made for literary productions of greater merit.

Therefore, with the advice and consent of the Donor, the Nominating Committee decided this summer to make no nominations for the year 1932 in the Class of Prose Fiction for which it had been announced that the prize would be given this year.

The Nominating Committee is now considering works of Prose Non-fiction published between January 1, 1930, and December 31, 1932, for the 1933 prize. In this they are following the procedure laid down in the original announcement; next year they will consider Poetry and the year after will turn again to Prose Fiction.

This statement is made at the request of the Donor and Committee to make clear our position to the interested public.

OLIVER LA FARGE, *Trustee*

Acknowledgments

Du Bois, W.E.B. "The Negro in Literature and Art." *Annals of the American Academy of Political and Social Science* 49 (September 1913): 862–67. Reprinted by permission of Sage Publications, Inc. Copyright 1913 Sage Publications.

Morris, Lloyd. "The Negro 'Renaissance.'" *Southern Workman* 59, No. 2 (February 1930): 82–86. Reprinted with the permission of the Hampton University Archives.

Woodson, Carter G. "Some Things Negroes Need to Do." *Southern Workman* 51, No.1 (January 1922): 33–36. Reprinted with the permission of the Hampton University Archives.

Dunbar-Nelson, Alice. "Negro Literature for Negro Pupils." *Southern Workman* 51, No. 2 (1922): 59–63. Reprinted with the permission of the Hampton University Archives.

"Negro Life and Its Poets." *Opportunity* 1, No. 12 (December 1923): 355.

Gregory, Montgomery. "Review of *Cane* by Jean Toomer." *Opportunity* 1, No. 12 (December 1923): 374–75.

Du Bois, W.E.B. and Alain Locke. "The Younger Literary Movement." *Crisis* 27 (February 1924): 161–63. Reprinted with the permission of the Crisis Publishing Company.

"The New Generation." *Opportunity* 2 (March 1924): 68.

Kerlin, Robert T. "A Pair of Youthful Negro Poets." *Southern Workman* 53, No. 4 (April 1924): 178–81. Reprinted with the permission of the Hampton University Archives.

"The Debut of the Younger School of Negro Writers." (Includes Carl Van Doren, "The Young Generation of Negro Writers") *Opportunity* 2 (May 1924): 143–45.

Gregory, Montgomery. "The Spirit of Phyllis Wheatley: A Review of *There is Confusion* by Jessie Redmon Fauset." *Opportunity* 2 (June 1924): 181–82.

Braithwaite, William Stanley. "The Negro in Literature." *Crisis* 28 (September 1924): 204–10. Reprinted with the permission of the Crisis Publishing Company.

Du Bois, W.E.B. "Fall Books." *Crisis* 29 (November 1924): 25–26. Reprinted with the permission of the Crisis Publishing Company.

Horne, Frank S. "Black Verse." *Opportunity* 2 (November 1924): 330–32.

Johnson, Charles S. "Review of *The Fire in the Flint* by Walter White." *Opportunity* 2 (November 1924): 344–45.

Overton, Grant. "Remarks re: *The Fire in the Flint* at Library, November 6, 1924." Transcription of Typed Manuscript. [Original manuscript in the James Weldon Johnson Collection, Beinecke Library, Yale University.]

Robeson, Paul. "Reflections on O'Neill's Plays." *Opportunity* 2 (November 1924): 368–70.

Johnson, Charles S. "Some Books of 1924." *Opportunity* 3 (February 1925): 58–59.

Munson, Gorham B. "The Significance of Jean Toomer." *Opportunity* 3 (September 1925): 262–63.

Locke, Alain. "American Literary Tradition and the Negro." *Modern Quarterly* 3, No. 3 (May-July 1926): 215–22.

Van Doren, Carl. "The Negro Renaissance." *Century* (March 1926): 635–37.

"Harlem: Mecca of the New Negro." *Survey Graphic* 6, No. 6 (1925): 621–724.

Van Vechten, Carl. Excerpt from *Nigger Heaven* (New York: Alfred A. Knopf, 1926): 3–16. Copyright 1926 by Alfred A. Knopf, Inc. and renewed 1954 by Carl Van Vechten. Reprinted by permission of the publisher.

"Opportunity Literary Contest." *Opportunity* 2 (August 1924): 228.

"An Opportunity for Negro Writers." *Opportunity* 2, No. 21 (September 1924): 258.

"Opportunity's Literary Prize Contest Awards." *Opportunity* 2 No. 21 (September 1924): 277, 279.

"Opportunity's Prize Contest." *Opportunity* 2, (October 1924): 291.

"The Last Warning." *Opportunity* 2 (December 1924): 355.

"The Contest." *Opportunity* 3, No. 29 (May 1925): 130–31.

"Out of the Shadow." *Opportunity* 3 (May 1925): 131.

"Contest Awards." *Opportunity* 3 (May 1925). Langston Hughes, "The Weary Blues," p. 143; Countee Cullen, "To One Who Said Me Nay," p. 143; John Matheus, "Fog," pp. 144–47; Helene Johnson, "Trees at Night," p. 147; G.D. Lipscomb, "Frames: A Play in One Act," pp. 148–53; "Gustavus Adolphus Stewart, "My Fellow Traveller," pp. 153–54.

"Contest Awards." *Opportunity* 3 (June 1925): 171–77. Zora Neale Hurston, "Spunk," p. 171; Sterling Brown, "Roland Hayes," pp. 173–74; Langston Hughes, "America," p. 175; Clarissa M. Scott, "Solace," p. 175.

"The Opportunity Dinner." *Opportunity* 3 (June 1925): 176–77.

"The Prize Winners." *Opportunity* 3 (June 1925): 186.

"Pot-Pourri: A Negro Renaissance." *Opportunity* 3 (June 1925): 187.

Moryck, Brenda Ray. "A Point of View: An Opportunity Dinner Reaction." *Opportunity* 3 (August 1925): 246–49, 251–52.

"The Contest." *Opportunity* 3, No. 34 (October 1925): 291–92.

"Opportunity's Second Annual Contest for Negro Writers Offers $1000.00 in Prizes." *Opportunity* 3 (October 1925): 308–309.

"The Contest." *Opportunity* 4 (March 1926): 81.

"A Contest Number." *Opportunity* 4, No. 42 (June 1926): 173.

"The Judges and the Entries." *Opportunity* 4 (June 1926): 174.

"Contest Awards." *Opportunity* 4 (June 1926). Arna Bontemps, "Golgotha Is a Mountain," p. 177; Arthur Huff Fauset, "Symphonesque," pp. 178–80, 198–200;

Frank H. Wilson, "Sugar Cain," pp. 181–84, 201–203; Lucy Ariel Williams, "Northboun'," p. 184.

Macy, John. "The Kingdom of Art." *Opportunity* 4 (June 1926): 185.

"The Awards Dinner." *Opportunity* 4 (June 1926): 186.

"Our Prize Winners and What They Say of Themselves." *Opportunity* 4 (June 1926): 188–89.

"The Third *Opportunity* Contest." *Opportunity* 4 (October 1926): 304–05.

"Opportunity's Third Annual Contest for Negro Writers Offers $1000.00 in Prizes." *Opportunity* 4 (October 1926): 318–19.

"The Contest." *Opportunity* 5, No. 6 (June 1927): 159.

"Contest Awards." *Opportunity* 5, No. 6 (June 1927): 179; Arna Bontemps, "The Return," p. 194; Sterling A. Brown, "When De Saints Go Ma'ching Home,"pp. 198–99; Helene Johnson, "Summer Matures," p. 199; Georgia Douglas Johnson, "Plumes," pp. 200–201, 217–18.

"The Contest Spotlight." *Opportunity* 5, No. 7 (July 1927): 204–5, 213.

Gordon, Eugene. "The Opportunity Dinner: An Impression." *Opportunity* 5, No. 7 (July 1927): 208–9.

"The *Opportunity* Contest." *Opportunity* 5, No. 9 (September 1927): 254.

"An *Opportunity* Award." *Opportunity* 9 (October 1931): 298.

"The New Opportunity Awards." *Opportunity* 9 (November 1931): 331.

"Essays and Stories." *Opportunity* 9 (November 1931): 365.

"The Judges." *Opportunity* 10, No. 1 (January 1932): 6.

"The Contest." *Opportunity* 10, No. 2 (February 1932): 38.

"The *Opportunity* Award." *Opportunity* 10, No. 5 (May 1932): 136.

"Charles W. Cranford: Winner of *Opportunity* Award." *Opportunity* 10, No. 5 (May 1932): 137.

W.E.B. Du Bois. "Truth and Beauty." *Crisis* 25, No. 1 (November 1922): 7–8. Reprinted with the permission of the Crisis Publishing Company.

Fauset, Jessie. "The Prize Story Competition." *Crisis* 26 (June 1923): 57–58. Reprinted with the permission of the Crisis Publishing Company.

Graham, Ottie B. "To a Wild Rose." *Crisis* 26 (June 1923): 59–63. Reprinted with the permission of the Crisis Publishing Company.

Spingarn, Amy E. "The Amy Spingarn Prizes." *Crisis* 28, No. 5 (September 1924): 199. Reprinted with the permission of the Crisis Publishing Company.

"The Amy Spingarn Prizes in Literature and Art." *Crisis* 28, No. 6 (October 1924): 247. Reprinted with the permission of the Crisis Publishing Company.

"To Encourage Negro Art." *Crisis* 29 (November 1924): 11. Reprinted with the permission of the Crisis Publishing Company.

"The Amy Spingarn Prizes in Literature and Art." *Crisis* 29 (November 1924): 1. Reprinted with the permission of the Crisis Publishing Company.

Seyboldt, Mark. "About the Short Story." *Crisis* 29 (December 1924): 78–79. Reprinted with the permission of the Crisis Publishing Company.

Seyboldt, Mark. "Play-Writing." *Crisis* 29 (February 1925): 164–65. Reprinted with the permission of the Crisis Publishing Company.

"The New Crisis." *Crisis* 30, No. 1 (May 1925): 7–9. Reprinted with the permission of the Crisis Publishing Company.

"The Amy Spingarn Prizes." *Crisis* 30, No. 3 (July 1925): 111. Reprinted with the permission of the Crisis Publishing Company.

"Krigwa." *Crisis* 30 (October 1925): 275–78. Reprinted with the permission of the Crisis Publishing Company.

"Krigwa, 1926." *Crisis* 31, No. 1 (November 1925): 7. Reprinted with the permission of the Crisis Publishing Company.

"Krigwa 1926." *Crisis* 31 (December 1925): 67–68. Reprinted with the permission of the Crisis Publishing Company.

"Krigwa, 1926." *Crisis* 31 (January 1926): 115. Reprinted with the permission of the Crisis Publishing Company.

W.E.B. Du Bois. "Krigwa." *Crisis* 32, No. 2 (June 1926): 59. Reprinted with the permission of the Crisis Publishing Company.

W.E.B. DuBois. "Prizes." *Crisis* 32, No. 6 (October 1926): 283. Reprinted with the permission of the Crisis Publishing Company.

"For a Prize Novel, $1000." *Crisis* 31 (March 1926): 217. Reprinted with the permission of the Crisis Publishing Company.

"Krigwa, 1927." *Crisis* 33 (January 1927). Reprinted with the permission of the Crisis Publishing Company.

"Krigwa, 1927." *Crisis* 33 (February 1927): 191–93. Reprinted with the permission of the Crisis Publishing Company.

"Krigwa, 1927." *Crisis* 34 (December 1927): 347. Reprinted with the permission of the Crisis Publishing Company.

Du Bois, W.E.B. "Economic Prizes." *Crisis* 36 (March 1929): 93. Reprinted with the permission of the Crisis Publishing Company.

"The Du Bois Literary Prize." *Crisis* 38 (April 1931): 137. Reprinted with the permission of the Crisis Publishing Company.

"The Donor of the Du Bois Literary Prize: An Autobiography." *Crisis* 38 (May 1931): 157. Reprinted with the permission of the Crisis Publishing Company.

"Proposed Rules of the Competition." *Crisis* 38 (May 1931): 157–58. Reprinted with the permission of the Crisis Publishing Company.

"To Publishers." *Crisis* 38 (December 1931): 432. Reprinted with the permission of the Crisis Publishing Company.

"The Du Bois Literary Prize." *Crisis* 40 (February 1933): 45. Reprinted with the permission of the Crisis Publishing Company.